WARMIA, MAZURIA
AND BIAŁYSTOK REGION

Białystok

WARSAW

MAZOVIA AND THE
LUBLIN REGION

Częstochowa

Zamość

Cracow

MAŁOPOLSKA
(LESSER POLAND)

GDAŃSK
Pages 230–249

**WARMIA, MAZURIA
AND BIAŁYSTOK REGION**
Pages 274–291

WARSAW
Pages 56–103

0 km   50

0 miles   50

**MAZOVIA AND THE
LUBLIN REGION**
Pages 108–125

EYEWITNESS *TRAVEL GUIDES*

POLAND

DK EYEWITNESS *TRAVEL GUIDES*

POLAND

Contributors: TERESA CZERNIEWICZ-UMER
MAŁGORZATA OMILANOWSKA
JERZY S. MAJEWSKI

DORLING KINDERSLEY
LONDON • NEW YORK • SYDNEY • DELHI
PARIS • MUNICH • JOHANNESBURG
www.dk.com

A DORLING KINDERSLEY BOOK

www.dk.com

Produced by Wydawnictwo Wiedza i Życie, Warsaw

CONTRIBUTORS Małgorzata Omilanowska, Jerzy S. Majewski
ILLUSTRATORS Andrzej Wielgosz, Bohdan Wróblewski,
Piotr Zubrzycki, Paweł Mistewicz
PHOTOGRAPHERS Krzysztof Chojnacki, Wojciech Czerniewicz,
Stanisława Jabłońska, Piotr Jamski, Euzebiusz Niemiec
CARTOGRAPHERS Ewa i Jan Pachniewiczowie,
Maria Wojciechowska, Dariusz Osuch (D. Osuch i spółka)

EDITOR Teresa Czerniewicz-Umer
DTP DESIGNERS Paweł Kamiński, Paweł Pasternak
PROOFREADER Bożena Leszkowicz
TECHNICAL EDITOR Anna Kożurno-Królikowska
DESIGNER Ewa Roguska i zespół
COVER DESIGN Paweł Kamiński

TRANSLATORS Mark Cole, Teresa Levitt,
Joanna Pillans, Iwona Sikorska, Vera Rich

Edited and typeset by Book Creation Services Ltd, London

Printed and bound by South China Printing Co. Ltd. (China)

First published in Great Britain in 2001
by Dorling Kindersley Limited
80 Strand, London WC2R 0RL

Copyright © 2001 Dorling Kindersley Limited, London

CONTENTS

INTRODUCING POLAND

The eagle, emblem of Poland, in
the Zygmunt Chapel, Cracow

Neo-Classical rotonda in the
Saxon Gardens, Warsaw

Horsedrawn carriages in Zakopane

**Lion from Namiestnikowski
Palace, Warsaw**

**Wawel Royal
Cathedral, Cracow**

INTRODUCING POLAND

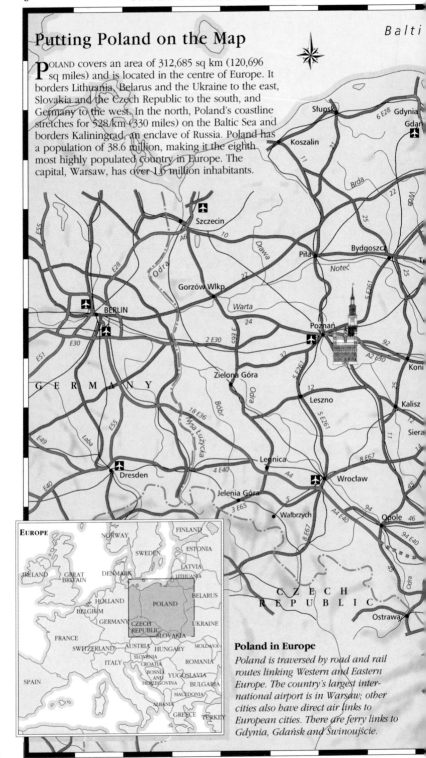

Putting Poland on the Map

POLAND covers an area of 312,685 sq km (120,696 sq miles) and is located in the centre of Europe. It borders Lithuania, Belarus and the Ukraine to the east, Slovakia and the Czech Republic to the south, and Germany to the west. In the north, Poland's coastline stretches for 528 km (330 miles) on the Baltic Sea and borders Kaliningrad, an enclave of Russia. Poland has a population of 38.6 million, making it the eighth most highly populated country in Europe. The capital, Warsaw, has over 1.6 million inhabitants.

Balti

Słupsk
Gdynia
Gdań
Koszalin
Szczecin
Piła
Bydgoszc
Noteć
Gorzów Wlkp.
Warta
BERLIN
Poznań
Koni
Zielona Góra
Leszno
Kalisz
Siera
Legnica
Wrocław
Dresden
Jelenia Góra
Wałbrzych
Opole
Ostrawa

G E R M A N Y

C Z E C H
R E P U B L I C

Poland in Europe

Poland is traversed by road and rail routes linking Western and Eastern Europe. The country's largest international airport is in Warsaw; other cities also have direct air links to European cities. There are ferry links to Gdynia, Gdańsk and Świnoujście.

EUROPE

NORWAY · FINLAND · SWEDEN · ESTONIA · LATVIA · LITHUANIA · IRELAND · GREAT BRITAIN · DENMARK · HOLLAND · BELARUS · POLAND · BELGIUM · GERMANY · CZECH REPUBLIC · UKRAINE · SLOVAKIA · FRANCE · SWITZERLAND · AUSTRIA · HUNGARY · MOLDAVA · SLOVENIA · CROATIA · ROMANIA · ITALY · BOSNIA AND HERZEGOVINA · YUGOSLAVIA · BULGARIA · MACEDONIA · SPAIN · ALBANIA · GREECE · TURKEY

◁ **Beskid Żywiecki Mountains**

a

RUSSIA
LITHUANIA
BELARUS
UKRAINE
SLOVAKIA

Nyoman
Kaunas
VILNIUS
Kaliningrad
Pregoła
Węgorapa
Suwałki
Hrodna
Nyoman
Łyna
Olsztyn
16
51
16
53
61
16
Drwęca
15
Ostrołęka
61
Łomża
64
8
Białystok
65
19
Narew
Ciechanów
60
Włocławek
10
Wkra
Płock
62
61
8
Wisła
60
WARSAW
2 E30
Siedlce
19
Biała Podlaska
Brest
Bug
Skierniewice
70
8 E67
Łódź
14
72
Pilica
Wisła
17
Radom
Wieprz
Piotrków Tryb.
12
9
Lublin
12
Chełm
17
Warta
74
19
Kielce
74
Zamość
Częstochowa
46
Tarnobrzeg
79
17
78
73
94 E40
Katowice
Wisła
Cracow
19
Tarnów
Rzeszów
4 E40
A4
Bielsko-
Biała
12
52
Nowy Sącz
Krosno
Przemyśl
9
28
28
94
47
49
E50
E50
E77
Košice
E50

0 km 100
0 miles 100

KEY

✈ Airport

⚓ Port

Motorway

Major road

Railway

National border

A PORTRAIT OF POLAND

GROWING NUMBERS OF *tourists visit Poland every year. Even so, it is still a relatively unknown country. To travellers crossing the lowlands from Eastern to Western Europe, there may not appear to be the diversity in landscape and buildings seen in other European countries. The pages that follow show the visitor the variety that Poland has to offer, in terms of its culture, history and landscape.*

Although it is situated in the plains of central Europe, Poland has a varied landscape. Alpine scenery predominates in the Tatra Mountains along the country's southern border, while the north is dominated by lakelands, which contrast with the landscape of the Baltic coast. For those who like unspoiled natural scenery, there are areas of primeval forests in Białowieża and extensive marshlands along the banks of the River Biebrza which are a haven for many rare bird and plant species. About 30 per cent of the area of Poland is woodland, including a number of vast forests covering more than 1,000 sq km (390 sq miles). Most of these consist of coniferous trees and mixed woodland, but there are also many forests of deciduous trees, mainly oak and hornbeam, or beech.

The Polish eagle

Many areas of great natural beauty are protected as national parks or reserves. Mountain lovers can make use of the well-developed infrastructure of hostels and other shelters, such as those found in the Beskid Sądecki or the Tatra Mountains; the more adventurous can explore the unfrequented and almost inaccessible Beskid Niski or Bieszczady. All areas have clearly marked hiking trails and well-equipped shelters *(schroniska)*. The countless lakes of Warmia and Mazuria, areas known as the Land of a Thousand Lakes *(Kraina Tysiąca Jezior)* are a haven for watersports enthusiasts, as are the waters of Pomerania and Wielkopolska. The lakes are popular with canoeists and in summer are dotted with rowing and sailing boats.

The Bzura, one of Poland's many unspoiled rivers

◁ **A rural chapel in winter**

A summer's day on a sandy Baltic beach

POPULATION AND RELIGION

Poland's inhabitants, who number almost 39 million, all but constitute a single ethnic group, with minorities accounting for less than 4 per cent of the population. The largest minorities are Belarussians and Ukrainians, who inhabit the east of the country, and Germans, who are concentrated mainly around the city of Opole in Silesia.

The vast majority of Poles are Catholic, but it would be wrong to identify Poles exclusively with the Roman Catholic Church. Large regions of the country, such as Cieszyn Silesia, have a substantial Protestant population, and followers of other denominations are also widely dispersed.

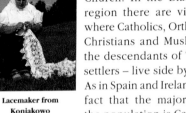

Lacemaker from Koniakowo

In the east of the country there are many Orthodox Christians; here, religious denomination does not necessarily coincide with ethnic identity, although Belarussians tend to be Orthodox while Ukrainians belong to the Greek Catholic (Uniate) Church. In the Białystok region there are villages where Catholics, Orthodox Christians and Muslims – the descendants of Tartar settlers – live side by side. As in Spain and Ireland, the fact that the majority of the population is Catholic continues to exert a major influence on the moral values of the country, as well as on its political life. An example of this is the many debates in the Sejm (the lower house of the Polish parliament) that have alternately limited and liberalized the right to abortion. Religion, however, is not a major factor in the way that Poles vote, as election results show. The political scene is almost equally divided between the supporters of the right and the post-communist left. Over the last ten years the Polish electorate has shown itself to be quite stable.

Pump room at the spa of Polanica-Zdrój

Religious belief is outwardly expressed by a deep reverence for religious symbols and rituals. Wayside crosses and shrines to the saints or the Virgin Mary add charm to the Polish countryside. The main religious festivals – Christmas, Easter, Corpus Christi and Assumption, as well as All Saints' Day, when almost everyone in Poland, regardless of their religious denomination, visits the graves of relatives – are solemnly observed. An unusual cult surrounds the Virgin. For centuries, believers from all over Poland and further afield have made the pilgrimage to the image of the Black Madonna in Częstochowa *(see pp156–7)*. Indeed, throughout Poland there are shrines to the Virgin, to whom miraculous powers have been ascribed. Another famous pilgrimage is made by Orthodox Christians to the holy mountain of Grabarka *(see p291)*. Poland is also visited by Jews from all over the world who come in remembrance of the millions who died there during the Holocaust under German occupation of the country during World War II.

Corpus Christi procession

CULTURAL VARIETY AND SHIFTING BORDERS

Magnificent buildings bearing witness to past splendours can be seen at almost every step. Most of these monuments are in Małopolska, Lubelszczyzna, Wielkopolska and Lower Silesia. Not all of them, however, belong to Polish culture, since the country's frontiers have changed many times over the centuries. A particularly important change came at the end of World War II, when the Allies approved a westward shift of Poland's borders. As a result, the inhabitants of the eastern areas, lost to Poland after the war, were resettled, and many were sent to the western regions, inhabited by Germans – who were in turn displaced.

Restored market square of the Old Town, Wrocław

A poster by Maria Pałasińska dedicated to Solidarity

The legacy of more than 100 years of partition rule is still visible in Poland's cultural landscape today. Russian, Prussian and Austrian administration left their mark not only on rural and urban architecture but also on the customs and mentality of the Polish people.

DEMOCRATIC CHANGE AND ECONOMIC DEVELOPMENT

The fall of communism in Poland came about largely thanks to the efforts of the trade union Solidarity (Solidarność), which was founded in 1980 but forced to go underground after the imposition of martial law. When the democratic opposition won the elections to the Sejm and the Senate in 1989, Poland again became a country with a parliamentary democracy and a market economy. This was important enough in itself, but it had wider implications too: by tackling its inefficient, crisis-ridden socialist economy, Poland had set the standard for economic reform in Central and Eastern Europe as a whole. Many Polish industries were priva-

Logo of the Polish stock exchange

tized, and the drastic reforms that were carried through over a number of years accelerated Poland's GDP to make it the fastest-growing in Europe. By the end of the 1990s, the Polish economy had become largely resistant to crisis.

The country has a substantial foreign trade deficit, but this is balanced by the surplus produced by an unofficial cross-border trade. There are, however, negative aspects of the reforms – among them the budget deficit and unemployment. The latter continues to be high. The problem of unemployment is somewhat mitigated by the illegal employment of workers, although this is usually confined to small firms. There is an ambitious programme of privatization, but it has not yet been fully completed, and many enterprises are still state-owned.

Heavy industry tends to be outdated, unprofitable and economically inefficient. There is an ongoing systematic programme of coal-mine closure, and former mineworkers have been forced to look for work elsewhere.

Session of the Sejm, the lower house of the Polish parliament

The Pazim, the tallest building in Szczecin

Political and economic changes have had their impact on Poland's towns and cities. Old buildings are being renovated, attention is being paid to the environment, new shops have appeared, and large out-of-town supermarkets and modern petrol (gas) stations have sprung up. New buildings – though not always architecturally distinctive – are going up everywhere. Market squares and main streets in many Polish towns have been pedestrianized. In many of the old towns that suffered damage during World War II – including Szczecin, Kołobrzeg, Głogów and Elbląg – buildings are now being reconstructed. Smaller towns, too – swelled by sprawling apartment housing after the war – are now acquiring more traditional buildings. Nonetheless, the vast concrete housing developments typical of the communist era still dominate many Polish townscapes.

Not surprisingly, this has brought considerable social and economic problems in its wake.

The archaic farming system is another candidate for restructuring. Polish farming is still based on traditional family smallholdings consisting of no more than a few acres of land. It is seriously under-mechanized and requires a disproportionate amount of manpower.

Many new public buildings – mainly office blocks – are springing up, too. Much of the new development is centred on the capital, Warsaw, although commercial investment is now slowly beginning to filter through to other cities, among them Cracow, Katowice, the Baltic conurbation of Gdańsk, Sopot and Gdynia, and Wrocław, Poznań and Łódź as well.

A fundamental part of the reform process is Poland's drive to join Western military and economic structures. In 1999, Poland became a member of NATO, and it is currently preparing to join the European Union. This requires harmonization of its legal and economic systems with those of the EU countries, providing a further powerful incentive to change.

The privatized Zakłady Metali Lekkich Kęty SA metalworks

The Landscape of Poland

POLAND's landscape is very varied. The south of the country is bounded by mountain ranges which, the further north you travel, gradually turn into areas punctuated by hills and low-lying ancient forests. Northern Poland, an area of great natural beauty, has been shaped by a succession of glaciers that moved southwards from Scandinavia. National parks and reserves have been established in many areas. The central regions of the country, consisting of lowlands, merge into picturesque lakelands and coastal plains.

A cabbage white on a meadow flower

FAUNA OF POLAND

The most typical Polish wildlife – including wild boar, deer and hare – is to be found in mixed and deciduous forests. Some species, such as bison and capercaillie, are found almost nowhere else in Europe. In the Carpathian and Sudety mountains, bears and lynxes may be seen.

Roman snail

MOUNTAINS

Nutcracker

The Tatra Mountains *(see pp164–5)* are the highest in Central Europe. Though covering a small area, they provide breathtaking alpine scenery. The High Tatras *(Tatry Wysokie)* are mainly granite, with jagged, rocky peaks. At 2,499 m (8,200 ft) above sea level, Rysy is the highest peak in Poland. The Western Tatras *(Tatry Zachodnie)*, consisting of sedimentary rock and crystalline shale, are inhabited by such rare animals as brown bears, marmots and chamois.

LAKELAND SCENERY

The lakelands that cover much of northern Poland consist of picturesque moraine woodland and thousands of lakes. Largest and most scenic are the Great Mazurian Lakes, in a district known as the Land of a Thousand Lakes *(Kraina Tysiąca Jezior)*. Abounding in forests, marshes and peat bogs, they are a haven for many bird species: the largest concentration of storks in Europe, swans, grebes, cranes and cormorants.

Crane

The crocus
(Crocus satinus) *blooms in early spring in mountain valleys and alpine meadows, mainly in the Tatras and Babia Góra ranges.*

Bog arum (Calla palustra) *is a poisonous perennial plant with a characteristic white leaf below a globular flower. It grows in peat bogs.*

The silver thistle
(Carlina acaulis) *is a protected plant. Its leaves form a rosette containing a basket-like flower with a covering of dry, silvery leaves.*

The great sundew
(Drosera anglica), *an insect-eating plant found in peat bogs, is a protected species in Poland.*

Deer, *which live in herds, are a relatively common sight in Poland's deciduous and mixed forests. They are hunted as game animals.*

Marmots, *rodents of the beaver family, live in the Tatra Mountains. They 'whistle' when disturbed.*

Wild boar, *widespread in Poland, are the ancestors of the domestic pig. Deciduous and mixed forests are their principal habitat.*

Moose *live in large forests, marshes and peat bogs, even near large cities. Large populations of them can be seen in Kampinoski National Park and in the Białystok region.*

THE LOWLANDS

Hoopoe

The apparent monotony of the lowlands is broken by elevations, meandering rivers, marshes and peat bogs. Most of the land is under cultivation, but there are also extensive forests. Białowieża Forest *(see p291)* shelters bison. Moose can be seen in the marshes and storks in the lakes.

THE COAST

Seagull

The sandy beaches of Poland's Baltic coast are among the finest in Europe. They are situated by sand dunes or cliffs, and were it not for river estuaries, it would be possible to walk along them for the entire length of the coast. Narrow sandy spits formed by the coastal currents and known as *mierzeje* are a characteristic feature of the shoreline.

The corn poppy *(Papaver rhoeas) is becoming increasingly rare as it is weeded out from cereal crops.*

Lyme grass (Elymus arenarius) *grows on the sand dunes. It has pointed leaves and its roots bind the sandy subsoil.*

Toadflax (Linaria vulgaris) *has narrow leaves and yellow-orange flowers with a characteristic spur. It grows in ditches and on wasteland.*

Marram grass (Ammophila arenarea) *has narrow grey-green leaves, and flowers between June and August. Like lyme grass, it helps to bind the sand dunes where it grows.*

Early Polish Architecture

A Romanesque capital

OVER THE CENTURIES, and particularly during World War II, Poland lost a great deal of its architectural heritage. However, major efforts on the part of both private individuals and the government have meant that many important buildings have been restored, and in some cases completely rebuilt. Royal and aristocratic palaces, churches, castles and entire streets of old towns can thus be admired today. Traditional wooden buildings are another interesting feature of Polish architecture.

Renaissance courtyard at Wawel Royal Castle

ROMANESQUE ARCHITECTURE

The Romanesque style of architecture seen in Polish cathedrals, palace chapels and monasteries flourished largely as a result of the country's conversion to Christianity in the 10th century. Unfortunately, few Romanesque buildings have survived intact. Among those that have are the collegiate church at Tum near Łęczycą *(see p229)* and the monastery at Czerwińsk *(see p114)*, both of which are decorated with stone carvings. The Romanesque style reached its apogee during the 12th century.

Semicircular presbytery

Triforium with decorative columns

Narrow windows that also served defensive purposes

The collegiate church at Tum near Łęczycą, *dating from the mid-12th century, is Poland's largest surviving Romanesque religious building.*

This 12th-century Romanesque doorway *is from the Cathedral of St Mary Magdalene* (see p190).

GOTHIC ARCHITECTURE

Gothic elements began to appear in late Romanesque architecture in the early 13th century; this transitional style can be seen in the abbeys at Wąchock, Sulejów and Koprzywnica. By the end of the century, the Gothic style was prevalent throughout Polish architecture. Many fortified castles were built at this time, more than 80 being founded by Kazimierz the Great. Notable examples are those at Będzin, Ogrodzieniec and Bobolice *(see pp158–9)*. Gothic churches and monasteries were also built throughout the country, fine examples surviving in Cracow and Wrocław. The oldest surviving wooden churches, such as that at Dębno, date from the same period. In Polish provincial architecture, the Gothic style persisted until the early 17th century.

The 15th-century church at Dębno *(see p165) is one of the oldest surviving wooden churches in Poland.*

The doorway of the early 15th-century Church of St Catherine *in Cracow has an ornamental stepped frame.*

THE RENAISSANCE AND MANNERISM

Renaissance architecture was introduced to Poland in the early 16th century by the Italian architect Bartolomeo Berrecci, who designed Wawel Royal Castle and the Zygmunt Chapel in Cracow. Many of the churches in Mazovia (as at Pułtusk and Płock) were influenced by the Italian Renaissance, as were the town halls in Poznań and Sandomierz. From the mid-16th century onwards, buildings in Pomerania were designed in the northern Mannerist style.

Decorative ceilings *such as those in the churches of Lubelszczyzna and Kalisz illustrate provincial interpretations of Renaissance and Mannerist forms.*

The Zygmunt Chapel (see p143) *is one of the finest examples of Renaissance architecture in Poland.*

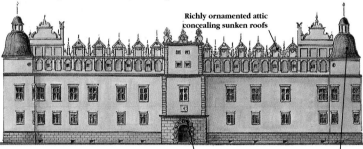

Richly ornamented attic concealing sunken roofs

Central gateways leading to a courtyard surrounded by cloisters

Corner lookout turret

Leszczyński Castle in Baranów Sandomierski (see p153) *is one of the few surviving late Renaissance buildings in Poland.*

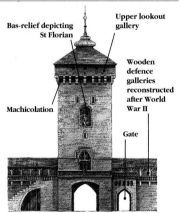

Upper lookout gallery

Bas-relief depicting St Florian

Wooden defence galleries reconstructed after World War II

Machicolation

Gate

The Florian Gate in Cracow (see p134), *a surviving city watchtower with Gothic fortifications, dates from the 13th to 15th centuries.*

ARCHITECTURE OF THE AGE OF THE TEUTONIC KNIGHTS

The Teutonic Knights, who ruled Eastern Pomerania and Prussia in the 13th and 14th centuries, left impressive brick-built Gothic buildings. The knights built defensive castles (such as those at Malbork, Gniew and Bytów) and city walls (as at Chełmno and Toruń), and founded numerous churches.

The imposing bulk of the Upper Castle, part of the Malbork Castle complex

Later Polish Architecture

BUILDINGS DATING FROM the Baroque era are quite a common sight in Polish towns and cities. Many distinctive 19th-century residences and architectural ensembles are also noteworthy, as in Łódź. Around 1900, at a period coinciding with that of Art Nouveau, attempts to build in a Polish national style produced particularly felicitous results. Folk architecture is another area of great interest. The best way to explore it is to visit the *skansens* (open-air museums) which exist in each region of the country.

Baroque cartouche with
the emblem of Poland

BAROQUE ARCHITECTURE

In the first half of the 17th century, architects of Italian descent started to introduce the early Baroque style to Poland. Nobles built imposing residences, chief among them Krzyżtopór Castle in Ujazd *(see pp44–5 and p152)*, in the Mannerist style, and the fortified early Baroque palace in Łańcut *(see pp172–3)*. Italian architects were also commissioned to design the Royal Palace in Warsaw, the country's new capital. The destruction wrought during the Polish-Swedish war was followed by a period of building in the late Baroque style. In Warsaw, the renowned Dutch architect Tylman van Gameren designed a large number of buildings, alongside Italian architects. During the rule of the Saxon kings in Poland, architects from Dresden designed many new buildings in Warsaw, as well as palaces like the one at Białystok *(see p290)*.

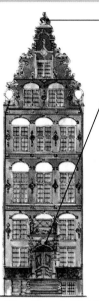

**High gable framed
by volutes**

**Pediment decorated with
coat of arms**

Edena House *in Gdańsk
is a fine example of the
Mannerist style.*

Kodeń Church, *with its broken
façade, is typical of the late
Baroque period.*

**Steep broken
roof**

**Bay window with a
decorative gable**

This country house in Koszuty *(see p211) is
a typical example of an aristocrat's country seat
in the Baroque style.*

**Porch in front of
main entrance**

**Corner
turrets**

NEO-CLASSICISM

Neo-Classicism appeared in Poland after the rule of Stanisław August Poniatowski, the country's last king. The Royal Palace and Łazienki Palace in Warsaw were built in the Neo-Classical style, as were many others including those at Lubostroń and Śmiełów. Features included landscaped gardens in the English manner.

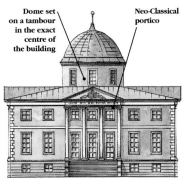

Dome set on a tambour in the exact centre of the building

Neo-Classical portico

Lubostroń Palace (see p221) *is a fine example of Palladianism, a refined Neo-Classical style imitating the work of the Italian Renaissance architect Andrea Palladio – in this case, his Villa Rotonda at Vicenza.*

The town hall in Łowicz *is an example of small-town public buildings in the Neo-Classical style of the early 19th century.*

HISTORICISM AND MODERNISM

The second half of the 19th century saw a proliferation of Neo-Gothic, Neo-Renaissance and Neo-Baroque buildings. In the 1880s there was a movement towards creating an architecture in the Polish national style, which gave rise to some very picturesque structures. Art Nouveau was short-lived in Poland, although it did leave a number of attractive buildings, primarily in Łódź.

The wooden chapel at Jaszczurówka *is an example of a building in the Polish national style.*

The Central School of Commerce *in Warsaw combines modern with traditional elements.*

TRADITIONAL ARCHITECTURE

Fine examples of wooden architecture can be found today at most *skansens*. Log cabins, often with thatched roofs, can still be seen in many villages in Poland.

Painted interior of a peasant dwelling in Zalipie

Beehive in human form

Windmill at the *skansen* (open-air museum) in Wdzydze Kiszewskie

The Literature of Poland

Stanisław Wyspiański

POLISH LITERATURE HAS always been inextricably linked to the historical development of the country, as the political situation, particularly over the last two centuries, has not always favoured freedom of speech. Many writers were forced to emigrate, while those who remained were often obliged to publish their works in other countries. Poland boasts four winners of the Nobel Prize for Literature: Henryk Sienkiewicz, Władysław S. Reymont, Czesław Miłosz and Wisława Szymborska.

THE MIDDLE AGES

POLISH WRITING originates in the 11th century. The earliest works were in Latin, often written by people from other regions who copied hagiographies and holy chronicles. The oldest Polish chronicle, by the Benedictine monk Gall Anonim, dates from the beginning of the 12th century. Native Polish writers soon appeared, and Polish literature expanded into all the literary forms known in Europe at the time. The first work in the Polish language was written in the second half of the 13th century. The earliest religious song in Polish, *The Mother of God (Bogurodzica)*, was probably written at the end of the 13th century, although it is not found in manuscript until the 15th century. The Polish *Holy Cross Sermons (Kazania świętokrzyskie)* date from around 1450.

Jan Kochanowski writing *Treny*, a lament for his daughter's death

RENAISSANCE AND BAROQUE

THE RENAISSANCE is regarded as the Golden Age of Polish literature, when both prose and poetry flourished. Mikołaj Rej (1505–69), the first significant writer in the Polish language, is generally regarded as the father of Polish literature. The most prominent poet of the time was Jan Kochanowski (1530–84), who wrote the first Polish tragedy, entitled *The Dismissal of the Greek Envoys (Odprawa posłów greckich)*. He was also the author of the humorous *Trifles (Fraszki)* and the sorrowful *Laments (Treny)*, a lament in the form of a cycle of 19 poems. Other notable figures among Poland's early poets are Mikołaj Sęp Szarzyński (1550–81) and Szymon Szymonowic (1558–1629).

The ancient Sarmatian culture had a great influence on Polish Baroque literature. The greatest works of the period are by Jan Chryzostom Pasek (1636–1701), who wrote highly colourful accounts both of great historical events and of the everyday life of the Polish nobility in the reign of Jan III Sobieski.

Romantic poet Adam Mickiewicz by Walenty Wańkowicz

THE ENLIGHTENMENT AND THE 19TH CENTURY

THE ENLIGHTENMENT, and particularly the reign of the last king of Poland, Stanisław August Poniatowski, was an important period in the development of Polish literature. The first Polish novel, *The Adventures of Mikołaj Doświadczyński (Mikołaja Doświadczyńskiego przypadki)*, was written by Bishop Ignacy Krasicki (1735–1801), a moralist and satirical poet.

POLISH CINEMA

The first Polish feature film was made as early as 1902, but it was not until after World War II that Polish film-makers achieved international renown. The best-known Polish film directors include Andrzej Wajda, whose *Man of Iron* won the Palme d'Or at the 1981 Cannes Film Festival, Kryzsztof Zanussi, Krzysztof Kieślowski *(Decalogue, Three Colours – Blue/White/Red)* and Roman Polański *(Chinatown)*, who has spent many years making films in the USA and France.

Scene from J. Hoffman's film *Colonel Michael*

Polish Romantic poetry played an important role in keeping nationalist sentiment alive. The outstanding writers of that time, Adam Mickiewicz, Juliusz Słowacki and Zygmunt Krasiński, wrote outside Poland. To this day, their work forms the canon of patriotic literature, whose jewel in the crown is Mickiewicz's *Pan Tadeusz*, which is both a nostalgic evocation of the vanishing traditions of the nobility and a vision of the emergence of more modern social attitudes. Also notable at this time was the comedy writer Aleksander Fredro, whose works include *Revenge (Zemsta)* and *Husband and Wife (Mąż i Żona)*.

Another writer who holds a prominent place in the history of Polish Romantic literature is Cyprian Kamil Norwid, regarded as the precursor of modernism. Eliza Orzeszkowa (1840–1910) and Bolesław Prus (1847–1912) are the principal figures in the next phase of the development of the Polish novel.

Monument to Aleksander Fredro in Wrocław

Another major writer of this time was Henryk Sienkiewicz (1846–1916), best known in Poland for his trilogy of historical novels describing events in 17th-century Poland and *The Teutonic Knights (Krzyżacy)*, which is devoted to the late 14th and early 15th centuries. Outside Poland, Sienkiewicz is better known for *Quo Vadis?*, which deals with the beginnings of Christianity and for which he was awarded the Nobel Prize for Literature in 1905.

20TH-CENTURY LITERATURE

FROM 1900 ONWARDS Young Poland *(Młoda Polska)*, a modern trend in Polish literature particularly associated with the artistic community of Cracow, began to emerge. A key role in this was played by Stanisław Wyspiański (1869–1907), author of the Symbolist play *The Wedding (Wesele)*, which was made into a film by Andrzej Wajda 70 years later. Also influential in Young Poland was a Bohemian group surrounding Stanisław Przybyszewski, a friend of Henrik Ibsen and Edvard Munch.

Another Nobel laureate was Władysław Reymont (1865–1925), who wrote society novels. He was awarded the Nobel Prize in 1924 for *The Peasants (Chłopy)*, which describes the lives of the inhabitants of a village near Łowicz. Between the wars, avant-garde writers such as Stanisław Ignacy Witkiewicz (aka Witkacy, 1885–1939), Bruno Schulz (1893–1942) and Witold Gombrowicz (1904–69) came to prominence.

Wisława Szymborska receiving the Nobel Prize for Literature

Polish literature after World War II spawned many famous writers, several of whom wrote from abroad for political reasons. Stanisław Lem wrote philosophical science fiction, which has been translated into many languages. His *Solaris* was made into a film by Andrei Tarkovsky. Tadeusz Różewicz, also well-known as a poet, and Sławomir Mrożek are prominent among playwrights. Hanna Krall and Ryszard Kapuściński are renowned for their documentary-writing. Andrzej Szczypiorski, who wrote *A Mass for Arras (Msza za miasto Arras)* and *The Beginning (Początek)* has also achieved international recognition. Contemporary poetry has a special place in Polish literature. Apart from Tadeusz Różewicz, its main exponents are Zbigniew Herbert, Ryszard Krynicki and Stanisław Barańczak. The best illustration of the achievements of contemporary Polish writers is the award of two recent Nobel Prizes: the 1980 prize, to Czesław Miłosz, and the 1996 prize, to the Cracow poetess Wisława Szymborska.

Nobel Prize winner Czesław Miłosz

The Music of Poland

POLAND HAS MADE a major contribution to the international music scene, as much through the works of great composers as through its renowned jazz musicians and colourful folk music. Polish classical composers such as Frédéric Chopin (1810–49), Stanisław Moniuszko (1819–72), Karol Szymanowski (1882–1937) and Wojciech Kilar (born 1932) have often been inspired by folk music, as have modern jazz and rock musicians. Poland has also given the world such outstanding musical performers as the tenor Jan Kiepura and the pianists Artur Rubinstein and Witold Małcużyński.

Frédéric Chopin in a portrait by Eugène Delacroix

EARLY MUSIC

ALTHOUGH THEY are not widely known, there is much of interest in the works of early Polish composers. Mikołaj z Radomia, a composer of the first half of the 15th century, produced both religious and secular works. In the Renaissance, composers such as Wacław z Szamotuł and Mikołaj Gomółka brought Polish music into the European mainstream. The first Polish opera stage was set up in the 17th century at the court of Władysław IV. Court and religious music flourished at that time, and the works of such composers as Adam Jarzębski, Stanisław S. Szarzyński and Marcin Mielczewski are still widely performed by Polish musicians today.

THE 19TH AND 20TH CENTURIES

THE MOST prominent Polish composer of the Romantic era was undoubtedly Frédéric Chopin (1810–49), who composed almost exclusively for the piano. Chopin contributed to the establishment of a Polish national style in music, and exerted a great influence on the development of European piano music. During his short life he composed a large number of preludes, mazurkas, polonaises, waltzes, études and other pieces. Many of Chopin's works contain elements of folk music. The Chopin Piano Competition, held in Warsaw, has been a regular event since 1927, and award-winners have gone on to become world-famous pianists.

Stanisław Moniuszko is regarded as the father of the Polish national opera. His most famous operas are *Halka*, inspired by highland folklore, and *The Haunted House (Straszny dwór)*, which evokes the traditions of the Polish nobility.

In the second half of the 19th century, the violinist Henryk Wieniawski and the pianist Ignacy Paderewski achieved world renown. The latter was also prominent in politics, serving for a time as Prime Minister of Poland.

Before World War I, the town of Zakopane was a major centre of Polish culture. It drew not only artists but also composers who sought inspiration from the landscape of the Tatra Mountains and the colourful folklore of the highland dwellers. Among composers associated with Zakopane is Mieczysław Karłowicz (1876–1909), noted especially for his symphonies. Karłowicz perished tragically in an avalanche in the Tatras at the young age of 33. Another frequent visitor to Zakopane was Karol Szymanowki, whose fascination with the folk music of the region inspired him to

JAN KIEPURA (1902–1966)

Jan Kiepura achieved international renown as an opera singer. He performed on the world's greatest stages, and from 1938 was with the Metropolitan Opera of New York. He gained popularity through his appearances in operettas and musicals, where he performed together with his wife, Marta Eggerth.

Stanisław Moniuszko

compose a number of works, including the ballet *Harnasie*.

One of the best-known modern composers is Krzysztof Penderecki (b. 1933), whose oeuvre includes epic symphonies, oratorios and operas. His opera *The Devils of Loudun (Diabły z Loudun)* has been performed all over the world. Other prominent composers of international standing are Andrzej Panufnik (1914–91), Witold Lutosławski (1913–94) and Henryk Górecki (b. 1933), whose works include the outstanding Symphony No. 3, which has topped the classical music charts for years. Other major composers of symphonic music are Wojciech Kilar (b. 1932) and Zbigniew Preisner (b. 1955), most widely known for their film music.

Folk band outside the Cloth Hall (Sukiennica) in Cracow

The composer and conductor Krzysztof Penderecki

JAZZ

JAZZ TRADITIONS in Poland go back to the time of the Second Republic. After World War II, jazz was deemed by the authorities to be "alien to the working class", and it was not until 1956 that jazz could be performed in public. An important jazz musician of that time was the pianist and composer Krzysztof Komeda (1931–69), who wrote the popular lullaby for Roman Polański's film, *Rosemary's Baby*.

During the 1960s, other jazz musicians came to prominence, including Adam Makowicz, Tomasz Stańko and Michał Urbaniak. Jazz clubs opened throughout the country, and the Warsaw Jazz Jamboree, first held in 1958, became the world's biggest jazz festival. Another renowned festival is Jazz on the Oder, held in Wrocław.

Many jazz musicians came to public recognition in the 1970s and 1980s, among them the pianist and saxophonist Włodzimierz Nahorny, the saxophonists Zbigniew Namysłowski and Janusz Muniak, and the pianist Sławomir Kulpowicz.

FOLK MUSIC

POLISH FOLK music is unusually colourful. Every region has its own specific tradition, and the music of the Tatra Mountains is unique. Folk bands play quite a basic range of instruments, the main one being the fiddle, and sometimes bagpipes or drums and basses. Depending on the region these instruments are supplemented by clarinets, horns, accordions and occasionally dulcimers.

The best way of getting to know and enjoy Polish folk music is to attend some of the concerts traditionally held during the summer months, such as the Kazimierz or Zakopane festivals. Here there is a chance to listen to live music being played and to watch the dance groups that perform in colourful folk costumes.

Polish vocal and dance groups have brought worldwide popularity to Polish folk music. The Mazowsze group, for example, gives stage performances that are inspired by the folk traditions of various regions.

The Warsaw Jazz Jamboree

The Traditional Nobility

Aristocratic figurine in porcelain

THE TRADITION OF THE Polish nobility was dominated by the idea of Sarmatism, which was based on the myth that the Polish aristocracy were descended from a warrior people called the Sarmatians. Sarmatism was influential in shaping the ideology of the ruling class, as well as its customs and lifestyle. A Sarmatian embraced the old order, was patriotic and Catholic, and at the same time valued freedom and privilege, lived life as a landowner and upheld family traditions. Sarmatism played an important part in art and literature, particularly memoirs.

*A **kulawka** was a special toasting goblet for drinking "bottoms up", as it could only be set down on its rim.*

Noblemen's houses *were typically single-storey buildings fronted by an imposing colonnade. Rooms flanked the central entrance hall.*

A TRADITIONAL BEVERAGE

Mead was a favourite drink of the Polish aristocracy. It is made by fermenting wort, a solution of honey and water that has been flavoured with herbs. The most popular type of mead is *trójniak*, in which honey makes up one-third of the total wort. The rarest is *półtorak*, with two parts honey and one part water. Although mead is no longer widely drunk, it is still produced today.

Stolnik mead

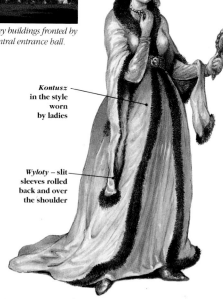

Turban

Headpiece with heron feathers

Kontusz in the style worn by ladies

Wyloty – slit sleeves rolled back and over the shoulder

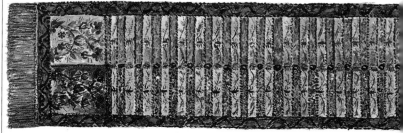

An election gathering, at which the nobility elected the king, is portrayed here. This was one of the greatest privileges exercised by the gentry.

COATS OF ARMS

The coats of arms of aristocratic families in Poland number no more than about 200. They were held in common by members of clans with different names. Aristocratic titles were not used at the time of the Republic (with the exception of the titles of Lithuanian princes), while magnate families looked to foreign rulers for titles. Polish heraldic symbols usually had their origins in individual symbols; they were therefore relatively simple and differed from those of Western Europe.

Fleur-de-lys

Gelątkowa

Ship

Szreniawa

POLISH NATIONAL DRESS

Required attire of the nobility in the Baroque era, its main elements were the żupan *(a kind of shirt) and the* kontusz *(an outer garment tied with a waist-band). Headgear took the form of either a* kołpak *(fur hat) or a square-bottomed* rogatiwka. *Men wore their hair short and sported a moustache, and sometimes a beard.*

Kołpak

Żupan

Wyloty

Kontusz sash

The kontusz was an outer garment with cutout sleeves, which were thrown over the shoulders.

The karabela was a traditional sword that had a single-sided blade and a highly ornamented handle, often with inlaid precious stones.

Coffin portraits of the deceased were painted in oils on metal plates cut to the shape of the cross-section of a coffin, to which they were attached during funerals.

Silk sashes known as kontuszy *were an indispensable part of a nobleman's attire. Several yards in length, they were worn wrapped around the waist and tied in a decorative knot, allowing the tassels to hang downwards.*

The Different Religions of Poland

ALTHOUGH THE MAJORITY of the Polish population today is Roman Catholic, in the course of the country's history its inhabitants have adhered to a variety of faiths. Besides Roman Catholics, there have been Orthodox Christians, Uniates and Jews (most of whom lost their lives in World War II), and, since the 16th century, Lutheran and Calvinist Protestants. When the Polish borders were redrawn after World War II, a large section of the Eastern Orthodox population found itself in Belarus or the Ukraine. At the same time, the western border moved further westwards, incorporating many German Protestant churches. The wide variety of Poland's ecclesiastical architecture bears witness to the many cultures and religions that have existed there.

Roadside shrine

The Convent of the Old Believers at Wojnowo *is one of the few places where this religious group can still be found.*

Orthodox Christians *today are found mainly in the eastern parts of the country, where many of their historic churches still stand.*

The Evangelical Reform Church in Warsaw *was built after the Reformation and used by the small group of Calvinist believers in Poland.*

The Basilica of the Holy Cross and the Birth of the Holy Mother *(Bazylika Krzyża Świelego i Narodzenia Matki Boskiej)* has the tallest church tower in Poland.

The cemetery at Kruszyniany*, one of the few Muslim burial grounds in Poland, is used by people of Tartar descent.*

The 'Church of Peace' (Kościół Pokoju) at Świdnica was one of three churches to be built specifically for Silesian Protestants after the Thirty Years' War, which ended in 1648.

OTHER DENOMINATIONS

Some of Poland's historic churches have changed denomination over the years – for instance, when Polish Catholics took over disused Protestant churches. Although the original interiors have generally not survived, the exteriors have often been carefully conserved. Some religious denominations no longer have followers in Poland, although their places of worship remain. An example is the Mennonite chapel in Gdańsk.

Old Mennonite chapel in Gdańsk

Open-air altar

Pauline monastery

Judaic artifacts in museums are poignant vestiges of the synagogues that were once so numerous in Poland. As a result of the Holocaust and the ensuing communist era, there are few Jews in Poland today.

CZĘSTOCHOWA PILGRIMAGE

The Monastery of Jasna Góra in Częstochowa is the most important Catholic shrine in Poland – and one of the greatest in the Christian world. The image of Our Lady of Częstochowa, also known as the Black Madonna, draws pilgrims all year round. The main pilgrimage, which attracts hundreds of thousands of believers from Poland and beyond, is held in the meadows at the foot of the monastery on 15 August each year.

The picturesque wooden churches of the Ukrainian Uniates, or Greek Catholics, built for the Lemk and the Boyk minorities, survive in the Carpathian Mountains. Their congregations were resettled in other areas during Operation Vistula after World War II.

Sports in Poland

POLISH SPORTSMEN AND women have come to prominence in athletics, canoeing, judo and wrestling. The athlete Irena Kirszenstein-Szewińska made Olympic history with her multiple world records in running and her seven Olympic medals. During the 1970s and early 1980s, the sporting events with the greatest mass appeal were association football matches, and the Polish national team scored a number of major international victories. While the popularity of football has waned somewhat, that of basketball is growing. Motorcycle speedway races attract numerous fans, and Poland is one of the few countries to host world ice sailing championships.

Junior World championships in Bydgoszcz

The Felix Stamm Boxing Championships

BOXING

THE POLISH Boxing Association was established in 1923 and the first championships took place the following year. Polish amateur boxers have frequently obtained impressive results, winning gold medals at Olympic tournaments. Two of the country's best-known boxers were Jerzy Kulej (middleweight) and Zbigniew Pietrzykowski (light heavyweight).

Currently, Polish amateur boxing has a relatively low profile and small audiences. By contrast, professional boxing seems to be growing in popularity once again.

CYCLING

THE FIRST bicycle race in Poland was held in Warsaw in 1869. Over the decades, the most popular contest has been the International Peace Race, which started in 1948 on the roads of Poland and Czechoslovakia, with East Germany included from 1952. The International Peace Race has lost some of the popularity that it once enjoyed. The most prestigious cycling event today is the Tour de Pologne, a race around Poland that takes place every year in early September and draws competitors from all over the world. As one of the more significant European cycling events, it attracts many cyclists who are in training for world championship races. Polish world championships in individual road races have been won by Joachim Halupczok, Janusz Kowalski, Lech Piasecki and Ryszard Szurkowski. Poland has won several world team races.

ATHLETICS

ATHLETICS, OFTEN regarded as the king of sports, goes back in Poland to the second half of the 19th century. Polish athletes competed for the first time on the world stage in the 1924 Olympic Games, held at the Colombes Stadium in Paris. Poland's first Olympic gold medal winner was Halina Konopacka, who won the discus at the 1928 Olympics in Amsterdam.

Poland reached its athletic peak in the late 1950s and early 1960s, the greatest name at the time being Irena Kirzenstein-Szewińska.

Poland currently hosts many international athletics events. Of the many long-established sporting events in Poland, the Janusz Kusociński Memorial Championships are probably the best known.

The Tour de Pologne, Poland's most prestigious cycle race

World speedboat championships in Żnin

SPEEDBOAT RACING

Speedboat racing in Poland goes back to the 1950s. The country's best-known representative in this sport is Waldemar Marszałek, who has won the world speedboat championship on many occasions. Another world speedboat champion in the 0–700 category is Tadeusz Haręza.

Action at a premier league football (soccer) match

FOOTBALL (SOCCER)

Polish football reached its peak in the 1970s and 1980s, when the Polish national team was highly placed in the world championships and players such as Boniek were household names. Polish teams also took medals in Olympic competitions. Although the standard of Polish football has

undoubtedly declined, league matches still attract large numbers of fans. The best-known premier league soccer teams are Stal Mielec, ŁKS Łódź, Widzew Łódź, Wisła Kraków, Pogoń Szczecin, Amika Wronki, Śląsk Wrocław, Legia Warszawa and Górnik Zabrze. The football season starts at the beginning of August and the Polish Cup finals are played in June.

SPEEDWAY

Dirt track motorcycle racing is extremely popular in Poland, and the country has had a number of successes in this field. Lack of Polish success during the 1980s, however, led to a decline in interest in the sport, but the upturn began again in 1989, as world speedway champions started once again to

frequent the country's speedway tracks.

Poland has often hosted the world speedway championships and its best-known tracks are in Bydgoszcz, Gorzów, Tarnów, Leszno, Toruń, Wrocław and Zielona Góra.

Polish speedway league races are extremely popular, and are second only to those in Britain. Since 1999, there have been extra first and second league races.

CANOEING

Poland has scored numerous successes in a variety of amateur and professional canoeing events. Many Polish canoeists have triumphed in world championships and won Olympic medals. Poland's best watersports facility for canoeing is Lake Malta in Poznań.

Speedway league duel between the Toruń and Bydgoszcz teams

POLAND THROUGH THE YEAR

Gingerbread heart

Tourists tend to visit Poland in the summer, between June and September. During that period, the most popular tourist spots are crowded, and a variety of open-air events, from street theatre festivals to re-enactments of medieval tournaments, take place throughout the country. The main music and drama festivals are held in spring and autumn. The best way of spending winter in Poland is skiing in the mountains. As the majority of Poles are Catholics, traditional Catholic feast days are the most important holidays. The celebrations that take place at Christmas, Easter, and Corpus Christi as well as other local church festivals are interesting spectacles for tourists.

SPRING

The OFFICIAL beginning of spring, 21 March, is an unofficial day of truancy among young people in Poland. The tourist season begins with the first warm days of spring.

MARCH

Topienie Marzanny *(23 Mar)* is the day when, in many areas, children throw small dolls – symbolizing winter – into rivers.

The International Poster Biennial *(even-numbered years)*, Warsaw.

Festival of Stage Songs, Wrocław. Polish and international performers take part.

International Dance Group Presentation, Kalisz.

International Festival of Alternative Theatre, Cracow.

APRIL

Palm Sunday (the Sunday before Easter) is the day when "palms" are blessed in the churches. The most colourful celebrations take place in villages in Kurpie and Małopolska – in particular Rabka, Lipnica Murowana and Tokarnia. During Holy Week (the week leading up to Easter), mystery plays are performed in churches around the country. The oldest and best-known spectacle is *Chwalebne Misterium Pańskie*, a passion play which has been performed in Kalwaria Zebrzydowska (*see p161*) since the 17th century. On **Holy Saturday**, Easter food is taken to church in baskets and blessed. Visits are also made to symbolic sepulchres in churches.

Easter Sunday is the most important Catholic holiday, when the grandest mass is held to mark the Resurrection.

Easter Monday (*Śmigus-dyngus*) is marked by the custom of people throwing water over one another.

Gdańsk International Guitar Festival (*every other year*), Gdańsk.

International Festival of Films for Children and Youth, Poznań.

Paka Cabaret Review, Cracow.

Passion play in Kalwaria Zebrzydowska

Performance at the Cracow Festival of Student Song

Festival of Theatre Schools, Łódź

MAY

International Labour Day *(1 May)*.

3 May The most important public holiday, marking the adoption of the first Polish constitution of 1791.

Festival of Student Song, Cracow. Performances by the best student vocalists and accompanists.

Chamber Music Days *(first 2 weeks in May)*, Łańcut. This is an international event.

International Book Fair *(last 2 weeks in May)*, Warsaw. One of the largest events of its kind in Europe.

Kontakt Theatre Festival *(last 2 weeks in May)*, Toruń.

Jazz on the Oder, Wrocław. Renowned jazz festival.

Poznań Jazz Fair, Poznań.

Short Film Festival, Cracow. The oldest film festival in the country.

AVERAGE HOURS OF SUNSHINE PER DAY

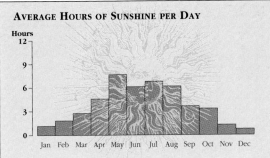

Hours

12 — 9 — 6 — 3 — 0

Jan Feb Mar Apr May Jun Jul Aug Sep Oct Nov Dec

Sunny days
The period from May to September has the greatest number of days of sunshine. April and September are often also sunny, while December has the least sunshine.

SUMMER

FROM THE END of June to the beginning of September, open-air events are held all over the country. Theatrical life in the towns and cities, by contrast, tends to slow down. Most open-air events are held in tourist areas.

Corpus Christi procession in Spicimierz

JUNE

Corpus Christi *(variable)*. Solemn processions are held throughout the country.
Midsummer's Night *(23 Jun)*.
Fishermen's Sea Pilgrimage *(29 Jun)*. Decorated fishing boats sail into the port of Puck across the bay.
Festival of Polish Song *(late Jun)*, Opole.
Mozart Festival *(late Jun–early Jul)*, Warsaw.
Malta – International Theatre Festival *(late Jun)*, Poznań.

Summer Film Festival *(late Jun)*, Łagów.
Festival of Folk Bands and Singers *(late Jun)*, Kazimierz Dolny.
Jewish Culture Festival *(Jun/Jul)*, Cracow.

JULY

Festival of Film Stars, Międzyzdroje.
Viking Festival, Wolin. Viking battles. Most of the boats arrive from Scandinavia.
International Street Theatre Festival *(mid-Jul)*, Jelenia Góra. There is also street theatre in Jedlnia Zdrój, Szczawno Zdrój and Wałbrzych in Lower Silesia, and in the cities of Gdańsk, Toruń, Cracow and Warsaw.
International Organ Festival *(mid-Jul)*, Kamień Pomorski.
Singing Poetry Festival *(mid-Jul)*, Olsztyn Castle.
Summer Jazz Days, Gdynia.
FAMA *(mid-Jul)*, Świnoujście. Student arts festival.
Piknik Country *(end of Jul)*, Mrągowo. International country music festival.

Street performers at the Dominican Fair in Gdańsk

AUGUST

Beskid Culture Week *(early Aug)*, Beskid region.
Dominican Fair *(first 2 weeks in Aug)*, Gdańsk.
Chopin Festival *(second week in Aug)*, Duszniki Zdrój.
Złota Tarka Traditional Jazz Festival *(mid-Aug)*, Iława.
Feast of the Assumption *(15 Aug)*. This is a religious holiday, but it is also the day on which Poles commemorate their victory over the Bolsheviks in 1920.
International Song Festival *(late Aug)*, Sopot.

Fishermen's sea pilgrimage in the bay of Puck

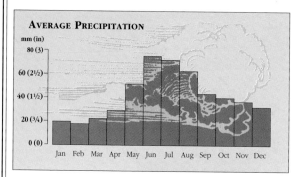

AVERAGE PRECIPITATION

mm (in)

80 (3)

60 (2½)

40 (1½)

20 (¾)

0 (0)

Jan Feb Mar Apr May Jun Jul Aug Sep Oct Nov Dec

Rainfall and snow
*Although autumn
showers are the most
unpleasant, the
heaviest rainfall
occurs in summer.
Heavy snow is usual
in winter.*

Autumn

FINE WEATHER continues in
Poland to the end of
October. Autumn comes
soonest in Pomerania,
Warmia and Mazuria, as well
as Suwalszczyna. The
transition from September to
October – when fallen leaves
create a riot of colour – is
known as the "golden Polish
autumn". It is also a time
when major cultural events
take place, as well as the
beginning of the new
academic year.

September

**Festival of Polish Piano
Music** *(early Sep)*, Słupsk.
Warsaw Autumn *(mid-Sep)*,
Warsaw. Contemporary music.
Wratislavia Cantans
(early Sep), Wrocław.
Oratorio and cantata festival.
**Laser and firework
displays**
(around 10 Sep), Olsztyn
near Częstochowa.

**Programme for the Polish
Feature Film Festival**

Festival of Science
(last 2 weeks in Sep),
Warsaw.
Days of Julian Tuwim,
Łódź. Various events,
including poetry readings.
Archaeology gala,
Biskupin.

October

**Borderlands Theatre
Festival** *(first week in
Oct)*, Cieszyn.
**Konfrontacje
Theatre Festival**,
Lublin.
**Lemk Cultural
Festival**, Gorzów
Wielkopollski.
**Warsaw Film
Festival**, Warsaw.
Jazz Jamboree *(third
week in Oct)*, Warsaw.
The Jazz Jamboree is
one of Europe's major
jazz festivals.
**Festival of Early
Music** *(late Oct)*. An
international festival

with venues in Warsaw,
Cracow and other cities.
**Polish Feature Film
Festival** *(end Oct)*. Gdynia.
Lithuanian All Saints' Day,
Puńsk. Poetry and music in
memory of the dead.

November

All Saints' Day *(1 Nov)*.
People visit the graves of
their relatives and light
candles there.
**All Saints' Day Jazz
Festival**, Cracow. The first
jazz festival in post-
communist Europe.
**"Etiuda" International
Film Festival** *(early Nov)*,
Cracow.
Independence Day
(11 Nov). The biggest
ceremonies in honour of
Polish independence in 1918
take place in Warsaw.
St Martin's Day
(11 Nov). In Wielkopolska
and Eastern Pomerania
people traditionally cook a
goose and bake pretzels
and croissants on St Martin's
Day. The holiday is marked
by major ceremonies in
Poznań, where St Martin is
the patron saint.
Głogów Jazz Meeting,
Głogów.

**Candles lit at a cemetery on
All Saints' Day**

Inauguration of the academic year

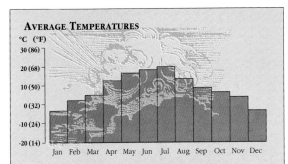

AVERAGE TEMPERATURES

°C (°F)

30 (86)
20 (68)
10 (50)
0 (32)
-10 (24)
-20 (14)

Jan Feb Mar Apr May Jun Jul Aug Sep Oct Nov Dec

Temperatures
Temperatures are highest in the summer, when they can exceed 30° C (86° F). In winter, temperatures can fall below zero (30° F), although this is usually short-lived.

WINTER

THE FIRST snow can fall in November, although snowless winters are becoming increasingly common. Subzero temperatures and hard frosts are not unusual. The coldest part of the country is Suwalszczyna, in the northeast corner.

DECEMBER

Christmas Crib Competitions (*first week in Dec*), held in Cracow market square.
Christmas Eve (*24 Dec*). The beginning of Christmas is marked with a celebratory meat-free dinner and midnight mass.
Christmas (*25 and 26 Dec*). Public holidays, with masses held in all churches.
New Year's Eve (*31 Dec*). Throughout Poland, people see in the New Year at balls and parties, and at celebrations in the main squares of most towns.

Cribs being brought to Cracow's Christmas Crib Competitions

JANUARY

New Year (*1 Jan*). Public holiday. A carnival begins and the season of balls opens.
Orthodox Church Music Festival (*mid-Jan*), Cracow.

FEBRUARY

Feast of St Mary Gromniczna (*2 Feb*). Wax candles known as *gromnici* are lit in churches.

End of Carnival The last Thursday before Lent is marked by eating doughnuts or other fried delicacies known as *faworki*. Splendid balls, concerts and shows are put on throughout the country to mark the last Saturday of the carnival.
International Festival of Sea Shanties, Cracow.

PUBLIC HOLIDAYS

New Year's Day (1 January)
Easter Monday (variable)
May Day (1 May)
Constitution Day (3 May)
Corpus Christi (variable)
Feast of the Assumption (15 August)
All Saints' Day (1 November)
Independence Day (11 November)
Christmas (25 and 26 December)

Winter cityscape, Gdańsk

THE HISTORY OF POLAND

POLISH BORDERS HAVE *changed almost continuously with the course of history. The origins of the Polish nation go back to the 10th century, when Slav tribes living in the area of Gniezno united together under the Piast dynasty, which then ruled Poland until 1370.*

Mieszko I, the first historic prince of this line, converted to Christianity in 966, bringing his kingdom into Christian Europe. The Piast dynasty ruled Poland with variable fortune and embroiled the nation in domestic quarrels for 150 years. After this dynasty died out, the great Lithuanian prince Jagiełło took the Polish throne and founded a new dynasty. The treaty with Lithuania signed at Krewa in 1385 initiated the long process of consolidation between these nations, culminating in 1569 with the signing of the Union of Lublin. In the 15th century the Jagiellonians achieved many military successes, forming the powerful Republic of Two Nations (Rzeczpospolita Obojga Narodów). After the Jagiellonian dynasty died out in 1572, the authorities introduced elective kings, with the nobility having the right to vote. Poland's political and

The Polish eagle

military weakness led to its partitioning by Russia, Prussia and Austria. In 1795 Poland was wiped off the map of Europe for more than 100 years. Attempts to wrest independence by insurrection were unsuccessful, and Poland did not regain its sovereignty until 1918. The arduous process of rebuilding and uniting the nation was still incomplete when, at the outbreak of World War II, a six-year period of German and Soviet occupation began. The price that Poland paid was very high: millions were murdered, including virtually its entire Jewish population. The country suffered devastation and there were huge territorial losses, which were only partly compensated by the Allies' decision to move the border westwards. After the war, Poland was subjugated by the Soviet Union and did not become a fully democratic nation until 1989.

Map of the Republic of Two Nations (Rzeczpospolita Obojga Narodów) in the 17th century

◁ **Stanisław August Poniatowski, the last king of Poland**

Poland under the Piast Dynasty

Crown of Kazimierz the Great

D URING THE 6TH century AD, Slav tribes began migrating from the east to what is today Polish territory. The Vistulanians (Wiślanie) settled around Cracow, and the Poles (Polanie) around Gniezno. The Polanie united under the rule of the Piast dynasty in the 10th century, and the conversion of Mieszko I (c.960–92) to Christianity in 966 led to the formation of the Polish state. After Mieszko, Bolesław the Brave (992–1025) acquired significant new territories. Later Piast kings ruled with variable fortune. On the death of Bolesław the Wry-Mouthed (1107–38), the nation was divided into districts, not to be reunified until the reign of Władysław the Elbow-High (1306–33). The country flourished under the rule of his son, Kazimierz the Great (1330–70).

POLAND IN THE YEARS 1090–1127

◼ *Polish territory*

Bishop Stanisław Szczepanów

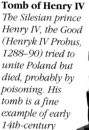

Prayer at the grave of St Wojciech
The Czech bishop Wojciech, who was martyred while on a mission to Prussia in 997, was the first Polish saint.

Tomb of Henry IV
The Silesian prince Henry IV, the Good (Henryk IV Probus, 1288–90) tried to unite Poland but died, probably by poisoning. His tomb is a fine example of early 14th-century Gothic sculpture.

MARTYRDOM OF ST STANISŁAW
An embroidery of 1504 from the chasuble in Kmita depicts the murder of Bishop Stanisław Szczepanów in 1079.

TIMELINE

950	1000	1050	1100	1
997 Martyrdom of Bishop Wojciech while on a mission to Prussia	**1000** Congress at Gniezno; convocation of the Polish church metropolis.		**1124–1128** Bolesław the Wry-Mouthed initiates the conversion of Western Pomerania to Christianity	
	1025 Coronation of Bolesław the Brave, first king of Poland			
	966 Adoption of Christianity	**1079** Martyrdom of Bishop Stanisław Szczepanów	**1138** Beginning of the division of Poland	

Coin minted in the reign of Bolesław the Brave

Vistulanian Plate
This Romanesque floor laid with plaster c.1170, preserved in the collegiate church in Wiślica, depicts a scene of adoration.

Bolesław the Bold

Kazimierz the Great
This 14th-century sculpture from the collection in the Collegium Maius in Cracow depicts Kazimierz the Great, who "found Poland of wood, and left it in stone".

Founding Document of the Cracovian Academy
Founded in 1364, the Cracovian Academy was the second university (after Prague) to be established north of the Alps.

VESTIGES OF THE PIAST DYNASTY

The Piast dynasty witnessed the development of Romanesque and early Gothic architecture. Romanesque churches have survived in Tum (*see p229*), Czerwińsk (*see p114*) and Tyniec (*see p145*). The abbeys in Sulejów, Wąchock (*see p152*) and Koprzywnica date from the 13th century. Some of the Gothic castles of Kazimierz the Great can be seen in the Jura region – for example at Będzin, Olsztyn and Bobolice (*see pp158–9*).

The Crypt of St Leonard
is a vestige of the Romanesque cathedral at Wawel Castle in Cracow (see pp138–9).

The castle at Będzin *is the best-preserved of all the Gothic castles built by Kazimierz the Great (see p205).*

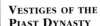

	1241 Victory at the Battle of Legnica against the Mongols		1320 Coronation of Władysław the Elbow-High and the unification of the Polish state	1340–1366 Kazimierz the Great conquers western Ruthenia (Ruś Halicko-Wołyńska)
1200	**1250**		**1300**	**1350**
	1226 Konrad Mazowiecki leads the Crusaders			1370 Louis of Hungary (Ludwik Węgierski) seizes the Polish crown

Coronation sword of Bolesław the Brave

The initials of Kazimierz the Great on the door of Wawel Cathedral

Poland under the Jagiellonians

Jagiellonian coat of arms

THE TREATY SIGNED in Krewa in 1385 uniting the Polish and the Lithuanian states proved to be a decisive moment in the history of Central Europe. The great Lithuanian prince Władysław Jagiełło received the hand of Jadwiga, the young and beautiful queen of Poland, and was crowned king of Poland. Jadwiga died in 1399, but the relationship between Poland and Lithuania established by the Union of Krewa was gradually strengthened. Jagiełło founded the Jagiellonian dynasty and, by the reign of Kazimierz the Jagiellonian in the mid-15th century, Poland and Lithuania had come to be the greatest power in Europe. The Jagiellonian kings also ruled the Czech nations and Hungary.

REPUBLIC OF TWO NATIONS IN THE YEARS 1386–1434

☐ Poland ☐ Lithuania

☐ Feudal territories

Second Treaty of Toruń
Signed in 1466, the treaty concluded the Thirteen Years' War with the Teutonic Knights, who lost nearly half their territory to Poland.

Ulryk von Jungingen, Grand Master of the Teutonic Order

Chapel at Lublin Castle
Ruthenian paintings in the Catholic Chapel of the Holy Trinity founded by Władysław Jagiełło reflect the multicultural nature of the Polish-Lithuanian state.

Plate showing Filippo Buonaccorsi
This sculpture commemorating the Italian humanist and educator of the young royals, who died in 1496, is by the eminent late Medieval sculptor Veit Stoss.

TIMELINE

1399 Death of Queen Jadwiga

1411 First Treaty of Toruń, establishing peace with the Teutonic Knights

1413 Treaty of Horodło, strengthening the bond between Poland and Lithuania

1440 Formation of the Prussian Union, in opposition to the Teutonic Knights

1385	1400	1415	1430

1385 Union of Krewa joins Poland and Lithuania

1410 Battle of Grunwald

1415 At the Council of Constanz, Paweł Włodkowic proclaims the theory of the sovereignty of all Christian and non-Christian peoples

Queen Jadwiga's sceptre

Virgin from Krużlowa
This statue, of around 1400, is a masterpiece of late Gothic sculpture.

Gothic Pax
The skill of medieval goldsmiths can be seen in this finely crafted cross.

Witold, the great Lithuanian prince

GOTHIC ARCHITECTURE

Many late Gothic buildings have survived in Poland. Among the most important are the Collegium Maius and the Barbican in Cracow *(see p133)*. After the formation of Royal Prussia, many parish churches were built in the towns lying within its territory, the largest being the Church of St Mary in Gdańsk *(see pp238–9)*.

The imposing twin-tower façade of the Church of St Mary reflects Cracow's former status (see p132).

BATTLE OF GRUNWALD

In one of the greatest medieval battles, on 15 July 1410, the combined forces of Poland, Lithuania and Russia routed the armies of the Teutonic Knights, who never regained their former might. The scene is depicted in this painting by Jan Matejko of 1878.

***Deposition* from Chomranice**
This Deposition *of Christ (c.1450) is held to be the apogee of Polish Gothic art.*

	1454 Act incorporating Prussia into the Crown of Poland	1473 Birth of Nicolaus Copernicus		1496 Piotrkowski Statute restricts the rights of commoners to acquire land
1445	**1460**	**1475**		**1490**
1444 Władysław of Varna dies at the Battle of Varna, fought against the Turks		1466 Second Treaty of Toruń		1492 Death of Kazimierz the Jagiellonian. First general Sejm (parliament)

Figure of St John by Veit Stoss, from the altar in the Church of St Mary, Cracow

Poland's Golden Age

Emblematic cockerel

IN THE 16TH CENTURY the Republic of Two Nations (Rzeczpospolita) formed by Poland and Lithuania was one of the largest European powers. In the western territories of the Polish Crown there was peace, relative prosperity and – rare elsewhere – religious tolerance. Under the Jagiellonians, and later under the first elective kings, art, education and the economy flourished. In the political sphere there was a significant movement to improve the Republic and institute reforms.

The so-called real union between Poland and Lithuania was concluded in Lublin in 1569. At that time, in terms of language, nationality and religion, the Republic was the most diverse state in Europe.

REPUBLIC OF TWO NATIONS, EARLY 16TH CENTURY

▨ *Poland*   ▨ *Lithuania*

☐ *Feudal territories*

Nicolaus Copernicus (1473–1543)
This Polish astronomer and humanist showed that the Earth revolves around the Sun.

Codex Behem
This illuminated manuscript of 1505 by Baltazar Behem, a writer and notary of Cracow, lists the city's privileges, statutes, and the guild laws.

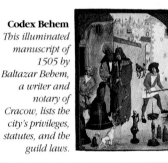

Representatives of the peoples of the East and West

Nobleman who brought the news of the Chancellor's death

OPATÓW LAMENT

The Renaissance tomb of Chancellor Krzysztof Szydłowiecki in the collegiate church at Opatów features a bas-relief sculpture depicting the mourning of the deceased, installed after 1532 (*see p152*). Around the table are friends of the Chancellor, humanists attached to the royal court and foreigners.

TIMELINE

1505 Adoption of the constitutional law of *Nihil Novi*

1520 Adoption of the Statute of Toruń, introducing serfdom

1525 Secularization of the defeated Teutonic Order. The elector Albrecht Hohenzollern, Duke of Prussia, makes an oath of fealty to the Polish king, Zygmunt the Old, in Cracow

1543 Copernicus famous tre is publishe

1500	1520	1540

1518 Bona Sforza arrives in Poland and marries Zygmunt the Old (Zygmunt Stary)

1521 The Polish army occupies Teutonic Prussia in the final war with the Teutonic Knights

Renaissance oven tile

Tomb of Stefan Batory
Despite his short reign, Batory was one of the most illustrious of the elective monarchs.

Union of Lublin

The federation of Poland and Lithuania established under the Union of Lublin in 1569 provided for a joint Sejm (parliament), king and foreign policy. However, each country had its own government, army, treasury and judiciary.

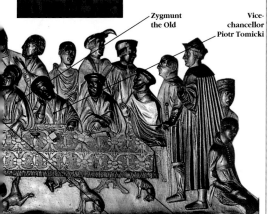

Zygmunt the Old

Vice-chancellor Piotr Tomicki

Jan Tarnowski, the deceased's son-in-law

Dogs, symbolizing the loyalty of the dead man's friends

Tapestry with Satyrs

The collection of tapestries at Wawel Castle (see p140) comprises over 160 splendid pieces. They were brought to the castle in the 16th century.

16TH-CENTURY ARCHITECTURE

The first instance of the Renaissance style in Poland dates from 1502. Often imitated but never equalled, the most splendid early Renaissance building was the Zygmunt Chapel in Wawel Cathedral (*see p143*), completed in 1533.

This castle in Książ Wielki, built by Santi Gucci between 1585 and 1589, is the most splendid example of Italian Mannerism in Poland.

The collegiate church in Pułtusk (see p113), built c.1560 by the architect Gianbattista of Venice, has barrel vaulting.

1557 Outbreak of the war with Russia over Livonia	**1563** Split of Polish Calvinists and isolation of the Polish Brethren, an extreme group of Reformationists		**1587** Zygmunt III Vasa is elected king of Poland	

1564 Jesuits arrive in Poland

Grotesque mask from Baranów Sandomierski

1560	**1580**	**1600**

1561 Secularization of the Livonian Branch of the Teutonic Order and incorporation of Livonia

1569 Union of Lublin

1579 The capture of Połock marks the start of Stefan Bathory's victory in the war against Russia

1596 The capital is moved from Cracow to Warsaw

The "Silver" 17th Century

THE 17TH CENTURY was dominated by the wars that the Republic of Two Nations waged against the Swedes, Russia and the Ottoman Empire. An uprising in the Ukraine in 1648 marked the beginning of a series of catastrophes. In 1655 the Republic of Two Nations was invaded and largely occupied by the Swedes.

Statue of Jan III Sobieski

Although it was short-lived, the Swedish occupation – known as the Deluge (*Potop*) – wreaked havoc. The final triumph of the Republic of Two Nations was the victory against the Turks at the Battle of Vienna in 1683, during the reign of Jan III Sobieski. The country eventually emerged from the wars without major territorial losses, but it was considerably weakened and its dominance was over.

REPUBLIC OF TWO NATIONS IN THE YEARS 1582–1648

☐ Poland ☐ Lithuania

☐ Feudal territories

A rebus on the main gate spells out "Krzyżtopór" with a cross (*Krzyz*) and an axe (*Topór*).

Siege of Jasna Góra, the Luminous Mountain
The run of Swedish victories ended in 1655 with the heroic Polish defence of the Pauline Monastery in Częstochowa.

Moat

Nobleman in a Dance with Death
The figure of a common Polish yeoman in traditional dress decorates the Chapel of the Oleśnicki family in Tarłów.

KRZYŻTOPÓR CASTLE

In the first half of the 17th century, dazzling residences were built in the Republic of Two Nations. The most splendid was the eccentric castle in Ujazd. Built at great expense, it stood for barely 11 years. It was demolished in 1655 by the Swedes and remains in ruins to this day (see p152).

TIMELINE

1604 First Moscow expedition of the false Demetrius	**1606** Zebrzydowski Rebellion	**1629** Truce with Sweden in Altmark	**1634** Władysław IV's victory over Russia, and peace in Polanów	**165** Beginning of the Swedis Delug
1600		**1620**		**1640**
1601 Outbreak of Northern War with Sweden		**1620** Battle against the Turks and Tartars at Cecora	**1632** Death of Zygmunt III Vasa	**1648** Death of Władysław IV, start of the Chmielnicki Uprising in the Ukraine

Zygmunt III Vasa

Baroque Monstrance
This monstrance, at Pelplin Cathedral in Pomerania, dates from 1646.

Shrine of St Stanisław
Relics of the patron saint of Poland are preserved in a shrine that was installed in Wawel Cathedral between 1626 and 1629.

The cloister walls around the courtyard are painted with real and legendary ancestors of the Ossoliński family.

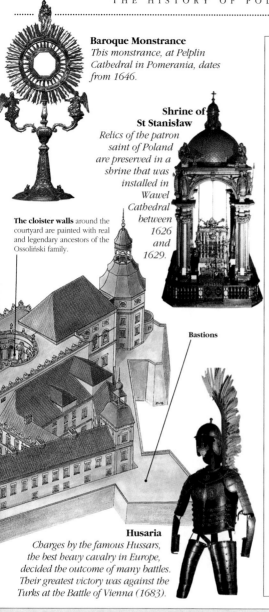

Bastions

Husaria
Charges by the famous Hussars, the best heavy cavalry in Europe, decided the outcome of many battles. Their greatest victory was against the Turks at the Battle of Vienna (1683).

17TH-CENTURY ARCHITECTURE

Many magnificent buildings in the late Mannerist and early Baroque styles were erected in the first half of the 17th century, during the reign of the Vasa dynasty. After the destruction wrought by the Swedish Deluge, there was no further artistic flowering until the reign of Jan III Sobieski. The early Baroque castles – for example, the Royal Palace in Warsaw *(see pp64–5)* – as well as numerous churches, of which the most impressive are the Jesuit churches in Cracow, Warsaw and Poznań, are all splendid examples of the architecture of this period.

The Bishops' Palace in Kielce (see p150) *is the best-preserved early Baroque residence.*

The Royal Chapel (see p239) *in Gdańsk, commissioned by Jan III Sobieski, was built by Tylman van Gameren and Andreas Schlüter in the Baroque style.*

1660 Peace treaty signed in Oliwa ends the Polish-Swedish War	**1667** Turks invade the southeastern borderlands	**1686** Signing of the Perpetual Peace with Russia	*Pair of cherubs*
	1660		1680	1700

1658 Polish Brethren exiled from Poland

1668 Abdication of Jan Kazimierz

1683 Jan III Sobieski's victory over the Turks at the Battle of Vienna

1699 Peace of Karłowice with Turkey

Mannerist window frame

Poland in the 18th Century

Order of Military Virtue

IN THE FIRST HALF of the 18th century, Poland was ruled by the Wettin dynasty of Saxony. Polish interests were gradually subordinated to those of neighbouring powers, and the election of Stanisław August Poniatowski as king, supported by the Tsarina Catherine the Great, sealed the nation's fate. Attempts to counteract Russian influence came to an end with the First Partition of Poland in 1772. The efforts of the patriotic faction and the achievements of the Four-Year Sejm changed little. The Second Partition followed in 1793, and when the uprising led by Tadeusz Kościuszko – the final attempt to save the country – was quashed, Poland lost its statehood for over 100 years.

REPUBLIC OF TWO NATIONS BEFORE THE PARTITIONS

▨ *Poland*   ▨ *Lithuania*

Rococo Statue from Lvov
In southeastern Poland, original altar statues by sculptors of the Lvov School can still be admired.

Stanisław August Poniatowski

Rococo Secretaire
This desk incorporates a clock cabinet and is decorated with painted panels depicting mythological scenes.

Portrait of Maria Leszczyńska
After the Polish king Stanisław Leszczyński lost the throne, his daughter Maria settled in Nancy and married Louis XV of France.

TIMELINE

1697 Coronation of August II, the Strong	**1717** "Dumb Sejm"	**1733** Election of August III	**1740** Opening of Collegium Nobilium, Warsaw
1704 Coronation of Stanisław Leszczyński, supported by the king of Sweden	**1721** End of Northern War		
1700	**1720**		**1740**
1700 Outbreak of Northern War	**1709** August II, the Strong returns to the throne	**1733** Stanisław Leszczyński is re-elected king	

Casing of a grenadier's cap

Tadeusz Kościuszko
This man fought in the American War of Independence and led the insurrection against the Russians in 1794.

August III
This Saxon king of the Wettin dynasty was an ardent lover of porcelain. His likeness was reproduced in Meissen.

18TH-CENTURY ARCHITECTURE

During the 18th century – the era of the late Baroque and Rococo – artists and architects from Saxony joined those who had already come to Poland from Italy. Many palaces, including Radziwiłł, were built in Warsaw and the provinces, such as Białystok *(see p290)*. Thanks to the patronage of Stanisław August Poniatowski, many Neo-Classical buildings were created, among them Łazienki in Warsaw.

The Palace on the Water
(see pp94–5) in Warsaw was the royal summer residence.

Hugo Kołłątaj

Prince Józef Poniatowski

Stanisław Małachowski, Speaker of the Sejm

CONSTITUTION OF 3 MAY

The Constitution of 3 May 1791 was a radical experiment in democracy and reform – the first such in Europe. It was, however, soon annulled as a result of the Federation of Targowica and the Russo-Polish war. Jan Matejko's painting shows members of the Sejm (parliament) marching on Warsaw Cathedral to swear allegiance.

Hugo Kołłątaj
A leading intellectual of the Polish Enlightenment, Kołłątaj collaborated on the Constitution of 3 May.

1764 Coronation of Stanisław August Poniatowski

1773 Convocation of National Education Commission

Coat of arms of Stanisław August Poniatowski

1794 Insurrection against the Russians

1795 Third Partition of Poland

1760

1780

1800

1756 Outbreak of the Seven-Year War

1772 First Partition of Poland

1788–1792 Deliberations of the Four-Year Sejm

1793 Second Partition of Poland

1791 Adoption of the Constitution of 3 May

Poland under the Partitions

Eclectic detail

Deprived of its independence, Poland became a territory for exploitation as though it were a colony. The hopes vested in Napoleon proved illusory. The transitory Grand Duchy of Warsaw lasted only eight years. The failure of the successive November and January insurrections (1831 and 1863) led to further restrictions by the tsarist rulers: landed property was confiscated and cultural and educational institutions dissolved. Many Poles tried to help the country from abroad. The collapse of the partitioning empires in World War I enabled Poland to regain its independence in 1918.

Republic of Two Nations Under the Partitions

☐ *Russian partition*

☐ *Austrian partition*

☐ *Prussian partition*

Patrol of Insurgents
This painting by Maksymilian Gierymski of around 1873 shows a scene from the January Insurrection. Several insurgents are patrolling the land.

Henryk Sienkiewicz's House in Oblęgorek
The small palace was given to the Nobel laureate Henryk Sienkiewicz in 1900 to mark the occasion of 25 years of his work as a writer.

Beggar waiting for alms

Emperor Franz Josef enjoying the loyalty of his subjects.

Timeline

1807 Grand Duchy of Warsaw established	**1831** Outbreak of the November Insurrection	**1845–1848** Construction of first Warsaw-Vienna railway line	**1846** Peasants' uprising
1795	**1820**		**1845**
1797 Formation of the Polish Legions in Italy	**1815** Dissolution of Grand Duchy of Warsaw at the Congress of Vienna		**1848** Uprising in Wielkopolska (Greater Poland)

Post-uprising mourning jewellery

Frédéric Chopin
This genius of a composer and pianist was born in Żelazowa Wola and left Poland for ever in 1830.

Stained-glass Window
The stained-glass windows designed by Stanisław Wyspiański for the Franciscan Church in Cracow are among the most beautiful works of Secessionist art in Poland.

THE GREAT EMIGRATION

In the 30 years following the failure of the November Insurrection, nearly 20,000 Poles left the country, the majority going to France. An important group of émigrés gathered around Prince Adam Czartoryski in Paris. Famous Poles in exile included the composer Frédéric Chopin and poets Adam Mickiewicz, Zygmunt Krasiński, Juliusz Słowacki and Cyprian Norwid.

Prince Adam Czartoryski, an exile in Paris, was considered the uncrowned king of Poland.

The inhabitants of Cracow greet the emperor

EMPEROR FRANZ JOSEF ENTERS CRACOW

Juliusz Kossak produced a series of paintings to commemorate the emperor's visit to Cracow in 1880. The city's inhabitants received him with great enthusiasm.

Prince Józef Poniatowski
Bertel Thorvaldsen designed this monument to Prince Józef Poniatowski, who died in 1813. Poniatowski was considered a Polish national hero.

1861 Founding of the National Sejm in Galicia

1873 Founding of the Academy of Sciences in Cracow

1903 Marie Curie (Maria Skłodowska-Curie) receives the Nobel Prize for Physics

1905 Henryk Sienkiewicz receives the Nobel Prize for Literature

1870

1895

1864 Final abolition of serfdom

1863 Start of the January Insurrection

Secessionist wall painting

1915 Russian troops leave Warsaw

Poland from 1918 to 1945

Eagle – emblem of the reborn Poland

$\mathbf{P}$OLAND REGAINED ITS independence in 1918, but for several years afterwards battles raged over its borders. In 1920, independence was again threatened by the Red Army. Despite domestic conflicts, Poland made considerable economic progress. The territories of the three areas previously held by Russia, Austria and Prussia were consolidated. The country's brief period of independence ended in 1939 with the German and Soviet invasions. Poland was occupied and its population persecuted, terrorized and partially exterminated. About 7 million Poles were killed, including 3 million Polish Jews *(see p160)*. An underground state operated, with the Home Army answering to the government in exile. Polish soldiers fought the Germans on all fronts.

POLAND IN 1938

▨ *Polish territory*

Volunteers fighting alongside the soldiers

Gdynia
Although Poland gained access to the sea, it had no port. Work on the construction of a new port at Gdynia began in 1922.

Interior of the Silesian Sejm
The industrialized region of Silesia had its own parliament in the interwar years, a sign of its importance.

MIRACLE ON THE VISTULA
This was the name given to Marshal Józef Piłsudski's victory at the Battle of Warsaw on 13–16 August 1920, which halted the Soviet march westwards and shattered the Bolshevik hope of a proletarian revolution throughout Europe.

TIMELINE

1918 Uprising against the Germans in Greater Poland. Warsaw is liberated from German occupation

1919 Start of the first Silesian uprising

1920 Miracle on the Vistula. Second Silesian uprising

1921 Germano-Polish plebiscite in Upper Silesia. Third Silesian uprising

1922 Murder of the president, Gabriel Narutowicz

1924 Złoty introduced to replace German Mark

1925 Start of the Germano-Polish trade war

1926 May Coup

1929 Start of the Great Depression

1915	1920	1925	1930

Magazine cover featuring the National Universal Exhibition in Poznań

Jósef Piłsudski

Jósef Piłsudski led the legions which were set up in the Austrian sector then dispersed. In 1918 he became the first leader of an independent Poland.

Plaque to the Victims of Execution

One of many plaques in Warsaw marking places of execution during World War II.

WARSAW UPRISING

On 1 August 1944 the underground Home Army (Armia Krajowa) launched an uprising in Warsaw against the occupying Germans. Its aim was to liberate the capital before the arrival of the Red Army. The Russians were waiting on the left bank of the river, allowing the Germans to suppress the outburst. The uprising lasted over two months and led to the complete destruction of the city as well as the loss of many lives.

In his film **Kanał**, *the director Andrzej Wajda showed the insurgents struggling through sewers beneath German-occupied districts of Warsaw.*

Father Ignacy Skorupka leads soldiers into attack

Bolshevik soldiers flee the battlefield

Hanka Ordonówna

She was one of the most popular actresses between the wars.

Monument to Those Murdered in the East

This monument commemorates all the Poles who were killed or deported after the Soviet invasion in 1939.

1935 Death of Marshal Piłsudski	1936 Start of the construction of the Central Industrial Region	1938 Poland annexes territory to the west of the River Olza		1943 Ghetto Uprising, Warsaw	*Occupying forces demolish the statue of Adam Mickiewicz*
		1942 Home Army formed. Anders' army evacuated from USSR			

1935	1940	1945
1939 Outbreak of World War II. German troops enter Poland, followed by Soviet forces. The Polish army is defeated and the country occupied	1940 The Russians murder Polish officers who were taken prisoner in Katyń	1944 Polish soldiers take the monastery at Monte Cassino, Italy. Warsaw Uprising. Formation of a pro-Soviet, Communist government in Lublin

Modern Poland

IN 1945 THE ALLIES agreed that Poland should be included in the Soviet zone of influence. The Big Three (Britain, the USA and Russia) also decided to alter Poland's borders. After rigged elections in 1947, the Communists took complete control. Despite successes in rebuilding the country, the socialist economy proved ineffective. The formation of Solidarity (Solidarność) in 1980 accelerated the pace of change, which was completed when Poland regained its freedom after the June 1989 elections.

1968 In March, conflicts occur between students and security forces. The authorities provoke incidents of an anti-Semitic and anti-intellectual nature

1945 After the terrible devastation of the war, the country is hauled out of the ruins by the effort of the whole nation

1947 Communists falsify the results of elections to the Sejm (parliament)

1955 30,000 delegates from 114 countries take part in the World Festival of Youth in Warsaw. This is the first time that the Iron Curtain has been briefly lifted

1966 Celebrations marking the millennium of Christianity in Poland, organized separately by Church and State

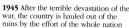

1953 Height of the persecution of the Catholic Church, trial of priests of the metropolitan curia of Cracow; Cardinal Stefan Wyszyński, Primate of Poland, is arrested

1958 First International Jazz Jamboree in Warsaw

1968 Polish forces take part in the armed intervention in Czechoslovakia

1946 Rigged referendum on abolishing the Senate, introducing agricultural reforms, nationalizing industry and the western border

1957 Premiere of *Kanał*, directed by Andrzej Wajda, one of the first films of the Polish School

1945 End of World War II

1956 In June, a workers' revolt in Poznań is bloodily suppressed. In October, after more demonstrations by students and workers, Soviet intervention is threatened. Władysław Gomułka becomes First Secretary of the Central Committee of the Polish United Workers' Party

1970 Bloody suppression of a strike and workers' demonstrations on the coast. Edward Gierek becomes First Secretary of the Central Committee of the Polish United Workers' Party

1979 First visit of John Paul II, the "Polish Pope", to his homeland. Both a religious and a political event, it rekindles Polish hopes of regaining freedom

1990 Lech Wałęsa is elected president of Poland

1999 Poland joins NATO

1980 Agreements signed in Gdańsk on 31 August end the strikes and allow the formation of the first Independent Autonomous Trades Unions. Lech Wałęsa becomes their leader

1997 The worst flood in a century devastates large areas of southern Poland

1981 Under the leadership of General Wojciech Jaruzelski, the Communist authorities introduce martial law. Solidarity goes underground

1990 Official end of the Polish People's Republic, adoption of Leszek Balcerowicz's radical market reforms

975	1980	1985	1990	1995	2000

975	1980	1985	1990	1995	2000

1976 Demonstrations against price rises, by workers in Radom and Ursus, are quashed. The opposition forms the Workers' Defence Committee. At the 21st Olympics in Montreal, Irena Kirszenstein-Szewińska wins gold for track and field sports for the third time

1989 At round-table talks, the opposition negotiates with the authorities about legalizing Solidarity and calling an election, in which the "civic society" then wins a landslide victory

2000 Cracow is European City of Culture

1997 On a visit to Warsaw, US president Bill Clinton announces that Poland is to join NATO

1984 Assassination of Father Jerzy Popiełuszko, Solidarity's pastor

The Rulers of Poland

A T THE TIME of its formation in 966, the Polish nation was ruled by the Piast dynasty. Bolesław the Brave, son of Mieszko I, was the first king of Poland. During the Period of Disunity from 1138, rulers bore only the title of prince. The first prince to be crowned king of Poland was Władysław I, the Elbow-High. After the death of Kazimierz the Great, the Polish crown passed to Louis of Hungary of the Angevin dynasty. The marriage of his daughter Jadwiga to the Lithuanian prince Jagiełło in 1384 established the Jagiellonian dynasty. From 1572 the Republic of Two Nations was ruled by elective kings with no hereditary rights. The last king was Stanisław August Poniatowski.

1386–1434
Władysław II
Jagiełło

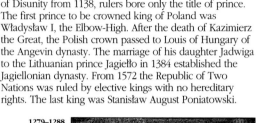

1279–1288
Leszek the
Black

1288–1290 Henry IV,
the Good

1290–1291
Przemysł II

1291–1305
Wacław II of Boh-
emia (from 1300)

1305–1306
Wacław III
of Bohemia

1079–1102 Władysław Herman

1229–1232 and **1241–1243**
Konrad I Mazowiecki

1058–1079 Bolesław II

1202 and **1228–1229**
Władysław III,
Spindleshanks

1025–1034 Mieszko II

1333–1370
Kazimierz III,
the Great

900	1000	1100	1200	1300	1400
PIAST DYNASTY		**PERIOD OF DISUNITY**			**JAGIELLONIA**
900	1000	1100	1200	1300	1400

1102–1107
Zbigniew
and
Bolesław III

1107–1138
Bolesław III

1306–1333
Władysław
I, the
Elbow-High

1370–1382
Louis of Hungary

1138–1146
Władysław II,
the Exile

1384–1399
Jadwiga

1146–1173
Bolesław IV,
the Curly

1434–1444 Władysław III
of Varna

1173–1177 and
1194–1202 Mieszko III,
the Elder

1447–1492 Kazimierz IV,
the Jagiellonian

1492–1501 Jan I Olbra

1177–1194 Kazimierz
II, the Just

1194–1210
and **1211–1227**
Leszek the White

c.960–992
Mieszko I
992–1025
Bolesław the
Brave (Bolesław
Chrobry),
crowned 1025

1031 Duke
Bezprym

1210–1211 Mieszko the Stumbler

1232–1238 Henry the Bearded

1238–1241 Henry the Pious

1034–1058
Kazimierz
the Restorer

1243–1279 Bolesław
V, the Bashful

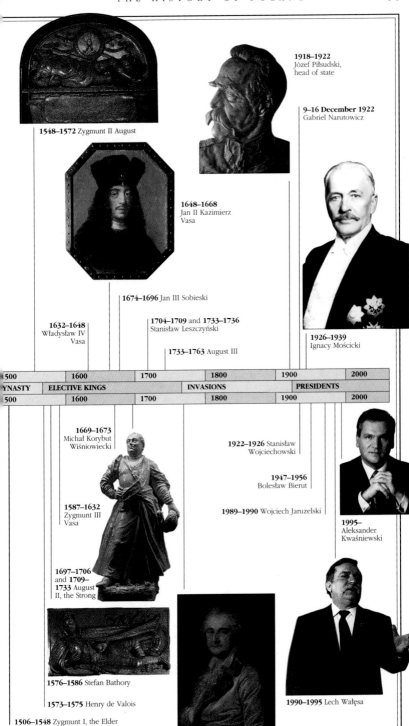

1548–1572 Zygmunt II August

1918–1922
Józef Piłsudski,
head of state

9–16 December 1922
Gabriel Narutowicz

1648–1668
Jan II Kazimierz
Vasa

1674–1696 Jan III Sobieski

1704–1709 and **1733–1736**
Stanisław Leszczyński

1632–1648
Władysław IV
Vasa

1733–1763 August III

1926–1939
Ignacy Mościcki

500	1600	1700	1800	1900	2000
YNASTY	ELECTIVE KINGS		INVASIONS	PRESIDENTS	
500	1600	1700	1800	1900	2000

1669–1673
Michał Korybut
Wiśniowiecki

1922–1926 Stanisław
Wojciechowski

1947–1956
Bolesław Bierut

1989–1990 Wojciech Jaruzelski

1587–1632
Zygmunt III
Vasa

1995–
Aleksander
Kwaśniewski

1697–1706
and **1709–**
1733 August
II, the Strong

1576–1586 Stefan Bathory

1573–1575 Henry de Valois

1506–1548 Zygmunt I, the Elder

1501–1506 Alexander the Jagiellonian

1990–1995 Lech Wałęsa

1764–1795 Stanisław August
Poniatowski

WARSAW AREA
BY AREA

Warsaw at a Glance

MOST PLACES OF INTEREST are located in the centre of Warsaw. This area not only forms the geographical heart of the city, but is also Warsaw's largest municipality. It is made up of seven smaller districts, Śródmieście being the central one. In the pages that follow, however, Warsaw is divided into three parts: the Old and New Towns, the Royal Route and the City Centre. The most interesting historical features of Warsaw are located along the Royal Route (Trakt Królewski), a series of roads linking the Old Town (Stare Miasto) and the Royal Castle (Zamek Królewski) with the Water Palace (Łazienki) and Wilanów, the palace of Jan III Sobieski, which stands just outside the city.

The Old Town Square, surrounded by town houses rebuilt after wartime destruction, is one of the most beautiful features of Warsaw. It teems with tourists and local people throughout the year. A statue of the Mermaid, symbol of Warsaw, was recently erected in the centre of the square.

The Palace of Culture is still the tallest building in Warsaw, despite the ongoing construction of skyscrapers in the city. The 30th floor has a viewing terrace as well as a multimedia tourist centre.

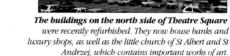

The buildings on the north side of Theatre Square were recently refurbished. They now house banks and luxury shops, as well as the little church of St Albert and St Andrzej, which contains important works of art.

0 m   500

0 yds   500

◁ **Royal Castle Square with Zygmunt's Column**

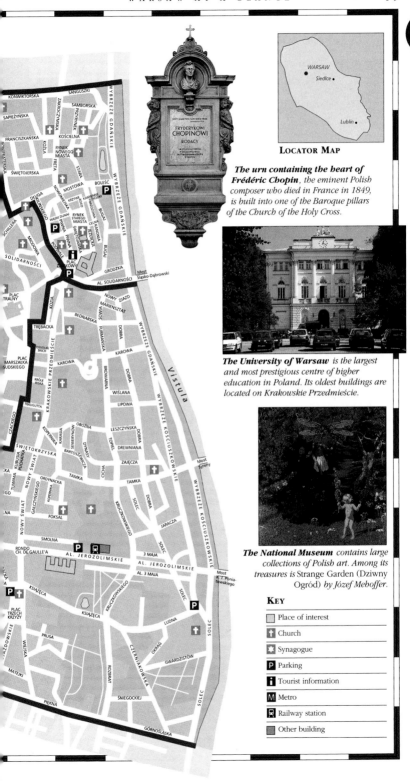

LOCATOR MAP

The urn containing the heart of
Frédéric Chopin, the eminent Polish
composer who died in France in 1849,
is built into one of the Baroque pillars
of the Church of the Holy Cross.

The University of Warsaw is the largest
and most prestigious centre of higher
education in Poland. Its oldest buildings are
located on Krakowskie Przedmieście.

The National Museum contains large
collections of Polish art. Among its
treasures is Strange Garden (Dziwny
Ogród) by Józef Mehoffer.

KEY

	Place of interest
✝	Church
✡	Synagogue
P	Parking
i	Tourist information
M	Metro
R	Railway station
	Other building

THE OLD AND NEW TOWNS

Traditional house decoration

HE OLD TOWN (Stare Miasto), partially surrounded by medieval walls, is the oldest district in Warsaw. It was founded at the turn of the 13th and 14th centuries, growing up around the castle of the Mazovian princes. Its medieval urban layout survives to this day. The pride of the Old Town is the market square with colourful town houses. Also of major interest are the Cathedral of St John and the Royal Castle, which was destroyed by German forces in 1944 and rebuilt between 1971 and 1984. Next to the Old Town is the more recent New Town (Nowe Miasto), which became a separate urban entity in 1408. The reconstruction of the Old Town and New Town, almost completely destroyed during the war, was an undertaking on a scale unprecedented in the whole of Europe. Today, these two districts are the most popular tourist attractions in Warsaw. The Old Town pulsates with life until late evening. There are many interesting little streets and an abundance of cafés, good restaurants and antique shops.

SIGHTS AT A GLANCE

Churches
Cathedral of St John p66 ❸
Church of the Holy Spirit ❽
Church of the Visitation of the Virgin Mary ⓯
Church of St Jacek ⓫
Church of St Kazimierz ⓮
Church of St Martin ❺
Jesuit Church ❹

Historic Streets and Squares
New Town Square ⓭
Old Town Square ❻
Ulica Freta ⓬

Historic Buildings and Monuments
The Barbican and City Walls ❼
Monument to the 1944 Warsaw Uprising ❿
Raczyński Palace ❾
Royal Castle pp64–5 ❷
Zygmunt's Column ❶

GETTING THERE
Both Old and New Towns are pedestrianized. The nearest bus stops to the Old Town are on Plac Zamkowy for buses E-1, E-3, 116, 122, 160, 174, 175, 180, 195, 303, 460, 495, 503, or at the beginning of the W-Z Route tunnel for trams 4, 13, 26, 32, 43 and 46 or buses 125, 170, 190 and 307. It is best to walk from the Old to the New Town. Alternatively, you can take buses 116, 122, 174, 175, 180, 195 and get off at Plac Krasińskiego or Ulica Bonifraterska.

KEY

▨	Street-by-Street map *pp62–3*
▨	Street-by-Street map *pp68–9*
🅿	Parking
ℹ	Tourist information

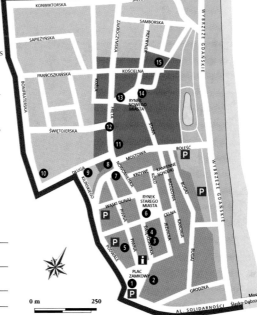

0 m   250

0 yds   250

◁ **The tower of the Church of St Martin overlooking the passage between Ulica Piwna and Ulica Świętojańska**

The Old Town

THE OLD TOWN SQUARE (Rynek Starego Miasta) is surrounded on all sides by town houses, rebuilt after World War II with great devotion. Today it is one of the most attractive places in Warsaw. From spring to autumn it is filled with café tables, and also becomes an open-air gallery of contemporary art. On the square and in neighbouring streets, especially Piwna and Jezuicka, there are numerous restaurants and bars that are reputed to be the best in Warsaw. The whole of the Old Town is not only a tourist attraction but also a favourite place for local people, who go to walk there, and for lovers to meet.

Church of St Martin
This striking modern cruci-fix incorporates a fragment of a figure of Christ that was burned during the 1944 Warsaw Uprising **5**

★ Cathedral of St John
After suffering damage during World War II, the cathedral was rebuilt in the Gothic style **3**

Jesuit Church
The Baroque-Mannerist sanctuary of Our Lady of Mercy, patron saint of Warsaw, was rebuilt after World War II **4**

Zygmunt's Column
This is the oldest secular monument in Warsaw **1**

★ Royal Castle (Zamek Królewski)
This former royal residence, rebuilt in the 1970s, is today the symbol of Polish independence **2**

PODWALE

PIEKARSKA

PIWNA

PLAC ZAMKOWY

ŚWIĘTOJAŃSKA

Palace Under the Tin Roof
This was the first house in Warsaw to have a tin, rather than tiled, roof.

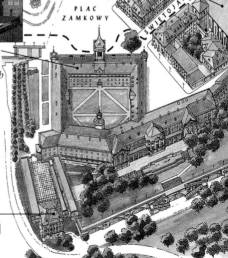

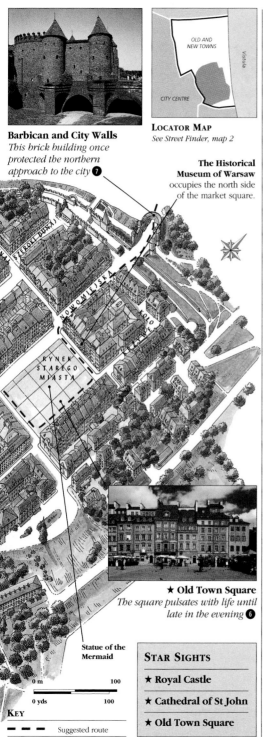

Barbican and City Walls
This brick building once protected the northern approach to the city ❼

LOCATOR MAP
See Street Finder, map 2

The Historical Museum of Warsaw occupies the north side of the market square.

Statue of Zygmunt III Vasa at the top of Zygmunt's Column

Zygmunt's Column ❶

Plac Zamkowy **Map** 2 D3. 🚌 *E-1, E-3, 116, 122, 125, 160, 170, 174, 175, 180, 190, 192, 195, 303, 307, 460, 495, 503.* 🚊 *4, 13, 26, 32, 43, 46.*

ZYGMUNT'S COLUMN, in the centre of Plac Zamkowy, is the oldest secular statue in Warsaw. It was erected in 1644 by Zygmunt III's son Władysław IV. The monument, which stands 22 m (72 ft) high, consists of a Corinthian granite column supported on a tall plinth and topped with a bronze statue of the ruler, who is depicted with a cross in his left hand and a sword in his right. The figure is the work of Clemente Molli, and the whole monument was designed by Augustyn Locci the Elder and Constantino Tencalla, two Italian architects working for the king. This monument, unusual in European terms, glorifies the secular ruler in a manner which had until then been reserved for saints and other religious subjects. Despite repeated damage and repairs, the statue retains its original appearance. The column on which it stands, however, has already been replaced twice. An older, fractured shaft can be seen on the terrace near the south façade of the Palace Under the Tin Roof.

★ **Old Town Square**
The square pulsates with life until late in the evening ❻

Statue of the Mermaid

0 m		100
0 yds		100

KEY

▬ ▬ ▬ Suggested route

STAR SIGHTS

★ **Royal Castle**

★ **Cathedral of St John**

★ **Old Town Square**

Royal Castle ❷

Tabletop from 1777

T HE DECISION to build the Royal Castle (Zamek Królewski) was made when Zygmunt III Vasa moved the capital from Cracow to Warsaw in 1596. It was built in the early Baroque style by the Italian architects Giovanni Trevano, Giacomo Rodondo and Matteo Castelli between 1598 and 1619, incorporating the earlier castle of the Mazovian princes. Successive rulers remodelled the castle many times. The late Baroque façade overlooking the River Vistula dates from the time of August III, and the splendid interiors from that of Stanisław August. Completely destroyed by the Germans during World War II, the castle was reconstructed from 1971 to 1988.

★ Ballroom
Decorated with 17 pairs of golden columns, the ballroom is one of the castle's most elaborate interiors.

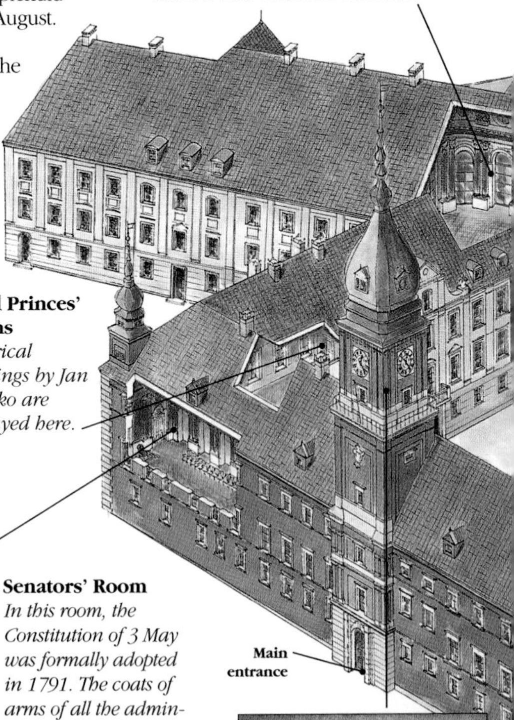

Royal Princes' Rooms
Historical paintings by Jan Matejko are displayed here.

Senators' Room
In this room, the Constitution of 3 May was formally adopted in 1791. The coats of arms of all the administrative regions and territories of the Republic are depicted on the walls. A reconstructed royal throne is also on show.

Main entrance

Zygmunt Tower
This tower, 60 m (197 ft) high, was built in 1619. It is crowned by a cupola with a spire. It is also known as the Clock Tower (Zegarowa), since a clock was installed in 1622.

STAR FEATURES

★ Ballroom

★ Marble Room

★ Canaletto Room

★ Marble Room
The interior dates from the time of
Władysław IV. The magnificent portraits of
Polish rulers by Marcello Bacciarelli are the
only later additions.

VISITORS' CHECKLIST

Plac Zamkowy 4. **Map** 2 D3.
((0 22) 657 21 70.
Reservations 9am–2pm Tue–Fri.
((0 22) 657 23 38. **FAX** (0 22)
657 22 71. ⊟ E-1, E-2, 116,
122, 125, 160, 170, 174, 175,
180, 190, 192, 195, 303, 307,
460, 495, 503. ⊟ 4, 13, 26, 32,
43, 46. ☐ 10am–4pm
Wed–Sat, 11am–4pm Sun.
Royal and Grand Apartments
☐ 15 Apr–Sep; 10am–6pm
Mon–Sat, 11am–6pm Sun. ● 1
Jan, Easter Sat & Sun, 1 May,
Corpus Christi, 1 Nov, 24, 25, 31
Dec. 🎫 (free on Sun except for
Royal and Grand Apartments).
🚻 👬 ⌨ except Sun. 🚫 no
flash photography. 🅿 ⌂

The Lanckoroński Gallery on the
second floor contains two paintings
by Rembrandt: *Portrait of a Young
Woman* and *Scholar at his Desk*.

Knights' Hall
The finest piece in this
beautiful interior is the
Neo-Classical sculpture
of Chronos by le Brun
and Monaldi.

**Apartment of Prince Stanisław
Poniatowski**
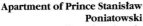
The Rococo panelling, thought to be
by the French cabinet-maker Juste-
Aurèle Meissonier, was taken from
the former Tarnowski Palace.

★ Canaletto Room

The walls of this room are decorated
with scenes of Warsaw by Canaletto,
the famous Venetian painter who was
one of the most commercially
successful artists of his day.

Cathedral of St John ❸

THE CATHEDRAL OF ST JOHN started life as a parish church at the beginning of the 15th century, only acquiring cathedral status in 1798. Over the years, successive rulers endowed it with new chapels and other elements. Important ceremonies have taken place here, including the coronation of Stanisław August Poniatowski in 1764 and the oath of allegiance to the Constitution of 3 May in 1791. Many famous Poles are buried in the cathedral, among them the Polish primate, Cardinal Stefan Wyszyński. Having been seriously damaged in World War II, the cathedral was rebuilt; its new façade was designed by Jan Zachwatowicz in the spirit of Mazovian Gothic architecture.

VISITORS' CHECKLIST

ul. Świętojańska 8. **Map** 2 D3.
(0 22) 831 02 89. E-1, E-3,116,
122, 160, 170, 175, 180, 195,
460, 503. 4, 13, 26, 32, 43, 46
10am–1pm, 3–6pm Mon–Fri,
10am–1pm Sat, 2–6pm Sun.
Crypt 10am–1pm, 3–6pm
Mon–Sat, 3–5pm Sun.

Narutowicz Crypt
Gabriel Narutowicz, first president of the Polish Republic, is interred in the cathedral with other distinguished Poles.

Choir Stalls
The choir stalls are a copy of those donated as a votive offering after Poland's victory in 1683 at the Battle of Vienna.

Main entrance

Baryczkowski Crucifix
This crucifix, famed for its miraculous powers, dates from the start of the 16th century and contains natural human hair.

Małakowski Family Tomb
This monument, carved in white marble, is based on a design by the Danish Neo-Classical sculptor Bertel Thorvaldsen.

Jesuit Church ❹

ul. Świętojańska 10. **Map** 2 D3.
Ⓒ (0 22) 831 16 75. 🚍 🚋 same as
Cathedral (p66).

THIS MANNERIST-BAROQUE
church was built for the
Jesuit order between 1609 and
1629, at the same time as the
monastery. Although it had a
somewhat chequered history, it
survived without major
changes until 1944, when it
was almost completely
destroyed. When it was rebuilt
after World War II, the church's
somewhat unusual architecture
was restored on the basis of
the original plans, which had
survived. Located in a narrow
space, it has a unique layout;
especially original is the way
in which the chancel is
flooded by light falling from
the lantern in the elliptical
dome over the apse. The
crypt, which contains a stonecutter's workshop, is in the
space once occupied by the
basements of the Gothic town
houses that stood on the site.

**Jesuit church, dedicated to the
Merciful Mother of God**

Church of
St Martin ❺

ul. Piwna 9/11. **Map** 2 D3.
Ⓒ (0 22) 831 02 21. 🚍 🚋 same as
Cathedral (p66).

THE EXISTING post-Augustan
church is the result of two
major reconstructions in the
Baroque style, carried out in
the years 1631–6 and in the
first half of the 18th century.
The latter phase of rebuilding
took place under the direction

of the architect Karol Bay, who
designed the interesting
undulating façade. The late
Baroque decoration of the
interior was destroyed in 1944.
Only a partially burned crucifix
survived. After the war, the
interior was minutely restored
to a design by Sister Alma
Skrzydlewska and the crucifix
incorporated into a modern
design. In the 1980s, the
church was a meeting place for
the political opposition to the
Communist government.

Old Town
Square ❻

Map 2 D3. 🚍 🚋 same as Cathedral
(p66). **Historical Museum of Warsaw**
Ⓒ (0 22) 635 16 25. 🕐 11 am–6pm
Tue, Thu, 10am–3:30pm Wed, Fri,
10:30am–4:30pm Sat–Sun. 🎟 (free
on Sun). **Museum of Literature**
Ⓒ (0 22) 831 76 91. 🕐 10am–3pm
Mon, Tue, Fri, 11am–6pm Wed, Thu,
11am–5pm Sun. 🎟 (free on Thu).

UNTIL THE END of the 18th
century, this rectangular
market square, 90 m (295 ft) by
73 m (240 ft), was the most
important place in Warsaw.
The houses around the square
were built by the most affluent
members of the community.
Most of them date from the
17th century, and it is these
that give the square its period
character. In the centre there
was once a town hall, a weigh
house and stalls, all
demolished in 1817. In their
place now stands a statue of
the Mermaid *(Syrenka)*.

Each row of houses bears the
name of one of the people
actively involved in the Four-
Year Sejm. On the north
side, Dekerta – named after
Jan Dekert, mayor of
Warsaw in the 18th century
– all the

houses are interconnected.
They are now occupied by the
**Historical Museum of
Warsaw**, which displays
typical interiors of
townspeople's homes and
craftsmen's workshops.

**The Barbican, standing on the site
of the former outer city gate**

The Barbican and
City Walls ❼

ul. Nowomiejska. **Map** 2 D2.

WARSAW IS ONE of the few
European capitals where
a large portion of the old city
wall survives. Construction of
the wall began in the first half
of the 14th century and
continued in phases up to the
mid-16th century. A double
circumvallation, reinforced
with fortresses and towers,
encircled the town. The
earliest part of the fortifications
is the Barbican, erected around
1548 by Gianbattista of Venice.
It was built on the site of an
earlier outer gate and was
intended to defend the
Nowomiejska Gate (Brama
Nowomiejska). The northern
part of this defensive building,
in the form of a dungeon
reinforced by four semicircular
towers, survived as the
external wall of a town house.
After World War II, parts of the
wall were rebuilt and the
Barbican, which had ceased to
exist for a long period, was
restored to its full scale.

Old Town Square, a favourite place both for local people and tourists

New Town

THE NEW TOWN took shape at the beginning of the 15th century along the route leading from Old Warsaw to Zakroczym. Of interest here are the Pauline, Franciscan, Dominican and Redemptorist churches and the Church of the Holy Sacrament, which were all rebuilt after World War II, and the colourful reconstructed town houses. Ulica Mostowa, the steepest street in Warsaw, leads up to the fortress that defended one of the longest bridges in 16th-century Europe.

★ **New Town Square**
A town hall once stood in the centre of this irregularly shaped square ⑬

Ulica Freta
This is the main thoroughfare in New Town. Freta means an uncultivated field or suburb ⑫

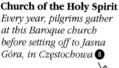

Church of the Holy Spirit
Every year, pilgrims gather at this Baroque church before setting off to Jasna Góra, in Częstochowa ⑧

★ **Church of St Jacek**
A feature of the unusually elongated interior is the 17th-century mausoleum of the Kotowski family ⑪

★ **Church of St Kazimierz**
This beautiful church is connected to the Convent of the Order of the Holy Sacrament ⑭

The Old Powder Magazine was once the bridge gate.

LOCATOR MAP
See Street Finder, map 2

0 m   100
0 yds   100

Church of the Visitation of the Virgin Mary
The oldest surviving church in New Town, Princess Anna of Mazovia funded its construction in the early 15th century ⓻

STAR SIGHTS

★ **Church of St Jacek**

★ **Church of St Kazimierz**

★ **New Town Square**

KEY

- - -   Suggested route

Church of the Holy Spirit ⓼

ul. Nowomiejska 23. **Map** 2 D2.
(*(0 22) 831 45 75*. 🚌 *116, 122, 174, 175, 180, 195, 303.*

THE LITTLE wooden Church of the Holy Spirit (Kościół św. Ducha) already existed in the 14th century. Repeatedly extended, it was burned down during the Swedish invasion in 1655. As the townspeople could not afford to rebuild the church, King Jan Kazimierz donated the site to the Pauline fathers from Częstochowa, who were renowned for defending their monastery at Jasna Góra (*see pp156–7*). In return, and at their own expense, the monks built a wall that enclosed the church and the monastery within Warsaw's defences.

The present church was built in 1707–17, based on a design by the architect Józef Piola. The work was directed by Józef Szymon Bellotti and later Karol Ceroni. The interior was completed in 1725.

Rebuilt after war damage, the church is known today – as it has been since 1711 – as the main starting point for pilgrimages to the shrine of the Virgin Mary at Jasna Góra.

In Ulica Długa, a small Neo-Classical house, just large enough for a newspaper kiosk, abuts the church. It was built at the beginning of the 19th century on the smallest plot in Warsaw; it occupies only a few square metres and has its own registry number.

Church of the Holy Spirit, facing down Ulica Mostowa

Façade of Raczyński Palace, which today is the Old Records Archive

Raczyński Palace ⓽

ul. Długa 7. **Map** 2 D2.
(*(0 22) 635 45 32.* 🚌 *116, 122, 174, 175, 180, 195, 303.*

RACZYNSKI PALACE (Pałac Raczyńskich), rebuilt in 1786 to a design by the royal architect Jan Chrystian Kamsetzer, houses the Old Records Archive. The most beautiful feature of this former residence is the early Neo-Classical ballroom – damaged in the war but restored afterwards – which is decorated with stuccowork and allegorical paintings on the theme of Justice.

The subject of the paintings was manifestly at odds with the sentiments of the residence's owner, Kazimierz Raczyński, who held high office in the royal court and was considered a traitor to his country by his contemporaries. In the 19th century, the palace was the seat of the Government Justice Commission, and in the interwar period, of the Ministry of Justice.

Particularly tragic events occurred here during World War II. Bullet marks in the wall of the building are evidence of the street execution of 50 local inhabitants who were arrested at random on 24 January 1944. But the worst crimes were committed here during the Warsaw Uprising. On 13 August 1944 a tank-trap exploded, killing some 80 insurgents, and on 2 September the Nazi SS killed several hundred injured people in the building, which was being used as a hospital.

Monument to the 1944 Warsaw Uprising

Monument to the 1944 Warsaw Uprising ⑩

pl. Krasińskich. **Map** 1 C2. 🚌 *116, 122, 174, 175, 180, 195, 303.*

THIS MONUMENT, unveiled in 1989, commemorates the heroes of the historic Warsaw Uprising. It consists of sculptures by Wincenty Kućma placed in an architect-ural setting by Jacek Budyń. The sculptures represent soldiers – one group defending the barricades, the other going down into the sewers. (The insurgents used the sewer system to move around Warsaw during the uprising.) The entrance to one such sewer is still to be found near the monument.

It was in front of this monument, during the celebrations marking the 50th anniversary of the uprising, that the President of the Federal Republic of Germany, Richard Herzog, apologized to the Polish nation for the unleashing of World War II by the Third Reich and the bloody suppression of the Warsaw Uprising.

Church of St Jacek ⑪

ul. Freta 8/10. **Map** 2 D2. 📞 *(0 22) 635 47 00.* 🚌 *116, 122, 174, 175, 180, 195, 303.*

AT THE BEGINNING of the 17th century, while the Jesuits were building a Baroque church in Old Town, the Dominicans started work on a Gothic chancel for the Church of St Jacek (Kościół św Jacka). They returned to the Gothic style partly because of the conservatism of Mazovian buildings and partly in an attempt to endow the church with the appearance of age, so as to create an illusion of the age-old traditions of the order – which had in fact only been set up in Warsaw in 1603. When work was interrupted by a plague that raged in Warsaw in 1625, the few remaining monks listened to confessions and gave communion through openings drilled in the doors. The work

Church of St Jacek from Ulica Freta

was completed in 1639. Next to it was erected the largest monastery in Warsaw.

Interesting features inside the church, rebuilt after World War II, include the beautiful vaulting above the aisles, the Gothic chancel, decorated with stuccowork of the Lublin type, and the 17th-century tomb-stones shattered in 1944. The Baroque tomb of Adam and Małgorzata Kotowski, by the Dutch architect Tylman van Gameren, is also noteworthy. The domed chapel in which it stands is decorated with portraits, painted on tin plate, of the donors, who became prosperous and were ennobled despite their humble origins.

Ulica Freta ⑫

Map 2 D2. 🚌 *116, 122, 174, 175, 180, 195, 303.* **Maria Skłodowska-Curie Museum** 📞 *(0 22) 831 80 92.* ⏰ *10am–4pm Tue–Sat, 10am–2pm Sun.* 🖼 ✔

THE MAIN ROAD in the New Town, Ulica Freta developed along a section of the old route leading from Old Warsaw to Zakroczym. At the end of the 14th century, buildings began to appear along it, and in the 15th century it came within the precincts of New Warsaw (Nowa Warszawa).

Several good antique shops and cafés are on this street. The house at No. 15, where Marie Curie was born, is now a museum dedicated to her and her achievements. Films about her life and the history of science are presented to groups on request.

MARIA SKŁODOWSKA-CURIE (1867–1934)

Maria Skłodowska (Marie Curie) was 24 years old when she left Warsaw to study in Paris. Within a decade she had become famous as the co-discoverer of radioactivity. Together with her husband, Pierre Curie, she discovered the elements radium and polonium. She was awarded the Nobel Prize twice: the first time in 1903, when she won the prize for physics jointly with her husband – becoming the first woman Nobel laureate – and the second in 1911 for chemistry.

The triangular-shaped New Town Square

New Town Square ⓭

Map 2 D2. 🚌 *116, 122, 174, 175, 180, 195, 303.*

THE HEART OF the New Town is the market square (Rynek Nowego Miasta). Once rectangular, it acquired its odd triangular shape after reconstruction. When the town hall, which stood in the centre of the square, was demolished in 1818, a splendid view of the Baroque dome which crowns the Church of St Kazimierz was opened up. Destroyed in 1944, the church was rebuilt in a manner reminiscent of the 18th century, though not exactly replicating the original. The façades of many buildings around the square are covered with Socialist Realist murals. A charming 19th-century well is to be found near Ulica Freta.

Church of St Kazimierz ⓮

Rynek Nowego Miasta 2. Map 2 D2. 🕿 *(0 22) 635 71 13.* 🚌 *116, 122, 174, 175, 180, 195, 303.* **Convent** ● *Church open to visitors.*

THE CHURCH AND Convent of the Order of the Holy Sacrament, designed by Tylman van Gameren, was built in 1688–92 by King Jan III Sobieski and Queen Maria Kazimiera. The remarkable domed building is distinguished by its clear Baroque architecture of classic proportions. The interior, which was damaged in the war, has since been renovated. Previously polychrome, it is now white. The most beautiful reconstructed feature is the tomb of Maria Karolina, Princesse de Bouillon, grand-daughter of Jan III Sobieski. It was installed in 1746 by Bishop Andrzej Załuski and Prince Michał Kazimierz Radziwiłł, a well-known reveller who once, unsuccess-fully, sought her hand in marriage. The tomb features a fractured shield and a crown falling into an abyss – ref-erences to the Sobieski coat of arms and the death of the last member of the royal line. At the rear of the convent a garden, unchanged since the 17th century, descends in tiers to the River Vistula below.

Tomb of Maria Karolina, Princesse de Bouillon

Church of the Visitation of the Virgin Mary ⓯

ul. Przyrynek 2. **Map** 2 D1. 🕿 *(0 22) 831 24 73.* 🚌 *175, 503.*

THE BRICK TOWER of the Church of the Visitation of the Virgin Mary (Kościół Nawiedzenia NMP) rises over the roofs of the houses on the bank of the River Vistula. This church is the oldest in the New Town. It was built at the beginning of the 15th century by the Mazovian princess, Anna, wife of Janusz I, the Elder, and is reputed to stand on the site of a pagan sacred spot.

Restoration carried out in the 19th century changed the building's appearance several times. Damaged, like so many other Polish buildings during World War II, it was subsequently rebuilt in the 15th-century Gothic style. The vaulting above the chancel was completed by medieval methods: that is, it was filled by hand, without the use of pre-fabricated moulds. In the cemetery next to the church there stands a modern statue of Walerian Łukasiński (1786–1868), founder of the National Patriotic Society.

From the terrace next to the church, there is a magnificent view of the Vistula valley.

Church of the Visitation of the Virgin Mary

THE ROYAL ROUTE

HE ROYAL ROUTE (Trakt Królewski) is so named because of the former royal residences that line it. It stretches from Belvedere Palace (Belweder), up to the Old Town, along Aleje Ujazdowskie, through Nowy Świat and on to Krakowskie Przedmieście. This part of Warsaw has been largely rebuilt after destruction suffered in World War II. On Aleje Ujazdowskie there are beautiful parks and little palaces surrounded by gardens, most of which now house embassies. The Neo-Classical Nowy

**Cardinal
Stefan Wyszyński**

Świat, its wide pavements decorated in summer with baskets of flowers, is lined with cafés and elegant shops. The most impressive buildings are on Krakowskie Przedmieście. This splendid location on the edge of the escarpment inspired powerful citizens to build large houses with gardens. Many churches and monasteries were also located here, as well as the president's residence and university buildings. In the street itself, there are statues of distinguished Poles. In summer, fêtes and bazaars are often organized along the Royal Route.

SIGHTS AT A GLANCE

Churches
Carmelite Church ③
Church of the Holy Cross ⑦
Church of St Anne ①
Church of the Visitation ⑤

Historic Buildings and Monuments
Gniński-Ostrogski Palace ⑨
Namiestnikowski Palace ④
Parliament ⑮
Staszic Palace ⑧
Statue of Adam Mickiewicz ②
University of Warsaw ⑥

Streets and Squares
Nowy Świat ⑩
Plac Trzech Krzyży ⑬
Aleje Ujazdowskie ⑭

Museums
National Museum pp80–81 ⑪
Polish Military Museum ⑫

GETTING THERE

You can get to the Royal Route by taking buses: 116, 122, 160, 174, 175, 180, 192, 195, 303, 460, 503, and on trams travelling along Aleje Jerozolimskie and the W-Z route.

KEY

Street-by-Street map *pp74–5*

P Parking

R Railway station

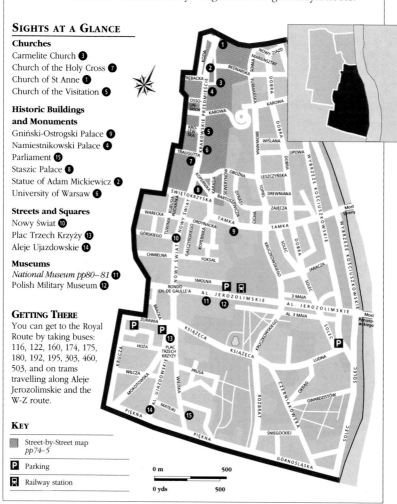

◁ *Mermaid (Syrena)*, a statue by Ludwika Nitschowa, on the Kościuszko Embankment

Krakowskie Przedmieście

KRAKOWSKIE PRZEDMIEŚCIE is undoubtedly one of the most beautiful streets in Warsaw. Rebuilt after the war, the magnificent palaces that lie along it now generally house government departments. There are also pleasant restaurants, bars and cafés. The street is lined with trees, green squares and little palaces with courtyards. On weekdays, Krakowskie Przedmieście is one of the liveliest streets in Warsaw, as two great institutions of higher education are situated here: the University of Warsaw and the Academy of Fine Arts.

Church of the Visitation
Also known as the Church of St Joseph, this is one of the few churches in Warsaw that was not destroyed during World War II. Its interior features are intact ❺

Carmelite Church
The Church of Our Lady of the Assumption and St Joseph the Bridegroom has a splendid early Neo-Classical façade crowned with a green globe representing the earth ❸

Namiestnikowski Palace
This former palace, rebuilt in the Neo-Classical style for the tsar's governor in the Kingdom of Poland, is now the president's residence ❹

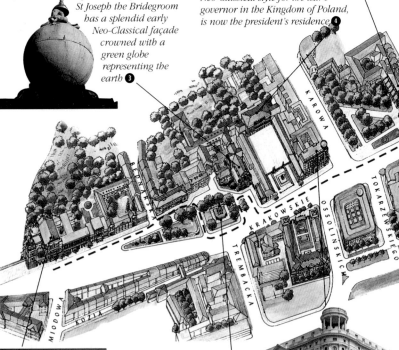

★ Church of St Anne
The Neo-Classical façade of the church is reminiscent of the style of the 16th-century Italian architect Andrea Palladio ❶

Statue of Adam Mickiewicz
The unveiling of the statue in 1898 was a great manifestation of patriotism ❷

Hotel Bristol
After its recent refurbishment, this hotel is the most beautiful and most luxurious, as well as the most expensive, in Warsaw.

Statue of Nicolaus Copernicus
This statue is situated at the
southern end of Krakowskie
Przedmieście.

LOCATOR MAP
See Street Finder, map 2

Staszic Palace
*This Neo-Classical palace
now houses the Polish
Academy of Sciences* **8**

★ **Church of the
Holy Cross**
*Inside this church
are urns contain-
ing the hearts of
Frédéric Chopin
and Władysław
Reymont, winner
of the Nobel Prize
for Literature* **7**

★ **University of Warsaw**
*The University of Warsaw
is the largest educational
institution in Poland.
Only some of the faculties
are situated at its main
site on Krakowskie
Przedmieście* **6**

KEY

– – – Suggested route

STAR SIGHTS

★ **Church of St Anne**

★ **Church of Holy Cross**

★ **University of Warsaw**

0 m   100

0 yds   100

Church of
St Anne **1**

ul. Krakowskie Przedmieście 68.
Map 2 D3. ☎ *(0 22) 826 89 91.*
🚌 *E-1, E-3, 116, 122, 125, 160,
170, 174, 175, 180, 190, 192,
195, 303, 307, 460, 495, 503.*
🚊 *4, 13, 26, 32, 43, 46.*

THIS GOTHIC CHURCH was
built for the Bernardine
order by Anna, widow of the
Mazovian prince Bolesław III,
in the second half of the 15th
century. It was extended
between 1518 and 1533.
Destroyed during the Swedish
invasion in the 1660s, it was
rebuilt in a Baroque style to a
design by Józef Szymon
Bellotti. The Gothic chancel
and the external walls were
retained. The Neo-Classical
façade, by Chrystian Piotr
Aigner and Stanisław Kostka
Potocki, is a later addition.

When the monastery was
closed in 1864, the church
became a religious academic
institution, a role that it
maintains to this day. The
relics of St Ładysław of
Gielniów, one of the patron
saints of Warsaw, are
preserved in a side chapel.
The magnificent interior of
the church has polychrome
paintings by Walenty
Żebrowski and a series of
Rococo altars. In the
monastery, part of which
dates from the 16th century,
the crystalline vaulting in the
cloisters has survived.

**Crystalline vaulting in the cloister
of the Bernardine monastery**

Statue of Adam Mickiewicz ❷

ul. Krakowskie Przedmieście.
Map 2 D4.

THIS STATUE OF Poland's most distinguished Romantic poet was unveiled in 1898, on the centenary of his birth. Erecting the statue during the period of intense Russification that followed the January Insurrection of 1863 was a great achievement on the part of the committee in charge of the project, led by Michał Radziwiłł and Henryk Sienkiewicz. The statue was designed by Cyprian Godebski, and the plinth by Józef Pius Dziekoński and Władysław Marconi. It was set up in a square off Krakowskie Przedmieście that was once lined with houses flanked by side streets. The houses were later demolished and the road widened. Only the statue of the Mother of God of Passau, dating from 1683, on the edge of the square, survives. It was made in the workshop of Szymon Belloti to a commission from Jan III Sobieski as an offering in thanks for a Polish victory at the Battle of Vienna and for the protection of the royal family.

The early Neo-Classical façade of the Carmelite Church

Statue of Adam Mickiewicz

Carmelite Church ❸

ul. Krakowskie Przedmieście 52/54.
Map 2 D4. 📞 (0 22) 826 05 31.
🚌 116, 122, 160, 174, 175, 180, 192, 195, 303.

THE BAROQUE CHURCH of Our Lady of the Assumption (Kościół Wniebowzięcia NMP) was built for the order of Discalced Carmelites in 1661–82, probably to a design by Józef Szymon Belloti, although the Neo-Classical façade is considerably later. Designed by Efraim Schroeger, it dates from 1782 and is one of the earliest examples of Neo-Classicism in Poland. Despite suffering war damage, the church, consisting of a nave with interconnecting side chapels and a transept, has many of its original features. The main altar, with sculptures by Jan Jerzy Plersch, is beautiful. Plersch also carved the sculptural group of the *Visitation of the Virgin*, a very sophisticated and Romantic piece which was transferred from an earlier Dominican church and can now be seen on the altar near the rood arch. Also noteworthy are the Baroque paintings, especially the two small works in the side altars near the chancel, by Szymon Czechowicz.

During the Northern War of 1705, Stanisław Leszczyński held peace negotiations with Charles XII in the church. From 1864, after the closure of the monastery, the monastic buildings housed a seminary.

Namiestnikowski Palace ❹

ul. Krakowskie Przedmieście 46/48.
Map 2 D4. 🚌 116, 122, 160, 174, 175, 180, 192, 195, 303, 460. ⬤ to the public.

THE PALACE OWES its elegant Neo-Classical form to refurbishment carried out by Chrystian Piotr Aigner in 1918–19. However, this work conceals much older walls, as a palace stood on this site as early as the mid-17th century.

Namiestnikowski Palace was home to several prominent familes, among them the Koniecpolskis, the Lubomirksis and, from 1685, the Radziwiłłs. From them the government of the Kingdom of Poland bought the palace in 1818 as the residence of the governor-general of the tsarist government. Among the people who lived here were General Józef Zajączek, viceroy of Tsar Alexander, and the much-hated General Iwan Paskiewicz. The wife of General Zajączek was a very colourful figure; she was a prima ballerina and shocked the town with her love affairs late into old age.

The palace escaped serious damage during World War II. After refurbishment, it was designated the seat of the Council of Ministers and witnessed many important political events: the signing of the Warsaw Pact in 1955, the treaty normalizing relations with Germany in 1970, and the Round Table Talks in 1989. Since 1994 the palace has been the residence of the president of the Republic of Poland.

Namiestnikowski Palace with a statue of Józef Poniatowski

Baroque ebony tabernacle in the Church of the Visitation

Church of the Visitation ➎

ul. Krakowskie Przedmieście 34.
Map 2 D4. 🚌 *111, 116, 122, 174, 175, 180, 192, 195, 303, 503.*

THE ORDER OF THE Visitation was brought to Poland by Maria Gonzaga, wife of Jan Kazimierz. Work on the Church of the Visitation (Kościół Wizytek) began in the same year but was interrupted, and not resumed until the 18th century, when the architect Karol Bay took control of the project. The façade, by Efraim Schroeger, was completed in 1763. Fortunately the church suffered no war damage, so its interior features have survived intact. The most splendid of these are the Rococo pulpit in the form of a ship and the sculptures on the high altar. Many fine paintings have also survived, including *The Visitation* by Tadeusz Kuntze-Konicz, *St Luis Gonzaga* by Daniel Szulc and *St Francis of Sales* by Szymon Czechowicz. The beautifully crafted ebony tabernacle, decorated with silver plaques by Herman Pothoff, was commissioned by Ludwika Maria and completed in 1654. Next to the church, the Baroque convent building and garden are still used by the Nuns of the Visitation today.

University of Warsaw ➏

ul. Krakowskie Przedmieście 26/28.
Map 2 D5. 📞 *(0 22) 620 03 81.*
🚌 *E-2, E-3, 111, 116, 122, 174, 175, 180, 192, 195, 303, 403, 503.*

THE NUCLEUS OF THE University of Warsaw (Uniwersytet Warszawski) grew from a summer palace known as the Villa Regia. In the first half of the 17th century, the palace belonged to the Vasa dynasty. From then on it underwent many phases of refurbishment, and in 1816 was chosen to house what was then the new university. After further alteration, the former palace acquired the late Neo-Classical appearance that it has today – as did the outbuildings to each side (designed by Jakub Kubicki in 1814–16), the main school (Corrazzi, commenced 1841), and the lecture hall and the former Fine Arts Department (both by Michał Kado, 1818–22). After the January Insurrection – when the university was run by the Russian authorities – a library was added (Stefan Szyller and Antoni Jabłoński, 1891–4). The Maximum Auditorium was built when the university passed back into Polish hands after the country regained its independence.

Today, the University of Warsaw is the largest educational establishment in Poland. The complex around Kazimierz Palace (Pałac Kazimierzowski), which houses several buildings, is now its administrative centre.

Church of the Holy Cross ➐

ul. Krakowskie Przedmieście 3.
Map 2 D5. 📞 *(0 22) 826 89 10.*
🚌 *E-2, E-3, 111, 116, 122, 174, 175, 180, 192, 195, 303, 403, 503.*

THE ORIGINAL Church of the Holy Cross (Kościół św Krzyża, 1626) was destroyed during the Swedish Deluge of the 1650s. The current Baroque missionaries' church was designed by Giuseppe Simone Bellotti and built between 1679 and 1696. The façade was completed in 1760.

The church is a splendid example of Varsovian church architecture of the late 17th century. During World War II, it suffered major damage and most of its interior was destroyed. The most interesting surviving feature is the altar in the south wing of the transept, designed by Tylman van Gameren. Many important ceremonies have taken place in the church, including the funerals of political thinker Stanisław Staszic (1755–1826), composer Karol Szymanowski (1882–1937) and painter Leon Wyczółkowski (1852–1936). Urns containing the hearts of composer Frédéric Chopin (1810–49) and novelist Władysław Reymont (1867–1925) are built into a pillar of the nave.

SVRSVM CORDA

Statue of Christ, Church of the Holy Cross

Monument to Nicolaus Copernicus in front of Staszic Palace

Staszic Palace ❽

ul. Nowy Świat 72. **Map** 2 D5. 🚌 *E-2, 111, 116, 122, 150, 155, 174, 175, 180, 192, 195, 303, 403, 503, 506.*

CONTRARY TO WHAT its name suggests, Staszic Palace (Pałac Staszica) never belonged to Stanisław Staszic, nor did he ever live here – although he did fund it. The palace was built by Antonio Corazzi between 1820 and 1823 in the late Neo-Classical style, as the headquarters of the Royal Society of Friends of Science. Since World War II it has housed the Polish Academy of Science and the Warsaw Scientific Society. The monument to astronomer Nicolaus Copernicus that stands in front of the building is by Bertel Thorvaldsen. It was unveiled in 1830.

Gniński-Ostrogski Palace ❾

ul. Okólnik 1. **Map** 4 D1. ☎ *(0 22) 826 59 35.* 🚌 *111, 116, 122, 150, 155, 174, 175, 180, 192, 195, 303, 506.* ◻ *1 May–30 Sep: 10am–5pm Mon, Wed, Fri, noon–6pm Thu, 10am–2pm Sat, Sun; 1 Oct–30 Apr: 10am–2pm Mon–Wed, Fri, Sat, noon–6pm Thu.* 🚭 ♿ 🎦
Concerts.

BUILT AFTER 1681, Gniński-Ostrogski Palace (Pałac Gnińskich-Ostrogskich) is one of Tylman van Gameren's grand masterpieces. The pavilion was erected on an elevated terrace above a cellar. According to legend, a golden duck lived under the palace, guarding its treasures.

Today the palace is home to the Frédéric Chopin Museum (Muzeum Fryderyka Chopina), which houses portraits, letters and autograph manuscripts, as well as the grand piano at which Chopin composed during the last two years of his life. It is also the home of the Chopin Society, and regular performances of Chopin's music take place here.

Nowy Świat ❿

Map 3 C1, 3 C2, 4 D1. 🚌 *E-1, E-2, 111, 116, 122, 150, 155, 174, 175, 180, 192, 195, 303, 403, 506.* 🚊 *7, 8, 9, 12, 22, 24, 25, 44.*

THE STREET KNOWN as Nowy Świat (New World) is a stretch of the medieval route leading from the castle to Czersk and on to Cracow, and thus forms part of the Royal Route. Buildings started to appear along a section of the road at the end of the 18th century. First came a small

number of Neo-Classical palaces; by the beginning of the 19th century they had been joined by late Neo-Classical town houses. At the end of the 19th century, Nowy Świat was an elegant street of restaurants, cafés, summer theatres, hotels and shops. After serious damage in World War II, only the Neo-Classical buildings were reconstructed, although later buildings were given pseudo-Neo-Classical features to preserve a uniformity of style.

Today, Nowy Świat is one of the most attractive streets in Warsaw, with wide pedestrian areas and cafés with pavement gardens. Blikle, the café at No. 33, boasts a 130-year tradition and the best doughnuts (*pączki*) in town. Kossakowski Palace, at No. 19, was remodelled by Henryk Marconi in 1849–51. Strolling along Nowy Świat it is worth turning down Ulica Foksal, where there are a number of 19th-century houses and small palaces. The most beautiful, at Nos. 1/2/4, was built for the Zamoyski family by Leandro Marconi in 1878–9. Today, it houses an up-market art gallery and the Association of Architects of the Polish Republic. At the roundabout on the intersection of Nowy Świat and Aleje Jerozolimskie stands the huge building of the former Polish United Workers' Party Central Committee. Transformed after the fall of communism into a "den of capitalism", it now houses banks, the Polish stock exchange and the offices of various companies.

Nowy Świat, a street of elegant shops and cafés

National Museum ⓫

See pp80–81.

Polish Military Museum ⓬

Aleje Jerozolimskie 3. **Map** 4 D2, 2 E5 and 6 E1. ((0 22) 629 52 71/2 ext. 34. ⬛ E-5, 101, 102, 111, 117, 158, 303, 517, 521. ⬛ 7, 8, 9, 12, 22, 24, 25, 44. ◯ 10am–4pm Wed–Sun. ▨ (free on Fri). **Outdoor exhibition** ◯ until dusk, free admission.

THE POLISH Military Museum (Muzeum Wojska Polskiego), established in 1920, contains a collection of Polish arms and armour spanning more than 1,000 years. The most interesting aspect of the permanent exhib-ition is the collection of armour from the Early Middle Ages to the end of the 18th century. It includes a rare gilded helmet that belonged to a Polish chieftain of the Early Christian era and numerous pieces relating to the greatest medieval battles fought on Polish territory.

Among the more unusual exhibits are medieval jousting armour and an impressive collection of 17th-century armour of the Husaria, the famous Polish cavalry, with eagle wings, leopardskins and a mounted cavalryman in full regalia. Heavy weapons from the two World Wars are displayed in the park next to the museum.

Plac Trzech Krzyży ⓭

Map 3 C2, 3 C3. ⬛ E-1, E-2, 108, 116, 118, 119, 122, 128, 151, 171, 180, 195, 403, 404, 503, 509, 513.

PLAC TRZECH KRZYŻY (Three Crosses Square) is something of a misnomer. Mounted on top of Baroque columns, two gilded crosses, commissioned by August II and made by Joachim Daniel Jauch in 1731, mark the beginning of Droga

Kalwaryjską (Road of Calvary). The third cross is held by St John Nepomuk, whose statue was erected in 1752 by Grand Crown Marshal Franciszek Bieliński to mark the completion of the project to pave the streets of Warsaw. A fourth cross crowns the dome of the 19th-century Church of St Alexander (Kościół św. Aleksandra). The oldest buildings around the square are two 18th-century town houses: No. 1 Nowy Świat, with an early Neo-Classical façade, and No. 2 Plac Trzech Krzyży, part of the complex of the Institute of the Deaf and Blind, established in 1817. New buildings recently erected round the square have restored something of its urban character.

Statue of St John Nepomuk

Aleje Ujazdowskie ⓮

Map 3 C3, 3 C4, 3 C5. ⬛ 107, 116, 119, 122, 159, 195, 382, 403, 404, 408, 415, 420, 503, 513, 520.

ALEJE UJAZDOWSKIE is one of the most beautiful streets in Warsaw – a good place for a stroll in the summer. While the east side is bordered by parks, the west is lined with elegant houses originally built for Warsaw's ruling classes but now largely occupied by embassies. There are also palatial houses;

No. 17 and No. 19, by architect Stanisław Grochowicz, are especially splendid. No. 17, built in 1903–4, has an eclectic façade. No. 1, formerly a barracks, houses the offices of the Council of Ministers.

Parliament ⓯

ul. Wiejska 2/4/6. **Map** 4 D3, 4 D4. ((0 22) 694 25 00. ⬛ 107, 108, 116, 118, 119, 122, 151, 159, 180, 195, 359. ◯ by prior arrangement.

THE PARLIAMENTARY tradition in Poland dates from 1453, but it was interrupted by the loss of Polish sovereignty at the end of the 18th century. Only after the restoration of Poland's independence in 1918 was its two-chamber parlia-ment – comprising the Sejm and the Senate – reconvened. Lacking a suitable building, representatives and senators gathered for a time in the former Institute for the Education of Young Ladies.

In 1925–8, a lofty semi-circular hall was built, with a debating chamber for the Sejm. It was designed by Kazimierz Skórewicz and decorated with Art Deco bas-reliefs by Jan Szczepkowski. After damage suffered in World War II, the parliamentary buildings were significantly extended in the spirit of the comparatively refined Socialist Realist style, to a design by Bohdan Pniewski.

In 1989, after the first free elections since World War II, the upper parliamentary chamber, abolished under communist rule, was restored. In 1999, a monument in honour of the Home Army was unveiled in front of the Sejm.

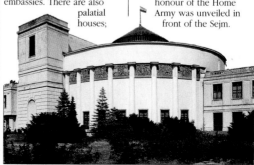

The semicircular parliament (Sejm) building, with Art Deco bas-reliefs

National Museum ⑪

W. Szymanowski,
The Kiss

THE NATIONAL MUSEUM (Muzeum Narodowe) was originally the Museum of Fine Arts, acquiring its present status in 1916. Despite wartime losses, today it has a large collection of works of art covering all periods from antiquity to modern times. Due to lack of space, not all the exhibits are on permanent display.

★ Virgin and Child
This important painting by Sandro Botticelli is the only work by the artist in Polish collections.

★ St Anne Fresco
This fresco of St Anne is one of the 10th-century wall paintings discovered by Polish archaeologists in Faras, Sudan.

Greek Vase
Some of the Greek vases displayed in the Gallery of Ancient Art are partly from a private collection.

Battle of Grunwald, a painting by Jan Matejko *(see pp40–41)*, is the most famous in the Gallery of Polish Art.

Ground floor

KEY

▨	Ancient Art
▨	Faras Collection
▨	Medieval Art
▨	Polish Paintings
▨	20th-century Polish Art
▢	Foreign Art
▨	Polish Decorative Art
▨	European Decorative Art
▨	L. Kronenberg Silver Room
▨	Temporary exhibitions
▢	Non-exhibition areas

Virgin from Wrocław
This "Beautiful Madonna" is an early 15th-century sculpture that exemplifies the International Gothic style.

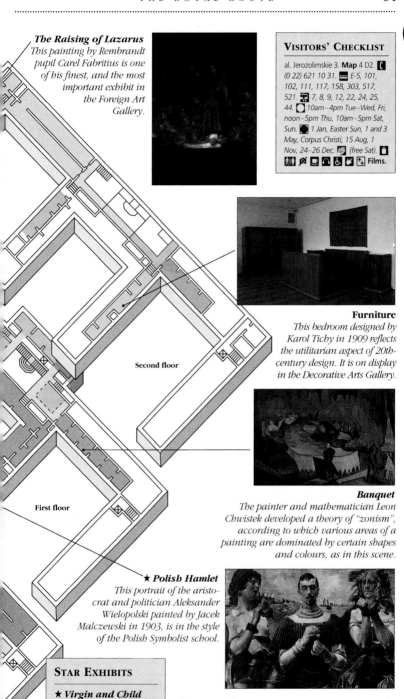

The Raising of Lazarus
This painting by Rembrandt pupil Carel Fabritius is one of his finest, and the most important exhibit in the Foreign Art Gallery.

Furniture
This bedroom designed by Karol Tichy in 1909 reflects the utilitarian aspect of 20th-century design. It is on display in the Decorative Arts Gallery.

Second floor

Banquet
The painter and mathematician Leon Chwistek developed a theory of "zonism", according to which various areas of a painting are dominated by certain shapes and colours, as in this scene.

First floor

★ Polish Hamlet
This portrait of the aristo-crat and politician Aleksander Wielopolski painted by Jacek Malczewski in 1903, is in the style of the Polish Symbolist school.

STAR EXHIBITS

★ *Virgin and Child*

★ *Polish Hamlet*

★ *St Anne Fresco*

GALLERY GUIDE
The collections are arranged on three floors. On the ground floor are the Galleries of Ancient Art, the Faras Collection and the Gallery of Medieval Art. On the first floor is the collection of Polish art. Foreign paintings can be seen on the first and second floors.

THE CITY CENTRE

FROM THE LATE 18TH to the mid-19th century, the area around Ulica Senatorska and Plac Teatralny was the commercial and cultural centre of Warsaw. Imposing Neo-Classical buildings with impressive colonnades are still to be seen there. The Grand Theatre (Teatr Wielki) on Plac Teatralny is one of the largest buildings of its type in Europe. The Saxon Gardens (Ogród Saski), stretching through the centre of the district, are what remains of a former royal park that adjoined the residence of the Saxon king August II. In the second half of the 19th

Nike Monument

century, the city's commercial centre moved to the area around Ulica Marszałkowska, prompted by the opening in 1845 of Warsaw's first railway station at the junction with Aleje Jerozolimskie. The city centre was completely transformed after the damage inflicted during World War II. Today, its principal landmark is the Palace of Culture and Science (Pałac Kultury i Nauki). The western part of the city centre is dominated by tower blocks. For tourists, the eastern side is of most interest. Here, several historic buildings have survived, dating from the 18th up to the early 20th century.

SIGHTS AT A GLANCE

Places of Worship
Capuchin Church ❸
Evangelical Church of the Augsburg Confession ⓬
Nożyk Synagogue ⓯

Buildings and Historic Monuments
Arsenal ❻
Branicki Palace ❷
Krasiński Palace ❺
Pac Palace ❹
Palace of Culture and Science ⓮
Primate's Palace ❶
Przebendowski-Radziwiłłów Palace ❼

Monuments and Commemorative Sites
Monument to the Heroes of the Ghetto ⓳
Path of Jewish Remembrance ⓲
Umschlagplatz Monument ⓱

Streets and Squares
Plac Bankowy ❽
Plac Teatralny ❾

Parks
Saxon Gardens ❿

Museums and Galleries
Ethnographical Museum ⓭
Pawiak Prison ⓰
Zachęta ⓫

KEY

▨	Street-by-Street map *pp84–5*
P	Parking
M	Metro

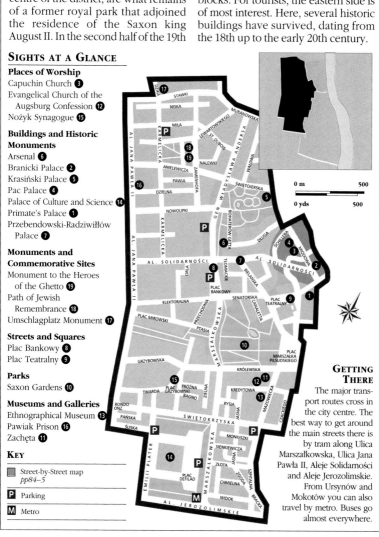

0 m   500
0 yds   500

GETTING THERE

The major transport routes cross in the city centre. The best way to get around the main streets there is by tram along Ulica Marszałkowska, Ulica Jana Pawła II, Aleje Solidarności and Aleje Jerozolimskie. From Ursynów and Mokotów you can also travel by metro. Buses go almost everywhere.

◁ **The Palace of Culture and Science by night, seen from Ulica Złota**

Ulica Miodowa

U LICA MIODOWA lies just outside the much-visited Old Town. Tourists rarely venture here, but it holds many attractions nonetheless. The street has three Baroque churches and several palaces – including the Neo-Classical Primate's Palace and the Rococo Branicki Palace – set behind spacious courtyards. The former Collegium Nobilium, the most famous Polish school for the children of the nobility in the 18th century, now houses the Academy of Dramatic Arts.

The Basilian church is hidden behind the palace façade. Byzantine-Ukrainian masses are celebrated here.

★ Pac Palace
The 19th-century interiors are decorated in the Gothic, Renaissance, Greek and Moorish styles ❹

Nike Monument

★ Capuchin Church
In accordance with the rule of poverty of the Capuchin order, the altars in this church have no gilt or polychrome decoration ❸

Branicki Palace
Rebuilt after World War II, the palace was crowned with sculptures derived from paintings by Canaletto ❷

LOCATOR MAP
See Street Finder, maps 1 & 2

The Field Cathedral of the Polish Armed Forces was built in the 17th century as a church for the Piarist order.

KEY

– – – Suggested route

0 m   50

0 yds   50

STAR SIGHTS

★ **Capuchin Church**

★ **Pac Palace**

The Primate's Palace, a building in the Neo-Classical style

Primate's Palace ❶

ul. Senatorska 13/15. **Map** 2 D3.
((0 22) 829 69 99. 116, 122, 174, 175, 180, 195, 303. ◖ *to the public.*

THE PRESENT-DAY appearance of the Primate's Palace (Pałac Prymasowski) reflects the refurbishments carried out by Efraim Schroeger in 1777–84 for the Primate of Poland, Antoni Ostrowski. Schroeger's work was then continued by Szymon Zug for the next primate, Michał Poniatowski. The unusual arrangement of the building, with its semicircular wings, is reminiscent of the designs of the most celebrated architect of the Italian Renaissance, Andrea Palladio (1508–80).

The Primate's Palace is generally considered to be the first Neo-Classical palace built in Poland. It was destroyed during World War II, then was rebuilt in 1949–52. Today it is used as an office building.

The superb Great Hall (Sala Wielka) is decorated with Ionic columns and delicate Neo-Classical stuccowork.

Branicki Palace ❷

ul. Miodowa 6. **Map** 2 D3. 116, 122, 174, 175, 180, 195, 303.
◖ *to the public.*

BRANICKI PALACE (Pałac Branickich) was built for Jan Klemens Branicki, adviser to August III. This powerful magnate was known both as a distinguished soldier and a connoisseur of fine art. Work began on the palace in 1740, to a design by Jan Zygmunt Deybel, and was completed by Giacopo Fontana.

Following almost complete destruction during World War II, this Rococo palace was rebuilt in 1947–53. The reconstruction was based on detailed historical research and 18th-century paintings.

Capuchin Church ❸

ul. Miodowa 13. **Map** 1 C3. 116, 122, 174, 175, 180, 195, 303.

THE CAPUCHIN church (kościół Kapucynów), or Church of the Transfiguration, was built by Jan III Sobieski in gratitude for the Polish victory over the Turks at the Battle of Vienna in 1683. Building began in the same year under the direction of Izydor Affaita – probably to designs by Tylman van Gameren and Agostino Locci the Younger – and was completed by Carlo Ceroni in 1692. The modest façade recalls the Capuchin church in Rome. The church houses urns containing the heart of Jan III and the ashes of the Saxon king, August II. In the crypt, there is a nativity scene with emotive figures.

Sarcophagus with the heart of Jan III Sobieski in the Capuchin church

Pac Palace ❹

ul. Miodowa 15. **Map** 1 C3.
((0 22) 634 96 00. **116, 122,
174, 175, 180, 192, 195, 303.
○ by arrangement.

THE BAROQUE Pac Palace
(Pałac Paca), formerly the
residence of the Radziwiłł
family, was designed and built
by Tylman van Gameren in
1681–97. One of the palace's
19th-century owners, Ludwik
Pac, commissioned the
architect Henryk Marconi to
redesign it; work was
completed in 1828. The
interiors were decorated in the
Gothic, Renaissance, Greek
and Moorish styles, and the
façade remodelled in the
Palladian manner. The palace
gate was modelled on a
triumphal arch and decorated
with Classical bas-relief
sculptures – the work of
Ludwik Kaufman, a pupil of
the celebrated Neo-Classical
sculptor Antonio Canova.
Today the palace houses the
Ministry of Health.

**Neo-Classical medallion on the
façade of Pac Palace**

Krasiński Palace ❺

pl. Krasińskich 5. **Map** 1C2.
((0 22) 635 62 09. **116, 122,
174, 175, 180, 195, 303.
○ during exhibitions.

KRASIŃSKI PALACE (Pałac
Krasińskich), in the
Baroque style, is regarded as
one of the most beautiful late
17th-century buildings in
Warsaw. It was designed by
Tylman van Gameren and
built between 1687 and 1700
for the mayor of Warsaw, Jan
Dobrogost Krasiński.

A triangular pediment
features ornamental reliefs
depicting the heroic deeds of
the Roman patrician Marcus
Valerius (known as Corvinus),

Krasiński Palace seen from the palace gardens

a legendary ancestor of Jan
Dobrogost Krasiński. The
reliefs are the work of
Andreas Schlüter, an
outstandingly gifted sculptor
and architect who later
designed the Arsenal and
Royal Castle in Berlin. Rebuilt
after war damage, the palace
now houses a collection of
antique prints and manuscripts
from the National Library.

Arsenal ❻

ul. Długa 52. **Map** 1 B3. **(** (0 22)
831 15 37. **E-2, 107, 111, 119,
125, 127, 170, 171, 190, 307, 406,
409, 410, 413, 414, 415, 420, 508,
512, 514, 515, 516, 522. **2, 4,
13, 15, 18, 26, 32, 35, 36, 43, 45, 46.
Archaeological Museum ○ 9am–
4pm Mon–Fri, 10am–4pm Sun.
Sat and 3rd Sun in the month.
(free on Sun).

THE ARSENAL was built in
1638–47, in the Baroque
style, by Władysław IV Vasa.
There, during World War II,
boy scout soldiers of the Grey
Ranks (the Szare Szeregi, who
were actively involved in the
resistance movement) released
21 prisoners from the hands of
the Gestapo; this brave action
is commemorated by a plaque.

The Arsenal now houses the
Archaeological Museum, with
exhibits from excavations
carried out within both the
country's pre-war and present-
day borders. Also on display
are objects from other
European countries, Asia, the
Americas and Africa. The
exhibition on prehistoric
Poland is highly recommended. By prior arrangement
visitors may make clay pots
using prehistoric methods.

Przebendowski-Radziwiłłów Palace ❼

al. Solidarności 62. **Map** 1 C3.
((0 22) 826 90 91. **E-2, 107,
111, 119, 125, 127, 170, 171, 190,
307, 406, 409, 410, 413, 414, 415,
420, 508, 512, 514, 515, 516, 522.
**2, 4, 13, 15, 18, 26, 32, 35, 36, 43,
45, 46. **Independence Museum**
(Muzeum Niepodległości) ○
10am–5pm Tue–Fri, 10am–4pm Sat,
Sun (free on Sun).

BEFORE WORLD WAR II, this
Baroque palace was in a
narrow shopping street. When
the East-West (W-Z) route was
constructed (1948–9), it was
suddenly surrounded by a
major traffic artery. The palace,
which has the most beautiful
mansard roofs in Warsaw and
an oval bow-fronted façade,
was built in 1728 to a design
by Jan Zygmunt Deybel. Since
1990 it has housed the Independence Museum (Muzeum
Niepodległości), which features
a collection of documents
relating Poland's history.

**The Baroque Przebendowski-
Radziwiłłów Palace**

Plac Bankowy ❽

Map 1 B3 and 1 B4. 🚌 E-2, 107,
111, 119, 125, 127, 170, 171, 190,
307, 406, 409, 410, 413, 414, 415,
420, 508, 512, 514, 515, 516, 522.
🚊 2, 4, 13, 15, 18, 26, 32, 35, 36,
43, 45, 46. **John Paul II Collection**
pl. Bankowy 1. 📞 (0 22) 620 27 25.
⏰ 10am–5pm Tue–Sun. 📷

TODAY PLAC BANKOWY (Bank
Square) is one of the
busiest places in Warsaw.
Once a quiet little square, it
was radically altered after the
construction of the East-West
route and Ulica Marszałkowska.
A statue of Feliks Dzierżyński,
the founder of the Soviet security service, was erected here,
and the square was renamed
in his honour. In 1989, to the
joy of local inhabitants, the
statue was removed and the
square's original name restored. Plac Bankowy was once
the site of the largest synagogue in Warsaw. It was
demolished after the collapse
of the Ghetto Uprising of 1943.
A tower block now stands on
the site. The most interesting
buildings are on the west side
of the square. The group of
Neo-Classical buildings zeal-
ously rebuilt after World War II
were designed by Antonio
Corazzi. The most impressive is
the three-winged palace of the
Commission for Revenues and
Treasury, which today serves
as a town hall. From the
junction with Ulica Elektoralna,
the fine building of the former
Bank of Poland (Bank Polski)
and Stock Exchange (Giełda)
can be admired. The building
now houses the John Paul II
Collection, donated by Janina
and Zbigniew Porczyński. It
consists of over 450 works by
famous artists and is
arranged
thematically.

Neo-Classical frieze on the façade of the Grand Theatre

Plac Teatralny ❾

Map 1 C4. 🚌 111.

BEFORE 1944, Plac Teatralny
(Theatre Square) was the
heart of Warsaw. The
enormous Neo-Classical
Grand Theatre (Teatr
Wielki) on the south side
was designed by
Antonio Corazzi and
Ludwik Kozubowski
and completed in
1833. The façade is
decorated with a
Neo-Classical frieze
by Paweł Maliński
depicting Oedipus
and his companions
returning from the
Olympian Games.
The theatre was
rebuilt and greatly
enlarged after
suffering war damage.
Two statues stand in
front of the building:
one depicts
Stanisław
Moniuszko, the

Bogusławski Monument

father of Polish opera (see
p24), and the other Wojciech
Bogusławski, who instigated
the theatre's construction.
Today it is the home of the
National Opera and the
National Theatre.
In 1848, the Russian
composer Mikhail Glinka
(1803–57) lived and worked in
the house at No. 2 Ulica
Niecała, just off Plac Teatralny.

Opposite the theatre, on the
north side of the square, stood
the small Church of St Andrew
and the enormous, repeatedly
extended Jabłonowski Palace,
which was refashioned as the
town hall in 1817–19. Close by
was Blank's Palace, a late
Baroque building, which
was owned by Piotr Blank,
a banker at the time of
Stanisław August
Poniatowski
(1764–95). At the
beginning of the Nazi
occupation of
Poland, the Germans
arrested Stefan
Starzyński, the
heroic mayor of
Warsaw, in this
building. During
the Warsaw
Uprising, the poet
Krzysztof Kamil
Baczyński died amid
its ruins. In the years
after World War II,
only Blank's
Palace was
rebuilt; Jabłon-
owski Palace and the church –
now the Church of St Brother
Albert and St Andrew – were
rebuilt only recently. The Nike
Monument, which once stood
in Plac Teatralny in memory of
Warsaw's resistance against
the Nazis, was moved to a
new site near the East-West
route, where it stands on a
high plinth.

Municipal government buildings on Plac Bankowy

Tomb of the Unknown Soldier in the Saxon Gardens

Saxon Gardens ❿

Map 1 C4, 1 C5. 🚌 *106, 107, 111, 119, 127, 160, 171, 460.* 🚋 *2, 4, 15, 18, 35, 36, 45.*

THE SAXON GARDENS (Ogród Saski) were laid out between 1713 and 1733 by August II, the Strong, to a design by Jan Krzysztof Naumann and Mateus Daniel Pöppelmann. Originally the royal gardens adjoining Morsztyn Palace, they became the basis for a Baroque town planning project in Warsaw known as the Saxon Axis (Osią Saską). In 1727 the Saxon Gardens became the first public park in Poland, and for two centuries they served as an alfresco "summer salon" for Varsovians. At the time of August III, Karol Fryderyk Pöppelmann built a Baroque summer theatre here; this stood until 1772. Between 1816 and 1827, James Savage refashioned the gardens in the English style. In 1870 they were graced by an enormous wooden summer theatre, which was destroyed in September 1939, at the start of World War II. The gardens are now adorned with 21 Baroque sandstone statues made by sculptors including Jan Jerzy Plersch in the 1730s. There were once many more statues here; some were removed to St

Baroque sculpture from the Saxon Gardens

Petersburg by Marshal Suvorov, who recaptured Warsaw during the uprising led by Tadeusz Kościuszko in 1794.

Saski Palace was destroyed at the end of 1944. All that remains today is the Tomb of the Unknown Soldier, where the body of a soldier who fell in the defence of Lvov (1918–19) was interred on 2 November 1925.

Zachęta ⓫

pl. Małachowskiego 3. Map 1 C5. 📞 *(0 22) 827 58 54.* 🚌 *106, 160.* 🕙 *10am–6pm Tue–Sun.* 🎫 *(free on Fri).*

THE ZACHĘTA building – now the National Gallery of Contemporary Art – was built in 1899–1903 for the Society for the Promotion of Fine Arts. It was designed by Stefan Szyller, the leading architect of Warsaw's Revival period, a 19th and early 20th century architectural movement. It was conceived as a monumental building in the Neo-Renaissance style, with four wings (only completed in 1995) and a glass-roofed inner courtyard.

As part of its endeavour to promote the work of contemporary Polish artists, the Society organized exhibitions, competitions and annual salons. It also purchased works of art. The Zachęta's permanent collections were transferred to the National Museum, and the building, as before, now serves as a venue for temporary exhibitions of modern art.

In 1922, Gabriel Narutowicz, the first president of the newly independent Polish Republic, was shot dead at the opening of an exhibition at the Zachęta. His assassin was Eligiusz Niewiadomskia, a Polish painter, critic and fanatic.

Evangelical Church of the Augsburg Confession ⓬

pl. Małachowskiego 1. Map 1 C5. 📞 *(0 22) 827 68 17.* 🚌 *106, 160.*

THE EVANGELICAL CHURCH of the Augsburg Confession (Kościół św Trójcy) was designed by Szymon Bogumił Zug and built in 1777–81. The Neo-Classical building is crowned by a dome 58 m (189 ft) high. For a long time the church was the highest building in Warsaw, and bore witness to the religious tolerance of the Polish nation and of Stanisław August Poniatowski (1764–95), the last king of Poland. The church is reminiscent of the

Façade of the Zachęta building (National Gallery of Contemporary Art)

The interior of the Evangelical Church of the Augsburg Confession

Pantheon in Rome; however, this ancient model was merely a starting point from which Zug developed a unique design. The interior of the church features a vast barrel-vaulted nave with rectangular transepts. The west front features a massive Doric portico which emphasizes the severity of the façade, regarded as one of the outstanding examples of Neo-Classical architecture in Poland. The interior, with its double tier of galleries supported by columns, has excellent acoustics and is used for choral and other concerts.

Ethnographical Museum ⑬

ul. Kredytowa 1. **Map**1 C5. ((0 22) 827 76 41/5. 🚍 106, 160. ○ 9am–4pm Tue, Thu, Fri, 11am–6pm Wed, 10am–5pm Sat, Sun. 🖽 (free on Wed).

THE ETHNOGRAPHICAL Museum (Muzeum Etnograficzne) is housed in a Neo-Renaissance building on the south side of Plac Małachowski. The former head office of the Land Credit Association, it was built in 1854–8, to a design by Henryk Marconi, an Italian architect who settled in Warsaw. It recalls the Libreria Sansoviniana in Venice, and is one of the city's finest 19th-century buildings. The museum contains permanent

displays of Polish folk costumes, folklore and arts and crafts, and collections of ethnic and tribal art from around the world, including Africa, Australia, the Pacific and Latin America. It also mounts occasional temporary exhibitions.

In a neighbouring building on Ulica Mazowiecka, behind a gate with bullet marks, is the glass-fronted Artist's House (Dom Artysty), which contains a modern art gallery. Also on Ulica Mazowiecka are several bookshops, the best of which are at the intersection with Ulica Święto-

Sacred figure, Ethnographical Museum

krzyska. Up until the beginning of World War II, Ziemiańska, a very famous café, was to be found at No. 22 Ulica Mazowiecka. This was where the cream of society and the artistic community met to exchange ideas and gossip over coffee.

Palace of Culture and Science ⑭

pl. Defilad 1. **Map** 3 A1, 3 B1. ((0 22) 656 62 01. 🚍 E-3, 101, 102, 105, 107, 109, 117, 119, 127, 128, 131, 150, 155, 158, 160, 171, 174, 175, 192, 406, 407, 409, 410, 412, 413, 414, 415, 420, 505, 506, 507, 508, 510, 512, 514, 515, 516, 517, 519, 521, 524. 🚎 2, 4, 7, 8, 9, 12, 15, 18, 22, 24, 25, 35, 36, 44, 45. Ⓜ Centre (Centrum) **Viewing platform** ○ 9am–6pm daily, all year round.

QUEEN JULIANA of the Netherlands is reputed to have described the Palace of Culture and Science (Pałac Kultury i Nauki) as "modest but tasteful". This enormous building – a gift from the people of Warsaw from the nations of the USSR – was built in 1952–5 to the design of a Russian architect, Lev Rudniev. At the time, this monument to "the spirit of invention and social progress" was the second tallest building in Europe. It resembles Moscow's Socialist Realist tower blocks, and although it has only 30 storeys, with its spire it is 230 m 68 cm (750 ft) high. Its volume is over 800,000 cubic m (28 million cubic ft) and it contains 40 million bricks. It is said to incorporate many architectural and decorative elements taken from stately homes after World War II. Despite the passage of time, this symbol of Soviet domination still provokes extreme reactions, from admiration to demands for its demolition.

Palace of Culture and Science, reminiscent of a Socialist Realist tower block

Interior of Nożyk Synagogue

Nożyk Synagogue ⑮

ul. Twarda 6. **Map** 1 A5. 🕻 *(0 22) 620 43 24.* 🚌 *106, 160, 460.*
Jewish Historical Institute
ul. Tłomackie 3/5. 🕻 *(0 22) 827 92 21.*

NOŻYK SYNAGOGUE was founded by Zelman and Ryfka Nożyk. In 1893 they donated the land on which it was to be built. Later they left half of their estate to the Orthodox Jewish community. The synagogue was built between 1898 and 1902. The interior has an impressive portico, crowned by a metal dome bearing the Star of David, which contains the Ark of the Covenant. In the centre of the nave is a raised pulpit known as a bema. The nave is surrounded by galleries that were originally intended for female worshippers.

Today, this is the only active synagogue in Warsaw. When it was built, it was hidden away in the heart of a housing estate, surrounded by high-rise tenement buildings. After the war, few of these were still standing. During the Nazi occupation, the synagogue was closed for worship and the German forces used it as a warehouse. Reopened in 1945, it was eventually (1977–83) restored to its original condition.

Of a total population of no more than 1,300,000, there were about 400,000 Jews in Warsaw before World War II; the city had the second largest Jewish population after that of New York. The northern part of Warsaw, which was inhabited pre-dominantly by Jews, was densely built up, with many tenement blocks. The languages spoken in the area were Yiddish, Hebrew and also Russian, spoken by Jews who had fled Russia.

Those interested in Jewish history and culture should also visit the historic – though somewhat overgrown – cemetery on Ulica Okopowa. The museum of the Jewish Historical Institute (Żydowski Instytut Historyczny), with a library, archives and Judaic museum, is also worth a visit.

Pawiak Prison ⑯

ul. Dzielna 24/26. **Map** 1 A2. 🕻
(0 22) 831 13 17. 🚌 *107, 148, 170, 180, 516.* 🚊 *16, 17, 19, 33, 47.* ◯
9am–5pm Wed, 9am–4pm Thu, Sat, 10am–5pm Fri, 10am–4pm Sun.
📷 🎫 🚻 🏛 🏧

PAWIAK PRISON was built in the 1830s by Henryk Marconi. It became notorious during the Nazi occupation, when it was used to imprison Poles and Jews arrested by the Germans. Now in ruins, Pawiak serves as a museum. In front of the ruin stands a long-dead tree, covered with obituary notices for prisoners who died there.

Tree with obituary notices in front of Pawiak Prison

Umschlagplatz Monument ⑰

ul. Stawki. **Map** 1 A1. 🚌 *109, 111, 148, 157, 170.* 🚊 *16, 17, 19, 33, 35, 47.*

THE UMSCHLAGPLATZ Monument, unveiled in 1988, marks the site of a former railway siding on

Umschlagplatz Monument on the Path of Remembrance

Ulica Dzika. It was from here that some 300,000 Jews from the Warsaw Ghetto and elsewhere were loaded onto cattle trucks and dispatched to almost certain death in the extermination camps. Among them was Janusz Korczak and his group of Jewish orphans. Living conditions in the Ghetto were indescribably inhuman, and by 1942 over 100,000 of the inhabitants had died. The monument, on which the architect Hanna Szmalenberg and the sculptor Władysław Klamerus collaborated, is made of blocks of black and white marble bearing the names of hundreds of Warsaw's Jews.

Path of Jewish Remembrance  18

ul. Zamenhofa, Stawki. **Map** 1 A1 and 1 B1. 🚌 109, 111, 148, 170, 180, 516. 🚊 16, 17, 19, 33, 35, 47.

THE PATH OF Jewish Remembrance (Trakt Męczeństwa i Walki Żydów), opened in 1988, runs between the Monument to the Heroes of the Ghetto and the Umschlagplatz Monument. It is marked by 16 blocks of granite bearing inscriptions in Polish, Hebrew and Yiddish and the date 1940–1943.

Stone on the Path of Jewish Remembrance

Each block is dedicated to the memory of the 450,000 Jews murdered in the Warsaw Ghetto in the years 1940–43, to the heroes of the Ghetto Uprising in 1943 and to certain individuals: Szmul Zygielbojm (1895–1943), a member of the Polish National Council in London, who committed suicide as an act of protest on hearing of the liquidation of the Warsaw Ghetto; Emanuel Ringelblum (1900–44), who established the Ghetto archives; Józef Lewartowski (1895–1942); Michał Klepfisz; Arie Wilner (1917–43); Mordechaj Anielewicz (1917–43), Commandant of the Jewish Fighting Organization; Mejer Majerowski (1911–43); Frumina Płotnicka (1914–43); Icchak Nissenbaum (1868–1942); Janusz Korczak; and the poet Icchak Kacenelson (1886–1944).

Monument to the Heroes of the Ghetto (detail)

Monument to the Heroes of the Ghetto 19

ul. Zamenhofa. **Map** 1 B2. 🚌 111, 180, 516.

THE MONUMENT to the Heroes of the Ghetto (Pomnik Bohaterów Getta) was erected in 1948, when the city of Warsaw still lay in ruins. Created by the sculptor Natan Rapaport and the architect Marek Suzin, it symbolizes the heroic defiance of the Ghetto Uprising of 1943, which was planned not as a bid for liberty but as an honourable way to die. It lasted one month.

Reliefs on the monument depict men, women and children struggling to flee the burning ghetto, together with a procession of Jews being driven to death camps under the threat of Nazi bayonets.

In front of this monument, on 7 December 1970, Willy Brandt, Chancellor of West Germany, knelt in homage to the murdered victims. Today, people come here from all over the world to remember the heroes of the Uprising.

GHETTO UPRISING

The Nazis created the Jewish ghetto on 16 November 1940. The area was carefully isolated with barbed wire fencing, which was later replaced with brick walls. Over 450,000 people were crowded into the ghetto: Jews from Warsaw and other parts of Poland as well as gypsies. In March 1942 the Germans began to liquidate the ghetto, deporting over 300,000 people to the death camp in Treblinka. The Ghetto Uprising, which began on 19 April 1943 and lasted one month, was organized by the secret Jewish Fighting Organization. Following the suppression of the Uprising, the Nazis razed the whole area to the ground.

Further Afield

THERE ARE MANY places of interest outside the centre of Warsaw. The most important lie along the Royal Route stretching from the Royal Castle in the north to Wilanów in the south, and also on the edges of the escarpment that runs down to the left bank of the River Vistula; here there are several country mansions with extensive parks. Most can be reached by tram or by bus.

Grave of Father Jerzy Popiełuszko, Church of St Stanisław Kostka

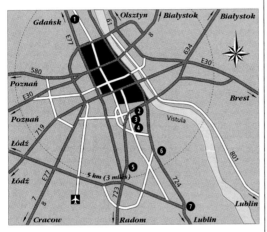

SIGHTS AT A GLANCE

Belvedere Palace **4**
Centre for Contemporary Art **2**
Church of St Anthony **6**
Church of St Stanisław Kostka **1**
Królikarnia Palace **5**
Łazienki Palace **3**
Wilanów **7**

KEY

■ City centre
■ Main road
═ Other road
≡ River
✈ Airport

Church of St Stanisław Kostka **1**

ul. Hozjusza 1. 🚋 (0 22) 839 45 72. 🚌 116, 121, 122, 157, 195, 303, 409, 413, 414, 415, 420, 508, 514, 515. 🚊 6, 15, 36, 45.

THE MODERNIST Church of St Stanisław Kostka (Kościół św. Stanisława Kostki), set among the villas of Żoliborz, is the burial place of Father Jerzy Popiełuszko, the pastor of the Solidarity movement, and because of this it is a place of pilgrimage for Poles. Popiełuszko was a national hero, renowned for his courageous sermons in defence of Poland's freedom. He was eventually murdered in 1984 by communist security agents. His grave is in the church cemetery; it is covered with a stone cross and surrounded by linked rocks arranged in the manner of a rosary. The church itself is distinguished by its openwork twin towers. Inside, there are Baroque paintings by the Silesian artist Michael Willmann.

Centre for Contemporary Art **2**

Aleje Ujazdowskie 6. **Map** 3 C5. 🚋 (0 22) 628 12 71. 🚌 116, 118, 119, 122, 138, 151, 180, 182, 187, 188, 195, 382, 403, 404, 408, 415, 420, 503, 513, 520. ○ 11am–5pm Tue–Thu, Sat, Sun, 11am–7pm Fri. 🎟 (free on Thu). ☑ ◙ 🚻 ⚕ ☕ ♿

THE CENTRE for Contemporary Art (Centrum Sztuki Współczesnej) organizes exhibitions of the work of artists from all over the world on a scale unequalled else-

Ujazdowski Castle, the home of the Centre for Contemporary Art

where in Europe. The centre is housed in Ujazdowski Castle, an early Baroque fortification built at the beginning of the 17th century for Zygmunt III Vasa and his son Władysław IV. The castle's layout was spacious – it had an internal cloistered courtyard and four towers – but its splendour was destined to be short-lived; the Swedish army sacked it in 1655 and it later changed hands repeatedly, being rebuilt many times. During World War II, Ujazdowski Castle was destroyed by fire. The ruins were completely removed in 1953 and rebuilding of the castle only began in the 1970s.

Refreshments are available in a room called the Qchnia Artystyczna, which is decorated in an original – if perhaps mad – manner and which commands exquisite views from the escarpment (see p317).

Łazienki Palace **3**

See pp94–95.

Belvedere Palace ❹

ul. Belwederska 52. 🚌 *116, 118, 119, 180, 195.* ⬤ *closed indefinitely for refurbishment.*

THE HISTORY of Belvedere Palace (Belweder) goes back to the 17th century. Its present appearance, however, dates from 1818, when it was refashioned by Jakub Kubicki for the Russian governor-general Prince Constantine (the much-hated brother of Tsar Alexander I) and his Polish aristocrat wife. On the night of 29 November 1830, a detachment of cadet officers, together with a number of students, attacked the palace, starting the November Insurrection.

After 1918, Belvedere Palace became the official residence of the presidents of Poland, including Marshal Józef Piłsudski (1867–1935), to whom an exhibition situated in the palace is devoted.

To the south of the palace, built on the site of the now demolished Ujazdowski Church, a terrace was built with a landscaped park at the foot of the escarpment. It was adorned with canals, a pool and several romantic pavilions in Greek, Egyptian and Gothic styles. These grounds are now part of Łazienki Park. This exceptionally beautiful Neo-Classical palace is best seen from the escarpment.

Królikarnia Palace ❺

ul. Puławska 113 a. 📞 *(0 22) 843 15 86.* 🚌 *167, 505, 514, 515, 516, 524.* 🚊 *4, 18, 19, 33, 35, 36.* ⬤ *10am–3:30pm Tue–Sun.* 🎟 *(free on Thu).* 📷 🚫 🎥 *no flash.* ♿

KRÓLIKARNIA PALACE (Pałacyk Królikarnia) owes its unusual name ("rabbit hutch") to the fact that it stands on the site of a rabbit farm and hunting grounds that belonged to August II in the 18th century. It is a square building covered with a dome, recalling Andrea Palladio's masterpiece, the Villa Rotonda, near Vicenza. This exquisite little Neo-Classical palace is set in a garden on the slope of the escarpment in the district of Mokotów. It was designed by Dominik Merlini for Karol de Valery Thomatis, the director of Stanisław August Poniatowski's royal theatres and a man reputed to have amassed a fortune at cards.

Today the palace houses the Xawery Dunikowski Museum, containing works by this renowned contemporary Polish sculptor.

Fatum, a sculpture by Xawery Dunikowski in Królikarnia Park

Baroque Church of St Anthony at Czerniaków

Church of St Anthony ❻

ul. Czerniakowska 2/4. 📞 *(0 22) 842 03 71.* 🚌 *131, 159, 180, 185, 187.*

THE BAROQUE Church of St Anthony (Kościół św Antoniego), built between 1687 and 1693 by the monks of the Bernardine order, was designed by Tylman van Gameren. The church stands on the site of the former village of Czerniaków, which belonged to Stanisław Herakliusz Lubomirski, the Grand Crown Marshal, who was nicknamed Solomon.

The relatively plain façade of this church belies its highly ornate interior, which includes trompe l'oeil paintings, stuccowork and altars by the painter Francesco Antonio Giorgiolo and the renowned sculptor Andreas Schlüter, among others.

The main theme of the paintings is the life of St Anthony of Padua; another person portrayed on the inside of the dome is Antonius Druzus, a legendary Roman ancestor of the Lubomirski lineage.

In a glass coffin under the high altar are the relics of St Boniface of Tarsus, who worked as an administrator for a Roman senator and was martyred in the year 300 AD. These treasured relics were presented to Stanisław Lubomirski by Pope Innocent XI in 1687.

Façade of the Neo-Classical Belvedere Palace, looking onto the gardens

Łazienki Palace ❸

ŁAZIENKI PARK is part of a great complex of heritage gardens. In the 17th century there was a royal menagerie along the foot of the escarpment. In 1674, Grand Crown Marshal Stanisław Herakliusz Lubomirski acquired the park and, engaging the services of Tylman van Gameren, he altered the southern part of the menagerie, building a hermitage and a bathing pavilion on an island. The pavilion gave the park its name (Łazienki meaning "baths"). In the second half of the 18th century, the park was owned by Stanisław August Poniatowski, who commissioned Karol Ludwik Agricola, Karol Schultz and later Jan Christian Schuch to lay it out as a formal garden. Lubomirski's baths were refashioned into a royal residence, Łazienki Palace, or Palace on the Water, which is now a museum.

Peacock
Just as in Stanisław August Poniatowski's time, visitors to Łazienki Park can admire the peacocks and take a boat ride on the lake, which is full of carp.

Old Orangery
In 1774–8, Dominik Merlini created the Stanisławowski Theatre in the Old Orangery. It is one of the few remaining 18th-century court theatres in the world.

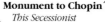

Monument to Chopin
This Secessionist monument was sculpted in 1908 by Wacław Szymanowski but not unveiled until 1926. Positioned at the side of a lake, it depicts Poland's most celebrated composer sitting under a willow tree, seeking inspiration from nature.

0 m　　　　　　100

0 yds　　　　　100

Temple of the Sibyl
This Neo-Classical building, based on an ancient Greek temple, dates from the 1820s. It is made of wood.

STAR SIGHTS

★ **Palace on the Water**

★ **Theatre on the Island**

★ Palace on the Water
Stanisław Lubomirski's 17th-century baths were converted (1772–93) into the Palace on the Water, Stanisław August Poniatowski's summer home.

Myślewicki Palace
Dominik Merlini designed the early Neo-Classical Myślewicki Palace in 1775–84 for Stanisław August Poniatowski's nephew, Prince Józef Poniatowski.

★ Theatre on the Island
The stage of the Theatre on the Island has a permanent backdrop imitating the ruins of a temple in the ancient city of Baalbek, Lebanon.

New Orangery
This building in cast iron and glass was designed by Józef Orłowski and Adam Loewe in 1860–61.

Wilanów ⑦

Detail from *Glory*

WILANÓW PALACE was built at the end of the 17th century as the city residence of Jan III Sobieski. This illustrious monarch, who valued family life as much as material splendour, commissioned Augustyn Locci to build a modest country house. Later the palace was extended and adorned by renowned architects and artists including Andreas Schlüter and Michelangelo Palloni.

Chinese Summerhouse
This small building stands in the English-style garden on the north side of the palace.

Great Crimson Room
The Great Crimson Room was created by Sigismund Deybel in 1730–33 for August II, the Strong, who rented the palace at that time.

Main Gateway
Dating from the time of Jan III Sobieski, the Main Gateway features allegorical figures representing War and Peace.

★ **Poster Museum**
A former riding school rebuilt in the 1960s now houses the Poster Museum, the first of its kind in Europe.

★ **Baroque Park**
*The oldest section of Wilanów's
gardens is behind the palace.*

VISITORS' CHECKLIST

ul. S.K. Potockiego 10/16.
(0 22) 842 07 95. W www.
wilanow-palac.art.pl E-2,
116, 130, 139, 164, 165, 180,
410, 414, 519, 522, 700, 710,
724, 806. **Palace**
9:30am–4pm Mon, Wed–Sat,
9am–4:30pm Sun. Jan. **Park**
9:30am until dusk. (free
on Thu).

0 m   50
0 yds   50

★ **Queen's
Antechamber**
*The walls are
covered with
original Baroque
fabric while the
ceiling has alle-
gorical paintings.*

Rear Façade of the Palace
*Open perspectives allow the rear
façade of the palace to be seen from
across the park, and even from the
adjoining fields of Morysin.*

**King's
Bedchamber**
*The bed canopy
is made of fabric
brought back by
Jan III Sobieski
from his victory
against the Turks
at the Battle of
Vienna in 1683.*

STAR FEATURES

★ **Queen's Antechamber**

★ **Poster Museum**

★ **Baroque Park**

WARSAW STREET FINDER

The coordinates given alongside the names of buildings and attractions in Warsaw refer to the street plan on pages 100–3. Map coordinates are also given alongside information about Warsaw hotels *(see pp298–9)* and restaurants *(see pp316–17)*. The first digit indicates the relevant page number;

Tourists in Warsaw

the letter and following number are grid references. On the plan opposite, Warsaw is divided into four sectors corresponding to the four maps on pages 100–103. The symbols that appear on the maps are explained in the key below. The plan of the city identifies the most important monuments and places of interest.

KEY

▨	Important monument
▨	Place of interest
▨	Other building
🚉	Railway station
M	Metro
P	Parking
ℹ	Tourist information
✚	Hospital or first aid station
🚓	Police station
✝	Church
✡	Synagogue
⊠	Post office
🚕	Taxi rank
=	Railway line
→	One-way street
▬	Pedestrianized street

SCALE OF MAPS 1–4

0 m	250
0 yds	250

Summer café garden in the Old Town

Marathon runners on Krakowskie Przedmieście

0 m	500
0 yds	500

Façade of the Neo-Classical Grand Theatre designed by Antonio Corazzi, on Plac Teatralny

Church of the Holy Spirit from Ulica Freta

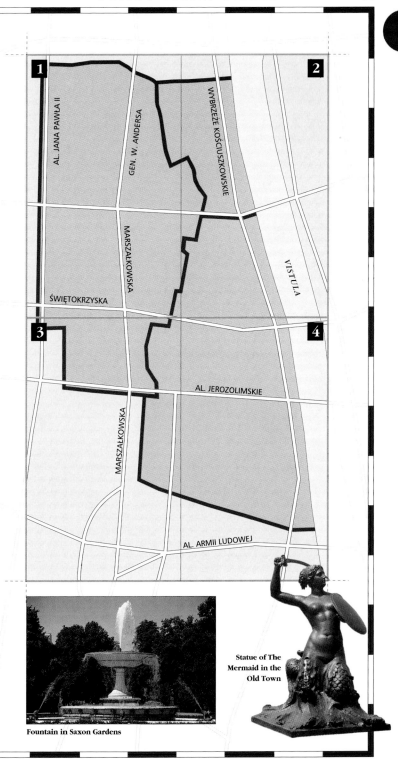

Fountain in Saxon Gardens

Statue of The Mermaid in the Old Town

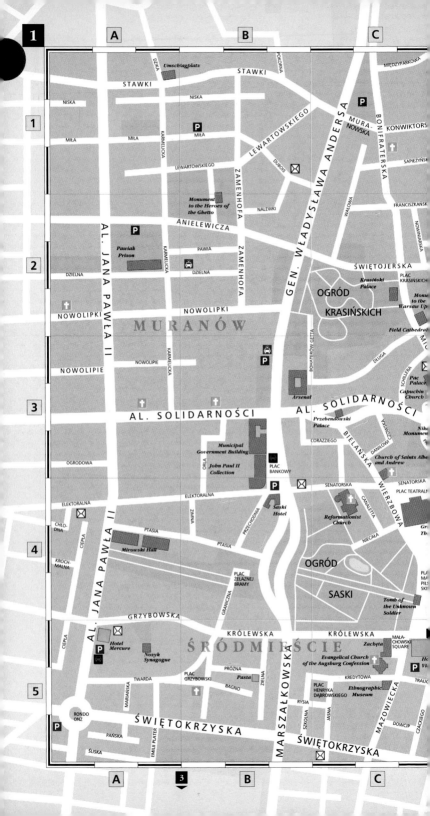

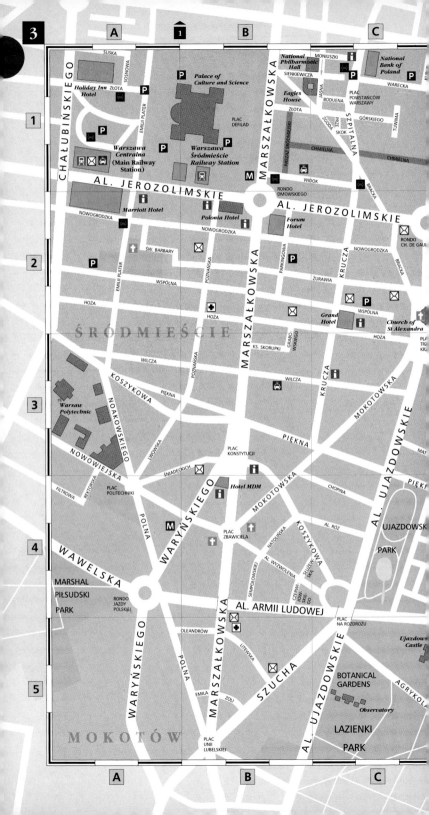

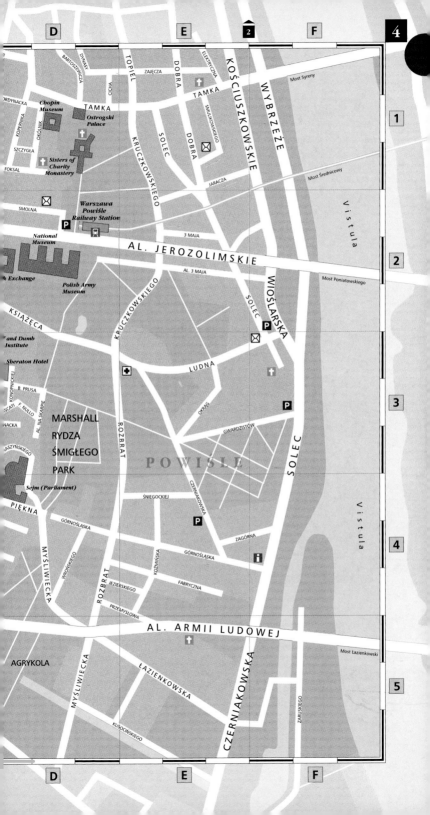

POLAND REGION
BY REGION

Poland at a Glance

WHILE SOUTHERN Poland consists of a band of mountains and uplands, Central Poland is a land of endless plains. In the north, a post-glacial landscape dominates, and the Baltic coast, though fairly cool, has beautiful sandy beaches. Its provinces also offer unblemished natural landscapes. The Tatra Mountains, the highest in Poland, are traversed by well-marked footpaths, from which fine views and a pure alpine environment can be enjoyed. For admirers of manmade structures, many historic buildings have survived in regional Poland, despite the country's stormy history.

*The **Gdańsk Crane** (see p237) is one of the largest European cranes dating from the Middle Ages. Restored after war damage, it stands as a symbol of the city's former commercial might.*

*Many of the attractive **sandy beaches** (see p259) on the Baltic Sea are backed by cliffs, which are vulnerable to storm damage.*

GDAŃSK
(See pp230–49)

POMERANIA
(See pp250–73)

**WIELKOPOLSKA
(GREATER POLAND)**
(See pp206–29)

SILESIA
(See pp174–205)

CRACOW
(See pp126–

***Raczyński Palace** (see pp212–13) at Rogalin is one of the most splendid residences in Greater Poland. The late Baroque palace now houses a museum of interiors and a valuable collection of paintings. It is surrounded by a beautiful park with ancient oaks.*

***The town hall in Wrocław** (see p191) is one of the most interesting late Medieval buildings in Central Europe. It is crowned with unusual finials and fine stone sculptures.*

0 km   75

0 miles   75

◁ **Panorama over the Vistula from Kazimierz Dolny**

The Mazurian Lake District (see pp284–5), *known as "The Land of a Thousand Lakes", is a wilderness, with great forests, extensive woods and marshlands, and brick-built houses, Gothic churches and castles. Its pure character, unspoilt by civilization, is appreciated by storks: more nest here than anywhere else in Europe.*

**IIA, MAZURIA AND
ŁYSTOK REGION**
(See pp274–91)

In Kazimierz Dolny (see p119), *under the Renaissance colonnades of the town houses in the market square, paintings are on display and wicker baskets offered for sale. Fortune-telling gypsies mingle among the tourists.*

WARSAW
(See pp56–103)

**MAZOVIA AND
THE LUBLIN REGION**
(See pp108–25)

**ŁOPOLSKA
(SER POLAND)**
e pp146–73)

The Cloth Hall in Cracow (see p131), *an unusual building in the centre of Main Market Square, once contained market stalls. Today it is filled with shops selling souvenirs and local folk art, and popular cafés. On the first floor there is a splendid gallery of 19th-century Polish art.*

Krasiczyn Castle (see p170), *dating from the early 17th century, is defended by sturdy towers. The walls have elaborate parapets.*

MAZOVIA AND THE LUBLIN REGION

I N THE NOSTALGIC LOWLAND *landscape of Mazovia, sandy roads wind through the fields, lines of windswept willows stand in isolation, and meadows stretch to the edge of valleys where swift rivers flow. For centuries, Podlasie was the borderland between the Poles and the eastern Slavonic peoples. The hilly Lublin region has many excellent examples of Renaissance and Baroque architecture.*

For centuries, Mazovia was, both culturally and economically, one of the least developed areas of the ethnically Polish lands of the Commonwealth of Two Nations. In the early Middle Ages it was the homeland of the Mazowie tribe. It was united with the state of the Polanie under Prince Mieszko I (963–92). The Principality of Mazovia came into existence in 1138, during the division of Poland, and it preserved its independence for 300 years. Mazovia was incorporated into the Kingdom of Poland in 1526 after the death of the last Mazovian princes, and in 1596, Sigismund III Vasa moved the capital of the Commonwealth of Two Nations from Cracow to Warsaw, in Mazovia.

Mazovia's cultural distinctiveness has been influenced by the presence of a politically active yet conservative petty yeoman-gentry. Even today, in the east of the region and in Podlasie, farmsteads, with humble cottages built in the style of mansions, can be seen.

Apart from Warsaw, the towns of Mazovia have always been modest, and this is evident even today in more recent buildings and modern urban planning.

After the Congress of Vienna (1815), Mazovia and the Lublin region formed part of the Congress Kingdom, under Russian rule. In 1918, the whole area was returned to the reborn Poland.

The Lublin area differs considerably from Mazovia, in both landscape and culture. Its architectural jewel is the delightful town of Kazimierz Dolny, on the banks of the Vistula.

Mazovia is a region of orchards

◁ **Neo-Gothic mansion of Zygmunt Krasiński in Opinogóra**

Exploring Mazovia and the Lublin Region

THE KAMPINOSKA FOREST (Puszcza Kampinoska), a national park, extends out from the suburbs of Warsaw. There are also large tracts of woodland, with wild animals, in the north and south of Mazovia. The Lublin region has a more diverse landscape. The gorge of the Vistula, around the town of Kazimierz Dolny, is one of the region's most beautiful sights. Roztocze and Zamość, widely described as the "pearl of the Renaissance", are also very picturesque. In Mazovia, the ruins of brick-built castles can be seen, and in both regions there are many country mansions. Żelazowa Wola is Frédéric Chopin's birthplace and nearby Łowicz is a well-known centre of folklore.

The house of the novelist Stefan Żeromski (1864–1925) in Naleczs

SIGHTS AT A GLANCE

SEE ALSO

• **Where to Stay** pp299–300.

• **Restaurants and Bars** pp317–318.

Landscape of Rostocz, in the Lublin uplands

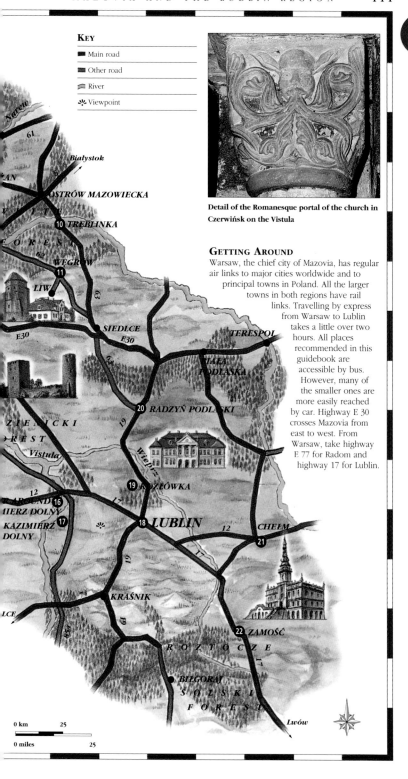

Detail of the Romanesque portal of the church in Czerwińsk on the Vistula

GETTING AROUND

Warsaw, the chief city of Mazovia, has regular air links to major cities worldwide and to principal towns in Poland. All the larger towns in both regions have rail links. Travelling by express from Warsaw to Lublin takes a little over two hours. All places recommended in this guidebook are accessible by bus. However, many of the smaller ones are more easily reached by car. Highway E 30 crosses Mazovia from east to west. From Warsaw, take highway E 77 for Radom and highway 17 for Lublin.

Narew

61

Białystok

AN

OSTRÓW MAZOWIECKA

V   I   S   T   U   L   A

10 *TREBLINKA*

F   O   R   E   S   T

62   *WĘGRÓW*

11

LIW

SIEDLCE

E30   E30

TERESPOL

63

BIAŁA PODLASKA

20 *RADZYŃ PODLASKI*

Z   I   E   N   I   C   K   I   19

O   R   E   S   T

Vistula

Wieprz

12

AROUND 16

MIERZ DOLNY

KAZIMIERZ 17

DOLNY

19 *KOZŁÓWKA*

17

18 *LUBLIN*   12   *CHEŁM*

21

19   17

74   *KRAŚNIK*

LCE   19

22 *ZAMOŚĆ*

R   O   Z   T   O   C   Z   E

17

BIŁGORAJ

S   O   L   S   K   I

F   O   R   E   S   T

Lwów

0 km   25

0 miles   25

The nave of the Renaissance cathedral in Płock

Płock ●

Road map D3. 🏛 126,000.
🚉 🚌 🛈 ul. Łukasiewicza 14 (0 24 264 15 97).

THIS CITY, BEAUTIFULLY situated on the high Vistula Bluff, is best known today for its large petrochemical plants. Its history, however, goes back many centuries. From 1075, Płock was the seat of the bishopric of Mazovia. Under Władysław I (1043–1102) and his heir Bolesław III Wrymouth (1102–1138), Płock was the capital of Poland and the favoured royal seat. From 1138 to the end of the 15th century, Płock was the place of residence of the Mazovian and Płock princes. In the 12th century, it was an important centre of political and cultural life in Poland.

The buildings of old Płock are relatively modest, although the small Neo-Classical houses, now restored, make a picturesque ensemble. Particularly noteworthy is the Neo-Classical **town hall**, built in 1824–7 to a design by Jakub Kubiecki. Here, on 23 September 1831 during the uprising against Russian rule, the final session of the insurgent Sejm of the Kingdom of Poland was held.

Another notable building is the large Neo-Gothic cathedral (1911–19) of the Mariavite Church of Poland. Also worth seeing are the Baroque church, the Classical toll-gates and the remains of the Gothic city walls.

⛪ Cathedral of Our Lady of Mazovia

ul. Tumska 3. [(0 24) 262 34 35. ◯ 4–5:30pm Mon–Fri, 10am–noon Sat.
The most interesting part of Płock is Tum Hill (Wzgórze Tumskie), with its Renaissance **Cathedral of Our Lady of Mazovia** and **castle** remains. The cathedral, built in 1531–5 was the first large Renaissance church in Poland. It was raised by Andrzej Krzycki, Bishop of Płock, later Primate of Poland and a noted scholar and poet. Giovanni Cini and Bernadino Zanobi de Gianotisa were the architects, with later rebuilding by Gianbattista of Venice. The interior of the cathedral is full of Renaissance and Baroque tombstones. A marble sarcophagus in the Royal Chapel houses the remains of Władysław I and his son Bolesław III. The grand Neo-Renaissance façade of the cathedral, with its twin towers, was built at the beginning of the 20th century to a controversial design by Stefan Szyller, who was in charge of the restoration work.

🏛 Diocesan Museum

ul. Tumska 3a. [(0 24) 262 26 23. ◯ 1 May–30 Sept: 10am–3pm Tue–Sat, 10am–2pm Sun & public hols; 1 Oct–30 Apr: 10am–3pm Sat, 11am–3pm Sun & public hols.
The Diocesan Museum (Muzeum Diecezjalne) contains a rich collection of cathedral treasures. Especially noteworthy are the gold vessels and liturgical textiles, particularly the chasubles, the oldest of which date from the 15th century. The museum also possesses woven sashes

The Neo-Classical town hall in the Old Market Square in Płock

from the old court dress of the nobility (see pp26–7). Sashes were often made into vestments.

🏛 Museum of Mazovia

ul. Tumska 2. [(0 24) 262 44 91. ◯ 1 May–30 Sep: 9am–4pm Tue–Thu, 10am–5pm Fri, Sat; 1 Oct–1 May: 9am–3pm Wed–Fri, 9am–4pm Sat, Sun.
The Museum of Mazovia (Muzeum Mazowieckie) is located in a former monastery and houses one of the largest collections of Art Nouveau in the world. Exhibits include reconstructions of domestic interiors, with works of art, furniture, textiles, and everyday objects of the period.

ENVIRONS: There are sports facilities on **Lake Włocławek**, a reservoir on the Vistula, and a stud farm at **Łąck**, 9 km (5 miles) from Płock.

Tum Hill from the Vistula, with the cathedral and Benedictine abbey

Ruins of the Gothic Castle of the Mazovian princes in Ciechanów

Ciechanów ❷

Road map E3. 47,000. 🚩 🚌
ℹ ul. Ściegiennego 2 (0 23 672 53 15).

ON THE EDGE of the town stand the Gothic ruins of the red-brick **Castle of the Mazovian princes**, built around 1420–30. After Mazovia was incorporated into the Kingdom of Poland, the widowed Queen Bona often stayed here. Today, the castle accommodates one of the exhibitions of the **Museum of the Mazovian Nobility** (Muzeum Szlachty Mazowieckiej).

In the town itself is the Gothic **Church of the Annunciation**, founded in the first half of the 16th century and rebuilt in the 17th, the parish **Church of the Nativity of the Blessed Virgin Mary**, dating from the 16th century, and the modest Neo-Gothic **town hall**, designed by Henryk Marconi in the mid-19th century. The low-rise apartment blocks with gable roofs near the railway station were built during the Nazi occupation. After the fall of Poland in September 1939 and the annexation of northern Mazovia to the Third Reich, the Nazis planned to settle German colonists in many towns here. Except for the castle and parish church, they intended to demolish the whole of Ciechanów and build it anew.

🏛 **Museum of the Mazovian Nobility**
ul. Warszawska 61a. 📞 (0 23) 672 53 46. 🕐 10am–4pm Tue–Sun. 🆓 (free on Sat).

Opinogóra ❸

Road map E3. 580. 🚩 🚌

OPINOGÓRA IS closely associated with Count Zygmunt Krasiński (1812–59), a leading poet of the Romantic movement. The miniature Neo-Gothic mansion, situated in an extensive landscaped park, was built as a wedding present for the poet, who moved here in 1843. According to local people, it was designed by the French architect Eugène Emmanuel Viollet-le-Duc, although art historians attribute it to Henryk Marconi. Today, the mansion houses the **Museum of Romanticism** (Muzeum Romantyzmu).

The romantic park in which the mansion is set also contains the parish church, with the mausoleum of the Krasiński family where the poet is buried. Noteworthy too is the marble tomb of Count Zygmunt's mother, Maria Krasińska, by Luigi Pampaloni, dating from 1841.

🏛 **Museum of Romanticism**
ul. Krasińskiego 5. 📞 (0 23) 671 70 25. 🕐 10am–4pm Tue–Sun.

Pułtusk ❹

Road map E3. 18,600. 🚌
ℹ Dom Polonii, ul. Szkolna 11 (0 23 692 90 02).

OF ALL THE SMALL TOWNS in Mazovia, Pułtusk has the most beautiful setting. Its historic centre, located on an island formed by an arm of the River Narwa, has one of the longest market squares in Europe. The town hall, with its Gothic brick tower, houses

the small **Regional Museum**. Of equal interest is the Gothic-Renaissance **collegiate church**, with barrel vaulting over the nave executed by Gianbattista of Venice in 1551 and 1556.

To the south of the market square rise the walls of the castle of the bishops of Płock. Destroyed and rebuilt a number of times, it incorporates Renaissance, Baroque and Neo-Classical elements. After restoration work in the 1980s the **House of the Polish Diaspora** (Dom Polonii) was set up here. Visitors can stay in the hotel and enjoy tennis, canoeing, rowing, horse riding and winter sledging parties. The old-time Polish kitchen, which serves home-made fruit and berry liqueurs and home-baked sourdough bread, is recommended. Also worth seeing in the old town is the 18th-century Jesuit Church of Saints Peter and Paul.

🏛 **Regional Museum**
Rynek 1. 📞 (0 23) 692 51 32. 🕐 10am–4pm Tue–Sun & public hols. 🆓 (free on Thu).

ENVIRONS: Near the town, on the right bank of the Narwa are water meadows and the **White Forest** (Puszcza Biała), which has a rich variety of plants and wildlife, including over 200 species of birds.

The town hall at Pułtusk, in one of Europe's longest market squares

The twin-towered basilica in Czerwińsk on the Vistula

Czerwińsk on the Vistula ❺

Road map E3. 🚶 *1,200.* 🚌

THE CHURCH and monastery in Czerwińsk on the Vistula, formerly owned by the Canons Regular and now by the Salesian order, are among the oldest buildings in Mazovia. The monastery was in existence by 1155 and the Romanesque **basilica** was probably built in the time of Bishop Aleksander of Płock in the mid-12th century. In spite of later Gothic and modern alterations, the main body of the building largely retains its original appearance. The basilica's nave and aisles each end in an apse – a characteristic feature of Romanesque churches. In 1410, the massed armies of Małopolska, Lithuania and Ruthenia gathered around the Gothic bell tower on their march to war against the Teutonic Knights.

ENVIRONS: A few miles west of Czerwińsk is the poor but nonetheless charming little town of **Wyszogród**, overlooking the Vistula. In the Middle Ages it had a castle (demolished at the end of the 18th century) and was the seat of a castellany. Evidence of the town's past glory survives in the church and partially preserved former Franciscan friary, founded in 1406 and rebuilt several times in the 17th and 18th centuries. There is also a Baroque parish church dating from 1779–89.

Żelazowa Wola ❻

Road map E3. 🚶 *60.* 🚌

THE ROMANTIC manor set in a verdant, well-tended park is the birthplace of the composer Frédéric Chopin (1810–49). At the time of his birth, however, it was no more than a thatched outbuilding in which Chopin's parents, Mikołaj and Justyna Tekla, rented a few rooms. In 1930–31, the building was converted into the **Chopin Museum** (Muzeum – Dom Urodzenia Fryderyka Chopina) and the park around it planted with trees and shrubs donated by horticulturalists from all over Poland. Inside were assembled all kinds of objects associated with the composer. During the German occupation, many of these were looted by the Nazis, the music of Chopin was banned and all pictures and busts of the composer were destroyed. After World War II, the manor was rebuilt, and in 1948 the museum was finally reopened once more to the public.

Concerts of Chopin's music are given in the house and garden, providing visitors with a unique opportunity to hear the music of the most inspired composer of the Romantic period in the atmosphere of an early 19th-century mansion.

Near Żelazowa Wola lies the village of **Brochów**, on the edge of the Kampinoska Forest (Puszcza Kampinoska). Frédéric Chopin was christened in the fortified Renaissance church here.

🏛 **Chopin Museum**
📞 *(0 46) 863 33 00.* 🔲 www.chopin.pl 🔲 *1 May–30 Sept: 9:30am–5pm Tue–Sun; 1 Oct–20 Apr: 10am–4pm Tue–Sun.* ⬤ *Mon.* **Concerts** *1 May–17 Oct: 11am & 3pm Sun.* 🎫

Woman from Łowicz dressed in regional costume

Łowicz ❼

Road map D3. 🚶 *31,000.* 🚉 🚌 ℹ️ *Stary Rynek 3 (0 46 830 91 10).*

THE RELATIVELY SMALL town of Łowicz, established in the 13th century, was the seat of one of the oldest castellanies in Poland. For several centuries, its castle (which is no longer standing) was the residence of the bishops of Gniezno, primates of Poland. The **collegiate church**, which was founded in the Middle Ages and rebuilt in the 17th century, contains many notable works of art. It also houses a number of tombs, the most

The manor in Żelazowa Wola, birthplace of Frédéric Chopin

illustrious occupant of which was Primate Jakub Uchański (d. 1581), whose tomb's most noteworthy features are a 16th-century alabaster carving by Jan Michałowicz of Urzedów and an early Neo-Classical frame by Ephraim Schroeger, dating from 1782–3.

The magnificent late Baroque high altar was made between 1761 and 1764 by Jan Jerzy Plersch to a design by Schroeger. It is considered by many to be one of the most original altars in Poland. The altar painting, crowned by an aureole and enclosed between the pilasters of a narrow frame, makes a great impression on churchgoers and tourists alike.

Near the collegiate church is the old **Piarist church** (kościół Pijarów) – the Piarists were a Catholic order. Its late Baroque undulating façade, which dates from around 1729, is extremely eye-catching. The interior of the building has Baroque altars by Jan Jerzy Plersch.

On the other side of Old Market Square, in the buildings of a former monastery and seminary for missionaries, is the **Łowicz Regional Museum** (Muzeum Ziemi Łowickiej) devoted to the folklore of the Łowicz area. Its exhibits include characteristic Łowicz costumes of the 19th and early 20th centuries, decorative paper cutouts and folk embroidery.

In the former chapel, built in 1689–1701 to designs by Tylman van Gameren and decorated with frescoes by Michelangelo Palloni, objects from the prehistoric Sarmatian culture are on display.

Łowicz comes alive at Corpus Christi, when in honour of this celebration local people dress in colourful traditional costumes to take part in a splendid procession that winds its way through the centre of town.

🏛 Łowicz Regional Museum
Stary Rynek 5/7. **📞** *(0 46) 837 39 28.* **🕐** *10am–4pm Tue–Sat.* **⬤** *Mon & public hols.*

⛪ Collegiate Church
Stary Rynek 27. **📞** *(0 46) 837 67 08.*

Temple of Diana in Arkadia, the landscaped park near Łowicz

Arkadia ❽

Road map D3. **🏯** *250.* **🚌**

NOT FAR FROM ŁOWICZ, on the road to Nieborów, lies Arkadia, a sentimentally romantic landscaped park. Laid out in 1778 by Princess Helena Radziwiłłowa, Arkadia's attractions include a lake with two islands and a number of romantic pavilions fancifully designed on historical or mythological themes by Szymon Bogumil Zug and Henryk Ittar.

Among ancient trees stand the Temple of Diana, the High Priest's House, the Margrave's Cottage with Greek arch, the Gothic Cottage, the Grotto of the Sybil and the Aqueduct.

On some of the pavilion walls, fragments of decorative carving and stonework salvaged from the destroyed Renaissance bishops' castle in Łowicz are mounted.

Nieborów ❾

Road map E3. **🏯** *950.* **🚌**

THE BAROQUE palace in Nieborów was built by Tylman van Gameren between 1690 and 1696 for Primate Michal S. Radziejowski, Archbishop of Gniezno. Radziejowski was a noted connoisseur of literature, music, art and architecture, and as such was a client worthy of Tylman. A symmetric garden was also laid out. Around 1766, at the wish of a later owner, Prince Michal K. Ogiiński, the building's façade was adorned with a Rococo figure portraying a dancing Bacchus, with a bunch of grapes and a garland on his head. Ogiiński is also famous for the construction of a canal, which, via the river system, linked the Black Sea to the Baltic.

Between 1774 and 1945, Nieborów Palace was the property of the aristocratic Radziwiłł family. It is famous for its fine furnishings, which include Antoine Pesne's portrait of the famous beauty Anna Orzelska, who was the natural daughter of Augustus II (1697–1733), and the antique head of Niobe, praised in the poetry of Konstanty Ildefons Gakzyiński (1905–53). This Roman head, which was carved in white marble after a Greek original of the 4th century BC, was presented to Princess Helena Radziwiłłowa by Catherine the Great.

A grand interior at Nieborów Palace

Monument to the victims of the death camps at Treblinka

Treblinka 🔟

Road map F3. 🚶 270. 🚃 🚌

In 1941, the nazis established a labour camp, Treblinka I, and in 1942 a death camp, Treblinka II. Around 800,000 people, mainly Jews brought from liquidated ghettos, were murdered here. Those brought to Treblinka II were taken off the trains and herded, without even being registered, to the gas chambers. Up until March 1943, the victims were buried in mass graves. After March 1943, the graves were dug up and the bodies burned. Thereafter all bodies were burned. In November 1943, Treblinka II was closed and the ground ploughed over and seeded. Today, the **Treblinka Museum of Struggle and Martyrdom** stands as a reminder of the past.

In 1964, two monuments were erected on the site of the camp. The monument at Treblinka II is large, spreading over 13 ha (30 acres). It gives an impression of "hundreds of thousands of human beings, coming from nowhere, in a spectral pilgrimage, going to their deaths". It is the work of the architect Adam Haupt and the sculptors Franciszek Duszenko and Franciszek Strynkiewicz.

🏛 **Treblinka Museum of Struggle and Martyrdom**
Kosów Lacki 76. ☎ (041) 787 90 76. ⏱ 15 Mar–31 Oct: 9am–7pm; 1 Nov–14 Mar: 9am–5pm. 📷 ✔

Węgrów 1️⃣1️⃣

Road map F3. 🚶 12,900. 🚌

Węgrów is a small town situated on the historical boundary between Mazovia and Podlasie. Its large, rectangular marketplace is distinguished by the Gothic-Baroque **parish church**, dating from 1703–6. Its interior is decorated with paintings by Michelangelo Palloni and fine Baroque images. The sacristy contains a mirror with a Latin inscription indicating that the legendary Pan Twardowski – the Polish Faust, who reputedly flew to the Moon on the back of a cockerel – used it in his practice of the black arts. Nearby stands a somewhat neglected **post-Reformation church**, dating from 1693–1706. Inside is an impressive Baroque monument to the founder, Jan Bonaventura Krasiński,

Armour, Museum of Arms, Liw

depicting Chronos and a female figure pointing to the spot where Krasiński is buried.

Environs: At **Liw**, 6 km (4 miles) west of Węgrów, the remains of a brick-built Gothic castle can be seen. The castle, erected in the 15th century, was surrounded by marshes, and the gates could be reached only by a causeway. It was twice stormed by Swedes in the 17th century. In 1782, a small house was erected on the rubble for the county chancellery. Today it houses a **Museum of Arms** (Muzeum Zbrojownia), which besides a display of weaponry contains portraits by the 18th-century Sarmatian School.

In **Stara Wieś** to the north is the palace of the Krasiński-Golicyny family, which has the finest examples in Poland of interiors in the English Gothic style.

🏛 **Museum of Arms**
Liw, ul. Batorego 2. ☎ (0 25) 792 57 17. ⏱ 10am–4pm Tue–Sat, 11am–4pm Sun & public hols.

Czersk 1️⃣2️⃣

Road map E4. 🚶 400. 🚌

Today, czersk is no more than a small village; in the distant past it was the capital of Mazovia. By 1413 – most probably due to a change in the course of the Vistula, which had suddenly moved away from Czersk – that role had passed to Warsaw. The spectacular ruins of the princely **castle** tower over the Vistula. The road to the fortress crosses a bridge over the moat. Here, three high towers still stand. In the 12th century, Prince Konrad Mazowiecki used one of its dungeons to imprison the small boy who later became Prince Bolesław the Shy of

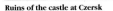

Ruins of the castle at Czersk

Cracow and Prince Henryk the Bearded of Wrocław.

ENVIRONS: Góra Kalwaria, 3 km (2 miles) north of Czersk, was once an important place of pilgrimage. Interesting features include the **market square**, with the **Church of the Exaltation of the Holy Cross** and the small Neo-Classical trade halls. The present **parish church** once belonged to the Bernardines. Before World War II, many Jews lived in Góra Kalwaria. Today, the Jewish cemetery serves as a memorial to that time.

An exhibit at the Centre for Polish Sculpture in Orońsk

Radom ⓭

Road map E4. 🚹 232,000. 🚉 🚌 🛈
ul. Sienkiewicza 4 (0 48 363 18 69).

THIS COMPARATIVELY large town was at one time best known for its arms industry, but today it is more readily associated with the workers' protests of 1976, which took place four years before the founding of Solidarity. Although Radom was rebuilt in the 19th century, several of its older buildings can still be viewed. Nothing, however, remains of the old town itself, which until 1819 was surrounded by a wall.

The most interesting feature of Radom is the Gothic **parish church** in Ulica Rwanska, which was built in 1360–70 and later remodelled. Two Baroque buildings – Esterka and Gaska – at Nos. 4 and 5 Rynek – house the **Gallery of Contemporary Art**; beside them stands the arcaded **town hall**, by Henryk Marconi. Also worth visiting are the **Bernardine monastery** and **church**,

which contain 30 tombs and memorial plaques, the oldest of which dates from the 16th century.
Wooden cottages, windmills and two 18th-century manors are displayed in the *skansen* at **Radom Rural Museum**.

🏛 **Radom Rural Museum**
ul. Szydłowiecka 30. 📞 (0 48) 362 55 91. 🌐 www.muzeum.radom.pl ⭕ 9am–5pm Tue–Fri, 9am–4pm Sat, Sun.

ENVIRONS: In parkland at **Oromsk**, 17 km (11 miles) from Radom, is the mansion of **Józef Brandt** (1841–1915), the noted painter of battle scenes. It is open to visitors, for whom a display of objects relating to the artist's life and work has been laid out. Another attraction is the **Centre for Polish Sculpture**, which is housed in a modern building within the park. International exhibitions and a sculpture biennale are held here.

Centre for Polish Sculpture
📞 (0 48) 618 45 16. @ crtoro@ polbox.com.pl ⭕ Apr–Oct: 8am–4pm Tue–Fri, 10am–5pm Sat, Sun; Nov–Mar: 7am–3pm Tue–Fri, 10am–3pm Sat, Sun.

Szydłowiec ⓮

Road map E4. 🚹 12,800. 🚌

THE MOST SIGNIFICANT features of this small town are the late Renaissance **town hall** and the Gothic-Renaissance **castle**, set on an island. The castle was built in 1510–16 and remodelled in the 17th century. Of its rich interior decoration, only traces remain. Of greater interest is the **Museum of Folk Musical**

Late Renaissance town hall in Szydłowiec

Instruments, the only museum of its kind in Poland.

🏛 **Museum of Folk Musical Instruments**
ul. Sowińskiego 2. 📞 (0 48) 617 12 43. ⭕ 1 May–31 Oct 8:30am–3:30pm Tue–Fri, Sun, 9:30am–5:30pm Sat; 1 Nov–30 Apr 8:30am–3:30pm Mon–Sun.

ENVIRONS: In **Chlewiska**, 11 km (7 miles) west of Szydłowiec, are the remains of an early 19th-century iron-works. A palace stands nearby.

Tower of the castle of the bishops of Cracow in Iłża

Iłża ⓯

Road map E4. 🚹 5600. 🚌

ALTHOUGH THE CASTLE of the bishops of Cracow has been in ruins since the beginning of the 19th century, its tower still dominates the town. It was built in the 14th century by Bishop Jan Grot. Later owners transformed it into an elegant Renaiss-ance residence. In 1637, Władysław IV came here in disguise. Hiding in the crowd, he wanted to get a secret look at the bride he had married by proxy, Cecilia Renata, daughter of Leopold II of Austria. Dazzled by her beauty, he quickly made his presence known. Unfortun-ately, the marriage did not prove a happy one.

A Tour around Kazimierz Dolny ⑯

THE ENVIRONS OF KAZIMIERZ DOLNY are renowned for their picturesque landscapes and rich heritage of historic buildings. Here the Vistula valley is cut by deep ravines, while from the gentle hills magnificent views unfold. It is tempting to linger in Nałęczów, with its popular spa, and in Puławy, where Czartoryski Palace stands in a landscaped park. The journey from Kazimierz Dolny to Janowiec can only be made by ferry; this provides an excellent opportunity for photographing both banks of the Vistula.

Gołąb ⑥
The Mannerist-Baroque church, which dates from 1628–36, has brick walls and fantastic decoration; beside it stands the Lorentine Chapel.

Sieciechów ⑦
The late Baroque Church of the Assumption of the Blessed Virgin towers over the buildings of the former Benedict-ine abbey. It was built between 1739 and 1769, though the walls contain Romanesque remains. The interior is adorned with paintings by Szymon Mankowski in the Rococo-Neo-Classical style.

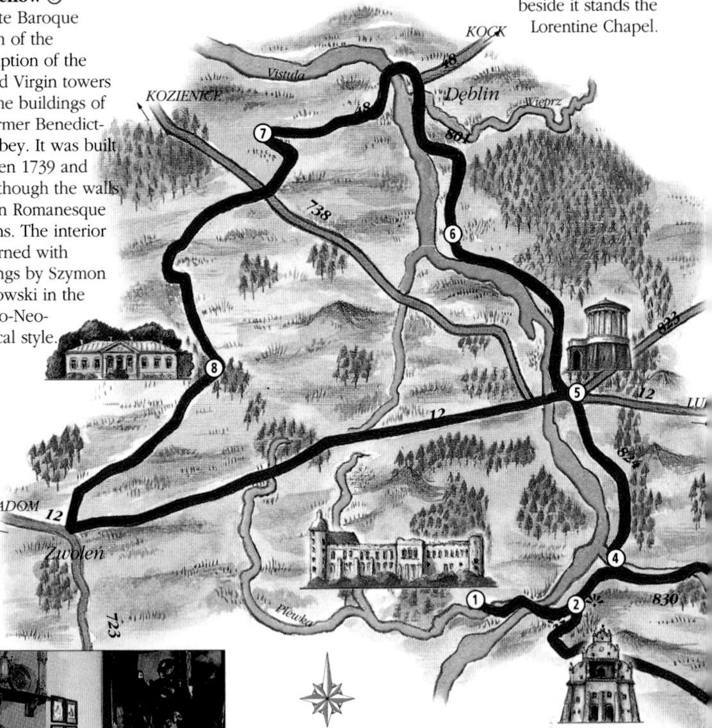

Czarnolas ⑧
This was the home of Jan Kochanowski (1530–84), the greatest poet of the Polish Renaissance. Little is left of his wooden manor, and the museum devoted to the poet's life and work is housed in the 19th-century mansion.

Janowiec ①
The extensive ruins of the castle that was built for the Firlej family in the 16th century now house a museum. It includes a small *skansen* where several wooden buildings, including an 18th-century manor and storehouse, have been re-erected.

0 km   5

0 miles   5

TIPS FOR DRIVERS

Tour length: 150 km (94 miles).
Stopping-off points: Good cafés
and restaurants are in Kazimierz
Dolny, Nałęczów and Puławy. The
ferry from Kazimierz to Janowiec
runs from May to Oct, every 30 mins.

Puławy ⑤
The former residence of the
Czartoryski family is set in a large
landscaped park, now sadly neglected. Many small ornamental
buildings, such as the Temple of
the Sybil and the Gothic House,
are to be seen here.

Bochotnica ④
In this hamlet stand the
ruins of a 14th-century
castle that, according to
legend, Kazimierz the
Great (1333–70) built for
Esterka, the beautiful
Jewish girl who became
his mistress.

Nałęczów ③
This health resort also
has a spa park, with a
pump room, baths and
Baroque palace. The
wooden cottage
housing the museum
of the novelist Stefan
Żeromski (1864–1925)
is open to visitors.

Kazimierz Dolny ②
During the summer, Kazimierz
Dolny swarms with tourists. It is a
popular weekend destination for
Varsovians. The town is well
provided with guesthouses, good
restaurants and cafés. There are also
handicraft stalls and young artists
offering their work for sale.

KEY

▬ Tour route

▭ Other road

⋇ Viewpoint

Bystra

③

LUBLIN

**St Christopher, House of Krzysztof
Przybyła, Kazimierz Dolny**

Kazimierz Dolny ⑰

Road map F4. 🏠 2,300. 🚌
🛈 Rynek 27 (0 81 881 00 46).
🎭 Festival of Folk Bands and Singers
(Jul); Film Summer (Aug).

K AZIMIERZ DOLNY is a delightful little town, the favourite
holiday resort of poets and
painters. The town was probably founded by Kazimierz the
Great. In the 16th and 17th
centuries, it grew rich from the
grain trade. The ruins of a
Gothic **castle** with a high
tower dominate the town. At its
foot can be seen the Renaissance **Parish Church of
Saints John the Baptist
and Bartholomew** built in
1610–13, which incorporates
the walls of an earlier Gothic
church. The interior has
provincial stuccowork
decoration in the vaulting
and early Baroque chapels.
　The most attractive part of
town is the **market square**,
flanked by several Mannerist
houses, with rich ornamental
coverings. Particularly attractive
are the **House of Mikołaj
Przybyła** and **House of
Krzysztof Przybyła**, at Nos.
12 and 13, dating from around
1615. There are also some
16th-century houses in Ulica
Senatorska, which leads down
to the Vistula, including the
Celej House, which dates from
around 1635. While strolling
through the town, note the
former synagogue, dating from
the 18th century, the granaries
on the banks of the Vistula,
and the pre-war villas.

Lublin

L UBLIN, THE LARGEST city in southeastern Poland, is well-endowed with historic buildings. It is also an important centre of academic life; its best-known seat of learning is the Catholic University of Lublin. Before World War II, the only Jewish college of higher education in Poland was located here. In 1944, after Lublin had been liberated from the Nazis, Poland's first communist government, convened at Stalin's behest, arrived here on the tanks of the Red Army.

Mannerist window frame

Historic houses round the Market Square in Lublin

Sightseeing in Lublin

The most attractive district of Lublin is the **Old Town** (Stare Miasto), situated on the edge of the escarpment. It is reached through **Cracow Gate** (Brama Krakowska), which has become a symbol of the city. This old part of Lublin is a maze of romantic lanes and alleys. The façades of the houses are decorated with Mannerist and Baroque ornamentation and have splendid attics. Many of the buildings have Socialist Realist paintings dating from 1954, when the whole town was renovated to celebrate the tenth anniversary of the establishment of the communist Lublin Committee (*see p51*).

At the centre of the Old Town is the **Market Square**, with Lublin's town hall. Here, the Crown Tribunal of the Kingdom of Poland once had its seat. In the 18th century, the town hall was rebuilt by Dominik Merlini in the Neo-Classical style. Today it houses the **Museum of the History of the Town Hall and Crown Tribunal of the Kingdom of Poland**. The most magnificent place of worship in the Old Town is the **Dominican church** (kóściół Dominik-anów), founded in 1342 and rebuilt in the 17th and 18th centuries. The finest of its 11 chapels is the mid-17th-century Mannerist-Baroque Firlej Chapel. Its ribbed dome is an ambitious confection ascribed to the

Cracow Gate, one of Lublin's symbols

mason Jan Wolff. The main street in Lublin, Krakowskie Przedmieście, is now a pedestrian precinct lined with elegant shops. In Plac Unii Lubelskiej are the **Capuchin church** (kóściół Kapucynów) and the **Church of Our Lady Victorious** (Kóściół Matki Boskiej Zwicięskiej), founded by Władysław Jagiełło (1386–1444) to commemorate his victory over the Teutonic Knights at the Battle of Grunwald in 1410 (*see pp40–41*).

The Jewish **cemetery** adjoining Ulica Kalinowszczyna, established in 1555, is evidence of the Jewish community that existed in Lublin for many centuries, celebrated in the novels of Nobel laureate Isaac Bashevis Singer (1904–91).

🏛 Museum of the History of the Town Hall and Crown Tribunal of the Kingdom of Poland
Rynek 1. 🄲 *(0 81) 532 68 66.* ◯ 9am–4pm Wed–Sat, 9am–5pm Sun.

Interior of the dome of the Firlej Chapel in the Dominican church

🔒 Cathedral of Saints John the Baptist and John the Evangelist
ul. Królewska 10. 🄲 *(0 81) 532 11 96.* The interior of this former Jesuit church is a triumph of Baroque art. Trompe l'oeil frescoes painted by Joseph Mayer in 1756–7 depict scenes set against a background of illusory architecture. The most beautiful frescoes are those in the cathedral treasury, depicting *Heliodorus Expelled from the Temple.*

Neo-Gothic façade of Lublin Castle

Visitors' Checklist

Road map F4.
342,000. for information
call (0 81) 94 36.
ul. Narutowicza 54
(0 81 532 44 12).
Lublin Folklore Meetings
(Jul); Festival of Music, Antiques,
Fine Arts (Sep–Oct).

Lublin Castle

pl. Zamkowy 1. **Muzeum Lubelskie**
(0 81) 532 50 01. 9am–4pm
Wed–Sat, 9am–5pm Sun.

Lublin's most important historic building is the **Chapel of the Holy Trinity** (Kaplica Świetej Trójcy). It forms part of Lublin Castle, which was built in the 14th century and remodelled in the Gothic style in 1823–6 for use as a prison. The interior of this Catholic chapel (*see p40*) is covered with Byzantine frescoes painted in 1418 by Orthodox artists. Among the saints and angels is a portrait of Władysław Jagiełło, the chapel's founder. The chapel is evidence of the cultural diversity of the Kingdom of Poland and the coexistence at this time of the Roman Catholic and Orthodox faiths.

The attentive visitor will notice graffiti left by vandals in the 16th century. In the museum laid out in the rest of the castle are exhibitions of Polish and foreign paintings, folk art and weaponry.

Frescoes in the Chapel of the Holy Trinity

Majdanek State Museum

Droga Męczenników Majdanka 67.
(0 81) 744 05 26. 1 Oct–30 Apr:
8am–3pm Tue–Sun; 1 May–30 Sep:
8am–6pm Tue–Sun. Free admission.

In 1941, the Nazis established a camp at Majdanek for Soviet prisoners of war; it later became a death camp. Of the half million people who passed through Majdanek 360,000 of them were murdered, many in mass executions. The camp has been preserved as a museum and memorial to the victims of extermination.

Lublin Rural Museum

Aleja Warszawska 96. (0 81) 533 31
37. 1 May–30 Sep: 9am–5pm daily;
1 Oct–30 Apr: 9am–4pm daily.

Rural buildings from villages, small towns and manorial estates, together with their furnishings, are to be seen in this *skansen*.

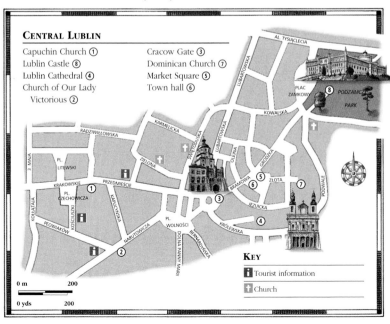

Central Lublin

Capuchin Church ①
Lublin Castle ⑧
Lublin Cathedral ④
Church of Our Lady
  Victorious ②

Cracow Gate ③
Dominican Church ⑦
Market Square ⑤
Town hall ⑥

Key

Tourist information
Church

0 m   200
0 yds   200

Kozłówka ⑲

Road map F4. 🏯 *800.* 🚌

THE MAGNIFICENT PALACE at Kozłówka is one of the best-preserved aristocratic residences in Poland. Built between 1735 and 1742 in the Baroque style by Giuseppe Fontana, its first owner was Michał Bieliński, Palatine of Chełm, who at the wish of Augustus II was married – albeit briefly – to one Aurora Rutkowska, who happened to be the king's illegitimate daughter by a Turkish lady named Fatima.

Kozłówka Palace later passed to the famous Zamoyski family, and was rebuilt in the Empire style and renamed **Zamoyski Palace**. In 1903, Konstanty Zamoyski established what in property law is called an "entail", in order to ensure that the palace would remain the undivided inheritance of the Zamoyski family.

Zamoyski was regarded by contemporaries as a "handsome man, outstanding for his good companionship and sense of humour". He was a great collector, a lover of music and a connoisseur of painting. He was educated in the France of Louis-Napoleon, and the style of the Second Empire is clearly visible in the rich décor of the palace interior, with its Neo-Rococo stuccowork, enormous ceramic stoves, chimneypieces in coloured

Picture gallery and White Staircase, Kozłówka Palace

marble, huge chandeliers, lambrequins, curtains, and furniture decorated with inlays and bronze – mainly excellent copies in Louis XV and Louis XVI style from the best French workshops.

Today, the palace is a **museum**. Fortunately, its entire contents have been preserved, making it Poland's finest collection not only of 19th-century art but also of everyday objects. (Do not miss the early 20th-century bathroom, which is most elegantly equipped, or the palace kitchens.)

Most impressive of all the exhibits is the collection of some 1,000 paintings, which almost completely cover the walls. These are not original works but high-quality copies of the masterpieces of European painting – the largest collection in Poland of its kind.

The palace chapel – which was modelled on the Royal Chapel at Versailles – was built between 1904 and 1909 by Jan Heurich junior, the pioneer of modern architecture in Poland. It contains a copy by Lorenzo Bartolini of the tomb of Zofia Zamoyska in the Church of Santa Croce in Florence.

An annexe of Kozłówka Palace is occupied by a unique gallery housing Socialist Realist art. The building is surrounded by a park which extends over 190,000 sq m (47 acres).

🏛 **Zamoyski Palace and Museum**
📞 *(0 81) 852 75 88.* 🕐 *Mar–Nov: 10am–3pm Tue, Thu, Fri; 10am–3pm Wed, Sat, Sun.* ⬤ *Dec–Feb.* 🎫

SOCIALIST REALIST ART, KOZŁÓWKA

Socialist Realism was a doctrinal art style that was developed in the Soviet Union in the Stalinist era. In Poland, it was current after World War II, from about 1949 to 1955. Its theoretical principles were unclear, and in practice what counted were the instructions given to the artists. The heroes of Socialist Realist works were party apparatchiks, buxom peasant women and muscular workers. A great number of such works, which were often to be seen on the roofs of public buildings and museum storehouses, can be seen in Kozłówka, where the largest collection in Poland of Socialist Realist art has been assembled.

Exhibition at Kozłówca

Radzyń Podlaski 🌐

Road map F4. 🏘 *16,800.*
🚉 *station 8 km (5 miles) from the town.* 🚌 ℹ️ *ul. Jana Pawła II 2 (0 83 352 15 35).*

IN ITS SPLENDOUR, **Potocki Palace** rivals Branicki Palace in Białystok, the "Versailles of Podlasie" *(see p290).* It was built for the ambitious Eustachy Potocki, who later became a general in the Lithuanian artillery. The palace was to be dazzling. It was reconstructed in 1750–58, in the Rococo style, by Giacopo Fontana and his talented team of artists. The painted decoration is by Jan Bogumił Plersch and the carving by Michał Dollinger and Chrystian Redler. The appearance of the palace, like the career of its owner, was calculated to have a great effect. With its elongated wings, it was different not only in form but also in character. Viewed from the courtyard, the unusual monumental wing, with its imposing gate-tower (visible even from the street), looks almost like a single-storey outbuilding. Similarly, the main block of the palace, which looks modest from the courtyard, overwhelms with its richness when viewed from the garden.

Dynamic Rococo carvings decorate the palace and adjacent orangery. The most interesting are the four groups of Hercules and the Lion, the Hydra, the Minotaur, and the Dragon.

Today, the palace houses various institutions.

In Radziń Podlaski itself is the **Church of the Holy Trinity** (Kościół Świętej Trójcy), built in 1641 by Jan Wolff, the illustrious mason of the Zamoyski family. The church contains the imposing red marble Renaissance tomb of Mikołaj Mniszech and his wife Zofia, possibly the work of Santi Gucci.

Chełm 🌐

Road map G4. 🏘 *69,000.* 🚉 🚌
ℹ️ *ul. Lubelska 20 (0 82 565 36 67).*
🎭 *International Choral Meetings (Apr).*

THE MOST INTERESTING aspect of Chełm is its network of underground tunnels, the remains of **chalk mines** (Podziemia). The tunnels are on three levels and descend to a depth of 30 m (100 ft); visitors may walk along them, candle in hand. In the 17th century, as many as 80 houses had an entrance to the workings. Mining ended in the 19th century. Above ground, the town's most impressive building is the **Piarist church**. It was built by Paolo Fontana in 1753–63 and has an undulant façade, elliptic nave and imposing dome. The Baroque interior is decorated with paintings by Joseph Mayer.

Interior of the Piarist church in Chełm

The best view of Chełm is from Castle Hill (Góra Zamkowa), where remains of a 13th-century princely castle can be seen. From here, the towers of Roman Catholic churches, the onion domes of a Greek Catholic and an Orthodox **church**, and a fine Baroque **synagogue** can be made out. A Jewish community, one of the earliest in Poland, settled here in the 12th century.

🏛 **Chalk Mines**
ul. Lubelska 55a. 📞 *(0 82) 565 25 30.* 🖥 *www.ptt.pl* ⏰ *8am–6pm Mon–Sat, 10am–4pm Sun; guided tours start at 11am, 1pm & 4pm.*

ENVIRONS: The **Polesian National Park** (Poleski Park Narodowy) lies 40 km (25 miles) northwest of Chełm. It forms part of the Łęczyńsko-Włodarskie Lake District and has many swamps, peat bogs and small lakes.

Rococo carvings on the orangery at Potocki Palace, Radzyń Podlaski

Zamość ②

Detail from building, Zamość

Z AMOŚĆ IS ONE of the best-preserved Renaissance towns in Europe. It was one of the first to be planned and built from scratch according to Italian concepts of the ideal town. The moving force behind this project was Jan Zamoyski (1541–1605), chancellor and commander-in-chief of the Crown, one of the most powerful and enlightened magnates of Poland's Golden Age, and the owner of Zamość. Bernardo Mornando was the architect and work began in 1581, continuing for more than ten years. A programme of restoration was carried out in the 1970s, and in 1992 UNESCO declared the town a World Heritage Site. Today, theatrical performances and many other cultural events take place in the Main Square.

★ Town Hall
With its fine ornamental tower and imposing fan staircase, the Town Hall is the focal point of Zamość.

★ Cathedral
The cathedral, designed by Bernardo Morandi in 1587, was completed in the 1630s. It was rebuilt in 1824–6. It has an unusual Mannerist façade and distinctively decorated vaulting.

Arsenal
The Arsenal, closely connected with the town's formidable fortifications, is today the Polish Army Museum.

Franciscan Church
In the 19th century, this large church was turned into a barracks and its Baroque gables pulled down.

VISITORS' CHECKLIST
Road map G5. 68,000.
Rynek Wielki 13 (0 84 639 22 92). **Regional Museum** *ul. Ormiańska 30.* (0 84) 638 64 94. 9am–4pm Tue–Sun. *International Meeting of Jazz Vocalists (Oct); Jazz on the Borderlands (May).*

Bastion Fortifications
The fortifications around Zamość allowed the town to resist a Cossack siege as well as the Swedish Deluge of the 1650s.

Former Church and Monastery of the Order of St John of God

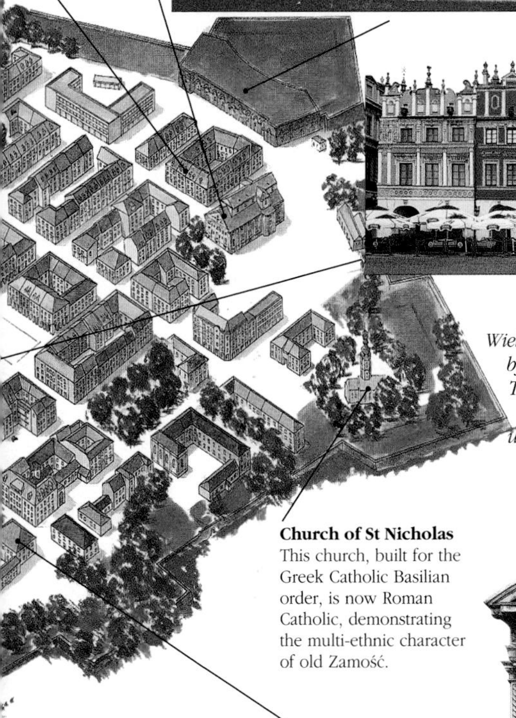

★ Main Market Square
The Main Market Square (Rynek Wielki) is surrounded on all four sides by arcaded houses two storeys high. They were built to a unified design, but many of their façades have unusual and elaborate decorations with an Oriental flavour.

Church of St Nicholas
This church, built for the Greek Catholic Basilian order, is now Roman Catholic, demonstrating the multi-ethnic character of old Zamość.

STAR SIGHTS

★ Main Market Square

★ Town Hall

★ Cathedral

Doorway of the Old Rectory
This magnificent rectory, adjoining the cathedral, is one of the oldest houses in Zamość.

CRACOW
·······················

RACOW IS ONE OF THE *most beautiful cities in Europe. Over the centuries, many important artists and architects came to work here, among them Veit Stoss from Germany, Bartolomeo Berrecci and Giovanni Maria Padovano from Italy, and Tylman van Gameren from Holland. Cracow has been spared major destruction, so it preserves the largest assemblage of historic buildings and monuments in Poland.*

The earliest mention of Cracow in the historical records dates from the middle of the 10th century; it had certainly been incorporated into the Kingdom of Poland before 992. In 1000 it became a see, and around 1038 it assumed the importance of a capital. Wawel Hill became the seat of government, and from 1257, when Bolesław the Chaste gave the city a new municipal charter, it began to spread and flourish at the foot of the hill. In 1364 the Cracow Academy was founded, increasing the city's importance on the European stage. During the 14th and 15th centuries, large sums of money were spent on the development of the city, as can be seen from the numerous Gothic churches and secular buildings that survive to this day.

At the beginning of the 16th century, Cracow came under the influence of the Renaissance. The Royal Castle, the Cloth Hall in the Main Market Square, and many private houses and mansions in the city were rebuilt in the Renaissance style. Cracow gradually lost its significance, and in 1596 the capital was moved to Warsaw, but it was in Wawel Cathedral that successive kings of Poland were crowned and entombed, and the city continued to acquire many magnificent buildings. Under the Partition of Poland *(see pp46–9)*, Cracow came under Austrian rule, which nevertheless permitted a relatively large degree of local autonomy. Hence it began to assume the role of the spiritual capital of all Poles, both in their native country and abroad. Cracow escaped significant damage during the two World Wars, and in 1978 UNESCO declared it a World Heritage site.

Memorial to Adam Mickiewicz, Poland's national poet, outside the Cloth Hall in the Main Market Square

◁ **Wawel Cathedral's Zygmunt Chapel, "the Pearl of the Renaissance north of the Alps"**

Exploring Cracow

A S MOST PLACES of interest in Cracow are located in its fairly
compact historic centre, the city is best seen on foot. A
good place to start is Wawel Hill (Wzgórze Wawelskie), with
its imposing Royal Castle and Gothic cathedral, in the crypt of
which many kings of Poland are interred. North of Wawel Hill
lies the old city of Cracow with its attractive market, the
Church of St Mary, the picturesque Cloth Hall and
many interesting old houses. To the south of
Wawel Hill is the Kazimierz district, with
its preserved Jewish quarter.

Outlying parts of
the city are served
by an extensive bus
and tram network.

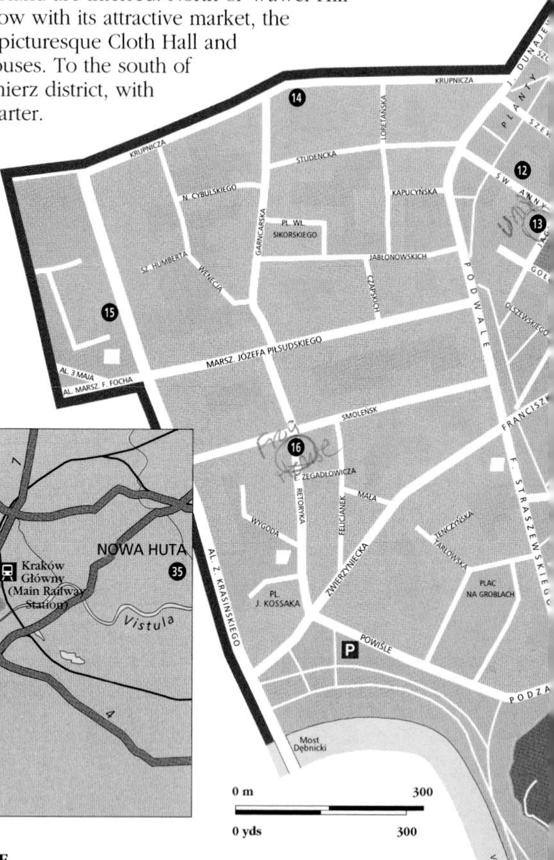

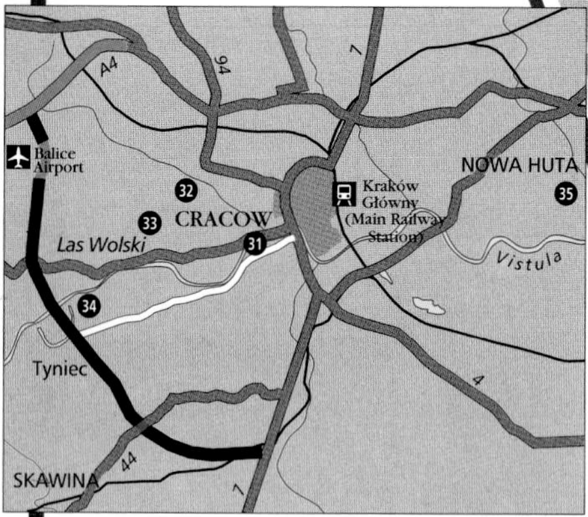

0 m   300

0 yds   300

SIGHTS AT A GLANCE

Churches

Benedictine Abbey
in Tyniec **34**

Camaldolite Monastery in
Bielany **33**

The Cathedral pp142–3 **26**

Church of Corpus Christi **28**

Church of St Anne **12**

*Church of St Mary
pp132–3* **3**

Church of Saints Peter
and Paul **19**

Cistercian Abbey
in Mogiła **35**

Dominican Church **4**

Franciscan Church **17**

Pauline Church on the Rock **27**

Piarist Church **10**

Premonstratensian Church **31**

**Buildings, Squares and
Streets**

Barbican **7**

City Hall Tower **2**

Decjusz Villa **32**

Fortifications on the Wawel **22**

Medical Society Building **5**

Plac Matejki **6**

Plac Szczepański **11**

Ulica Floriańska **8**

Ulica Grodzka **18**

Ulica Kanonicza **20**

Ulica Retoryka **16**

Museums and Galleries

Cathedral Museum **23**

Cloth Hall **1**

Collegium Maius **13**

Czartoryski Museum **9**

Józef Mehoffer Museum **14**

"Lost Wawel" Exhibition **24**

National Museum **15**

The Royal Castle pp140–41 **25**

Stanisław Wyspiański
Museum **21**

Synagogues and Cemeteries

Old Synagogue **29**

Remuh Cemetery and
Synagogue **30**

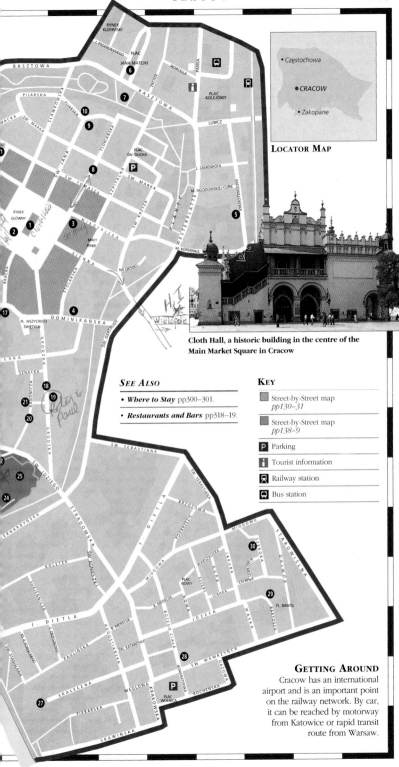

Cloth Hall, a historic building in the centre of the
Main Market Square in Cracow

LOCATOR MAP

- Częstochowa
- **CRACOW**
- Zakopane

SEE ALSO

- *Where to Stay* pp300–301.
- *Restaurants and Bars* pp318–19.

KEY

	Street-by-Street map *pp130–31*
	Street-by-Street map *pp138–9*
P	Parking
i	Tourist information
	Railway station
	Bus station

GETTING AROUND

Cracow has an international
airport and is an important point
on the railway network. By car,
it can be reached by motorway
from Katowice or rapid transit
route from Warsaw.

Main Market Square

THIS HUGE market square (Rynek Główny) was laid out when Cracow received its new municipal charter in 1257. One of the largest in Europe, it seethes with life all year round. In summer, pedestrians find themselves negotiating the maze of café tables that fill the square, along with a host of shops, antique dealers, restaurants, bars and clubs. There are also many interesting museums, galleries and historic sights, including some splendid Renaissance and Baroque houses and mansions.

★ Church of St Mary
The façade of this church has for centuries stood as a symbol of Polish architecture ❸

★ Cloth Hall
This beautiful Renaissance building replaced an earlier Gothic market hall. The upper floor houses part of the National Museum ❶

City Hall Tower
The Gothic tower is the only remaining part of the former City Hall. A café has been opened in the basement ❷

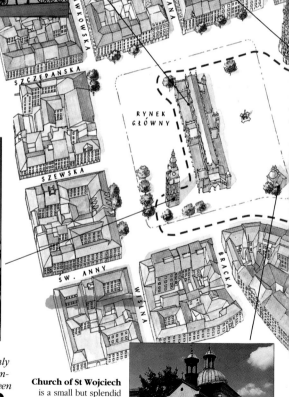

RYNEK GŁÓWNY

Church of St Wojciech is a small but splendid Romanesque church. It predates the planning of the vast Main Market Square and is all but lost in it.

KEY

– – – Suggested route

LOCATOR MAP
See pp128–9.

The Church of St Barbara, dating from the late 14th century, contains many treasures, including a 15th-century Gothic pietà.

House known as "At the Sign of the Lizards"

0 m 50

0 yds 50

STAR SIGHTS

★ Church of St Mary

★ Cloth Hall

Frenzy, by Władysław Podkowiński (1866–95), in the National Museum

Cloth Hall ❶

Rynek Główny 1/3. 🚌 100, 152, 192, 194. 🚊 1, 2, 6, 7, 8, 12, 15, 18.
Gallery of Polish Painting
📞 (0 12) 422 11 66. ◻ 1 Jan–30 Sep: 10am–6:30pm Tue–Wed, Fri–Sun, 10am–6pm Thu; 1 Oct–31 Dec: 10am–6:30pm Tue–Wed, Fri, 10am–6pm Thu, 10am–3pm Sat, Sun. 🖼 (free on Sun). 🚫 ✔ 🅿

S ET IN THE centre of the Main Market Square, the Cloth Hall (Sukiennice) replaces an earlier Gothic trade hall dating from the second half of the 14th century. Destroyed in a fire then rebuilt by Giovanni Maria Padovano, it owes something of its present appearance to Tomasz Pryliński's Romantic-style restoration (1875–9). Today, the ground floor is filled with cafés and souvenir shops; on the upper floor is the Gallery of Polish Painting, with a collection of 19th-century paintings by, among others, Marcello Bacciarelli, Piotr Michałowski, Jan Matejko and Jacek Malczewski.

City Hall Tower ❷

Rynek Główny 1. 🚌 100, 152, 192, 194. 🚊 1, 2, 6, 7, 8, 12, 15, 18.
Branch of the Historical Museum of Cracow 📞 (0 12) 422 15 04.
◻ May–Sep: 10am–5pm Wed–Fri, 10am–4pm Sun. 🖼 🅰

T HE GOTHIC TOWER, crowned by a Baroque cupola, that dominates the Main Market Square is the only remaining vestige of the City Hall, built in the 14th century and pulled down in the first half of the 19th. Today the tower contains a branch of the Historical Museum. Aspects of the city's history are also documented in the Museum of the History of the Market, in the crypt of the neighbouring Church of St Wojciech.

Church of St Mary ❸

See pp132–3.

Dominican Church ❹

ul. Stolarska 12. 📞 (0 12) 429 47 74.
🚊 1, 2, 7, 12, 18. ◻ during services.

T HE ORIGINS of the Dominican church (kościół Dominikanów) go back to the second half of the 13th century. Rebuilt a number of times, by the middle of the 15th century it had become the magnificent Gothic building that still stands today. A number of mortuary chapels were also added; many of them are major works of Renaissance and Baroque art in their own right, with rich decorations and furnishings. Of particular note are the Baroque chapel of the Zbaraski family, at the west end of the north aisle, and the Mannerist chapel of the Myszkowski family, in the first bay of the south aisle. The church was badly damaged by a great fire that swept through the city in 1850, destroying almost all of its wooden furnishings, although it was promptly restored.

Shrine of St Jack in the Dominican church

Church of St Mary ❸

THE IMPOSING Church of St Mary (Kościół Mariacki) was built by the citizens of Cracow to rival the Royal Cathedral on Wawel Hill. Building began in 1355, but work on the vaulting and the chapels continued until the mid-15th century, and the lower tower was not completed until the early 16th. At this time, sermons were preached in German; in the Middle Ages, the bishops of Cracow were German-speaking. This great basilica, with its rows of side chapels, contains an exceptional number of important works of art.

★ Crucifix
The large sandstone crucifix by Veit Stoss is a fine example of 15th-century sculpture.

Hejnał Tower
The famous trumpet call – the Hejnał – is sounded hourly from the tower. The call is unfinished, in memory of a medieval trumpeter, shot while sounding the alarm. The Hejnał is broadcast live by Polish radio daily at noon.

Main entrance

Baroque Porch
This pentagonal porch was built in the mid-18th century to a design by Francesco Placidi.

Ciborium
This large ciborium, in the form of a Renaissance church, was made by Giovanni Maria Padovano in about 1552.

STAR SIGHTS

★ Altar of the Virgin

★ Crucifix

**Gothic
stained-glass
window made
around 1370**

**Visitors'
entrance**

★ **Altar of the Virgin**
*The great Gothic
polyptych is 12 m (39 ft)
long and 11 m (36 ft)
high. It was carved by Veit
Stoss in 1477–89.*

**Stained-glass window, Medical
Society Building**

Medical Society Building ⑤

ul. Radziwiłłowska 4. ☎ (0 12) 422
75 47. 🖥 www.tlk.krakow.pl 🚊 1,
3, 7, 9, 19, 22. ⬤ 10am–3pm
Mon–Fri.

THE MEDICAL Society Building
(Gmach Towarzystwa
Lekarskiego) was designed by
Władysław Kaczmarski and
Józef Sowiński and built in
1904. It would hardly merit
mention were it not for its
interior décor, the creation of
Stanisław Wyspiański, one of
the most talented artists of the
Young Poland movement. He
was responsible for the interior
decoration of individual rooms
and furnishings inspired by
folk art, as in the magnificent
stained-glass window *Apollo*
and *The Solar System*.

Plac Matejki ⑥

🚌 100, 115, 124, 152, 192, 194,
501, 502 🚊 3, 4, 5, 7, 13, 14,
15, 19.

THIS TYPICAL Cracovian
square was laid
out at the end of the
19th century. The
Church of St
Florian (Kościół
św. Floriana), on
the corner of Ulica
Warszawska, is
considerably
older. Its present
appearance is the
result of frequent
rebuilding – in
particular a Neo-
Baroque

reconstruction in the early
years of the 20th century. The
original church on this site
was built in the early 13th
century. At the end of the
19th century, huge monu-
mental public buildings and
splendid private houses were
erected around the square.
The Academy of Fine Arts, at
No. 13, designed by Maciej
Moraczewksi and built
between 1879 and 1880, is
particularly impressive.

The Grunwald Monument
in the centre of the square
was unveiled in 1910 to mark
the 500th anniversary of the
Battle of Grunwald *(see p41)*,
in which the armies of the
Teutonic Knights were routed. The huge sculpture of
Władysław Jagiełło is by
Antoni Wiwulski.

Barbican ⑦

ul. Basztowa. ☎ (0 12) 422 98 77.
🚌 100, 115, 124, 152, 192, 194. 🚊
3, 4, 5, 7, 13, 14, 15, 19. ⬤ 10am–
5pm Wed–Fri, 10am–4pm Sat, Sun
(summer only). 📷 (free on Sat).

THE BARBICAN (Barbakan) is
one of the remaining
elements of Cracow's
medieval fortifications. The
double ring of walls that once
surrounded the city was built
in stages from 1285 to the
beginning of the 15th century.
Most of the circumvallation
was pulled down in the 19th
century. The Barbican was
built in 1498–9, when the
city's defences were strengthened in response to advances
in military tactics and equipment. It protected the Florian
Gate, to which it was connected by an underground
passage. The latter's route is
indicated by a change in the
colour of the paving stones.

The 15th-century Barbican, based on Arab designs

The Florian Gate, Ulica Floriańska

Ulica Floriańska ❽

🚌 100, 115, 124, 152, 192, 194. 🚊
3, 4, 5, 7, 13, 14, 15, 19. **Matejko's
House** 📞 (0 12) 422 59 26. ◯
9am–3:30pm Tue, Thu, Sat, Sun,
9am–6pm Fri. 🎫 (free on Sun). 🅿 🚻

THIS CHARMING street in the
old town is full of restaurants, cafés and shops. It leads
from the Main Market Square
to the Florian Gate and was
once part of the Royal Route,
along which rulers would ride
on their way from Warsaw to
their coronation in Cracow.
   Matejko's House (Dom
Matejki), at No. 41, is the
birthplace of the painter Jan
Matejko (1838–93). It is also
the house where he spent
most of his life. On display
here is a collection of Matejko's
paintings – also his studio, full
of artist's materials.
   A little further on, at No. 45,
is **Jama Michalika**, a café that
was extremely fashionable in
the late 19th to early 20th
centuries. The fine Art
Nouveau décor by Karol Frycz
can still be seen.
   The **Florian Gate** at the end
of the street, is one of the few
surviving remnants of the city's
medieval fortifications, along
with a section of the city wall
and three towers.

Czartoryski Museum ❾

ul. św. Jana 19. 📞 (0 12) 422 55 66.
🚌 100, 115, 124, 152, 192, 194.
🚊 3, 4, 5, 7, 13, 14, 15, 19. ◯
Oct–Apr: 10am–3:30pm Tue–Thu,
Sat, Sun; May–Sep: 10am–6pm Tue–
Sat, 10am–3:30pm Sun. 🎫 (free on
Sun). 📷 🅿 🚻

THE RELATIVELY small
Czartoryski Museum has
one of the most interesting art
collections in Poland.
Assembled in Puławy at the
end of the 18th century by
Izabella Czartoryska *(see
p119)*, it was the private
collection of the Czartoryski

Leonardo da Vinci, *Lady with an
Ermine*, **Czartoryski Museum**

family. The collection was
later taken to Paris and then
to Cracow, where it was put
on public view. It includes
remarkable examples of
handicrafts and carving, but
most significant are the
paintings – foremost among
them Leonardo da Vinci's
Lady with an Ermine (c.1485)
and Rembrandt's *Landscape
with Good Samaritan* (1638).

Piarist Church ❿

ul. Pijarska 2. 📞 (0 12) 422 22 55.
🚌 100, 115, 124, 152, 192, 194.
🚊 3, 4, 5, 7, 13, 14, 15, 19.
◯ during services only.

THE EXCEPTIONALLY beautiful
Rococo façade of the
Piarist church (kościół
Pijarów), which stands at the
top of Ulica św Jana, was
built to the design of
Francesco Placidi between
1759 and 1761. It conceals
the façade of the older
Baroque church of 1718–28
designed by Kacpra Bażankę.
The interior has stuccowork
by Chrystian Bol and paintings by Franz Eckstein.

Plac Szczepański ⓫

🚌 100, 124, 152, 192, 194, 502.
🚊 4, 7, 13, 14, 15, 32. **Fine Arts
Society Building** 📞 (0 12) 422 66
16. ◯ 8:15am–8pm daily. 🎫
The Bunker 📞 (0 12) 423 12 43.
◯ 11am–6pm Tue–Sun. 🎫

PLAC SZCZEPAŃSKI is always
full of cars. Nonetheless,
it contains a number of
interesting buildings that
house the arts and is well
worth exploring.
   At No. 1, the **Old Theatre**
(Teatr Stary) is the oldest
theatrical building in Poland.
It opened in 1798 and has
since been rebuilt twice –
most recently between 1903
and 1905, when it was
remodelled by Franciszek
Mączyński and Tadeusz
Stryjeński in the Art Nouveau
style. The frieze on the façade
is by Józef Gardecki.
   Exhibitions are regularly
held at the **Fine Arts Society
Building** (Pałac Sztuki) at
No. 4. Built by Franciszek

Mączyński in 1901, this too is in the Art Nouveau style. Interesting exhibitions of contemporary art are also on display for viewing at **The Bunker** (Bunkier), a Brutalist building erected in the 1960s, located at No. 3a.

Baroque shrine of St John of Cantinus in the Church of St Anne

Church of St Anne ⑫

ul. św. Anny 11. **C** (0 12) 422 53 18. 🚊 1, 6, 7, 8, 14, 15. 🕐 during services.

IN THE NARROW Ulica św. Anny, it is impossible to miss the imposing Baroque façade of the twin-towered Church of St Anne (Kościół św Anny). The architect was Tylman van Gameren. In designing the façade, he took into account the fact that any view of it would be acutely foreshortened by virtue of the narrowness of the street.

The church building was erected between 1689 and 1703, although work on the decoration was not completed until much later.

The interior has murals by Karol and Innocenti Monti and a fine high altar by Baldassare Fontana. The painting of St Anne that adorns it is by Jerzy Eleuter Siemigonowski. Also notable

are the Baroque choir stalls, decorated by Szymon Czechowicz, and the pulpit, which was carved by Antoni Frączkiewicz.

In the south transept is the shrine and reliquary of St John of Cantinus, a 15th-century theologian and the patron of St Anne's. The church was built after the saint's beatification.

Collegium Maius ⑬

ul. Jagiellońska 15. **C** (0 12) 422 05 49. 🚊 1, 6, 7, 8, 14, 15. 🕐 11am–2:30pm Mon–Fri, 11am–1:30pm Sat. 🎟 (free on Sat).

THE COLLEGIUM MAIUS is the oldest surviving college of the Jagiellonian University, which grew from the Cracow Academy established by Kazimierz the Great in 1364. Queen Jadwiga, wife of Władysław Jagiełło, bequeathed her personal fortune to the Academy, and after her death in 1399 it was refounded as the Jagiellonian University. In the second half of the 15th century it acquired new premises, which incorporated the walls of several older buildings. The present appearance of the Collegium Maius is largely due to a 19th-century restoration in a Romantic style, although the building's Gothic structure survives. Copernicus (see p273) undoubtedly walked in the cloistered courtyard when he was a student here. In the **Jagiellonian University Museum** are numerous exhibits documenting the rich history of the university.

Auditorium of the Collegium Maius, with Renaissance coffered ceiling

Józef Mehoffer Museum ⑭

ul. Krupnicza 26. **C** (0 12) 421 11 43. 🚊 4, 7, 8, 12, 13, 14, 15. 🕐 1 May–30 Sep: 11am–6pm Tue–Fri, 10am–3:30pm Sat, Sun; 1 Oct–30 Apr: 10am–3:30pm Tue, Fri, 10am–6pm Wed, 10am–3:30pm Sat, Sun. 🎟 (free on Sun).

THIS SMALL museum is located in the house where Józef Mehoffer (1854–1946), the leading Art Nouveau stained-glass artist, lived. It contains furnishings made by Mehoffer as well as examples of his artistic output, including the captivating Portrait of the Artist's Wife. The well-known artist and writer Stanisław Wyspiański (1869–1907) also lived in the house.

National Museum ⑮

al. 3 Maja 1. **C** (0 12) 633 97 67. 🚌 103, 104, 119, 144, 152, 173, 179, 192. 🚊 15, 18. 🕐 10am–3:30pm Tue, Thu–Sun, 10am–5pm Wed. 🎟 (free on Sun). 🖥

THE ENORMOUS edifice that dominates this part of the city is the main building of Cracow's National Museum. Building began in the 1930s but was not finished until 1989.

The exhibits are divided into three main sections. The first is devoted to the applied arts. The second comprises an interesting collection of militaria and objects of historical interest, such as the military jacket of Józef Piłsudski (see p51). The third has an important collection of 20th-century painting and sculpture. The work of the artists of the Young Poland movement is particularly well represented. The display also features pieces by schools that were active in the interwar years, and some fine examples of the art of the postwar period.

Model of the Monument to Adam Mickiewicz in the National Museum

Ulica Retoryka ⑯

🚌 *103, 104, 119, 144, 152, 164, 173, 179, 192.* 🚊 *15, 18.*

TAKE A WALK down Ulica Retoryka and it is impossible to miss the remarkable houses that were designed and built here by Teodor Talowski (1857–1910) in the late 19th century.

The architect had an exuberant imagination and a lively sense of humour; the houses that he designed are in an unusual mixture of the Neo-Gothic and Neo-Mannerist styles. They have startling ornamentation, sometimes artificially damaged so as to bestow a patina of age.

At No. 1, for example, is the house **"At the Sign of the Singing Frog"**. Close by is the house **"At the Sign of the Donkey"**, with a motto in Latin that translates as "Every man is master of his own fate". The architect gave to his own house the motto "Festina lente", or "Make haste slowly".

"At the Sign of the Singing Frog"

Franciscan Church ⑰

pl. Wszystkich Świętych. 🛈 *(0 12) 422 53 76.* 🚊 *1, 6, 7, 8, 12, 18.* 🕐 *10am–4:30pm Mon–Sat, 1–3pm Sun; also during services.*

THE ORIGINS of the Gothic Franciscan church go back to the 13th and 15th centuries, although rebuilding in the 17th and 19th centuries

Stained-glass window in the Franciscan church

has considerably altered its appearance. The church, however, is renowned more for its interior decoration than for its architecture and attracts many visitors from all over the world.

A number of interesting features from different ages have been preserved, although the most notable are the Art Nouveau murals and stained-glass windows by Stanisław Wyspiański, dating from around 1900. The chancel and transept are decorated with a vertiginous scheme featuring entwined flowers, heraldic motifs and religious scenes. The stained-glass windows are monumental compositions of great expressive power and represent one of the highest achievements of the Secessionist stained-glass movement. Particularly noteworthy is *Let there be Light (see p49)*, which shows the figure of God the Father creating the world.

The cloisters are lined with murals that include the Gallery of Cracovian Bishops, in which the finest portrait is that of Bishop Piotr Tomicki, painted by Stanisław Samostrzelnik some time before 1535.

Ulica Grodzka ⑱

🚊 *1, 6, 7, 8, 10, 12, 18.*

MANY INTERESTING buildings give this picturesque, winding street leading from the Main Market Square to the Wawel a historical atmosphere. At No. 53 is the cloistered courtyard of the **Collegium Iuridicum**, a law college founded in the 15th century and rebuilt in 1718. A little further along rises the façade of the Church of Saints Peter and Paul, with the white stone tower of the 13th-century Romanesque **Church of St Andrew** (Kościół św Andrzeja) gleaming behind it. The walls of the latter conceal an earlier, late 11th-century

The Church of St Andrew in Ulica Grodzka

building. The interior was radically altered around 1702 by Baldassare Fontana.

The adjacent Baroque building is the former Catholic **Church of St Martin** (Kościół św Marcina). Built between 1637 and 1640 for the Discalced Carmelites, it is now in the hands of the Evangelical Church of the Augsburg Confession.

Church of Saints Peter and Paul ⑲

ul. Grodzka 56. 🛈 *(0 12) 422 65 73.* 🚊 *1, 6, 7, 8, 10, 12, 18.* 🕐 *9am–5:30pm Mon–Sat, 1–5:30pm Sun; also during services.* 📷

THE CHURCH of Saints Peter and Paul (Kościół św św Piotra i Pawła) is one of the most beautiful early Baroque churches in Poland. It was built for the Jesuits soon after their arrival in Cracow.

Work began in 1596, but after a structural disaster in 1605, the church was almost completely rebuilt to the design of an architect who remains unknown to this day.

The church is enclosed by railings topped with the twelve figures of the apostles dating from 1715–22. The interior of the building contains fine stuccowork by Giovanni Battista Falconi and rich Baroque furnishings. The high altar and the organ screen, designed by

Kacper Bażanka, are particularly noteworthy.

Among the many funerary monuments there is none more striking than the black and white marble tomb of Bishop Andrzej Tomicki, dating from 1695–6.

Baroque façade of the Jesuit Church of Saints Peter and Paul

Ulica Kanonicza 🟢

🔲 *1, 6, 8, 10.* **Archdiocesan Museum** 🔲 *(0 12) 421 89 63.* ⬜ *10am–4pm Tue–Fri, 10am–3pm Sat, Sun.* **St Vladimir Foundation** 🔲 *(0 12) 421 99 96.* ⬜ *noon–4pm Thu– Sun.* **Cricoteka** 🔲 *(0 12) 422 83 32.* ⬜ *10am–4pm Mon–Fri.*

U LICA KANONICZA is named after the canons of the Cracow Chapterhouse, who once had their houses here. Most of the houses were established in the Middle Ages, but in the course of later rebuilding they were embellished with Renaissance, Baroque and Neo-Classical elements. They constitute one of the most important groups of historical buildings in Cracow today.

The finest of these houses is considered to be the **Deanery**, at No. 21. Its present form dates from rebuilding in the 1580s – a project probably undertaken by the Italian architect Santi Gucci – which did, however, preserve the arcaded courtyard and the mysterious decoration of the façade.

During the 1960s, Karol Wojtyła – later Pope John Paul II – lived in this house. The adjacent house at No. 19, with a modest Neo-Classical façade, contains the **Arch-diocesan Museum**, which

has many valuable religious artifacts and a reconstruction of the room at No. 21 where the future pontiff lived.

The house at No. 15 also dates from the 14th century, although its present form is a result of rebuilding during the Renaissance era. The house is the headquarters of the **St Vladimir Foundation**, and an interesting collection of icons from disused Greek-Catholic and Orthodox churches in southeastern Poland can be seen here.

A visit to **Cricoteka**, at No. 5 Ulica Kanonicza, is a different kind of artistic experience. Cricoteka was the home of the famous avant-garde theatre group Cricot 2, founded by Tadeusz Kantor (1915–90) in 1956. A painter, stage-set designer and producer of "happenings", Kantor was an extremely versatile artist, and the shows he staged at Cricoteka – for example, *Wielopole, Wielopole* and *The Dead Class* – brought him universal renown. His company continued his work after his death. The Gothic house contains no stage – just archives and documents that relate the history of the theatrical company.

***Helenka*, a pastel portrait by Stanisław Wyspiański**

Stanisław Wyspiański Museum 🟡

ul. Kanonicza 9. 🔲 *(0 12) 422 83 37.* 🔲 *1, 6, 7, 8, 10, 12, 18.* ⬜ *10am–3pm Tue–Wed, Fri–Sun, 10am–6pm Thu.* 🆓 *(free on Sun).*

A DMIRERS OF THE stained glass in the Franciscan church and the Medical Society Building should visit this museum. Many of Wyspiański's works are here; designs for stained-glass windows, stage sets, textiles, pastels and a maquette, *The Polish Acropolis* – Wyspiański's vision for the transformation of the Wawel.

Monumental portal of the Deanery in Ulica Kanonicza

The Wawel

O N THE WAWEL, the Vistulanians once built a citadel. It was replaced by a succession of buildings, including the Renaissance castle and Gothic cathedral that stand there today. Once the site of coronations and royal burials, the Royal Cathedral is regarded by Poles as a spiritual shrine. The Royal Castle beside it, at one time the hub of cultural and political life in Poland, is a symbol of national identity.

★ **Royal Castle (Zamek Królewski)**
The Royal Castle, once home to the Jagiell-onian kings, has survived without major damage. It incorporates the walls of older Gothic buildings ㉕

Fortifications on the Wawel
The Wawel's systems of fortification have been demolished and renewed several times since the Middle Ages – right up to the 20th century ㉒

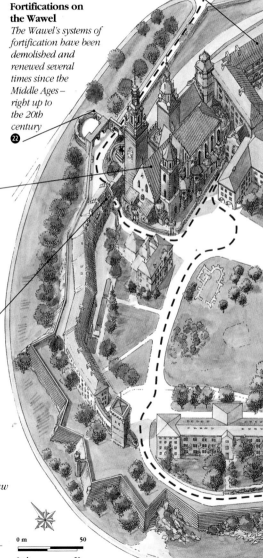

★ **Cathedral**
The Gothic cathedral, lined with royal burial chapels from different ages, has some extraordinarily valuable furnishings ㉖

Cathedral Museum
On display are important artifacts from the cathedral treasury, including the magnificent robe of Stanisław August Poniatowski (1764–95) ㉓

KEY

– – – Suggested route

0 m   50

0 yds   50

LOCATOR MAP
See pp128–9.

Fortifications on the Wawel ㉒

Wawel. 1, 6, 7, 8, 10, 12, 18.

THE WAWEL was fortified from early times. Of the oldest Gothic fortifications only fragments remain, but three towers raised in the second half of the 15th century survive; they are known today as the Senatorial Tower, the Sandomierz Tower and the Thieves' Tower. Of the fortifications dating from the 16th to 17th centuries the most interesting is the Vasa Gate. Since 1921 it has been crowned with a monument to the 18th-century national hero Tadeusz Kosciuszko. The Wawel continued to play a defensive role into the 19th century, and a relatively well-preserved system of fortifications dating from the late 18th to mid-19th centuries can still be seen today.

Sandomierz Tower, one of three towers on the Wawel

Cathedral Museum ㉓

Wawel 3. (0 12) 422 51 55. 1, 6, 7, 8, 10, 12, 18. 10am–3pm Tue–Sat (10am–4pm in summer).

THIS MUSEUM is located in buildings near the cathedral and contains a valuable collection of pieces from the cathedral treasury. Here visitors can admire liturgical vessels and vestments; one of the finest is the chasuble of Bishop Piotr Kmita, which dates from 1504 and is ornamented with

Embroidered hood of Bishop Trzebicki's cope, Cathedral Museum

quilted embroidery depicting scenes from the life of St Stanisław *(see pp38–9)*. The museum also contains such historic items as replicas of funeral regalia, royal swords and trophies from battles won.

"Lost Wawel" Exhibition ㉔

Wawel 5. (0 12) 422 16 97. 1, 6, 7, 8, 10, 12, 18. 9:30am–3pm Mon, Wed, Thu, 9:30am–4pm Fri, 9.30am–3pm Sat, 10am–3pm Sun. 16–30 Mar. (1 Jun–30 Sep: free on Wed; 1 Oct–31 May: free on Sun).

FOR ANYONE who is interested in archaeology, this exhibition is a real delight. The display charts the development of the Wawel over a considerable period of time, and includes a virtual image of the Wawel buildings as they existed in the early Middle Ages, archaeological finds from Wawel hill, and a partially reconstructed early Romanesque chapel dedicated to the Blessed Virgin (Saints Felix and Adauctus). Built at the turn of the 11th century, the chapel was discovered during research work carried out in 1917.

Chapel of the Blessed Virgin, part of the "Lost Wawel" exhibition

"Lost Wawel" Exhibition
On display are various finds from archaeological excavations on the Wawel hill ㉔

STAR SIGHTS

★ **Royal Castle**

★ **Cathedral**

The Royal Castle ㉕

THE ROYAL CASTLE in Wawel, one of the most magnificent Renaissance residences in Central Europe, was built for Zygmunt I, the penultimate ruler of the Jagiellonian dynasty. The four-winged palace, built in 1502–6 but incorporating the walls of a 14th-century building that stood on the site, was designed and constructed by the Italian architects Francisco Fiorentino and Bartolomeo Berrecci. After the royal court was transferred to Warsaw, the palace fell into neglect, and during the era of the Partitions it served as a barracks. At the beginning of the 20th century it was restored and turned into a museum.

Head from the ceiling of the Audience Hall

Tapestry from *The Story of Noah*
These biblical tapestries were commissioned in the 16th century.

Oriental Collection
The nucleus of this collection consists of the spoils of war taken by Jan III Sobieski after his victory over the Turks at the Battle of Vienna in 1683.

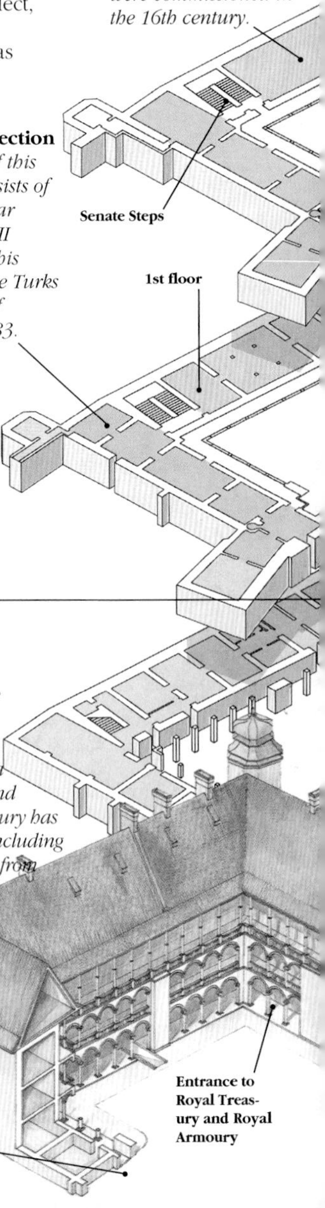

Senate Steps

1st floor

CASTLE GUIDE
The area open to visitors consists of part of the ground floor of the Royal Castle, where items from the Royal Treasury and Royal Armoury are displayed, as well as the halls on the first and second floors of the east and north wings. The castle's Oriental collection fills the ground floor of the west wing.

Royal Treasury and Armoury
The Royal Armoury has a rich collection of arms and armour. The Royal Treasury has many precious objects, including this 11th-century chalice from the abbey at Tyniec.

KEY

- ☐ Royal apartments
- ☐ Royal Treasury
- ☐ Royal Armoury
- ☐ Oriental Collection
- ☐ Non-exhibition space

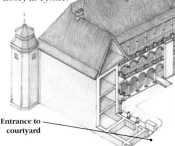

STAR FEATURES

★ **Audience Hall Ceiling**

★ **Chamber of the Birds**

Entrance to Royal Treasury and Royal Armoury

Entrance to courtyard

★ Chamber of the Birds
The chamber is part of a suite furnished in the early Baroque style for Zygmunt III Vasa.

VISITORS' CHECKLIST

Wawel 5. **☎** *(012) 422 16 97.*
🚆 *1, 6, 7, 8, 10, 12, 18.* ⏰
9:30am–3pm Tue–Thu, Sat,
9:30am–4pm Fri, 10am–3pm
Sun. 🎟 *(free on Wed).* 📷

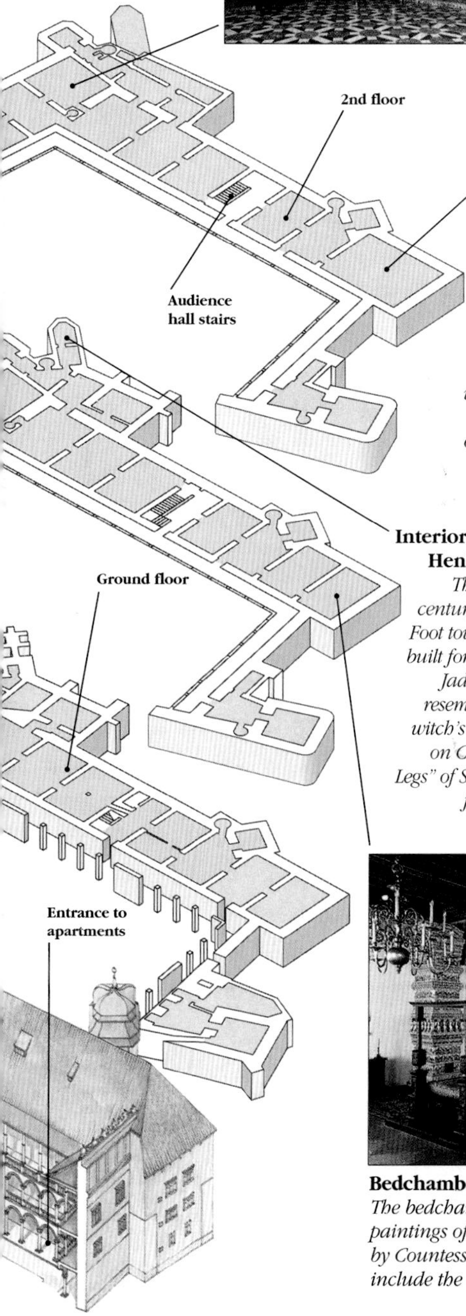

2nd floor

★ Audience Hall Ceiling
The Audience Hall has a Renaissance coffered ceiling featuring the carved wooden heads of rulers, burgesses and knights. Of almost 200 heads that once decorated the ceiling, 30 survive.

Audience hall stairs

Interior of the Hen's Foot
The 14th-century Hen's Foot tower was built for Queen Jadwiga. It resembles the witch's "House on Chicken-Legs" of Slavonic folklore.

Ground floor

Entrance to apartments

Bedchamber
The bedchamber is adorned with Italian paintings of the 14th and 15th centuries donated by Countess Karolina Lanckorońska. They include the enchanting Angel *by Simone Martini.*

The Cathedral

THE CATHEDRAL of Saints Stanisław and Wacław, which stands on the Wawel in Cracow, is one of the most important churches in Poland. Before the present cathedral was erected (1320–64), two earlier churches stood on the site. The cathedral has many fine features, including a series of chapels founded by rulers and bishops, the most beautiful being the Renaissance Zygmunt Chapel. There are royal tombs in both the cathedral and the Crypt of St Leonard, a remnant of the Romanesque Cathedral of St Wacław begun in 1038.

The top of the clock tower is decorated with statues of saints.

Zygmunt Bell
This is the largest bell in Poland. It was made in 1520, weighs almost 11 tonnes and has a diameter of over 2 m (6 ft).

Main entrance

★ **Tomb of Kazimierz the Jagiellonian**
This royal tomb in the Chapel of the Holy Cross, completed in 1492, is one of the last commissions that the German sculptor Veit Stoss fulfilled in Poland.

Shrine of St Stanisław
The silver coffin containing the relics of St Stanisław, the bishop of Cracow to whom the cathedral is dedicated, was made in 1669–71 by Pieter van der Rennen, a goldsmith from Gdańsk.

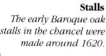

Stalls
The early Baroque oak stalls in the chancel were made around 1620.

High
altar

★ Zygmunt Chapel
The chapel containing the tombs of the two last Jagiellonian kings is the jewel of Italian Renaissance art in Poland. The tomb of Zygmunt the Old was made after 1530 by Bartolomeo Berrecci. That of Zygmunt August was made in 1574–5 by Santi Gucci.

Royal tombs
These Baroque sarcophagi were made for members of the royal Vasa dynasty. The cathedral is the final resting place of most of the Polish kings, as well as national heroes and revered poets.

STAR FEATURES

★ Tomb of
Kazimierz
the Jagiellonian

★ Zygmunt Chapel

Crypt of the Pauline Church on the Rock, pantheon to Polish creativity

Pauline Church on the Rock ㉗

ul. Skałeczna 15. **C** *(0 12) 421 74 18.*
🚌 103, 124, 128, 302. **🚋** 18, 19,
22. **○** 8am–4pm Mon–Sat. **Crypt of Honour** **○** 8am–noon and after 2pm (ask at the gate if closed). 🚫

THE IMPRESSIVE Baroque Pauline Church on the Rock (Kościół Paulinów na Skałce), with its adjoining monastery complex, was built in 1733–42 by Gerhard Müntzer in collaboration with Antoni Solari. The present church was preceded by two earlier buildings. It was at the foot of the altar of the Romanesque church, the first to be built on the site, that St Stanisław, Bishop of Cracow, was murdered (see pp38–9).

The interior includes Baroque stuccowork by Jan Lehnert. The crypt was converted by Teofil Żebrawski into a pantheon to Polish writers and artists. Among the eminent people who lie here are the painters Jacek Malczewski (1854–1929) and Henryk Siemiradzki, the writers and poets Józef Ignacy Kraszewski, Adam Asnyk (1839–97) and Wincenty Pol (1807–72), and the artist and writer Stanisław Wyspiański.

Return along Ulica Skałeczna towards Ulica Augustiańska and take a look at the beautiful Gothic Convent and Church of St Catherine (Kościół św Katarzyny), begun in the mid-14th century. It once belonged to the Augustinian order, but was deconsecrated and used as a warehouse. Of the original features only the high altar remains. The 15th-century Hungarian Chapel (Kaplica Węgierska) next door is connected by a covered bridge over Ulica Skałeczna to the Baroque Augustinian convent.

Church of Corpus Christi 28

ul. Bożego Ciała 25. ☎ (0 12) 656 28 63. 🚃 502. 🚊 6, 8, 10, 19, 22. ◌ 9am–noon, 1:30–7pm and during services Mon–Sat.

THE MIGHTY GOTHIC Church of Corpus Christi was built as the parish church of the new town of Kazimierz, which was founded to the south of the castle by Kazimierz the Great in the 14th century. Work on the church began around 1340, continuing into the early 15th century. The basilica-like interior contains some fine works of art in the Baroque style, including the magnificent high altar of 1634–7 with the painting of *The Birth of Christ* by Tomasso Dolabella, a fine mid-18th-century pulpit, and stalls dating from 1632, originally built for the monks (although the church has been in the care of canons since the 15th century). The monastery is on the north side of the church.

Old Synagogue 29

ul. Szeroka 24. 🚃 184, 198. 🚊 3, 9, 13. **Museum of Jewish History** ☎ (0 12) 422 09 62. ◌ 9am–3pm Wed, Thu, Sat, Sun, 11am–6pm Fri. 🖼

THE OLD SYNAGOGUE was built by Matteo Gucci in

Gothic-Renaissance bema in the Old Synagogue

the mid-16th century in the Renaissance style. It replaced an earlier Gothic synagogue that was destroyed by fire in 1557. In the Hall of Prayer you will find a reconstructed bema and Ark of the Covenant.

The synagogue houses a branch of the Historical Museum. The displays contained within consist of some finely crafted artifacts which were used in Jewish rituals, and documents relating to the history of Cracovian Jews and their martyrdom during the Nazi occupation in World War II.

Tomb in Remuh Cemetery from the first half of the 17th century

Remuh Cemetery and Synagogue 30

ul. Szeroka 40. ☎ (0 12) 266 60 57. 🚃 184, 198. 🚊 3, 9, 13. ◌ 9am–4pm Mon–Fri. 🖋

THIS SMALL AND humble prayer house known as the Remuh is one of two Jewish synagogues in Cracow that are still in use. It was built around 1557 by Izrael ben Józef for his son Mojżesz Isserles, a famous scholar and rabbi, known as Remuh. The Renaissance building was later extended, although its basic outline remains as it was. Inside, the Renaissance Ark of the Covenant and the bema, rebuilt as a replica of the original, have survived.

Behind the synagogue is one of the most important Jewish cemeteries in Europe.

Despite the damage that the cemetery suffered during World War II, many of the tombstones have survived. Many of the oldest, dating from the second half of the 16th century, have been unearthed from beneath the soil. Fragments of shattered tombstones have been built into the cemetery wall abutting Ulica Szeroka.

The town houses of the former Jewish quarter still stand along this road; among them is the family home of Helena Rubinstein, founder of the cosmetics business. This part of town was immortalized in Steven Spielberg's film *Schindler's List*. The district now has shops and kosher restaurants where in the evening real klezmer bands can be heard.

Many other buildings of interest relating to the district's Jewish past have survived in neighbouring streets. They include the Tempel Synagogue at Ulica Miodowa 24, the Izaak Prayer House at Ulica Jakuba 25, and, at Ulica Józefa 38, the Gothic-Renaissance Wysoka Prayer House.

Premonstratensian Church 31

ul. Kościuszki 88. ☎ (0 12) 422 99 70. 🚊 1, 2, 6.

THE PREMONSTRATENSIAN Church (Kościół Norbertanek) and Convent on the banks of the Vistula at Zwierzyniec was founded in 1162. The present appearance of the small nave church is the result of rebuilding in 1595–1604. The extensive convent also dates from the early 17th century.

The Chapel of St Margaret (Kaplica św Małgorzaty), an octagonal building in the early Baroque style, was erected nearby, on Ulica św Bronisława. Behind the chapel is the Church of Our Saviour (Kościół Najświętszego Salwatora). Built in the second half of the 12th century, it was remodelled at the beginning of the 17th, when it was reduced to a small nave church with a tower at the west end.

Decjusz Villa from the garden, the arcaded loggia flanked by towers

Decjusz Villa ㉜

al. 28 Lipca 1943 r. 17a. **C** *(0 12) 425 33 90.* **W** *www.villa.unet.pl* *102, 152, 192. Concerts every third Sun in the month.*

I N THE CHARMING residential district of Wola Justowska stands the Decjusz Villa, a manor house whose origins go back to the late Middle Ages.

It was rebuilt around 1530 in the Renaissance style for Justus Ludwik Decjusz, and acquired its present shape around 1620, when it was extended for Stanisław Lubomirski, Palatine of Cracow. It was then remodelled in the early Baroque style.

Visitors who want to make sure they get the best view of the Decjusz Villa, an impressive three-storey arcaded loggia that is flanked by towers, should view it from the garden. Today the villa houses the European Academy. There is a good restaurant in the basement.

Camaldolite Monastery in Bielany ㉝

ul. Konarowa 1–16. **C** *(0 12) 429 71 45.* *109, 209, 239, 249, 269.* *to men: during services; to women: 2 and 7 Feb, 25 Mar, Easter, Whitsun, 19 Jun, the first Sun after 15 Aug, 8 Sep, 25 Dec.*

S EEN FROM afar, this monolithic Mannerist-Baroque monastery set on Srebrna Góra (Silver Mountain) appears to be a tempting tourist attraction. However, the monks, who are the monastery's sole inhabitants, are committed to absolute silence and no contact with the outside world. Visits are therefore severely restricted, especially for women.

The monastery was founded in the early 17th century by Valentin von Säbisch and completed by Andrea Spezza. It is richly adorned with Baroque features, and from the windows of the chapel it is possible to glimpse the monks' dwellings, to which visitors are not admitted.

Removed from the world: the Camaldolite Monastery at Bielany

Benedictine Abbey in Tyniec ㉞

ul. Benedyktyńska 37. **C** *(0 12) 267 59 77 or 267 55 26.* *112.* *6am–6:30pm.*

T HIS IMPRESSIVE Benedictine abbey is set on a high chalky outcrop overlooking the River Vistula. The history of the abbey goes back to the mid-11th century. Originally, a Romanesque basilica stood on the site. It was replaced in the 15th century by a Gothic church. The present Baroque abbey was built in 1618–22.

Although in the course of its stormy history the church has lost many fine and valuable features, it still retains its monumental Baroque altars. Some elements of the original Romanesque building have survived in the underground parts of the abbey adjacent to the church.

Cistercian Abbey in Mogiła ㉟

ul. Klasztorna 11. **C** *(0 12) 644 23 31.* *113, 123.* *6am–7pm.*

B EHIND THE FINE Baroque façade of the church, which was designed and erected by Franciszek Moser in 1779–80, lies a much older interior. Founded by Bishop Iwo Odrowąż, the Cistercian abbey was built in the 13th century. The consecration of the church took place in 1266. The interior of the early Gothic basilica, which contains a number of Renaissance paintings by Stanisław Samostrzelnik, has survived alongside later, mainly Baroque, features.

Other interesting parts of the abbey are the Gothic cloisters and the chapter house, which contains paintings by the 19th-century artist Michał Stachowicz. These depict the legend of Wanda, whose patriotism led her to throw herself into the Vistula. Her tomb, situated under a tumulus, is located nearby.

Benedictine abbey, Tyniec, perched on a chalky outcrop above the Vistula

MAŁOPOLSKA (LESSER POLAND)

Małopolska is the country's *most picturesque and varied region. Attractions such as the ski resort of Zakopane, hiking trails in the Tatra Mountains, the magical Black Madonna of Częstochowa and a lively folk tradition make it Poland's most popular tourist destination. Cracow, not only the regional capital but the spiritual and historic capital of the nation, is one of the noblest cities in Europe.*

In the 9th century, the Vistulanians established a Polish state in Małopolska. Their capital was Cracow, or Wiślica. In 990, Małopolska became part of the Polanian duchy of Mieszko I, and in 1039, Prince Kazimierz the Restorer made Cracow the centre of his realm of power. For centuries, Małopolska was the heart of Poland. However, its importance began to wane at the end of the 16th century, when the capital of the Republic was moved to Warsaw.

After the Partitions of Poland, Małopolska went into a gradual decline. While Galicia, its southern part, came under Austrian rule, its northern part was incorporated into the Russian empire. When Galicia gained autonomy within the Austro-Hungarian Empire, Galician towns, and especially Cracow, became important centres of Polish culture, retaining their identity despite a succession of annexations. Not until 1918, when Poland at last regained its independence, did Małopolska again become part of the Polish state.

The Małopolska region is dotted with picturesque towns, ruined castles, palaces, country mansions, great monasteries and pretty wooden churches. The eastern fringes of the region are distinguished by their Uniate Orthodox churches. There are also many monuments to the Jewish population that was present in Małopolska before 1945.

In many parts of the region, folk customs survive and flourish, nowhere more than in the Podhale region; in Zakopane, the regional capital of Podhale, folklore and folk art are a local industry.

The Galician small town of Stary Sącz, at the foot of the Sądecky Beskidy Mountains

◁ **Wooden house in the forest, beneath the towering Tatra Mountains**

Exploring Małopolska

M ALOPOLSKA, IN THE south of Poland, is the country's main tourist region. Apart from Cracow, the greatest attractions for visitors are the mountain ski resort of Zakopane, which is the winter sports capital, and the picturesque Tatra Mountains. In summer many hikers are drawn to the region, and its mountains are traversed by well-marked hiking trails. There are numerous welcoming hostels for those in need of overnight shelter. Parts of the Beskid Niski Mountains are almost without human habitation, so that it is still possible to walk for several days without encountering a single living soul. Spiritual relief can be found deep within the forests, where walkers may be surprised to encounter pretty wooden churches.

Interior of a cottage in Zalipie, with traditional decoration

GETTING AROUND

Cracow and Rzeszów can be reached by air. The larger towns all have good rail links with the rest of the country. Some small villages can only be reached by bus or car. The E77 highway goes north and south from Cracow, while the E40 goes eastwards through Tarnów, Rzeszów and Przemyśl. Parallel to it, but further south, major road 48 connects Nowy Sącz with Biecz, Krosno and Sanok.

KEY

- ▬ Motorway
- ▬ Major road
- ▬ Other road
- ≋ River
- ❊ Viewpoint

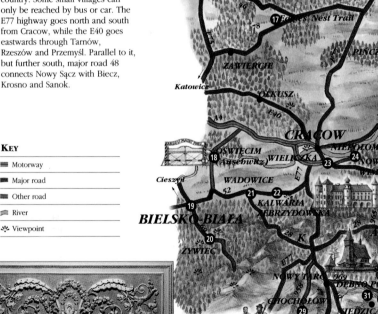

A detail of Neo-Classical decorative moulding in the palace at Łańcut

SIGHTS AT A GLANCE

Niedzyce Castle overlooking the artificial lake on the Dunajec

SEE ALSO

• **Where to Stay** pp302–3.

• **Restaurants and Bars** pp319–21.

The Henryk Sienkiewicz Museum in Oblęgorek

Oblęgorek **❶**

Road map E5. 🏯 *950*. 🚌

T HE WRITER Henryk
Sienkiewicz *(see p23)*
received a small manor house
in Oblęgorek as a gift from
the nation in 1900. It is an
eclectic building with a tall
circular tower. The interior is
as it was when Sienkiewicz
lived and worked here. Today
it houses the **Henryk
Sienkiewicz Museum**.

Henryk Sienkiewicz is the
best-known Polish novelist.
He received the Nobel Prize
for Literature for one of his
historical novels – *Quo Vadis?*
– in 1905.

**🏛 Henryk Sienkiewicz
Museum**
🎟 *(041) 303 04 26.* ⏱ *10am–4pm
Wed–Sun.* 🎫 *(free on Fri).*

Kielce **❷**

Road map E5. 🏯 *209,000*. 🚉 🚌
ℹ *Rynek 1 (041) 367 64 36).* **FAX** *(041)
345 86 81.* 🌐 www.
um.kielce.p/um_polish/tur.html

I N A CITY WHOSE beauty has
been defaced by buildings
that went up after World War
II, the **Bishops' Palace** stands
out like a jewel. It is an
exceptionally fine example of
a well-preserved aristocratic
town house of the first half of
the 17th century *(see p45)*.
The early Baroque façades with
four corner towers have been
preserved almost intact, as has

the decoration of the rooms
on the first floor. The marble
doorways and beamed ceilings
are original.

The palace was built in
1637–41, probably by the royal
architect Giovanni Trevano,
under the direction of Tomasso
Poncino, for the Bishop of
Cracow, Jakub Zadzik. During
the reign of Zygmunt III, this
exceptional clergyman was in
charge of the Republic's
foreign policy, successfully
making peace with Russia and
establishing a long-standing
ceasefire with Sweden. His role
as a bishop, however, was
inglorious. He contributed to
the shameful decision to
condemn the Polish Brethren

during the Sejm of 1641. These
events are illustrated on the
palace ceilings, which were
painted in 1641.

The period interiors form
part of the **National Museum**
in the palace. There is also an
excellent gallery of Polish
painting here.

Next to the palace is the
cathedral, built on the site of
an earlier church of 1632–5,
the time of Bishop Zadzik.

Several dozen wooden
village buildings from the
area around Kielce are laid
out over an area of 4.2 sq km
(1.6 sq miles) in the **Kielce
Rural Museum**.

🏛 National Museum
pl. Zamkowy 1. 🎟 *(041) 344 40 14.*
🌐 www.kielce.uw.gov.pl/muzeum
⏱ *9am–4pm Mon, Wed–Sun,
10am–6pm Tue.* 🎫
🏛 Kielce Rural Museum
Temporary exhibition ul. Jana
Pawła II 6. 🎟 *(041) 344 92 97.*
⏱ *10am–3pm Sun–Fri.* 🎫 *(free on
Sun).* ***Skansen*** in Tokarnia 🎟 *(041)
315 41 71.* ⏱ *Apr–Oct: 10am–5pm
Tue–Sun; Nov–Mar: 9am–2:30pm
Mon–Fri.* 🎫

ENVIRONS: The ruins of a
13th-century castle dominate
the town of **Chęciny**, 15 km
(9 miles) to the west of
Kielce. **Paradise Cave**
(Jaskinia Raj), to the north of
Chęciny, contains spectacular
stalactites and stalagmites.

The Dining Hall in the Bishops' Palace in Kielce

Holy Cross Mountains ❸

Road map E5. 🚃 🚌 ℹ️ *(041) 367 64 36 or 367 60 11.*

IN GEOLOGICAL TERMS, the Holy Cross Mountains (Góry Świętokrzyskie) – part of the Małopolska uplands – are among the oldest in Europe. Eroded over many thousands of years, they are neither high nor steep, but they are exceptionally rich in minerals, which have been exploited since ancient times. The remains of prehistoric mines and furnaces have been found here. The Łysogóry range, with Mount Łysica at a mere 612 m (2,000 ft), the highest peak in the mountains, lies within the

Broken rock on the Kysogóry slopes, Świętokrzyski National Park

Świętokrzyski National Park. The primeval forest of fir trees that once covered the range was seriously damaged by acid rain in the 1970s and 1980s, so that only vestiges remain today. In ancient times Łysa Góra, the second-highest peak in the Holy Cross Mountains, was a pagan place of worship. Its slopes are covered with *gołoborza*, heaps of broken rock. Legend tells of the witches' sabbaths that are said to have taken place here.

The **Benedictine abbey in Święty Krzyż** on the summit of Łysa Góra was built in the 12th century and extended during the rule of the Jagiellonian dynasty. The church, which replaces an earlier Romanesque church, was built in 1782–9 and has predominantly Baroque and Neo-Classical features. The interior is decorated with paintings by the 18th-century artist Franciszek Smuglewicz. The cloisters and vestry, with late Baroque frescoes, date from the 15th century. The domed chapel of the Oleśnicki family, dating from the 17th century, is the abbey's most outstanding feature. Kept in the chapel since 1723, the relic of the Holy Cross attracts crowds of pilgrims. In the crypt beneath

Ruins of the Baroque Bishops' Palace at Bodzentyn

the chapel is a glass coffin containing the supposedly mummified body of Prince Jeremi Wiśniowiecki. In his novel *With Fire and Sword* Henryk Sienkiewicz portrayed this magnate as a saviour, and hero of the battles against Ukrainian insurgents in 1648. History judges him less kindly: a seasoned soldier, an unimaginative politician and a brute, who by passing sentences of impalement earned himself the nickname Pałej (The Impaler).

Bodzentyn, north of Łysogóry, is worth a visit for its 18th-century Gothic parish church. The Renaissance altar comes from Wawel Cathedral in Cracow. The stately ruins of the Bishops' Palace can also be seen in the town.

ŚWIĘTOKRZYSKI NATIONAL PARK

The Łysogóry range constitutes the major part of the park. Natural features of particular interest include *gołoborza*, created by the fragmentation of quartzite sandstone, and vestiges of the primeval fir forest. On Chełmowa Góra, native Polish larch can be seen.

KEY

- -- Hiking trail
- 🚘 Road
- 🅿️ Car park
- ℹ️ Tourist information
- 🔭 Viewpoint

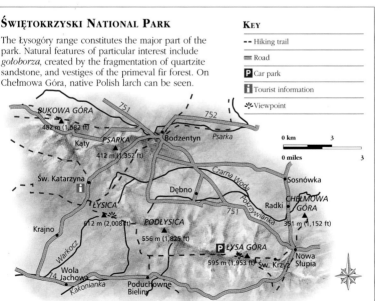

Wąchock ❹

Road map E4. 🏘 *3,300.* 🚉 🚌

WĄCHOCK IS A NEAT town with a very well-preserved **Cistercian abbey**. It was founded in 1179 by Gedka z Gryfitów, Bishop of Cracow. The church, built in the early 13th century, has Romanesque and Gothic features. The architect is unknown, although the inscription "Simon" that can be seen on the façade is thought to be his signature. The interior is decorated with mural paintings and contains tombstones and altars. The most important Romanesque interiors of the abbey – those of the chapter house and the rooms off the cloisters – have been preserved almost intact to this day. The abbey was remodelled between 1636 and 1643, the façade being given the appearance of a palace with the addition of arcades and an enormous tower.

Opatów ❺

Road map E5. 🏘 *7,100.* 🚌

THE COLLEGIATE CHURCH of St Martin (Kolegiata św. Marcina), built in the first half of the 12th century, is among the best-preserved of the major Romanesque churches in Poland. The massive façade has two quadrilateral towers and representations of dragons and plants on its borders. The interior contains interesting furnishings and tombs, the most eminent being the tomb with the bronze effigy of Krzysztof Szydłowiecki, the

Collegiate Church of St Martin in Opatów

royal chancellor who became the owner of Opatów. The tomb dates from 1533–6 and bears a relief known as the Opatów Lament *(see pp42–3)*. The marble tombstone of Anna Szydłowiecka carved by Bernardino de Gianoti in 1536 is also noteworthy.

The curious holes and ruts in the walls of the church are an unusual mark of the past. Noblemen would use the church walls to sharpen their sabres, which they would often do on horseback. This explains why the holes are so high.

Ujazd ❻

Road map E5. 🏘 *1,600.* 🚌
ℹ *(0 15) 860 12 39.* **Krzyżtopór Castle** 📞 *(0 15) 860 11 33.*

THE MAIN ATTRACTION in Ujazd are the ruins of

Krzyżtopór Castle, built for the palatine Krzysztof Ossoliński, probably by Agostino Locci the Elder in 1627–47. It is one of the most eccentric residences of its time in Europe *(see pp44–5)*. Having been attacked during the Swedish Deluge *(see p44)*, the castle fell into neglect. The palace was enormous and for 300 years its walls provided the surrounding villages with vast amounts of building material. However, the magnificent ruins are still extremely impressive.

ENVIRONS: Ossolin, situated 15 km (9 miles) to the east of Ujazd, is the town from which the Ossoliński family came. The historic remains here are much more modest. It survived an explosion in 1816, inflicted by subsequent owners who sought to blow

The stately ruins of Krzyżtopór Castle in Ujazd

it up in search of the treasure rumoured to be hidden there.

The Mannerist and Baroque collegiate church in **Klimontów**, 13 km (8 miles) east of Ujazd, and begun in 1643, is something of an architectural curiosity. The elliptical nave with galleries is an unusual combination, and the columns sunk into niches hollowed out in the pillars make a mockery of the principles of tectonics.

Sandomierz ➐

Road map F5. ⬛ *23,000.* ▣ ⬛
ℹ *PTTK, Rynek 25/26 (0 15 832 37 21 or 832 26 82).* **Underground Tourist Route** *ul. Oleśnickich 1.* ▣ *(0 15) 832 30 88.* ◯ *May–Sep: 10am–5:30pm daily; Oct–Apr: 10am until dusk daily.*

THE BEST VIEW of this small, ancient town is from the River Vistula. In 1138, Sandomierz became the capital of an independent duchy, and from the 14th century until the Partitions of Poland it was a regional capital. Part of the network of underground passages that runs beneath the town is open to tourists.

The main entrance to the old town is **Opatów Gate**. The charming, slightly sloping **Market Square** is surrounded by elegant houses. In the centre stands the town hall, with its splendid Renaissance parapet. It houses the **Regional Museum**. The most important building in the town is the **cathedral**, built around 1360 on the site of an earlier Romanesque cathedral and later altered. The 15th-century Ruthenian-Byzantine frescoes in the chancel depict scenes from the lives of Christ and the Virgin.

The **Church of St James** (Kościół św Jakuba) is an exceptionally fine late Romanesque aisled basilica. Built in brick, it was begun in 1226. Its ceramic decoration and beautiful portal are evidence that it was built by master craftsmen from Lombardy. The remains of 49 Dominican friars murdered by Tartars in 1260 lie in the Martyrs' Chapel.

Opatów Gate, defending the old town of Sandomierz

🏛 Diocesan Museum
ul. Długosza 9. ▣ *(0 15) 832 23 04.* ◯ *1 Apr–31 Oct: 9am–4pm Tue–Sat, 1:30–4pm Sun; 1 Nov–31 Mar: 9am–4pm Wed–Sat, 1:30–3pm Sun.*
The museum is in the Gothic house of Jan Długosz (1415–80), the celebrated chronicler of Poland. It features religious paintings and sculptures from the Middle Ages to the 19th century, including *Madonna with the Christ Child* and *St Catherine* by Lucas Cranach the Elder.

🏛 Regional Museum
Castle ▣ *(0 15) 644 57 57/58.* ◯ *May–Sep: 10am–5pm Tue–Sun; Oct–Apr: 9am–4pm Tue–Fri, 9am–3pm Sat, 10am–3pm Sun.*
Town Hall *Rynek 10.* ▣ *(0 15) 832 22 65.* ◯ *May–Sep: 9am–4pm Tue–Sun; Oct–Apr: 9am–4pm Tue–Fri, 9am–3pm Sat, 10am–3pm Sun.*
The Regional Museum is split between the town hall and

the recently refurbished Gothic and Renaissance castle. The museum contains archaeological, ethnographic and historical displays.

Baranów Sandomierski ➑

Road map E5. ⬛ *1,500.* ▣ *3 km (2 miles) from the centre.* ⬛

LESZCZYŃSKI CASTLE, built in Baranów Sandomierski for the Leszczyński family in 1591–1606, is one of the finest examples of Mannerist architecture in the whole of Poland. The castle consists of four wings arranged around a rectangular arcaded courtyard. The grand exterior staircase and the façades, with their elaborate attics giving the impression of a massive (but in fact delicate) curtained wall, are striking. The square tower in the central façade serves a purely decorative purpose. On account of its architectural ornamentation, featuring spheres, rosettes and strange creatures, the castle is thought to have been designed by Santi Gucci. The **Sulphur Basin Museum** on the ground floor contains furniture, suits of armour and other interesting objects from the castle's heyday, as well as exhibits relating to the history of sulphur exploitation in the huge quarries nearby.

🏛 Sulphur Basin Museum
ul. Zamkowa 20. ▣ *(0 15) 811 80 40.* ◯ *9am–3pm Tue–Sun, 9am–4pm & public hols.* ▣

Staircase in the courtyard of Leszczyński Palace in Baranów Sandomierski

**The Camaldolite church
in Rytwiany**

Rytwiany ⑨

Road map E5. 🏛 *950.* 🚌 🚍

THE MAIN attraction of
Rytwiany is the early
Baroque **Camaldolite church**
that stands next to the monastery. It was built in 1624–5
by the Tęczyński family and is
considered to be one of the
finest examples of Camaldolite
architecture in Europe. In
accordance with the rules of
the order, the entrance to the
sanctuary leads through a
narrow passageway, with the
tiny houses of the monks lying
behind the monastery walls.
The clock in the church tower
marked the times for different
activities in the monastery. The
modest appearance of the
façade contrasts with the
exuberant interior: stuccowork
is complemented by colourful
frescoes painted by the prior,
Venante da Subiaco. The
church is hidden deep in the
forest in a vast clearing,
unfortunately beyond the
reach of most tourists.

For the intrepid traveller, the
ruins of the 15th-century
Gothic castle of Wojciech
Jastrzębiec, Archbishop of
Gniezno, which stand on the
edge of the village, are also
worth visiting.

Kurozwęki ⑩

Road map E5. 🏛 *840.* 🚌

THE 14TH-CENTURY Gothic
castle that once stood in
the small village of Kurozwęki
was one of the earliest stone
fortresses in Małopolska.

Today, only vestiges remain,
incorporated in the large
Rococo-Neo-Classical castle
that now stands on the site,
surrounded by a neglected
park and with stables nearby.
The castle was built for an
influential Poraj family, who
were at the height of their
power in the times of Zawisza,
Chancellor and Bishop of
Cracow (died c.1382), known
for his sumptuous lifestyle.

ENVIRONS: In **Raków,** 12 km
(7 miles) north of Kurozwęki,
is the Protestant church of the
Polish Brethren. It is contemporary with the establishment
of Raków Academy in the
17th century.

Szydłów ⑪

Road map E5. 🏛 *1,100.* 🚍 🖼
Jousting tournament (early Jun).

THE ATTRACTIVE medieval
town of Szydłów is
reached by crossing a bridge
over a moat and passing
through one of the old town
gates. In the 16th century this
was a flourishing town, and
in 1528 it even had its own
sophisticated water supply.
By the mid-17th-century,
however, it was falling into
decline. Features of interest
are the **town walls**, 2 m (6 ft)
thick and 680 m (2,230 ft)
long, with spiked battlements,
and the Market Square,
dominated by the parish
Church of St Władysław
(Fara św Władysława),
initially in the Gothic style but
rebuilt in the 17th century.

Also worth a visit are the
Gothic **castle** of
Kazimierz the

Great, with its **Regional
Museum**, and the 16th-
century **synagogue**, with
Renaissance parapets and
Baroque wall paintings.

🏛 **Regional Museum**
ul. Szkolna 8. 📞 *(0 41) 354 51 46.*
🕐 *7am–3:30pm Tue, Thu, Fri,
10am–2pm Sat, Sun.*

**Cracow Gate, the Gothic south
gate into the old town of Szydłów**

Grabki Duże ⑫

Road map E5. 🏛 *410.* 🚌

BETWEEN 1742 and 1750, the
architect Francisco Placidi
built a Rococo palace here for
the castellan Stanisław
Rupniewski. At the time, the
unusual shape of the building
aroused suspicions that the
castellan intended it to be for
a harem. Rupniewski loved
women, so did nothing to
contradict the gossip.

The nucleus of the "harem"
is a central hall covered with
a fanciful roof. This is
surrounded by four single-
storey
wings that

The castle in Kurozwęki, with its severe Neo-Classical façade

The palace of Stanisław Rupniewski in Grabki Duże, said to be for a harem

once contained small apartments. The design of the palace is not dissimilar to that of a windmill.

Busko Zdrój

Road map E5. ⛪ *18,400.* 🚌 🚉
ℹ *al. Mickiewicza 3 (041 378 17 33 or 378 24 74).* 🎭 *K. Jamroz Music Festival (Jun, Jul).*

SPRINGS WITH healing properties were discovered here in 1776, but it was not until the beginning of the 19th century that they began to be exploited. In 1836 a sanatorium was opened and a **park** laid out. The Neo-Classical **bath house** dates from 1836–8; visitors may sample the waters in the pump room. The spa itself is valued for its rare sulphur and salt springs and for its therapeutic mud.

Wiślica ⓮

Road map E5. ⛪ *610.* 🚌

THIS SLEEPY VILLAGE may have been the capital of the Vistulanians in the 11th century. The Market Square, which is planted with trees, is unexpectedly dominated by the enormous Gothic **collegiate church**, founded by Kazimierz the Great after 1350. The chancel is decorated with Ruthenian-Byzantine frescoes dating from 1397–1400 which are now barely visible. The floor is that of an earlier Romanesque church; the figures engraved

within it date from the second half of the 12th century and may perhaps represent the Piast princes *(see p39)* who founded the church.

Pińczów ⓯

Road map E5. ⛪ *12,400.* 🚌
ℹ *ul. Pałeki 26 (0 41 357 20 20 or 357 20 44).* 🎭 *Days of Ponidzie (Jun).*

IN THE 16TH CENTURY, the town of Pińczów was an important centre of artistic and intellectual life. It is dominated by the castle built in the 15th century for Cardinal Zbigniew Oleśnicki. Oleśnicki was a politician and confidant of Władysław II and Kazimierz IV, as well as being a patron of the medieval Polish chronicler Jan

Długosz. During the Renaissance, the castle was remodelled for the Myszkowski family by Santi Gucci. It was dismantled before 1799, the result being that little remains today.

Between 1556 and 1586, the humanistic Calvinist college was active in Pińczów – just as the printing house of the Polish Brethren was to be a few decades later. A beautiful Renaissance house decorated with sgraffito is sometimes identified as the Polish Brethren's printing house: it is not, but it still merits the visitor's attention.

The **Chapel of St Anne** (Kaplica św Anny), on the top of the hill, is an unusual Mannerist building. It was founded in 1600 by Zygmunt Myszkowski and built, it is thought, by Santi Gucci.

In nearby Mirów, the **Franciscan church** and the 17th-century Mannerist-Baroque **parish church**, which has early Baroque vaulting and rich furnishings, are both worth a visit. In the vestibule of the parish church, a marble tombstone of a middle-class woman, Anna Jakubczyńska, who died in 1618, attracts the visitor's attention.

Also worth seeing is the late Renaissance **synagogue**, which is the last remaining trace of the Jews who once lived in Pińczów.

The parish and Franciscan church in Mirów, near Pińczów

Częstochowa ⑯

THE MONASTERY of Jasna Góra in Częstochowa is the most famous shrine of the Virgin in Poland and the country's greatest place of pilgrimage – for many, its spiritual capital. The image of the Black Madonna of Częstochowa, to which miraculous powers are attributed, is Jasna Góra's most precious treasure. Founded in 1382 by Pauline monks who came from Hungary at the invitation of Władysław, Duke of Opole (who probably brought the image of the Black Madonna to Częstochowa), the monastery withstood several sieges, including the legendary 40-day siege by the Swedes in 1655 *(see p44).*

Knights' Hall
The hall contains a series of late 17th-century paintings depicting major events in the monastery's history.

Refectory
The ceiling is decorated with rich frescoes by the 17th-century painter Karl Dankwart. In 1670, a wedding reception was held here for the Polish king Michał Korybut Wiśniowiecki and his bride, Eleanor.

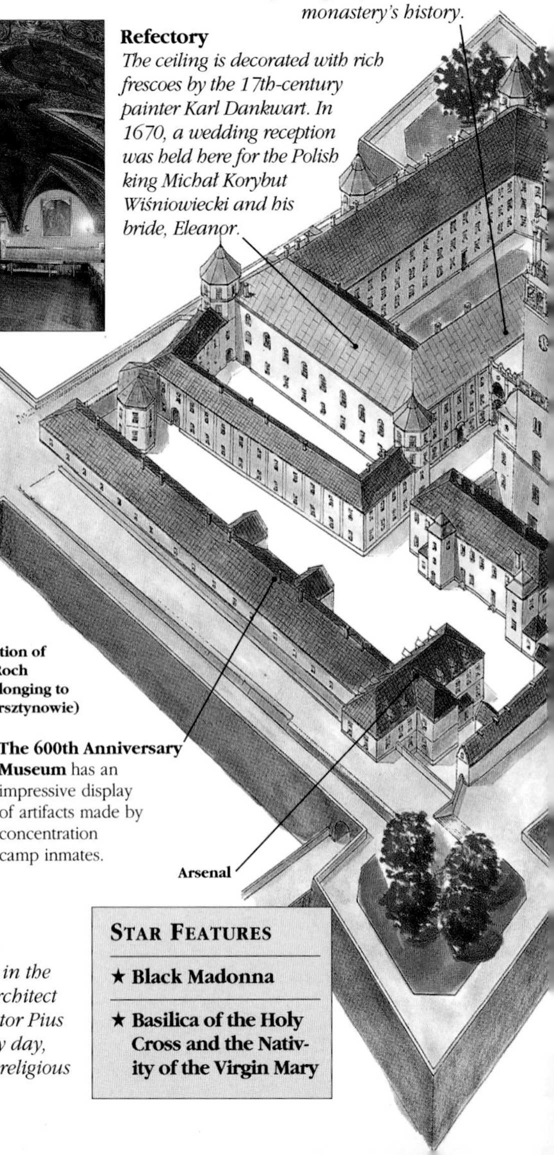

Bastion of St Roch (belonging to Morsztynowie)

The 600th Anniversary Museum has an impressive display of artifacts made by concentration camp inmates.

Arsenal

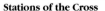

Stations of the Cross
The 14 Stations of the Cross standing on artificial rocks in the moat were created by the architect Stefan Szyller and the sculptor Pius Weloński in 1900–13. Every day, groups of pilgrims attend a religious service here.

STAR FEATURES

★ **Black Madonna**

★ **Basilica of the Holy Cross and the Nativity of the Virgin Mary**

★ Black Madonna
The most important icon of the Catholic faith in Poland, depicting the Virgin with the Christ Child, was probably painted in 1434 on top of an older Byzantine icon – the original Black Madonna, which was damaged by robbers in 1430.

VISITORS' CHECKLIST

Road map D5. 👥 *255,000.* 🚉
🚌 ℹ *al. Najświętszej Marii Panny 65 (0 34 324 13 60).* **Tourist Information Centre in Jasna Góra, Pauline Monastery** *ul. Kordeckiego 2 (0 34 365 38 88).* **Jasna Góra** ◯ *5am–9:30pm.* **Black Madonna of Częstochowa** *(unveiling times) May–Sep: 6am, 1pm Mon–Fri, 6am, 2pm Sat, Sun; Oct–Apr: 6am, 3pm daily.* **Treasury, Arsenal, 600th Anniversary Museum** ◯ *May–Sep: 9am–5pm; Oct–Apr: 9am–4pm.* 🎵 *"Gaude Mater" International Festival of Religious Music (early May).*

Outdoor altar,
where services are held for the crowds of pilgrims.

Treasury
Gold and silver vessels, church vestments, tapestries and votive offerings are among the items on display.

Chapel of the Last Supper
This chapel was designed by Adolf Szyszko-Bohusz in the 20th century.

Confessional

Monastery Gates
The Lubomirski Gate, the Stanisław August Gate, the Gate of the Sorrowful Virgin Mary and the Bank (or Jagiellonian) Gate all lead to the monastery hill.

★ Basilica of the Holy Cross and the Nativity of the Virgin Mary
The present basilica dates from 1692–1728. The Baroque decoration of the high altar and of the ceiling, the latter by Karl Dankwart, is rich in detail.

Eagles' Nests Trail ⑰

THE CRACOW-Częstochowa upland is a limestone mountain range formed in the Jurassic period. Perched on rocky outcrops, some of the castles, most of which were built in the Middle Ages and ruined during the Swedish Deluge of the 1650s *(see p44)*, resemble eagles' nests. Ojców National Park, with Pieskowa Skała Castle, encompasses some of the most beautiful upland areas. This castle was once the stronghold of kings, but at the end of the Middle Ages it passed into the hands of bandits – Piotr Szafraniec and his son Krzysztof – who lured rich merchants to their deaths. Today all is peaceful: tourist trails, rock-climbing and beautiful scenery.

Olsztyn ①
Every autumn, thousands of spectators gather to watch as a magnificent firework display and laser show illuminate the stately ruins of the castle.

Mirów ②
The castle once belonged to the Myszkowski family. It is perched on a rocky ridge, turning the natural lie of the land to defensive advantage.

```
0 km        5
0 miles        5
```

TIPS FOR HIKERS

Length of trail: *190 km (118 miles).*
Stopping-off points: *Many bars and restaurants are to be found along the trail. There is a restaurant and café in Pieskowa Skała Castle.*

Bobolice ③
Today, jousting tournaments and outdoor games take place in the surroundings of the splendid ruins of the castle built by Kazimierz the Great in the 14th century.

Ogrodzieniec ④
In the 16th century the castle belonged to the Boner family of Cracow. With its gate, towers and galleries, it is one of the most picturesque castles on the trail.

Błędowski Desert ⑤
This miniature desert is 320 sq km (123 sq miles) of drifting sand and dunes. Unique in Central Europe, it is slowly becoming choked with vegetation.

Olkusz ⑥
The town is well endowed with historic buildings. It owes its prosperity to silver and lead mining.

Pieskowa Skała ⑦
The well-preserved castle with its arcaded courtyard and bastions dominates the Prądnik valley. It is situated on an inaccessible rock surrounded by spectacular scenery.

Ojców National Park ⑧
The Prądnik valley has a karst landscape; there are outcrops of limestone, a multitude of gorges and caves with bats. The most famous rock is the pillar known as Hercules' Club.

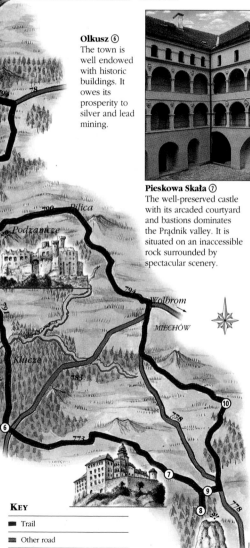

Grodzisko ⑨
The obelisk with a stone elephant is an unusual monument. It was made in 1686 and stands next to the Church of the Assumption.

Imbramowice ⑩
This small village has a late Baroque Premonstratensian convent built in the 18th century.

KEY

■ Trail

■ Other road

❊ Viewpoint

Gate and unloading platform, Birkenau extermination camp

Oświęcim (Auschwitz) ⑱

Road map D5. 🏘 43,000. 🚉 🚌

ALTHOUGH THE NAME Oświęcim means little to foreigners, its German equivalent, **Auschwitz**, evokes fear in almost everyone. It was here that the Nazis established their largest concentration and extermination camp. Auschwitz is synonynous with death, cruelty, the annihilation of the Jews and the Holocaust. It is a massive graveyard. No visitor can leave unmoved.

The Auschwitz camp, known as Auschwitz I, opened in June 1940 when the first Polish political prisoners arrived. In March 1941 a much larger camp at **Birkenau** (Brzezinka in Polish), Auschwitz II, was started, 3km (2 miles) from Oświęcim. Auschwitz III, a labour camp, was built nearby in Monowice in 1943. The Nazis brought in people, overwhelmingly Jews, from all over Europe. The gas chambers, which had the capacity to kill thousands daily, started working ceaselessly in 1942. Trains drew up to the ramp where people would be herded out for selection for extermination (the fate of the majority), forced labour or medical experiments. Those selected for extermination would be gassed and their bodies incinerated in one of the four crematoria. Apart from Jews, numbers of Poles, Soviet prisoners of war, gypsies and homosexuals died here.

For the Poles, Auschwitz is a particular symbol of their own suffering and martydom. St Maksymilian Kolbe died in the Death Block from starvation after volunteering his life for

that of a fellow prisoner. Soviet forces liberated the camp in January 1945. They found 7,650 sick and dying prisoners when they arrived.

Above the entrance to Auschwitz are inscribed the words "Arbeit macht frei" ("Work makes free"). The camp has been preserved as a memorial, and the prison blocks that survive have been turned into a **museum** charting the history of the camp and of persecution in wartime Poland. In all, between 900,000 and 1.5 million Jews and others were murdered in the extermination camps here. The camp is a UNESCO World Heritage Site.

🏛 Oświęcim-Brzezinka Museum

ul. Więźniów Oświęcimia 20. 📞 (0 33) 843 20 22. 🖳 www.auschwitz.org.pl
🕐 16 Dec–29 Feb: 8am–3pm; Mar, 1 Nov–15 Dec: 8am–4pm; Apr, Oct: 8am–5pm; May, Sep: 8am–6pm; Jun–Aug: 8am–7pm. 🅳

Bielsko-Biała ⑲

Road map D6. 🏘 174,000. 🚉 🚌
ℹ ul. Stojałowskiego 19 (0 33 819 00 50/60). 🖳 www.mcibielsko.pl

THE CITY WAS created by joining the Silesian town of Bielsko and the Galician town of Biała. It was once an important centre for the production of textiles and wool, as an interesting early 20th-century complex of buildings testifies.

Many streets contain miniature versions of old Viennese houses. The **Castle of the Sułkowski princes**, built in the Middle Ages and altered in the 19th century, is also of interest. The unusual hilltop Church of St Nicholas (Kościół św Mikołaja) began as a modest 15th-century Gothic church and was extensively remodelled in 1907–10.

Bielsko-Biała is a good starting point for excursions into the Beskid Śląski Mountains. The chair lift from the suburbs takes visitors to the Szyndzielnia peak, 1,026 m (3,365 ft) up.

Żywiec ⑳

Road map D6. 🏘 32,000. 🚌 🚉
ℹ Rynek 12 (0 33 861 43 10).

THE TOWN OF ŻYWIEC is widely associated with one of the best Polish brands of beer, which is brewed locally. It is also a good

Lake Żywiecki, a man-made reservoir on the River Soła

Arcaded courtyard of the Renaissance castle in Żywiec

starting point for excursions into the Beskid Żywiecki Mountains. Lake Żywieckie, with its water-sports facilities, is another tourist attraction. This is also a town of thriving folk traditions; a particular high point is Corpus Christi, when women dressed in traditional costumes take part in a festive procession. Local monuments include the **Market Square**, surrounded by old houses, the 19th-century **town hall** and the **Church of the Nativity of the Virgin Mary** (Kościół Narodzenia Najświętszej Marii Panny), built in 1582–3. Not far from the Market Square is the **Gothic Church of the Holy Cross** (Kościół św Krzyża).

The most important buildings in the town are the Renaissance **castle** and the 19th-century **palace**, started in the 16th century for Mikołaj Komorowski. In the mid-17th century, Jan Kazimierz, King of Poland, was the owner of Żywiec. When he abdicated in 1668, he lived here briefly before leaving Poland.

In the early 19th century, the town became the property of the Habsburgs, who built a palace next to the castle. Marrying into the Polish aristocracy, the last of the Habsburgs were strongly connected with Poland.

⚜ **Castle**
ul. Kościuszki 5. 📞 (0 33) 861 21 24.
🕐 9am–4pm Tue–Sun.

Wadowice ㉑

Road map D6. 🚶 *19,400*. 🚌 🚏

K AROL WOJTYŁA, who became Pope John Paul II in 1978, was born in Wadowice on 18 May 1920. His childhood home, a modest two-room flat, has been turned into a small museum, called the **House of John Paul II**, with objects relating to his early life. He was christened in the **Church of the Presentation of the Virgin Mary** (Kościół Ofiarowania NMP), near the Market Square. The late Baroque church, built in 1791–8, replaces an early Gothic church, of which only the chancel remains. The tower, with Baroque cupola, was built by Tomasz Pryliński in the late 19th century.

🏨 **House of John Paul II**
ul. Kościelna 7. 📞 (0 33) 823 26 62.
🕐 May–Nov: 9am–1pm, 2–6pm; Oct–Apr: 9am–12pm, 2–5pm Tue–Sun.

Kalwaria Zebrzydowska ㉒

Road map D6. 🚶 *4,400*. 🚌 🚏

K ALWARIA ZEBRZYDOWSKA is not only the oldest **calvary** in Poland but one of the most unusual. It was commissioned in 1600 by Mikołaj Zebrzydowski, the ruler of

Herod's Palace, one of the stations of Kalwaria Zebrzydowska

Cracow and an ardent Catholic, whose plan it was to replicate the layout of Jerusalem.

The calvary consists of 40 chapels, set on the surrounding hills and built between 1605 and 1632. The most distinctive are the work of the Flemish architect and goldsmith Paul Baudarth. Some have unusual shapes: the House of the Virgin Mary takes the form of the Mystic Rose, and the House of Caiaphas that of an ellipsis. Their façades have Dutch ornamentation. The large Baroque monastery church dates from 1702; the monastic buildings were constructed by Baudarth and Giovanni Maria Bernadoni in 1603–67.

For nearly 400 years, Kalwaria Zebrzydowska has attracted thousands of pilgrims. Passion plays are performed here during Holy Week and the Feast of Assumption is celebrated in August.

Bernardine church in Kalwaria Zebrzydowska

The underground Chapel of St Kinga in the salt mine at Wieliczka

Wieliczka ㉓

Road map D5. 🏘 *17,600.* 🚆 🚌

WIELICZKA IS FAMOUS for its ancient **salt mine**, which was opened 700 years ago and is still being exploited today. Unique in the world, it has been listed by UNESCO as a World Heritage Site.

Only 2 km (1½ miles) of the network of underground galleries and chambers are open to the public. They reach a depth of 135 m (442 ft) and have a stable temperature of 13–14° C (55–57° F). The two-hour visit takes in ancient underground chambers, saline lakes, wooden mining machines and underground buildings. The most impressive of these is the Chapel of St Kinga, with altarpieces, chandeliers and sculptures made of salt. Additional figures carved in salt, the oldest dating from the 17th century, can be seen in other chambers. The Staszic Chamber has the highest ceiling, at 36 m (115 ft). At the end of the German occupation, the Nazis tried to establish an aircraft factory in the mines. There is also an underground sanatorium where respiratory diseases are treated.

The Salt Mine Castle at Ulica Zamkowa 8 is also worth a visit. From the 13th century right up until 1945 it was a base for the management of the salt mine. Today it houses a museum with – among other things – a splendid collection of antique salt mills.

Salt Mine

ul. Daniłowicza 10. 📞 *(0 12) 278 73 02.* 🌐 *www.kopalnia.pl* 🕐 *16 Apr–15 Oct: 7:30am–6:30pm; 16 Oct–15 Apr: 8am–4pm.* ● *1 Jan, Easter, 1 Nov, 4 Dec, 24–26 Dec, 31 Dec.* 📷

Niepołomice ㉔

Road map E5. 🏘 *7,300.* 🚆 🚌

IN THE 14TH CENTURY, the **royal castle** at Niepołomice was the hunting base of Kazimierz the Great. Between 1550 and 1571 it was converted into a Renaissance palace by Zygmunt August. The entrance gate, dating from 1552, was once decorated with a Jagiellonian eagle; the plaque, with the Latin inscription "May the King Win and Live", hints at its former splendour. The monarchs loved hunting in the **game park** nearby. In 1525 Zygmunt I brought "in a wooden trunk a great bear from Lithuania". The bear hunt ended unhappily. Confronted by the angry animal, the pregnant Queen Bona Sworza turned and fled, falling from her horse and suffering a miscarriage.

At the castle in 1551, Queen Bona Sworza's son, Zygmunt August, sat at the deathbed of his sweetheart wife, Barbara Radziwiłłowna. Their marriage had caused a moral and political scandal and Queen Bona was unjustly suspected of poisoning her daughter-in-law.

Today, the forest is much smaller than it was in the time of the Jagiellonians. It is still, however, a sizeable nature reserve with plenty of secluded areas, and bison are raised there.

Zalipie ㉕

Road map E5. 🏘 *710.* 🚌 🚆 *6 km (4 miles) from the village.*

ZALIPIE HAS A UNIQUE folk art tradition: cottages, barns, wells and fences are painted with colourful floral, animal, geometric and other motifs. Domestic interiors and furnishings are also decorated. The painters are predominantly the women of the village. Every year in June, a competition called the Painted Cottage is organized and exhibitions of paintings are held.

Painted cottage in Zalipie

The Gothic-Renaissance town hall in Tarnów

Tarnów

Road map E5. 118,000. Rynek 2 (0 14 621 04 32).

Tarnów received its municipal charter in 1330; the medieval layout of the old town is perfectly preserved and many ancient houses are still standing. Those around the arcaded **Market Square** are among the finest. The **town hall**, in the centre, dates from the 15th century and was remodelled in the second half of the 16th century by Giovanni Maria Padovano. The Renaissance attics and elegant portal date from that time.

The late Gothic **Cathedral of the Nativity of the Virgin Mary** (Katedra Narodzenia NMP) was built in 1400 and has been extended many times. It is the grandest building in Tarnów, its Gothic portal decorated with sophisticated iconography. Its **Diocesan Museum** is worth a visit.

The monuments, stalls, epitaphs and tombstones within are mostly those of the Tarnowski family, who at one time owned the town. The large tombs belonging to Grand Hetman Jan Tarnowski and his son Jan Krzysztof were fashioned by Giovanni Maria Padovano between 1561 and 1570.

The portraits of the deceased are remarkable. The marble bas-reliefs depict Jan Tarnowski's victories in battle at Orsza, Obertyn and Starodub. Tarnowski, a friend of the poet Jan Kochanowski, was known as a charismatic and witty commander as well as a renowned author of military theory.

Diocesan Museum
pl. Katedralny 6. (0 14) 621 99 93. www.diecezja.tarnow.pl 10am–3pm Tue–Sat, 9am–2pm Sun.

The castle in Dębno, which houses a Museum of Period Interiors

Dębno near Brzeska

Road map E6. 1,400.

This small, well-proportioned castle surrounded by a moat was built in 1470–80 for the castellan and royal chancellor Jakub Dębiński. It survives in an excellent state of preservation. The **Museum of Period Interiors** installed in the castle re-creates the atmosphere of noble houses of the 15th to 18th centuries.

Not only the living quarters but also the castle's kitchen, pantry and wine cellar are included in the exhibition.

Museum of Period Interiors
(0 14) 665 80 35. Mar–Dec: 10am–5pm Tue, Thu, 9am–3pm Wed, Fri, 11am–3pm Sat, 11am–5pm Sun. Jan–Feb.

Nowy Wiśnicz

Road map E6. 1,900.

The enormous **castle** and the **Monastery of the Discalced Carmelites** overlook this town from the hills above. The **parish church** stands in the Market Square below. Each of these early Baroque buildings was raised by Stanisław Lubomirski, Palatine of Cracow, in the 17th century. This rich and wise magnate earned renown in the Battles of Chocim against the Turks, and grew so strong that he "felt more powerful than the king". Twice the emperor bestowed a dukedom on him. The castle, which previously belonged to the Kmita family, was extended by Lubomirski after 1615. It has corner towers, an arcaded courtyard and an unusual entrance gate, framed by enormous volutes. Now a prison, the monastery is not open to visitors. The façade of the parish church is one of the most unusual pieces of architecture in Poland, combining Baroque elements in a Mannerist way.

Lubomirski Castle, towering above the town of Nowy Wiśnicz

Old cottages along the main street of Chochołów

Chochołów 🕖

Road map D6. 🏠 *1,100.* 🚌

A LONG THE MAIN STREET of the 16th-century village stand traditional wooden cottages, the best examples of highland architecture in the whole Podhale region. One of the cottages, at No. 75, is open to the public. It dates from 1889 and has "white" and "black" rooms, a vestibule and a cellar. It also houses the **Museum of the Chochołów Insurrection**, which took place in 1846 against Austrian rule.

Chochołów has a curious local custom that involves cleaning the walls of the building once a year until they are white.

🏛 **Museum of the Chochołów Insurrection**
Chochołów 75. ⬜ *10am–2pm Wed–Sun.*

Zakopane 🕚

Road map D6. 🏠 *29,000.* 🚆 🚌
ℹ *ul. Kościuszki 17 (0 18 201 22 11).* 🔲 www.zakopane.pl
📷 *Autumn in the Tatras; International Festival of Mountain Folklore (end Aug).*

F OR OVER 100 YEARS, the Polish people have regarded Zakopane as their country's winter capital, on a par with alpine resorts as an upmarket winter sports centre. The municipal authorities are currently making preparations for the Winter Olympics that are due to be held here in 2006.

Many tourists are also appreciative of Zakopane in the summer months. While

Entrance to the Villa Koliba Museum

Zakopane, railway line from Kuźnic to Kasprowy Wierch

some go hiking in the mountains, most are content to admire the scenery from the windows of their cable cars gliding to the summit of Mt Kasprowy Wierch or from the funicular railway ascending Mt Gubałówka. Later in the day, many of the tourists gather in Krupówki, the town's central pedestrianized area, which is lined with cafés, restaurants, exclusive souvenir shops and art galleries.

Walking down Krupówki it is impossible to resist the market near the funicular railway station. On sale can be found leather *kierpce* (traditional highland moccasins), woollen highland pullovers, wooden *ciupagi* (highlanders' sticks with decorative axe-like handles), and also *bryndza* and *oscypek* (regional cheeses made from sheep's milk).

Villa Atma, the wooden house where the composer Karol Szymanowski *(see p24)* lived from 1930 to 1936 now houses a museum

PANORAMA FROM MOUNT GUBAŁÓWKA
The finest panorama of the Tatra Mountains from the northern, Polish side of the range is from Mt Gubałówka or Głodówka pod Bukowiną. The Tatras, the highest mountains in Central Europe, with alpine landscapes, lie within Polish and Slovak national parks. The main attractions for tourists include the excursion to the Lake Morskie Oko (Eye of the Sea) and the ascent by cable car to the summit of Mount Kasprowy Wierch. In summer, hikers can follow the many designated trails. In winter, the mountains offer favourable conditions for skiing.

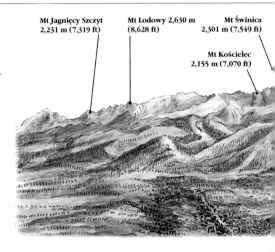

Mt Jagnięcy Szczyt 2,231 m (7,319 ft)

Mt Lodowy 2,630 m (8,628 ft)

Mt Świnica 2,301 m (7,549 ft)

Mt Kościelec 2,155 m (7,070 ft)

dedicated to this eulogist of the Tatra Mountains. It is worth a visit as it is in typical Zakopane style.

Villa Atma
ul. Kasprusie 19. *(0 18) 201 34 93.*
10am–3pm Tue, Thu, Sat, Sun, noon–6pm Fri.

Dębno Podhalańskie ③

Road map E6. 790.

The Convent of the Order of St Clare in Stary Sącz

T HE LARCH TIMBER **Parish Church of St Michael the Archangel** (Kościół parafialny św Michała Archanioła) is one of the most highly regarded examples of wooden Gothic architecture in Europe. The ceiling, walls and furnishings are covered with colourful geometric, figural and floral motifs painted in around 1500. A magnificent domed tower rises over the church.

Wooden Gothic church in Dębno Podhalańskie

Dunajec Raft Ride ②

See pp166–7.

Stary Sącz ③

Road map E6. 8,800.
(0 18) 443 55 97. www.sacz.pl
Early Music Festival (Jun–Jul).

T HIS CHARMING Galician town has a picturesque cobbled Market Square surrounded by small houses that in summer are bedecked with flowers. Were it not for the presence of cars, tourists and modern shops, one might imagine that time had stood still here. The town's finest buildings include the **Convent of the Order of St Clare** (Klasztor sw Klarysek), founded in 1208 by the Blessed Kinga. The Gothic church was consecrated in 1280 and the vaulting dates from the 16th century. Its altars, with stuccowork ornamentation made by Baldassare Fontana in 1696–9, and a pulpit from 1671 showing a depiction of the Tree of Jesse, complement the modern decoration of the church.

ENVIRONS: Nowy Sącz is situated 8 km (5 miles) northeast of Stary Sącz. In the large **Market Square** stands the Neo-Baroque **town hall** of 1895–7. The town's major buildings are the old collegiate church, now the parish Church of St Marguerite (Kościół parafialny św Małgorzaty), founded by Zbigniew Oleśnicki in 1466, and a fine synagogue.

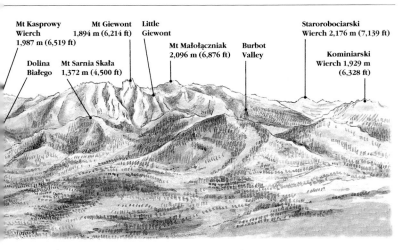

| Mt Kasprowy Wierch 1,987 m (6,519 ft) | Mt Giewont 1,894 m (6,214 ft) | Little Giewont | | | Starorobociarski Wierch 2,176 m (7,139 ft) |

Dolina Białego

Mt Sarnia Skała 1,372 m (4,500 ft)

Mt Małołączniak 2,096 m (6,876 ft)

Burbot Valley

Kominiarski Wierch 1,929 m (6,328 ft)

Dunajec Raft Ride ㉜

T HE PIENINY MOUNTAINS form a small range famous for its spectacular landscapes cut through by the Dunajec valley. The raft ride on the river that flows through the limestone mountain gorges is one of the best-known tourist attractions in Poland. At first the rafts move with deceptive calm, but as they approach the gorge behind the cloister ruins the water becomes rougher as the river twists and winds. This lasts for about 8 km (5 miles), after which the water once again flows more slowly. The exhilarating ride ends in Szczawnica, a well-known health resort.

Niedzica Castle ①
The castle was built in 1330 for the Hungarian Berzevicy family. It now houses the Museum of the Spisz Region.

Czorsztyn Castle ②
The castle once guarded the Polish border with Hungary. Its ruins perch on a precipitous outcrop of rock.

0 km 1
0 miles 1

KEY

- - Raft ride route
▬▬ Tour route
▬▬ Other road
☆ Viewpoint

Dunajec Dam ③
Despite protests, the building of this dam went ahead. On the day of its opening in 1997, it saved the Dunajec valley from a disastrous flood.

Krynica ㉞

Road map E6. 🏔 *13,000.* 🚉 🚌
ℹ️ *ul. Piłsudskiego 8 (0 18 471 56 54).* 🌐 *www.krynica.pl* 🎭 *Jan Kiepura Festival (Aug–Sep); concerts by spa orchestras (all year round).*

W ELL-EQUIPPED with sanatoria and pump rooms, Krynica is one of the largest health resorts in Poland. Fashionable and luxurious pre-war boarding houses stand next to old wooden villas. The best known is "Patria", built by Bohdan Pniewski in the Art

One of Nikifor's paintings on view at the Nikifor Museum

Nouveau style, and owned by singer Jan Kiepura (1902–66). The **New Sanatorium** near the pedestrian promenade (Deptak) is also worth a visit. Completed in 1939, it retains its original furnishings and décor. The Great Pump Room nearby is always very popular with visitors.

The town is surrounded by tree-covered mountains. Mt Jaworzyna, at 1,114 m (3,654 ft) the highest peak in the area, can be reached by cable car, departing from Czarny Potok. In winter, the mountain turns into a skier's paradise. The local ski trails are the longest in Poland. Remote areas of the mountains are inhabited by lynxes, wolves and bears, so caution should be exercised away from the established trails.

The work of amateur painter Nikifor (d. 1968) is displayed in the "Romanówka" villa, now the **Nikifor Museum**.

🏛 **Nikifor Museum**
Bulwary Dietla 19. 🕿 *(0 18) 471 53 03.* ◯ *10am–1pm and 2–5pm Tue–Sun.*

Biecz ㉟

Road map E6. 🏔 *4,900.* 🚉 🚌 *City bus from Gorlice.* 🎭 *Pogórze Folklore Days.*

I N THE 16TH CENTURY this small town was one of the most important centres of cloth manufacture in Poland. It is dominated by the **town hall tower**, built in 1569–81, and the **Parish Church of Corpus Christi** (Kościół farny Bożego Ciała). One of the most magnificent late Gothic churches in all of Małopolska, it was built at the turn of the 15th century in a style that seeks to reconcile the Gothic tradition with the new canons of the Renaissance. The first pharmacy in the Carpathian foothills was located in the **Renaissance house** at Ulica Węgierska 2, dating from 1523; it now houses a division of the **Regional Museum**.

🏛 **Regional Museum**
ul. Kromera 3. 🕿 *(0 13) 447 10 93.* ◯ *1 May–30 Sep: 8am–5pm Tue–Sun, 8am–4pm Sat; 1 Oct–30 Apr 8am–3pm Tue–Sat, 9am–2pm Sun.*

Szczawnica ⑧

This well-known health resort is mainly a centre for the treatment of respiratory diseases. It is also the disembarkation point for the Dunajec river raft ride.

Ostra Skała ⑦

After Ostra Skała (Sharp Rock) the River Dunajec turns sharply as it flows through the narrowest part of the gorge.

TIPS FOR VISITORS

Raft ride: 2–2½ hours.
Length: 18 km (11 miles).
📞 (0 18) 262 97 21 or 262 97 93. @ splyw@flisacy.com.pl
Starting point: Sromowce Wyżne – Kąty. May–Nov: daily.

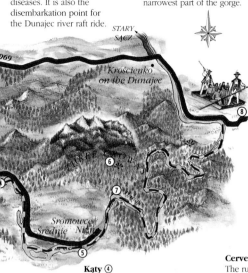

Trzy Korony ⑥

Trzy Korony (Three Crowns) is the most beautiful massif in the Pieniny range. In 1287, the Blessed Kinga took refuge from the Tartars in the Castle of the order of St Clare, whose ruins stand on one peak.

Cerveny Kláštor ⑤

The ruins of the Red Monastery can be seen on the Slovak side of the Dunajec.

Kąty ④

Departure point for the raft ride.

View of the Parish Church of Corpus Christi in Biecz

ENVIRONS: In the village of **Harklowa** is a late Gothic wooden church dating from the turn of the 15th century.

Krosno ㊱

Road map F6. 🏠 49,000. 🚉 🚌
ℹ️ ul. K. Pużaka 49 (0 13 432 77 07).
🎭 Krosno Fair (Jun); Krosno Music Autumn (Oct).

KROSNO WAS ONCE the centre of the Polish oil industry, but there is more to the town than its industrial past. The finest historical monument is the Oświęcim Chapel in the Gothic Franciscan church. Completed in 1647, the chapel is decorated with exquisite stuccowork by Giovanni Battista Falconi. It contains the tombs of the half-siblings Anna and Stanisław, whose love ended in tragedy. The Market Square is surrounded by old arcaded houses, the most interesting of which is No. 7, with its Renaissance doorway.

ENVIRONS: In **Odrzykoń**, 10 km (6 miles) north of Krosno, stand the ruins of Kamieniec Castle. Kamieniec was the setting for *Revenge* (1834), the most popular comedy by the 19th-century writer Count Aleksander Fredro *(see p23)*, the plot of which involves a dispute over the hole in the wall dividing the courtyard of the castle.

In the **geological park** not far from the castle stands a group of sandstone and shale structures known as Prządki (The Spinners), which have unusual, sometimes quite startling shapes.

Iwonicz Zdrój and **Rymanów**, 15 km (9 miles) east of Krosno, are very popular health resorts. At **Dukla** are the Baroque Mniszcha Palace, which today houses a historical museum, and the 18th-century Bernardine church with the charming Rococo tomb of Maria Amalia Brühla Mniszkowa, with its peaceful effigy.

In **Bóbrka**, 12 km (7 miles) south of Krosno, an industrial *skansen* has been created in what is certainly one of the oldest oil wells in the world, established in 1854.

Bieszczady Mountains Tour ⑳

THE BIESZCZADY MOUNTAINS, together with the neighbouring Beskid Niski, are the wildest in Poland. Tourists return with blood-curdling tales of encounters with bears and wolves, or the discovery of a skeleton in the forest undergrowth. Needless to say, these stories are often exaggerated. Before World War II, the region was densely populated by Ukrainians and ethnic groups known as the Boyks and the Lemks. After the war, because of fighting and resettlements, it became deserted, and farming largely disappeared from the region by the 1970s. Pastures and burnt-out villages became overgrown as the forest encroached and wild animals returned to the mountains.

Komańcza ⑦
Cardinal Stefan Wyszyński, Primate of Poland, was sent into exile to this village, deserted after World War II. He was interned by the communist authorities in 1955–6.

Połonina Wetlińska ⑥
Known as "połoniny", these elongated ranges with picturesque alpine meadows above forest level are a characteristic feature of the Bieszczady Mountains. The most interesting, 1,250 m (4,100 ft) up, are Caryńska and Wetlińska.

Bieszczady National Park ⑤
The highest and wildest part of the mountains falls within Bieszczady National Park, which covers an area of 2,700 sq km (1,042 sq miles). In summer, many tourists walk the hiking trails. The main tourist base is in the small village of Ustrzyki Górne.

TYLAWA

BIESZCZADY MOUNTAIN ANIMALS

The lynx, emblem of Bieszczady National Park, is not the only feline to make its home in these mountains. Wildcats also live here. They are rarely seen because they are very shy, concealing themselves in the forest undergrowth. Carpathian deer, with a population of 5,000, are more often encountered. Roe deer are also abundant and relatively tame. Wolves, a protected species numbering about 100 here, are more cautious. Bison, kings of the Polish forest, number up to 120, and brown bear may also be seen. The Bieszczady Mountains are also popular with ornithologists for the many species of birds of prey: eagles, including the golden eagle, falcon and hawk.

A wild mountain wolf

Zagórz ①
Zagórz, dominated by the ruins of the 18th-century Baroque fortified Church of Discalced Carmelites, is the starting point of hiking trails into the Bieszczady Mountains.

Równia ④
The most beautiful Orthodox churches in the Bieszczady Mountains are vestiges of the numerous villages of the Boyks and the Lemks.

TIPS FOR DRIVERS

Tour length: *106 km (66 miles).*
Stopping-off points:
Restaurants, boarding houses and inns can be found in Polańczyk, Lesko, Wetlin, Ustrzyki Dolne and Ustrzyki Górne. In the summer season, bars also open.

Solina ③
The highest dam in Poland – 82 m (269 ft) high and 664 m (2,178 ft) long – was built at Solina. The reservoir that was created is ideal for sailing. The dam is surrounded by magnificent forests with nature reserves.

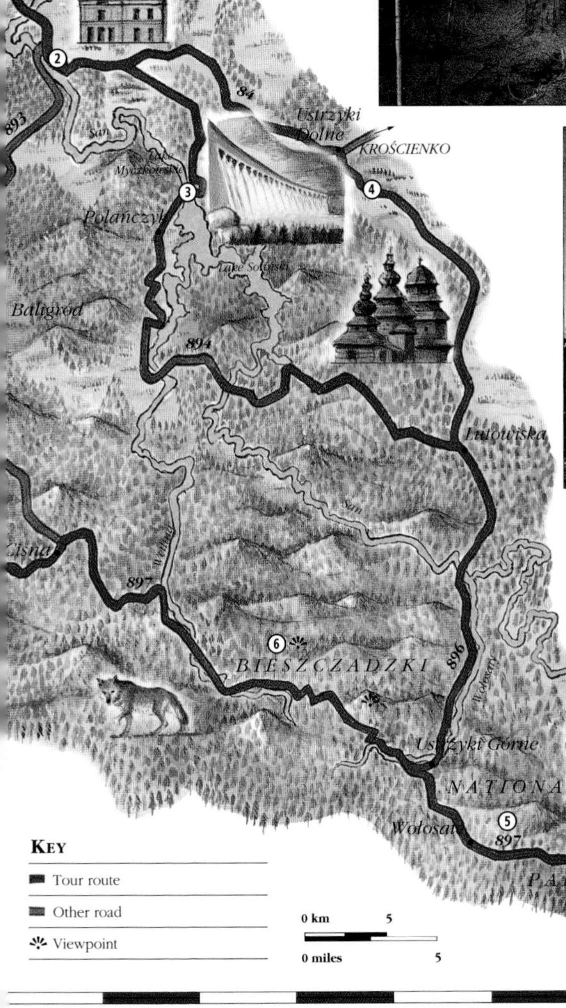

Lesko ②
This charming town has many fine buildings, including a castle and a 16th-century parish church. The Baroque synagogue houses a museum, and the Jewish cemetery is also of interest.

KEY

▬ Tour route

▭ Other road

☆ Viewpoint

0 km 5

0 miles 5

The Divine Tower, one of four towers in Krasiczyn Castle

Krasiczyn ❸

Road map F6. 🏠 *440.* 🚌 **Castle** 📞 *(0 16) 671 83 21.* 🌐 *www. krasiczyn.motronik.com.pl* ⏱ *summer: 10am–4pm Tue–Sun; winter: 9am–3pm Tue–Sun.* 🏨

KRASICZYN CASTLE is one of the most magnificent castles in the old Ruthenian territories of the Polish crown. Building began in 1592 on the site of an earlier castle by Stanisław Krasicki, castellan of Przewór. It was continued by his son Marcin and completed in 1608. The architect was Galeazzo Appiani.

The castle takes the form of an arcaded courtyard, with a tall clock tower over the gate and four stout cylindrical towers at the corners. The Divine Tower contains a chapel. The Papal Tower is crowned by a dome and decorated with a parapet symbolizing the papal tiara. The Royal Tower has a crown-shaped dome, and the Tower of the Gentry is topped with sword pommels.

The Baroque sgraffito on the walls is striking. Mythological scenes are depicted on the upper tier; the central tier is filled with portraits of the kings of Poland from the 14th-century Jagiellonian monarchs to Jan III Sobieski, King of Poland at the time, and portraits of nobles. In the lowest tier are medallions with the busts of Roman patricians. Little of the original decoration of the interior survives, as it

was destroyed by fire in 1852, on the eve of the marriage of a later owner, Duke Leon Sapieha. The castle is open to visitors; the residential section contains a hotel and restaurant.

ENVIRONS: In Krzywcza, 10 km (6 miles) west of **Krasiczyn** stand the ruins of the castle of the Kącki family. About 12 km (7 miles) south of Krasiczyn, in **Posada Rybotycka**, can be seen the only stone fortified Uniate church in Poland. In **Kalwaria Pacławicka**, the 18th-century Franciscan monastery has about a dozen chapels marking the Stations of the Cross. Passion plays are performed here on Good Friday and many processions and plays are organized during the year for different church festivities.

The funeral of the Virgin enacted in a passion play in Kalwaria Pacławicka

Przemyśl ❸

Road map F6. 🏃 *71,000.* 🚉 🚌 ℹ *ul. Władycze 3 (0 16 675 16 64).* 🌐 *www.um.przemysl.pl* 🛶 *Canoe rally (Apr, May); Gitariada International Festival (Jul).*

THE HISTORY of Przemyśl, picturesquely laid out on a hill and the banks of the River San, goes back to prehistoric

times. In the Middle Ages it was a regional capital and lay on a busy trade route. The object of dispute between Poland and Ruthenia, it became part of Poland in 1340, later passing into Austrian control.

During World War I, the strongly fortified city successfully held out against the besieging Russian army. The **fortifications** from that time survive. From 1939 to 1941 the River San, which flows through the city, constituted a border between territory held by the Soviet Union and Germany.

The city's Catholic and Orthodox churches, together with its synagogues, are evidence of its multicultural history. Today, a Ukrainian minority lives alongside the city's Polish population.

The **cathedral**, remodelled in 1718–24, is predominantly in the Baroque style; of its earlier Gothic form only the chancel remains. Notable features of the interior include the Renaissance tomb of Bishop Jan Dziaduski, by Giovanni Maria Padovano, and the late Gothic alabaster figure of the Virgin from Jacków. Near the cathedral are the Baroque Church of the Discalced Carmelites and the former Jesuit church, now Uniate, dating from 1627–48. The castle, founded by Kazimierz the Great in the 1340s, stands on a hill above the city. The top of its tower offers a panorama of the city and the San valley.

Przemyśl, on the banks of the River San

Orsetti House, a palace in the Renaissance style, in Jarosław

Jarosław 40

Road map F5. 42,000.
Jarosław Museum in the Orsetti House (0 16) 621 54 37.
www.jaroslaw.pl/biuletin
10am–2pm Wed, Thu, 10am–3:30pm Fri (Apr–Oct: 10am–6pm Fri). (free on Sun). Early Music Festival (Aug).

THE CITY OF JAROSŁAW owes its wealth to its location on the River San and the trade route linking the east with western Europe. In the 16th and 17th centuries, the largest fairs in Poland were held here. When Władysław IV attended a fair in Jarosław, he mingled with an international crowd and conversed with merchants from as far away as Italy and Persia. The **Orsetti House**, built in the style of an Italian Renaissance palazzo, testifies to the wealth of the city's merchants. Built in the 16th century and extended in 1646, it is crowned with a Mannerist parapet. The **town hall**, with coats of arms on the corner towers, stands in the centre of the broad **Market Square.**

Leżajsk 41

Road map F5. 14,500.
(0 17) 242 61 47. www.lezajsk.um. gov.pl Organ recitals in the basilica (Jun–Sep, 7pm; booking required).

THE MAJOR ATTRACTIONS of Leżajsk are its Bernardine basilica and monastery, built by the architect Antonio Pellacini and the organ recitals that take place in the basilica,

which was built in 1618–28. Its interior decoration and the furnishings, such as the oak stalls, pulpit and high altar, are mostly the work of the monks themselves. The basilica was established by Łukasz Opaliński, who earned renown by his defeat of the lawless magnate Stanisław Stadnicki in mortal combat.

The west end of the nave is filled with the complex organ, completed in 1693 and said to be the finest in Poland. The central theme of the elaborate Baroque casing is Hercules' fight with the Hydra, the nine-headed monster of Greek mythology. Not only is this a symbol of the age-old struggle of virtue against vice but also of Polish victory over the Turks, who were threatening Europe at the time.

The Jewish cemetery in Leżajsk is a place of pilgrimage for Jews from all over the world, who come to visit the tomb of Elimelech, the great 18th-century Orthodox rabbi.

Łańcut 42

See pp172–173.

Rzeszów 43

Road map F5. 151,000.
ul. Asnyka 6 (0 17 852 46 12). rzeszowturista@intertele.pl

THE DOMINANT BUILDING in this town is the Gothic **Church of Saints Stanisław and Adalberg** (Kościół św św Stanisława i Wojciecha), dating from the 15th century and with a later Baroque interior. The former Piarist **Church of the Holy Cross** (Kościół św Krzyża), extended in 1702–07 by Tylman van Gameren, and the Baroque monastery and **Bernardine church** of 1624–9 are also worth a visit. The latter contains the unfinished mausoleum of the Ligęz family, with eight alabaster statues carved by Sebastian Sala around 1630.

The remains of the old **castle** of the Ligęz family can still be seen. It later passed into the ownership of the Lubomirskis, who surrounded it with bastions in the 17th century. The Market Square, with an eclectic town hall remodelled in 1895–8, is another interesting feature.

Highlights of the **Muzeum Miasta Rzeszowa** include the gallery of 18th- to 20th-century Polish painting and the collection of glass, china and faïence.

Muzeum Miasta Rzeszowa
ul. 3 Maja 19. (0 17) 853 60 83.
10am–5pm Tue, Fri, 10am–3pm Wed, Thu, 9am–2pm Sun. (free on Sun).

Fair in Leżajsk, a centre of folk pottery

Łańcut ⑫

THE TOWN OF ŁAŃCUT was purchased by Stanisław Lubomirski in 1629. Securing the services of the architect Maciej Trapola and the stuccoist Giovanni Battista Falconi, this powerful magnate went about building a fortified residence in the town. It was completed in 1641. After 1775 the palace, by then owned by Izabella Lubomirska, was extended and the interiors remodelled. The Neo-Classical Ballroom and the Great Dining Room were created during this period, and the magnificent gardens with their many pavilions laid out. In the 19th century, ownership of the palace passed to the Potocki family. From 1889 to 1914, the penultimate owners, Roman and Elżbieta Potocki, modernized the residence. The palace, now a museum, attracts numerous visitors.

★ Column Room
The statue in this room is that of the young Henryk Lubomirski, carved by Antonio Canova in around 1787.

Mirror Room
The walls are lined with Rococo panelling brought back to Łańcut by Izabella Lubomirska – probably from one of her visits to France.

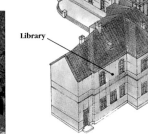

Library

Carriage
The largest collection of carriages in Poland is displayed in the coach house. It comprises 120 different types of coaches, carriages and other horse-drawn vehicles.

STAR FEATURES
★ **Theatre**
★ **Ballroom**
★ **Column Room**

★ Theatre
The small court theatre was built around 1800. Its present appearance is the result of remodelling carried out by the eminent Viennese workshop of Fellner & Helmer.

Sculpture Gallery
Many pieces, mostly 19th-century, make up the collection on display; among them is this statue of Psyche carried by Zephyrs, a copy of a piece by John Gibson.

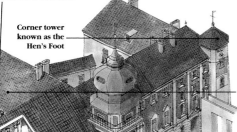

Corner tower known as the Hen's Foot

The main entrance

Neo-Rococo Clock
This typically French Neo-Rococo gilt clock is mounted in the mirror that hangs over the fireplace in the Billiard Room.

★ Ballroom
The Neo-Classical ballroom was designed by Christian Piotr Aigner in 1800. The stuccowork is by Fryderyk Baumann.

Façade
The palace façades are fundamentally Baroque. The rustication of the lower storey, however, is typical of French Renaissance style – part of the remodelling that the palace underwent at the end of the 19th century.

SILESIA

ILESIA'S GREAT WEALTH *of architectural monuments, its eventful history and its beautiful and varied landscape distinguish it from other regions of Poland. The region's well-preserved historic towns and the many hiking trails in the picturesque Sudeten Mountains make it an area that invites long exploration.*

The stormy history of Silesia (Śląsk) and the great variety of cultural influences that have flourished here have given this region a rich heritage. It belonged initially to the Bohemian crown and passed into Polish control around 990. When Poland split into principalities, Silesia began to gain independence. Divided into smaller independent duchies, it returned to Bohemian rule in the 14th century. After 1526, together with other Bohemian territories, it became part of the Habsburg Empire. During the Reformation, most of its inhabitants were converted to Lutheranism. The Thirty Years' War (1618–48) inflicted devastation on Silesia, bringing in its wake the repression of Protestantism. While Jesuits and Cistercians erected magnificent Baroque monasteries at that time, under the terms of the Peace of Westphalia of 1648, Protestants were limited to building the three "peace churches". The Habsburgs lost Silesia to Prussia in 1742. Although the main language was German, many areas, especially the Opole region and Upper Silesia, were inhabited by an influential Polish minority. After World War I, as a result of the Silesian Uprisings of 1919–21, the eastern part of Upper Silesia, together with Katowice, was included within Polish borders. After 1945, nearly all of historical Silesia joined Poland, and its German population was deported. Poles who had been resettled from Poland's eastern provinces (which had been annexed by the Soviet Union) took their place.

Silesia is an enchanting region, not only for the breathtaking beauty of its mountain landscapes but also for its outstanding architecture. The medieval castles built to defend ancient borderlands, the grand Renaissance manor houses and impressive Baroque residences, the great Gothic churches and stately monasteries – all these provide ample attractions and a historic atmosphere.

A hint of spring: melting snow in the Karkonosze Mountains

◁ **Książ Castle, near Wałbrzych, seat of the Hochberg family, looks out over an autumnal landscape**

Exploring Silesia

THE MOST ATTRACTIVE part of the region is Lower Silesia. A good starting point for exploration is Wrocław, the provincial capital and a city full of historic buildings as well as interesting 20th-century architecture. From here, the area of Kotlina Kłodzka, with the fantastically shaped Table Mountains, is within easy reach. Not far away lies Jelenia Góra, a good base for hiking in the Karkonosze Mountains in summer or for skiing on the nearby slopes in winter. The visitor to Silesia will also find beautiful palaces and churches in almost every village. Many fine residences, however, are gradually falling into ruin.

Sheep in the alpine pastures of the Beskid Śląski Mountains

SEE ALSO

- *Where to Stay* pp303–5.
- *Restaurants and Bars* pp321–3.

KEY

▰▰	Motorway
▬▬	Main road
▬▬	Other road
≈	River
☆	Viewpoint

SIGHTS AT A GLANCE

GETTING AROUND

There are rail links between all the major Silesian
cities, so that is possible to travel by train from
Wrocław to Jelenia Góra, Legnica, Głogów, Świdnica,
Wałbrzych and Kłodzk. There are also good connections between Katowice, Opole and Wrocław, and
trains also stop in Brzeg. Although smaller towns are
accessible by bus, the service can be very infrequent,
so that outside the major cities the best way to travel is
by car. Parts of the motorway that will run through
Silesia have already been opened.

The Baroque plague column in the
Market Square in Świdnica

The house of Gerhard Hauptmann in Jagniątków

0 km   25

0 miles   25

The Baroque-Neo-Classical palace of the Talleyrand family in Żagań

Żagań ❶

Road map B4. 🏠 28,000. 🚉 🚌

THE ORIGINS of Żagań go back as far as the 13th century. A particularly happy episode in the history of this pretty town on the River Bóbr was the period from 1845 to 1862, thanks to the beautiful Dorothea Talleyrand-Périgord, the youngest daughter of Peter Biron, Duke of Kurland.

Dorothea was something of a social magnet. She was a friend of Maurice Charles de Talleyrand, one of Louis Napoleon's ministers, and his nephew's wife. Her circle attracted the most eminent composers and writers of the day, among them Franz Liszt and Giuseppe Verdi. Her residence was the **palace** built for Albrecht von Wallenstein, a commander in the Thirty Years' War (1618–48). Dorothea had alterations made, and the palace's present Neo-Classical appearance and the lay-out of the rooms were commissioned by her in the mid-19th century. It now houses the **Cultural Institute**.

Other prominent buildings in the town are the Franciscan **Church of Saints Peter and Paul** (Kościół św św Piotra i Pawła), built in the Gothic style and dating from the 14th century. The enormous **Church of the Assumption** (Kościół Wniebowzięcia NMP), which once belonged to the Augustinians, also merits attention. It was built in stages from the late 13th to the early 16th century, although the finely furnished interior dates from the 1830s. The library of the monastery

next to the church contains works by the 18th-century painter George Wilhelm Neunhertz and items connected to the German astronomer Johannes Kepler, who worked in Żagań between 1628 and 1630.

🏛 **Cultural Institute**
ul. Szprotawska 4. 🅲 *(0 68) 377 34 61.* ⭘ *by appointment only.* ♿
🛕 **Church of Saints Peter and Paul**
ul. Łużycka.
🛕 **Church of the Assumption**
pl. Klasztorny. 🅲 *(0 68) 377 59 82.*

Głogów ❷

Road map B4. 🏠 75,000. 🚉 🚌
🚹 *ul. Poczdamska 1 (0 76 833 31 34).* 🌐 *www.glogow.com.pl* ♫ *Jazz in Głogów (Oct, Nov).*

THIS TOWN on the Odra River was established about 1,000 years ago but fell into ruin during World War II. Two Gothic churches, the collegiate Church of the

Architecture old and new: a street in the old town in Głogów

Assumption, set on an island in the Odra, and the Church of St Nicholas in the old town, have not been rebuilt. However, the beautiful Jesuit Baroque **Church of Corpus Christi** (Kościół Bożego Ciała), built in 1694–1724 to a design by Giulio Simonetti, has been reconstructed. Its original twin-tower façade was added in 1711 by Johann Blasius Peintner. The picturesque town hall with its slender tower owes its present form to remodelling carried out by Augustus Soller in 1831–4. It too has been reconstructed. On the bank of the Odra stands the castle of the dukes of Głogów, with an original 14th-century medieval tower and Gothic cellars, and later Baroque walls. It houses the **Archaeological and Historical Museum**. Among the exhibits are a collection of instruments of torture.

🏛 **Archaeological and Historical Museum**
ul. Brama Brzostowska 1.
🅲 *(0 76) 834 10 81.* ⭘ *10am–5pm Wed–Sun.*
🛕 **Church of Corpus Christi**
ul. Powstańców. 🅲 *(0 76) 833 36 01.*

Lubiąż ❸

Road map B4. 🏠 2,300. 🚉
Malczyce. 🚌 **Abbey. Lubiąż Foundation** 🅲 *(0 71) 389 71 66.* ⭘ *Apr–Nov: 9am–6pm daily; Oct–Mar: 10am–3pm daily.* ♿

THE GIGANTIC Cistercian monastic complex situated on the high bank of the River Odra comes into view from a great distance. Cistercian monks first settled in Lubiąż in 1175. They built a Romanesque church followed by a Gothic basilica, of which the twin-tower façade and ducal chapel remain. The present abbey dates from 1681–1715. After World War II, it was used as a warehouse for unsold books, mostly works by Lenin. Its restoration began in the mid-1990s. An exhibition of Silesian sculpture as well as certain rooms of the monastery, including the

Refectory of the Cistercian Abbey in Lubiąż

refectory and the Ducal Hall, are now open to the public.

The ceiling of the refectory is decorated with paintings by Michael Willmann, whose work is also to be seen on the altars of the parish church in Lubiąż. The great Ducal Hall is a magnificent example of the late Baroque style, its purpose being to glorify the faith and the feats of the Habsburg dynasty.

Legnica ❹

Road map B4. 🏚 105,000. 🚊
🛈 Rynek 29 (0 76 851 22 80).

LEGNICA, AFTER WROCŁAW and Opole Silesia's third-largest city, became the capital of the independent duchy of Legnica in the 13th century. Today it is a large administrative centre and copper-mining town, as evidenced by the displays in the **Copper Museum**.

The **Parish Church of John the Baptist** (Fara św Jana Chrzciciela) is one of the most beautiful Baroque shrines in Silesia, built for the Jesuits in 1714–27. The presbytery of the original church was converted

into a chapel, the Mausoleum of the Silesian Piasts (1677–8).

In the northern part of the old town stands the **Dukes' Castle**. It has medieval origins and was remodelled many times. The fine Renaissance gate was added by George von Amberg in 1532–3. From here, Ulica Mariacka leads to the Gothic **Church of the Virgin Mary** (Kościół NMP), dating from the 14th century and remodelled in the first half of the 15th.

In the Market Square stand the Baroque town hall of 1737–46, which houses a theatre, and the Gothic **Cathedral of Saints Peter and Paul** (Katedra św św Piotra i Pawła), built in the 14th century and preserving a 13th-century baptismal font. In the centre of the Market Square are eight narrow arcaded houses known as the **Herring Stalls** and, at No. 40, a 16th-century house known as **By the Quail's Nest House**, with sgraffito decoration.

🏛 Copper Museum
ul. Partyzantów 3. 🄲 (0 76) 862 49 49.
🄾 11am–5pm Wed–Sun. 🄼 (free on Wed).

🏠 Parish Church of John the Baptist
ul. Partyzantów 25. 🄲 (0 76) 862 29 95.
🏠 Church of the Virgin Mary
pl. Mariacki 1. 🄲 (0 76) 854 34 40.
🄾 1 May–30 Sep: 11am–6pm Tue–Fri, 10am–3pm Sat; 1 Oct–30 Apr: by appointment only.
🏠 Cathedral of Saints Peter and Paul
pl. Fryderyka Chopina.
🄲 (0 76) 862 25 61.

Legnickie Pole ❺

Road map B4. 🏚 1,300. 🚌

IT WAS AT Legnickie Pole that a great battle between the Poles, led by Henry II, the Pious, and the Tartars took place on 9 April 1241. Despite the Turks' defeat of the Poles and the death of their commander, Poland prevented westward Tartar expansion. The **Museum of the Battle of Legnica** details this event.

The Benedictine abbey, dating from 1727–31 and built by Kilian Ignaz Dientzenhofer in the Baroque style, is the greatest attraction of this small village. The abbey church, dedicated to St Jagwida, has an elliptical nave and undulating vaulting covered with trompe l'oeil paintings by Cosmas Damian Asam. Its furnishings are equally fine.

🏛 Museum of the Battle of Legnica
🄲 (0 76) 858 23 98. 🄾 11am–5pm Wed–Sun.

The Baroque façade of the Benedictine abbey church in Legnickie Pole

Tower of the Baroque Church of Peace in Jawor

Jawor are the 14th-century Church of St Martin (Kościół św Marcina), and the late 15th-century Church of St Mary (Kościół Mariacki). The best place to finish a walk around the town is the Market Square, which is surrounded by arcaded Baroque houses.

🏛 **Gallery of Silesian Ecclesiastical Art**
ul. Klasztorna 6. █ *(0 76) 870 30 86 or 870 23 21.* ◻ *Oct–Mar: 10am– 4pm Wed–Sun; Apr–Sep: 10am–5pm Wed–Fri, 10am–4pm Sat, Sun.*

Jawor ❻

Road map B4. 🏃 *15,500.* 🚃 🚌

THE CAPITAL of an independent duchy in the Middle Ages, Jawor is dominated by a castle that is a vestige of those times. Reconstruction has robbed the castle of much of its original splendour, but other buildings, which were painstakingly restored after World War II, enhance the town's historic atmosphere.

The most picturesque building is the large **Church of Peace** (Kościół Pokoju). It was one of three Protestant "peace churches" erected in Silesia after the Peace of Westphalia that marked the end of the Thirty Years' War (1618–48). It was built by Andreas Kempner, to a design by Albrecht von Säbisch, in 1654–6. With the church in Świdnica *(see p185)*, it is among the world's largest timber-framed structures. Other notable buildings in

Złotoryja ❼

Road Map B4. 🏃 *17,400.* 🚃 🚌
ℹ *Rynek 1 (0 76 878 37 78).*
@ *ofir@bbk.pl* 🏅 *World Gold-Panning Championships (Aug).*

DERIVED FROM THE Polish word *złoto*, meaning gold, the town's name reflects the fact that the gold-rich sands of the River Kaczawa, which flows through Złotoryja, have been exploited since the Early Middle Ages. Even today gold-seekers flock to contests organized by the local gold-panning association.

Features of interest in Złotoryja include the Gothic **Church of St Mary** (Kościół NMP), which has a 13th-century presbytery, and the remains of the town walls.

ENVIRONS: The volcanic **Wilcza Góra Geological Park**, also known as Wilkołak, lies 2 km (1¼ miles) south of Złotoryja. Unusual basalt formations known as "basalt roses" can be seen in the western part of the park.

Gothic doorway of Grodziec Castle

Grodziec ❽

Road Map B4. 🏃 *500.* 🚃 *Złotoryja.* 🚌

AN IMPOSING fortification crowning a basalt hill, Grodziec Castle was built in the 15th century in the Gothic style as the seat of the dukes of Legnica. It was extended in 1522–4 and over the next four centuries it was destroyed several times, once during the Thirty Years' War (1618–48). It was rebuilt in the Romantic style in 1906–8.

The walls, which follow the contours of the hill, are irregular. The castle's tower and living quarters survive.

At the bottom of the hill is the magnificent, although neglected, palace built for the Frankenberg family by Johann Blasius Peintner in 1718–27. Its overgrown surroundings were once attractive gardens.

Lwówek Śląski ❾

Road Map B4. 🏃 *9,300.* 🚃 🚌
ℹ *ul. Sienkiewicza 42 (0 75 782 34 77).* @ *it-lwowek@wp.pl*
Ⓦ *www.sudety.it.pl or www.lwowek.home.pl* ◻ *8am–5pm Mon–Fri, 9am–2pm Sat.*

LWÓWEK ŚLĄSKI is a small town set on a precipice overlooking the River Bóbr, in the foothills of the Izerski Mountains. Remnants of the stone walls that once surrounded the settlement can be seen all around.

The centrepiece of the town is its Gothic-Renaissance

Gold-panning competition in Złotoryja

Gothic-Renaissance town hall in Lwówek Śląski

town hall. Built in the 15th century, it was extended in 1522–5 and restored in 1902–5, when the delightful arcades around the building were added. Several town houses of historical interest stand in the Market Square.

The twin-towered **Church of the Assumption** (Kościół Wniebowzięcia) has an imposing Romanesque façade which dates from the 13th century. The tympanum over the portal depicts the Coronation of the Virgin. The main body of the church was not added until the turn of the 16th century. The Gothic chapel on the south side, which dates from 1496, has vaulting with beautiful 16th-century frescoes.

The ruins of another Gothic church also survive in Lwówek Śląski. The church was built by Franciscan monks but fell into disuse in 1810.

ENVIRONS: The castle at **Płakowice**, 2 km (1¼ miles) south of Lwówek Śląski, is one of the finest Renaissance castles in Silesia. It was built in 1550–63 for the von Talkenberg family.

Czoch Castle ⑩

Road Map A4. ▦ *Sucha*. ☎ *(0 75) 721 15 53.* ◷ *10am–3pm daily, but always telephone in advance to arrange a guide.*

CZOCH CASTLE (Zamek Czocha) is one of Silesia's major tourist attractions. Standing in a picturesque location on the banks of Lake Leśniańskie, it can be seen for miles around.

The castle dates from the 14th century, and because it was destroyed and rebuilt several times over many centuries, incorporates a range of architectural styles. It was most recently renovated in the early part of the 20th century, when the Gütschoff family of Dresden had their dilapidated family seat rebuilt by Bodo Ebhardt in 1904–14. Ebhardt's Romantic vision restored Zamek Czocha to its former glory and the castle has since been used as the setting for several films.

Lubomierz ⑪

Road Map B4. ▦ *1,800.* ▯ ▤ ▯ *pl. Wolności 21 (0 75 783 35 73).* ▨ *Review of Polish Comedy Films (Aug).*

A SLEEPY LITTLE TOWN in the foothills of the Izerskie Mountains, Lubomierz boasts a picturesque **market square** lined with large arcaded houses. The Baroque Benedictine church built by Johann Jakob Scheerhof in 1727–30 dominates the town.

Many Polish films have been shot in the streets of Lubomierz. The popular comedy film *Sami swoi* ("Just Our Own") brought it the greatest renown. The film follows the fortunes of displaced persons from Poland's eastern territories – which were lost to the Soviet Union after World War II – as they settle in the town, itself a former German territory ceded to Poland.

🏛 The Kargul and Pawlak Museum
pl. Wolności 21. ☎ *(075) 783 35 73.* Ⓦ *www.sami-swoi.com.pl* ◷ *10am–4pm Tue, 11am–4pm Wed–Sun.* ▨
This museum is housed in Płóciennik House, built in the 16th century and reconstructed around 1700. Its collection includes items used during the making of Sylwester Chęciński's film *Sami swoi*.

The imposing outline of Czoch Castle in Sucha

The Foothills of the Karkonosze Mountains ⑫

THE KARKONOSZE MOUNTAINS, the highest in the Sudeten (Sudety) chain, draw holidaymakers all year round. There are many footpaths and good facilities for hikers throughout the summer, while in winter skiers come to enjoy the exhilarating pistes. The upper parts of the Karkonosze Mountains are a national park and are recognized by UNESCO as a World Biosphere Reserve.

In the lower parts of the mountains are several small towns that are attractive to tourists, such as Karpacz and Szklarska Poręba, as well as Cieplice and Sobieszów in the administrative district of Jelenia Góra *(see p184)*.

Cieplice ①
This popular spa town has a number of fine Baroque buildings, including Schaffgotsch Palace and its Cistercian and Protestant churches. There is also a natural history museum.

Szklarka Waterfall ②
A forest of fir trees provides a scenic setting for the 15-m (45-ft) waterfall.

Piechowice

JAKUSZYCE ← E 65 ③ ②

Szklarska Poręba ③
This health resort is a good starting point for excursions into the Karkonosze Mountains. It is also famous for its glassworks – handmade crystal artifacts are available in local kiosks.

Jagniątków ④
A picturesque villa was built here by the Nobel Prize-winning author Gerhart Hauptmann for his second wife in 1900–02. It now houses a gallery of paintings illustrating scenes from Hauptmann's works.

Miłków ⑥
A Baroque palace and church surrounded by stone walls covered in penitentiary crosses are the main attractions of this village.

Sobieszów: Chojnik Castle ⑤
Situated on a high escarpment, this 14th-century castle was built for Duke Bolko II. In the 15th and 16th centuries it was renovated by the Schaffgotsch family, but in 1675 was gutted by a fire after being struck by lightning.

Mysłakowice ⑧

The village is noted for its Neo-Gothic palace, which once belonged to Kaiser Friedrich Wilhelm IV, for a church designed by Karl Friedrich Schinkel and for Tyrolean-style houses built by religious refugees fleeing persecution in the Tyrol.

Interior of the Cistercian Church of St Mary in Krzeszów

TIPS FOR DRIVERS

Tour length: *About 70 km (46 miles).*

Stopping-off points: *Bars and restaurants can be found in Szklarska Poręba, Cieplice and Karpacz. The Spiż restaurant in Miłków is recommended.*

Other attractions: *Karpacz also has a chair lift to Kopa, which is one hour's walk from Mt Śnieżka. Another chair lift from Szklarska Poręba goes to Szrenica.*

KEY

◾ Scenic route

◾ Other road

☆ Viewpoint

0 km   5

0 miles   5

Karpacz ⑦

The buildings of this popular health resort are concentrated along a single street 7 km (4½ miles) long. The wooden Romanesque church here was brought from Vang, in Norway, in 1842–4.

Krzeszów ⓭

Road map B5. 🚹 *1,300.*
🚉 *Kamienna Góra.* ⛪ **Church of St Mary, Church of St Joseph and Mausoleum of the Silesian Piasts**
📞 *(0 75) 742 33 25.* ◷ *9am–6pm daily.* ♿

THIS TINY VILLAGE in the Góry Kamienne Mountains has one of the most picturesque groups of historic buildings in Poland. Benedictine monks settled here in 1242, followed by Cistercian monks in 1292. They were responsible for building the Church of St Joseph (Kościół św Józefa), which has frescoes by Michael Willmann, in 1690–96. They also built the abbey **Church of St Mary** (Kościół NMP Łaskawej) in 1727–35. The interior is decorated with vertiginous trompe l'oeil paintings by Georg Wilhem Neunhertz; sculptures by Anton Dorazil and Ferdinand Maximilian Brokoff make the pilasters, cornices and vaulting appear to float in mid-air. The figures of saints on the stalls in the chancel are of particular interest.

Behind the presbytery is the **Mausoleum of the Silesian Piasts** (Mauzoleum Piastów Śląskich), with the Gothic tombs of Bolko I (d. 1301) and Bolko II (d. 1368), dukes of Świdnica-Jawor. Figures of their wives, Agnieszka and Beatrycza, stand opposite the tombs. On the wall is an epitaph by the son of Bolko II, the last member of the Piast dynasty.

Arcaded houses around the Market Square in Jelenia Góra

Jelenia Góra ⑭

Road Map B4. 🏘 89 000. 🚉 🚌
ℹ️ pl. Piastowski 36 (0 75 755 88 44
or 755 88 45). ◯ 9am–5pm Mon–Fri,
10am–2pm Sat. ℹ️ pl. Ratuszowy 2
(0 75 767 69 25). 🅦 www.sudety.it.pl
◯ 9am–5pm Mon–Fri, 10am–2pm
Sat, Sun. 🎭 International Street
Theatre Festival (Jul); Jelenia Góra
(Sep); Cieplice Spring (May).

SITUATED AT THE foot of the
Karkonosze Mountains,
Jelenia Góra is a favourite
tourist destination and a
major starting point for
mountain hikers. The
town was granted city
status at the end of the
13th century. It was
once renowned for its
textiles – delicate batiste
and voile that were
exported as far as Africa
and America. It was also
one of the main
centres of engraved
glassware, examples
of which can be seen in the
Regional Museum.

Silesian glassware

The town's historic centre is
the Market Square, with a
Baroque town hall
surrounded by arcaded town
houses. In Ulica Maria
Konopnicka, east of the
Market Square, is the **Church
of Saints Erasmus and
Pancras** (Kościół św św
Erazma i Pankracego), a
Gothic basilica of the late
14th to early 15th centuries.
The line of the old defensive
walls here is marked by a
chapel that was once a keep.
In Ulica 1 Maja, on the
same axis, is the Church of
Our Lady, with two
penitentiary crosses *(see
p185)* set into the outer walls.
The street then leads to the
Baroque former Protestant
Church of the Holy Cross

(Kościół św Krzyża), known
also as the Church of Peace.
The town boundaries of
Jelenia Góra were expanded
in 1976 and now include the
spa of Cieplice, with its
Natural History Museum,
and the town of Sobieszów
(see pp182–3), which includes
the **Karkanosze National
Park Natural History
Museum**.

🔒 Church of Saints
Erasmus and Pancras
pl. Kościelny. 📞 (0 75) 752 21 60.
This Gothic basilica of the
first half of the 14th
century features late
Gothic vaulting
dating from about
1550 and a Baroque
altar depicting the
Transfiguration.

🔒 Church of the
Holy Cross
ul. 1 Maja. 📞 (0 75) 752 42 11.
This church (Kościół
św Krzyża), built by Martin
Franze in 1709–18, is
modelled on St Catherine's in
Stockholm. A triple tier of
galleries lines the interior and
frescoes by Felix Anton
Scheffler and Jozef Franz
Hoffman cover the ceilings.
The altar, which is structurally
integrated with the organ loft,
is particularly striking.

🏛 Regional Museum
ul. Matejki 28. 📞 (0 75) 752 34 65.
🅦 www.kustosz.com.pl
◯ 9am–3:30pm Tue, Thu, Fri,
9am–5pm Wed, Sat, Sun.
📷 (free on Wed).
The Regional Museum
contains the largest
collection of decorative
glassware in Poland. A
traditional Karkonosze
hut nearby houses an
ethnographical exhibition.

🏛 Natural History
Museum
Jelenia Góra – Cieplice, ul. Wolności 268.
📞 (0 75) 775 15 06. ◯ May–Sep:
9am–6pm Tue, 9am–4pm Wed–Fri,
9am–5pm Sat, Sun; Oct–Mar:
9am–4pm Tue–Sun.

🏛 Karkanosze National
Park Natural History
Museum
ul. Chałubińskiego 23.
📞 (0 75) 755 33 48. ◯ 10am–4pm
Tue–Sun.

Bolków ⑮

Road Map B4. 🏘 5,800. 🚉 🚌

THE GREAT TOWERING **Castle
of the Dukes of
Świdnica-Jawor** is the main
feature of this small town. It
was built in stages from the
mid-13th to the mid-14th
century. Sacked and destroyed
several times, in the 16th
century it was rebuilt in the
Renaissance style by Jakob
Paar. Today the castle is a
local history **museum**. The
Gothic Church of St Jadwiga
(Kościół św Jadwigi) is also
worth a visit. In the old town,
several fine houses survive.

🏛 Castle Museum
ul. Księcia Bolka. 📞 (0 75) 741 32 97.
◯ Apr–Oct: 9am–4pm Tue–Sat,
9am–6pm Sun; Nov–Mar: 9am–4pm
Tue–Sun.

ENVIRONS: In **Świny**, 2 km
(1¼ miles) north of Bolków,
are the haunting ruins of a
castle. The upper part was
built in the 14th century. The
lower wing is a 17th-century
late Baroque palace.

**The crenellated tower of
Bolków Castle**

Książ

Road Map B5. **Castle** Wałbrzych,
ul. Piastów Śl. (*(0 74) 843 26 18.*
◻ *1 Apr–30 Sep: 10am–6pm
Tue–Sun; 1 Oct–31 Mar: 10am–4pm
Tue–Sun.* ● *Mon.*
Palm House Wałbrzych-Lubiechowo,
ul. Wrocławska 158. (*(0 74) 840 08 80.*
◻ *I Jun–31 Aug: 10am–8pm
Tue–Sun; 1 Sep–31 May: 10am–6pm
Tue–Sun.* ● *Mon.* 🖼

KSIĄŻ CASTLE, on the
outskirts of Wałbrzych, is
the largest residential building
in Silesia. This huge edifice was
built on a rocky hilltop
overlooking the surrounding
wooded countryside. The late
13th-century Gothic **castle** of
Prince Bolko I was rebuilt in
the mid-16th century for the
Hochberg family of Meissen,
who remained its owners until
World War II. One of the most
powerful Silesian families, they
extended the building several
times, particularly in
1670–1724 and 1909–23. The
Hochbergs' reputation was
coloured by several scandals.
The penultimate owner of the
castle was Hans Henry XV von
Pless. After divorcing his wife,
Princess Daisy, he married a
much younger Spanish
woman, Clotilda. She gave
birth to a daughter, but then
left the elderly prince for his
son Bolko.

During World War II
attempts were made to
convert the castle into headquarters for the German
leader Adolf Hitler by drilling
tunnels into the rocky hill.
Today part of the castle
houses a museum, a hotel
and a restaurant. The grounds
are now the **Książ Nature
Park**. The stables and palm
house, still in use,
are open to
visitors.

Książ Castle, set high above the River Pełcznica

**High altar in the Church of Saints
Stanisław and Wenceslas**

Świdnica ⑰

Road Map B5. 🏙 *63,000.* 🚊 🚌

FOR ALMOST 100 years from
1292, Świdnica was the
capital of the independent
duchy of Świdnica-Jawor. It
minted its own coins and was
renowned for its beer, which
was exported to many cities
in central Europe. The town's
mercantile traditions are well
illustrated in the **Museum of
Silesian Trade** that is housed
in the town hall.

From the pretty market
square, with its fine Baroque
plague column *(see p177)*,
Ulica Długa, the main street,
leads to the 14th-century
**Church of Saints Stanisław
and Wenceslas** (Kościół św
św Stanisława i Wacława), a
Gothic building with the
highest tower in Silesia. The
interior is richly furnished and
decorated in styles ranging
from Gothic to Baroque. The
altar canopy was
made by Johann
Riedl in 1694. The
town's most
impressive
building,

however, is the **Church of
Peace** (Kościół Pokoju). With
that in Jawor *(see p180)*, it is
one of two surviving Protestant
"peace churches" built after the
Peace of Westphalia that ended
the Thirty Years' War (1618–
48). The timber-framed church,
designed by Albrecht von
Säbisch, was built in 1656–7.
Its undistinguished exterior
conceals an unusual interior,
with a two-tiered gallery, fine
paintings and furnishings.

🏛 **Museum of Silesian
Trade**
Rynek 37. (*(0 74) 852 12 91.*
◻ *10am–3pm Tue–Fri, 11am–5pm
Sat, Sun.* 🖼 *(free on Fri).*
🔒 **Church of Saints
Stanisław and Wenceslas**
pl. Kościelny. (*(0 74) 852 12 91.*
◻ *daily* 🖼
🔒 **Church of Peace**
pl. Pokoju. (*(0 74) 852 28 14.*
◻ *9am–1pm and 3–5pm Mon–Sat,
3–5pm Sun.*

ENVIRONS: **Jaworzyna**, 10 km
(6 miles) northwest of
Świdnica, has Poland's largest
museum of steam locomotives.

**Penitentiary cross in Łaziska,
Upper Silesia**

PENITENTIARY
CROSSES

As a form of punishment,
criminals in the Middle
Ages sometimes had to
make a stone cross and
place it at the scene of
their crime or near a
church. Depictions of the
implement used to carry
out the deed (such as a
crossbow) or a part of the
victim's body (such as the
feet) were engraved on
the cross.

Renaissance gate of Grodno Castle in Zagórze Śląskie

Zagórze Śląskie ⑱

Road Map B5. 🏛 430. 🚇 🚉

T HE MAIN ATTRACTION in this small village is **Grodno Castle**. Built by Bolko I at the end of the 13th century, it was altered by later owners and then fell into ruin, but was saved by major restoration work in 1907–29.

Today the castle houses a museum, whose more curious exhibits include the skeleton of a young woman. For the murder of her husband, she was condemned to death by starvation by her own father.

♣ **Grodno Castle**
🎫 (0 74) 845 33 60. ⏰ 10am–3pm Tue–Fri, 10am–4pm Sat, Sun.

ENVIRONS: A few kilometres south of Zagórze Śląskie are underground **tunnels** dug secretly in the final year of World War II by prisoners of the Gross-Rosen (Rogoźnica) concentration camp.

🚇 **Walim Tunnels (Sztolnie w Walimiu)**
🎫 (0 74) 845 73 00.

🆆 www.pcet.com.pl *(website for all underground tunnels in Poland).* ⏰ *9am–5pm Tue–Fri, 9am–6pm Sat, Sun (summer: until 8pm Sat, Sun).*
🚇 **Osowiec Tunnels (Sztolnie w Osówce)**
🎫 (0 74) 845 62 20. ⏰ 10am–4pm daily. Entry on the hour. 🎟 *(extra charge for groups of fewer than five).*

Mt Ślęza ⑲

Road Map B5.

M T ŚLĘŻA IS A conical peak visible from great distances all around. Used as a location for religious rituals during the Bronze Age (3500–1500 BC), it is crowned with a stone circle and mysterious statues of unknown origin stand beside the road that leads to the summit. The best view of the surrounding countryside is from the terrace of the Neo-Romanesque **church** built on Mt Ślęza in 1851–2. The hill of neighbouring **Wieżyca** has at its summit a tower erected in honour of the German statesman Otto von Bismarck in 1906–7, and is also a good vantage point from which to view the entire area.

In Sobótka, at the foot of Mt Ślęza, a former hospital built by Augustinian monks houses the **Ślęza Museum**. The best place to stay, or stop for lunch, is the hotel Zamek Górka, located in a Gothic-Renaissance Augustinian presbytery that later became the palace of the von Kulmiz family.

🏛 **Ślęza Museum**
Sobótka, ul. św Jakuba 18.
🎫 (0 71) 316 26 22. ⏰ 9am–4pm Wed–Fri and last Tue in the month, 10am–5pm Sat, Sun.

Wojnowice ⑳

Road Map B4. 🏛 400. 🚇
🚉 Mrozów. 🎫 (0 71) 317 07 16.

W OJNOWICE PRESENTS a rare opportunity to see a genuine and well-preserved Silesian Renaissance **manor house**. It was built in the early 16th century for Nikolaus von Scheibitz and soon after was acquired by the Boner family, who converted it into a Renaissance castle with a small arcaded courtyard. Compact and moated, it is now a hotel, with an excellent restaurant *(see p322)*. It is a superb place for a short break.

Moated Renaissance manor house in Wojnowice

Trzebnica ㉑

Road Map C4. 🏛 12,100.
🚉 Oborniki Śląskie. 🚇

I N 1203 JADWIGA, wife of Henry I, brought an order of Cistercian monks from Bamberg, in southern Germany, to Trzebnica. Jadwiga was buried here and, after her canonization in 1267, the monastery became an important place of pilgrimage. The entire complex underwent major rebuilding in the second half of the 17th century, obliterating its Romanesque

Country track in Ślęza

architecture, although the tympanum of the main portal retains a fine relief of around 1230 representing the Old Testament figures David and Bathsheba. The Gothic chapel of St Jadwiga contains her Baroque-style tomb, dating from 1677–8. The figure of the saint was carved by Franz Josef Mangoldt in 1750.

Coronation of the Virgin in the portal of the Chapel of St Jadwiga

Oleśnica ㉒

Road Map C4. 🏘 38,000. 🚇 🚌

THE MOST impressive building in the town is the **Castle of the Dukes of Oleśnica**. While the Gothic interior is original, the exterior, with its circular corner tower, is the result of successive stages of rebuilding from 1542 to 1610 by the Italian architects Francesco Parr and Bernardo Niuron. The castle retains ornamental gables in the attic rooms in the wings and the unusual galleries

supported on brackets overlooking the courtyard. Attached to the castle is the **palace** of Jan Podiebrad, built in 1559–63.

A pleasant way of rounding off a visit to Oleśnica is to walk through the old quarter to the Gothic **Church of St John the Evangelist** (Kościół św Jana Ewangelisty). Beside the presbytery is a Baroque chapel built in memory of the dukes of Wurtemberg, and containing the Renaissance tombs of Jan and Jerzy Podiebrad. Other attractive elements include the stylish Mannerist pulpit from 1605 and the Gothic stalls from the late 15th and early 16th centuries. Remnants of castle walls, with the tower of the Wrocławski Gate, and the Neo-Classical town hall, rebuilt after World War II, are other features of interest.

Wrocław ㉓

See pp188–197.

Brzeg ㉔

Road Map C5. 🏘 39,000. 🚇 🚌

THE ATTRACTIVE TOWN of Brzeg, on the River Odra, has an illustrious history. It received its charter in 1245, and from 1311 to 1675 was the capital of the duchy of Legnica-Brzeg. The town's most impressive building

Renaissance sculpture on the gate tower of Brzeg Castle

is without doubt the **Castle of the Dukes of Legnica-Brzeg**. It was built originally in the Gothic style and a 14th-century Gothic chapel survives, in whose presbytery a mausoleum to the Silesian Piasts was built in 1567. The castle was transformed into a Renaissance palace in the second half of the 16th century. The three-winged complex features a circular courtyard and a tower over the entrance gate dating from 1554. The walls are decorated with busts of all the ancestors of Duke Jerzy II and his wife Barbara von Brandenburg. Today the castle houses the **Museum of the Silesian Piasts**.

Other buildings of interest are the **town hall**, erected in 1570–7, the 14th-century **Church of St Nicholas** (Kościół św Mikołaja) and the late Baroque Jesuit church, which was built in 1734–9.

🏛 **Museum of the Silesian Piasts**
pl. Zamkowy 1. 🕾 (077) 416 32 57.
Ⓦ www.zamekbrzeg.pl
🕐 10am–4pm Tue, Thu–Sun, 10am–6pm Wed.

ENVIRONS: A few kilometres from Brzeg is the small village of Małujowice, or Mollwitz, where on 10 April 1741 a major battle was fought in the Austro-Prussian war. The Gothic church there contains unusual 14th-century frescoes and Renaissance ceilings.

Courtyard of the Castle of the Dukes of Oleśnica

Wrocław ㉓

T̶HE CITY OF WROCŁAW bears the stamp of several cultures. It was founded by a Czech duke in the 10th century and a Polish bishopric was established here in 1000. Later it became the capital of the duchy of Silesian Piasts, and then came under Czech rule in 1335. In 1526, with the whole Czech state, it was incorporated into the Habsburg Empire, and in 1741 was transferred to Prussian rule. The fierce defence that German forces put up here in the last months of World War II left almost three quarters of the city in ruins. However, reconstruction has largely healed the ravages of the past.

Emblem of the Golden Deer House in Market Square

Baroque pietà in the Church of the Holy Name of Jesus

⌗ Wrocław University

pl. Uniwersytecki 1. **Aula Leopoldina**
【 (0 71) 375 22 15.
ⓦ www.uni.wroc.pl
◯ 10am–3:30pm Thu–Tue.

Wrocław University was established as an academy by Emperor Leopold I in 1702 and in 1811 became a university. Many of its alumni have gained renown. They include eight Nobel laureates, among them the nuclear physicist Max Born (1882–1970). Since 1945 it has been a Polish centre of learning and university.

The centrepiece of this imposing Baroque building is the assembly hall, the Aula Leopoldina, of 1728–41. The decoration includes stucco-work, gilding and carvings by Franz Josef Mangoldt and paintings by Christoph Handke glorifying wisdom, knowledge and science, and the founders of the academy.

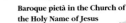

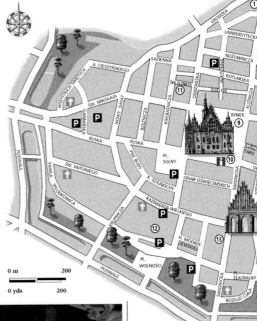

The richly ornamented interior of the university assembly hall

⛪ Church of the Holy Name of Jesus

pl. Uniwersytecki 1.
【 (0 71) 343 63 82.
The Church of the Holy Name of Jesus (Kościół Imiena Jezus), built for the Jesuits in 1689–98, is an important example of Silesian Baroque church architecture. The modest exterior conceals a breathtaking interior, built in 1722–34 by Krzysztof Tausch. The vaulting was decorated by the Viennese artist Johann Michael Rottmayer in 1704–6.

♣ Plac Biskupa Nankera

The buildings in this square date from various periods. The Gothic **Church of St Vincent** (Kościół św Wincentego), at No. 5, was erected in the 13th to the 15th centuries. The late 17th-century Baroque monastery is now part of the University of Wrocław.

The group of Baroque monastic buildings at No. 16 encloses the small 13th-century **Church of St Clare** (Kościół św Klary). The church was used by the Piasts as a

The Baroque Hochberg Chapel beside the Church of St Vincent

🏛 National Museum

pl. Powstańców Warszawy 5.
📞 (0 71) 372 51 50. ⏰ Apr–Oct: 10am–4pm Tue, Wed, Fri–Sun, 9am–5pm Thu; Nov–Mar: 10am–4pm Tue, Wed, Fri, Sun, 9am–5pm Thu, 11am–5pm Sat. 🎫 (free on Thu).

The ground floor contains examples of Silesian and Gothic art, including the tombstone of Henry

IV, the Good dating from 1300. The first floor has 16th and 17th-century paintings, including works by the Silesian artist Michael Willmann (1630–1712) and wooden sculptures by Thomas Weissfeldt (1630–1712). The second floor is devoted to the work of modern Polish artists.

Façade of the National Museum

🏛 Panorama of Racławice

ul. Purkyniego 11. 📞 (0 71) 344 16 61.
⏰ 9am–4pm Tue–Sun. 🎫 ♿
The Panorama of Racławice depicts the Battle of Racławice of 4 April 1794, when the Poles defeated the Russians. It is 120 m (400 ft) long and 5 m (16 ft) high and took the artists Jan Styka and Wojciech Kossak nine months to paint. It was unveiled in Lviv, in the Ukraine, in 1894. Brought to Poland in 1946, it was finally put on display in Wrocław in 1985, in a specially built rotunda.

Rotunda containing the Panorama of Racławice

mausoleum, and it still contains Gothic ducal tombs. Next door, at No. 17, is the Gothic **Church of St Maciej** (Kościół św Maciej), which dates from the 14th and early 15th centuries and was once owned by the Knights Hospitallers of the Red Star. The pavilion of the gallery at No. 8, on the opposite side of the street, contains 13th-century walls of the **House of the Nuns of Trebnica**, the oldest surviving secular building in the city.

CENTRAL WROCŁAW

Bernadine Church and Monastery ⑥
Church of the Holy Name of Jesus ②
Church of St Elizabeth ⑪
Church of Saints Wenceslas, Stanisław and Dorothy ⑬
Kameleon Store ⑧
Main Market Square ⑨
National Museum ④
Panorama of Racławice ⑤
Plac Biskupa Nankera ③
Royal Palace ⑫
Cathedral of St Mary Magdalene ⑦
Town Hall ⑩
Wrocław University ①

KEY

🛈 Church	
🛈 Tourist information	
🅿 Parking	

Wrocław Old Town

FOR THOSE WHO ENJOY exploring on foot, the old town of Wrocław is a delightful place. The restored buildings located around the large Main Market Square have been given over to an assortment of bars, restaurants and cafés with al fresco seating, while the churches nearby contain a wealth of religious art and ecclesiastical furnishings. The impressive Gothic town hall has a finely decorated interior.

On summer evenings the Main Market Square in the old town comes alive as local people and tourists alike gather there, some to gossip and exchange news, others to attend the concerts and many cultural events that are held in the square.

modernist architecture, an office building of 1912–13 by an equally renowned architect, Hans Poelzig.

Detail of the ornamental façade of the House of the Seven Electors

Late Gothic portal of the Bernadine church

🏛 Bernadine Church and Monastery

ul. Bernardyńska 5. **Museum of Architecture** ☎ *(0 71) 344 82 78.* ◻ *10am–3:30pm Wed–Sat, 11am–5pm Sun.* 📷

This impressive group of monastic buildings (Kościół i Klasztor pobernardyński) was constructed by Bernadine monks in 1463–1502. Having been rebuilt from their wartime ruins, they now house Poland's only Museum of Architecture. The monastery is of interest for its late Gothic cloisters and the Church of St Bernard of Siena, a towering Gothic basilica with a typically Baroque gable.

🏛 Cathedral of St Mary Magdalene

ul. św Marii Magdaleny. ☎ *(0 71) 344 19 04.* ◻ *9am–noon, 4–6pm daily.*

The great Gothic Cathedral of St Mary Magdalene (Katedra św Marii Magdaleny) was erected between about 1330

and the mid-15th century, incorporating the walls of a 13th-century church that had previously stood on the site. Inside the basilica is a Renaissance pulpit of 1579–81 by Friedrich Gross, a Gothic stone tabernacle and tombstones of various periods. The portal on the north side is a fine example of late 12th-century Romanesque sculpture. It was taken from a demolished Benedictine monastery in Olbina and added in 1546 *(see p18).* The tympanum, depicting the Dormition of the Virgin, is now on display in the National Museum.

Detail of the Cathedral of St Mary Magdalene

🏛 Kameleon Store

ul. Szewska 6.

The Kameleon store (Dom Handlowy Kameleon) is an unusual building on the corner of Ulica Szewska and Ulica Oławska. Its semicircular bay, formed of rows of windows, juts out dramatically. It was built by the German architect Erich Mendelsohn as a retail store for Rudolf Petersdorf in 1927–8. Nearby, at the intersection of Ulica Łaciarskiej and Ofiar Oświęcimskich, is another interesting example of

🏛 Main Market Square

Medal Museum Rynek 6. ☎ *(0 71) 344 93 83.* 🌐 www.muzeum.miejskie.wrocław.pl @ muzeum_miejskie@age.pl ◻ *May–Nov: 11am–5pm Wed–Sat, 10am–6pm Sun; Dec–Apr: 11am–4pm Wed–Sat, 10am–5pm Sun.*

Wrocław's Main Market Square is the second-largest in Poland, after that in Cracow. In the centre stand the town hall and a group of buildings separated by alleys. The houses around the square date from the Renaissance to the 20th century. Some still have their original 14th and 15th-century Gothic vaults. The most attractive side of the square is the west, with the late Baroque **House of the Golden Sun**, at No. 6, built in 1727 by Johann Lucas von Hildebrandt and now the Medal Museum, as well as the **House of the Seven Electors**, its paintwork dating from 1672. Also to the south is the Griffin House, at No. 2, built in 1587–9. It has a galleried interior courtyard. On the east side, at Nos. 31 and 32, is the Secessionist **Phoenix store** of 1904 and, at No. 41, the **Golden Hound**, a rebuilt town house of 1713. The north side was rebuilt after World War II. Just off the corner of the market square, fronting the Church of St Elizabeth (Kościół św Elżbiety), are two small acolytes' houses, the Renaissance Jaś, of around 1564, and the 18th-century Baroque Małgosia.

🏛 Town Hall

ul. Sienkiewicza 14/15. **Historical Museum** 📞 (0 71) 344 57 30.
Rynek Stary Ratusz Museum of Bourgeois Art 📞 (0 71) 344 14 34.
Ⓦ www.muzeum.miejskie.wroclaw.pl
🕐 For both museums. May–Oct: 11am–5pm Wed–Sat, 10am–6pm Sun; Nov–Apr: 10am–4pm Wed–Sat, 10am–5pm Sun.

The town hall is one of the most important examples of Gothic architecture in central and eastern Europe. Its present appearance is the result of rebuilding that took place between 1470 and 1510.

The town hall's southern façade was embellished with Neo-Gothic stone carvings in around 1871. Inside are impressive vaulted halls, the largest being the triple-aisled Grand Hall on the ground floor, and several late Gothic and Renaissance doorways. Outside the entrance to the town hall is a plaque commemorating the comedy writer Aleksander Fredro (1793–1876), made in 1879 by Leonard Marconi and transferred to Wrocław from Lviv in 1956 *(see p23)*.

Gothic gables of the east façade of the town hall

🔒 Church of St Elizabeth

ul. św Elżbiety. 📞 (0 71) 343 72 04.
The large tower dominating the market square is that of the Church of St Elizabeth (Kościół św Elżbiety), one of the largest churches in

Wrocław. The Gothic basilica was built in the 14th century on the site of an earlier church, although the tower was not completed until 1482. It became a Protestant church in 1525. Since 1946 it has been a garrison church.

The church has suffered damage from a succession of wars, fires and accidents. A fire in 1976 destroyed the roof and the splendid Baroque organ. Fortunately, more than 350 epitaphs and tombstones have survived, forming a remarkable exhibition of Silesian stone-carving from Gothic to Neo-Classical times.

Church of St Elizabeth with Jaś and Małgosia, acolytes' houses

⚓ Royal Palace

ul. Kazimierza Wielkiego 34/35.
Ethnographical Museum
📞 (0 71) 344 33 13. 🕐 Nov–Mar: 10am–4pm Tue, Wed, Fri–Sun, 9am–4pm Thu; Apr–Oct: 10am–4pm Tue, Wed, Fri–Sun, 9am–5pm Thu.
🎫 (free on Sat).
Plac. Wolnosci 7a. **Archaeological Museum** 📞 (0 71) 344 15 71.
🕐 Nov–Mar: 10am–4:30pm Wed, Fri–Sun, 9am–4:30pm Thu; Apr–Oct: 10am–4:30pm Wed, Fri, 9am–4:30pm Thu, 10am–5:30pm Sat, Sun.

The Baroque palace, enclosed by a court of annexes, was built in 1719. After 1750, when Wrocław came under Prussian rule, it was a residence for the Prussian kings. On the side facing Plac Wolńci, only a side gallery remains of the Neo-Renaissance palace built in 1843–6. The Royal Palace contains the Archaeological Museum and Ethnographical Museum, the latter illustrating Silesian folk history and art.

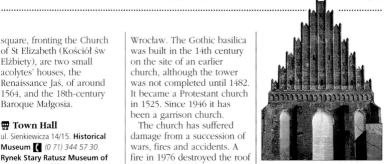

The Church of Saints Wenceslas, Stanisław and Dorothy

🔒 Church of Saints Wenceslas, Stanisław and Dorothy

ul. Świdnicka 20.
📞 (0 71) 343 27 21.
Dedicated to three saints, the Czech St Wenceslas, the Polish St Stanisław and the German St Dorothy, this church (Kościół św św Wacława, Stanisława i Doroty) was built in 1351 to cement relations between the three nationalities in Wrocław. The church's unusually narrow interior is Baroque. The Rococo tombstone of Gottfried von Spaetgen stands in the nave.

OSSOLINEUM

The National Ossoliński Institute was founded by Count Józef Maksimilian Ossoliński in Vienna in 1817. In 1827 it moved to Lwów (later Lviv), where it assembled collections of manuscripts, prints, etchings and drawings, promoted scientific research and engaged in publishing. After World War II most of the collections were transferred to the National Museum in Wrocław, while the manuscripts were housed in the Baroque monastery of the Knights Hospitallers of the Red Star.

The Baroque monastery that houses the Ossolineum

Ostrów Tumski and Piasek Island

OSTRÓW TUMSKI was once an island in the River Odra, and it is here that the history of Wrocław began. According to legend, the city was founded by Duke Vratislav of Bohemia. In the year 1000 a bishopric was established and the island grew into a centre of ducal power. After the city moved to the left bank of the Odra in 1292, the island remained the base of ecclesiastical authority. In the 19th century the northern arm of the Odra was filled in and Tumski ceased to be an island. Tumski Bridge connects it to Piasek Island, a small sandbank that since the first half of the 12th century has been the location of a monastery for canons regular.

Statue of St John Nepomuk

Church of the Holy Cross (Kościół św Krzyża)
This Gothic church is set on two levels. The upper church is reached via a portal enclosed by a double arch.

Church of St Martin

Tumski Bridge
The present bridge was built in 1888–92. The figures of St Jadwiga and St John the Baptist guarding it are by Gustav Grunenberg.

ŚW. MARCINA

MOST MŁYŃSKI

ŚW. JADWIGI

★ Church of St Mary on Piasek (Kościół NMP na Piasku)
The interior of the church was restored after World War II.

0 m ___ 250
0 yds ___ 250

STAR SIGHTS

★ Cathedral of St John the Baptist

★ Church of St Mary on Piasek

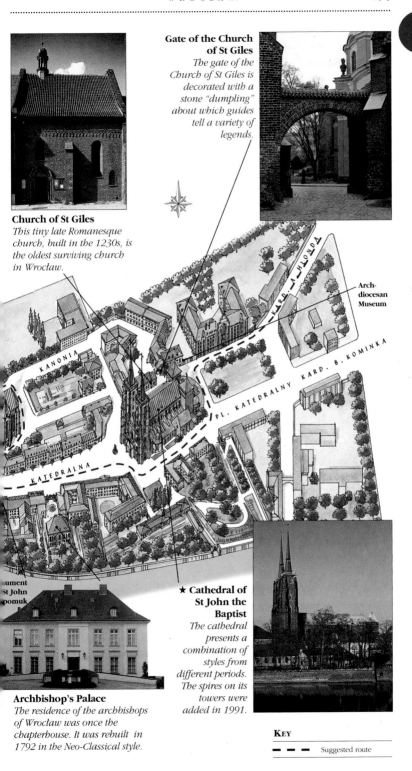

Gate of the Church of St Giles
The gate of the Church of St Giles is decorated with a stone "dumpling" about which guides tell a variety of legends.

Church of St Giles
This tiny late Romanesque church, built in the 1230s, is the oldest surviving church in Wrocław.

Arch-diocesan Museum

KARD. A. HLONDA

KANONIA

PL. KATEDRALNY   KARD. B. KOMINKA

KATEDRALNA

...ument
...St John
...pomuk

★ **Cathedral of St John the Baptist**
The cathedral presents a combination of styles from different periods. The spires on its towers were added in 1991.

Archbishop's Palace
The residence of the archbishops of Wrocław was once the chapterhouse. It was rebuilt in 1792 in the Neo-Classical style.

KEY

‑ ‑ ‑   Suggested route

Exploring Ostrów Tumski and Piasek Island

WROCŁAW'S ISLANDS, BATHED by the River Odra, are peaceful places for a stroll away from the bustle of the city. The cathedral, the islands' principal landmark, preserves its valuable interior despite having suffered the ravages of World War II. The Archdiocesan Museum is a rich repository of Gothic art. A walk through the islands' many narrow streets and alleys can be followed by a visit to the Botanical Gardens.

The Gothic Church of the Holy Cross, built on two levels

Gothic portal of the Church of St Mary on Piasek

🔒 Church of St Mary on Piasek
ul. Najświętszej Marii Panny 1.
The rather forbidding bulk of the Church of St Mary on Piasek (Kościół NMP na Piastu) dominates Piasek Island. The church was constructed for canons regular in the second half of the 14th century on the site of a 12th-century Romanesque building whose tympanum is built into the wall over the sacristy in the south aisle.

The Church of St Mary suffered extensive damage in World War II, but some impressive features survive. The asymmetrical tripartite rib vaulting over the aisles is unusual. The church also houses a fine collection of Gothic altars brought here from other churches in Silesia.

🔒 Church of St Martin
ul. św Marcina 7.
The first ecclesiastical building raised on the site now occupied by the Church of St Martin (Kościół św Marcina) was a stronghold chapel erected at the turn of

the 11th century. The present church dates from the late 13th century but was rebuilt after World War II because it had suffered major damage. The present building consists of an octagonal nave and an unfinished presbytery.

🔒 Church of the Holy Cross
pl. Katedralny. 🔔 (0 71) 322 25 74.
The two-tiered Church of the Holy Cross (Kościół św Krzyża) was established in 1288 by Henry IV, the Pious. Building continued in the 14th century, and the south tower was not completed until 1484. The lower church has been used by Uniates since 1956. The upper church, a narrow nave with a transept, was badly damaged during World War II, when most of its interior fittings were lost. The tombstone dedicated to the church's founder has been moved to the National Museum, but the original tympanum, depicting the ducal couple admiring the heavenly Throne of Grace, can be seen in the north aisle. The 15th-century triptych over the high altar comes from a church in Świny.

♣ Archbishop's Palace
ul. Katedralna 11. ● to visitors.
The present Archbishop's residence, once the home of the canons of the cathedral, is a relatively plain building that was reconstructed from a more splendid Baroque edifice in 1792. The old bishop's palace, which stands at Ulica Katedralna 15 nearby, is a fine Neo-Classical building dating from the second half of the 18th century, although three 13th-century wings from the earlier palace remain.

🔒 Cathedral of St John the Baptist
pl. Katedralny. 🔔 (0 71) 322 25 74.
◻ daily. **Tower** ◻ 1 Apr–30 Sep: 10am–4pm Mon–Sat.
The Cathedral of St John the Baptist (Archiatedra św Jana Chrzciciela) presents a combination of styles from different periods. The presbytery was built some time between 1244 and 1272;

Ulica Katedralna, with the Cathedral of St John the Baptist

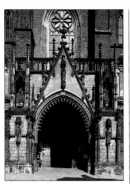

Portal of the Cathedral of St John the Baptist on Ostrów Tumski

THE BRIDGES OF WROCŁAW

Situated on the River Odra, the city of Wrocław boasts more than 100 bridges crossing numerous streams, canals and inlets. The oldest is the Piasek Island bridge, dating from 1845. The best known is Grunwaldzki Suspension Bridge, dating from 1908–10, which under German rule was named the Kaiserbrücke.

Grunwaldzki Suspension Bridge

the basilica was built in the first half of the 14th century and the west tower was completed even later. Three quarters of the cathedral were destroyed in World War II, and most of the present building is the result of post-war reconstruction. The east end, with its interesting chapels accessible from the presbytery, survives in its original form. The Chapel of St Elizabeth in the south aisle was built in the Roman Baroque style by Giacomo Scianzi in 1680. The interior of the chapel is also the work of Italian artists: the tomb of Cardinal Frederyk, a Hessian landowner whose burial chapel this became, is by Domenico Guidi. The altar is by Ercole Ferrata.

The presbytery contains a late Gothic polyptych of 1522, which was brought from Lubin, and Baroque choir stalls from a church of the Premonstratensian order.

🏛 Archdiocesan Museum

pl. Katedralny 16. 📞 (0 71) 327 11 78.
🕐 9am–3pm Tue–Sat, 10am–3pm Sun and public hols.

The Archdiocesan Museum (Muzeum Archidiecezjalne) stands among a group of buildings dating from three historical periods. The earliest is the Gothic-Renaissance chapterhouse built in 1519–27, which has fine portals and arcades. The later Baroque chapterhouse was completed in 1756. The purpose-built Neo-Gothic museum, libraries and archives of the archdiocese

were built in 1896. The museum contains an important and growing collection of Silesian religious art going back to the Gothic period. In addition to altars and sculptures, it has on display one of the earliest cabinets in the world, dating from 1455.

Archdiocesan Museum on Ostrów Tumski

❀ Botanical Gardens

ul. H. Sienkiewicza 23.
📞 (0 71) 322 50 45 ext. 40.
🕐 1 Jun–31 Oct: 8am–6pm daily.

Wrocław boasts the most attractive botanical gardens in

Poland. They were established in 1811 by two professors from the University of Silesia in Katowice, and after being totally destroyed in World War II were reverently re-created. The gardens' central area contains ponds fashioned from what was an arm of the River Odra when Ostrów Tumski was still an island. The gardens contain palms, an alpine garden, cactuses and a 19th-century model of the geology of the Silesian town of Wałbrzych. On a walk through the gardens 7,000 plant species can be seen and a bust of the Swedish botanist Carolus Linnaeus (1708–78), dating from 1871, stands among the greenery. A branch of the gardens, with an extensive arboretum, has been established in Wojsławice, near Niemcza.

The Botanical Gardens on Ostrów Tumski

Around Central Wrocław

MANY PLACES OF INTEREST lie within walking distance of central Wrocław. A relaxing day can be spent at the zoo, the museums of natural history, geology and mineralogy and in Szczytnicki Park. The Jewish cemetery gives a fascinating insight into Poland's past. There are also several notable 20th-century buildings, such as the People's Hall and the 1920s Mieszkanie i Miejsce Pracy housing estate.

Museum, which was set up in 1820. Since 1904 the exhibits have been displayed in a purpose-built wing of this Art Nouveau building.

Some of the exhibits in the Mineralogy Museum

🏛 Geology and Mineralogy Museums
ul. Cybulskiego 30. **Geology Museum** ☎ *(0 71) 320 13 27.*
🕐 *9am–3pm Mon–Wed, 9am–5pm Thu, Fri.* **Mineralogy Museum**
☎ *(0 71) 320 12 06.* 🕐 *10am–3pm Tue–Fri.*

A vast building in a style typical of the German Third Reich houses two interesting museums, both run by departments of the University of Wrocław. The Geology Museum contains a wealth of different rocks and fossils, while the Mineralogy Museum delights visitors with its colourful displays of minerals from all over the world.

🏛 Natural History Museum
ul. Sienkiewicza 21.
☎ *(0 71) 322 18 80.*
[W] *www.biol.uni.wroc.pl/muzsekr/index*
🕐 *10am–3pm Tue, Wed, Fri, Sat, 10am–6pm Thu, Sun.*

This museum, which is extremely popular with children, has a substantial collection of animals and plants from all continents. The collections of tropical butterflies, shells and mammal skeletons are the largest in Poland. Some date back to the 18th century, and formed the beginnings of the University's Zoological

🐾 Zoo
ul. Wróblewskiego.
☎ *(0 71) 348 30 24.*
[W] *www.zoo. wrocław.pl* @ *lutra@ zoo.wrocław.pl*
🕐 *9am–4pm daily.*

Wrocław has one of the largest and best laid-out zoos in Poland, thanks to its long-standing directors Hanna and Antoni Gucwińscy, who for many years presented a TV programme on animal photography. The zoo, founded in 1865, is situated above the River Odra opposite Szczytnicki Park. While walking among the animal paddocks it is worth taking a look at the old pavilions, which feature a variety of architectural styles.

🏛 People's Hall
ul. Wróblewskiego. ☎ *(0 71) 347 51 00.*
🕐 *9am–7pm, except during trade fairs and sports events.*

The People's Hall (Hala Ludowa), originally known as the Century Hall, was intended to be the centre-piece of an exhibition commemorating the centenary of Poland's victory over Napoleon at Lipiec. It was designed by Max Berg and built in 1911–13. At the time of its construction, it was regarded as one of the finest modern buildings in Europe. The centre of the hall is covered by a reinforced concrete dome with a radius of 65 m (200 ft). It is lit by a sophisticated method – the openwork design inside the stepped tambour consists of rows of windows that can be shaded or uncovered as required. The auditorium can accommodate up to 5,000 people. The hall has functioned as a concert hall and theatre, and today is used for sports events and trade fairs. Around the hall are some of the pavilions of the Historical Exhibition. It is also worth walking through the

Ostrich in a paddock at Wrocław Zoo

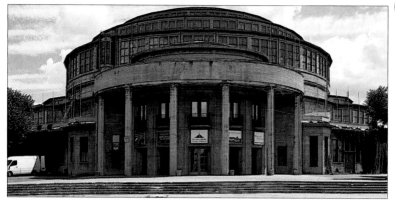

The former Century Hall designed by Max Berg

old exhibition grounds and seeing the oval pond, which is surrounded by shady pergolas. A steel needle 96 m (316 ft) in height made by Stanisław Hempel, stands outside the main entrance. It was erected here in 1948.

♣ Szczytnicki Park

North of the exhibition area is an extensive park whose history dates back to the 18th century. It was originally the site of the residence of Duke Friedrich Ludwig von Hohenlohe-Ingelfingen, but that building was destroyed during the Napoleonic Wars (1799–1815), after which the area was remodelled as a landscaped park.

One of Szczytnicki Park's distinctive features is its delightful Japanese garden, which has been painstakingly restored with the help of Japanese gardening experts.

The footbridges and pathways that run among the pavilions and plants make a charming setting for a leisurely walk. Look out for the rose garden and a small 12th-century wooden church that was brought over from Stare Koźle and reconstructed.

House designed by Hans Scharoun on the Mieszkanie i Miejsce Pracy housing estate

▦ Mieszkanie i Miejsce Pracy Housing Estate

The Mieszkanie i Mejsce Pracy housing estate is a unique landmark in the development of residential architecture in the 1920s. The houses were examples of different residential buildings designed for the Exhibition of Living and Working Space organized by the Deutscher Werkbund movement in 1929. Many prominent German architects took part in the project. The most impressive building is an apartment block (at Ulica Kopernika 9) designed by Hans Scharoun, architect of several buildings in Berlin, including the National Library and the Berlin Philharmonic Orchestra's Concert Hall. Modern architecture enthusiasts should also visit Sępolno, which was built in 1924–8 and is a fine example of a garden city.

✠ Jewish Cemetery

ul. Ślężna 37/39. ☎ (0 71) 367 82 36. ◯ 8am–6pm daily. ✉ Noon Sun. ⬤ Jewish holidays.

This is one of the few Jewish cemeteries in Poland that escaped destruction at the hands of the Nazis during World War II. Opened in 1856, it was the burial place of many celebrated citizens of Wrocław, including the socialist politician Ferdinand Lassalle, the painter Clara Sachs and the parents of Sister Theresa Benedicta of the Cross, who was born in Wrocław as Edith Stein.

Japanese garden in Szczytnicki Park

Façade of the Cistercian church in Henryków

altar, with *The Birth of Christ in the Vision of St Bernard of Clairvaux* by Michael Willmann, and the large, highly ornamented choir stalls. A plague column outside the church depicts the four archangels.

Other points of interest are the extensive monastery and the scenic park laid out at the rear of the monastery in the early 18th century. A summerhouse stands in the park.

Henryków ㉕

Road Map C5. 🏠 *1,400.* 🚪 🚌
Cistercian Church pl. Cystersów 1.
📞 *(0 74) 810 50 69.* 📮

THE SMALL TOWN of Henryków is known for its **Cistercian church**, founded in 1227 by Henryk the Bearded. A series of allotments surrounding the abbey separate the church and monastery from the street, so that access to the church is by way of a series of gates. The church, originally in the Gothic style, was rebuilt in the early 14th century and remodelled in the Baroque style by Matthias Kirchberger in 1687–1702. Prominent features of the Baroque interior are the high

Kamieniec Ząbkowicki ㉖

Road Map B5. 🏠 *4,700.* 🚪 🚌

THE SMALL TOWN of Kamieniec Ząbkowicki is dominated by the 14th-century Gothic church and Baroque monastery of its Cistercian abbey, which was founded in 1272.

There is also a Gothic **castle**, perched on a hill but well worth the effort of a climb to visit. It was commissioned by Marianna Orańska in the 1870s, and after her death was completed for her son, Duke Albrecht of Prussia. The architect was Karl Friedrich Schinkel. A massive residence with large circular external

towers and two internal piazzas, the castle has an ideal symmetry. Its magnificent ballroom has palm vaulting supported on a single central basalt column.

Unfortunately the palace's once superb art collection and library were destroyed just after World War II. Today the castle, while not yet wholly reconstructed, is open as a hotel. It stands in an attractive overgrown park.

Kłodzko Valley ㉗

See pp200–201.

Gothic town walls and tower in Paczków

Paczków ㉘

Road Map B5. 🏠 *8,400.* 🚪 🚌
ℹ️ *Rynek 13/14 (0 77 431 61 77).*

COMPLETELY SURROUNDED by a medieval wall set with towers and gates, Paczków has been dubbed the "Carcassone of Silesia" after

Neo-Gothic castle in Kamieniec Ząbkowicki

the medieval walled city in southwest France. Paczków was founded in 1254, and the old town retains its original street layout. It contains many distinctive town houses, a Neo-Classical town hall and the Church of St John (Kościół św Jana), an originally Gothic church that was rebuilt in the Renaissance style in 1529–36 and fortified for defensive purposes.

Otmuchów ㉙

Road Map C5. 🚶 *5,400.* 🚉 🚌

OTMUCHÓW HAS a picturesque setting between two lakes, Lake Głębinowskie and Lake Otmuchówskie. In spring and summer the town is filled with flowers, partly as the result of the spring flower festival that is held here.

From the 14th century until 1810 Otmuchów belonged to the bishops of Wrocław. Its historic buildings are all in close proximity around the sloping Market Square. On the lower side is the Renaissance town hall, built in 1538, with a later tower. On the upper side is the Baroque parish church of 1690–6, and the Palace of the Bishops of Wrocław. The adjacent palace, known as the Lower Castle, was the bishops' secondary residence.

The Beautiful Well in Nysa, with Baroque wrought ironwork

Nysa ㉚

Road Map C5. 🚶 *48,000.* 🚉 🚌
🛈 *ul. Bracka 4 (0 77 435 50 31).* @ nysa@www.nysa.pl 🖳 www.nysa.pl

NYSA, FOUNDED in 1223, was once the capital of the dukes of Wrocław and the see of the duchy of Nysa (Niesse). In the 16th and 17th centuries it became the residence of the Catholic bishops of Wrocław, who were driven there from Ostrów Tumski during the Reformation. After 1742 the Prussians enclosed the town with ramparts. Despite suffering massive destruction during World War II, Nysa retains a number of interesting buildings. The town centre is dominated by the Gothic **Church of Saints James and Agnieszka** (Kościół św św Jakuba i Agnieszki), with a separate belfry dating from the early 16th century. The well beside it, covered with unusual wrought ironwork, is known as the Beautiful Well and dates from 1686. Of Nysa's many churches, the finest are the **Church of Saints Peter and Paul** (Św Św Piotra i Pawła) and the Jesuit **Church of the Assumption** (Wnieboziécia NMP). Also of interest are the bishop's palace and manor, which stand beside a group of Jesuit buildings. The palace houses a local history museum.

🔒 Church of Saints James and Agnieszka
pl. Katedralny 7.
📞 *(0 77) 433 25 05.*
A number of side chapels containing the tombs of bishops flank the lofty nave of this 14th–15th-century church (Kościół św Jakuba i św Agnieszki). The high altar only survived World War II because it was removed and hidden in the mountains.

🔒 Church of Saints Peter and Paul
ul. św Piotra. 📞 *(0 77) 431 05 13.*
This late Baroque church (Kościół św św Piotra i Pawła) was built by Michael Klein and Felix Anton Hammerschmidt in 1719–27 for the Canons Regular of the Holy Sepulchre. Its original furnishings are intact. Entry is via the office of the seminary situated in the monastery.

🔒 Church of the Assumption
pl. Solny. ⭕ *daily.*
Jesuits were brought to Nysa by Bishop Karol Habsburg. This Baroque Jesuit church (Kościół Wnieboziécia NMP), built in 1688–92, has a magnificent twin-towered façade. The interior features paintings by Karl Dankwart. It is one of a group of buildings known collectively as the Carolinum College.

🏛 Town Museum
pl. Bpa Jarosława 11.
📞 *(0 77) 433 20 83.*
⭕ *8am–5pm Tue, 8am–3pm Wed–Fri, 10am–3pm Sat, Sun.*
The Town Museum is located in the former bishop's palace, dating from 1660–80. It contains a fine collection of European painting, including pictures from the studios of Lucas Cranach the Elder (1472–1553) and Hugo van der Goes (c.1440–82).

Renaissance town hall in Otmuchów

Kłodzko Valley ㉗

THE EXCEPTIONALLY BEAUTIFUL Kłodzko Valley is renowned for its architecture and spas as well as for its scenery. A border region for many centuries, it is dotted with castles. Many dignitaries, attracted by its favourable climate and its mineral springs, built splendid residences here. The area has several well-equipped hiking trails, particularly on Gory Stołowe (Table Mountains), and a number of ski resorts.

Góry Stołowe ②
The Table Mountains are an unusual geological phenomenon – the strange shapes of the sandstone and marl hills were created by erosion. At Szczeliniec Wielki and Błędne Skały, fissures form natural mazes.

Wambierzyce ①
The village is an ancient place of pilgrimage. The Pilgrimage Church dates from 1695–1710, although its oval nave was built in 1715–20. In the village and nearby hills are more than 130 Stations of the Cross.

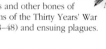

Kudowa Zdrój ③
The Chapel of Skulls (Kaplica czaszek) near Kudowa Zdrój was built in 1776. It contains 3,000 skulls and other bones of victims of the Thirty Years' War (1618–48) and ensuing plagues.

Duszniki Zdrój ④
Features of interest in this health spa are the Baroque pulpit in the Church of Saints Peter and Paul (Kościół św św Piotra i Pawła), by Michael Kössler, and the Museum of the Paper Industry.

Polanica Zdrój ⑤
Founded in the early 19th century, this spa is considered to be the most attractive in the whole Kłodzko Valley.

TIPS FOR DRIVERS

Tour length: 216 km (135 miles).
Stopping-off points:
Restaurants are easy to find in spa towns such as Kudowa Zdrój and Lądek Zdrój and in Kłodzko or Bystryca Kłodzka.
Other attractions: Bear's Cave at Jaskinia Niedźwiedzia, near Kletno; pre-booking ☎ (0 74) 814 12 50. Underground walk in Kłodzko ☐ 9am–5:40pm.
⬤ Mon, Thu.

Kłodzko ⑪
The large 18th-century castle commands a panoramic view over the town. There is also a Gothic bridge with Baroque carving and an underground passage.

Lądek Zdrój ⑩
This picturesque resort has luxurious mineral baths and a historic market square. For the energetic, the ruins of Karpień Castle are within walking distance.

Kletno ⑨
Bear's Cave, the largest in the Sudeten range, has 3 km (2 miles) of subterranean passages on four different levels with stalactites and stalagmites in a variety of shapes.

Międzygórze ⑧
This delightful resort at the foot of the Śnieżnik massif in the Wilczka River Valley is an ideal starting point for mountain hiking.

Bystrzyca Kłodzka ⑦
The town's Museum of Fire-Making is devoted to the manufacture of matches and cigarette lighters. The Gothic church that towers over the old town has an unusual double-nave interior.

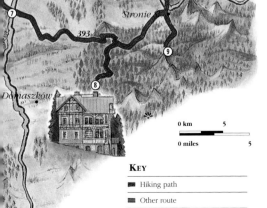

Gorzanów ⑥
The Renaissance-Baroque palace in Gorzanów dates from the 16th century. Its present form is the result of extensions carried out in the 17th century.

0 km 5

0 miles 5

KEY

■ Hiking path

■ Other route

☼ Viewpoint

Opole ③①

Road Map C5. 🏔 *123,000.* 🚉 🚌
🎵 *Festival of Polish Song (Jun).*

THE ORIGINS OF Opole, on the River Odra, go back to the 8th century. Once the seat of the Piast duchy, from 1327 it was ruled by Bohemia, from 1526 by Austria, and from 1742 by Prussia. Although it has been part of Poland only since 1945, it has always had a sizeable Polish population. The town hall was built in 1936 in imitation of the Palazzo Vecchio in Florence. Other notable buildings include the **Cathedral of the Holy Cross**, a Gothic church with a Baroque interior, and the late Gothic Franciscan church, containing the tombs of the dukes of Opole. On Piaseka Island, near the amphitheatre in the park, stands the Piast Tower, all that remains of the Gothic ducal castle.

🏛 **Regional Museum**
ul. św Wojciecha 13.
📞 *(0 77) 454 46 11.*
🕐 *8am–4pm Tue–Fri, 10am–3pm Sat, noon–5pm Sun.*

Góra Świętej Anny ③②

Road Map C5. 🚉 *Leśnica.*

GÓRA ŚWIĘTEJ ANNY is a place of pilgrimage for Catholics and a centre of commemoration of the Silesian uprisings of 1919–21. The great Pilgrimage Church of St Anne was built here by the Gaschin-Gaszyński family in the second half of the 17th century. The Stations of the Cross that make up the 18th-century Calvary are placed around the church and monastery. The Calvary still draws large numbers of pilgrims.

During the Third Silesian Uprising in May and June 1921, two major battles were fought in the mountains near Góra Świętej Anny. They are commemorated by a commanding monument carved by Xawery Dunikowski in 1955 that stands on the mountainside above a gigantic amphitheatre built in 1930–4. A **museum** contains records relating to the uprising.

🏛 **Museum of the Uprising**
Góra Świętej Anny. 📞 *(0 77) 461 54 66.*
🕐 *9am–3pm Tue–Sun.* ♿

Romanesque Rotunda of St Nicholas in Cieszyn

Cieszyn ③③

Road Map D6. 🏔 *36,000.* 🚉 🚌
🎵 *Viva il Canto Festival of Vocal Music (Jun); Na Granicy Theatre Festival (Oct); Cieszyńska Jazz Autumn Festival (Sep–Oct).*

THIS DELIGHTFUL town on the Czech-Polish border was founded in the 9th century. From the 13th to 17th centuries it was the capital of a Silesian duchy and in 1653 fell under Habsburg rule. On a hill where a castle once stood is the 11th-century Romanesque **Rotunda of St Nicholas** (Rotunda św Mikołaja), the Piast Tower, in the Gothic style, and a hunting palace built by Karol Habsburg in 1838.

The Market Square has some fine town houses and a Neo-Classical town hall. Cieszyn also features a number of churches, foremost among them being the Protestant **Church of Grace** (Kościół Łaski), of 1709.

The town is well kept, with a number of pedestrianized streets. Czech as well as Polish is heard in its homely pubs, bars and restaurants.

Pszczyna ③④

Road Map D6. 🏔 *37,000.* 🚉 🚌

PSZCZYNA, WHICH is located on the edge of the ancient Pszczyna Forest, derives its name from a residence that was built within the walls of a Gothic castle in the area. For many centuries the building, conveniently situated next to the forest and its wildlife, was used as a hunting lodge.

The town hall in the Market Square in Opole

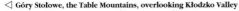

◁ **Góry Stołowe, the Table Mountains, overlooking Kłodzko Valley**

From 1846 Pszczyna was ruled by the Hochbergs of Książ *(see p185)*. The **palace** was rebuilt for them in 1870–76 in the French Neo-Renaissance style.

Today the palace houses a **museum** with an interesting and well-stocked armoury, a collection of hunting trophies and a fine array of period furniture. The centrepiece of the palace is the extraordinary Hall of Mirrors, which contains two vast mirrors, each with a surface area of some 14 sq m (150 sq ft).

Gliwice, one of 14 towns comprising the Upper Silesian Industrial Region

🏛 Palace Museum
ul. Brama Wybrańców 1.
📞 (0 32) 210 30 37.
W www.muzeum.pszczyna.top.pl
🕐 Nov–Mar: 9am–3pm Wed, 9am–2pm Thu, Fri, 10am–2pm Sat, 10am–3pm Sun; Apr–Oct: also 10am–2pm Tue. ● 15–31 Dec and 1 and 3 May, Easter, Corpus Christi, 1 and 11 Nov.

Portrait of Princess Daisy in the Palace Museum in Pszczyna

Upper Silesian Industrial Region ③⑤

Road Map D5. 🚊 🚌

THE VAST CONURBATION of 14 towns that make up the Upper Silesian Industrial Region (Górnośląski Okręg Przemysłowy) was created by the coal-mining industry, which has been active in the area since the 18th century. The conurbation's hardworking inhabitants have their own unique dialect, which is spoken especially by the older generation.

After World War I and following the three Silesian uprisings of 1919–21, almost the entire region was incorporated into Poland. Although the towns, with their mines, steelworks and power stations, seem unappealing, the region is of interest to tourists. Katowice, the capital, has particularly interesting buildings dating from the interwar years. In Kościusz Park stands a wooden church of 1510 that was moved here from Syryna, a Silesian village, as well as the **Archdiocesan Museum** and **Museum of Silesia**. The museum in Bytom has some interesting works of art. In Chorzowa the main attraction is a park with a funfair. The **Upper Silesian Ethnographic Park** has a display of the traditional buildings of Upper Silesia.

🏛 Archdiocesan Museum
Katowice, ul. Jordana 39.
📞 (0 32) 251 67 03. 🕐 2–6pm Tue–Thu, 2–5pm Sun.
The museum has a collection of ecclesiastical art, the most outstanding piece being *Head of a Monk* by José de Ribera (1591–1652).

🏛 Museum of Silesia
Katowice, ul. Korfantego 3.
📞 (0 32) 58 56 61 or 253 01 29.
🕐 10am–5pm Tue–Fri, 11am–4pm Sat, Sun.
Among the displays to be enjoyed at the Silesian Museum is a collection of 19th and 20th-century Polish painting.

🏛 Coal Museum
Będzin, ul. Świerczewskiego 15.
📞 (0 32) 267 77 07.
Castle and Palace 🕐 9am–3pm Tue, Thu–Sun, 10am–4pm Wed; Apr–Sep 9am–3pm Tue, Thu–Sat, 10am–5pm Wed, 10am–4pm Sun.
Będzin Castle was founded by Kazimierz the Great. Constructed from roughly hewn boulders, it was erected in stages between 1250 and 1350. In 1834 it was restored in the romantic Neo-Gothic tradition by Franciszek Maria Lanci. The castle now houses the fascinating Coal Museum. Another branch of the museum is to be found in the Mieroszewski Palace.

Będzin Castle, now the home of the Coal Museum

WIELKOPOLSKA (GREATER POLAND)

WIELKOPOLSKA (GREATER POLAND) *is the cradle of Polish state-hood. It was here in the mid-10th century that the Polonians, the strongest of the Polish tribes, set up an enduring state structure. It was also in this region that the Piast dynasty, the first Polish dynasty, emerged to rule the country in the 10th century. The first two capitals of Poland, Gniezno and Poznań, lie in Wielkopolska.*

During the Thirty Years' War of 1614–48, the region of Wielkopolska was settled by large numbers of dissenting Germans, particularly from neighbouring Silesia. The Protestant faith of the incomers set them apart from the existing inhabitants, who were Catholics.

During the Partitions of Poland, Wielkopolska was divided. Under the terms of the Congress of Vienna of 1815, the larger western part fell under Prussian rule, and the smaller eastern part came under Russian control. In the second half of the 19th century the Prussian part of Wielkopolska was subjected to repeated but unsuccessful campaigns of Germanization. Polish activists fought back in the courts and laid the economic foundations for the Polish section of the population. At the end of 1918, insurrection broke out in the western part of Wielkopolska and almost the entire region as it had been before the Partitions was reincorporated into the Polish state.

The inhabitants of Wielkopolska have a long-standing reputation for thrift and orderliness. The years of Soviet domination that followed World War II strained these qualities to the limit, although the local state-owned farms worked more efficiently than those in other parts of the country and many palaces and country mansions have survived in better condition than was the case elsewhere.

Poznań, the capital of Wielkopolska, abounds in historic buildings, as do other towns in the region. Almost every town, however small, contains something of interest. Wielkopolska maintains its identity: to this day the customs preserved in many of the region's towns and villages are distinct from those in other parts of Poland.

Old windmills in a typical Wielkopolska setting

◁ **Anger, one of the vices depicted on the Romanesque columns of the Premonstratensian Church in Strzelno**

Exploring Wielkopolska

W IELKOPOLSKA'S EXTENSIVE territory is mainly low-lying, but the landscape is far from monotonous. In the northern part of the region is a hilly area, with vast forests and lakes, that is ideal country for a walking or cycling holiday. Besides Poznań, the regional capital, other towns of interest include Gniezno, seat of an archbishopric and the first capital of Poland. In the area around Gniezno traces of the rise of Polish statehood can be seen on Ostrów Lednicki, in Strzelno, and in Kruszwica on Lake Gopło.

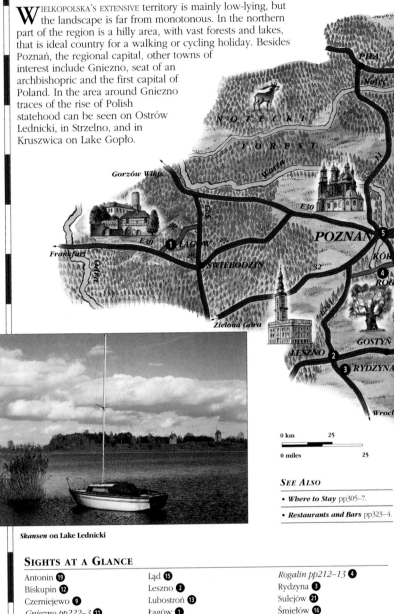

| 0 km | 25 |
| 0 miles | 25 |

SEE ALSO

• *Where to Stay* pp305–7.

• *Restaurants and Bars* pp323–4.

Skansen on Lake Lednicki

SIGHTS AT A GLANCE

KEY

- ▰ Motorway
- ▰ Major road
- ▰ Other road
- ≈ River
- ✹ Viewpoint

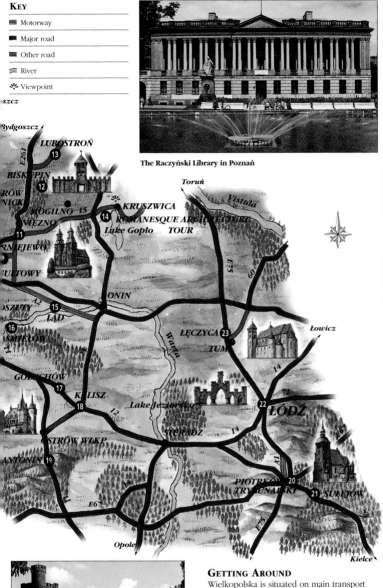

szcz

Bydgoszcz

LUBOSTROŃ ⑬

E261

BISKUPIN ⑫

**RÓW
NICK**

MOGILNO 15

KRUSZWICA

⑭ **ROMANESQUE ARCHITECTURE**

GNIEZNO ⑪   *Lake Gopło*   **TOUR**

RNIEJEWO

UŁTOWY

Toruń

Vistula

E75

60

The Raczyński Library in Poznań

ONIN

A2

OSZUTY

LĄD ⑮

⑯ **ŚMIEŁÓW**

Warta

ŁĘCZYCA ㉓

TUM

Łowicz

14

GOŁUCHÓW

⑰

KALISZ

⑱   12   *Lake Jeziorsko*

ŁÓDŹ
㉒

72

SIERADZ

14

A1

OSTRÓW WLKP.

ANTONIN ⑲

14

**PIOTRKÓW
TRYBUNALSKI** ⑳

SULEJÓW ㉑

E67

E75

Opole

Kielce

GETTING AROUND

Wielkopolska is situated on main transport routes between eastern and western Europe. The efficient express train service from Berlin to Poznań takes just under 5 hours, and the journey from Warsaw by express train takes about 4 hours. All the larger towns of the region have rail connections, while smaller ones can be reached by bus. Roads are generally good, although Poznań suffers from almost permanent traffic jams. Poznań can also be reached by air, although the number of international connections is limited.

Façade of Kórnik Castle

Łagów ❶

Road Map B3. 🏘 *1,600.* 🚉 🚌
ℹ *ul. Kościuszki 3 (0 68 341 20 10).*
🎬 *Lubuskie Film Festival (Jun).*

Ł AGÓW, SITUATED in
woodland between lakes
Łagów and Ciecz, is known
for its film festival.
The tower of the 14th-
century **castle** built by the
Knights Hospitallers affords a
magnificent view of the
surrounding countryside, as
does the 19th-century tower
of the Neo-Classical Church
of St John the Baptist (Kościół
św Jan Chrzciciela), dating
from 1726. Around the town
are also remains of the 15th-
century town walls, with their
gate towers, the Polish Gate
and Marchian Gate.

**ENVIRONS: Łagów Nature
Park**, near the town, contains
protected areas of woodland
and wild flowers.
About 16 km (10 miles) east
of the town are the remains
of a system of **fortifications**
erected by the Germans just
before World War II. Its
surviving corridors and
bunkers are now inhabited by
thousands of bats.

Leszno ❷

Road Map B4. 🏘 *63,000.* 🚉 🚌
ℹ *Słowiańska 24 (0 65 529 81
91).* 🎬 *Days of Leszno (May);
Summer of Folklore (Aug).*

I N THE 17TH century the town
gave asylum to religious
dissidents fleeing the ravages
of the Thirty Years' War
(1618–48) in Silesia. Apart
from Lutheran Protestants,
they included a group known
as the Bohemian Brethren,
who founded the Arian
Academy that gained
renown across
Europe. One of its
members was Jan
Amos Komeński
(Commenius),
a prominent
philosopher of
the Reformation.
The town was
destroyed by fire in
1707, so that none
of its monumental

Palace in Rydzyna, former seat of the Sułkowski family

buildings dates from earlier
than the 18th century. The
Baroque **town hall** was built
just after the fire to a design
by Pompeo Ferrari. Beside
the market square is the
distinctive Baroque **parish
church**, built by Jan Catenaci
at the turn of the 18th
century. It has a delightful
façade and interior with
Baroque altars and tombs.
Ferrari also designed the
former Lutheran **Church of
the Holy Cross** (Kościół
luterański św Krzyża), which
was built after 1707.
The **Regional Museum's**
finest collection is in the Polish
Portrait Gallery, and features
18th-century coffin portraits of
the Bohemian Brethren.

🏛 **Regional Museum**
pl. Metziga 17.
📞 *(0 65) 529 29 86 or 529
61 40.* ⏰ *noon–5pm Tue,
9am–2pm Wed–Fri,
10am–2pm Sat, Sun.*
● *Mon.*
Judaic section
ul. Estkowskiego 6.
📞 *(0 65) 529 61 45.*
⏰ *10am–5pm Tue,
9am–5pm Wed–Fri,
10am–2pm first Sat,
Sun in the month.*
● *Mon and day after
public holiday.*

Leszno's Baroque town hall

Rydzyna ❸

Road Map B4. 🏘 *2,200.* 🚌 🚉

T HIS SMALL TOWN is
dominated by the **palace**,
built in the 15th century. Its
present late Baroque
appearance dates from after
1737; further building work
was carried out by Karl Martin
Frantz in 1742, when
paintings by Wilhelm
Neunhertz were added to the
ballroom ceiling. The
ballroom was destroyed by
fire in 1945.
The ceiling was painted in
honour of the palace's owner,
Prince Józef A. Sułkowski. A
member of a noble family of
relatively low rank, he was
catapulted to success at the
court of August III, but fell
from the king's favour in 1738
and was replaced by Henryk
Brühl. The palace remained
in the possession of the
Sułkowskis into the early 20th
century, when it was sold to
the Prussian rulers. It is now a
hotel *(see p307)*.
The Market Square is lined
with Baroque houses, the
town hall and two Baroque
churches: the **Parish Church
of St Stanisław** (Kościół św
Stanisława) designed by Karl
Martin Frantz and Ignacy
Graff in 1746–51, and the
Protestant church, dating
from 1779–83, also by Graff.

Rogalin ❹

See pp212–13.

Poznań ❺

See pp214–19.

A room with coffered ceiling and ornate floor in Kórnik Castle

Kórnik ❻

Road Map C3. 🏛 *6,000.* 🚊 🚌

SET ON AN island and surrounded by a landscaped park, Kórnik Castle is one of the most picturesque castles in Poland. Its present appearance dates from the 19th century, when it was rebuilt in the English Neo-Gothic style by Karl Friedrich Schinkel. There have also been some subsequent alterations.

The castle's original interior survives: the Moorish Hall is decorated in the style of the Alhambra Palace in southern Spain and in the Dining Room the ceiling is covered with the coats of arms of all the Polish knights who fought at the Battle of Grunwald (1410). An inscription in Turkish on the ceiling of one hall is an expression of thanks to Turkey, which refused to recognize the partition of Poland. The castle also contains a collection of 18th- and 19th-century porcelain and other pieces.

The castle became the repository of the art treasures that were once kept at

Suit of armour, Kórnik Castle Museum

Czartoryski Palace in Puławy *(see p119)*. In order to acquire the library at Puławy, Tytus Działyński persuaded his son Jan to marry Izabella, heiress to the Czartoryski fortune.

The castle has an extensive library and a museum. The museum's collections include a display of 16th- to 19th-century Polish and foreign paintings, as well as sculpture, drawings and an intriguing array of militaria, including a complete suit of armour. The **Kórnik Library** contains manuscripts of Polish poets' works and a substantial collection of prints and maps. There is also a park that

contains an arboretum with many rare species of trees, and a walk here is a relaxing way to round off a visit.

🏛 Kórnik Library
ul. Zamkowa 5. 📞 *(0 61) 817 00 33 or 817 19 30.* 🖥 www.bkpn.poznan.pl ⏲ *1 Oct–30 Nov, 1 Mar–30 Apr: 9am–3:30pm Tue–Sun; 1 May–30 Sep: 9am–5pm Tue–Sun.* ⚫ *Mon, public hols, Easter, 1 Sep, 1 Dec–28 Feb.* 📷

ENVIRONS: There are several holiday villages scattered along the shores of lakes Kórnik and Bniń, to the south of Kórnik. The best known of them is **Zaniemyśl**, which boasts both a bathing beach and a holiday camp among its attractions. On Edward Island there is a 19th-century wooden pavilion built in the style of a Swiss chalet.

Koszuty ❼

Road Map C3. 🏛 *400.* 🚊 🚌

IN AN ENCHANTING 18th-century country house, set in a landscaped garden, the interior of a Wielkopolska landowner's mansion has been reconstructed and is now the **Środa Land Museum**.

🏛 Środa Land Museum
📞 *(0 61) 285 10 23.* ⏲ *9am–3pm Tue–Fri, 10am–2pm Sat.*

ENVIRONS: The town of **Środa Wielkopolska**, which is situated just 6 km (4 miles) east of Koszuty, has an interesting Gothic collegiate church dating from the 15th–16th centuries.

Country house in Koszuty dating from the 18th century

Raczyński Palace, Rogalin ❹

Rococo clock

RACZYŃSKI PALACE, in the village of Rogalin, is one of the most magnificent buildings in Wielkopolska. It was begun in around 1770 for Kazimierz Raczyński, Palatine of Wielkopolska and Grand Marshal of the Crown. It was designed in the Baroque style, but during construction the architectural ornamentation was abandoned. The imposing main building, however, retains its late Baroque solidity. In 1782–3 curving colonnades were added and complemented by annexes in the classic Palladian style. A drawing room and grand staircase designed by Jan Chrystian Kamsetzer were added in 1788–9.

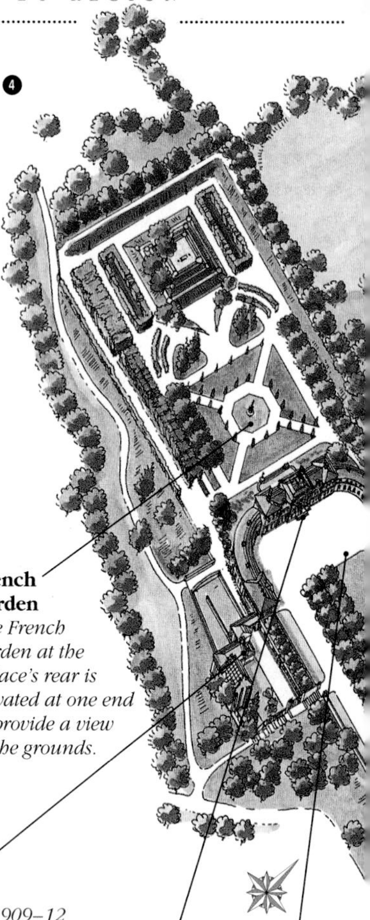

French Garden
The French garden at the palace's rear is elevated at one end to provide a view of the grounds.

★ Art Gallery
A pavilion built in 1909–12 contains a collection of European and Polish paintings dating from about 1850 to the early 20th century, including works by Claude Monet and Jan Matejko.

The entrance courtyard is approached by a tree-lined drive and flanked by coach houses and stables. It also has riding stables on the northeast side.

0 m   100

0 yds   100

STAR FEATURES

★ Palace

★ Art Gallery

★ Palace
The main building of the late Baroque palace was given a more fashionable Neo-Classical character by the addition of curving colonnades.

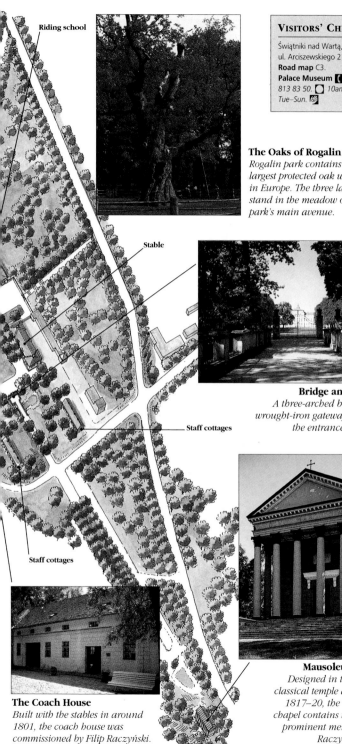

Riding school

VISITORS' CHECKLIST

Świątniki nad Wartą,
ul. Arciszewskiego 21.
Road map C3.
Palace Museum C (0 61)
813 83 50. 10am–4pm
Tue–Sun.

The Oaks of Rogalin
Rogalin park contains one of the largest protected oak woodlands in Europe. The three largest trees stand in the meadow off the park's main avenue.

Stable

Bridge and Gateway
A three-arched bridge and a wrought-iron gateway open onto the entrance courtyard.

Staff cottages

Staff cottages

Mausoleum Chapel
Designed in the style of a classical temple and built in 1817–20, the mausoleum chapel contains the tombs of prominent members of the Raczyński family.

The Coach House
Built with the stables in around 1801, the coach house was commissioned by Filip Raczyński.

Poznań ⑤

POZNAŃ IS THE CAPITAL of Wielkopolska and its largest city. A stronghold by the name of Polan stood here in the 8th century, and in the 10th century it was the capital of the emerging Polish state. In 968 it became the seat of the first bishopric in Poland. Poznań has many historic buildings, the finest of which are the cathedral and those in the old town. A visit to the late 19th-century quarter is also rewarding. Today Poznań is Poland's second financial centre after Warsaw and a major centre of commerce. Annual trade fairs attended by producers and traders from all over the world have been held here since 1921.

Interior of the former Dominican Church of the Heart of Jesus

🔒 Church of the Heart of Jesus
ul. Szewska 18.
📞 (0 61) 852 50 76.
The Church of the Heart of Jesus (Kościół Serca Jezusowego), built in the 13th century, is the oldest church in the old town. It was a Dominican church until 1920, when it passed to the Jesuits. During the German occupation in World War II, a repository was set up here for Polish books removed from the libraries of Poznań.

🏛 Old Market Square
The **Old Market Square** (Stary Rynek) is the heart of the old town. It is surrounded by town houses with colourful façades, among which stands the Renaissance town hall. The ground floors of the buildings around the square are filled mainly by banks, cafés and restaurants, and the streets leading off the square contain elegant shops. From spring to autumn the square bustles with life, and the outdoor cafés with their tables and colourful sunshades are permanently busy. Local artists display their paintings, while children play on the steps of the town hall. The square is also a venue for cultural events.

Some of the houses in the Old Market Square were destroyed during the battles for Poznań in 1945, and

were rebuilt after World War II, but others escaped serious damage. They include Mielżyński Palace, which dates from 1796–8, and **Działyński Palace**, both in the Neo-Classical style.

🏛 Działyński Palace
Stary Rynek 78. 📞 (0 61) 852 89 29.
🌐 www.bkpn.poznan.pl
The palace was built in the late 18th century for Władysław Gurowski, Grand Marshal of Lithuania. The elegant Neo-Classical façade is crowned with a large eagle and set with figures of Roman soldiers made by Anton Höhne in 1785–7. It is worth going inside to see the columned Red Room upstairs. The building is now used as a library, theatre, exhibition and concert hall.

The Old Market Square in Poznań

CENTRAL POZNAŃ

The façade of Działyński Palace

🏛 Town Hall

Stary Rynek 1. **Museum of the History of Poznań** 📞 (0 61) 852 56 13. ⬜ 9am–4pm Mon, 9am–3pm Tue, Fri, noon–6pm Wed, 10am–3pm Sun. ⬛ Thu, Sat.

Poznań's town hall is one of the finest municipal buildings

in Europe. It was built in 1550–60 by the Italian architect Giovanni Battista di Quadro. The façade has three tiers of arcades, topped by a grand attic and a large tower and decorated with portraits of the kings of Poland.

The greatest tourist attraction is the clock tower, where at noon each day two clockwork goats emerge from doors twelve times to butt heads. The Great Hall, or Renaissance Hall, on the first floor was lavishly decorated to reflect the affluence of the city's municipal leaders. The coffered ceiling is covered with an intricate series of paintings. Other important collections can be seen in the Royal Hall and the Court-room. The centrepiece of the Old Market Square is the Baroque **Proserpine Fountain** of 1766, depicting the abduction of the ancient Roman fertility goddess Proserpine by Pluto, ruler of the underworld. Nearby stands a copy of a stone **pillory** of 1535 and a 20th-century fountain with the figure of a Bamberka, a peasant woman from the Poznań area (see p216). It commemorates the Catholic settlers who were sent to Poznań at the beginning of the 18th century from Bamberg, in southern Germany. Soon they became Polonized, although many of the city's inhabitants still claim to be descendants of the Bamberg settlers.

🏛 Church of Saints Mary Magdalene and Stanisław

ul. Klasztorna 11. 📞 (0 61) 852 69 50.

Construction work on this Baroque church, which was originally built for use as a Jesuit chapel, began in 1651 and continued for more than 50 years. Several architects, craftsmen and artists had a role in this extended project, among them Tomasso Poncino, Bartołomiej Wąsowski and Jan Catenaci.

The most impressive aspect of the church is probably its monolithic interior. Gigantic columns along the walls lead the eye towards the illuminated high altar, which was designed and constructed in 1727 by Pompeo Ferrari.

The Baroque buildings of a former Jesuit monastery and college stand close to the church. They were built for the brotherhood in 1701–33. Today, however, they are used for secular business by the members of Poznań's town council.

The Renaissance town hall, with its three tiers of loggias

KEY

🏛 Church

ℹ Tourist information

🅿 Parking

Exploring Poznań

POZNAŃ HOLDS MUCH of interest beyond the old town. The Bernadine church in Plac Bernadyński has a remarkably narrow twin-towered façade built in the 18th century by Jan Steyner. It is matched by the former Lutheran Church of the Holy Cross (Kościół św Krzyża), dating from 1777–83. Walking

Bamberka statue in Poznań

towards the main railway station, you go through the town centre and across Plac Wolności, a square lined with shops and banks, then following Ulica św Marcina, where the old Kaiser's palace is located. The trade fair area can be seen on the other side of the railway.

♠ Przemysław Castle

Góra Przemysława 1. **Museum of Applied Art** ((0 61) 852 20 35.
◯ 10am–4pm Tue, Wed, Fri, 10am–5pm Sat, 10am–3pm Sun.

Little remains of the castle built by Przemysław II in the 13th century. The reconstructed castle that now stands on the site houses the Museum of Applied Art, which holds a collection of everyday objects, decorative artifacts and religious items dating from the Middle Ages to the present. The Baroque **Franciscan church** on Ulica Góra Przemysława dates from the early 18th century. Frescoes by the Franciscan painter Adam Swach decorate the nave.

🏛 National Museum

al. Marcinkowskiego 9.
((0 61) 856 80 00. @ mnoffice @man.poznan.pl ◯ noon–6pm Tue, 10am–5pm Wed–Sat, 11am–4pm Sun. (free on Sat).
The National Museum is housed in what was originally the Prussian Friedrich

Statue of Hygeia, Greek goddess of health, outside the Raczyński Library

Museum, a Neo-Renaissance building of 1900–1903. Its collections of Polish painting are among the best in Poland.

The Gallery of Polish Art includes medieval art of the 12th to 16th centuries and 17th to 18th-century coffin portraits *(see p27)*. The best examples of painting of the Young

Poland movement are the canvases of Jacek Malczewski (1854–1929). The Gallery of European Art contains works from various collections, including that of Atanazy Raczyński, brother of the philanthropist Count Edward Raczyński *(see p212)*. The most outstanding are by Dutch and Flemish painters including Joos van Cleve and Quentin Massys. Italian, French and Spanish painters, including Francisco de Zurbarán, are also represented.

📖 Raczyński Library

pl. Wolności 19. ((0 61) 852 94 42.
◯ 9am–7pm Mon–Fri.
With its façade of columns, the Raczyński Library combines grandeur with elegance, and cannot be compared with any other building in Poznań. The idea for a library was initiated by Count Edward Raczyński in 1829. The aim of this visionary aristocrat was to turn Poznań into a "New Athens"; the library was to be a centre of culture and "a shrine of knowledge".

Although the library's architect is unknown, it is thought to have been built by the French architects and designers Charles Percier and Pierre Fontaine. A seated **figure of Hygeia**, the ancient Greek goddess of health, with the features of Konstancja z Potockich, wife of Edward Raczyński, was installed in front of the library in 1906.

Another element of the "New Athens" of Poznań was to be a gallery (now non-existent) for the outstanding art collection owned by Edward Raczyński's brother, Atanazy *(see p212)*.

📖 Former Kaiser District

After the Second Partition of Poland in 1793, Poznań came under Prussian rule. In the second half of the 19th century, Prussia heightened its policy of Germanization in Wielkopolska. One of its instruments was the Deutscher Ostmarkenverein ("German Union of the Eastern Marches"), which the

The somewhat severe Neo-Renaissance façade of the National Museum

Poles called the "Hakata" colonization commission from the acronym of the initials of its founders. When the city's ring of 19th-century fortifications was demolished, a decision was made to use the new space for government buildings. Designed by the German town planner Josef Stübben, they were built in 1903–14 and today stand amid gardens, squares and avenues, with a theatre, the colonization commission, a post office and the royal academy (now the university). Dominating the scene is the Kaiserhaus, designed by Franz Schwechten. The castle was rebuilt by the Germans, but little survives of its original splendour apart from a marble imperial throne and the décor of some of the rooms. The chairs from the Great Hall are now in the Sejm (parliament) in Warsaw. Today the Kaiserhaus accommodates the Kaiserhaus Cultural Centre.

Beside it, in Plac Mickiewicza, stands the Monument to the Victims of June 1956, which takes the form of two large crosses. The monument was unveiled in 1981 to commemorate the violent suppression of the workers' uprising in Poznań in 1956 *(see p52)*.

The Opera, built in 1910, is flanked by statues of lions

churches face each other across a small square. One is the Discalced Carmelites' Church of St Joseph, built by Cristoforo Bonadura the Elder and Jan Catenaci in 1658–67. It contains the tomb of Mikołaj Jan Skrzetuski, who died in 1668 and on whom Henryk Sienkiewicz *(see p23)* based the hero of his historical saga *With Fire and Sword*.

The other is the small Gothic Church of St Adalbert, forming a pantheon with practically the same function as the Pauline Church on the Rock in Cracow *(see p143)*. In the crypt are the remains of great figures in the history of Wielkopolska. They include Józef Wybicki (1747–1822), who wrote the Polish national anthem, and the Australian traveller and scientist

Paweł Edmund Strzelecki (1797–1873). A striking contrast to the rest of the building is the ultramodern glass, concrete and stainless steel entrance to the crypt, which was designed by Jerzy Gurawski in 1997.

The modern entrance to the crypt of the Church of St Adalbert

Monument to the Victims of June 1956

Hill of St Adalbert

The hill is said to be the spot where, 1,000 years ago, St Adalbert gave a sermon before setting off on his campaign to evangelize the Prussians. On the summit two

THE POZNAŃ TRADE FAIR

The trade fair area is in the city centre, the main entrance lying opposite Dworcowy Bridge. The Poznań International Trade Fair has been held here every year since 1921. It takes place in June, and for its duration the surrounding area is filled with an international throng of businessmen. If you visit at this time you will find that the local cafés and restaurants are often full and hotel accommodation can be extremely hard to come by.

The symbol of the Trade Fair is a steel needle erected over the lower part of the Upper Silesian Tower in 1955, the main part having been destroyed during World War II. When the tower was built in 1911, to a design by Hans Poelzig, it was considered by admiring critics to be a masterpiece of modern architecture in reinforced concrete.

The needle rising over the Poznań International Trade Fair

Poznań Cathedral

T HE FIRST CHURCH, a pre-Romanesque basilica, was built in
Poznań in 966, shortly after Poland adopted
Christianity, and the first rulers of Poland were buried
there. In 1034–8 the basilica was destroyed during
pagan uprisings and the campaign of the
Czech prince Bøetislav. It was
then completely rebuilt in the
Romanesque style. It was
remodelled in the Gothic
and Baroque periods, and
after suffering war
damage was restored to
its earlier Gothic form.
Vestiges of the pre-
Romanesque and
Romanesque churches
can be seen in the crypt.

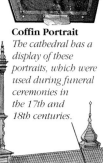

Coffin Portrait
*The cathedral has a
display of these
portraits, which were
used during funeral
ceremonies in
the 17th and
18th centuries.*

**Tomb of the
Górka Family**
*The tomb of the
Górkas, a prominent
Wielkopolska family,
was made in the
Chapel of the Holy
Cross by Girolamo
Canavesi in 1574.*

Main entrance

STAR FEATURES

★ **Golden Chapel**

★ **Tomb of Bishop
Benedykt Izdbieński**

High Altar
*The late Gothic polyptych on the
high altar was probably carved in
the workshop of Jacob Beinhart in Wrocław and
painted in the Pasje studio of Upper Silesia.
It was brought to the cathedral in 1952.*

Gothic Church of St Mary, with the cathedral in the background

★ Tomb of Bishop Benedykt Izdbieński
The tomb was made by Jan Michałowicz of Urzędów, the most celebrated sculptor of the Polish Renaissance, in 1557–62.

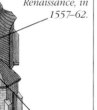

★ Golden Chapel
The chapel, built in 1834–41, contains the tombs of two of Poland's first rulers, Mieszko I and Bolesław the Brave. Their statues were carved by Chrystian Rauch.

Ostrów Tumski Island

Ostrów Tumski Island is the oldest part of Poznań. In the 10th century it was the site of one of the first capital cities of the Polish state.

Today the island is dominated by the Gothic towers of the cathedral, which contains many fine works of art. Near the cathedral stands the small Gothic **Church of St Mary** (Kościół halowy NMP), which was built in the years 1431–48 for Bishop Andrzej Bniński by Hanusz Prusz, a pupil of the notable late medieval architect Heinrich Brunsberg.

Also of interest is the **Lubrański Academy**, the first institute of higher education to be established in Poznań. It was founded in 1518 by Bishop Jan Lubrański. Behind its inconspicuous façade lies a small arcaded Renaissance courtyard. The academy acquired its greatest renown in the early 16th century. One of its alumni was Jan Struś, a scientist and a prominent physician during the years of the Polish Renaissance.

In the gardens on the other side of Ulica ks. l. Podsadzego stand a number of canons' and vicars' houses which are charming in appearance – if a little neglected. One of them contains the collections of the **Archdiocesan Museum**.

The late Gothic **Psalter**, which was built in around 1520 by Bishop Jan Lubrański, is another of Ostrów Tumski Island's notable buildings. Its fine stepped and recessed gables are enclosed by ogee arches.

Arcaded courtyard of Lubrański Academy

🏛 Archdiocesan Museum
ul. ks. l. Podsadzego 2.
📞 *(0 61) 852 61 95.* 🕐 *9am–3pm Mon–Sat.*

The superb collection of religious art on display in the Archdiocesan Museum includes examples of medieval painting and sculpture, pieces of Gothic embroidery and some fine *kontusz* sashes *(see pp26–7)*. The most important pieces in the museum are probably the *Madonna of Ołobok*, a Romanesque-Gothic statue dating from about 1310–29, and a fascinating group of coffin portraits *(see p27)*.

Façade of the Baroque and Neo-Classical palace in Gułtowy

Gułtowy ❽

Road Map C3. 🏘 990. 🚉 🚌
📞 (0 61) 852 61 56.
⭕ appointment only.

THE PRETTY Baroque and
Neo-Classical palace at
Gułtowy was built in 1779–83
for Ignacy Bniński to a design
by an unknown architect and
subsequently altered by Ignacy
Graff. The most striking feature
of its interior is the two-tiered
ballroom decorated with
delicate trompe l'oeil paintings
dating from about 1800.

Czerniejewo ❾

Road Map C3. 🏘 2,600. 🚉 4.5 km
(3 miles). 🚌 **Palace Hotel** 📞 (0 61)
427 30 30.

CZERNIEJEWO HAS one of the
finest Neo-Classical palaces
in Wielkopolska. It was built
for General Jan Lipski in
1771–80, and the monumental
four-columned portico was
added in 1789–91. Situated in a
large park and connected to the
town by a wide scenic avenue,
it makes a grand impression.
Within, the unusual circular
ballroom is probably its finest
feature. Today the palace is a
hotel, a restaurant and a
conference venue.

Ostrów Lednicki ❿

Road Map C3. 🚌 🚉 🛳 15 Apr–31
Oct: 9am–5pm Tue–Sat, 10am–5pm
Sun; Nov, 1 Feb–14 Apr: 9am–3pm
Tue–Sat, 10am–3pm Sun. 📞 (0 61)
427 47 80 ext. 23. ⚫ Mon, Dec, Jan.

THE SMALL ISLAND in Lake
Lednickie has special
significance as the place
where Poland is believed to
have adopted Christianity. In
the 10th century a fortified
town stood on the island,
surrounded by earth ramparts
enclosing the earliest known
Christian buildings in Poland.
Archaeologists have
uncovered the foundations of
a rotunda and a rectangular
hall identified as a baptistery
and palace. The remains of a
church were also found.

The town is assumed to
have been the seat of the
Piasts (see pp38–9). The
baptism of Poland, by which
the country adopted
Christianity, is believed to
have taken place in this
baptistery in 966.

🏛 Museum of the First Piasts

Dziekanowice 32. 📞 (0 61) 427 47 80.
W www.info.poznan.pl ⭕ 15 Feb–14
Apr, Nov: 9am–3pm Tue–Sat,
10am–3pm Sun and public hols; 15
Apr–30 Apr, 1 Jul–31 Oct: 9am–5pm
Tue–Sat, 10am–5pm Sun and public
hols; 1 May–30 Jun: 9am–6pm
Tue–Sat, 10am–6pm Sun and public
hols. ⚫ 1 Dec–14 Feb. 🚫

Gniezno ⓫

See pp222–3.

Biskupin ⓬

Road Map C3. 🏘 320. 🚌 ℹ (0 52)
302 50 25. W www.biskupin.pl 🚫
Archaeology Gala (Sep).

THE REMAINS OF A 2,500-year-
old Iron Age fortified
settlement can be seen on an
island in Lake Biskupinskie.
The settlement was built
entirely of wood and was
inhabited for about 150 years
by people of the Lusatian
culture. It was surrounded by
a stockade and a wall of
earth and wood 6 m (18 ft)
high. Access was over a
bridge and through a
gateway. The wall enclosed
more than 100 houses built in
13 terraces, and the streets
were paved with wood. The
population was about 1,000.

When the water level rose,
the lake flooded the houses
and covered the settlement
with a layer of silt, so that the
site was abandoned. It was
rediscovered in 1934 by a local
teacher, Walenty Szwajcer. It is
the earliest known settlement
in Poland and one of the most
interesting prehistoric sites in
the whole of Europe.

Some of the buildings have
been reconstructed and there
are pens with small ponies,
goats and sheep similar to
those that the inhabitants
would have raised. The
annual Archaeology Gala
features exhibitions – of Iron
Age hairstyles and archery,
for example – and workshops
where artifacts identical to
those used when the fort was
inhabited are made by
prehistoric methods.

Reconstructed fortifications of the Iron Age lake settlement in Biskupin

Lubostroń ⑬

Road Map C3. 🏯 *790.* 🚌
📞 *(0 52) 384 46 23.*

I N 1795–1800 Fryderyk Jozef Skorzewski, a landowner, commissioned Stanisław Zawadski to build a palace in the Neo-Classical style here. It has a square floor plan with a central rotunda and columned porticos on all four sides, and is an outstanding imitation of the Villa Rotonda built in Vicenza, Italy, by the celebrated Italian Renaissance architect Andrea Palladio.

Lubostroń Palace has a rather severe and monu-mental appearance, but its interior is one of the finest surviving examples of Polish Neo-Classical architecture. It is decorated with a bas-relief depicting the history of the Wielkopolska region.

The palace is set in land-scaped grounds which date from about 1800. Today it is used for conferences and also has guest rooms for hire.

Lubostroń Palace viewed from the courtyard

Romanesque Architecture Tour ⑭

See pp224–5.

Interior of the Baroque church in Ląd

Ląd ⑮

Road Map C3. 🏯 *530.* 🚌

L ĄD WAS SETTLED by Cistercian monks after 1193. The monastery retains a number of Romanesque and Gothic buildings, one of which contains a Gothic fresco of about 1372 commemorating the benefactors of the church. The Baroque church is considerably later. The twin-towered façade by Giuseppe Simone Belloti does not do justice to the ornately decorated nave, which was built in 1730–33. Commissioned by the abbot Mikołaj A. Łukomski, Pompeo Ferrari designed a single interior space covered by a large dome rising to a height of 36 m (119 ft); the paintings by Georg Wilhelm Neunhertz depict the Church Fathers during the land seizures and give visual expression to the methods by which the Counter-Reformation would triumph in Poland: by teaching and persuasion rather than by military.

ENVIRONS: In Ciążeń, 5 km (3 miles) west of Poznań, is a late Baroque bishop's palace, now owned by Poznań University Library. **Nadwarciański Nature Reserve** nearby is one of the world's most scenic refuges for wading and aquatic birds.

Śmiełów ⑯

Road Map C3. 🚌

T HE NEO-CLASSICAL PALACE in Śmiełów, built by Stanisław Zawadski for Andrzej Ostroróg Gorzeński in 1797, is associated with the Romantic poet Adam Mickiewicz, who stayed here in 1831, hoping to cross into the annexed part of the country where the November Insurrection against Russian rule was taking place.

His plan failed, but the palace at Śmiełów, with its fine landscaped grounds, became the backdrop to Mickiewicz's love for Konstanta Łubieńska. Today, fittingly, the palace houses the **Adam Mickiewicz Museum**, dedicated to the poet's life and works and containing exhibits from the age of Romanticism.

🏛 **Adam Mickiewicz Museum**
Żerków. 📞 *(0 62) 740 31 64.*
⬜ *1 Oct–30 Apr: 10am–4pm Tue–Sun; 1 May–30 Sep: 10am–4pm Tue–Sat, 10am–6pm Sun.*
🎟 *(free on Sat).*

Neo-Classical palace in Śmiełów, today the Adam Mickiewicz Museum

Gniezno ⓫

THE 14TH-CENTURY Gothic Cathedral of the Assumption (Archikatedra Dnieąnieńska Wniebowzłcia NMP) stands on the site of two earlier churches. The first was a pre-Romanesque church built some time after 970, and the second a Romanesque church dating from the mid-11th century. When Princess Dąbrowka, wife of Mieszko I, was buried here in 977, Gniezno was the first capital of the Polonians. Its importance increased further when in 997 the relics of St Adalbert were laid in the church. From 1025 to the 14th century Poland's royal rulers were crowned in the cathedral.

Potocki Chapel
The chapel of Archbishop Teodor Potocki was built by Pompeo Ferrari in 1727–30. It is decorated with Baroque paintings by Mathias Johannes Mayer.

Baroque towers were reconstructed after the originals of 1779.

★ Epitaph of Archbishop Zbigniew Oleśnicki
This epitaph was carved in red marble by the late Gothic sculptor Veit Stoss in 1495.

★ Bronze Doors
The bronze doors of the cathedral, made in the late 12th century and depicting scenes from the life and martyrdom of St Adalbert, are among the finest examples of Romanesque art in Europe.

St Adalbert

St Adalbert (St Wojciech in Polish) was a bishop from Prague. In 977, at the suggestion of Bolesław the Brave, he left Poland for the heathen lands of Prussia, where he converted the inhabitants to Christianity but was martyred. Bolesław bought the saint's body from the Prussians, giving them in return its weight in gold, and laid the remains in Gniezno.

Pope Sylvester II acknowledged the bishop's martyrdom and canonized him.

In 1038, when the Czech prince Bœtislav invaded the city, the cathedral was sacked and the saint's relics taken to Prague.

Baptism of the Prussians, a scene from the cathedral doors

VISITORS' CHECKLIST

Road Map C3. 68,400. ul. Dworcowa (0 61 426 21 11). ul. Dworcowa (0 61 426 38 93). ul. Łubieńskiego 11 (0 61 426 37 01). **Cathedral** ul. Łaskiego 9. (0 61) 426 38 98. 9am–6pm services, noon–1pm. Bronze Doors

Exploring Gniezno

Besides its magnificent cathedral, Gniezno has many historic buildings and fine museums, making for a pleasant walk around the city. **Gniezno Archdiocesan Museum**, next to the cathedral, contains religious artifacts, including paintings, sculpture, textiles and coffin portraits (see p27). A smart street leads off the Market Square to the Gothic **Church of St John** (Kościół św Jana), which has 14th-century murals. It is hard to imagine that this small town was once the capital of the Polish nation. The history of the city is told in the **Museum of the Origins of the Polish State**, in Piast Park. In the park are the remains of a late medieval fortified town.

🏛 Gniezno Archdiocesan Museum

ul. Kolegiaty 2. (0 61) 426 37 78. 1 Apr–31 Oct: 9am–4pm Tue–Sun; 1 Nov–31 Mar: 9am–3pm Tue–Fri. (free for clergy). This is an interesting museum containing religious art, including some artifacts from the cathedral treasury.

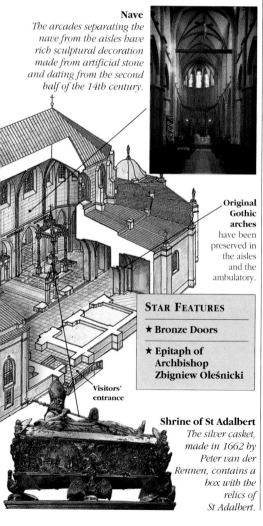

Nave

The arcades separating the nave from the aisles have rich sculptural decoration made from artificial stone and dating from the second half of the 14th century.

Original Gothic arches have been preserved in the aisles and the ambulatory.

STAR FEATURES

★ **Bronze Doors**

★ **Epitaph of Archbishop Zbigniew Oleśnicki**

Visitors' entrance

Shrine of St Adalbert

The silver casket, made in 1662 by Peter van der Rennen, contains a box with the relics of St Adalbert.

Monument to Bolesław the Brave

🏛 Museum of the Origins of the Polish State

ul. Kostrzewskiego 1. (0 61) 426 46 41. www.mppp.home.pl Jul–Apr: 10am–5pm Tue–Sun; May–Jun: 9:30am–5:30pm Tue–Sun. This interesting archaeological museum documents the early history of the town of Gniezno and the period when it was the capital of Poland.

Romanesque Architecture Tour ⓮

Romanesque column in Strzelno

S ADLY, FEW BUILDINGS survive in Wielkopolska from the earliest days of the Polish nation in the 10th century. For hundreds of years most building in Poland was in wood, and more durable brick or stone architecture was rare. A tour of pre-Romanesque and Romanesque buildings in Wielkopolska might start at Gniezno, then take in Trzemeszno and Mogilno. The finest Romanesque architecture in Poland is to be found in Strzelno – examples are the Rotunda of St Procopius and the Church of the Holy Trinity, with its remarkable Romanesque pillars. Another town of interest is Kruszwica, setting for the legend of King Popiel and home to the "Mouse Tower" of that tale.

Gniezno ①
By the 14th century, Gniezno's Romanesque church had been replaced by a Gothic cathedral, but the bronze doors of the earlier building survive (see pp222–3).

Trzemeszno ②
In the 12th century an order of Augustinian canons regular settled here on the site of a pre-Romanesque basilica and Benedictine monastery that had been demolished in 1038. In 1782–91 the church was rebuilt in the Baroque style.

POZNAN

15

Mogilno ③
The Benedictine church probably dates from the 11th century. After many phases of rebuilding it finally acquired a Baroque façade, although many Romanesque elements remain, in particular the crypt.

Strzelno ④
The Rotunda of St Procopius in Strzelno dates from the turn of the 13th century. In the Church of the Holy Trinity 12th-century carvings, discovered in 1946, depict personifications of the virtues and vices of Christian tradition.

TIPS FOR DRIVERS

Tour length: About 100 km (60 miles).
Stopping-off points: Every town mentioned has restaurants and cafés as well as accommodation available. There is a tourist hostel in Strzelno.

Lake Gopło ⑦

This narrow lake is surrounded mostly by marshy meadows. It is home to many birds, including bitterns, marsh harriers, lapwings and wild geese.

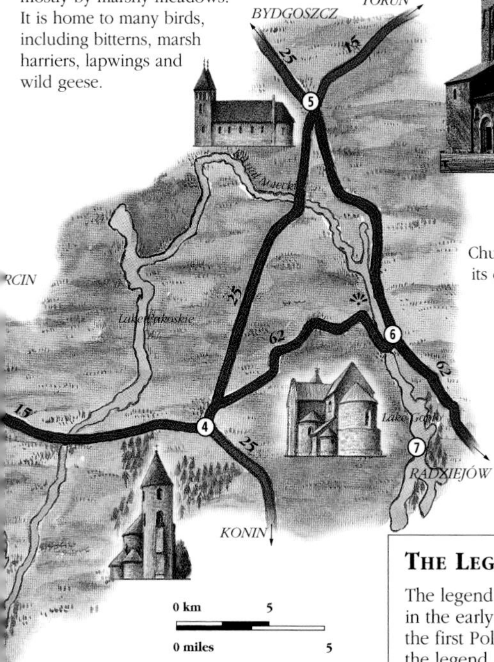

Kruszwica ⑥

Kruszwica was briefly the seat of a bishopric and the mid-12th-century Church of St Peter may well have been its cathedral. The shell and the interior of the church are built of granite ashlars, which remarkably survive almost in their original state.

KEY

■ Tour route

■ Other road

✵ Viewpoint

THE LEGEND OF KING POPIEL

The legend of King Popiel was recorded in the early 12th century by Gall Anonim, the first Polish chronicler. According to the legend, Siemowit Piast, founder of the Piast dynasty, was a peasant from Kruszwica. The Polonians, terrified by the atrocities committed by their king, Popiel, decided to depose him and chose Siemowit Piast as his successor. Popiel fled to his tower but the rebels turned into mice and devoured him. The Gothic tower overlooking Lake Gopło in Kruszwica is called the "Mouse Tower" but was in fact built in the 14th century, a few hundred years after these events were said to have taken place.

The Mouse Tower

Inowrocław ⑤

The most historic building in this health resort is the Church of Our Lady, dating from the turn of the 13th century, built in the time of the dukes of Inowrocław.

Castle in Gołuchów, home of the Działyński family

Gołuchów ⑰

Road Map C4. 🏛 1,500. 🚌

THE CASTLE AT Gołuchów looks as if it belongs in the Loire Valley, in France, alongside the other Renaissance châteaux for which that region is celebrated. Although the castle at Gołuchów was built in the mid-16th to 17th centuries, its present exterior dates only from 1872–85, commissioned by the owners, Izabella Czartoryska and her husband, Jan Działyński. Izabella was the daughter of Adam Czartoryski, a Polish émigré leader in Paris, and was educated in France; her wish was to turn the residence into a "paradise on earth" according to her own tastes. She also built a museum that was open to the public. Initial plans for the renovation of the castle were made in around 1871 by the French architect Eugène Viollet-le-Duc. The rest of the castle was designed by his son-in-law, Maurice August Ouradou, after plans by Polish architects. Today the **castle museum** contains European and Oriental works of art from the collection of the Działyński family.

🏛 **Castle Museum**
ul. Działyńskich.
📞 (0 62) 761 70 13.
🕐 10am–3pm Tue–Sun. 🅿 🖥

ENVIRONS: In **Dobryczy**, 23 km (14 miles) to the west of Gołuchów, is the Neo-Classical residence of Augustyn Gorzeński, a freemason, built in 1798–9.

Kalisz ⑱

Road Map C4. 🏛 105,000. 🚌 🚉
🛈 ul. Garbarska 2 (0 62 764 21 84).
@ citosir@poczta.onet.pl
ⓦ www.kalisz.pl
🎭 Theatre Festival (May); International Jazz Festival (Nov–Dec).

KALISZ, A SETTLEMENT on the amber route between the Baltic Sea and Rome, has ancient origins. It is mentioned as Calisia by Ptolemy in his *Geography* of AD 142–7. However, a town did not grow up here until the 13th century, and it did not really develop until the 15th century, when Kalisz became a provincial capital. During the Partitions of Poland, Kalisz was the furthest outpost of the Russian empire. In 1914, just after the start of World War I, it was severely bombarded by Prussian artillery. Its rebuilding began in 1917, and the present city centre, with town houses surrounding the **Market Square**, the **town hall** and the Bogusławski Theatre, dates from that time. A substantial number of earlier buildings survive. These include the Gothic **Cathedral of St Nicholas** (Katedra św Mikołaja), the late Baroque collegiate **Church of the Assumption** (Kościół Wniebowzięcia NMP), and the neighbouring Mannerist **church**, formerly a **Jesuit college**. The group of Bernadine monasteries and

Bernadine church in Kalisz

the late Renaissance **Church of the Annunciation** (Kościół Nawiedzenie NMP) are also worth a visit.

🏛 Cathedral of St Nicholas
ul. Kanonicka 5. 📞 (0 62) 757 39 19 or 757 59 74.

Antoni Radziwiłł's hunting lodge in Antonin

Antonin ⑲

Road Map C4. 👥 320. 🚌 🚉
🎵 Chopin Festival (Sep).

WHEN DUKE Antoni Radziwiłł asked Karl Friedrich Schinkel to build him a hunting lodge, it was an unusual commission for the architect. The small larchwood building, dating from 1822–4, has a cruciform plan and an octagonal centre. The octagonal hall is surrounded by galleries supported by a large central pillar. It was here that, in 1827, Frédéric Chopin taught Wanda, Duke Radziwiłł's daughter, with whom he fell in love. Unfortunately the piano on which the great composer played was chopped up for firewood by soldiers of the Red Army who were billeted in the lodge. It now houses a **Centre for Culture and Art**, and is the venue for concerts and festivals in honour of Chopin, as well as hunting balls.

🎪 Centre for Culture and Art
Pałac Myśliwski. 📞 (0 62) 734 81 14. 🕙 10am–6pm Tue–Fri, by arrangement Sat, Sun.

ENVIRONS: In the village of Bralin, 36 km (22 miles) north of Antonin, is a delightful wooden church called Na Pólku, dating from 1711.

Piotrków Trybunalski ⑳

Road Map D4. 👥 80,000. 🚉 🚌
ℹ️ pl. Czarnieckiego 10 (0 44 649 51 96).

BEFORE THE PARTITION of Poland, this was the town where sessions of the royal court and parliament were held, and after 1578 it was the seat of the Crown Tribunal. The town flourished and many magnificent churches bear witness to those times. Above **Tribunal Square** (Rynek Trybunalski) rises the brick tower and Baroque roof of the Gothic **Parish Church of St Jacob**. Synods and official ceremonies were conducted here. The large **Jesuit church**, dating from 1695–1727, contains remarkable trompe l'oeil paintings by Andrzej Ahorn, himself a Jesuit and a self-taught painter. The scheme includes a painting of a monk looking into the church through a painted grille. Other interesting churches include the **Piarist church and monastery**, now a Protestant church, a 17th-century **Dominican monastery complex** and the former **Dominican Church of Saints Jacek and Dorothy** (Kościół św św Jacka i Doroty), with Rococo interior. There is also a

Detail from the castle in Piotrków Trybunalski

Regional Museum located in a Gothic-Renaissance castle that is essentially a large brick tower designed as a residence. The most interesting part of the museum is the exhibition of grand interiors of the 16th to 20th centuries.

🏛 Regional Museum
pl. Zamkowy 4. 📞 (0 44) 647 52 72. 🕙 10am–5pm Tue, 10am–4pm Wed–Sat, 10am–3pm Sun.

🏛 Church of St Jacob
ul. Krakowskie Przedmieście 1. 📞 (0 44) 646 51 40.

🏛 Jesuit church
ul. Pijarska 4. 📞 (0 44) 647 01 51.

Sulejów ㉑

Road Map D4. 👥 5,700. 🚌

IN 1177 A CISTERCIAN abbey was founded here by Kazimierz the Just for Burgundian friars. The church was consecrated in 1232. It is in the Romanesque-Gothic style and has remained almost unaltered across the centuries, although the interior does contain Baroque altars and paintings in the same style.

The Romanesque portal in the west front bears what are said to be sword marks made by knights who in 1410 went to war with the Teutonic Knights. The monastery fell into ruin, although the remaining parts of it have been renovated and are now a hotel and **museum**. Near the abbey is a large artificial lake made in the 1970s on the River Pilica. It is a popular holiday spot.

🏛 Regional Museum
📞 (0 44) 616 20 11. 🕙 9am–4pm Mon–Fri. 📷

Cistercian abbey in Sulejów

Łódź ㉒

THE CENTRE OF THE Polish textile industry, Łódź developed at an astonishing rate as the industry thrived. Its population grew from just 15,000 in 1850 to more than half a million in 1914. It was a place of great contrasts, which were vividly documented in the novel *The Promised Land* (1899) by the Nobel Prize-winning author Władysław Reymont. The contrasts can still be seen in the architecture of the city, where vast fortunes and abject poverty existed side by side. Factories and opulent mansions sprang up in their hundreds, contrasting with the ramshackle homes of the factory workers.

VISITORS' CHECKLIST

Road map D4. 🏙 793,000.
🚉 🚌 **Railway information**
📞 *(0 42) 94 36*. **Coach
information PKS** 📞 *(0 42) 631
97 06.* 🛈 *ul. Traugutta 18
(0 42) 633 71 69).* 🎭 *Kódi
Festival (c.15 May).*

Exploring Łódź
The city's main thoroughfare is Ulica Piotrkowska, which is several kilometres long. Its most important section stretches from **Plac Wolności** to Aleje Piłudskiego. It is Poland's longest pedestrianized street and is lined with shops, cafés, restaurants and banks.

Behind the town houses, the brick factory buildings still stand, many of them now converted into stores. A noteworthy example is the one at **Piotrkowska 137/139**, built in 1907 for the cotton manufacturer Juliusz Kindermann by the architect Gustav Landau-Gutenteger, and featuring a gold mosaic frieze depicting an allegory of trade. In Plac Wolności is a

Stained-glass window in Poznański Palace

Monument to Tadeusz Kościuszko of 1930, rebuilt after its destruction in 1939 and a favourite meeting place for the city's youth. Beside it

stands the modest Neo-Classical **town hall**, which dates from 1827, when the foundations of industry were being laid in Łódź.

The city's **cemeteries** – the Catholic and Protestant cemeteries in Ulica Srebrzyńska and the Jewish cemetery in Ulica Bracka – contain some exceptionally interesting monuments that bear witness to the variety of cultures and nationalities that existed in Łódź before 1939, when it was a city with one of the largest Jewish populations in Europe. The grand mausoleums were built for local industrialists, who before 1914 were the wealthiest people in the Russian empire.

The **Leopold Kindermann Villa** at Ulica Wólczańska 31/33 is another Art Nouveau building designed by Gustav Landau-Gutenteger. It was built in 1902 and features fine

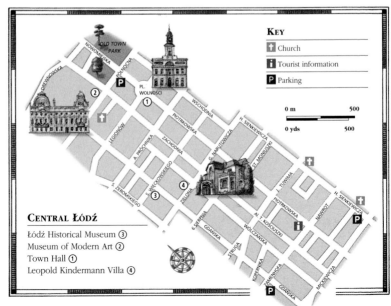

CENTRAL ŁÓDŹ
Łódź Historical Museum ③
Museum of Modern Art ②
Town Hall ①
Leopold Kindermann Villa ④

KEY

✝ Church

🛈 Tourist information

🅿 Parking

0 m   500
0 yds   500

stained-glass windows. Today it houses an art gallery.

At the turn of the 20th century the townscape of Łódź was dominated by the industrialists' palaces. The finest surviving examples are the residences of the textile factory-owner Izrael Kalmanowicz Poznański, at Ogrodowa 15 and Gdańska 36, and a remarkable palace at Plac Zwyciéstwa 1 that rivals the one built by Karol Scheibler, the merchant celebrated as the "cotton king" of Poznań.

Romanesque basilica at Tum, near Łęczyca

🏛 Łódź Historical Museum

ul. Ogrodowa 15. 📞 (0 42) 654 00 82.
🌐 www.poznanskipalace.pl
🕐 10am–2pm Tue, Thu–Sun, 2–6pm Wed. 🈺

The museum is located in Poznański Palace, beside a large group of brick factory buildings. Alongside the palace stands a former spinning mill, a vast Neo-Renaissance edifice designed by Hilary Majewski in 1876. The eclectic palace, which has twin cupolas, was built in stages from 1888 onwards. Notable features of the interior are the grand staircase, the series of private apartments and reception rooms, which have recently been restored, and the *belle époque* furniture.

Moorish stove in the Scheibler Palace, Łódź

The museum contains exhibits associated with the pianists Władysław Kędra and Artur Rubinstein, who was born in Łódź.

🏛 Museum of Modern Art

ul. Więckowskiego 36. 📞 (0 42) 633 97 90. 🌐 www. muzeumsztuki.lodz.pl
🕐 10am–5pm Tue, 11am–5pm Wed, Fri, noon–7pm Thu, 10am–4pm Sat, Sun.

The Museum of Modern Art is housed in another of Izrael Poznański's palaces, this one built in imitation of a Florentine Renaissance palazzo.

Besides work by Poland's foremost modern painters, the museum also contains a collection of modern art, including works by Hans Arp, Piet Mondrian, Joseph Beuys and Max Ernst.

The devil Boruta at Łęczyca royal castle

🏛 Museum of Cinematography

pl. Zwycięstwa 1. 📞 (0 42) 674 09 57.
🌐 www.kinomuzeum.lodz.art.pl
🕐 10am–3pm Tue–Fri, 11am–3pm Sat, Sun.

Situated in the eclectic palace of Karol Scheibler, the museum contains a rich collection of films and film posters from the earliest days of cinematography to modern times. It also documents the works of Łódź's renowned film school, whose graduates include major names in Polish cinema – the directors Andrzej Wajda, Roman Polański, Krzysztof Kieślowski and Jerzy Skolimowski, and the much-praised cameraman Witold Sobociński.

Łęczyca ㉓

Road map D3. 🏠 140. 🚊 🚌

THE ROYAL CASTLE at Łęczyca, built in 1357 by Kazimierz the Great, was the third fortified building to be raised in the town. Little is known about the first. The second was the seat of the rulers of another duchy.

The castle, with its brick tower, served as a jail for imprisoned aristocrats. The **Regional Museum** within it contains artifacts from prehistoric times to the present. The main attraction is the unusual exhibition dedicated to the devil Boruta, legendary guardian of the treasure hidden in the castle's cellar.

🏛 Regional Museum

ul. Zamkowa 1. 📞 (0 24) 721 24 49 or 721 25 43. 🕐 10am–5pm Tue, 10am–4pm Wed–Fri, 9am–2pm Sat, Sun.

ENVIRONS: In **Tum**, 3 km (2 miles) from Łęczyca, is the best-preserved Romanesque church of significant size in Poland. This granite building, consecrated in 1161, was remodelled several times, but its current form is close to its original one. It consists of a triple-nave basilica with two circular and two square towers and an apse at the west and east ends. The west apse has a remarkable Romanesque fresco of *Christ in Glory*, painted in 1161.

GDAŃSK

....

GDAŃSK IS AMONG THE *finest cities of northern Europe, distin guished by beautiful buildings and a history that stretches back more than 1,000 years. For many centuries the wealth-iest city in Poland, it was in 1939 the place where the first shots of World War II were fired. The end of the conflict brought destruction, but Gdańsk recovered as settlers moved in from other parts of Poland.*

The earliest mention of Gdańsk occurs in 997. For more than 300 years it was the capital of a Slav duchy in Pomerania, and in 1308 it was taken over by the Teutonic Knights. Under their rule, the city grew.

In 1361 Gdańsk became a member of the Hanseatic League (a trade association of Baltic towns), further bolstering its economic development. From 1466 until the Second Partition in 1793, the city belonged to Poland; it was the country's largest Baltic port and an important centre of the grain and timber trade between Poland and the rest of Europe.

A wealthy city, Gdańsk played a pivotal role in the Polish Republic *(see p42)*. It also became a major centre of the arts – goldsmiths fashioned fine jewellery for the royal courts of Europe, and the city's gemstone and amber workshops won great renown. From 1793 it was incorporated into Prussia, only becoming a free city under the Treaty of Versailles after World War I. It was almost totally destroyed during World War II, but a post-war rebuilding programme has restored many of the city's finest buildings and much of its historic atmosphere.

Today Gdańsk, attractively set between the coast and wooded hills, is renowned for its mercantile traditions and its openness to the world. Together with the coastal resort of Sopot and the port of Gdynia *(see p263)*, it forms the conurbation known as Trójmiasto ("the Tri-city").

View of the main town of Gdańsk

◁ **The Gdańsk Crane, the largest medieval port crane in Europe**

Exploring Gdańsk

THE MOST IMPÓRTANT buildings in terms of the history of Gdańsk are to be found in the city centre, which can be reached by taking a bus or tram to the Main Station (Dworec Główny), the Highland Gate (Brama Wyżynna) or the Podwale Przedmiejskie, and continuing on foot from there. The bus, tram or urban railway (SKM) are all useful for travelling to outlying parts of the city. You can also take the SKM to reach Oliwa in the northwest, which has a fine group of cathedral buildings, one of which contains a famous organ, and a good park for walking.

View of Ulica Długie Pobreże on the River Motława

GETTING THERE

Gdańsk has good transport links. There are rail services to and from all the major cities in Poland – the express train from Warsaw takes just 4 hours. There is an international airport at Rębiechowo, near Gdańsk. It is also easy to reach Gdańsk by car, whether from Warsaw (route E77), central Poland (route E75), Szczecin (route E28) or Berlin (route 22).

KEY

▨ Street-by-Street map
   See pp234–5

▨ Street-by-Street map
   See pp240–41

P Parking

ℹ Tourist information

▨ Railway station

⛴ Pier

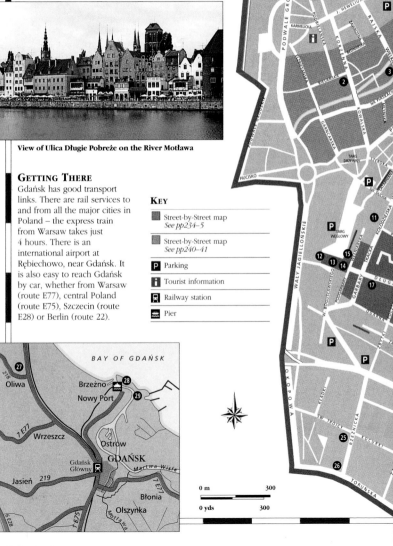

0 m   300

0 yds   300

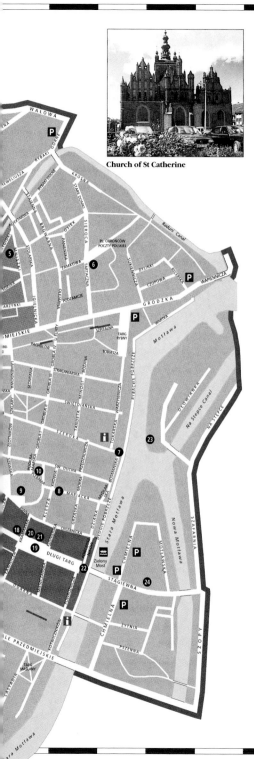

Church of St Catherine

Locator Map

Sights at a Glance

Museums and Galleries

Churches

Historic Buildings

Major Streets and Districts

See Also

Street-by-Street: Along Raduna Canal

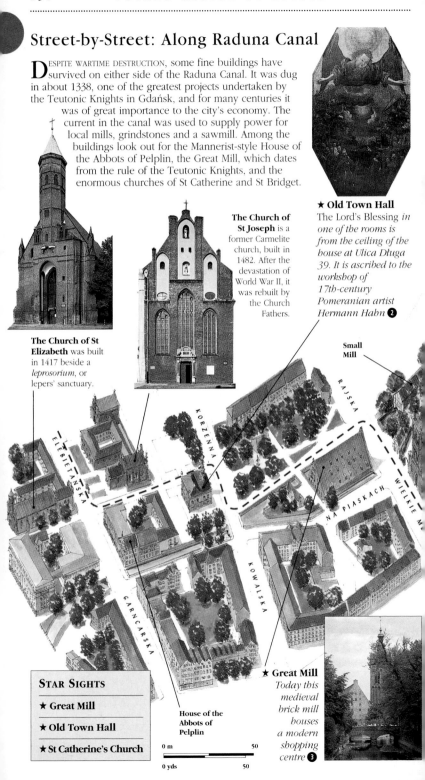

ESPITE WARTIME DESTRUCTION, some fine buildings have survived on either side of the Raduna Canal. It was dug in about 1338, one of the greatest projects undertaken by the Teutonic Knights in Gdańsk, and for many centuries it was of great importance to the city's economy. The current in the canal was used to supply power for local mills, grindstones and a sawmill. Among the buildings look out for the Mannerist-style House of the Abbots of Pelplin, the Great Mill, which dates from the rule of the Teutonic Knights, and the enormous churches of St Catherine and St Bridget.

The Church of St Joseph is a former Carmelite church, built in 1482. After the devastation of World War II, it was rebuilt by the Church Fathers.

★ **Old Town Hall**
The Lord's Blessing *in one of the rooms is from the ceiling of the house at Ulica Długa 39. It is ascribed to the workshop of 17th-century Pomeranian artist Hermann Hahn* ❷

The Church of St Elizabeth was built in 1417 beside a *leprosorium*, or lepers' sanctuary.

Small Mill

ELŻBIETAŃSKA

KORZENNA

RAJSKA

NA PIASKACH

WIELKIE M

KOWALSKA

GARNCARSKA

★ **Great Mill**
Today this medieval brick mill houses a modern shopping centre ❸

House of the Abbots of Pelplin

STAR SIGHTS
★ Great Mill
★ Old Town Hall
★ St Catherine's Church

0 m   50

0 yds   50

LOCATOR MAP
See pp232–3

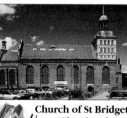

Church of St Bridget
This church was used as a place of worship by Solidarity members ⑤

★ **St Catherine's Church**
The memorial to astronomer Johannes Hevelius (1611–87) was installed in 1780 by Daniel G. Davisson, his great grandson ④

KEY

- - - Suggested route

Monument to the Shipyard Workers ①

Plac Solidarności Robotniczej.
🚃 🚊 *to dworec PKP.*

THE MONUMENT was built a few months after the famous Gdańsk Shipyard workers' strike of 1980 and the creation of the independent Solidarity trade union *(see p53)*. It was erected in honour of the shipyard workers who were killed during the strike and demonstrations of December 1970; it stands 30 m (100 ft) from the spot where the first three victims fell. Its three stainless steel crosses, 42 m (130 ft) high, were both a warning that such a tragedy might happen again and a symbol of remembrance and hope.

The monument was designed by the ship-yard workers and a group of artists including Bogdan Pietruszka, Wiesław Szyślak, Robert Pepliński and Elżbieta Szczodrowska. It was built by a team of workers from the shipyard. In the 1980s, the cross was the rallying point for Solidarity demonstrations, which were suppressed by the police.

Monument to the Shipyard Workers

Old Town Hall ②

ul. Korzenna 33/35.
📞 *(0 58) 301 10 51.* @ sekreteriat @nck.org.pl ♿ 🖥 🚻 ☕

BUILT BY ANTONIS van Opbergen in 1587–95, the Old Town Hall in Gdańsk is an outstanding example of Dutch Mannerist architecture. It is a compact, plain building with no distinctive ornamentation, and is equipped with a defence tower. The stone doorway was probably made by Willem van der Meer. Beneath each bracket are two distorted masks personifying vice, and two smiling, chubby masks, personifying virtue. Within the town hall, the painting, sculpture and furniture are very interesting, although little is left of the original decorative scheme of 1595. The painted ceiling in one of the rooms is by Hermann Hahn, a 17th-century Pomeranian artist. It was removed from a house at Ulica Długa 39 and transferred to the Old Town Hall some time after 1900. The theme of the ceiling paintings is allegorical: the central one depicts *The Lord's Blessing* and a figure of Zygmunt III Vasa also appears.

GDAŃSK SHIPYARD

The Gdańsk Shipyard is known throughout the world as the birthplace of Solidarity *(see p53)*. In December 1970, a shipyard workers' strike and protests in the city were crushed by the authorities. The next strike, in 1980, led to the establishment of the Independent Solidarity Trade Union. The strike leader was Lech Wałęsa, who was to become President of Poland (1990–5). Since 1989, in free market conditions, the shipyard has proved commercially unviable.

Main entrance to the Gdańsk Shipyard

The Great Mill from the Raduna Canal

Great Mill ❸

ul. Wielkie Młyny 16. ☐ 10am–6pm Mon–Fri, 10am–1pm Sat.

T HE GREAT MILL (Wielki Młyn) was one of the largest industrial buildings in medieval Europe. It was constructed during the rule of the Teutonic Knights, being completed in around 1350. It is built in brick and is crowned by a tall, steeply pitched roof.

At the front of the building stood a two-storey bakery with a chimney set against the gable of the mill which reached the height of its roof. Beside the mill stood 12, later 18, large poles to which millstones were attached for grinding various types of grain. The mill was destroyed by fire in 1945, but was restored after World War II. This remarkable old building now contains a modern shopping centre.

Church of St Catherine ❹

ul. Wielkie Młyny.
⊞ (0 58) 301 15 95.

T HE CHURCH OF St Catherine (Kościół św Katarzyny) is the oldest and also the most important parish church in the old town. It was built in 1227–39 by the dukes of Gdańsk-Pomerania and underwent major rebuilding in the 14th century.

Most of the Gothic, Mannerist and Baroque furnishings that the church once contained were pillaged or destroyed in 1945. The most notable surviving pieces are the paintings by Anton Möller and Izaak van den Blocke, the Baroque memorials to various townspeople and the tombstone of the astronomer Johannes Hevelius, dating from 1659.

The tower, 76 m (250 ft) high, was first built in 1486. Demolished in 1944 and later rebuilt, it is once again a major landmark. It is well worth climbing to the top of the tower; the effort is rewarded by wonderful views of the city. The presbytery on the east side of the church has a fine late Gothic gable.

Gothic tower of the Church of St Catherine

Church of St Bridget ❺

ul. Profesorska 17.
⊞ (0 58) 301 31 52.

T HE CHURCH OF St Bridget (Kościół św Brygidy) was well known in Poland in the 1980s as a place of worship and sanctuary for members of Solidarity. It was built on the site of a 14th-century chapel dedicated to St Mary Magdalene, where in 1374 the remains of the visionary St Bridget were displayed as they were being taken from Rome to Vadstena in Sweden. Soon afterwards a monastery for the Sisters of St Bridget was founded here. The church built beside it was completed in around 1514.

The brick shell of the Gothic church contrasts with the more recent belfry, built in 1653 by Peter Willer. The church's stark interior is an effective foil for the modern altars, tombstones and sculptures that it now contains. The most impressive of these are the high altar and the monument to Father Jerzy Popiełuszko, who was murdered in 1984 by Polish security service officials.

Polish Post Office ❻

pl. Obrońców Poczty Polskiej 1/2.
Post Office Museum ⊞ (0 58) 301 76 11. ☐ 10am–4pm Wed–Sat, 10:30am–2pm Sun. 🎫 (free on Sun).

T HE POLISH POST Office was the scene of some of the most dramatic events of the first days of World War II. At daybreak on 1 September 1939, German troops attacked the Polish Postal Administration that had its base here, in what was then the free city of Gdańsk. For 15 hours the postal workers resisted the onslaught, but they were finally overwhelmed. On 5 October more than 30 of them were executed by Nazi soldiers at the Zaspa Cemetery. Their heroism is commemorated in the Post Office Museum and by a monument depicting an injured postal worker atop scattered mail, handing over his rifle to Nike, Greek goddess of victory. It was designed by Wincenty Kućma in 1979 and bears an epitaph written by Maria and Zygfryd Korpalski in 1979.

Monument to Father Jerzy Popiełuszko in the Church of St Bridget

Ulica Mariacka, once the haunt of writers and artists

Gdańsk Crane ❼

ul. Szeroka 67/68. **Maritime Museum**
☎ (0 58) 301 69 38 and 301 86 11.
W www.trojmiasto.pl ○ 10am–6pm
Tue, Wed, Fri–Sun, noon–6pm Thu.

THE GDAŃSK CRANE (Żuraw), icon of the city, is one of its finest buildings and a medieval structure almost unique in Europe. Built in the 14th century and then renovated in 1442–4, when it acquired its present appearance, it combined the functions of a city gate and a port crane.

The crane, an entirely wooden structure, is set between two circular brick towers. It was operated by men working the huge treadmills within, and was capable of lifting weights of up to 2 tonnes to a height of 27 m (90 ft). The crane was used not only to load and unload goods but also in fitting masts to ships.

The crane was destroyed by fire in 1945. As part of the rebuilding programme after World War II it was repaired and reconstructed, together with its internal mechanism. It is now part of the collection of the Central Maritime Museum *(see p245)*. The

Crane Tower looks out over Ulica Długie Pobrzeże, which runs alongside the River Motława. Once known as the Long Bridge, it was originally a wooden footbridge that functioned as a quay where ships from all over the world tied up. Today a fleet of yachts and small pleasure boats offering trips around the harbour in the Port of Gdańsk is moored here.

Ulica Mariacka ❽

ULICA MARIACKA, regarded as Gdańsk's finest street, runs eastwards from the Church of St Mary to Długie Pobrzeże, terminating at the Mariacka Gate on the riverfront. Rebuilt from the ruins that resulted from World War II, the street contains outstanding examples of traditional Gdańsk architecture. Here, town houses that were once owned by wealthy merchants and goldsmiths have tall, richly ornamented façades; others are fronted by external raised terraces with ornamented parapets. It is small wonder that this picturesque street has for centuries inspired writers and artists.

The neighbourly porch gossip that once upon a time filled the evening air is sadly no more. Today, however, the street is a favourite haunt of lovers as well as tourists, most of whom are looking for picturesque subjects to photograph or browsing through the amber jewellery for which Ulica Mariacka is now celebrated. During the long summer evenings, a number of musicians provide free open-air concerts, and the welcoming street cafés stay open until late at night.

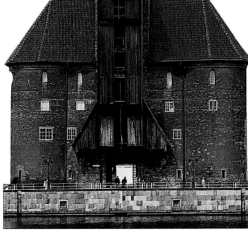

The Gdańsk Crane, a medieval building almost unique in Europe

Church of St Mary ❾

Tᴴᴇ ᴄʜᴜʀᴄʜ ᴏꜰ ꜱᴛ ᴍᴀʀʏ (Kościół Mariacki) is the largest medieval brick-built church in Europe. Building work began in 1343 and took 150 years to complete. The final stage of construction, involving the 100-m (325-ft) long nave, was carried out by Henryk Hetzel. From 1529 to 1945, when it was destroyed, St Mary's was a Protestant church. Like so many other parts of Gdańsk, it was rebuilt after World War II. The interior contains furnishings in the Gothic, Mannerist and Baroque styles. Look out for the memorial tablets to prominent local families.

★ Astronomical Clock
The clock, made by Hans Dürunger in 1464–70, shows the hour and also the days, dates of moveable feasts and phases of the moon. At noon a procession of figures representing Adam and Eve, the Apostles, the Three Kings and Death appears.

★ Tablet of Charity
This ornate panel, made by Anton Möller in 1607, once hung over the church collection box. Its purpose was to encourage churchgoers to be generous.

★ Tablet of the Ten Commandments
This panel of around 1480–90 depicts each of the Ten Commandments in two scenes, illustrating obedience to and disregard of the laws.

Sᴛᴀʀ Fᴇᴀᴛᴜʀᴇꜱ

★ **Tablet of the Ten Commandments**

★ **Astronomical Clock**

★ **Tablet of Charity**

The Beautiful Madonna of Gdańsk
The Chapel of St Anne contains this 15th-century figure of the Virgin and Child by an unknown artist.

VISITORS' CHECKLIST

ul. Podkramarska 5.
▌ (0 58) 301 39 82. ◯ 8am–
6pm daily. **Tower** ◯ 1 May–31
Aug: 10am–6pm daily; 30 Sep–
30 Apr: 10am–4pm daily. ◙

Gothic Sacrarium
The sacrarium, in the shape of an open-work tower decorated with pinnacles, is over 8 m (26 ft) high.

Epitaph to Valentin von Karnitz
The memorial tablet to Valentyn von Karnitz, of around 1590, has many Dutch Mannerist features. The centre painting depicts the biblical tale of the Lamentation of Abel.

Royal Chapel ⑩

ul. św Ducha 58.
▌ (0 58) 302 1423.

THE ROYAL CHAPEL (Kaplica Królewska) was built by Jan III Sobieski as a place of worship for Catholics of the parish of St Mary's, which had become a Protestant church in 1529. The chapel was built in 1678–81 to designs by the great royal architect Tylman van Gameren.

The carving in the Kaplica Królewska is by Andreas Schlüter the Younger. The chapel itself is enclosed within a chamber and is situated on a raised floor. The interior is less ostentatious than the façade.

The Arsenal seen from Targ Węglowy

Arsenal ⑪

ul. Targ Węglowy 6. **National College of Visual Arts**
▌ (0 58) 301 28 01.

THE ARSENAL is the finest example of the Dutch Mannerist style in Gdańsk. It was built, probably to plans by Antonis van Opbergen in collaboration with Jan Strakowski, in 1600–9.

Today the ground floor of the former weapons and ammunition store is filled with shops, while the National College of Visual Arts occupies the upper storeys. The building has a finely decorated façade, with fascinatingly original carvings by Wilhelm Barth.

Street-by-Street: Długi and Długa Targ

DŁUGI TARG AND Ulica Długa, its continuation, are the most attractive streets in Gdańsk. Długi Targ leads westwards from the Green Gate on the River Motława to join Ulica Długa, which runs as far as the Golden Gate. These two pedestrianized streets are lined with old town houses that were once the residences of the city's wealthiest citizens. Most of the Main City's principal buildings, including the town hall and Artus Court, are on Długi Targ. Together the streets formed an avenue that was used for parades, ceremonies and sometimes public executions and from 1457 for the processions that accompanied royal visits – which is why the two streets were known as the Royal Way.

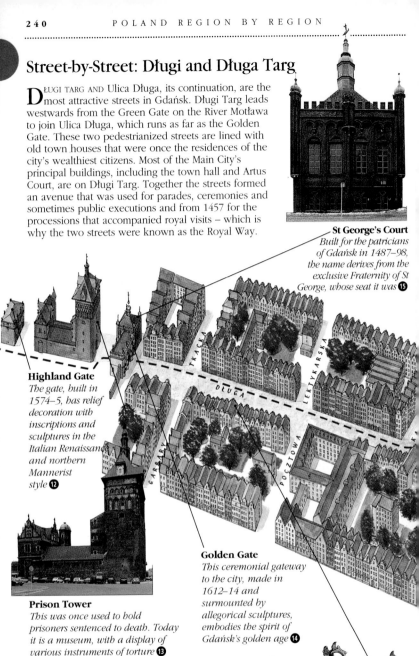

St George's Court
Built for the patricians of Gdańsk in 1487–98, the name derives from the exclusive Fraternity of St George, whose seat it was **15**

Highland Gate
The gate, built in 1574–5, has relief decoration with inscriptions and sculptures in the Italian Renaissance and northern Mannerist style **12**

Prison Tower
This was once used to hold prisoners sentenced to death. Today it is a museum, with a display of various instruments of torture **13**

Golden Gate
This ceremonial gateway to the city, made in 1612–14 and surmounted by allegorical sculptures, embodies the spirit of Gdańsk's golden age **14**

★ Uphagen House
The interior of this recently restored town house features 17th-century Rococo panelling, which survived wartime destruction **17**

STAR SIGHTS
★ **Main Town Hall**
★ **Artus Court**
★ **Uphagen House**

★ Main Town Hall
The Allegory of Justice *by Hans Vredeman de Vries decorates the main council chamber, also known as the Red Room* ⑱

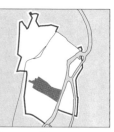

LOCATOR MAP
See pp232–3.

★ Artus Court
The bench of the Brotherhood of St Christopher, in this meeting house for dignitaries, is adorned with the story of Lot and his daughter by Laurentius Lauenstein ⑳

Ulica Długa
Rebuilt after wartime destruction, this is the main street of old Gdańsk ⑯

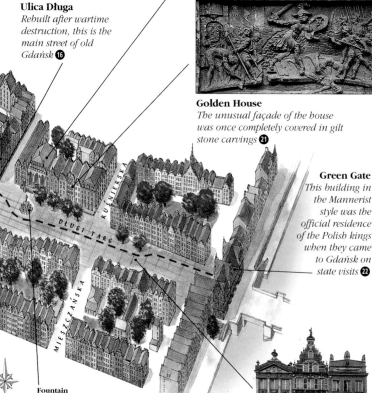

Golden House
The unusual façade of the house was once completely covered in gilt stone carvings ㉑

Green Gate
This building in the Mannerist style was the official residence of the Polish kings when they came to Gdańsk on state visits ㉒

KUŚNIERSKA

DŁUGI TARG

CZA

MIESZCZAŃSKA

Fountain of Neptune

0 m   300

0 yds   300

KEY

– – –   Suggested route

Długi Targ
When the street was rebuilt after World War II, the houses and their stepped terraces were reconstructed ⑲

The Highland Gate, part of the new fortifications of 1571–6

Highland Gate ⑫

ul. Wały Jagiellońskie.

THE HIGHLAND GATE marks the beginning of the Royal Way that, following Ulica Długa and Długi Targ, descends eastwards to the Green Gate *(see p240)*. It was built by Hans Kramer of Saxony as part of the fortifications that were erected along the western limits of the city in 1571–6. Originally built in brick, the gate acquired its present appearance in 1588, when the Flemish architect Willem van den Blocke faced it with stone on its western side, making it look as if it were made of masonry blocks.

The upper level is decorated with cartouches containing coats of arms: that of Poland, held by two angels (on the breast of the eagle the coat of arms of Stanisław August, a bull calf, is visible) are flanked by the Prussian coat of arms, borne by unicorns, and those of Gdańsk, borne by lions.

Prison Tower ⑬

ul. Długa–Przedbramie.
📞 (0 58) 301 49 45. **Branch of the Museum of the History of Gdańsk.** ☐ 10am–3:30pm Tue–Fri, 11am–3:30pm Sat, Sun.
🎟 (free on Sun).

THE CURRENT EXTERIOR of the Prison Tower, in a mixture of architectural styles, is the result of several rebuildings. The tower was originally built as part of the now-destroyed Ulica Długa Gate that was erected in the second half of the 14th century as part of the medieval fortifications of the Main Town.

In the 15th and 16th centuries the tower was heightened several times and the surrounding buildings altered accordingly. When the new fortifications were built in 1571–6 the entire complex lost its purpose. It began to be used as a prison, court and torture chamber.

It was remodelled for its new purpose in 1604 by Antonis van Opbergen, who gave it a northern Mannerist form, and by Willem van der Meer, who added decorative detail. The tower was the scene of many blood-curdling interrogations. There is a whipping post on the western wall, which was also the site of many executions. At the turn of the 20th century, in accordance with the new functions of the buildings, a stonecutter's workshop was installed in the courtyard.

Golden Gate ⑭

ul. Długa.

THE GOLDEN GATE was built in 1612–14 on the site of the medieval Ulica Długa Gate. The architect, Abraham van den Blocke, devised the new construction in the style of a classical Roman triumphal arch through which the Royal Way would enter the city of Gdańsk.

The arches of the gate are framed by Ionic columns in the lower tier surmounted by composite columns in the upper tier. The gate is crowned with statues carved by Piotr Ringering in 1648 and reconstructed after the originals were damaged in World War II. The statues on the outer side of the gate, facing away from the city, depict peace, freedom, prosperity and glory, while those on the inner side, facing the city, represent prudence, piety, justice and harmony. The carved decoration is complemented by inscriptions in both Latin and German on the theme of civic virtue. The whole gate was designed and constructed in the Neo-Classical style but with Mannerist elements.

The Golden Gate, so called because of the gilding on its façade

St George's Court ⑮

ul. Targ Węglowy 27. ⬤ to visitors.

THE FRATERNITY of St George, an association of archers and the oldest of its kind in medieval Gdańsk, originally met in Artus Court. However, in 1487 the fraternity acquired its own premises, St George's Court, which was built under the direction of Hans Glothau in the Flemish style. It was completed in 1494.

The first floor contained an archery range and storerooms for archery equipment. Members of the fraternity met in the Great Hall on the first floor. The hall was also used for ceremonies, meetings and banquets and for the performance of plays.

In 1566 it was crowned by a figure of St George and the Dragon, which was removed and is now on display in the National Museum (the figure on the small tower is a copy). In the 19th century the building housed the School of Fine Art. Today Artus Court is the premises of the Gdańsk branch of the Association of Polish Architects.

Looking down Ulica Długa from the Golden Gate to Długi Targ

Ulica Długa ⑯

TODAY, AS IN THE past, Ulica Długa ("Long Street") is the Main Town's principal thoroughfare. The houses that line the street were once inhabited by the foremost burghers of Gdańsk, and virtually every one has its own colourful history. Although the oldest surviving houses on the street date from the Middle Ages, most were built during the heyday of the Hanseatic League.

With their narrow façades crowned by a variety of elements – from coats of arms and symbols to animals, allegorical figures and the heroes of classical mythology – the houses on Ulica Długa are typical of the architecture of Gdańsk. Unfortunately when they were modernized in the mid-19th century, all the stepped terraces that originally fronted the entrances to the houses were removed.

After the carnage of World War II, almost every building on Ulica Długa was left in ruins. Many of the houses were later reconstructed, but only the finest buildings were rebuilt in architectural detail.

The Red Room in the Main Town Hall

Uphagen House ⑰

ul. Długa 12. ☎ (0 58) 301 23 71. **Section of the Museum of the History of Gdańsk** ◯ 1 Apr–30 Sep: 11am–6pm Tue, Thu, 10am–4pm Wed, 10am–5pm Fri, Sat, 11am–5pm Sun; 1 Oct–31 Mar: 10am–3:30pm Tue–Sat, 11am–3:30pm Sun. 🎟 (free on Wed).

THE HOUSE THAT originally stood at Ulica Długa 12 was acquired by Johann Uphagen, a town councillor, in 1775. He had it demolished, and a new residence was built in its place. The architect, Johann Benjamin Dreyer, completed the project in 1787. The result was an attractive building combining Baroque, Rococo and early Neo-Classical features.

The sole ornamentation of the restrained façade is the Rococo decoration to the door, which is inscribed with the initial A, for Abigail, the owner's wife. The interiors, with Rococo and Neo-Classical elements, are splendid.

The Rococo doorway of Uphagen House

Main Town Hall ⑱

ul. Długa 47. **Museum of the History of Gdańsk** ☎ (0 58) 301 48 71. ◯ 10am–3:30pm Tue–Sat, 11am–3:30pm Sun. 🎟 (free on Sun). ♿ 👪

THE CITY'S FIRST town hall was built after 1298 on the orders of Świętopełk II, Duke of Gdańsk-Pomerania. It functioned as an office of the Hanseatic League.

Work on the current building was begun in 1327. An elegant tower was added in 1486–8, during one of several phases of rebuilding. After a fire in 1556, this Gothic town hall was remodelled in the Mannerist style. The interior was lavishly decorated in 1593–1608 by the most prominent painters and craftsmen of the day, including Hans Vredeman de Vries, Izaak van den Blocke and Simon Herle. Their combined genius produced one of the finest town halls in all of northern Europe, proof of the city's wealth and power. It also served as a royal residence.

The highlight of the town hall is without doubt the Red Room, which was once the Great Council Chamber. The Renaissance fireplace is by Willem van der Meer and the centrepiece of the ceiling paintings is the *Apotheosis of Gdańsk* by Izaak van den Blocke. After being destroyed in 1945, the town hall was rebuilt and many of its furnishings reconstructed. It now houses the Museum of the History of Gdańsk.

Długi Targ ⑲

DŁUGI TARG, a broad short street that runs on from Ulica Długa and terminates at the Green Gate on the River Motława, is the final part of the Royal Way leading from the Golden Gate through to the city centre. It also functioned as a marketplace as well as a site for the public execution of aristocratic prisoners. The townhouses on Długi Targ, like those elsewhere in the old town, were destroyed in 1945 but have been restored. Today the square is filled with souvenir shops. Its focal point is the Fountain of Neptune, which was installed outside Artus Court in 1633.

Fountain of Neptune in Długi Targ

St George killing the Dragon, a carving of 1485 in Artus Court

Artus Court ⑳

ul. Długi Targ 44. **Museum**
📞 (0 58) 346 33 58.
🕐 10am–3:30pm Tue–Sat,
11am–3:30pm Sun (1 Apr–30 Sep:
until 5pm). 🚫 📷 🏠 🚻

ARTUS COURT was a meeting place for the wealthy burghers of Gdańsk, who were inspired by the chivalrous traditions of King Arthur and the Knights of the Round Table. Similar fraternities were set up throughout Europe, and they were particularly fashionable in the cities of the Hanseatic League. Visitors to the court came to discuss the issues of the day and to enjoy the fine beer that was served there in unlimited quantities. The first Artus Court in Gdańsk was established in the 14th century, but the original building was destroyed by fire in 1477. The present building opened in 1481. Its rear elevation preserves the building's original Gothic style, but the façade was twice rebuilt, first in 1552 and again in 1616–17 by Abraham van den Blocke. The interior furnishings were renewned several times, funded mainly by individual fraternities, who would gather for meetings seated on benches along the walls of the court. Despite wartime destruction, reconstruction has succeeded in recreating something of the court's historic atmosphere. A highlight of the interior is the intricately decorated 16th-century Renaissance tiled stove, 12 m (40 ft) high.

Golden House ㉑

ul. Długi Targ 41. ⬤ *to the public.*

THE GOLDEN HOUSE, also known as Speimann House or Steffens House after its owners, was built in 1609–18 for Jan Speimann, mayor of Gdańsk and a wealthy merchant and patron of the arts, and his wife Maria Judyta. The architect was Abraham van den Blocke, who also executed some of the stone carving. The most impressive feature of the house is its façade, which is covered in intricate gilt carvings, and which fortunately escaped the fires that ravaged the building in 1945.

Today the building houses the Maritime Institute. Local people claim that it is haunted; in one of the corridors the shining figure of the former lady of the house, Maria Judyta Speimann, is said to appear and can be heard whispering the words "A just deed fears no man".

Green Gate ㉒

ul. Długi Targ 24. 📞 (0 58) 305 55 53.

WITH ITS PINNACLED roof and elaborate decorative stonework, the Green Gate hardly resembles the usual city gate – it is more like a mansion. There is good reason for this, because the gate was intended to serve as a residence for visiting royalty. In the event it was used in this way only once – when Maria Louisa Gonzaga arrived in Gdańsk from France in order to marry Władysław IV in 1646.

The gate was designed in the Mannerist style by the architect Johann Kramer from Dresden, and built in 1564–8 by Regnier from Amsterdam. Its windows provide a magnificent view of Ulica Długi Targ and the town hall in one direction, and the River Motława and Spichlerze Island in the other.

The Green Gate, not only a city gate but also a royal residence

Central Maritime Museum ㉓

IN THE 17TH CENTURY Poland strove to be "master of the Baltic Sea" and her seafarers were dedicated to maintaining Poland's maritime presence. The themes of the displays in the Maritime Museum are Gdańsk's seafaring traditions and navigation on the Vistula. Exhibits include a reconstruction of scenes from a sailor's life aboard the Swedish ship *Solen*, sunk at the Battle of Oliwa in 1627 and recently raised from the seabed in the Gulf of Gdańsk.

VISITORS' CHECKLIST

ul. Szeroka 67/68 i Ołowianka 9/11.
☎ (0 58) 301 69 38. ▥ 106, 111, 138, 158. ◻ 8am–4pm Tue–Sun. ▨

ORP Bałtyk
The ship's wheel from ORP Bałtyk, Poland's largest naval vessel before 1939, is part of the display in the Gdańsk Crane.

Chandler's Workshop
The Oliwa Warehouse contains reconstructed workshops that once equipped the navy.

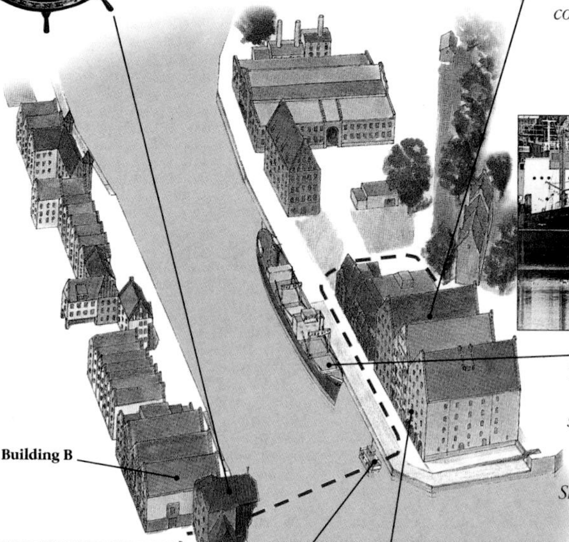

Sołdek
The Sołdek, *the first Polish oceangoing ship to be built after World War II, was built in the Gdańsk Shipyard in 1948. Its holds are now used for exhibitions.*

Building B

Ferry
An easy way from one building to another is by ferry.

MUSEUM GUIDE
The museum consists of a number of buildings on either side of the River Motława. There is a Polish naval exhibition in the Gdańsk Crane. Building B contains a collection of boats from distant parts of the world. The exhibition in the granaries is dedicated to the presence of Poland and Gdańsk at sea from the Middle Ages to the present.

KEY

– – – – Suggested route

STAR FEATURE

★ Grain Warehouse

★ The Grain Warehouse
The collection of naval weapons exhibited here includes 17th-century cannons from Polish and Swedish ships.

Spichlerze Island ㉔

📖 *106, 111, 112, 120, 121, 138, 158, 166, 186.* 🚋 *8, 13.*

Once joined to the mainland, Spichlerze Island was created when the New Motława Canal was dug in 1576. A centre of trade developed here at the end of the 13th century. What was then a relatively small number of granaries had grown to more than 300 by the 16th century. Each granary had a name and each façade was decorated with an individual emblem. The purpose of digging the canal, and thus of surrounding the district with water, was not only to protect the granaries against fire but also to safeguard their contents against thieves.

Everything was destroyed in 1945. Today a main road bisects the island, and the charred stumps that can still be seen in many places are all that remain of the granaries. The name signs on some ruins – such as Arche Noah ("Noah's Ark") on Ulica Żytniej ("Wheat Street") – remain legible. Reconstruction began several years ago. The first granaries to be rebuilt were those between the Motława and Ulica Chmielna ("Hop Street"). One of them is now the headquarters of ZUS, the Polish social security organization. Restoration of a group of buildings on Ulica Stągiewna was completed in 1999. Two 16th-century Gothic castle keeps, survivors of World War II, are in this street. They are known as the Stągwie Mleczne ("Milk Churns").

Chapel of St Anne, near the Church of the Holy Trinity

Church of the Holy Trinity ㉕

ul. św Trójcy 4. 📞 *(0 58) 763 05 70 or 763 05 72.* 📖 *106, 111, 112, 116, 120, 121, 138, 158, 166, 178, 186.* 🚋 *8, 13.*

The imposing Church of the Holy Trinity (Kościół św Trójcy) was built by Franciscan monks in 1420–1514. In 1480, the Chapel of St Anne was constructed alongside the church. Protestantism quickly spread to Gdańsk, and one of its most ardent proponents in the region was the Franciscan friar Alexander Svenichen. When congregations declined because of Svenichen's activities, the Franciscans decided in 1556 to hand the monastery over to the city as

Monkey from the stalls of the Church of the Holy Trinity

a theological college. The head of the Franciscan order did not agree with the Gdańsk friars' decision to cede the monastery but the order's petitions to the Polish kings to have the property returned bore no result. As a result, the church was transferred to the Protestants. The grammar school that was established here later became the widely celebrated Academic Grammar School. It also came to house the first library in Gdańsk. However, centuries later in 1945 it was returned to the Catholics, after the violence of World War II had reduced it to a ruin.

The aisled church has a distinctive exterior with ornamental Gothic spires. They crown the elongated presbytery, the façade and the walls of the adjacent Chapel of St Anne. The presbytery, which was occupied by the friars, was separated from the aisles by a wall. Interesting features of the interior are the many tombstones that are set into the floor and the numerous works by Gdańsk artists. The very fine Gothic stalls were made by local craftsmen in 1510–11. Their carved decorations depict a wide variety of subjects, among them animals including a monkey, a lion fighting a dragon and several birds.

The church contains the oldest surviving pulpit in Gdańsk – it dates from 1541 and is another remarkable example of local wood carving. In the north aisle can be seen the marble tomb made by Abraham van den Blocke in 1597 for Giovanni Bernardo Bonifacio, Marquis d'Orii, a restless spirit and champion of the Reformation who founded the Gdańsk library. "Bones long since thrown ashore here finally rest from their earthly wanderings" reads the poetic Latin inscription.

Beside the church is a half-timbered galleried house dating from the 17th century.

The Milk Churns, two medieval keeps on Spichlerze Island

National Museum ㉖

THE NATIONAL MUSEUM is laid out mainly in a former Gothic Franciscan monastery of 1422–1522. It contains a wealth of artifacts, from wrought-iron grilles to sculpture and painting. The museum's most prized piece is *The Last Judgement* by the Flemish painter Hans Memling (c.1430–94). Some historians claim that it was plundered by privateers from Gdańsk from a ship bound for Italy.

VISITORS' CHECKLIST

ul. Toruńska 1. **(** (0 58) 301 70 61. 🚌 106, 111, 112, 116, 120, 121, 138, 158, 166, 178, 186. 🚋 8, 13. ◯ 1 Jun–15 Sep: 9am–4pm Tue–Fri, 10am–5pm Sat, Sun; 16 Sep–31 May: 9am–4pm Tue–Fri, 10am–4pm Sat, Sun. 🎟

★ The Last Judgement
The central panel of Hans Memling's 1467 triptych depicts The Last Judgement, *while the left-hand side panel represents the Gates of Heaven and the right-hand one shows the torments of Hell.*

MUSEUM GUIDE
The exhibits on the ground floor include Gothic art and gold jewellery. The first floor has more recent paintings. The upper floor displays temporary exhibitions.

"The Griffin's Talons"
This bison-horn cup was made in the 15th century and belonged to a sailing fraternity.

Longcase Clock
A Rococo clock made c.1750 is decorated with scenes from the biblical story of Tobias and the Raising of the Copper Snake.

KEY
- ☐ Pomeranian medieval art
- ☐ Gold jewellery and goldwork
- ☐ Metalwork
- ☐ Gdańsk and northern European furniture, 15th–18th centuries
- ☐ Ceramics
- ☐ Dutch and Flemish painting
- ☐ Gdańsk painting, 16th–18th centuries
- ☐ Polish painting, 19th and 20th centuries
- ☐ 19th-century Gdańsk artists (temporary exhibitions)
- ☐ Furniture-making in Gdańsk and eastern Pomerania in the 18th century
- ☐ The Last Judgement

STAR FEATURE

★ The Last Judgement

Oliwa Cathedral ㉗

O LIWA, A DISTRICT to the northwest of Gdańsk, was once the base of wealthy Cistercians, who built a cathedral and monastery here. The present cathedral, built in the 14th century in the Gothic style, replaced the original 13th-century Romanesque church that was destroyed by fire in 1350. While the exterior has survived without major alteration, the interior has been redecorated in the Baroque style. Its famous organ can be heard in recitals. The monastery buildings are now occupied by branches of the Diocesan, Ethnographical and Contemporary Art museums. Oliwa Park, with lakes and wooded hills, is a pleasant place for a walk.

Mannerist Stalls
The stalls in the chancel, decorated with bas-reliefs of the Apostles, were made in 1604.

The former high altar, built in 1604–6, has a depiction of the Holy Trinity.

Tomb of the Kos Family
The tomb was carved in around 1599, probably by the prominent Gdańsk sculptor Willem van den Blocke.

Main entrance

★ Organ Loft
The organ loft was made by local Cistercian monks in 1763–88. The organ, made by Jan Wulff and Fryderyk Rudolf Dalitz and completed in 1793, was the largest in Europe at the time.

STAR FEATURES

★ Organ Loft

★ High Altar

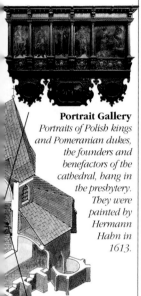

Portrait Gallery

*Portraits of Polish kings
and Pomeranian dukes,
the founders and
benefactors of the
cathedral, hang in
the presbytery.
They were
painted by
Hermann
Hahn in
1613.*

★ **High Altar**
*Thought to be by
Andreas Schlüter, it was
decorated by Andreas
Stech with images
of the Virgin and
St Bernard, patrons of
the monastery at Oliwa.*

**The Monument to the Defenders
of Westerplatte**

Westerplatte ❷❽

🚌 106, 158. Ferries in summer
season at Green Gate. **Guardhouse
No 1 Museum** ul. Mjr. H. Sucharskiego.
☎ (0 58) 343 69 72. ⭕ May–Jun:
10am–5pm daily.

I T WAS AT WESTERPLATTE that
the first shots of World War
II were fired, at dawn on
1 September 1939. The
German battleship *Schleswig
Holstein* opened fire on Polish
ammunition dumps in the
Free City of Gdańsk. Although
the Germans expected the
capture of the Westerplatte to
take a matter of hours, the
182-man garrison under Major
Henryk Sucharski resisted for
seven days, their heroism
becoming a symbol of Polish
resistance in the struggle
against the Nazi invasion.

Today ruined barracks and
concrete bunkers, together
with a huge Monument to the
Defenders of Westerplatte
unveiled in 1966, bear witness
to that struggle.

Wisłoujście Fortress ❷❾

ul. Stara Twierdza. ☎ (0 58) 343 14 05.
🚌 106. ⭕ for restoration until
2002.

F ORTIFICATIONS WERE first built
on this strategic point at
the mouth of the River Vistula
in the time of the Teutonic
Knights. Work on the
construction of a brick tower
began in 1482. From here, a
duty was levied on passing
ships using a simple
enforcement method that was
impossible to avoid – a chain
was stretched across the river,
preventing the ship's passage,
and released only when the
captain had made the
required payment. Equipped
with a brazier in which a fire
was lit, the tower was also
used as a lighthouse.

In 1562–3 the tower was
surrounded by a system of
defences, and afterwards was
repeatedly fortified and
refortified as military
technology advanced. In
1586–7 the entire complex
was reinforced by four
bastions, designed by Antonis
van Op bergen and Jan
Strakowski, and an outer
moat was added. This was
followed by the addition of a
ditch in 1624–6. Also in the
17th century, 15 tall barrack
buildings were added around
the now-ageing tower.

Over the following years,
constant building, often
by prominent fortification
engineers of the time, steadily
enlarged the fortress. It
withstood several sieges
and was often used to
accommodate visiting royalty.

Wisłoujście Fortress, which once defended the mouth of the River Vistula

POMERANIA

EAUTIFUL BEACHES AND THE *resorts of the Baltic are Pomerania's main attractions, which every summer draw large numbers of holiday-makers in search of sand and sun. A less crowded but equally attractive aspect of the region are the Drawsko Lakes and the alpine scenery of Szwajcaria Kaszubska, west of Gdańsk.*

Polish Pomerania is divided into the two regions of Western and Eastern Pomerania, each with an ethnically diverse population. The border between the two regions is in the districts of Bytów and Lębork.

Christianity was introduced to Western Pomerania by Bishop Otto of Bamberg, who founded a bishopric in Wolin in 1140. The Duchy of Pomerania, established in the 12th century, maintained its independence for several centuries and secured its economic development through the strength of its port cities, which were part of the Hanseatic League. The Thirty Years' War (1618–48) and the death of the last duke of the Gryfici dynasty brought this independence to an end. Most of Western Pomerania came under the rule of Brandenburg, while Szczecin and the surrounding area was engulfed by Sweden until 1713. In the 18th and 19th centuries, Western Pomerania became first Prussian, then German, territory. It was returned to Poland in 1945.

Eastern Pomerania was Christianized in the 10th century. Although it originally belonged to Poland, it became an independent duchy from the 12th century. Overrun by the Teutonic Knights in 1306, it then enjoyed strong economic development. In 1466, after the Second Peace of Toruń, areas of Eastern Pomerania, including Royal Prussia, were ceded to Poland. However, during the Partitions of Poland *(see p46)*, Eastern Pomerania became part of Prussia. It was finally returned to Poland in 1919. Gdańsk was given the status of a free city and only became part of Poland in 1945.

Pomerania's landscape was formed by the movement of glaciers. Its hilly countryside with small, clear lakes and its varied Baltic coastline make the region outstandingly beautiful.

Malbork Castle, the great fortress of the Teutonic Knights, on the River Nogat

◁ **Wild cliffs on Pomerania's Baltic coast**

Exploring Pomerania

POMERANIA IS ONE of Poland's most attractive regions, and in summer resorts such as Międzyzdroje, Kołobrzeg, Ustka, Łeba and Sopot teem with sunbathers and watersports enthusiasts. The most popular holiday spots are on the Hel Peninsula, where swimmers can choose between the open waters of the Baltic Sea or the calm of the Gulf of Gdańsk. For sightseeing at a slower pace there are the villages of Kashubia. The shady, tree-lined lanes in the region of Słupsk and Koszalin make for enjoyable cycle tours, while the clean rivers are attractive for canoeing. Those with an interest in history will not be disappointed with the great variety of historic buildings, from castles and cathedrals to small village churches and the stately houses of old seaside resorts.

A half-timbered house, typical of the Gdańsk region, in Różyny

GETTING AROUND

Szczecin and Gdańsk can be reached by air *(see pp352–3)*. The best way to tour Pomerania is by car. The E28 connects Gdańsk with Słupsk, Koszalin and Szczecin. Parallel to it but further to the south is route 22, which is part of the old German A1 from Berlin to Kaliningrad (Królewiec). The E75 goes south from Gdańsk to Gniew. All larger towns and cities have rail links. In the Gulf of Gdańsk there are also ferries to Sopot and Hel.

SIGHTS AT A GLANCE

SEE ALSO

• *Where to Stay* pp308–10.

• *Restaurants and Bars* pp325–6.

Fishermen's buoys on a Baltic beach

SŁOWIŃSKI
NATIONAL PARK

8

WŁADYSŁAWOWO

Lake Łebsko

ŁUCK   **11**   216

ŁEBA   213

HEL PENINSULA

USTKA

SŁUPSK   **7**

12   GDYNIA

13   SOPOT

GDAŃSK

KASHUBIA   **10**
228

W   I   S   L   A
E   S   T   U   A   R   Y

BYTÓW   **9**

Elbląg

KOŚCIERZYNA

MALBORK

MIASTKO

WDZYDZE
TUCHOLSKIE

Brda

PELPLIN   **14**

15

GNIEW   **16**

17

T   U   C   H   O   L   S   K   I   E

SZCZECINEK

CHOJNICE   W   O   O   D   S

KWIDZYN

TUCHOLA   240

GRUDZIĄDZ   16

SĘPÓLNO
KRAJEŃSKIE

18   Olsztyn

Lake Koronowo

CHEŁMNO   **19**

E261

Wisła

20   Drwęca   **22**

BYDGOSZCZ   TORUŃ   GOLUB-
DOBRZYŃ

21

25

23   CIECHOCINEK

Inowrocław   E75

| 0 km | | 50 |
| 0 miles | | 50 |

The lakes of Szwajcaria Kaszubska in autumn

KEY

■ Major road

■ Other road

≋ River

☆ Viewpoint

Szczecin ❶

SZCZECIN, ON THE RIVER ODRA, is a major port even though it is more than 65 km (40 miles) from the sea. It serves both oceangoing vessels and river traffic, and is linked with Berlin by the Odra and by canals. A castle and a fishing village existed here in the 9th century. Szczecin was granted a municipal charter in 1243 and soon after it joined the Hanseatic League. It became the capital of a Pomeranian duchy and in 1673–1713 was overrun by the Swedes. Under Prussian rule it became a major port. The city suffered severely during World War II; post-war restoration has been confined to its more important buildings.

The Gate of Prussian Homage, once known as the Royal Gate

The Castle of the Dukes of Pomerania, rebuilt in the Renaissance style

Exploring Szczecin

The old town of Szczecin is picturesquely laid out on a steep escarpment. The large **Castle of the Dukes of Pomerania** was founded in the mid-13th century and was rebuilt in the Renaissance style by Guglielmo di Zaccharia in 1575–7. It consists of five wings, with two interior courtyards and two towers. The east wing dates from the 17th century. After damage suffered during World War II, the castle was almost completely rebuilt and its once-magnificent interior re-created. The basement of the east wing houses the **Castle Museum**. In a Baroque building near the castle is the main section of the **National Museum**. From the

castle balcony overlooking the Odra, the **Tower of the Seven Cloaks**, the only remaining part of the city's medieval fortifications, can be seen. Across the road is the **Gate of Prussian Homage**, formerly the Royal Gate, one of a pair that was built under Swedish rule in 1726–8. The architect was Gerhard Cornelius de Wallrawe, and the sculptor Berhold Damart. North of the castle is the red-brick late Gothic **Church of Saints Peter and Paul** (Kościół św św Piotra i Pawla), while further along the banks of the Odra is **Ulica Wały Chrobrego**. This boulevard, an impressive municipal project of 1902–13, was known in German times as the Hakenterrasse

("Haken's Terrace") in honour of the mayor who initiated it. One of the buildings on the boulevard houses the **Maritime Museum**. From the terraces, with their decorative pavilions and a statue of *Hercules Fighting the Centaur* by Ludwig Manzel, there is a fine view of the harbour below.

North of the castle stands **Loitz House**, a sumptuous late Gothic town house built for the Loitz banking family in 1547. Further down, among the newly built townhouses in the old style, is the mainly 15th-century Baroque **town hall**. It houses the **Szczecin History Museum**. The **Cathedral of St James** (Katedra św Jakuba) was also rebuilt after almost complete wartime destruction; only the presbytery and west tower survived the bombing. It was originally erected in stages from the late 13th to the 15th centuries, with the involvement of the renowned architect Heinrich Brunsberg. The cathedral has several Gothic altars originating from other churches in Pomerania. From the cathedral it is possible to

View of Ulica Wały Chrobrego, with the Maritime Museum and local government offices in the distance

walk southwards towards the Gothic Church of St John (Kościół św Jana), founded by the Franciscans, or to wander through the part of the city stretching out to the west that was built in the late 19th century. Many town houses and villas in a variety of styles have been preserved here, and the area has numerous bars and restaurants.

🏛 National Museum

ul. Staromłyńska 27. 🄲 (0 91) 433 50 66. 🅆 www.muzeum.szczecin.pl ◐ Oct–May: 10am–5pm Tue, Thu, 9am–3:30pm Wed, Fri, 10am–4pm Sat, Sun; Apr–Sep: until 5pm. 🈚 (free on Thu).

Loitz House, once the home of a family of bankers

The museum's extensive collections comprise artifacts mainly from Western Pomerania. Of particular interest are the displays of Gothic ecclesiastical art and jewellery and the costumes of Pomeranian princes.

🏛 Maritime Museum

ul. Wały Chrobrego 3. 🄲 (0 91) 433 60 18. 🅆 www.muzeum.szczecin.pl ◐ Oct–Apr: 10am–4pm Tue–Sun; May–Aug: 10am–5pm Tue–Sun. 🈺 Mon. 🈚

The museum's principal theme is the history of seafaring in the Baltic. The archaeological displays include amber and silver jewellery and a medieval boat. There are also models of ships, nautical instruments and an ethnographical section. Boats and fishing vessels are displayed in a *skansen* behind the museum.

🏛 Castle Museum

ul. Korsarzy 34. 🄲 (0 91) 433 88 42. 🅆 www.zamek.szczecin.pl ◐ 9am–6pm Tue–Sun.

This museum is housed in the former crypt of the dukes of Pomerania. It contains the tin coffins of the last of the Gryfici dynasty, and a special exhibition on the history and the restoration of the castle.

Portal of the Cathedral of St James

🏛 Szczecin History Museum

ul. Mściwoja 8. 🄲 (0 91) 488 02 49. ◐ 10am–5pm Tue, Thu, 9am–3:30pm Wed, Fri, 10am–4pm Sat, Sun. 🈚

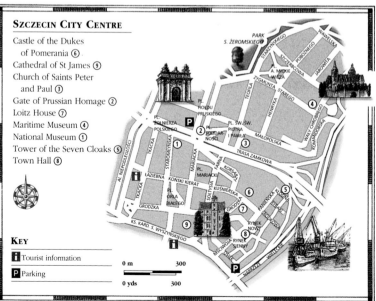

Szczecin City Centre

Castle of the Dukes of Pomerania ⑥
Cathedral of St James ⑨
Church of Saints Peter and Paul ③
Gate of Prussian Homage ②
Loitz House ⑦
Maritime Museum ④
National Museum ①
Tower of the Seven Cloaks ⑤
Town Hall ⑧

Key

🛈 Tourist information

🅿 Parking

0 m	300
0 yds	300

Around Wolin ❷

WOLIN'S FORESTS, deserted sandy beaches and picturesque, sometimes dramatic, coastal cliffs delight walkers and inspire photographers. Wolin also has plenty to offer those with an interest in historic buildings – the cathedral in Kamień Pomorski is one of the finest in Poland.

Wolin National Park ④
Apart from its beaches and lakes, the park is known for its bison, which can be seen in a special reserve. The bird life includes the rare sea eagle.

Międzyzdroje ③

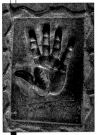

This renowned health resort was created in 1830. It has a seafront promenade and a pier from which the cliffs can be admired. It is also a good base for hiking in Wolin National Park.

Świnoujście ②
The town straddles Poland's two islands – Wolin and Uznam. The only way of moving between the two parts of the town is by ferry. It has a large port, wide beaches and the elegant buildings of a coastal resort.

Wolin ①
In the Early Middle Ages this small town was a major Baltic port. Today it is the venue for the Viking Festival that takes place every July as a reminder of the settlement's historic importance (see p33).

Stargard Szczeciński ❸

Road map B2. 🏛 71,000.
🚉 🚌 🛈 ul. Łokietka 3a (0 92 577 66 36).

WITH ITS OWN port in the Szczecin Lagoon at the mouth of the River Ina, Stargard Szczeciński once rivalled Szczecin as a merchant town of the Hanseatic League.

Almost three quarters of the old town was destroyed during World War II, although the Gothic defensive walls with their towers and gates survived. The town's finest building is the Gothic **Church of St Mary** (Kościół Mariacki), which was founded in the late 13th century but only given its present appearance by Heinrich Brunsberg in the mid-15th century. The rich decoration of glazed and moulded brick is striking. The magnificent town hall, built in the 16th century and remodelled in 1638, has a gable with intricate tracery. A pleasant

Interior of the Gothic Church of St Mary in Stargard Szczeciński

way to round off a trip to Stargard Szczeciński is to visit the café in the former salt granary, a Gothic building overlooking a spur of the Ina.

The **Regional Museum** has some militaria and an archaeological and ethnographical display.

🏛 **Regional Museum**
Rynek Staromiejski 3. 📞 (0 92) 577 25 56. ☐ 10am–4pm Tue–Sat, 10am–2pm Sun; Apr–Sep: until 6pm.

Drawsko Lakes ❹

Road map B2.

THE DRAWSKO LAKES are an oasis of quiet, unspoiled scenery. Their crystal-clear waters teem with fish and, in season, the forests are carpeted with mushrooms. The area is ideal for a canoeing or rowing holiday.

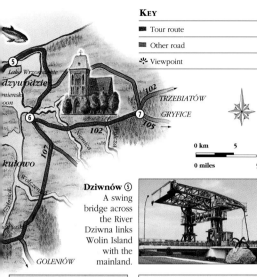

KEY

■ Tour route

▦ Other road

✤ Viewpoint

TRZEBIATÓW

GRYFICE

0 km   5

0 miles   5

Kamień Pomorski ⑥
The town was the seat
of a bishopric from 1176.
Its widely admired
cathedral contains a
well-preserved collection
of fine late Gothic
murals as well as
famous organs.

Dziwnów ⑤
A swing
bridge across
the River
Dziwna links
Wolin Island
with the
mainland.

GOLENIÓW

TIPS FOR DRIVERS

Tour length: 103 km (65 miles).
Stopping-off points: Plenty of
good cafés and restaurants are to
be found in Kamień Pomorski
and Międzyzdroje.
Additional features: Golf
course at Kołczewie. Bison
reserve ⭕ 1 Jun–15 Sep:
10am–6pm Tue–Sun; 16 Sep–
31 May: 9am–3pm Mon, Fri.

Świerzno ⑦
The modest timber-frame palace here was built for the Fleming
family in 1718–30. In the 17th century the family
also founded the timber-framed church that stands nearby.

**Lake Drawsko, the second-deepest
lake in Poland**

The largest of the lakes is
Drawsko, on whose shores
stands Stare Drawsko, with
ruins of a once-impressive
14th-century Teutonic
Knights' castle. In the
delightful spa town of
Polczyn Zdrój the mineral
springs are surrounded by a
park and there are some
elegant early 20th-century
sanatoria. **Złocieniec** has an
outstanding example of
Baroque architecture in the
form of a palace that was
built here in 1704–45.

Kołobrzeg ❺

Road map B1. 👥 46,000.
🚉 🚌 ℹ ul. Dubois 20 (0 94 352 23
11 or 352 32 87).
Ⓦ www.kolobrzeg.pl ⭕ 7:30am–
3:30pm Mon–Fri. 🎵 Kołobrzeg
Summer Music Festival.

THE FINE SANDY
beaches of
Kołobrzeg make it one
of the most popular
health resorts on the
Baltic coast. It has a
full complement of
hotels, sanatoria,
holiday homes and
fried-fish stalls, but it
is also a working
fishing port. In the
past it
was a
fortified
coastal town
of strategic
significance.

**The sturdy brick-built lighthouse
in Kołobrzeg harbour**

In summer the long
promenade, leading to the
lighthouse, is crowded with
holiday-makers. The brick-built
Cathedral of the Virgin Mary
(Katedra NMP) was begun in
1255 and later altered and
extended. Among the
remarkable objects it
contains is a chandelier
made by Johann
Apengheter of Lübeck
in 1327 depicting the
Virgin and St John the
Baptist. The Neo-Gothic
town hall was built by
the Berlin architect Karl
Friedrich Schinkel in
1829–32. It is surroun-
ded by alleys lined
with old houses.
The **fortress**,
now in ruins,
was unsuccess-
fully besieged
by Napoleon's
troops in 1807.

Darłowo ❻

Road map B1. 🏛 *15,300.* 🚌 🚉

Dᴀʀłᴏᴡᴏ, ꜱᴇᴛ 2.5 km (1½ miles) inland on the banks of the River Wieprza, is one of the most attractive towns of coastal Pomerania. In summer the waterfront district swarms with tourists and the fish stalls do a brisk trade, but the town's real charm lies in its old riverside district, where there are many historic buildings. The most prominent of these is the Gothic **Castle of the Dukes of Pomerania**. Founded in the 14th century, it was rebuilt several times and partially demolished in the 19th century; its surviving parts now house a museum.

The castle is associated with Erik of Pomerania, the warlike Duke of Słupsk, whose royal blood enabled him, in 1397, to hold the thrones of Denmark, Sweden and Norway. His turbulent rule was marked by constant warfare. He was finally deposed and returned to Darłowo, where he established the Duchy of Słupsk, crowning himself and, as Erik I, retaining his rule over Gotland. He was buried in the Church of St Mary (Kościoł Mariacki), and his sarcophagus, made in 1888, can be seen here in the sepulchral chapel. Erik may also have been the founder of the late Gothic **Chapel of St Gertrude** (Kaplica św Gertrudy) on Ulica Tynickiego, an unusual twelve-sided building.

Shifting dunes in Słowiński National Park

Słupsk ❼

Road map C1. 🏛 *99,000.* 🚌 🚉
🛈 *al. Wojska Polskiego 16 (0 59 842 43 26).* @ *it.slupsk@parr.slupsk.pl*
🎵 *International Festival of Organ Music (Jun–Aug).*

Fʀᴏᴍ 1368 ᴛᴏ 1648, this town on the River Słupia was the capital of the Duchy of Western Pomerania. The Renaissance ducal castle was built by Antonio Guglielmo di Zaccharia in 1580–87. Today it is the **Museum of Central Pomerania**, which, besides items of local interest, has the country's largest collection of portraits by the painter and writer Stanisław Ignacy Witkiewicz (1885–1939), better known as Witkacy.

The watermill opposite the castle, dating from about 1310, is one of the oldest in Poland. Now a branch of the museum, it houses an ethnographical collection. In the Dominican Church of St Hyacinth (Kościoł św Jacka) nearby are the black marble and alabaster tombs of Bogusław de Croy, the last of the dukes of Pomerania, and his mother, the Duchess Anna de Croy. They were carved by Kasper Gockhaller of Gdańsk

in 1682. The 14th-century Church of St Mary (Kościoł Mariacki) is also of interest.

🏛 Museum of Central Pomerania
ul. Dominikańska 5/9.
📞 *(0 59) 842 40 81–2.* 🖥 *www.mars. slubsk.pl/mps* 🕐 *1 May–15 Sep: 10am–6pm Tue–Sun; 16 Sep–30 Apr: 10am–4pm Wed–Sun.*

Effigy of Anna de Croy in the Church of St Hyacinthus

Słowiński National Park ❽

Road map C1. 🚌 📞 *(0 59) 811 72 04.* 🖥 *www.mos.gov.pl/kzpn*

Słᴏᴡɪ́ɴꜱᴋɪ ɴᴀᴛɪᴏɴᴀʟ ᴘᴀʀᴋ is renowned for its large, shifting sand dunes, which move at a rate of about 9 m (30 ft) a year, leaving the stumps of dead trees behind them. The area was once a gulf, of which the glacial lakes Łebsko and Gardno are vestiges. The park, a World Biosphere Reserve, is a haven for wild birds; more than 250 species, including the rare sea eagle, are found here.

The park's highest point, Rowokół, offers a fine view of the dunescape. At its foot is the village of Smołdzino, with a small Baroque church founded by Duchess Anna de Croy in the 17th century.

In the hamlet of Kluki, on Lake Łebsko, is a *skansen* dedicated to the ancient local Slovincian culture. Fishing equipment and agricultural implements are exhibited in

The castle of Erik of Pomerania, Duke of Słupsk, in Darłowo

the farmsteads. An electric train runs to the park from Rąbka, near the resort of Łeba. The town of Nowęcin, also near Łeba, has a Neo-Gothic palace built for the Wejher family in 1909. It now houses a hotel and restaurant.

Corner tower of the Gothic castle of the Teutonic Knights in Bytów

Bytów ⑨

Road map C1. *17,000.* *ul. Zamkowa 2 (0 59 822 55 97).* www.infotur-bin.info.pl

BYTÓW, WITH NEARBY Lębork, was the westernmost outpost of the territory held by the Teutonic Knights. The town, which after its conquest in 1466 was established as a Polish fiefdom, was ruled by the dukes of Pomerania, and later by Brandenburg and Prussia. It has been part of Poland since 1945.

Few of Bytów's historic buildings survive. The most interesting is the **castle** of the Teutonic Knights, which was built in 1390–1405 and was one of the first castles in Europe to be adapted for the use of firearms. It has four circular corner towers and a residential wing was added in about 1570. It houses the **Museum of Western Kashubia**, which contains a collection of artifacts relating to the ancient Kashubian culture.

Timber-framed fishermen's cottages in Jastarnia, on the Hel Peninsula

Museum of Western Kashubia
ul. Zamkowa 2. *(0 59) 822 26 23.* *16 Sep–30 Apr: 10am–4pm Tue–Fri, 10am–3pm Sat, Sun; 1 May–15 Sep: 10am–6pm Tue–Sun.*

Kashubia ⑩

See p262.

Hel Peninsula ⑪

Road map D1. *Jastarnia, ul. Sychty 47 (0 58 675 21 78).*

THE NARROW Hel Peninsula is about 34 km (22 miles) long and in width ranges from just 200 m (650 ft) to 3 km (2 miles). It is made up of sandbanks formed by sea currents; in the 18th century it was no more than a chain of islets. The peninsula is now the Nadmorski Park Krajobrazovy, an area of outstanding natural beauty. When the railway line to Hel was completed in 1922, resorts began to spring up on the peninsula. Their main attraction was the double beach – one part facing the sea, the other the Gulf of Gdańsk. At the base of the peninsula is the town of **Władysławowo**, named after Władysław IV, who founded a now-vanished fortress here. Today the town's boundaries embrace many resorts, such as Jastrzębia Góra, Cetniewo and Chałupy. **Jastarnia** is the most popular resort, as it still retains many of its original fishermen's cottages. The most elegant resort is **Jurata**, established in 1928; modernist hotels dating from the 1930s can also be seen here. At the very end of the peninsula is the fishing port and tourist resort of **Hel**, with its towering lighthouse and timber-framed fishermen's cottages. The former Protestant church, built in the 15th century, is now the **Fisheries Museum**. From Hel, passenger and tourist boats cross to Gdynia and Gdańsk.

Fisheries Museum
Hel, ul. Żeglarska. *(0 58) 675 05 52.* *mid-Jun–mid-Sep: 9am–6pm daily; mid-Sep–mid-Jun: 9am–4pm daily.*

The narrow Hel Peninsula, separating Puck Bay from the Baltic Sea

Kashubia ⑩

A TRIP TO the part of Kashubia known as Szwajcaria Kaszubska ("Kashubian Switzerland") is a chance to experience the culture of a people who have inhabited this area for centuries. The Kashubian Museum in Kartuzy has a collection of original embroidery, toys and snuffboxes carved from horn, in Chmielno are working potteries and in Wdzydze Kiszewskie is a *skansen* with traditional Kashubian cottages.

Kartuzy ①
The town takes its name from the Carthusians, who founded a monastery here in the 1380s. The collegiate church still stands. The Kashubian Museum re-creates the daily life of the region.

Chmielno ②
This village has several workshops producing traditional Kashubian pottery. Potters can be seen at work, and their products are for sale.

Kashubian Park Krajobrazowy ③
The national park in Szwajcaria Kaszubska offers some breathtaking views from the summit of its moraine hills.

Wdzydze Kiszewskie ④
As well as traditional peasant farmsteads, this *skansen* has a windmill, an inn, a school and a small church.

0 km 5
0 miles 5

Wieżyca ⑥
At 331 m (1,090 ft) above sea level, this is the highest point in Kashubia. Its slopes are popular for skiing in winter.

Kościerzyna ⑤
Although not in itself a scenic town, Kościerzyna is a good stopping place on a tour of Kashubia. A monument to Józef Wybicki, author of the Polish national anthem, stands in the town.

TIPS FOR DRIVERS

Tour length: *120 km (75 miles).*
Stopping-off points: *There are bars and restaurants in Kartuzy, Chmielno and Kościerzyna.*
Places of interest: *Kashubian Museum, Kartuzy.* [C] *(0 58) 681 03 78.* [ ] *8am–4pm Tue–Fri, 8am–3pm Sat, 10am–2pm Sun; outside holiday season 8am–4pm Tue–Fri, 8am–3pm Sat. Kashubian Pottery Museum, Chmielno.* [C] *(0 58) 684 22 89.* [ ] *9am–6pm daily; Nov–Mar: until 4pm.*

KEY

▬ Tour route

▬ Other road

☆ Viewpoint

◁ **Breakwaters along the Baltic Coast**

The three-masted training ship
Dar Młodzieży **moored in Gdynia**

Gdynia ⑫

Road map D1. 👥 *248,000.* 🚃 🚌
ℹ️ *ul. 3 maja 27 (0 58 621 75 24 or
628 54 66).* 🔗 *www.gydnia.pl* 🎭
*Days of the Sea (Jun); Festival of Polish
Feature Films (Oct).*

GDYNIA, UNTIL 1918 a small
fishing village, is one of
the most recently developed
towns in Poland. When, after
World War I, Poland regained
independence but did not
control the port of Gdańsk, the
authorities decided to
build a major port at Gdynia.
During World War II Gdynia
and its shipyard were used by
the German Kriegsmarine,
and the town was renamed
Gotenhafen by the Germans.
A landmark in Gdynia's post-
war history came in
December 1970, when
striking workers were fired on
by the militia. In 1980 a
monument in their honour
was erected.

A walk along the Northern
Pier offers an overview of the
port at work and a sight of
the town's most important
landmarks. By the quay are
two floating museums, the
ships *Błyskawica* and *Dar
Pomorza*. The *Błyskawica*
is a destroyer that saw action
in World War II alongside
Allied forces in Narvik,
Dunkirk and during the
Normandy landings. *Dar
Pomorza* is a three-masted
training vessel, built in 1909
and decommissioned in 1981.
It was replaced by the *Dar
Młodzieży*, which can
sometimes also be seen
moored in the port. At the
end of the pier is a statue of
the writer Joseph Conrad
(1857–1924), who was born
in Poland as Teodor Josef
Konrad Korzeniowski.
Beyond the pier stands
the **Marine Museum
and Aquarium**.

You can walk
along Gdynia's
seafront promenade
all the way to the
islet of Kępa
Redłowska.
A wander
around the city's
shopping area,
with its boutiques
and bars, is equally
enjoyable.

**Fish: street
ornament in
Gdynia**

⚓ ORP Błyskawica
al. Zjednoczenia.
📞 *(0 58) 626 37 27.* ⏱ *Jun–Aug:
10am–1:30pm, 2–5:30pm Tue–Sun;
Sep–May: 10am–1:30pm, 2–4:30pm
Tue–Sun.*

⚓ Dar Pomorza
al. Zjednoczenia.
📞 *(0 58) 620 23 71.* ⏱ *Sep–May:
10am–4pm Tue–Sun; Jun–Aug:
10am–6pm daily.*

**🏛 Marine Museum and
Aquarium**
al. Zjednoczenia. 📞 *(0 58) 621 70 21.*
⏱ *Sep–May: 10am–5pm Tue–Sun;
Jun–Aug: 9am–7pm.*

Sopot ⑬

Road map D1. 👥 *43,000.* 🚃 🚌
ℹ️ *ul. Dworcowa 4 (0 58 551 00 02).*
🔗 *www.kms.sopot.pl* ⏱ *9am–5pm
Mon–Fri.* 🎭 *International Festival of
Song (Aug).*

SOPOT IS THE MOST popular
resort on the Baltic coast.
It was established as a sea-
bathing centre in 1824 by
Jean Georges Haffner, a
physician in the Napoleonic
army who chose a spot on
the coast that since the 17th
century had been favoured by
the wealthy burghers of
Gdańsk for their mansions. Its
heyday came in the interwar
years, when it attracted some
of the richest people
in Europe. The pier
is a continuation of
the main street,
Ulica Bohaterów
Monte Cassino,
colloquially known
as Monciak. The pier is
512 m (1,680 ft long)
and the bench running
all the way around it
is the longest in
Europe. The pier is
filled with bars,
restaurants and cake
shops as well as
antique shops and
boutiques selling
amber. It is a pleasant
place to enjoy a beer and the
sea air. An alternative is coffee
at the Grand Hotel, built in
1924–7, which overlooks the
beach. This splendid Neo-
Baroque building once
housed a casino.

The town's narrow streets
hide many delightful
guesthouses. In the wooded
hills behind the town is the
Opera Leśna ("Opera in the
Woods"), built in 1909 and
the venue of the International
Song Festival (see p33).

The Grand Hotel in Sopot, overlooking the beach and the Gulf of Gdańsk

Malbork ⑭

MALBORK, THE CASTLE of the Teutonic Knights, was begun in the 13th century. In 1309 it was made capital of an independent state established by the order. The first major phase of building was the Assembly Castle, a fortified monastery later known as the Upper Castle. The Middle Castle was built some time after 1310, and the Palace of the Grand Master was begun in 1382–99 by Konrad Zöllner von Rotenstein. In 1457 the castle was taken by Poland and used as a fortress. It was restored in the 19th century, and again after World War II.

The well in the courtyard of the High Tower

Summer Refectory
It has double rows of windows and late Gothic palm vaulting supported on a granite central column. The Winter Refectory adjoins it on its eastern side.

★ Palace of the Grand Master
The grandeur of the four-storey palace was almost without equal in medieval Europe.

Upper Castle

★ Golden Gate
Built in the late 13th century, this is enclosed by a porch. The keystone in the vaulting is carved with the figure of Christ.

Church of St Mary
is presently being restored and is closed to visitors.

Cloistered Courtyard
The inner courtyard of the Upper Castle is surrounded by slender Gothic arches with triangular vaulting.

STAR SIGHTS

★ **Palace of the Grand Master**

★ **Golden Gate**

Lower Castle
These partly reconstructed farm buildings, abutting the former Chapel of St Lawrence, have been converted into a hotel.

VISITORS' CHECKLIST

Road map D1. 🏠 *40,000.* 🚌
🚉 🛈 *ul. Piastowska 15 (0 55 272 92 46).* **Castle Museum**
ul. Starościńska 1. 📞 *(0 55) 272 26 77.* 🕐 *1 May–30 Sep:*
9am–5pm Tue–Sun; 1 Oct–30 Apr: 9am–3pm Tue–Sun.
Courtyard 🕐 *1 hour longer.* 📷
📷 🍴 🚻 ♿ **Son et Lumière**
show *1 May–15 Oct; after dusk.*

Battlements
A good view of the towers and walls surrounding the castle can be had from the east side.

Teutonic Knight
The Teutonic Knights, or the Knights of the Teutonic Order of the Hospital of St Mary in Jerusalem, had a strict monastic code. In battle they were distinguished by the black crosses on their white cloaks.

Chapel of St Anne
Built in 1331–44 beneath the choir of the Church of St Mary, this contains the tombs of eleven Grand Masters.

The Altar of St Mary in the south aisle at Pelplin

Pelplin ⓯

Road map D2. ⓧ 8,500. 🚉 🚌
ℹ️ pl. Grunwaldzki 2 (0 58 536 14 54).

THE BEAUTIFUL Cistercian abbey at Pelplin is one of the finest examples of Gothic architecture in Poland. Work on the monastery began in 1276, when the Cistercians came to Pelplin.

The brick-built church, now a **cathedral**, dates largely from the 14th century, although its late Gothic vaulting was not completed until the late 15th and early 16th centuries. The imposing triple-naved basilica has no tower, and the west and east fronts are almost identical. The interior contains an outstanding collection of finely crafted furnishings, including

Gothic stalls with a rare carving of the Holy Trinity in which the Holy Ghost is depicted not as the customary dove but as a man. Other fine pieces include the 17th-century Mannerist and Baroque altar and a pulpit supported on a figure of Samson in combat with a lion. There are several paintings by Hermann Hahn, including a large *Coronation of the Virgin* on the high altar. The monastery was dissolved in 1823, and in 1824 the church became the **Cathedral of the Virgin Mary** (Katedra NMP). The monastery buildings now accommodate the **Diocesan Museum**, whose carved gallery contains a handsome collection of ecclesiastical art as well as illuminated manuscripts. The most highly prized exhibits are a Madonna cabinet from Kolonówka, a rare original Gutenberg Bible of 1435–55 and a 17th-century musical manuscript, the *Pelplin Tabulature for Organ*. A range of goldwork and liturgical objects are also displayed in the cathedral treasury.

Samson fighting a lion, Pelplin Cathedral

🔔 **Cathedral of the Virgin Mary**
ul. Mestwina 4. 📞 (0 58) 536 17 07.
🕐 9am–4pm Mon–Sat, and during services. ✉️

🏛️ **Diocesan Museum**
ul. ks. Biskupa Dominika 11.
📞 (0 58) 536 12 21. 🕐 11am–4pm Tue–Sat, 10am–5pm Sun.
⚫ on religious feast days.

Gniew ⓰

Road map D2. ⓧ 7,200. 🚉 🚌
🎫 Gniewniki (Jun); International Tournament for the Sword of Sobieski (Aug).

THIS PRETTY LITTLE town on the bank of the River Vistula retains a medieval atmosphere. Founded by the Teutonic Knights in 1276, it was later the seat of a commander of the order and in 1466 became part of Poland.

The town's narrow alleys lead into the **Market Square**, which is lined with arcaded buildings. While most date from the 18th century, some, like the town hall, have Gothic elements. Traces of the 14th to 15th-century fortifications that once protected Gniew from invaders still remain.

The Gothic **Church of St Nicholas** (Kościół św Mikołaja) towers over the town. Probably built in the first half of the 14th century, it retains its magnificent

Gniew seen from the River Vistula, framed by the Church of St Nicholas and the Castle of the Teutonic Knights

Kwidzyn Cathedral, seat of the bishops of Pomerania in the 13th century

interior, which includes Gothic vaulting and Mannerist, Baroque and Neo-Gothic altars.

The town's most distinctive feature is the **castle** of the Teutonic Knights. This imposing fortress was begun in 1283 and completed in the mid-14th century. The castle has a regular plan, with four corner turrets and the remains of a mighty keep in the northeastern corner.

In summer the castle hosts festivals, jousting tournaments and reconstructions of medieval banquets.

🏛 Castle Museum
ul. Zamkowa 2. 📞 (0 58) 535 35 29.
🕐 9am–5pm Tue–Sun.
⛪ Church of St Nicholas
ul. Okrzei 4. 📞 (0 58) 535 20 16.

Kwidzyn 🔟

Road map D2. 🏘 37,000. 🚉 🚌 🚹
ul. Piłsudskiego 21 (0 55 279 41 67 or 279 58 12). 🌐 www.nm.kwidzyn.pl

FROM 1243 UNTIL 1525, the small town of Kwidzyn was the capital of the Pomezania bishopric, one of four to be established in the territory ruled by the Teutonic Knights. After the order was dissolved, the town passed in turn to Prussia, Germany and Poland.

The **cathedral** standing on a high escarpment and the **castle** attached to it are fine examples of Gothic architecture. The cathedral was built in the 14th century on the site of an earlier church, of which only the

narthex (a portico or porch separated from the nave by a screen) remains. The porch dates from 1264–84.

In 1862–4 the cathedral was remodelled in the Neo-Gothic style by Friedrich August Stüler. The interior of this vast pseudo-basilica has Gothic murals, which unfortunately were excessively repainted in the 19th century. Many of the earlier furnishings are still in place, including a late Gothic bishop's throne of about 1510 and Baroque altars and tombs. The presbytery gives access to the tiny cell of the Blessed Dorothy of Mątowy, who ordered that she be immured there in 1393. By the north nave is the Baroque chapel of Otto Frederick von Groeben, which contains a tomb depicting the deceased accompanied in death by his three wives.

The castle resembles a knights' fortress, although it was in fact the seat of a chapter. It was built in 1322–47 and partially demolished in the 18th century. Among the interesting features of the castle are the well tower and

the exceptionally tall latrine tower, which is connected to the castle by a gallery supported on large arches.

Grudziądz 🔞

Road map D2. 🏘 101,000. 🚉 🚌

GRUDZIĄDZ, SITUATED on an escarpment overlooking the River Vistula, was once a major port. It was founded by the Teutonic Knights and became part of Poland in 1466. As a result of the Partitions of Poland, it became part of Prussia from 1772 and in 1918 was returned to Poland. Despite the damage it suffered during World War II, the town has some fine buildings. The Gothic **Church of St Nicholas** (Kościoł sw Mikołaja) was begun in the late 13th century and completed in the second half of the 15th. It contains a late Romanesque font from the 14th century. The former Benedictine abbey, including the Palace of the Abbesses of 1749–51, is also of interest. Part of the abbey now houses a museum and art gallery.

The huge complex of **harbour granaries**, 26 brick buildings built side by side along the waterfront, fulfilled a defensive function as well as being used for storage. From the town side they are hardly noticeable, but seen from the river the granaries appear to surround the entire hillside. They were built mostly in the 17th and 18th centuries, but some are significantly older.

🏛 Grudziądz Museum
ul. Wodna 2/5. 📞 (0 56) 465 90 63. 🌐 www.grudziadz.pl
🕐 10am–6pm Tue, 10am–3pm Wed, Thu, 1–6pm Fri, 10am–2pm Sun.

The granaries in Grudziądz

Chełmno ⑲

T HE LANDS OF Chełmno that Konrad, Duke of Mazovia, presented to the Teutonic Knights in 1228 were the beginning of the vast state established by the order. The knights' first city, Chełmno, was founded in 1233 and was initially intended to be the capital of their state but this honour went to Malbork *(see p264)*. The civic laws of Chełmno became a model for other cities.

VISITORS' CHECKLIST

Road map D2. 🏘 *21,200.* 🚌 *ul. Dworcowa.* 📞 *(0 56) 686 21 56.* 🌐 *www.chelmno.pl* ℹ *Rynek 28 (0 56 686 21 04).*

Exploring Chełmno

Chełmno's medieval street plan and 13th to 15th-century fortifications survive virtually intact. The town walls are set with 23 towers and a fortified gate, the **Grudziądz Gate**, which was converted into a Mannerist chapel in 1620. The town's finest building is the **town hall**, a late Renaissance building of 1567–72 with traces of earlier Gothic elements. It houses the Chełmno Museum. At the rear of the town hall is an iron measuring stick equalling 4.35 m (just over 14 ft) and known as the Chełmno Measure, or *pręt*. The Baroque building on Ulica Franciszkańska, dating from the turn of the 18th

The late Renaissance town hall in the Market Square

century, once housed the **Chełmno Academy**, which was founded in 1692.

Six Gothic churches have been preserved in Chełmno. The largest of these is the **Church of the Assumption** (Kościół Wniebowz-ięcia NMP) of 1280–1320, a fine aisled building containing early Gothic frescoes and stone carvings. Two monastery churches, the **Church of St James** (Kościół św Jakuba) and the **Church of Saints Peter and Paul** (Kościół św Piotra i Pawła), date from the same period. The Abbey of the Cistercian Nuns, established in the late 13th century, is an exceptional group of buildings. It was later transferred to Benedictine

Baroque high altar in the Church of the Assumption, Chełmno

monks and then passed to the Catholic sisters who run a hospital here today. The entrance on Ulica Dominikańska leads through to an internal courtyard, which in turn gives access to the **Church of St John the Baptist** (Kościół św Jana Chrzciciela), built in 1290–1340. It has two

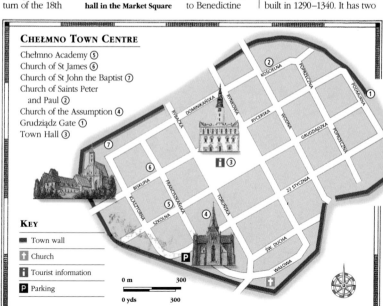

CHEŁMNO TOWN CENTRE

Chełmno Academy ⑤
Church of St James ⑥
Church of St John the Baptist ⑦
Church of Saints Peter and Paul ②
Church of the Assumption ④
Grudziądz Gate ①
Town Hall ③

KEY

▪ Town wall

✝ Church

ℹ Tourist information

🅿 Parking

0 m   300

0 yds   300

storeys, the lower one having two naves, and the upper a single nave that was reserved for the choir of the Order of Teutonic Knights.

🏛 Chełmno Museum

Rynek. 📞 (0 56) 686 16 41.
🕐 10am–4pm Tue–Fri, 10am–3pm Sat, 10am–1pm Sun. 🌐

ENVIRONS: In Chełmża, 23 km (14 miles) north of Chełmno, stands the Gothic Cathedral of the Holy Trinity, which was built originally in 1251–1359 and rebuilt after 1422.

Bydgoszcz ⑳

Road map C2. 🏠 373 000. 🚉 🚌
ℹ️ ul. Zygmunta Augusta 10 (0 52 322 84 32 or 322 23 50).
🔲 www.bydgoszcz.pl 🎭 Bydgoszcz Music Festival (Sep); Musica Antiqua Europae Orientalis (every 3 years, Sep).

BYDGOSZCZ LIES at the confluence of the River Brda and the Bydgoszcz Canal, which then flow into the Vistula. The city was only briefly part of the state of the Teutonic Knights, after which its fate was linked with that of the rest of Poland. It was the scene of dramatic events on 3 September 1939 when the town's German minority attempted to stage a coup. The Nazis entered the town and massacred thousands of the Polish population.

The **old town** of Bydgoszcz is set on a bend of the Brda. It has several monumental town houses, the late Gothic church of Saints Nicholas and Martin (Kościół św św Mikołaja i Marcina) and two monasteries: a Bernadine monastery with a church of 1545–52, and the

Church and Convent of the Poor Clares (Kościół Klarysek), which today houses a **Regional Museum**. The half-timbered **granaries** on the banks of the Brda, built in the 18th and 19th centuries, was used for the salt and wheat that the town traded and to store the beer for which it was renowned.

🏛 Regional Museum

ul. Gdańska 4. 📞 (0 52) 322 75 76.
🕐 10am–6pm Tue, Wed, Fri, 10am–4pm Thu, 12–4pm Sat, Sun. 🌐

Toruń ㉑

See pp270–3.

Golub-Dobrzyń ㉒

Road map D2. 🏠 12,800. 🚉
🚌 🎭 International Jousting Tournament (Jun).

THIS PICTURESQUE town was originally two separate settlements, one on either side of the River Drwęca. During the Partitions, Golub was part of Prussia and Dobrzyń part of Russia. Golub's principal feature is the large **castle** built by the Teutonic Knights in 1293–1310. From 1466 Golub was part of Poland, and in the 17th century the castle became the residence of Queen Anna Vasa of Sweden, sister of Zygmunt III Vasa. The castle was rebuilt for her in 1616–23 in the Renaissance style. Highly educated and with an interest in botany and natural medicine, Anna Vasa was an unusual woman for her time. She remained a spinster, reputedly because of her ugly appearance. Today the castle

The castle built by the Teutonic Knights in Golub-Dobrzyń

hosts such events as jousting tournaments and oratory competitions, as well as New Year's balls, at which revellers say that the ghost of Queen Anna appears. By ironic coincidence, the Miss Poland beauty contests are also held here.

🏛 Castle Museum

ul. Zamkowa. 📞 (0 56) 683 24 55.
🕐 Jun–Sep: 9am–7pm daily; Oct–May: 9am–5pm daily.

Graduation tower for the production of salt in Ciechocinek

Ciechocinek ㉓

Road map D3. 🏠 11,000. 🚉 🚌
ℹ️ (0 54 283 31 11). 🔲 www. ciechocinek.pl 🎭 Festival of Kujawy and Dobrzyń folklore (Jun); International Festival of Roma Song and Culture (Jul).

CIECHOCINEK IS one of Poland's best-known spa towns, which grew and prospered thanks to its iodine-rich salt springs. It is not strictly part of Pomerania but of Kujawy, and has always been a Polish town. The town came into being in 1824, when Stanisław Staszic started to build saltworks and the first of three salt graduation towers. The "towers" are huge wooden frames filled with thorny brushwood which, washed with brine, accumulates salt crystals. Each "tower" is more than 1.7 km (1 mile) wide. Other features of Ciechocinek are the group of baths built in a variety of styles between 1845 and 1913, a fine park with a flower clock, a pump room designed by Edward Cichocki, a bandstand and open-air theatre, and numerous elegant boarding houses, sanatoria and hotels dating from the start of the 20th century.

Toruń ❷

Stained glass

Toruń's principal claim to fame is as the birthplace of the astronomer Nicolaus Copernicus *(see p273)*, but it is also renowned for its architecture. The city was founded by the Teutonic Knights in 1233 and quickly became a major centre of trade; in 1454, when its citizens rebelled against the knights' rule, it passed to the kings of Poland. The old town of Toruń, picturesquely situated on the banks of the River Vistula, retains its medieval street plan, and has a rare calm, since most of the streets are closed to traffic.

Star House, an early Baroque town house in the Old Market Square

The Wilam Horzyca Theatre

🎭 Wilam Horzyca Theatre

pl. Teatralny 1. 📞 *(0 56) 622 50 21.*
The delightful theatre, in the Art Nouveau style with Neo-Baroque elements, was built in 1904 by the Viennese architects Ferdinand Fellner and Hermann Helmer. The Kontakt Theatre Festival is held here each year in early summer, bringing together theatre performers from all over Europe and drawing large and enthusiastic audiences to its performances.

⛪ Church of the Virgin Mary

ul. Marii Panny. 📞 *(0 56) 622 31 39.*
The Gothic Church of the Virgin Mary (Kościół NMP) was built for Franciscan monks in 1270–1300. It has an unusually richly ornamented east gable. Late 14th-century wall paintings can be seen in the south aisle, while in the north aisle is a 16th-century Mannerist organ loft, the oldest in Poland. By the presbytery is the mausoleum of Anna Vasa *(see p269)*, sister of Zygmunt III, made in 1636. She was of royal blood but could not be buried at Wawel Castle because she was of the Protestant faith.

The elaborate east end of the Church of the Virgin Mary

🏛 Old Market Square

The Old Market Square is the city's finest open space and still the vibrant heart of its historic district. The centrepiece is the town hall, but on all four sides of the square there are fine buildings. On the south side, at No. 7, is the Meissner Palace, built in 1739 for Jakob Meissner, mayor of Toruń, and given a Neo-Classical façade in 1798. Many of the town houses retain their original details, such as that at No. 17, with a portal made in 1630. The most attractive house in the square is Star House, at No. 35 on the east side, built in 1697. It has a richly ornamented façade, with stuccowork motifs of fruit and flowers. In the square stands a monument to Nicolaus Copernicus made by Friedrich Tiecek in 1853, and a fountain with the figure of a raftsman who, according to legend, rid the citizens of Toruń of a plague of frogs by playing his fiddle.

The town hall in the Old Market Square

VISITORS' CHECKLIST

Road map D2. 🏠 *203,000.*
🚊 *Toruń Główny, ul. Kujawska 1
(0 56 94 36).* 🚉 *Toruń Miasto,
pl. 18 Stycznia.* 🚌
🛈 *ul. Piekary 37/39
(0 56 621 09 31).*
🎭 *Theatre Festival (Jun);
Probaltica Baltic Arts and Music
Festival (mid–May).*

🏛 Town Hall

Rynek Staromiejski 1. **Regional Museum** 📞 *(0 56) 622 70 38.*
◻ *9am–4pm Tue–Sun.* **Tower**
◻ *May–Oct: 10am–4pm.* 🎟

The town hall, an imposing three-storey building with internal courtyard, was built in 1391–9. In 1602–5 the Gdańsk architect Antonis van Opbergen added the third storey and gave the building a Mannerist appearance. The lower parts of the tower date from the 13th century. Standing 42 m (138 ft) high, it commands a fine view over the city. The town hall now houses a museum featuring Gothic art, 19th-century paintings and local crafts.

The building's original interiors are also noteworthy, especially the vaulting of the former bakery and wool stalls on the ground floors of the east and west wings. The basement accommodates a restaurant and a popular pub, *Pod Aniołem.*

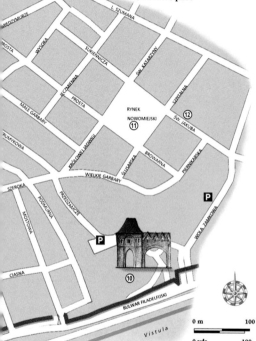

KEY

▬	City walls
🛈	Tourist information
P	Parking

TORUŃ CITY CENTRE

The Church of the Virgin Mary seen from the top of the town hall tower

Exploring Toruń

Toruń gingerbread

ORUŃ SURVIVED World War II relatively unscathed. It has well-preserved city walls and a series of gates that once opened onto the quayside. Granaries dating from the 15th to the 19th centuries still line the streets leading down to the river. The Cathedral of Saints John the Baptist and John Evangelist and the richly ornamented Palace of the Bishops of Kujawy are two of Toruń's finest buildings and the Copernicus Museum stands as a memorial to the city's most famous son.

Church of the Holy Spirit

Rynek Staromiejski. *(0 56) 655 48 62.*
The Baroque Church of the Holy Spirit (Kościoł św Ducha) in the Old Market Square was built in the mid-18th century for the Protestant community of Toruń. It was begun by Andreas Adam Bähr, and completed by Ephraim Schroeger.

Copernicus House

ul. Kopernika 15/17. *(0 56) 622 67 48.*
Oct–Apr: 10am–4pm Tue–Sun; May–Sep: 10am–6pm Tue–Sun.
These two neighbouring Gothic town houses from the 15th century are outstanding examples of Hanseatic merchants' houses. The meticulously painted façades and fine carving of the arched gables bear witness to the city's former wealth. The house at No. 17 was that of Mikołaj Kopernik, a merchant and the father of the boy who was to become the famous astronomer. The house, although it may not be the one in which the younger Mikołaj was born, is now a museum.

The Crooked Tower, part of the fortifications on the River Vistula

Crooked Tower

ul. Pod Krzywą Wieżą.
The Crooked Tower is one of Toruń's greatest attractions. It is part of the town's old fortifications system, and was probably built in the first half of the 14th century. Although it leans significantly from the perpendicular, the ceilings that were added later are perfectly level – so that beer glasses can be set down on the tables in the pub that it now houses with no danger of their sliding off.

Gothic Granary

ul. Piekary 4.
The most remarkable of the many Gothic granaries still standing in Toruń is that on the corner of Ulica Piekary and Ulica Rabiańska. Although the granary was rebuilt in the 19th century, it retains its towering ornamental gable with fine pointed arches.

Palace of the Bishops of Kujawy

ul. Żeglarska 8.
The palace was built by the Bishop Stanisław Dąmbski in 1693. In the 19th century it was converted into a hotel and then into a mess for military officers. Subsequent restoration work undid the damage inflicted by these conversions and returned the building to its former elegance. It is now the Academy of Fine Arts.

Cathedral of Saints John the Baptist and John the Evangelist

Cathedral of Saints John the Baptist and John the Evangelist

ul. Żeglarska. *(0 56) 622 32 62.*
The origins of the Cathedral of Saints John the Baptist and John the Evangelist (Kościoł św św Janóv) go back to 1250. The oldest surviving part of the cathedral is the presbytery. The nave, with its numerous side chapels, was completed by Hans Gotland in about 1500, long after the tower had been finished in 1433. The interior is a treasury of art. The

A room in the Copernicus House

NICOLAUS COPERNICUS

Nicolaus Copernicus (Mikołaj Kopernik; 1473–1543), astronomer, mathematician, economist, doctor and clergyman, was born in Toruń. For most of his life he lived in Warmia. He wrote treatises on economics, but gained the greatest renown for his astronomical observations. His heliocentric theory of the universe, which he expounded in *De Revolutionibus Orbium Celestium* (1543), posited the fact that the planets rotate around the Sun.

Renaissance epitaph to Copernicus in Toruń

presbytery contains some fine 16th-century mural paintings. There are also altars, chandeliers, stained-glass windows, sculpture and many paintings. In one of the side chapels in the south aisle is the Gothic font where Nicolaus Copernicus was baptized and a memorial to him of about 1580. He was buried in Frombork Cathedral *(see p278)*.

♟ Castle of the Teutonic Knights
ul. Przedzamcze.
Little more than ruins remain of the castle that the Teutonic Knights built in Toruń. Before the castle at Malbork *(see pp264–5)* was built, Toruń was the knights' capital.

The castle was built in the 13th century and extended in the 14th. However, it was destroyed in 1454 when the people of Toruń rose up in rebellion against the knights. Only the latrine tower – a tower

overhanging a stream that acted as a sewer – were left standing, although part of the cellars and cloisters survive. The late Gothic house that was built on the site in 1489, probably with materials scavenged from the castle, was the meeting house of the Brotherhood of St George.

♞ New Market Square
The new town emerged as a separate civic entity in 1264. Although it does not have as many historic buildings as the old town, there is a good deal of interest here. In summer the square is filled with fruit and vegetable stalls. In the centre, where the town hall once stood, is a former Protestant church, built in 1824, probably by the German architect Karl Friedrich Schinkel. It has been converted into a gallery of contemporary art. Fine houses, some with ornate façades like that of the Baroque house at No. 17, surround the square. On the corner of Ulica Królowej Jadwigi and the square is the Golden Lion pharmacy, a brick-built house originating

in the 15th century. At the corner of Ulica Ślusarska is the *Blue Apron Inn*, with a Baroque façade of about 1700, today a popular café.

♟ Church of St James
ul. św Jakuba. ☎ (0 56) 622 29 24.
The Gothic Church of St James (Kościoł św Jakuba) was built in the first half of the 14th century as the new town's parish church. It was first used by Cistercian monks, and then by Benedictines. It contains wall paintings of the second half of the 14th century. In the south aisle is a late 14th-century Gothic Crucifix in the form of the Tree of Life, in which the figure of Christ is nailed to the branches of a tree containing the figures of the prophets. Above the rood beam is a rare depiction of the Passion of about 1480–90, consisting of 22 scenes of the Stations of the Cross.

Gothic tower of the Church of St James in the new town

🏛 Ethnographical Museum
ul. Wały gen. Sikorskiego 19.
☎ (0 56) 622 80 91. ⏰ May–Sep: 9am–4pm Mon, Wed, Fri, 10am–6pm Tue, Thu, Sat, Sun; Oct–Apr: 10am–4pm Sat, Sun, 9am–4pm Tue–Fri. 🎟 (free on Mon).
The museum contains fishing implements and folk art. There is also a *skansen*, in which wooden houses from the region of Kujawy, Pomerania and Ziemia Dobrzyńska are displayed.

Latrine tower, the surviving part of the Castle of the Teutonic Knights

WARMIA, MAZURIA AND BIAŁYSTOK REGION

K NOWN AS THE LAND OF A THOUSAND LAKES, *northeastern Poland is blessed with vast forests and undulating moraine hills as well as a large number of lakes and rivers. There are no major industrial areas. Its three regions, Warmia, Mazuria and Białostoc-czyzna, are ethnically diverse and have had very different histories.*

Warmia, the western part of the region, was once inhabited by the early Prussians, and in the 13th century was taken over by the Teutonic Knights, who established a bishopric here. Warmia became part of Poland in 1466. Under the Partitions it was transferred to Prussia, and was not returned to Poland until 1945. Warmia has many historic churches.

Mazuria and the Iława Lake District at its southern and eastern fringes were also once controlled by the Teutonic Knights. When the order was secularized in 1525, the region became known as ducal Prussia and was ruled by the Hohenzollern family, although until 1657 it was a Polish fiefdom. The area's subsequent history is linked to that of Germany, and it did not become part of Poland again until

1945. Many castles were built by the Knights and some Prussian mansions can be seen here today.

The Suwałki and Augustów lakelands and Białostocczyzna form the region's eastern part, which once belonged to the kingdom of Lithuania. The area was covered in primeval forests, and three – the Augustów, Knyszyńska and Białowieża forests – remain today. The Biebrza valley contains Poland's largest stretches of marshland and peat swamps and offers plenty for naturalists. Those interested in religious culture are also well served: the Orthodox church in Grabarka, the old monastery of the Orthodox order of St Basil in Supraśl, the mosque in Kruszyniany and the synagogue in Tykocin represent a panoply of faiths.

View from the belfry of Frombork Cathedral

◁ **Sunset over the lakelands of northeast Poland**

Exploring Warmia, Mazuria and Białystok Region

NORTHEASTERN POLAND is an ideal place for a longer holiday. It is suitable for watersports such as sailing trips on the Mazurian Lakes or canoeing expeditions down the Czarna Hańcza or Krutynia rivers, and there are also plenty of opportunities for cycling tours. For unspoiled primeval scenery, the Białowieża Forest National Park with its bison reserve and the Biebrza marshes, with their population of nesting birds, are almost without equal.

Szczurkowo, a village where storks outnumber people

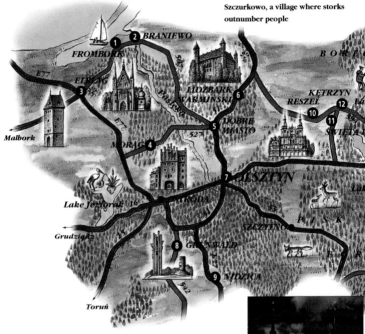

SIGHTS AT A GLANCE

Baroque façade of the Jesuit church in Święta Lipka

GETTING AROUND

The main road is Highway No. 16 from Grudziądz via Olsztyn to Augustów. Highway E77 goes from the south to Elbląg, highway 51 runs from Olsztyn to the border with the Russian Kaliningrad District, while highway 19 links Augustów with Białystok. Charter flights depart from Szymany, the region's only airport, near the town of Szczytno, and there are also connections with some airports in Germany. There are rail links with all major towns, and buses link other towns in the region.

The forests of Suwalszczyzna, carpeted with mushrooms

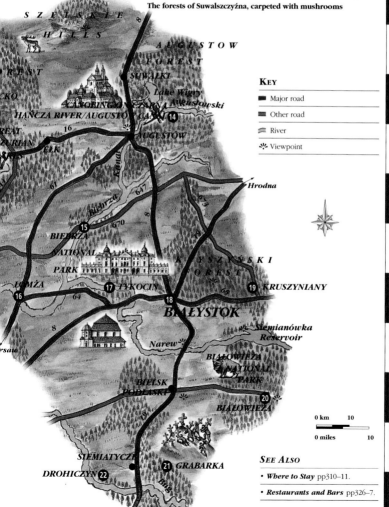

KEY

■ Major road

■ Other road

≈ River

☀ Viewpoint

SEE ALSO

- **Where to Stay** pp310–11.
- **Restaurants and Bars** pp326–7.

Frombork ●

THE HISTORY OF THIS FORTIFIED town goes back to the second half of the 13th century, when it became a Warmian chapter (diocesan capital). The Gothic cathedral, which was erected in 1342–88, has an unusual form, with no towers on its west end, giving it the appearance of a Cistercian monastery, and an eight-bay nave that allowed each member of the chapter to have a separate altar. There are also several canons' stalls in the chancel. The cathedral is surrounded by defensive walls set with towers and pierced by a large main gate in its south side. In the cathedral grounds are a bishop's palace and chapterhouse.

VISITORS' CHECKLIST

Road map D1. **Cathedral**
ul. Katedralna. ◯ 9:30am–
4:30pm Mon–Sat. **Copernicus
Tower** ◯ 9:30am–6pm daily.
Museum 【 (0 55) 243 72 18.
◯ 9am–4pm Tue–Sun.
Planetarium 【 (0 55) 243 73 92.
◯ 9am–4pm daily. **Summer
organ recitals** noon and 3pm.

Altar of St Anne
The Altar of St Anne, in the north aisle, has as its focal point this subtle painting of 1639 by the Gdańsk artist Bartholomäus Strobel.

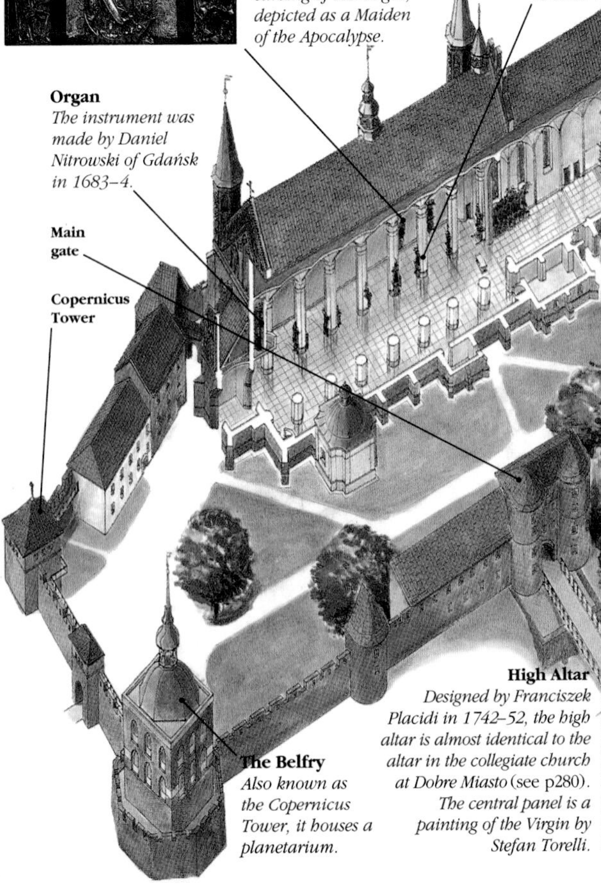

Former High Altar
Commissioned by Bishop Łukasz Watzenrode, uncle of Nicolaus Copernicus, the high altar was made in Toruń in 1504. It is in the form of a polyptych and is now in the south aisle. The central panel has a carving of the Virgin, depicted as a Maiden of the Apocalypse.

Bishop's Palace
The palace now houses the Copernicus Museum.

Organ
The instrument was made by Daniel Nitrowski of Gdańsk in 1683–4.

Main gate

Copernicus Tower

The Belfry
Also known as the Copernicus Tower, it houses a planetarium.

High Altar
Designed by Franciszek Placidi in 1742–52, the high altar is almost identical to the altar in the collegiate church at Dobre Miasto (see p280). The central panel is a painting of the Virgin by Stefan Torelli.

Braniewo ❷

Road map D1. 🏛 17,100.
🚌 🚉

THE FORTIFIED town of Braniewo was founded by the Teutonic Knights in 1250. It was the seat of the bishops of Warmia and later became the diocesan capital of Warmia. A member of the Hanseatic League, the town was a busy port and grew prosperous through the linen trade. During the Counter-Reformation it played an important role as the first Jesuit centre in Poland: the Hosianum Jesuit College was founded here in 1565, and a papal college set up in 1578.

Just 8 km (5 miles) of the Russian border, Braniewo has become an important transit point for travellers crossing from one country to the other. Although it suffered severe damage during World War II, several fine buildings are still to be seen here.

⛪ Church of St Catherine
ul. Katedralna. [(0 55) 243 24 29.
The nave of the Gothic Church of St Catherine (Kościół św Katarzyny) dates from 1343–81 and the vaulting and tower from the 15th century. War damage reduced the church to little more than ruins, but it has been extensively restored.

Church of St Catherine
in Braniewo

⛪ Church of St Anthony
ul. Królewiecka.
[(0 55) 243 23 88.
The Neo-Classical Church of St Anthony (Kościół św Antoniego) was built in 1807–37 by the German architect Karl Friedrich Schinkel. Originally Protestant, it is now a Catholic church.

🗼 Tower of the Bishop's Castle
ul. Gdańska. ⬤ to the public.
The tower, built in the 13th century as a town gate, led from the Castle of the Bishops of Warmia to a close connecting it to the town walls.

Elbląg ❸

Road map D1. 🏛 127,000. 🚌 🚉
🛈 ul. 1 Maja 30 (0 55 232 73 73).
@ portur@elblag.com.pl

ONCE A LARGE port on a par with Gdańsk, Elbląg is today known for its large ABB engineering plant, its

Postmodern houses in the old town of Elbląg

restored old town and as the home of EB beer, which is enjoyed throughout Poland. Founded in 1246 by the Teutonic Knights, the town was part of the Polish Republic from 1466 to 1772, when under the Partitions it passed to Prussian rule. After the devastation caused by World War II, only the most important old buildings of Elbląg were rebuilt. The Brama Targowa tower is all that remains of the former Gothic fortifications that surrounded the town.

In the old town, just a few town houses, on Ulica Wigilijna, survive. Today a programme of rebuilding is under way; new houses in the style of the old Hanseatic merchants' houses, with stairways and their typical gables, are revitalizing the old town. The quarter is well provided with friendly bars and good restaurants.

⛪ Church of the Virgin Mary
ul. Kuśnierska 6. [(0 55) 232 53 86 or 236 16 33. ⬤ 10am–6pm Mon–Sat, 10am–5pm Sun.
This Gothic church with a double aisle was built for Dominican monks in the 14th century. After World War II it became the EL art gallery.

⛪ Church of St Nicholas
ul. Mostowa 18. [(0 55) 232 69 79 or 232 45 85.
The Church of St Nicholas (Kościół św Mikołaja) was begun in the 13th century and completed in 1510. The interior includes a font from 1387 by Bernhuser, a *Crucifixion* ascribed to Jan van der Matten and a late Gothic altar with the Adoration of the Magi.

The EL art gallery in the Church of the Virgin Mary

THE ELBLĄG CANAL

The Elbląg Canal is one of the most extraordinary feats of hydraulic engineering in Poland. A network of canals and locks connecting a number of lakes, it was built in 1848–72 by the Dutchman Georg Jacob Steenke. Including its branches, its total length is 212 km (133 miles). Ingenious slipways enable barges to be hauled overland from one lake to another where the difference in the water levels is too high for conventional locks to be built: there are five slipways along the 10-km (6-mile) section between

Buczyniec and Całuny, and from the canalside ships can be seen being hauled along them. You can book a boat trip along the canal that will take you through the Vistula valley and Iława Lake District.

Portait by Gerrit Honthorst in the Herder Museum in Morąg

Morąg ❹

Road map D2. 🏠 14,900. 🚊 🚌

MORĄG, LOCATED in the lakelands of Iławski Morąg, was founded by the Teutonic Knights – like all other towns in the region. It received its municipal charter in 1327. Despite joining the Prussian Union, Morąg remained part of the state of the Teutonic Knights, and up until 1945 its history was linked to that of ducal Prussia. In the town are the remains of a 14th-century Teutonic castle, a Gothic town hall that was rebuilt after World War II, and the Church of St Joseph (Kościół św Józefa), built in the 14th century and extended in the late 15th, with Gothic polychromes from that time.

Morąg is the birthplace of the German philosopher Gottfried von Herder (see below). A **museum** dedicated to him is housed in a Baroque palace dating from 1717–19 that once belonged to the Dohn family.

🏛 **Johann Gottfried von Herder Museum**
ul. Dąbrowskiego 54.
📞 *(0 89) 757 28 48.* ⭕ *9am–5pm Tue–Sun.* 🈯

Dobre Miasto ❺

Road map E2. 🏠 11,000. 🚊 🚌

DOBRE MIASTO, founded in 1329, owes its historical importance to the fact that in 1347 it became the seat of a college of canons of the diocese of Warmia. The vast Gothic collegiate church that they established was constructed in the second half of the 14th century.

Its interior has two Gothic side altars as well as a Baroque high altar identical to that made by Franciszek Placidi for Frombork Cathedral *(see p278)*. The church also has richly decorated Baroque stalls, which have remarkable Gothic steps carved into them in the shape of lions.

Interior of the Gothic collegiate church in Dobre Miasto

The Gothic cloisters of the Bishop's Castle in Lidzbark

Lidzbark Warmiński ❻

Road map E1. 🏠 17,200. 🚊 🚌

FROM 1350 TO 1795 Lidzbark was the main residence of the bishops of Warmia, and one of the region's major towns. Picturesquely set on a bend of the River Łyna, the town is dominated by the medieval Bishops' Castle. The massive edifice with corner towers was built in the second half of the 14th century. Of special interest are the Palace of Bishop Grabowski and the Great Refectory in the east wing, the Rococo chapel and armoury in the south wing, the Small Refectory in the west wing and the bishops' apartments in the north wing. The cloistered courtyard has murals. The astronomer Nicolaus Copernicus *(see p273)* lived here as secretary and physician to his uncle, Bishop Łukasz von Wantzenrode, in 1503–10. The castle now houses the **Warmia Museum** and a bar and art gallery in its cellars.

On the opposite bank of the Łyna, in the historic town centre, stands the fine **Gothic Church of Saints Peter and Paul** (Kościół św św Piotra i Pawła). There are also remnants of the city walls, and the main gate, the Brama Wysoka, still stands. The former Protestant church (now Orthodox) nearby was built in 1821–3 by Karl Friedrich Schinkel.

JOHANN GOTTFRIED VON HERDER (1744–1803)

The German writer and philosopher Johann Gottfried von Herder, who was born in Morąg, was one of the great figures of the Enlightenment. He studied theology in Königsberg (Kaliningrad) before entering the priest-hood. He saw the importance of nations in the making of history and the role of culture and language in preserving national identity. While living in Riga, he recorded Latvian folk songs.

🏛 Regional Museum

pl. Zamkowy 6. **[** (0 89) 767 21 11.
◯ 1 May–30 Sep: 9am–5pm
Tue–Sun; 1 Oct–30 Apr: 9am–4pm
Tue–Sun. **◖** Mon.
On display is a selection of
Warmian art and a unique
collection of icons from the
Convent of the Old Believers'
in Wojnowo (see p284).

🔒 Church of Saints Peter and Paul

ul. Kościelna 1. **[** (0 89) 767 40 95.

**The High Gate, part of the
defences of Olsztyn old town**

Olsztyn **➐**

Road map E2. 🏘 158,000. 🚉 🚌
ℹ ul. Piastowska 4 (0 89 535
38 38 or 527 29 12). **◯** 8:30am–
4pm Mon–Fri, 9am–noon Sat.
🎭 Olsztyn Blues Nights; Castle
Poetry Readings (Jul).

OLSZTYN IS THE LARGEST city
in Warmia and Mazuria
and the main town of the two
regions. It is a centre of both
academic and cultural life as
well as a major city. It is also
associated with several
sporting heroes,
particularly in
speedway and
aerobatics. It hosts the various
events that make up the
Olsztyn Summer Arts festival
(see p33).

The Gothic Castle of the
Warmian Chapter, which was
built in the 14th century,
formed the beginning of the
city. The castle was built on a
hill on the banks of the Łyna.
It was a four-sided fortress of
modest proportions with
residential quarters in the
north wing and a service
wing to the south. The palace
in the east wing was added in
1756–8. The finest part of the
building is the refectory,
which has intricate crystalline
vaulting. On the wall of the
cloister is a remarkable
diagram of an equinox
probably drawn by Nicolaus
Copernicus, who combined
his duties as an administrator
of the chapter in Olsztyn with
his astronomical obser-
vations. The castle now
houses the **Museum of
Warmia and Mazuria**, which
has a special section
dedicated to Nicolaus
Copernicus. The first floor
contains an ethnographical
and natural history collection.

The castle's fortifications
were linked to the city walls,
which were built after 1353
on the far side of the moat.
The moat today has an open-
air theatre that is used for
concerts in summer.

In the picturesque old town
of Olsztyn, set on a slope, are
remnants of the walls and the
High Gate. The quaint little
Market Square surrounded by
arcaded houses was built
during the post-war
reconstruction of the city,
but the houses retain their
original cellars, which today
are given over to bars,
restaurants and cafés.
Standing in the middle of the
square is a Baroque town
hall, whose wings were
added in 1927–9.

Another important building
in the Market Square is the
Gothic **Cathedral of St
James** (Katedra św Jakuba),
most probably built between
1380 and 1445. The
exceptionally fine crystalline
vaulting was added in the
early 16th century.

🏛 Museum of Warmia and Mazuria

ul. Zamkowa 2. **[** (0 89) 527 95 96.
@ muzeum@mailbox.olsztyn.pl
◯ 1 May–3 Sep: 9am–5pm
Tue–Sun; 4 Sep–30 Apr: 10am–4pm
Tue–Sun.

🔒 Cathedral of St James

ul. Staszica 12. **[** (0 89) 527 32 80.

ENVIRONS: Barczewo, 10 km
(6 miles) east of Olsztyn, is
the birthplace of Feliks
Nowowiejski (1877–1946),
composer of the Rota, a
patriotic Polish anthem. His
family home contains a
small **museum** dedicated
to his life.

🏛 Feliks Nowowiejski Museum

ul. Mickiewicza 13.
[(0 89) 514 85 49.
◯ 9–11am Tue,
noon–5pm Wed,
9am–2pm Fri,
9am–1pm Sat.
◖ Mon, Thu,
Sun.

The Castle of the Warmian Chapter in Olsztyn

**The monument to the Battle of
Grunwald outside the town**

Grunwald ❽

Road map E2. 🏛 *420.* 🚌
🎪 *Battle of Grunwald (15 Jul).*

THE FIELDS between
Grunwald and Stębark
(Tannenberg in German)
were the scene of one of the
greatest battles of the Middle
Ages. On 15 July 1410, the
forces of the Teutonic Knights
met a combined force of
Poles and Lithuanians. Some
14,000 cavalry plus infantry
commanded by Ulrich von
Jungingen, the Grand Master
of the Teutonic Knights, faced
24,000 Polish-Lithuanian
cavalry and several thousand
infantry led by Władysław II
Jagiełło. The knights suffered
a resounding defeat, and the
Grand Master himself was
killed. Historians believe that
during World War I, in
August 1914, the German

Field Marshal Hindenburg
deliberately chose this site for
his victorious battle against
the Russians in order to
negate the memory of that
defeat. The monument to the
medieval Battle of Grunwald
that stands on the site was
designed by Jerzy Bandura
and Witold Cęckiewicz and
unveiled in 1960. Nearby is a
small **museum** with a
collection of documents
about the battle and
archaeological finds from the
site. For several years the
battle's anniversary has been
marked by re-enactments of
the engagement as it is
described in chronicles.

🏛 **Museum of the Battle of
Grunwald in Stębark**
Stębark 1. 📞 *(0 89) 647 22 27.*
⊙ *8am–6pm daily.*

Nidzica ❾

Road map E2. 🏛 *15,200.* 🚇 🚌
🎪 *Nidzica Festival (May).*

THE MAIN FEATURE of Nidzica
is the Teutonic Castle,
which overlooks the town
from a hill. It was built in the
late 14th century and altered
in the 16th century. Reduced
to ruins, it was rebuilt in the
19th century and again after
World War II. Part of it is
now a hotel. Some of the
town's medieval fortifications
also survive.

ENVIRONS: The **Tartars' Stone**
lies 2 km (just over 1 mile)
south of Nidzica. This large

rock, with a circumference
of 19 m (63 ft), marks the
spot where, according to
legend, the leader of the
Tartars was killed in
1656, thus sparing
Nidzica from
invasion in 1656.

**Castle for the Bishops of Warmia,
built to repulse Lithuanian attacks**

Reszel ❿

Road map E1. 🏛 *5,400.* 🚌

THIS LITTLE TOWN was once a
major Warmian city. It was
granted a municipal charter in
1337 and in the second half of
the 14th century a Gothic
**Castle for the Bishops of
Warmia** was built here. The
castle's tower commands a
splendid view over the town.
The castle is now a hotel and
also houses a **gallery** of
contemporary art.

There are two churches: the
Gothic Church of Saints Peter
and Paul, built in the 14th
century with late 15th-century
vaulting, and
the former
Church of
St John

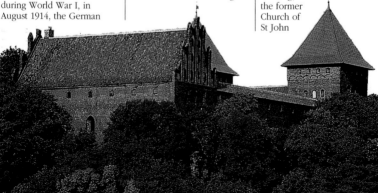

The Gothic Castle of the Teutonic Knights in Nidzica

Trompe l'oeil paintings in the pilgrimage church in Święta Lipka

the Baptist, now an Orthodox church, built in 1799–1800 in the Baroque style.

🏛 Castle Gallery
ul. Podzamcze 4. 📞 (0 89) 755 07 59.
⭕ May–Sep: 9am–5pm Tue–Sun; Oct–Apr: 10am–4pm Tue–Sun.

Święta Lipka ⓫

Road map E2. 🏠 190. 🚌
🎵 Święta Lipka Music Evenings (Jun–Aug).

ŚWIĘTA LIPKA HAS one of the most important **shrines** of the cult of the Virgin in Poland. The name of the town means "holy lime" (or linden tree) and the legend that grew up concerns a miraculous sculpture of the Virgin that was carved by a prisoner in the 15th century and hung from a roadside lime tree. A chapel containing the statue of the Virgin, destroyed during the Reformation, was built around it. The land was part of ducal Prussia. In 1619 a temporary chapel was built here, followed in 1687–93 by a proper church, which was cared for by the Jesuits. In 1694–1708 cloisters and outside chapels were added and the façade and belfry were completed in 1729.

During the Counter-Reformation Święta Lipka was a Catholic stronghold within Protestant ducal Prussia. Large donations were made for decorating the church, resulting in one of the finest and most intriguing examples of Baroque art in Poland.

The interior contains frescoes, including trompe l'oeil paintings in the dome by Mathias Mayer, and the high altar has an image of the Virgin dating from about 1640. The figure organ built in 1721 by Johann Mosengel of Królewiec (Königsberg) is a great attraction for both tourists and pilgrims. In summer, several organ recitals are given every day, and during some of them the figures in the organ loft are set in motion.

Kętrzyn ⓬

Road map E1. 🏠 30,000. 🚆 🚌

FROM THE 14TH century Kętrzyn was the seat of the Prosecutor of the Teutonic Knights, who built the castle that can still be seen today. Kętrzyn then passed to Prussia and later Germany, but retained a sizeable Polish population. The original Polish name for the town was Rastembork; in 1946 it was renamed in honour of the Polish national activist Wojciech Kętrzyński. The old town was almost entirely flattened during World War II: only the town walls and the Church of St George (Kościół św Jerzego) survived. Its exterior is modest, but the interior is impressive – its finest decoration being the crystalline vaulting of around 1515.

ENVIRONS: Ten km (6 miles) east of Kętrzyn is **Gierłoż**, location of the "Wolf's Lair", Adolf Hitler's headquarters in 1940. It consisted of dozens of reinforced concrete bunkers built in woodland. There was also an airfield, railway lines and a power station. Here, on 20 July 1944, the German officer Claus von Stauffenberg made an unsuccessful attempt on Hitler's life. The lair was never discovered by Allied intelligence, and the bunkers were blown up by the withdrawing Germans in January 1945.

Crystalline vaulting in the Church of St George in Kętrzyn

The Great Mazurian Lakes ⑬

T HE GREAT MAZURIAN LAKES are the largest in Poland and a
popular holiday spot in summer. Despite this, the
countryside remains largely unspoiled, and many rare plants
and birds thrive here. The lakes are interlinked by rivers and
canals, and are suitable for yachting or canoeing trips.
Another way to see the region is to take a cruise aboard a
ship of the Mazurian Shipping Company or to drive along
the roads that wind among the lakeside trees.

The district is a paradise for ramblers and for those who
delight in discovering secret spots. Its woods conceal
overgrown bunkers built by the Germans in World War II.

Sztynort, once the residence of
the Prussian Lehndorff family,
stands on a large peninsula.
Some of the oak trees in the
park surrounding the house are
three centuries old.

Ryn

*The castle that towers over
the town was built by
Konrad Wallenrod, Grand
Master of the Teutonic
Knights, for his brother
Frederick in 1394. It was
rebuilt in the English
Gothic style in 1853.*

Mikołajki

*The summer capital of the Mazurian Lake District is
the location of its main yachting marina. A variety
of vessels – from sailing dinghies, yachts and canoes
to motorboats – are available for hire.*

Wojnowo

*The church, cemetery
and convent at
Wojnowo were built by
the Old Believers, who
fled Russia in the 18th
and 19th centuries.*

**The Pranie Forester's
House Museum** honours
the poet Konstanty
Ildefons Gałczynski
(1905–53), who spent the
last days of his life here.

Giżycko
In the woods beside the town, on an isthmus between the lakes, is the grim Prussian Boyen Castle, which was built in 1844.

VISITORS' CHECKLIST

Road map F1, F2, E2.
Giżycko, Pisz, Ruciane Nida.
i *Mikołajki (0 87 421 68 50).*
Mazurian Shipping Company
Giżycko. **(** *(0 87) 428 53 32.*
Pisz Regional Museum
(*(0 87) 423 22 64.* ○ *1 Oct–30 Apr: 8am–3pm daily; 1 May–30 Sep: 8am–4pm daily.* ● *Mon.*

Lake Niegocin
Like most others in the region, the lake is popular with watersports enthusiasts and swimmers. Holiday resorts and campsites are scattered around the lakes.

Lake Sniardwy is not very deep but, covering an area of 106 sq km (40 sq miles), it is the largest in Poland.

Water Lilies
Several varieties of water lily can be seen in the region's lakes.

0 km   10

0 miles   10

KEY

■ Major road

■ Minor road

☆ Viewpoint

WILD SWANS

Lake Łuknajno, which is listed by UNESCO as a World Biosphere Reserve, has become one of Poland's finest nature reserves for wild swans. The fact that the lake is shallow – its average depth does not exceed 1.5 m (4 ft) – makes it easy for the birds to feed on the weed that grows on the lakebed. In 1922 eggs laid by the swans of Lake Łuknajno were used to regenerate Berlin's swan population. Lake Łuknajno attracts wildlife photographers from all over the world, lured by the chance of an unforgettable shot. To safeguard the natural habitat, boats are not allowed on the lake.

A swan on Lake Łuknajno

The local history museum in Pisz features a granite column with a human face known as the Prussian Woman.

Canoeing on the Czarna Hańcza and Augustów Canal ⑭

THIS IS ONE of the most beautiful canoeing routes in Poland. In some places the narrow, winding River Czarna Hańcza is as swift as a mountain stream; in others its course slows as its banks widen. The route downstream passes swamps and lakes and goes through locks on the Augustów Canal that have remained almost unchanged since the time that they were built at the beginning of the 19th century. Canoe trips may be made individually or in organized groups.

Lake Wigry ①
Lake Wigry, in Wigry National Park, is the largest lake in the Suwałki region. Part of the "silent zone", it has numerous islands.

Camaldolite Monastery ②
This monastery stands on the peninsula in Lake Wigry. The monastery buildings have been converted into a hotel. Beyond, the Czarna Hańcza River flows from the lake.

The Czarna Hańcza River ③
The most beautiful stretch of the Czarna Hańcza, beyond the village of Wysoki Most, takes a meandering route. All around is the Augustów Forest.

Rygol ④
Here the river forks, its right arm joining the Augustów Canal. Canoeists may stray off the route and follow the canal leading to the border with Belarus, but they must turn back at the last lock before the border, which is closed.

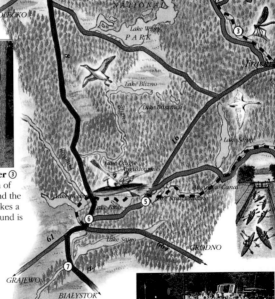

Locks ⑤
The Augustów Canal connects the River Niemen with the River Biebrza and, further on, with the Vistula, passing through several locks on the way. Built in 1823–39, the canal was a great engineering achievement.

◁ **One of the many clear lakes in northeast Poland**

**Typical landscape of the
Augustów lake district**

Augustów ⑥

Augustów is a major tourist
town with many hotels,
guesthouses and rest
centres. There is a
large yachting marina
on the canal.

Białobrzegi ⑦

Canoeing trips
usually end in
Augustów, but
canoeists may
continue along the
Augustów Canal
through Białobrzegi
southwards to the swamps
on the River Biebrza.

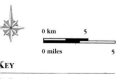

0 km   5

0 miles   5

KEY

■ Canoeing route

■ Main road

■ Other road

✣ Viewpoint

Meadows covered by the floodwaters of the River Biebrza

Biebrza
National Park ⑮

Road map F2. 🚐 ℹ️ *Osowiec
National Park Management (0 86 272
06 20 or 272 01 34).* @ *biebrza@
polbox.com* 🎟️ *tickets available in the
management office, foresters' lodges
and gamekeepers' cottages.*

BIEBRZA NATIONAL PARK is one
of the wildest places in
Europe, untouched by human
activity. It stretches for 70 km
(50 miles) along the banks of
the River Biebrza and contains
Poland's largest swamps, which
are home to a wide variety of
wildlife. A close encounter with
a moose is a distinct possibility.
The greatest attraction of the
swamps, however, is their rich
bird life; over 260 species live
here, and bird-watchers from
afar come to the swamps to
observe them. The most
interesting swamp for bird life
is **Red Swamp** (Czerwone
Bagno), part of a strictly
protected nature reserve
accessible only by means of a
wooden walkway. Walkways
have also been installed in
other parts of the park. A walk
along the red tourist trail holds
a range of attractions –
although you may have to
wade through mud to reach
them. Visitors may hire a guide
and tour the swamps in a punt,
or descend the River Biebrza in
a canoe, for which a ticket and
the permission of the park
management are required.

In **Osowiec**, in the middle
of the swamps, there is a
beaver reserve. Nearby stand
the partly blown-up walls of a
Russian redoubt. Although it
was impregnable, the
Russians, fearful of the
German offensive, abandoned
it in 1915.

Łomża ⑯

Road map F2. 🏃 *62,000.* 🚉 🚐

ŁOMŻA IS A LARGE provincial
town with many
distinguished buildings. Its
Gothic **cathedral**, built in
the 16th century by the last
dukes of Mazovia, has a
number of notable features:
in particular, the cellular and
star vaulting of its interior,
the silver reliefs on the high
altar, and the tombs of
Andrzej Modliszewski, mayor
of Łomża, his wife and their
son. The tombs are the work
of Santi Gucci. The Capuchin
church and regional museum
are also of interest.

ENVIRONS: In **Nowogród**, set
on a high bank of the River
Narew, 15 km (9 miles)
northwest of Łomża, is a
skansen in which the houses
and other buildings of a
typical Kurpie village are
displayed. Opened in 1927, it
is one of the oldest *skansens*
in Poland.

**Star vaulting over the nave of
Łomża Cathedral**

The synagogue in Tykocin, now a Regional Museum

Tykocin ⑰

Road map F2. 👥 *1,800.* 🚌
🛈 *ul. Złota 2 (0 85 718 16 27).*

THE TOWN OF Tykocin was granted a municipal charter in 1425. In 1659 it was given to Stefan Czarnecki, hero of the bitter wars with Sweden, in recognition of his service to the king and to Poland. It later passed to the royal field commander Jan Klemens Branicki. The town owes its present appearance to renovation – financed by Branicki – that was carried out after a fire in 1741.

In the centre of the Market Square there stands a Baroque monument to Stefan Czarnecki that was carved between 1761 and 1763 by the court sculptor Pierre Coudray. The **parish church** on the east side of the square was built a little earlier, in 1750. The Baroque **synagogue**, which dates from 1642, is a relic of the town's former Jewish population. Inside, the walls are inscribed with religious quotations in Hebrew and Aramaic. The synagogue now contains the **Tykocin Museum**.

🏛 **Tykocin Museum**
ul. Kozia 2. 📞 *(0 85) 718 16 26.*
🕐 *May–Sep: 10am–5pm Tue–Sun;*
Oct–Apr: 10am–3pm Tue–Sun. 📷

Białystok ⑱

Road map F2. 👥 *272,000.* 🚉 🚌
🛈 *ul. Wyszyńskiego 2/77 (0 85 742 83 74).* 🎭 *Białystok Days (around 20 Jun).*

BIAŁYSTOK IS THE largest town in northeast Poland. Its population is both Polish and Belarussian, something that can easily be read in the cityscape: the domes of the Orthodox church rise up next to the towers of the Catholic church, and there are many Belarussian cultural institutions. Białystok was once owned by the Branicki family; indeed, the layout of the town is dominated by their former residence, **Branicki Palace**.

The Baroque palace was built by Tylman van Gameren in the 17th century and extended by Jan Zygmunt Deybel – who gave it the appearance of a royal mansion – between 1728 and 1758. It was modelled on the Palace of Versailles, and a formal park, with terraces, canals, fountains, summer houses and numerous sculptures, was laid out around it. Like other members of the high aristocracy, Jan Klemens Branicki, royal field commander and an extremely wealthy man in his own right, maintained his own private army. He was also a connoisseur of art.

Statue by J.C. Redler at Branicki Palace in Białystok

In political circles, however, he was unpopular, opposing reform and contributing to the ruin of Poland. Parts of the palace now house the town's medical academy.

Another interesting building is the **Church of St Roch** (Kościół św Rocha), a delicate construction in reinforced concrete, designed by Oskar Sosnkowski, and built beween 1927 and 1946. The Baroque town hall in the Market Square houses a **Regional Museum**.

♣ **Branicki Palace**
ul. Kilińskiego 1. 📞 *(0 85) 742 20 21.*
🛐 **Church of St Roch**
ul. Dąbrowskiego 1. 📞 *(0 85) 652 10 58 or 652 06 33.*
🏛 **Regional Museum**
Rynek Kościuszki 1. 📞 *(0 85) 742 14 40.*
🕐 *10am–5pm Tue–Sun.*

Kruszyniany ⑲

Road map G2. 👥 *110.*

KRUSZYNIANY AND nearby **Bohoniki** count among their inhabitants the descendants of the Tartars who settled here in the 17th century. Although they became fully integrated into the community a long time ago, their Muslim faith and customs live on. Descendants of the Tartars also live in the Podlasie villages of Nietupy, Łużyny and Drahle. Kruszyniany has a charming wooden **mosque**, originating in the 18th century and rebuilt in 1843. The tombstones in the Muslim graveyard face Mecca.

Wooden mosque in Kruszyniany, built by the descendants of the Tartars

Białowieża National Park ⑳

Road map G3. 🚌 🚻 *PTTK, ul. Kolejowa 17 (0 85 681 26 24).*

THE BIAŁOWIEŻA Forest, covering almost 1,500 sq km (580 sq miles), is the largest natural forest remaining in Europe. It lies partly in Poland and partly in Belarus. The larger – Belarussian – part is virtually inaccessible to tourists; the Polish part became a national park in 1932. Many parts of the park have pre-served their natural character – that of a primeval forest. The areas of greatest interest may be visited only with a guide. Recently, thanks to the efforts of ecologists, the park's borders have been extended on the Polish side.

The forest has an impressive abundance of flora and fauna. There are several thousand species of plants and 11,000 species of animals, including many very rare birds, such as the capercaillie, black stork and golden eagle. Larger mammals include elk, deer, roe deer, wild boar, wolf, lynx and, most famously, the European bison.

On the road running through the forest there is a bison-breeding centre and enclosures where bison, deer, wild boar and Polish ponies can be seen. The park also has a **forest museum**, whose exhibits were once housed in a brick hunting lodge used by the tsars. It was torched by German forces in 1944. Only an Orthodox church remains.

Białowieża National Park has been listed by UNESCO as a World Biosphere Reserve.

🏛 Białowieża Forest Museum

Palace Park Botanical Gardens. 📞 *(0 85) 681 23 06.* 🕐 *Apr–Sep: 9am–4pm daily; Oct–Mar: 9am–3pm daily.*

Grabarka ㉑

Road map F3. 🚶 *50.* 🚐 *Nurzec.* 🚌 **Orthodox convent.** 📞 *(0 85) 655 27 92 or 655 00 10.*

FOR POLAND'S Orthodox Christians, there is no more important place of pilgrimage in the country than the Holy Mountain outside Grabarka. The story goes that in 1770, when the plague was ravaging the town, the inhabitants of Grabarka were directed by a heavenly sign to erect a cross on the hill. The

Part of the forest of crosses on the Holy Mountain outside Grabarka

plague passed and the hill became a hallowed site.

To this day its slopes are covered with hundreds of votive crosses. The original wooden church, destroyed by an arsonist in 1990, was replaced by a brick-built church. The Orthodox convent next to it is the only one in Poland.

Drohiczyn ㉒

Road map F3. 🚶 *21,000.* 🚌 🚻 *ul. Kraszewskiego 13 (0 85 655 70 69).*

DROHICZYN, SET ON a high bank of the Bug River, is today a small, quiet town. As early as the 13th century, however, it was a major centre of trade, and in 1520 it became the provincial capital of Podlasie. In 1795, with the Third Partition of Poland, it was demoted to the status of an ordinary village.

The oldest surviving church in the town is the Baroque **Franciscan church**, dating from 1640–60. The cathedral, originally a Jesuit church, dates from 1696–1709. Nearby stands the former **Jesuit monastery**, later taken over by the Piarists. The striking **Benedictine church**, begun in 1744, has a typically Baroque undulating façade and elliptical interior. The **Orthodox church**, originally Greek Catholic, dates from 1792. To the east of the town, along the winding Bug River, lies a park, the **Podlasie Bug River Gorge**.

Baroque façade of the Benedictine church in Drohiczyn

EUROPEAN BISON

The European bison *(Bison bonasus)* is the largest mammal native to Europe. The weight of an adult bull may reach 1,000 kg (2,200 lb). The largest population of bison ever recorded – 1,500 animals – was in Białowieża in 1860. Hunting these animals has always been restricted, but in World War I (1914–18) the species faced extinction. In 1929, several bison were brought to Poland from zoos in Sweden and Germany to be bred in their natural habitat. The first were set free in Białowieża National Park in 1952. Today bison can also be seen in the other great forests of Poland, including Borecka, Knyszyńska and Niepołomice *(see p162)*.

The European bison

TRAVELLERS'
NEEDS

WHERE TO STAY

ONLY A FEW years ago the standard of Polish hotels was much lower than that of their Western European counterparts. Since 1989, however, many new luxury hotels have been built and many existing hotels have been modernized. Nonetheless, there is still a dearth of good, affordable hotels. Recently, many palaces and manor houses that would otherwise have fallen into ruin have been transformed into comfortable small hotels. They are to be found all over Poland. While some offer luxurious suites, others provide rooms with period interiors at a moderate price. Cheap beds are also provided by PTTK hostels, mountain lodges and private guesthouses, and there are many campsites.

A list of selected hotels all over Poland, from the small and modest to the large and luxurious, including those run by international hotel chains, is to be found on pages 298–311.

Porter at the Hotel Bristol in Warsaw

Part of the elegant lobby of the Grand Hotel in Sopot

HOTELS

AT THE UPPER end of the scale is a small number of luxury hotels with fine period interiors. These hotels were established in the 19th century or at the beginning of the 20th. The most elegant – and expensive – in this category is the Hotel Bristol in Warsaw. The Hotel Francuski in Cracow and Pod Orłem in Bydgoszcz may also be included in this group. The most common type of hotel is the architecturally mediocre modern building; against these, others such as the imposing Warsaw Sheraton, tend to stand out. Before 1989, the largest network of hotels in Poland was run by a state-owned company called Orbis. Today it faces increasing international competition.

For comfort at reasonable prices, the best are perhaps the small modern hotels with all conveniences and a pleasant family atmosphere. Recommended in this category are the Hanza in Gdańsk, in the historic part of the city, and the Vivaldi in Poznań. Recently converted buildings are equally recommended: among these are the Villa Hestia in Sopot, once the eclectic home of a pre-war millionaire from Gdańsk, which has just a small number of rooms, and the Jelonek in Jelenia Góra, a tastefully renovated Baroque tenement house.

MANOR HOUSES AND PALACES

THOSE WHO PREFER staying in historic mansions can choose from a number of such establishments all over Poland. Most – the former property of wealthy landlords or rich factory owners – were reduced to ruin in the communist era, so they are not filled with valuable paintings, fine antique furniture and the trappings of a comfortable lifestyle characteristic of old mansions. Some palaces have been thoroughly renovated, and their interiors refurbished

The entrance to the Hotel Francuski in Cracow

One of the lounges in the luxurious Hotel Bristol in Warsaw

◁ **Outdoor cafés in the Market Square of the Old Town of Warsaw**

The modern Mercure-Fryderyk Chopin Hotel in Warsaw

with great attention paid to the needs and comfort of guests. They are usually quite expensive. Most of the grander hotels have peaceful settings among trees in a beautiful park. Others, at the cheaper end of the scale, tend to be furnished in a more basic manner, with functional rather than comfortable beds often bought from a socialist department store. This type of hotel will not have a swimming pool, lift or nightclub.

RESERVATIONS

WHEN PLANNING to visit a major town or city, a resort or a well-known tourist area, it is best to book a hotel in advance. Finding a room once you arrive can be difficult. In Warsaw, hotel accommodation is particularly scarce in June and July, from September to November and around public holidays. In Cracow, the tourist season lasts the whole year. In Poznań, accommodation is hard to find during the trade

fairs that take place here throughout the year. Rooms in resorts are hard to find during the holiday season. Accommodation in mountain resorts also tends to be scarce over Christmas and during the skiing season.

FACILITIES

RECENT PROGRAMMES of renovation and modernization mean that there has been a great improvement in the general standard of accommodation available in Poland. In many hotels, rooms have en suite toilets and showers or baths. Most have television and some have a video recorder. Generally, rooms tend not to be very large.

Some hotels offer an inexpensive laundry service; superior-standard hotels provide a 24-hour service and minibar. Guests should check out before noon. Those who wish to leave later may deposit their luggage in reception. Most hotel staff speak English.

PRICES AND REDUCED RATES

HOTEL TARIFFS at the upper end of the scale are relatively high and change according to the season. The most expensive hotels are located in Warsaw and Poznań, closely followed by those in other major cities. During the trade fairs, accommodation prices in Poznań are usually much higher than at other times.

Hotels in small towns are generally cheaper, as are the more out-of-the-way manor

houses or palace hotels. Most hotels offer reduced rates at weekends and special rates for children.

Hotels belonging to international chains such as the Intercontinental or Forum offer a range of reduced rates. It is also acceptable to negotiate a reduction when booking. Budget accommodation is provided in the form of hotels that have been converted from hostels for workers, soldiers or students.

The restaurant of the Grand Hotel in Cracow

HIDDEN EXTRAS

IN MOST HOTELS, VAT (which currently varies from 7 to 22 per cent) and service are included in the price. As in other countries, international telephone calls made from hotel rooms can be quite expensive because the hotel charges a commission on top of the cost of the call. Breakfast is usually charged as an extra. Buffet breakfasts or pre-prepared breakfast sets are particularly popular. Tipping staff is not customary except in the more expensive hotels.

As a general rule there is no reduction for single travellers – the same price will be charged for a double room regardless of whether occupied by one or two guests. However, if there are many vacancies, some hotels may offer a double room for the same rate as they would charge for a single room.

The Hotel Neptun on the coast in Łeba

The Hotel Amber in Międzyzdroje, located right on the beach

ROOMS AND FLATS TO LET

Rooms in private houses in towns and resorts are usually easy to find, even during the tourist season. In towns, the best way of obtaining information on private accommodation is from a tourist information centre. In a resort, it is better to explore and find a room on your own, comparing standards and prices. On the coast or at lakeside resorts, rooms may be hard to find outside the tourist season as many guesthouses only operate in summer. Accommodation agencies should provide a range of options from which to choose. When booking a room through an agency, payment must be made in cash. Cash is also the generally accepted form of payment in guesthouses.

AGRITOURISM

Agritourism, a type of ecological tourism connected with the countryside, has been developing since the beginning of the 1990s. As well as taking a room and enjoying home-cooked food and such things as fresh cow's milk, tourists may participate in daily farming tasks. At many farms, tourists can ride on horseback or in a horse-drawn carriage. Prices vary depending on the standard of accommodation and services provided. Addresses of agritourist farms are available from tourist agencies. Such magazines as *Podróże, Voyage* and the tourist supplement issued with the Saturday edition of *Gazeta Wyborcza* may also be useful.

The Kadyny Palace Hotel

YOUTH HOSTELS

Poland has an excellent network of youth hostels. In most tourist areas they operate all year round. In summer, empty school buildings are converted into temporary hostels. Permanent hostels usually have shared rooms and a communal bathroom and kitchen. Due to their popularity, it is advisable to book at least two or three days in advance.

On Fridays and Saturdays, as well as in spring and autumn, rooms in youth hostels are more difficult to find because they tend to be booked by school excursion groups. Hostels are usually closed from 10am to 4pm or 5pm, and again after 10pm.

The price per night is low, especially if you share a room with several other people. Holders of International Youth Hostel Federation cards are entitled to considerable reductions, even on these low rates.

MOUNTAIN LODGES

Hiking along marked mountain trails has long been popular in Poland and is one of the most important areas of tourism. The network of mountain lodges is very extensive; indeed, it is possible to walk the length and breadth of the Carpathian and Sudeten mountains staying only in mountain hostels.

Standards vary from modest to quite comfortable. It is advisable to book in advance, although after nightfall the staff cannot refuse to let you in, even if all the rooms are occupied. At worst you will end up sleeping on the floor. Mountain lodges usually have bathrooms, and buffets serving hot meals. It is also possible to hire equipment.

When hiking along Poland's southern border, hikers may stay in lodges on the Czech and Slovak side of the border and pay in Polish currency.

The Ornak alpine lodge in the Tatra Mountains

One of Poland's many campsites

are better equipped and offer lounges, bungalows, playgrounds for children, and football pitches. At bivouacs, conditions are basic.

CAMPSITES

WHILE A FEW campsites are open all year round, most operate only from the beginning of May to the end of September. Standards do vary. Campsites can be found on the periphery of most large towns and cities as well as in some smaller towns, and at almost all tourist spots on the coast, beside lakes, rivers and in the mountains. In summer, some campsites are so crowded that tents almost touch one another, and it is usually quite noisy late into the night. All campsites are fenced in and have resident staff. Lighting, electricity (220 V), as well as running water, mobile toilets and showers are also provided. The large ones that operate throughout the year

DISABLED TRAVELLERS

NEWLY BUILT AND recently renovated hotels and guesthouses usually have special facilities for disabled people, such as wheelchair access and chairlifts. Rooms with facilities for the disabled are also increasingly widely provided. However, provision for special needs is by no means universal, so it is advisable to contact the hotel beforehand to check what facilities for disabled people, if any, are provided.

TRAVELLING WITH CHILDREN

CHILDREN ARE WELCOME in most hotels and guest-houses; Polish culture is on the whole child-friendly.

Extra beds in parents' rooms are usually provided on request. Many hotels offer special rates for children, and some make no charge for children up to the age of 3 or even, in some cases, 14. This cannot be assumed to be the case, however, so when booking it is definitely advisable to enquire.

Most hotel restaurants also serve special meals for children, although high chairs are rarely provided. Crèches and childcare facilities can be hard to find, so again, if childcare is required it is essential to check in advance.

Typical mountain lodge with rooms to let

Choosing a Hotel

THE HOTELS LISTED below have been selected on the basis of their location, standard and price in relation to the facilities offered. They are listed by region, the coloured tabs in the margins corresponding with those by which the regions of Poland are identified throughout the guide. For the street map of Warsaw see pages 100–103. For the road map of Poland, see the back flap.

	NUMBER OF ROOMS	CREDIT CARDS ACCEPTED	FACILITIES FOR CHILDREN	PRIVATE PARKING	RESTAURANT

WARSAW

ROYAL ROUTE (TRAKT KRÓLEWSKI): *Europejski* ⓩⓩⓩⓩ ul. Krakowskie Przedmieście 13. **Map 2 D4.** 📞 *(0 22) 826 50 51.* **FAX** *(0 22) 826 11 11.* @ europe@orbis.pl Ⓦ www.orbis.pl The Europejski is the oldest hotel in Warsaw. Rebuilt after World War II, it unfortunately does not have its original interiors. The rooms are not very spacious. 🚪 📺 🛎	238	AE DC MC V		▪	●
ROYAL ROUTE (TRAKT KRÓLEWSKI): *Grand* ⓩⓩⓩⓩ ul. Krucza 28. **Map 3 C2.** 📞 *(0 22) 583 21 00.* **FAX** *(0 22) 621 97 24.* @ wagrand@orbis.pl Ⓦ www.orbis.pl The Grand lives up to its name: it is a large hotel built at the end of the 1950s for visiting heads of state and other officials. 🚪 📺 🛎 ♨	314	AE DC MC V		▪	●
ROYAL ROUTE (TRAKT KRÓLEWSKI): *Le Royal Meridien –Bristol* ⓩⓩⓩⓩ ul. Krakowskie Przedmieście 42/44. **Map 2 D4.** 📞 *(0 22) 625 25 25.* **FAX** *(0 22) 625 25 77.* @ bristol@it.com.pl Ⓦ www.lemeridien-bristol.com This most elegant and exclusive hotel opened in 1900. Its Secessionist interior, designed by Otto Wagner of Vienna, has been renovated. The Paderewski Suite is especially fine. 🚪 🛗 ♨ 🟰 🛎 📺 🟥 ♨	206	AE DC MC V	●	▪	●
ROYAL ROUTE (TRAKT KRÓLEWSKI): *Sheraton* ⓩⓩⓩⓩ ul. Prusa 2. **Map 4 D3.** 📞 *(0 22) 657 61 00.* **FAX** *(0 22) 657 62 00.* @ sherato1@warsaw.com.pl Ⓦ www.sheraton.com This large luxury hotel has an excellent location and a range of facilities, including conference rooms, restaurants, cafés and a jazz bar. It is oriented towards VIPs and business people. On the upper floor there are suites with valet service. 🚪 🛗 🟰 📺 🟥 🛎 🟥	350	AE DC MC V	●	▪	●
CITY CENTRE (ŚRÓDMIEŚCIE): *Mercure–Fryderyk Chopin* ⓩⓩⓩⓩ al. Jana Pawła II 22. **Map 1 A5.** 📞 *(0 22) 620 02 01.* **FAX** *(0 22) 620 87 79.* @ mercure@perytnet.pl This large French-owned luxury hotel has rooms furnished in a smart modern style. The excellent restaurant Le Balzac specializes in French cuisine. 🚪 🛗 🟰 📺 🟥	250	AE DC MC V	●	▪	●
CITY CENTRE (ŚRÓDMIEŚCIE): *Victoria Inter-Continental* ⓩⓩⓩⓩ ul. Królewska 11. **Map 1 C5.** 📞 *(0 22) 657 80 11.* **FAX** *(0 22) 657 80 57.* @ victoria@polbox.pl Ⓦ www.interconti.com This was once the most luxurious hotel in Warsaw, with good restaurants and conference rooms. The rooms are furnished in a mid-1970s style and have modern en suite bathrooms. 🚪 🛗 🟰 🟰 🛎 🟥 📺 🟥	365	AE DC MC V	●	▪	●
FURTHER AFIELD: *Karat* ⓩⓩⓩ ul. Słoneczna 37. 📞 *(0 22) 601 44 11.* **FAX** *(0 22) 849 52 94.* A hotel in a residential street with relatively large, well-equipped rooms. Prices are reasonable. 🚪 📺 🛎 🛗	37	AE DC MC V	●	▪	●
FURTHER AFIELD: *Polonia* ⓩⓩⓩ al. Jerozolimskie 45. **Map 3 B2.** 📞 *(0 22) 628 72 41.* **FAX** *(0 22) 628 66 22.* @ hotel.polonia@syrena.com.pl Built at the beginning of the 20th century in the Beaux Arts style, this hotel housed a variety of embassies after World War II, when much of Warsaw was in ruins. Unfortunately, an unsympathetic renovation in the 1960s completely deprived the rooms of their distinctive style. 🚪 📺 🛎	224	AE DC MC V	●	▪	●
FURTHER AFIELD: *Zajazd Napoleoński* ⓩⓩⓩ ul. Płowiecka 83. 📞 *(0 22) 815 30 68.* **FAX** *(0 22) 815 22 16.* This is a comfortable hotel in the style of a classic Polish manor house. The interiors recall the Napoleonic era. 🚪 🛎 📺	24	AE DC MC V		▪	●

Price categories for a standard double room per night with bath or shower, breakfast, service and VAT included (in PLN):

ⓩ under 150
ⓩⓩ 150–300
ⓩⓩⓩ 300–450
ⓩⓩⓩⓩ 450–600
ⓩⓩⓩⓩⓩ over 600

CREDIT CARDS ACCEPTED
One or more of the following credit cards are accepted: American Express (AE), Diners Club (DC), MasterCard (MC), VISA (V).

FACILITIES FOR CHILDREN
Such facilities include cots, high chairs and sometimes childcare.

PRIVATE PARKING
The hotel has its own car park or parking spaces. These may not be on the same premises.

RESTAURANT
This is not necessarily recommended, although particularly good hotel restaurants are also listed in the restaurant section.

	NUMBER OF ROOMS	CREDIT CARDS ACCEPTED	FACILITIES FOR CHILDREN	PRIVATE PARKING	RESTAURANT
FURTHER AFIELD: *Syrena MDM* ⓩⓩⓩⓩ pl. Konstytucji 1. **Map 3 B4.** ☎ *(0 22) 621 62 11.* **FAX** *(0 22) 621 41 73.* @ hotel.MDM@syrena.com.pl Ⓦ www.syrena.hotel.pl This large hotel is located in a building dating from the height of the socialist era. Having been modernized, all rooms are pleasantly, if modestly, furnished and have clean, bright bathrooms. 🛏 ♿ TV 🔒 ≋	120	AE DC MC V	●	■	●
FURTHER AFIELD: *Solec* ⓩⓩⓩⓩ ul. Zagórna 1. **Map 4 F4.** ☎ *(0 22) 625 44 00.* **FAX** *(0 22) 621 64 42.* @ solec@orbis.pl Ⓦ www.orbis.pl This standard two-storey hotel was built in the 1970s. 🛏 ▯ TV 🔒 ≋	147	AE DC MC V	●	■	●
FURTHER AFIELD: *Forum* ⓩⓩⓩⓩⓩ ul. Nowogrodzka 24/26. **Map 3 B2.** ☎ *(0 22) 621 02 71.* **FAX** *(0 22) 625 04 76.* @ waforum@orbis.pl Ⓦ www.orbis.pl *or* Ⓦ www.interconti.com The Forum, built by the Swedes in the mid-1970s, is Warsaw's largest hotel. The tiny rooms are furnished in the style typical of the era of the Polish People's Republic. The recently renovated bathrooms, however, are clean and bright. 🛏 ♿ ☰ TV 🔒	733	AE DC MC V		■	●
FURTHER AFIELD: *Holiday Inn* ⓩⓩⓩⓩⓩ ul. Złota 48/54. **Map 3 A1.** ☎ *(0 22) 620 65 34 or 697 39 99.* **FAX** *(0 22) 697 38 99.* @ bc.holiday@orbis.pl Ⓦ www.holiday-inn.com This large, modern hotel is situated in the centre of Warsaw, next to the Central Railway Station. Comfortably equipped rooms. 🛏 ♿ ☰ TV 🔒 🍴	336	AE DC MC V	●	■	●
FURTHER AFIELD: *Jan III Sobieski* ⓩⓩⓩⓩⓩ pl. Zawiszy 1. ☎ *(0 22) 579 10 00.* **FAX** *(0 22) 658 13 66.* @ hotel@sobieski.com.pl Ⓦ www.sobieski.com.pl When it was built, this Postmodern hotel attracted much controversy. In fact, it is one of the best in Warsaw. Its rooms are spacious and immaculate and the best overlook the quiet garden on the restaurant roof. The hotel is a member of Polish Prestige Hotels. 🛏 ♿ ▯ ☰ TV 🔒 🍴	413	AE DC MC V	●	■	●
FURTHER AFIELD: *Marriott* ⓩⓩⓩⓩⓩ al. Jerozolimskie 65/79. **Map 3 A2.** ☎ *(0 22) 630 63 06.* **FAX** *(0 22) 830 03 11.* @ marriott@it.com.pl Ⓦ www.marriott.com A hotel in central Warsaw that occupies the upper 20 storeys of a 40-floor skyscraper. It has luxuriously appointed rooms and suites, a range of facilities, restaurants, banqueting suites and conference rooms for business people, and a casino. 🛏 TV ♿ ≋ 🔒 🍴	521	AE DC MC V	●	■	●
FURTHER AFIELD: *Residence St. Andrews Palace* ⓩⓩⓩⓩⓩ ul. Chmielna 30. **Map 3 B1.** ☎ *(0 22) 826 96 35.* @ office@residence.com.pl Ⓦ www.residence.com.pl This luxury guesthouse has suites with fully equipped kitchens, and is arranged in a newly renovated historic residence house of 1905. The rooms are furnished with replica antique pieces. 🛏 TV 🔒	24	AE DC MC V	●	■	●
MAZOVIA AND THE LUBLIN REGION					
JABŁONNA: *Pałac w Jabłonnie* ⓩⓩ ul. Modlińska 105. **Road map E3.** ☎ *(0 22) 621 57 37.* This hotel was once the palace of the Poniatowski family. It has a historic atmosphere and a quiet location. 🛏 ▯ TV	24			■	●
JANÓW PODLASKI: *Pensjonat Uroczysko Zaborek* ⓩ Kolonia 28. **Road map F3.** ☎ *and* **FAX** *(0 83) 341 30 68.* @ pensjonat@zaborek.com.pl Ⓦ www.zaborek.com.pl This small hotel is located in a historic wooden manor house. The old windmill next to the hotel has been converted into an elegant suite. 🛏 ▯	24			■	●

Price categories for a standard
double room per night with
bath or shower, breakfast,
service and VAT included
(in PLN):
ⓩ under 150
ⓩⓩ 150–300
ⓩⓩⓩ 300–450
ⓩⓩⓩⓩ 450–600
ⓩⓩⓩⓩⓩ over 600

CREDIT CARDS ACCEPTED
One or more of the following credit cards are accepted: American
Express (AE), Diners Club (DC), MasterCard (MC), VISA (V).
FACILITIES FOR CHILDREN
Such facilities include cots, high chairs and sometimes childcare.
PRIVATE PARKING
The hotel has its own car park or parking spaces. These
may not be on the same premises.
RESTAURANT
This is not necessarily recommended, although particularly
good hotel restaurants are also listed in the restaurant section.

		NUMBER OF ROOMS	CREDIT CARDS ACCEPTED	FACILITIES FOR CHILDREN	PRIVATE PARKING	RESTAURANT

KAZIMIERZ DOLNY: *Hotel Łaźnia*   ⓩ
ul. Senatorska 21. **Road map** F4. 【 *(0 81) 881 02 98.* FAX *(0 81) 881 02 49.*
This charming, quiet hotel is located in the renovated historic town baths.
The hot apple pie served in the hotel restaurant is especially
recommended. 🔧 TV ◉

| | 6 | AE DC MC V | | ◼ | ● |

KAZIMIERZ DOLNY: *Spichlerz Kobiałki*   ⓩⓩⓩ
ul. Krakowska 61. **Road map** F4. 【 *and* FAX *(0 81) 881 00 36.*
This unusual hotel is located in a converted granary on the River Vistula.
The complex includes a villa of 1920 with luxurious rooms.
🔧 TV 🍴 ◉

| | 39 | AE DC MC V | ● | ◼ | ● |

LUBLIN: *Orbis Unia*   ⓩⓩⓩⓩ
al. Racławickie 12. **Road map** F4. 【 *(0 81) 533 20 61.* FAX *(0 81) 533 30 21.*
@ unia@orbis.pl Ⓦ www.orbis.pl
A good hotel situated in the city centre. The pleasant rooms have
newly renovated bathrooms. 🔧 TV ◉

| | 110 | AE DC MC V | | ◼ | ● |

PĘCICE: *Dwór Polski*   ⓩⓩⓩ
Pęcice near Komorowa. **Road map** E3. 【 *and* FAX *(0 22) 759 01 29.*
This 18th-century manor house is ideal for a relaxing break and is
also perfect for banquets. Reservation necessary. 🔧 TV ◉

| | 8 | AE DC MC V | | ◼ | ● |

PUŁTUSK: *Dom Polonii*   ⓩⓩ
ul. Szkolna 11. **Road map** E3. 【 *(0 23) 692 90 00.* FAX *(0 23) 692 36 20.*
@ info@dompolonii.pultusk.pl Ⓦ www.dompolonii.pultusk.pl
The Dom Polonii hotel is located in the castle of the bishops of
Płock *(see p113)*. Set on a hill beside the Narew River, it towers
over Pułtusk. The hotel's three restaurants serve traditional Polish dishes
with home-smoked meats, homemade preserves and bread baked on the
premises. 🔧 TV 🍴 🛏 ◉

| | 86 | AE DC MC V | ● | ◼ | ● |

RADZIEJOWICE: *Pałac w Radziejowicach*   ⓩⓩ
ul. Sienkiewicza 4. **Road map** E3. 【 *(0 46) 857 71 75.* FAX *(0 46) 857 71 13.*
The Creative Workshop of the Ministry of Culture and National Heritage,
located in this building, formerly a palace of the Radziejowski family,
includes a hotel, whose rooms are in the main part and a wing of the
building as well as in the chalet. The standard and prices of the rooms
vary. Reservation necessary. 🔧 TV ◉

| | 29 | AE DC MC V | | ◼ | ● |

WOLA SUCHOŻEBRSKA: *Dworek Ziemiański*   ⓩⓩ
Wola Suchożebrska near Suchożebrów. **Road map** F3. 【 *(0 25) 633 90 89.*
This hotel in a small manor house has tastefully arranged interiors, full of
old photographs and other pieces. Meals are served on Ćmielów
porcelain. The beds are made up with starched linen and guests awake
to the sound of cocks crowing. 🔧 TV

| | 4 | | ● | ◼ | ● |

ZAMOŚĆ: *Hotel Zamojski*   ⓩⓩ
ul. Kołłątaja 2/4/6. **Road map** G5. 【 *and* FAX *(0 84) 639 28 86 or 639 25 16.*
@ zamosc@orbis.pl Ⓦ www.orbis.pl
This newly opened hotel in the centre of town is elegant, luxurious and
comfortable. 🔧 TV 🛏

| | 53 | AE DC MC V | | ◼ | ● |

CRACOW

Logos   ⓩⓩ
ul. Szujskiego 5. **Road map** D5. 【 *(0 12) 632 33 33.* FAX *(0 12) 632 42 10.*
@ logos-kr@interkom.pl Ⓦ www.interkom.pl/logos
This modern building blends perfectly with its historic surroundings.
Located just off Main Market Square, the hotel offers comfortable,
attractively furnished rooms at reasonable prices.
🔧 TV 👤 🛏 🍴 📶

| | 49 | AE DC MC V | ● | ◼ | ● |

Polonia

ul. Basztowa 25. **Road map** D5. **C** *(0 12) 422 12 33.* **FAX** *(0 12) 422 16 21.*
@ polonia@bci.krakow.pl **W** www.hotel-polonia.com.pl
The Polonia occupies an old building with newly renovated rooms at reasonable prices in the city centre. There are suites with antique furniture.

zł zł — 69 — AE DC MC V

Polski Pod Białym Orłem

ul. Pijarska 17. **Road map** D5. **C** and **FAX** *(0 12) 422 11 44.*
@ hotel.polski@podorlem.com.pl **W** www.podorlem.com.pl
This small hotel is situated next to the Florian Gate. The rooms are gradually being renovated.

zł zł — 54 — AE DC MC V

Royal

ul. św Gertrudy 26–29. **Road map** D5. **C** *(0 12) 421 49 79 or 421 35 00.*
FAX *(0 12) 421 58 57.*
The Royal is recommended for those who are on a budget but appreciate an interesting location. The renovated building, at the foot of Wawel Castle, dates back to the times of Austro-Hungarian rule.

zł zł — 115 — AE DC MC V

Saski

ul. Sławkowska 3. **Road map** D5. **C** *(0 12) 421 42 22.* **FAX** *(0 12) 421 48 30.*
@ info@hotelsaski.com.pl
Located in the historic city centre, just off Main Market Square, this monumental hotel offers rooms of varied standard. Not all have en suite bathrooms, but the stylish antique suites are worth their price.

zł zł — 60 — AE DC MC V

Alef

ul. Szeroka 17. **Road map** D5. **C** and **FAX** *(0 12) 421 38 70.*
@ alef@alef.pl **W** www.alef.krakow.pl
The Alef is a tiny hotel with five tastefully furnished suites and a private family atmosphere. It is located in a small residence house in the heart of the Jewish district, near the Old Synagogue.

zł zł zł — 5 — AE DC MC V

Fortuna

ul. Czapskich 5. **Road map** D5. **C** and **FAX** *(0 12) 422 31 43.*
@ info@hotel-fortuna.com.pl **W** www.telendreson.com.pl
The Fortuna is a small hotel near the Planty (parks), in a renovated 19th-century residence house with modern conveniences.

zł zł zł — 30 — AE DC MC V

Pod Różą

ul. Floriańska 14. **Road map** D5. **C** *(0 12) 422 12 44.* **FAX** *(0 12) 421 75 13.*
@ pod-roza@hotel.com.pl
Dating from the mid-19th century, this hotel has luxurious, finely furnished rooms and an excellent location.

zł zł zł — 53 — AE DC MC V

Elektor

ul. Szpitalna 28. **Road map** D5. **C** *(0 12) 423 23 17.* **FAX** *(0 12) 423 23 27.*
@ elektor@bci.krakow.pl
This luxury hotel has suites of the highest standard, and is in a newly renovated residence located near the Słowacki Theatre. Particularly recommended for business people.

zł zł zł zł — 15 — AE DC MC V

Forum

ul. Konopnickiej 28. **Road map** D5. **C** *(0 12) 261 92 12.* **FAX** *(0 12) 269 00 80.*
@ krforum@orbis.pl **W** www.orbis.pl or **W** www.interconti.com
This enormous hotel with its large comfortable rooms is situated opposite Wawel Castle, on the banks of the Vistula. The rooms overlooking the river command excellent views. It offers a range of facilities, such as shops and various services.

zł zł zł zł — 276 — AE DC MC V

Francuski

ul. Pijarska 13. **Road map** D5. **C** *(0 12) 422 51 22.* **FAX** *(0 12) 422 52 70.*
@ francuski@bci.krakow.pl **W** www.orbis.pl
This high-class hotel, opened in 1910, has a lot of atmosphere. Gilding, cut glass and mirrors are ubiquitous, and antique furniture graces the rooms.

zł zł zł zł — 42 — AE DC MC V

Grand

ul. Sławkowska 5/7. **Road map** D5. **C** *(0 12) 421 72 55.* **FAX** *(0 12) 421 83 60.*
@ grand@kr.onet.pl **W** www.grand.pl
A beautiful building dating from the 1860s, the Grand is almost on Main Market Square. Mirrors line the restaurant walls and it has a glass roof. It is expensive, but worth the price.

zł zł zł zł — 56 — AE DC MC V

For key to symbols see back flap

	NUMBER OF ROOMS	CREDIT CARDS ACCEPTED	FACILITIES FOR CHILDREN	PRIVATE PARKING	RESTAURANT

MAŁOPOLSKA (LESSER POLAND)

BARANÓW SANDOMIERSKI: *Zamkowy*   ZL ZL ZL

| | 33 | | ● | ■ | ● |

ul. Zamkowa 20. **Road map** E5. **C** and FAX (0 15) 811 80 40.
@ hotel.zamkowy@baranow.motronik.com.pl W www.baranow.motronik.com.pl
This magnificent Renaissance castle *(see p153)* has luxurious suites as well as less expensive rooms in a nearby building. ▮ TV ▮

BIELSKO-BIAŁA: *Prezydent*   ZL ZL ZL ZL

| | 36 | AE DC V | ● | ■ | ● |

ul. 3 Maja 12. **Road map** D6. **C** (0 33) 822 72 11. FAX (0 33) 815 02 73.
@ prezydent@pol.pl W www.polhotels.com/prezydent
This large hotel is situated in the city centre in a building of the era of Emperor Franz Josef. It has newly renovated bathrooms, period interiors and a *belle époque* atmosphere. ▮ TV ▮ ▮

CZĘSTOCHOWA: *Orbis Patria*   ZL ZL ZL

| | 102 | AE DC MC V | ● | ■ | ● |

ul. Popiełuszki 2. **Road map** D5. **C** (0 34) 324 70 01. FAX (0 34) 324 63 32.
@ patria@orbis.pl W www.orbis.pl
The Orbis Patria is a large hotel at the foot of Jasna Góra. Rooms overlook the monastery. ▮ TV ▮ ▮ ▮

KIELCE: *Hotel Exbud*   ZL ZL ZL

| | 76 | AE MC V | ● | ■ | |

ul. Manifestu Lipcowego 34. **Road map** E5. **C** (0 41) 332 63 93.
FAX (0 41) 332 64 40.
This large modern hotel is a member of Polish Prestige Hotels. TV ▮ ▮ ▮

KOŚCIELISKO: *Pensjonat Górski Pałacyk*   ZL

| | 28 | | ● | ■ | |

ul. Salamandra 16. **Road map** D6. **C** and FAX (0 18) 207 09 26.
W www.gorskipalacyk.com.pl
This small, well-appointed guesthouse has several rooms and suites. An excellent base for hiking in the mountains. Families welcome. ▮ TV ▮ ▮

KRASICZYN: *Zamkowy*   ZL ZL

| | 44 | AE DC MC V | ● | ■ | ● |

Krasiczyn. **Road map** F6. **C** and FAX (0 17) 225 26 72.
@ hotel.krasiczyn@motronik.com.pl W www.krasiczyn.motronik.com.pl
The hotel, in a coach house, forms part of a Renaissance castle *(see p170)*. The newly renovated rooms are of a high standard. Groups may book the hunting lodge, which has a suite of rooms and small kitchen. ▮ TV ▮

ŁAŃCUT: *Zamkowy*   ZL

| | 13 | AE DC MC V | | ■ | |

ul. Zamkowa 1. **Road map** F5. **C** (0 17) 225 26 71. FAX (0 17) 225 26 72.
The hotel is located in a wing of the palace *(see pp172–3)*. Most of the rooms have not yet been renovated and are inexpensive. Luxury suites, at a higher price, are also available. ▮ TV

NIDZICA: *Zamek w Niedzicy*   ZL ZL

| | 13 | AE DC MC V | | ■ | |

Niedzica. **Road map** E6. **C** and FAX (0 18) 262 94 89.
The Gothic-Renaissance castle *(see p282)* has been open to tourists for several years. Guests may stay in the castle or in Celnica. There is no restaurant, but meals are prepared to order. ▮

NOWY SĄCZ: *Beskid*   ZL ZL ZL

| | 78 | AE DC MC V | | ■ | ● |

ul. Limanowskiego 1. **Road map** E6. **C** (0 18) 443 57 70. FAX (0 18) 443 51 44.
@ resbeskid@orbis.pl W www.orbis.pl
The Beskid is a large modern hotel in the centre of the town, near the railway station. ▮ TV ▮ ▮ ▮

PASZKÓWKA: *Pałac Wężyków*   ZL ZL ZL

| | 43 | AE DC MC V | | ■ | ● |

Paszkówka 37. **Road map** D6. **C** (0 33) 879 30 33. FAX (0 33) 879 32 61.
@ palac@paszkowka.kra.pl
This Neo-Gothic palace has recently been converted into a luxury hotel. There are comfortable rooms located in the granary and the palace itself has elegant suites and conference rooms. ▮ TV ▮ ▮ ▮

PRZEMYŚL: *Hotel Gromada* — ⓩⓩ | 117 | AE DC MC V
ul. Wybrzeże Marszałka J. Piłsudskiego 4. **Road map** F6.
C *(0 16) 676 11 12.* **FAX** *(0 16) 676 11 13.* **W** www.gromada.pl
This newly built luxury hotel is located on the River San. The rooms command a good view of the town. 🛏 ♿ 🅿 ▤

RZESZÓW: *Hotel Rzeszów* — ⓩⓩ | 300 | AE DC MC V
ul. Cieplińskiego 2. **Road map** F5. **C** *(0 17) 852 34 41.* **FAX** *(0 17) 853 33 89.*
@ rzeszow@hotelesemako.com.pl
This hotel has a good restaurant, serving among other things such unusual dishes as ostrich sirloin in cream sauce. 🛏 📺

RZESZÓW: *Hotel Prezydencki* — ⓩⓩⓩ | 58 | AE DC MC V
ul. Podwisłocze 46. **Road map** F5. **C** *(0 17) 853 33 89.* **FAX** *(0 17) 852 34 41.*
Quite a good modern hotel, although it has an unattractive appearance and is located among high-rise buildings. 🛏 📺 ⇄

SIENIAWA: *Pałac w Sieniawie* — ⓩⓩ | 28 | AE DC MC V
ul. Kościuszki 32. **Road map** F5. **C** *(0 16) 621 09 69.* **FAX** *(0 16) 621 61 01.*
This Baroque mansion has been turned into an elegant hotel with an enchanting ballroom and dining room. The tastefully decorated rooms have antique furniture and comfortable bathrooms. The extensive park is pleasant for long walks. 🛏 📺

WOLA ZRĘCZYCKA: *Bella Vita* — ⓩⓩ | 19 | AE DC MC V
Wola Zręczycka near Gdowa. **Road map** E6. **C** *(0 12) 278 66 98.*
This 19th-century wooden manor house is an excellent base for hunters and for those planning to visit Cracow or Wieliczka. 🛏 📺 🅿

ZAKOPANE: *Orbis Giewont* — ⓩⓩⓩ | 44 | AE DC MC V
ul. Kościuszki 1. **Road map** D6. **C** *(0 18) 201 20 11.* **FAX** *(0 18) 201 20 15.*
@ giewont@orbis.pl **W** www.orbis.pl
This large monumental hotel is situated in the town centre and was built during World War II. 🛏 📺

ZAKOPANE: *Orbis Kasprowy* — ⓩⓩⓩⓩ | 286 | AE DC MC V
Polana Szymoszkowa 1. **Road map** D6. **C** *(0 18) 201 40 11.*
FAX *(0 18) 201 52 72.* @ kasprowy@zakopane.top.pl
This modernist hotel was built in the 1970s on the slopes of Mount Gubałówka, near skiing routes. 🛏 📺 ♨ 🍴 🅿 ♿ 🏊

SILESIA

JELENIA GÓRA: *Jelonek* — ⓩⓩ | 11
ul. 1 maja 5. **Road map** B4. **C** *(0 75) 764 65 41.* **FAX** *(0 75) 752 62 66.*
@ igora@orbis.pl **W** www.orbis.pl
This small, quiet hotel in a Baroque residence is situated near the main promenade. Newly opened, it has very clean, well-equipped rooms. 🛏 📺

JELENIA GÓRA: *Orbis Jelenia Góra* — ⓩⓩⓩⓩ | 188 | AE DC MC V
ul. Sudecka 63. **Road map** B4. **C** *(0 75) 764 64 81.* **FAX** *(0 75) 752 62 66.*
This high-class, comfortable, modern hotel has a wide choice of services and a view over Karkonosze Mountains. 🛏 📺 🅿 ⇄ ♨ 🍴

KAMIENIEC ZĄBKOWICKI: *Castel* — ⓩ | 20
Kamieniec Ząbkowicki. **Road map** B5. **C** *(0 74) 817 32 04.*
Located in a splendid Silesian castle, this romantic hotel was once owned by the Hohenzollern dynasty *(see p198).* 🛏 🅿

KARPACZ: *Karkonosze* — ⓩⓩ | 12 | AE DC MC V
ul. Wolna 4. **Road map** B5. **C** *(0 75) 761 82 77.* **FAX** *(0 75) 741 80 33.*
@ hkarkonosze@gip.com.pl
This small mountain hotel has luxuriously equipped rooms and a family atmosphere. The three suites, with communal lounge, kitchen and en suite bathrooms, are relatively inexpensive. The hotel has its own piste, with artificial snow when necessary. 🛏 ♿ 🅿

KARPACZ: *Rezydencja* — ⓩⓩⓩ | 28
ul. Parkowa 6. **Road map** B5. **C** *(0 75) 761 80 20.* **FAX** *(0 75) 761 95 13.*
@ www.sudety.info.pl/rezydeneja
This luxurious mountain hotel is situated in the centre of Karpacz. It was built in the early 20th century, with tiers of balconies and tasteful renovation. In summer, guests may ride along one of the longest toboggan runs in Poland. 🛏 📺

Price categories for a standard double room per night with bath or shower, breakfast, service and VAT included (in PLN):

ⓩ under 150
ⓩⓩ 150–300
ⓩⓩⓩ 300–450
ⓩⓩⓩⓩ 450–600
ⓩⓩⓩⓩⓩ over 600

CREDIT CARDS ACCEPTED
One or more of the following credit cards are accepted: American Express (AE), Diners Club (DC), MasterCard (MC), VISA (V).

FACILITIES FOR CHILDREN
Such facilities include cots, high chairs and sometimes childcare.

PRIVATE PARKING
The hotel has its own car park or parking spaces. These may not be on the same premises.

RESTAURANT
This is not necessarily recommended, although particularly good hotel restaurants are also listed in the restaurant section.

	NUMBER OF ROOMS	CREDIT CARDS ACCEPTED	FACILITIES FOR CHILDREN	PRIVATE PARKING	RESTAURANT

KATOWICE: *Orbis Silesia* ⓩⓩⓩⓩ | 194 | AE DC MC V | | ■ | ● |
ul. Piotra Skargi 2. **Road map** D5. 📞 *(0 32) 259 62 11 or 18.*
FAX *(0 32) 259 61 40.* @ silesia@orbis.pl W www.orbis.pl
This large hotel is located in the town centre and has conference rooms, restaurants and shops. 🔧 TV ♿

KATOWICE: *Orbis Warszawa* ⓩⓩⓩⓩ | 287 | | | ■ | ● |
ul. Roździeńskiego 16. **Road map** D5. 📞 *(0 32) 200 44 44 or 200 44 12.*
FAX *(0 32) 200 44 11.* @ warsaw@orbis.pl W www.orbis.pl
This large, comfortable hotel was built in the 1970s on the fringe of the city centre. 🔧 TV ♿ ▤ 🏊 🍴

KOBIERZYCE: *Pałac Kobierzyce* ⓩⓩ | 17 | AE DC MC V | ● | ■ | ● |
ul. al. Pałacowa 1. **Road map** C4. 📞 *(0 71) 311 19 86.* **FAX** *(0 71) 311 14 59.*
This Renaissance palace, 15 km (9 miles) from Wrocław, has modern rooms with en suite bathrooms. Guests may go horse riding in the large park. 🔧 TV ♿ 🍴

KRASKÓW: *Pałac Krasków* ⓩⓩ | 35 | AE DC MC V | ● | ■ | ● |
Krasków near Marcinowic. **Road map** B4. 📞 *(0 74) 858 51 01.* **FAX** *(0 74) 858 52 52.*
@ palac@hotel-palac-kraskow.com.pl W www.hotel-palac-kraskow.com.pl
This hotel is in the former Baroque palace of the Sedlitz family. The rooms are furnished with antiques. Cheaper rooms are available in the annexe and mill house. It has an excellent restaurant serving international dishes. 🔧 TV ♿

KROBIELOWICE: *Pałac Krobielowice* ⓩⓩ | 22 | | | ■ | ● |
Krobielowice near Kątów Wrocławskich. **Road map** B4.
📞 and **FAX** *(0 71) 316 66 48.* @ info@palackrobielowice.com W www.palackrobielowice.com
This hotel is in a bewitching Renaissance-Baroque palace, and its interiors are furnished with antiques. In the garden is the mausoleum of the former owner of the palace, Gebhard Bücher, the Prussian field marshal who contributed to the defeat of Napoleon at the Battle of Waterloo. 🔧 TV 🔋

ŁOMNICA: *Pałac Łomnica* ⓩⓩ | 11 | AE DC MC V | ● | ■ | ● |
ul. Karpnicka 3. **Road map** B5. 📞 *(0 75) 713 04 60.* **FAX** *(0 75) 713 05 33.*
A small, comfortable hotel in a Neo-Classical palace that stands next to a larger late Baroque palace. A short distance away are the former residences of Louisa, Queen of the Netherlands, in Wojnowice, Frederick Wilhelm III, King of Prussia, in Mysłakowice, and of Princess Elizabeth of Hesse and Jagwida, Queen of Bavaria, in Karpniki. 🔧 🔋

OPOLE: *Piast* ⓩⓩⓩ | 25 | AE DC MC V | ● | ■ | ● |
ul. Piastowska 1. **Road map** C5. 📞 *(0 77) 454 97 10.* **FAX** *(0 77) 454 97 17.*
This small hotel is in a pre-war building situated on Piaseka Island, not far from the amphitheatre where the annual Festival of Polish Song is held. 🔧 TV ♿ 🔋

PROMNICE: *Noma-Residence* ⓩⓩⓩⓩ | 13 | AE DC MC V | | ■ | ● |
Promnice-Kobiór. **Road map** D5. 📞 and **FAX** *(0 32) 219 46 78.*
@ promnice@noma2.com.pl W www.promnice.com.pl
The Noma-Residence is a very comfortable hotel in a picturesque shooting lodge, formerly owned by the dukes of Hochberg-Pszczyńscy. The rooms are furnished with antiques and the service is of a high standard. The excellent restaurant is an additional attraction. The hotel is a member of Polish Prestige Hotels. 🔧 TV 🔋

SOBÓTKA: *Zamek Górka* ⓩ | 24 | AE DC MC V | | ■ | ● |
ul. Zamkowa 12. **Road map** B4. 📞 and **FAX** *(0 71) 316 21 33.*
This pseudo-medieval castle, a fairytale building with many towers and pretty, well-preserved interiors, houses a modestly appointed hotel. The castle, once owned by the Kulmitz family, is surrounded by a landscaped park. Many tourists on their way to the sacred Mount Sobótka stay here. 🔧 🔋

Sucha: *Zamek Czocha* ⓩ 35
Near Leśna. **Road map** A4. 📞 *(0 75) 721 11 85.* w www.czocha.z.pl
This magnificent castle *(see p181)*, set on the lakeside, is not
particularly luxurious and some of the cheaper rooms have no
en suite bathrooms. However, the castle has a memorable atmosphere
and is said to be haunted. 🔧 TV

Szczyrk: *Meta* ⓩⓩⓩ 8 AE DC MC V
ul . Skośna 4. **Road map** D6. 📞 *and* FAX *(0 33) 817 88 74.*
The Meta is an alpine lodge in the Austrian style with all comforts and
large suites. It is situated next to the chairlift station to Mount Skrzyczne,
where the longest downhill skiing routes in Poland start. 🔧 TV 🔲 ▤

Szklarska Poręba: *Husarz* ⓩⓩⓩ 6 AE DC MC V
ul. Kilińskiego 18. **Road map** D5. 📞 *(0 75) 717 33 63.*
Built in 1895, this hotel is in a former hunting lodge, with an antique-
furnished interior. It is surrounded by a large park. TV 🔲 ♿

Świerklaniec: *Pałac Kawalera* ⓩⓩ 20 AE DC MC V
ul. Parkowa 30. **Road map** D5. 📞 *and* FAX *(0 32) 284 44 90.*
This comfortable hotel occupies the only part of the Neo-Baroque
residence of the Donnersmarck dynasty to be preserved. 🔧 TV

Woszczyce: *Dwór Szczepańskich* ⓩⓩⓩ 12 AE DC MC V
Woszczyce. **Road map** C5. 📞 *(0 32) 221 55 62.* @ dwor@dsw.com.pl w www.dsw.com.pl
Located in a small, picturesque manor house this comfortable hotel has
rooms decorated in period styles. The restaurant is excellent. 🔧 TV ▤ 🔲

Wrocław: *Dwór Polski* ⓩⓩⓩ 28 AE DC MC V
ul. Kiełbaśnicza 2. **Road map** C4. 📞 *and* FAX *(0 71) 372 34 15 or 322 34 19.*
@ dworpol@wr.onet.pl w www.wroclaw.com/dworpol.htm
Located in a historic residence in the old part of Wrocław, this
luxurious hotel deserves its fame. The local restaurants specializing
in traditional Polish cuisine *(see pp322–3)* are also well known. 🔧 TV ♿

Wrocław: *Hotel Exbud* ⓩⓩⓩ 49 AE DC MC V
ul. Kiełbaśnicza 24. **Road map** C4. 📞 *(0 71) 341 09 16.* FAX *(0 71) 343 91 49.*
@ recepcja@exbud-hotel.wroc.pl w www.exbud-hotel.wroc.pl
The Hotel Exbud is a small, modern hotel located in a rebuilt
19th-century town house in the old part of the city. The rooms overlook
an impressive atrium with glazed roof. There is a restaurant on the
ground floor and a winter garden on the roof. 🔧 TV ▤ 🔲 ♿

Wrocław: *Maria Magdalena* ⓩⓩⓩ 82 AE DC MC V
ul. św Marii Magdaleny 2. **Road map** C4. 📞 *(0 71) 341 08 98.* FAX *(0 71) 341 09 20.*
@ hotel@hotel-mm.com.pl w www.hotel-mm.com.pl
This small, comfortable hotel is in the old part of the city, next to the
Church of St Mary Magdalene. 🔧 TV ▤ 🏊 🔲 ♿

Wrocław: *Park Plaza* ⓩⓩⓩ 177 AE DC MC V
ul. Drobrzewa 11/13. **Road map** C4. 📞 *(0 71) 320 84 00.* FAX *(0 71) 320 84 59.*
@ hpwroclaw@bph.pl w www.polhotels.com or www.bph.com.pl
This large and luxurious hotel is the newest in Wrocław. It is situated on the
River Odra, with a view of the city's historic buildings. 🔧 TV ▤ 🔲 ♿ 🔲

Wrocław: *Art Hotel* ⓩⓩⓩⓩ 72 AE DC MC V
ul. Kiełbaśnicza 20. **Road map** C4. 📞 *(0 71) 342 42 49.* FAX *(0 71) 342 39 29.*
@ recepcja@arthotel.wroc.pl w www.arthotel.wroc.pl
This comfortable hotel is in renovated Gothic-Renaissance and Neo-Gothic
buildings in the old part of Wrocław. The atrium has been converted into a
shopping mall. The hotel is a member of Polish Prestige Hotels. 🔧 TV ▤ 🔲 ♿

Wrocław: *Orbis Wrocław* ⓩⓩⓩⓩ 292 AE DC MC V
ul. Powstańców Śląskich 5/7. **Road map** C4. 📞 *(0 71) 361 46 51.*
FAX *(0 71) 361 66 17.* @ hwroclaw@orbis.pl w www.orbis.pl
This large, luxurious hotel was built in the 1980s and is situated
in the city centre near the railway station. 🔧 TV ▤ 🏊 🔲 ♿

WIELKOPOLSKA (GREATER POLAND)

Antonin: *Pałac Radziwiłłów* ⓩ 14
ul. Pałacowa 1. **Road map** C4. 📞 *and* FAX *(0 62) 736 16 51.* w www.ckis@kalisz.pl
The famous hunting lodge of the Radziwiłł family *(see p227)* has inexpensive
but quite basic rooms. 🔧 TV 🔲

Price categories for a standard double room per night with bath or shower, breakfast, service and VAT included (in PLN):
ⓏⓁ under 150
ⓏⓁⓏⓁ 150–300
ⓏⓁⓏⓁⓏⓁ 300–450
ⓏⓁⓏⓁⓏⓁⓏⓁ 450–600
ⓏⓁⓏⓁⓏⓁⓏⓁⓏⓁ over 600

CREDIT CARDS ACCEPTED
One or more of the following credit cards are accepted: American Express (AE), Diners Club (DC), MasterCard (MC), VISA (V).
FACILITIES FOR CHILDREN
Such facilities include cots, high chairs and sometimes childcare.
PRIVATE PARKING
The hotel has its own car park or parking spaces. These may not be on the same premises.
RESTAURANT
This is not necessarily recommended, although particularly good hotel restaurants are also listed in the restaurant section.

		NUMBER OF ROOMS	CREDIT CARDS ACCEPTED	FACILITIES FOR CHILDREN	PRIVATE PARKING	RESTAURANT
CZERNIEJEWO: *Pałac Czerniejewo* ⓏⓁⓏⓁ		38			■	●
GĘBICE: *Pałac* ⓏⓁ		23	AE DC MC V		■	●
KOBYLNIKI: *Pałac Kobylniki* ⓏⓁ		11	AE DC MC V		■	●
KRZEŚLICE: *Pałac w Krześlicach* ⓏⓁⓏⓁⓏⓁ		20	AE DC MC V	●	■	●
LESZNO: *Akwawit* ⓏⓁⓏⓁ		64	AE DC MC V		■	●
ŁAGÓW: *Zamek Joannitów* ⓏⓁ		14			■	●
ŁÓDŹ: *Grand* ⓏⓁⓏⓁⓏⓁⓏⓁ		153	AE DC MC V			●
OJERZYCE: *Country* ⓏⓁⓏⓁ		18	AE DC MC V	●	■	●
PIETRONKI: *Pałac Pietronki* ⓏⓁ		16			■	●
POZNAŃ: *Dorrian* ⓏⓁⓏⓁⓏⓁ		19	AE DC MC V		■	●

CZERNIEJEWO: *Pałac Czerniejewo* ⓏⓁⓏⓁ
ul. gen. Lipskiego 5. **Road map** C3. ☎ *(0 61) 427 30 30.* FAX *(0 61) 429 12 30.*
@ recepcja@palac-czerniejewo.ig.pl Ⓦ www.palac-czerniejewo.ig.pl
The Pałac Czerniejewo is a beautiful complex of Neo-Classical buildings with accommodation ranging from elegant suites to more modest rooms in the annexe. The rooms in the stable and coach house have no en suite bathrooms. It is also possible to stay in the Neo-Gothic palace in nearby Arcugów. 🖥

GĘBICE: *Pałac* ⓏⓁ
Pępowo Gębice. **Road map** B3. ☎ and FAX *(0 65) 573 61 50.*
This is a small palace with rather elaborate interiors. It is set in a park. The restaurant serves good cuisine. 🖥 📺 ♿ 🍴 ⚙

KOBYLNIKI: *Pałac Kobylniki* ⓏⓁ
Near Obrzycko. **Road map** B3. ☎ and FAX *(0 61) 292 19 07.* Ⓦ www.palackobylniki.com.pl
This hotel is located in a palace with towers built by Zygmunt Gorgolewski for Tadeusz Twardowski, lord of the manor. It is by no means a luxury establishment, but guests may go hunting and horse riding. 🖥 📺

KRZEŚLICE: *Pałac w Krześlicach* ⓏⓁⓏⓁⓏⓁ
Near Pobiedziska. **Road map** C3. ☎ *(0 61) 815 33 70.* FAX *(0 61) 817 75 38.*
@ adam@palace.pl Ⓦ www.palace.pl
The hotel is located in a beautifully renovated Neo-Gothic palace of the second half of the 19th century. The comfortable rooms have individual character and well-chosen antique furniture. This is a perfect place for those who appreciate silence and elegance, and an excellent base for sightseeing in Poznań, 25 km (15 miles) from Krześlice. 🖥 📺 📺

LESZNO: *Akwawit* ⓏⓁⓏⓁ
ul. św Józefa 5. **Road map** C4. ☎ *(0 65) 529 37 81.* FAX *(0 65) 529 37 82.*
@ hotel@akwawit.com.pl Ⓦ www.akwawit.com.pl
The Akwawit is a modern though not very tastefully appointed hotel, with indoor swimming pools and a 120-m (400-ft) water slide. The price includes the use of the pool and fitness club. 🖥 ♿ ⚙ 🏊

ŁAGÓW: *Zamek Joannitów* ⓏⓁ
ul. Kościuszki 3. **Road map** B3. ☎ and FAX *(0 68) 341 20 10.*
This hotel, with all modern comforts, is located in a medieval castle of the Knights Hospitallers (*see p210*). 🖥 📺 📠

ŁÓDŹ: *Grand* ⓏⓁⓏⓁⓏⓁⓏⓁ
ul. Piotrkowska 72. **Road map** D4. ☎ *(0 42) 633 99 20.* FAX *(0 42) 633 78 76.*
@ logrand@orbis.pl
Built in 1888, the Grand is a large hotel situated in the city's main street. 🖥 📺 ⚙ 📺

OJERZYCE: *Country* ⓏⓁⓏⓁ
Near Kupienin. **Road map** B3. ☎ and FAX *(0 68) 382 57 02.*
The Country is an elegant, luxurious hotel in a Neo-Renaissance palace situated near the Berlin to Poznań road. Its excellent restaurant serves Polish and German dishes. 🖥 📺

PIETRONKI: *Pałac Pietronki* ⓏⓁ
Near Chodzież. **Road map** C2. ☎ *(0 67) 284 54 70.* FAX *(0 67) 282 00 70.*
Located in the Neo-Classical Palace of the Counts of Bniński, this hotel was built in 1901. 🖥 📺

POZNAŃ: *Dorrian* ⓏⓁⓏⓁⓏⓁ
ul. Wyspiańskiego 29. **Road map** C3. ☎ *(0 61) 867 45 22.* FAX *(0 61) 867 45 59.*
@ dorrian@post.pl Ⓦ www.polhotels.com or Ⓦ www.poltravel.com
The Dorrian is a modern, low-rise hotel in the centre of Poznań. 🖥 📺 ♿ ⚙ 🍴

POZNAŃ: *Park* — ⓏⓁⓏⓁⓏⓁ — 100
ul. Majakowskiego 77. **Road map** C3. ☎ *(0 61) 879 40 81.* FAX *(0 61) 877 38 30.*
@ hppoznan@beph.pl
The Park is a comfortable hotel surrounded by a garden. It is a member
of Polish Prestige Hotels. ▯▯▯▯▯▯
AE DC MC V

POZNAŃ: *Vivaldi* — ⓏⓁⓏⓁⓏⓁ — 200
ul. Winogrady 9. **Road map** C3. ☎ *(0 61) 853 21 77.* FAX *(0 61) 853 29 77.*
@ vivaldi@vivaldi.pl ᴡ www.vivaldi.pl
This small hotel combines comfort with charm and a relaxed atmosphere.
It is a member of Polish Prestige Hotels. ▯▯▯▯▯▯▯
AE DC MC V

POZNAŃ: *Poznań* — ⓏⓁⓏⓁⓏⓁⓏⓁ — 495
pl. Wl. Andersa 1. **Road map** C3. ☎ *(0 61) 858 70 00.* FAX *(0 61) 833 29 61.*
@ hpoznan@orbis.pl ᴡ www.orbis.pl
The largest hotel in Poznań, it has upper floors commanding a
magnificent panorama of the city. The lobby epitomizes the style of
1970s Poland. ▯▯▯▯▯▯▯
AE DC MC V

PRZYBYSZEWO: *Pałac w Przybyszewie* — ⓏⓁⓏⓁ — 13
Przybyszewo near Leszna. **Road map** B4. ☎ and FAX *(0 65) 533 82 00.*
This hotel is in an eclectic mid-19th century palace. There are riding
stables nearby. ▯▯
AE DC MC V

ROKOSOWO: *Zamek Rokosowo* — ⓏⓁ — 22
Rokosowo near Łęki Małej. **Road map** C4. ☎ *(0 65) 573 33 08.* FAX *(0 65) 573 33 04.*
This hotel is located in a romantic castle built in 1847–50 for Count Józef
Mycielski. The interiors are beautifully furnished with antiques and
the rooms have comfortable, renovated bathrooms. ▯▯▯
AE DC MC V

RYDZYNA: *Zamek w Rydzynie* — ⓏⓁⓏⓁⓏⓁ — 50
pl. Zamkowy 1. **Road map** B4. ☎ *(0 65) 529 50 40.* FAX *(0 65) 529 50 26.*
@ zamek@zamek-rydzyna.com.pl ᴡ www.zamek-rydzyna.com.pl
This hotel is located in the Baroque palace of the Sułkowski family
(see p210) and is set in a park. It has tastefully renovated interiors and a
magnificent ballroom. The hotel is a member of European Castle
Hotels & Restaurants. ▯▯▯
AE DC MC V

SULEJÓW PODKLASZTORZE: *Hotel Sulejów Podklasztorze* — ⓏⓁⓏⓁ — 51
ul. Jagiełły 1. **Road map** D4. ☎ *(0 44) 616 20 11.* FAX *(0 44) 616 20 02.*
@ podklasztorze@pro.onet.pl ᴡ www.trybunalskie.pro.onet.pl
This modern hotel is out of the ordinary and is located in a monastery
housing relics dating from the 13th century. ▯▯▯▯
AE DC MC V

UNIEJÓW: *Zamek Uniejów* — ⓏⓁ — 20
Uniejów. **Road map** D3. ☎ *(0 63) 288 81 45.* FAX *(0 63) 288 90 86.*
This hotel is in a Gothic-Renaissance castle on the River Warta. The events
that take place here, as well its restaurant, attract many tourists. ▯▯▯

ZIELONA GÓRA: *Qubus* — ⓏⓁⓏⓁⓏⓁ — 56
ul. Ceglana 14a. **Road map** B3. ☎ *(0 68) 324 34 44.* FAX *(0 68) 324 34 54.*
@ zielonagora@qubushotel.com.pl ᴡ www.qubushotel.com
This modern hotel in the town centre belongs to the Qubus chain. ▯▯
AE DC MC V

GDAŃSK

Novotel — ⓏⓁⓏⓁⓏⓁ — 152
ul. Pszenna 1. **Road map** D1. ☎ *(0 58) 301 56 11 or 18.* FAX *(0 58) 300 29 50.*
@ ngdansk@orbis.pl ᴡ www.orbis.pl
Built in the 1970s, this hotel has a unique location on the historic
Spichlerze Island. Conventional facilities. ▯▯▯▯▯
AE DC MC V

Hanza — ⓏⓁⓏⓁⓏⓁⓏⓁ — 60
ul. Tokarska 6. **Road map** D1. ☎ *(0 58) 305 34 27.* FAX *(0 58) 305 33 86.*
@ hotel@hanza-hotel.com.pl ᴡ www.hanza-hotel.com.pl
This elegant, modern hotel on the Motława is in the heart of historic
Gdańsk. It is a member of Polish Prestige Hotels. ▯▯▯▯▯▯
AE DC MC V

Helvelius — ⓏⓁⓏⓁⓏⓁⓏⓁ — 281
ul. Heweliusza 22. **Road map** D1. ☎ *(0 58) 321 00 00.* FAX *(0 58) 321 00 20.*
@ helvelius@orbis.pl ᴡ www.orbis.pl
Built in the 1970s and situated in the old part of the city, this skyscraper
is one of the best hotels in Gdańsk. It provides a good range of services
and commands a magnificent view of historic Gdańsk. ▯▯▯▯▯
AE DC MC V

Price categories for a standard double room per night with bath or shower, breakfast, service and VAT included (in PLN):
ⓩ under 150
ⓩⓩ 150–300
ⓩⓩⓩ 300–450
ⓩⓩⓩⓩ 450–600
ⓩⓩⓩⓩⓩ over 600

CREDIT CARDS ACCEPTED
One or more of the following credit cards are accepted: American Express (AE), Diners Club (DC), MasterCard (MC), VISA (V).

FACILITIES FOR CHILDREN
Such facilities include cots, high chairs and sometimes childcare.

PRIVATE PARKING
The hotel has its own car park or parking spaces. These may not be on the same premises.

RESTAURANT
This is not necessarily recommended, although particularly good hotel restaurants are also listed in the restaurant section.

		NUMBER OF ROOMS	CREDIT CARDS ACCEPTED	FACILITIES FOR CHILDREN	PRIVATE PARKING	RESTAURANT
Holiday Inn ⓩⓩⓩⓩ ul. Podwale Grodzkie 9. **Road map** D1. 🕻 *(0 58) 300 60 00.* ☎ *(0 58) 300 60 03.* 🌐 www.holidayinn.pl/gdansk The Holiday Inn has small, modern rooms and is located in a shopping and office complex near the railway station. 🛏 📺 ♿ 🏊 🍴 🔞 🍽		143	AE DC MC V	●	■	●
POMERANIA						
BYTÓW: *Zamek w Bytowie* ⓩ ul. Zamkowa 2. **Road map** C1. 🕻 *and* ☎ *(0 59) 822 20 94.* 🌐 www.awinet.com.pl/hotzam This is not a particularly luxurious hotel but it is housed in a Teutonic castle where jousting tournaments are held. 🛏 📺		30	AE DC MC V	●	■	●
BYDGOSZCZ: *City* ⓩⓩⓩⓩ ul. 3 Maja 6. **Road map** C2. 🕻 *(0 52) 325 25 00.* ☎ *(0 52) 325 25 05.* @ city@city-hotel.pl 🌐 www.cityhotel.bydgoszcz.pl The City is a very good modern hotel of a high standard, situated in the city centre. The hotel's own Chopin Restaurant specializes in international cuisine; the fish dishes are recommended. 🛏 📺 ♿ 🔞		130	AE DC MC V		■	
BYDGOSZCZ: *Pod Orłem* ⓩⓩⓩⓩ ul. Gdańska 14. **Road map** C2. 🕻 *(0 52) 583 05 30.* ☎ *(0 52) 584 02 24.* @ podorlem@orbis.pl 🌐 www.orbis.pl Built in 1898, the Pod Orlem is a large hotel situated in the city centre. It is of a luxurious standard and has renovated interiors. It is a member of Polish Prestige Hotels. 🛏 📺 🔞 🍽 ♿		74	AE DC MC V		■	●
GDYNIA: *Orbis Gdynia* ⓩⓩⓩⓩ ul. Armii Krajowej 22. **Road map** D1. 🕻 *(0 58) 666 30 40.* ☎ *(0 58) 620 86 51.* @ gdynia@orbis.pl 🌐 www.orbis.pl Built in the 1980s, this large comfortable hotel is clean and modern, though somewhat expensive and anonymous. 🛏 📺 ♿ 🏊 🍽 🔞		297	AE DC MC V		■	●
JURATA: *Bryza* ⓩⓩⓩ ul. Świętopełka 1. **Road map** D1. 🕻 *(0 58) 675 23 43.* ☎ *(0 58) 675 24 26.* This luxurious hotel with its range of facilities is favoured by business people. It is situated on the Hel Peninsula and overlooks the sea. 🛏 ♿ 🔞 🏊 🍴 🍽 🏊 🔞		64	AE DC MC V		■	●
KAMIEŃ POMORSKI: *Hotel pod Muzami* ⓩ ul. Gryfitów 1. **Road map** A1. 🕻 *and* ☎ *(0 91) 382 22 40.* This small hotel is located in a historic residence of the first half of the 18th century. Simple, modest, but comfortable. 🛏 📺		12	AE DC MC V		■	●
KAMIEŃ POMORSKI: *Staromiejski* ⓩ ul. Rybacka 3. **Road map** A1. 🕻 *(0 91) 382 26 44.* ☎ *(0 91) 382 26 43.* The Staromiejski is a comfortable hotel in historic buildings around the Market Square, right on Kamień. 🛏 📺		38	AE DC MC V	●	■	●
KRĄG: *Podewils–Zamek Rycerski* ⓩⓩ Near Ostrów. **Road map** C1. 🕻 *(0 94) 318 82 91.* ☎ *(0 94) 316 91 11.* @ krag@podewils-hotel.pl 🌐 www.podewils-hotel.pl The hotel is located in a picturesque castle beside a lake in parkland. The atmosphere is warm and homely. Its excellent restaurant serves traditional Polish dishes; the cutlet served on rye bread is recommended. 🛏 📺 🍽		104	AE DC MC V		■	●
KROKOWA: *Zamek* ⓩⓩ ul. Zamkowa 1. **Road map** C1. 🕻 *(0 58) 774 21 12.* ☎ *(0 58) 774 21 10.* @ krokowa@z.pl 🌐 www.zkrokowa.z.pl The Zamek is a hotel in the newly renovated castle of the Pomeranian von Krokow family. The interior is furnished with Dutch antiques and has Baroque staircases. The restaurant is recommended. The surrounding park is just one of numerous attractions. 🛏 ♿ 🔞		21	AE DC MC V		■	●

ŁEBA: *Neptun*
ul. Sosnowa 1. **Road map** C1. ☎ *(0 59) 866 14 32.* **FAX** *(0 59) 866 23 57.*
🖩 www.leba.pl
This 19th-century hotel, in the style of a small medieval castle, is situated right on the coast. The comfortable rooms and private beach are its greatest attractions. 🛏 TV ⊚

Złzłzłzł | 32 | AE DC MC V

MACIEJEWO: *Hotel w Maciejewie*
Near Maszewo. **Road map** A2. ☎ *(0 91) 418 12 85.* **FAX** *(0 91) 418 11 30.*
@ palace@pomerania.com.pl 🖩 www.pomerania.com.pl
This comfortable hotel is in a 19th-century Neo-Gothic palace on Lake Lechickie, 50 km (31 miles) from Szczecin. It has a good restaurant, located in the former ballroom. 🛏 TV 🎿 🔲 ⊚

Złzł | 25 | AE DC MC V

MALBORK: *Zamek*
ul. Starościńska 14. **Road map** D1. ☎ and **FAX** *(0 55) 272 33 67.*
This hotel is located in one of the buildings of the great Castle of the Teutonic Knights *(see pp264–5)*. An overnight stay here is ideal for seeing one of the *son et lumière* shows that take place in the courtyard. 🛏 TV

Złzł | 42 | AE DC MC V

MIĘDZYZDROJE: *Nautilius*
Promenada Gwiazd 8. **Road map** A1. ☎ *(0 91) 328 09 99.* **FAX** *(0 91) 328 23 30.*
@ 18255346@pro.onet.pl
The Nautilius is a newly renovated hotel in a building dating from 1913, located on a typical seaside promenade. 🛏 TV

Złzł | 17 | AE DC MC V

MIĘDZYZDROJE: *Amber Baltic*
Promenada Gwiazd 1. **Road map** A1. ☎ *(0 91) 328 10 00.* **FAX** *(0 91) 328 10 22.*
@ office@vi-hotels.com 🖩 www.vi-hotels.com
This luxurious hotel on the coast, with private beach, is patronized by the stars of the Polish film and entertainment industry. The recommended Chopin Restaurant specializes in international cuisine. 🛏 TV 🎿 🔲 ▤ 🔲

Złzłzł | 190 | AE DC MC V

NOSOWO: *Pałac*
Near Biesiekierz. **Road map** B1. ☎ and **FAX** *(0 94) 318 03 80.* 🖩 www.maxmedia.pl/nosowo
This modest hotel is located in a dilapidated palace. It does, however, have pleasant surroundings. ⊚

Zł | 15 | AE DC MC V

NOWĘCIN: *Dwór*
Nowęcin. **Road map** C1. ☎ *(0 59) 866 16 15.* **FAX** *(0 59) 866 19 47.*
@ hoteldwornowecin@poczta.onet.pl 🖩 www.maxmedia.pl/dwor
This charming small palace is situated in picturesque forests near Łeba. The rooms have antique furniture. The restaurant specializes in traditional Polish cuisine, in particular dishes prepared according to old recipes. 🛏 TV

Złzł | 30 | AE DC MC V

PUCK: *Admirał*
ul. Morska 5. **Road map** D1. ☎ *(0 58) 673 11 97.* **FAX** *(0 58) 673 27 97.*
The Admiral is a small, clean hotel in a charming 19th-century residence in the town centre, with a somewhat old-fashioned atmosphere. The restaurant is the best in the neighbourhood. 🛏 TV

Złzł | 6 | AE DC MC V

RYNKÓWKA: *Grabowy Dwór*
Near Rychława. **Road map** D2. ☎ and **FAX** *(0 52) 332 84 29.*
This small guesthouse is in a 19th-century Neo-Gothic palace, situated in the Tuchola Forest. 🛏 TV ⊚

Złzł | 4 | | |

RZUCEWO: *Jan III Sobieski*
Near Żelistrzewo. **Road map** D1. ☎ and **FAX** *(0 58) 673 88 05.*
@ rzucewo@zameksobieski.pl 🖩 www.zameksobieski.pl
Situated on Puck Bay, this Neo-Gothic palace of 1840–45 was recently converted into a luxurious hotel. It has period rooms, a two-floor library, a vaulted lobby and a well-stocked wine cellar. It is also within easy reach of Gdańsk and Sopot. 🛏 TV

Złzł | 29 | AE DC MC V

SOPOT: *Grand Orbis SA*
ul. Powstańców Warszawy 12. **Road map** D1. ☎ *(0 58) 551 00 41.*
FAX *(0 58) 551 61 24.* @ sogrand@orbis.pl 🖩 www.orbis.pl
Before World War II this hotel was patronized by aristocrats and tycoons, who would frequent the casino. After the war, it drew many famous singers performing at the annual International Festival of Song in Sopot. Today it is a hotel of medium standard, but it is still attractive on account of its architecture and its convenient location overlooking the beach, near Sopot's famous pier.
🛏 🎿 ⊚ 🔲 🔲

Złzłzł | 112 | AE DC MC V

Price categories for a standard
double room per night with
bath or shower, breakfast,
service and VAT included
(in PLN):

ⓏⓁ under 150
ⓏⓁⓏⓁ 150–300
ⓏⓁⓏⓁⓏⓁ 300–450
ⓏⓁⓏⓁⓏⓁⓏⓁ 450–600
ⓏⓁⓏⓁⓏⓁⓏⓁⓏⓁ over 600

CREDIT CARDS ACCEPTED
One or more of the following credit cards are accepted: American
Express (AE), Diners Club (DC), MasterCard (MC), VISA (V).
FACILITIES FOR CHILDREN
Such facilities include cots, high chairs and sometimes childcare.
PRIVATE PARKING
The hotel has its own car park or parking spaces. These
may not be on the same premises.
RESTAURANT
This is not necessarily recommended, although particularly
good hotel restaurants are also listed in the restaurant section.

		NUMBER OF ROOMS	CREDIT CARDS ACCEPTED	FACILITIES FOR CHILDREN	PRIVATE PARKING	RESTAURANT

SOPOT: *Villa Hestia*   ⓏⓁⓏⓁⓏⓁⓏⓁ
ul. Władysława IV 3/5. **Road map** D1. 📞 and **FAX** *(0 58) 551 21 00.*
@ villa@hestia.pl W www.villa.hestia.pl
This well-run guesthouse is in an eclectic, renovated villa and houses
an exclusive restaurant and Gdańsk business club. The interior is
furnished with carefully chosen antiques. 🚗 TV 🔲 🍴

Number of rooms: 5 — AE DC MC V — Private Parking ■ — Restaurant ●

STRZEKĘCINO: *Bursztynowy Pałac*   ⓏⓁ
Near Świeszyn. **Road map** B1. 📞 and **FAX** *(0 94) 316 12 27.*
W www.hotel-bursztynowy-palac.pl
The hotel is located in the White Palace and neighbouring Amber Palace.
The charming interiors and comfortable rooms make this a relaxing place
to stay. Horse riding and a tennis court are available. 🚗 TV 🍴 🔲 🏊

Number of rooms: 30 — AE DC MC V — Facilities ● — Private Parking ■ — Restaurant ●

SZCZECIN: *Panorama*   ⓏⓁⓏⓁ
ul. Radosna 60. **Road map** A2. 📞 *(0 91) 460 76 07.* **FAX** *(0 91) 460 76 07.*
@ hotel@panorama-bg.pl
The Panorama is a modern, comfortable hotel in a renovated building
surrounded by a park. 🚗 TV 🔲 🔲 🍴

Number of rooms: 140 — AE DC MC V — Facilities ● — Private Parking ■ — Restaurant ●

SZCZECIN: *Park*   ⓏⓁⓏⓁⓏⓁ
ul. Plantowa 1. **Road map** A2. 📞 *(0 91) 359 55 95.* **FAX** *(0 91) 359 45 94.*
The Park is a small, quiet hotel located in a restored building
set in park grounds. 🚗 TV 🍴

Number of rooms: 15 — AE DC MC V — Private Parking ■ — Restaurant ●

SZCZECIN: *Radisson*   ⓏⓁⓏⓁⓏⓁⓏⓁⓏⓁ
pl. Rodła 10. **Road map** A2. 📞 *(0 91) 359 55 95.* **FAX** *(0 91) 359 45 94.*
@ info@szzzh.rdsas.com W www.radisson.com.pl
The Radisson is the most luxurious hotel in Western Pomerania.
Large and modern, it is situated in the city centre. There are
two excellent restaurants, the more expensive Renaissance and the
Europe, with a good lunchtime buffet. 🚗 TV 🔲 ▤ 🏊 🍴

Number of rooms: 368 — AE DC MC V — Facilities ● — Private Parking ■ — Restaurant ●

TORUŃ: *Helios*   ⓏⓁⓏⓁⓏⓁ
ul. Kraszewskiego 1/3. **Road map** D2. 📞 *(0 56) 619 85 50.* **FAX** *(0 56) 619 62 54.*
@ helios@orbis.pl W www.orbis.pl
A standard Orbis hotel built in the 1960s, situated near the historic
old city. The bathrooms are newly renovated. 🚗 TV 🔲

Number of rooms: 108 — AE DC MC V — Private Parking ■ — Restaurant ●

WARMIA, MAZURIA AND BIAŁYSTOK REGION

AUGUSTÓW: *Zajazd Turystyczny Hetman*   ⓏⓁⓏⓁ
ul. Sportowa 1. **Road map** F2. 📞 and **FAX** *(0 87) 644 53 45.*
Recently renovated, this hotel has a beautiful location beside Lake Necko.
🚗 TV 🔲

Number of rooms: 36 — AE DC MC V — Private Parking ■

BIAŁYSTOK: *Cristal*   ⓏⓁⓏⓁ
ul. Lipowa 3. **Road map** F2. 📞 *(0 85) 742 50 61.* **FAX** *(0 85) 742 58 00.*
@ cristal@cristal.com.pl W www.cristal.com.pl
A large hotel in the city centre, with a very good restaurant; the duck
with apples is recommended. The hotel is a member of Polish
Prestige Hotels. 🚗 TV 🔲 ⚡ 🍴 🔲

Number of rooms: 87 — AE DC MC V — Private Parking ■ — Restaurant ●

ELBLĄG: *Elzam*   ⓏⓁⓏⓁⓏⓁ
pl. Słowiański 2. **Road map** D1. 📞 *(0 55) 234 81 11.* **FAX** *(0 55) 232 40 83.*
The Elzam, in the town centre, dates from the socialist era. It has, however,
been renovated and can now be described as luxurious. 🚗 🔲 🔲 ▤

Number of rooms: 112 — AE DC MC V — Facilities ● — Private Parking ■ — Restaurant ●

GUTKOWO: *Żejmo*   ⓏⓁⓏⓁ
Near Olsztyn. **Road map** E2. 📞 *(0 89) 523 88 00.* **FAX** *(0 89) 523 88 01.*
Situated beside Lake Żbik, the Żejmo is the newest hotel in Warmia. The
great thatched roof is covered with 120,000 bundles of Mazurian reeds.
🚗 TV 🔲 🔲 ⚡ 🔲 ▤

Number of rooms: 142 — AE DC MC V — Facilities ● — Private Parking ■ — Restaurant ●

KADYNY: *Palace Hotel*
Near Tolmicko. **Road map** D1. █ *(0 55) 231 61 20.* FAX *(0 55) 231 62 00.*
W www.poltravel.com *or* W www.polhotels.com
The Palace is an elegant and restful hotel in the former buildings of a
stud once owned by Emperor Wilhelm II. Today the silence is broken
only by the sound of horses in the neighbouring stud farm. 🔲 █ 🏊
ZL ZL ZL | 38 | AE DC MC V

KARNITY: *Zamek*
Near Miłomłyn. **Road map** D2. █ *(0 89) 647 34 65.* FAX *(0 89) 647 34 64.*
Located in an impressive mid-19th century Neo-Gothic castle, this hotel
has a picturesque location on Lake Kocioł. 🔲 TV █
ZL ZL | 34 | AE DC MC V

KLEKOTKI: *Młyn Klekotki*
Near Godkowo. **Road map** D1. █ *(0 55) 249 72 08.* @ klekotki@polbox.com
This clean, elegant and modest hotel is located in a recently renovated
water mill. 🔲 TV 🍴
ZL ZL | 28

MIKOŁAJKI: *Gołabiewski*
ul. Mrągowska 34. **Road map** E2. █ *(0 87) 421 65 17.* FAX *(0 87) 421 60 10.*
This, the largest hotel in the Great Mazurian Lakes region, caters both
for tourists and business people. 🔲 TV █ 🛏 🏊 🍴
ZL ZL | 410 | AE DC MC V

MIKOŁAJKI: *Mazur*
pl. Wolności 6. **Road map** E2. █ *(0 87) 421 69 41.* FAX *(0 87) 421 69 43.*
This newly built hotel occupies the former town hall, a historic building
that was completely reconstructed. There is a yachting marina next to
the hotel. 🔲 🛏 █
ZL ZL | 34 | AE DC MC V

MRĄGOWO: *Mrongovia*
ul. Giżycka 6. **Road map** E2. █ *(0 89) 741 32 21 or 29.* FAX *(0 89) 741 32 20.*
@ mragov@orbis.pl W www.orbis.pl
This large, low-rise hotel on the shore of Lake Czos is good value for
families. A cheaper alternative is to rent a bungalow beside the hotel.
🔲 TV 🛏 🏊 🍴 █
ZL ZL | 254 | AE DC MC V

OGONKI: *Stara Kuźnia*
Near Węgorzewo. **Road map** F1. █ *and* FAX *(0 87) 427 00 90.* W www.mazury.com.pl
This small hotel is situated in an old forge on the picturesque shore of
Lake Święcajty. 🔲 TV █
ZL ZL | 9 | AE DC MC V

OLSZTYN: *Park*
ul. Warszawska 119. **Road map** E2. █ *(0 89) 524 06 04.* FAX *(0 89) 524 00 77.*
@ hpolsztyn@beph.pl
A large hotel on the Warsaw road, the Park is a standard modern
building that is luxuriously appointed. Guests may go horse riding.
🔲 TV 🍴 🛏 🛏 🏊
ZL ZL | 100 | AE DC MC V

OSIEKA: *Biały Książę*
Near Bartoszyce. **Road map** E1. █ *(0 89) 762 62 66.* FAX *(0 89) 762 20 46.*
This small hotel is in a renovated 19th-century palace with a comfortable
atmosphere and a good restaurant serving Polish dishes. 🔲 TV █
ZL ZL | 24

RESZEL: *Zamek w Reszlu*
ul. Podzamcze 3. **Road map** E1. █ *and* FAX *(0 89) 755 07 59.*
This small, modest hotel in the former Castle of the Bishops of Warmia
(see p282) is of an average standard though quite attractive. Well-
known Polish painters come here to paint in the open air. The castle
also houses a museum and hosts concerts, literary events and
art exhibitions. 🔲 TV
ZL | 12

SORKWITY: *Zamek*
ul. Zamkowa 15. **Road map** E2. █ *and* FAX *(0 89) 742 81 89.*
@ palace@cso.com.pl
This hotel in the former Neo-Gothic castle of the Mirbach family,
situated in a park by the lake, has a varied range of rooms. There
are also 4-bed camping huts to let. 🔲 TV █
ZL | 10

WIGRY: *Dom Pracy Twórczej*
Near Stary Folwark. **Road map** F1. █ *and* FAX *(0 87) 563 70 19.*
The hotel is located in a former Camaldolite monastery on Lake Wigry
(see p288), which is one of the most beautiful lakes in Poland. Some rooms
are located in what were the monks' living quarters. Open-air painting
events, concerts and art seminars are held here. This is a perfect place
for those seeking isolation and a peaceful atmosphere. 🔲 █
ZL | 49

For key to symbols see back flap

WHERE TO EAT

POLISH FOOD still suffers from a poor international image, but new restaurants serving national dishes as well as delicacies from different parts of the world have recently been established in Poland. Generally, it is not difficult to find a good restaurant in a large town or city, although the prices are often exorbitant. In smaller towns, on

The sign of Cracow's Chimera restaurant

the other hand, a little exploration may be required, but will often reveal a restaurant serving good, inexpensive food.

The restaurants and bars listed on pages 316–27 have been selected on the basis of the quality of their cuisine and service. Many are hotel restaurants, because in Poland, as elsewhere, this is where the best cuisine is often to be found.

The Kubicki restaurant in Ulica Wartka, Gdańsk

MEALS

THE TRADITIONAL Polish breakfast has a high calorie content. It consists of boiled or fried eggs, smoked meats, cheese and, in the winter, soup. Today, soup rarely appears at the breakfast table, although sausage and pâté are still normal sights. In town centres, tourists may have difficulty finding establishments serving breakfast. Only some bars and restaurants serve morning meals. Hotel restaurants, by contrast, customarily serve breakfast.

Traditionally, the evening meal – consisting of soup, a main course (usually a meat dish), and a dessert – is the most important meal of the day. Polish restaurants are gradually adopting a lighter cuisine, adding to traditional menus such dishes as salads, although this is not very common. Tourists may have problems finding good restaurants in small towns, where the choice is likely to be limited to soups, snacks and pork chops.

EATING OUT

MANY TOURISTS are surprised to find that, compared to other countries, Poland has a relatively small number of restaurants. This is because there is no great tradition of eating out, since most Polish people simply cannot afford to do it on a regular basis. Restaurant customers are therefore chiefly business people, commercial travellers and tourists.

In large towns and cities, particularly in Warsaw, there is a severe shortage of mid-price restaurants; nearly all restaurants are on the expensive side and the price of alcohol is exorbitant.

In Poland, lunch is served from noon and it is possible

to have your midday meal at any time in the afternoon. Restaurants then stay open until the late evening. In large towns and cities, they may keep their dining rooms open until the last guests are ready to leave, although the kitchens usually close at 10pm.

In more upmarket restaurants, be aware that customers are expected to be well dressed, although men are not usually required to wear a tie.

Most restaurants in large towns and cities accept credit cards. Elsewhere this is not the case and it is customary to pay in cash. Information on paying with credit cards is included in the list of restaurants on pages 316–27.

The Pod Aniołami restaurant in Cracow

U Wnuka, an inn in Zakopane

TYPES OF RESTAURANTS

VERY GOOD RESTAURANTS with gourmet menus can only be found in the largest cities, and even then they are not very numerous. In the countryside, the exceptions to the rule are restaurants in luxurious hotels, especially those located in castles or palaces. In most cities – and most especially in Warsaw – it is difficult to find a restaurant that serves good food at reasonable prices. In some cities it is possible to find bars serving so-called "home food", and it is often possible to have a good and inexpensive meal in a small town or village.

Cracow in particular is renowned for its good restaurants. Those in Poznań and Wrocław are also recommended, and Zakopane is famous for its regional cuisine.

CHEAP FOOD

THERE ARE SOME traditional establishments where it is possible to eat cheaply in Poland: bars. Unfortunately, few bars can be recommended, since most of them serve pre-prepared and often frozen food. In some places a "milk bar", a relic from Communist times, can be found and here a portion of pancakes or Russian ravioli (*pierogi*) costs very little.

There are also salad bars, where in addition to salads, which are sold by weight, sandwiches or soup are also served. Most pubs include one or two hot dishes on the

menu. A traditional Polish café serves only drinks and desserts. Newly opened bars in large towns and cities go beyond this, offering a selection of additional light dishes, such as soups, spaghetti, salads and warm vegetable dishes, but this variety comes at a high price.

The Tsarina restaurant in Warsaw

FAST FOOD

IN RECENT YEARS, Poland has experienced a real invasion of fast-food outlets in the form of McDonald's, Burger King and Pizza Hut. Many Polish fast-food establishments also offer takeaway hamburgers and portions of pizza. In

coastal resorts and the Great Mazurian Lakes region, fish is served from seasonal fish stalls. Other options include open-air barbecues serving roast sausages, or stalls serving Vietnamese and Turkish dishes.

PRICES

PRICES IN POLISH restaurants vary in the extreme. In a luxurious, renowned restaurant in a large town or city, especially in Warsaw, a three-course meal without wine may cost as much as 150–200 PLN. Elsewhere a comparable meal should cost not more than 70 PLN, and in smaller towns as little as 20–30 PLN.

Alcohol is relatively expensive in Poland, and the price of imported liquor is exorbitant.

The prices given on the menu include VAT and service. Beyond this, it is customary to leave a tip of 10 per cent. Very often, menu prices apply just to the main dish; an extra charge is made for potatoes, salads, and other side dishes, and they will appear on the bill as separate items. In the case of fish and meat dishes, such as a joint of pork, the price on the menu refers to a portion of 100 g (just under ¼ lb). When ordering, it is advisable to specify the weight of the portion, since the bill will show only the price of the whole meal.

Tables outside the Leśny Dwór restaurant in Wrocław in summer

What to Eat in Poland

Bread roll

POLISH CUISINE is deeply rooted in the multicultural tradition of that part of the country that, apart from Poles, was inhabited by Jews, Belarussians, Lithuanians and Ukrainians. Polish cuisine has also been influenced by neighbouring Russia, Germany, the Czech Republic and Austria, and has sometimes been inspired by Italian, French and even Oriental traditions. Poles are especially fond of aromatic smoked meats and herring, prepared in several different ways. Soup is a regular component of most meals and there is also a lot of meat, usually served with side dishes or sweet and sour sauces. Polish cuisine is famous for its excellent *pierogi* (ravioli), pancakes, stuffed *pyzy* (noodles) and fruit dumplings.

Śledzie
Herring in cream, with onion and apple, is a favourite starter.

Bigos
A national Polish dish, made up of cooked cabbage, mushrooms and different kinds of meat.

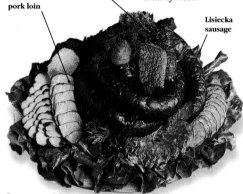

Roast pork joint

Smoked pork loin

Lisiecka sausage

Gołąbki
Cabbage leaves stuffed with rice and meat, served with tomato sauce.

Pierogi
Ravioli in several variations – stuffed with meat, sauerkraut and mushrooms, or with cottage cheese or fruit.

SMOKED MEATS
Traditionally prepared Polish meats are famous worldwide. Varieties include gruba krakowska, *a thick Cracovian sausage flavoured with garlic;* kabanosy, *sticks of dry smoked pork sausage thinly sliced; and* myśliwska, *a juniper-flavoured "hunters' sausage". The excellent Polish ham, sirloin or* baleron *(boned ham, boiled and smoked in a bladder) are other delicacies.*

Borsch
This is a well-known soup made with beetroot stock.

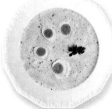

Żurek
Soup based on rye flour, with mushrooms, sausage and hard-boiled eggs.

Grzybowa
A traditional wild mushroom soup served with noodles.

Trout
Pan-fried or grilled, trout is a favourite freshwater fish in Poland.

Wiejska Kiszka
Black pudding, also known as kaszanka, *stuffed with buckwheat and served hot.*

Cracovian-style Duck
Stewed duck with mush-rooms served with a portion of Cracovian buckwheat.

Golonka
Roast knuckle of pork served with stewed cabbage and mashed potato.

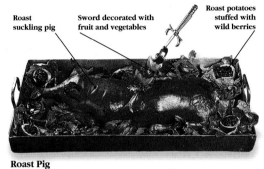

Roast suckling pig   Sword decorated with fruit and vegetables   Roast potatoes stuffed with wild berries

Roast Pig
Traditionally served at large receptions. The pig is roasted whole and stuffed with spicy or sweet buckwheat.

Pork Chop
A traditional pork chop cooked in breadcrumbs and usually served with potatoes and cabbage.

Zrazy Zawijane
Beef olives stuffed with pickles; served with buck-wheat and beetroot purée.

Stuffed Pork
Roast pork with prune stuffing.

CAKES AND PASTRIES

Polish cakes tend to be heavy and filling. The most popular is yeast cake. Poppy seeds mixed with nuts, almonds and raisins are a favourite filling for cake rolls. Poles are also fond of cheesecake, gingerbread and apple pie, as well as deep-fried frosted doughnuts with candied rose filling.

Gingerbread   Cheesecake

Polish doughnut   Poppy seed cake

Kremówka
A cream cake made famous by Pope John Paul II, who used to eat it as a young boy in his home town of Wadowice.

Choosing a Restaurant and Bar

T HE RESTAURANTS in this guide have been selected for their good
cuisine and interesting location. They are listed by region, the
coloured tabs in the margins corresponding with those by which
the regions of Poland are identified throughout the guide. For
the street map of Warsaw see pages 100–103. For the road map
of Poland, see the inside back cover.

	CREDIT CARDS ACCEPTED	VEGETARIAN DISHES	GOOD WINE LIST	GARDEN OR TERRACE

WARSAW

OLD AND NEW TOWNS (STARE I NOWE MIASTO): *Barbakan*   ㉵㉵
ul. Freta 1. **Map 2 D2.** ☎ *(0 22) 831 45 20.*
A good, relatively cheap restaurant specializing in Polish cuisine. The
menu includes simple dishes such as *pierogi* (ravioli) or *golonka* (knuckle
of pork), and excellent fish delicacies.

| AE DC MC V | ● | ■ | ● |

OLD AND NEW TOWNS: *Fukier*   ㉵㉵㉵㉵
Rynek Starego Miasta 27 (Old Market Square). **Map 2 D3.** ☎ *(0 22) 831 10 13.*
ⓦ www.it.pl/fukier
Cosy, antique interiors and Magda Gessler's masterly cooking skills
guarantee an excellent though by no means cheap dinner. Polish national
dishes predominate but there are also delicacies from other parts of
Europe. The delicious wild mushroom soup is recommended.

| AE DC MC V | ● | ■ | ● |

OLD AND NEW TOWNS: *Tsarina*   ㉵㉵㉵㉵
ul. Jezuicka 1/3. **Map 2 D3.** ☎ *(0 22) 635 74 74.*
Specializing in sophisticated Russian gourmet cuisine, this is a very
expensive and extremely stylish restaurant. Excellent *bliny* (pancakes)
with caviar, a very good Georgian-style goose and *ucha*, fish soup served
by three waiters who, having laced the soup with vodka, extinguish the
burning pieces of birch in the tureen.

| AE DC MC V | ● | ■ | |

ROYAL ROUTE (TRAKT KRÓLEWSKI): *Studio Buffo*   ㉵㉵
ul. Konopnickiej 6. **Map 4 D3.** ☎ *(0 22) 626 89 07.*
This restaurant specializes in traditional Polish cuisine by Maciej Kuroń, a
well-known chef who appears on television and in magazines.

| AE DC MC V | ● | ■ | |

ROYAL ROUTE (TRAKT KRÓLEWSKI): *Lalka*   ㉵㉵㉵㉵
ul. Prusa 2 (in the Sheraton Hotel). **Map 4 D3.** ☎ *(0 22) 657 67 06.*
A luxurious restaurant with excellent cuisine that is a mixture of Polish
and French influences. 🛉

| AE DC MC V | ● | ■ | |

ROYAL ROUTE (TRAKT KRÓLEWSKI): *Malinowa*   ㉵㉵㉵㉵
ul. Krakowskie Przedmieście 42/44 (in the Hotel Bristol). **Map 2 D4.**
☎ *(0 22) 625 25 25.* @ bristol@it.com.pl ⓦ www.lemeridien-bristol.com
In this restaurant, very expensive but considered to be the best in
Warsaw, the speciality is French cuisine. 🛉

| AE DC MC V | ● | ■ | |

CITY CENTRE (ŚRÓDMIEŚCIE): *El Popo*   ㉵㉵
ul. Senatorska 27. **Map 1 C4.** ☎ *(0 22) 827 23 40.*
@ siesta@siesta.com.pl ⓦ www.siesta.com.pl
The best Mexican restaurant in Warsaw, recommended for a proper
taco feast. 🛉

| AE DC MC V | ● | ■ | |

CITY CENTRE (ŚRÓDMIEŚCIE): *Prohibicja*   ㉵㉵
ul. Podwale 1. **Map 2 D3.** ☎ *(0 22) 635 62 11.*
A small restaurant with a bar and café, popular for its simple, delicious
food and for its friendly proprietors. It is frequented by Polish film stars.

| AE DC MC V | ● | ■ | ● |

CITY CENTRE (ŚRÓDMIEŚCIE): *La Boheme*   ㉵㉵㉵
pl. Teatralny (inside the National Theatre). **Map 1 C4.** ☎ *(0 22) 692 06 81.*
ⓦ www.laboheme.com.pl
A restaurant specializing in sophisticated French cuisine as well as
traditional Polish dishes. The kitchen sells some of its products in a
nearby bar, which serves snacks and takeaways. 🛉

| AE DC MC V | ● | ■ | |

CITY CENTRE (ŚRÓDMIEŚCIE): *Zachęta*   ㉵㉵㉵
pl. Małachowskiego 3. **Map 1 C5.** ☎ *(0 22) 828 05 84.*
Italian dishes served in an extravagant interior with décor in the
form of bent metal plates, cables with colourful lights and other
similarly bizarre objects.

| AE DC MC V | ● | ■ | ● |

		CREDIT CARDS ACCEPTED	VEGETARIAN DISHES	GOOD WINE LIST	GARDEN OR TERRACE

Price categories are for a three-course meal for one without wine, including VAT (in PLN).

ⓩ under 40
ⓩⓩ 40–70
ⓩⓩⓩ 70–100
ⓩⓩⓩⓩ over 100

CREDIT CARDS ACCEPTED
The following credit cards are accepted: American Express (AE), Diners Club (DC), MasterCard (MC), VISA (V).

VEGETARIAN DISHES
The menu includes dishes suitable for vegetarians.

GOOD WINE LIST
A wide choice of different wines.

GARDEN OR TERRACE
Meals served outdoors, weather permitting.

FURTHER AFIELD: *Lokomotywa* — ⓩ — AE DC MC V — ● — — ●
ul. Krucza 17. **Map 3 C3.** ((0 22) 621 78 74.
A restaurant designed like an old locomotive, with techno-style interior and real home cooking – for example, *pierogi* (ravioli) or *racuchy* (apple pancakes).

FURTHER AFIELD: *Flik* — ⓩⓩ — AE DC JCB MC V — ● — ■ — ●
ul. Puławska 43. ((0 22) 849 44 06. Ⓦ www.iexperts.com/flik
Masterful cuisine at reasonable prices served in spacious, bright interiors. Salmon in pancakes, roast duck with fruit and perfectly prepared fish – for example a pikeperch on a potato pancake with apples – are considered to be the restaurant's finest specialities. For a cheap snack, there is Mały Flik, on the lower floor. 🏃

FURTHER AFIELD: *Mekong* — ⓩⓩ — AE DC MC V — ● — ■ —
ul. Wspólna 35. **Map 3 B2.** ((0 22) 621 18 81.
@ siesta@siesta.com.pl Ⓦ www.siesta.com.pl
One of the best Chinese restaurants in Warsaw. The Szechuan-style pork is recommended.

FURTHER AFIELD: *Qchnia Artystyczna* — ⓩⓩ — AE DC MC V — ● — — ●
al. Ujazdowskie 6 (inside Ujazdowski Castle). **Map 3 C5.** ((0 22) 625 76 27.
@ qchnia@waw.pdi.net
This attractively decorated restaurant in Ujazdów Castle serves high-quality dishes at reasonable prices. The international cuisine includes sophisticated salads, tasty herrings, excellent sirloin in cherry sauce and pancakes that melt in the mouth.

FURTHER AFIELD: *Santorini* — ⓩⓩ — AE DC MC V — ● — — ●
ul. Egipska 7. ((0 22) 672 05 25. @ siesta@siesta.com.pl Ⓦ www.siesta.com.pl
A restaurant with cosy interiors, surprisingly laid out in an inconspicuous building, serving excellent cuisine from different regions of Greece.

FURTHER AFIELD: *Kosmiczny Krab* — ⓩⓩⓩ — AE DC MC V — — ■ —
ul. Koszykowa 54. ((0 22) 630 88 55.
A restaurant serving a range of European food. The décor has a space theme. 🏃

FURTHER AFIELD: *Belvedere* — ⓩⓩⓩⓩ — AE DC MC V — — ■ — ●
New Orangery in Łazienki Palace, entrance on ul. Parkowa. ((0 22) 841 48 06 or 841 22 50. @ restauracja@belvedere.com.pl Ⓦ www.belvedere.com.pl
The Belvedere restaurant is in a fine location in Łazienki Park, in a beautiful conservatory filled with tropical plants, with excellent French cuisine to match.

MAZOVIA AND THE LUBLIN REGION

GRÓJEC: *La Terrazza* — ⓩⓩ — AE DC MC V — ● — ■ — ●
ul. Graniczna 1 B. **Road map E4.** ((0 48) 664 58 17. @ terrazza@laterrazza.pl
An authentic Italian restaurant run by cooks from the southern Apennines. Traditional cuisine and a wide choice of dishes have earned it wide popularity.

KAZIMIERZ DOLNY: *Restauracja-Grill w Domu Michalaków* — ⓩ — AE DC MC V — ● — — ●
ul. Nadrzeczna 24. **Road map F4.** ((0 81) 881 05 79. @ michalak@man.pulawy.pl
Despite the implication of its name, the restaurant is not limited to serving chargrilled meat and fish. The salad bar serves a range of salads and good soup. 🏃

KAZIMIERZ DOLNY: *Zielona Tawerna* — ⓩⓩ — AE DC MC V — — ■ — ●
ul. Nadwiślańska 4. **Road map F4.** ((0 81) 881 03 08. FAX (0 81) 882 10 60.
The restaurant specializes in international cuisine. The meat dishes, including excellent sirloin steak served in a pumpkin shell, are especially recommended. 🏃

For key to symbols see back flap

<table>
<tr><td>
Price categories are for a three-course meal for one without wine, including VAT (in PLN).
ⓩ under 40
ⓩⓩ 40–70
ⓩⓩⓩ 70–100
ⓩⓩⓩⓩ over 100
</td>
<td>
CREDIT CARDS ACCEPTED
The following credit cards are accepted: American Express (AE), Diners Club (DC), MasterCard (MC), VISA (V).
VEGETARIAN DISHES
The menu includes dishes suitable for vegetarians.
GOOD WINE LIST
A wide choice of different wines.
GARDEN OR TERRACE
Meals served outdoors, weather permitting.
</td>
</tr>
</table>

		CREDIT CARDS ACCEPTED	VEGETARIAN DISHES	GOOD WINE LIST	GARDEN OR TERRACE
LUBLIN: *Piwnica u Biesów* Rynek 18. **Road map** F4. 【 *(0 81) 532 16 48.* In this restaurant, named the Devil's Cellar, the attractions are such dishes as *Golonka Boruty* (the Devil Boruta's Knuckle of Pork) and *Schab Sinobrodego* (Bluebeard's Pork Chop). There is good live music in the evening at weekends.	ⓩ	AE DC MC V	●	■	●
LUBLIN: *Hades* ul. Peowiaków 12. **Road map** F4. 【 *(0 81) 532 87 61.* Ⓦ www.hades.lublin.pl A fashionable restaurant with good cuisine, specializing chiefly in Polish delicacies. The menu also includes some original dishes invented by famous restaurant guests. The pork, herring in cream and particularly the steak tartare, prepared in several different ways, are recommended. 🏃	ⓩⓩ	AE DC MC V		■	
LUBLIN: *Oberża Artystyczna Złoty Osioł* ul. Grodzka 5a. **Road map** F4. 【 *(0 81) 532 90 42.* @ zlotyosiol@poczta.fm This restaurant, located in the very centre of the old town of Lublin, has an intimate interior, where art exhibitions are organized. The dishes have such extraordinary names as "Donkey's Ear" or "Young Breasts": clarification from the waiter will be needed.	ⓩⓩ	AE DC MC V	●	■	●
LUBLIN: *Resursa* ul. Krakowskie Przedmieście 68. **Road map** F4. 【 *(0 81) 534 29 91.* Excellent Polish cuisine in a traditional style. Magnificent beef steaks and shish kebabs.	ⓩⓩ	AE DC MC V	●	■	
LUBLIN: *Piwnica* ul. M. Skłodowskiej-Curie 12. **Road map** F4. 【 *(0 81) 534 39 19.* A modest restaurant specializing in Mediterranean cuisine. The excellent assorted Italian cold meats are recommended.	ⓩⓩⓩ	AE DC MC V		■	
PŁOCK: *Zajazd Rybaki* ul. Mostowa 5/7. **Road map** D3. 【 *(0 24) 264 56 57.* Ⓦ www.zajazd-rybaki.plo.pl or Ⓦ www.hotelguide.com The restaurant is located in a historic building on the River Vistula. The speciality is Polish dishes, including trout in beef stock. 🏃	ⓩ	AE DC MC V	●	■	●
SEROCK: *Pod Złotym Linem* ul. Wierzbica 9. **Road map** E3. 【 *(0 22) 782 74 73.* One of the best fish restaurants in Poland, with a regular clientele that comes from Warsaw for Sunday lunch. The restaurant serves chiefly freshwater – and freshly caught – fish. Specialities are tench and perch in cream. 🏃	ⓩⓩ	AE DC MC V			●
ŚWIDNIK: *Świdniczanka* al. Niepodległości 7. **Road map** F4. 【 *(0 81) 751 29 30.* A cheap restaurant with good cuisine. The Świdnik-style pork chop and the carp in cream are recommended.	ⓩ		●		
<div align="center">**CRACOW**</div>					
Chimera ul. św Anny 3. **Road map** D5. 【 *(0 12) 423 21 78, ext 104.* @ kontact@chimera.com.pl Ⓦ www.chimera.restauracje.com Polish dishes, including roast pork, are served on the ground floor. The salad bar in the basement serves light, healthy food.	ⓩⓩ	AE DC MC V	●	■	●
Chłopskie Jadło ul. św Agnieszki 1. **Road map** D5. 【 *(0 12) 421 85 20.* @ chlopskiejadlo@restauracje.com Ⓦ www.chlopskiejadlo.restauracje.com A fine restaurant, with interiors in the style of a peasant's hut, serving Polish dishes such as black pudding and *pierogi* (ravioli). Fish dishes are served in the part of the restaurant called *Baba Ryba* (Woman Fish).	ⓩⓩ				

Hawełka

Rynek Główny 34. **Road map** D5. (*(0 12) 422 47 53.* @ hawelka@kki.com.pl
This establishment, named after its 19th-century founder, consists of two
restaurants under one roof. The relatively inexpensive restaurant on the
ground floor specializes in Cracovian cuisine, including an excellent
Cracovian-style duck. On the first floor is a very expensive restaurant
serving sophisticated dishes.

ⓩⓩ | AE DC MC V

Mesa kapitana Cook'a

ul. Zamoyskiego 52. **Road map** D5. (*(0 12) 656 08 93.* W www.gwc.net/mesa
This fish restaurant is located in Podgórze, far from the centre of Cracow and
thus out of the way of the crowds of tourists. Recommended dishes are the
crab soup, *pierogi* (ravioli) with salmon, and bran pancakes with salmon.

ⓩⓩ | AE DC MC V

Orient Express

ul. Poselska 22. **Road map** D5. (*(0 12) 422 66 72.*
The interior is in the style of a 19th-century restaurant car on the Orient
Express. The menu features international dishes, including beef cooked
in the Flemish style and delicious pancakes.

ⓩⓩ | AE DC MC V

Paese

ul. Poselska 24. **Road map** D5. (*(0 12) 421 62 73.*
@ paese@fema.krakow.pl W www.paese.fema.krakow.pl
The best Polish restaurant specializing in Corsican cuisine. The menu
includes a selection of excellent fish and seafood dishes.

ⓩⓩ | AE DC MC V

Pod Aniołami

ul. Grodzka 35. **Road map** D5. (*(0 12) 421 39 99.*
The restaurant is located in medieval cellars, decorated with a selection of
historic objects. The menu features traditional Polish dishes, highlanders'
delicacies in particular. You can try *oszczypki* (a special kind of cheese
prepared by Polish highlanders) or *żurek*, highlander style (a sour soup).

ⓩⓩ | AE DC MC V

Wentzl

Rynek Główny 19. **Road map** D5. (*(0 12) 429 57 12.*
W www.wentzl.restauracje.com
The restaurant has traditions dating back to the 18th century.
Today, as in the past, it serves dishes typical of the Austro-Hungarian
empire. The speciality is *maczanka* Cracovian style, rolled pork with
cumin and onion sauce.

ⓩⓩ | AE DC MC V

A Dong

ul. Brodzińskiego 3. **Road map** D5. (*(0 12) 656 48 72.*
W www.gwc.com.pl/adong
One of the best Asian restaurants in Poland. Chinese and Vietnamese
dishes predominate, but the menu also includes Far Eastern cuisine. The
Peking duck is recommended.

ⓩⓩⓩ | AE DC MC V

Alef

ul. Szeroka 17. **Road map** D5. (*(0 12) 421 38 70.* W www.alef.pl
An excellent restaurant located in the centre of an old Jewish district of
Kazimierz and specializing in Jewish cuisine. Diners may sample such
delicacies as stuffed carp, goose livers or *czulent* (a Hungarian dish)
while listening to "Klezmer" band players.

ⓩⓩⓩ | AE DC MC V

Lemon

ul. Floriańska 53. **Road map** D5.
A small, cosy Serbian restaurant serving grilled dishes, such as shish
kebab and *pljeskavica* (a traditional Serbian soup).

ⓩⓩⓩ | AE DC MC V

Cyrano de Bergerac

ul. Sławkowska 26. **Road map** D5. (*(0 12) 411 72 88.* W www.cyranodebergerac.pl
This French restaurant run by Pierre Gaillard, a chef from Lyon, France, is
relatively expensive, but the quality fully justifies the prices. The fish
dishes are particularly recommended.

ⓩⓩⓩⓩ | AE DC MC V

MAŁOPOLSKA (LESSER POLAND)

BIELSKO-BIAŁA: *Patria*

ul. Wzgórze 19. **Road map** D6. (*(0 33) 812 24 08.*
The menu at this restaurant, with its interesting Secessionist interior,
features Polish dishes as well as delicacies from other countries. The
Danie Królewskie (Royal Dish) consists of three large portions of different
kinds of meat, served with rice and fruit. 🍴

ⓩ | AE DC MC V

Price categories are for a three-course meal for one without wine, including VAT (in PLN):

ⓩ under 40
ⓩⓩ 40–70
ⓩⓩⓩ 70–100
ⓩⓩⓩⓩ over 100

CREDIT CARDS ACCEPTED
The following credit cards are accepted: American Express (AE), Diners Club (DC), MasterCard (MC), VISA (V).

VEGETARIAN DISHES
The menu includes dishes suitable for vegetarians.

GOOD WINE LIST
A wide choice of different wines.

GARDEN OR TERRACE
Meals served outdoors, weather permitting.

	CREDIT CARDS ACCEPTED	VEGETARIAN DISHES	GOOD WINE LIST	GARDEN OR TERRACE
BIELSKO-BIAŁA: *Zajazd Klimczok* ⓩ ul. Bystrzańska 94. **Road map** D6. 🕻 *(0 33) 814 15 67.* A wooden inn with a fireplace in the dining room. On the menu are traditional Polish and regional dishes, with Silesian cuisine predominating. 🛉	AE DC MC V			●
BRZESKO: *Zajazd Okocim* ⓩ ul. Wesoła 4. **Road map** E5. 🕻 *(0 14) 663 17 61.* This inn, located in a converted early-20th-century building decorated with paintings from Zalipie, serves cheap, simple food. There is a wide choice of Polish dishes, including *pierogi* (ravioli) or Zalipie-style *żurek* (sour soup). 🛉	AE DC MC V	●		●
GŁOGOCZÓW: *Chłopskie Jadło* ⓩ Głogoczów 196. **Road map** D6. 🕻 *(0 90) 31 58 13.* @ chlopskiejadlo@restauracje.com Ⓦ www.chlopskiejadlo.restauracje.com This restaurant is one of the greatest culinary revelations of recent years in Poland. As its name (which translates as Peasants' Fare) suggests, country dishes are its speciality. There are *pierogi* (ravioli) and simple tasty soups, especially *żurek* (sour soup) and cabbage soup, as well as excellent meats.	AE DC MC V	●		●
GŁOGOCZÓW: *Nowina* ⓩ Głogoczów 1 – Dwór. **Road map** D6. 🕻 *(0 12) 273 12 26.* This restaurant, located in a small manor house, is a competitor for Chłopskie Jadło. Old Polish cuisine, including mutton steak and Lithuanian *kołduny* (dumplings stuffed with meat) is the speciality. For several years, Novina has topped the list of the best restaurants in Poland. 🛉	AE DC MC V	●		●
KIELCE: *Winnica* ⓩ ul. Winnicka 4. **Road map** E5. 🕻 *(0 41) 344 45 76.* The Winnica is a cheap, good restaurant, serving Polish and Ukrainian dishes. 🛉	AE DC MC V			●
ŁAŃCUT: *Pałacyk* ⓩ ul. Paderewskiego 18. **Road map** F5. 🕻 *(0 17) 225 20 43.* This restaurant is located in a late-19th-century villa, with period interiors decorated with hunters' trophies. The cuisine is a mixture of Polish and Oriental fare.	AE DC MC V	●	■	●
NOWY SĄCZ: *Ratuszowa* ⓩ Rynek 1. **Road map** E6. 🕻 *(0 18) 443 56 15.* Located in the basement of the town hall, this restaurant specializes in traditional Polish dishes. The *pierogi* (ravioli), *gołąbki* (cabbage leaves stuffed with meat and rice), spare ribs, and above all, *golonka* (knuckle of pork) in honey are recommended.	AE DC MC V	●	■	●
NOWY SĄCZ: *Kupiecka* ⓩⓩ Rynek 10. **Road map** E6. 🕻 *(0 18) 442 08 31.* Located in picturesque vaulted cellars, this restaurant serves mainly international dishes. The steaks and the fish dishes, such as trout in horseradish sauce, are recommended. 🛉	AE DC MC V	●	■	
PRZEMYŚL: *Karpacka* ⓩ ul. Kościuszki 5. **Road map** F6. 🕻 *(0 16) 678 64 88.* Good, inexpensive, traditional Polish cuisine. The simple dishes include *pierogi* (ravioli) with cabbage and mushrooms and *golonka* (knuckle of pork). 🛉	AE DC MC V	●		
PRZEMYŚL: *Wyrwigrosz* ⓩ pl. Dominikański 25. **Road map** F6. 🕻 *(0 16) 678 58 58.* Ⓦ www.wyrwigrosz.pl This is both a popular pub and a restaurant serving good food. The menu is mostly inspired by Oriental cuisine.	AE DC MC V	●		●

SIENIAWA: *Pałacowa* ㉿㉿ AE DC MC V
Sieniawa 122. **Road map** F5. (*(0 16) 622 73 73.*
The Baroque palace of the Sieniawski family houses a small hotel and a pleasant restaurant. It specializes in Polish cuisine and offers an excellent selection of wines. ⚐

SUCHA BESKIDZKA: *Karczma Rzym* ㉿ AE DC MC V
Rynek 1. **Road map** D6. (*(0 33) 874 27 97.*
A traditional inn specializing in Silesian cuisine. The Strzyżawa-style *żurek* (a sour soup) is highly recommended.

WISŁA: *Wiślańska Strzecha* ㉿
ul. Stellera 8–19. **Road map** D6. (*(0 33) 855 27 54.*
For a fast, tasty and very cheap meal, this is ideal. On the menu feature simple Silesian and traditional Polish dishes.

ZAKOPANE: *Dworek Bawarski* ㉿ AE DC MC V
ul. Bogdańskiego 5. **Road map** D6. (*(0 18) 206 65 11.*
This restaurant serves Bavarian dishes. On the menu are potato salads, Bavarian-style knuckle of pork and roast meat in wine sauce. ⚐

ZAKOPANE: *Poraj* ㉿ AE DC MC V
ul. Krupówki 50. **Road map** D6. (*(0 18) 206 37 65.*
The restaurant was established in 1887. It is famous for tasty snacks, particularly *awanturki* (little crudités). Excellent *bigos* (sauerkraut with mushrooms and different kinds of meat), tripe and, in season, fried mushrooms are also available.

ZAKOPANE: *Redykołka* ㉿ AE DC MC V
ul. Kościeliska 1. **Road map** D6. (*(0 18) 206 63 32.* W www.zakopane.onet.pl/redyk.htm
This restaurant, located in a wooden hut, serves typical highlanders' dishes, especially lamb. The waitresses wear traditional Zakopane dress. ⚐

ZAKOPANE: *U Wnuka* ㉿ AE DC MC V
ul. Kościeliska 8. **Road map** D6. (*(0 18) 206 61 47.*
Excellent highlanders' dishes are served in small rooms in this 150-year-old wooden house. The *kwa śnica* (a sour soup of the region) and the spare ribs are delicious. For dessert, the pancakes with berries are recommended. A highlanders' band provides live music at weekends.

ZAKOPANE: *Bąkowo Zohylina* ㉿㉿ AE DC MC V
ul. Piłsudskiego 28a. **Road map** D6. (*(0 18) 201 20 45.*
@ zohylina@zakopane.top.pl W www.zohylina.zakopane.top.pl
Excellent regional cuisine including *oszczypki* (cheeses), spare ribs, knuckle of pork, roast lamb and game. ⚐

ZAKOPANE: *Zbyrcok* ㉿㉿ AE DC MC V
ul. Krupówki 29. **Road map** D6. (*(0 18) 201 32 10.*
Typically of Zakopane, this restaurant has wooden interiors, the waitresses wear regional dress and the menu features *kwa śnica* (a sour soup of the region), delicious roasted duck and *placki po zbójnicku* (potato pancakes).

SILESIA

GŁOGÓW: *Złoty Lew* ㉿㉿ AE DC MC V
ul. Grodzka 2. **Road map** B4. (*(0 76) 835 24 49.*
A restaurant with a wide choice of dishes for a range of tastes, from snails and frogs' legs to simpler fare. ⚐

JELENIA GÓRA: *Karczma Grodzka* ㉿㉿㉿
ul. Grodzka 5. **Road map** B4. (*(0 75) 764 63 59.*
A restaurant with antique interiors and excellent regional cuisine. The *pierogi* (ravioli) with cabbage and the *chłopskie jadło* (peasants' food) are recommended. ⚐

KARPACZ: *Thai* ㉿㉿ AE DC MC V
ul. Obrońców Pokoju 7a (in the Promyk Hotel). **Road map** B5. (*(0 75) 761 61 96.*
W www.karpacz.com.pl/promyk
A small restaurant with a beautiful view serving Oriental, chiefly Thai, dishes.

KATOWICE: *Chopin* ㉿㉿㉿ AE DC MC V
ul. Kościuszki 169. **Road map** D5. (*(0 32) 205 24 68.*
An elegant and cosy restaurant serving a selection of French and Polish dishes. The *rolada śląska* (stuffed rolled meat) with dumplings is popular and highly recommended.

<table>
<tr><td>

Price categories are for a three-course meal for one without wine, including VAT (in PLN).

ⓩ under 40
ⓩⓩ 40–70
ⓩⓩⓩ 70–100
ⓩⓩⓩⓩ over 100

</td><td>

CREDIT CARDS ACCEPTED
The following credit cards are accepted: American Express (AE), Diners Club (DC), MasterCard (MC), VISA (V).
VEGETARIAN DISHES
The menu includes dishes suitable for vegetarians.
GOOD WINE LIST
A wide choice of different wines.
GARDEN OR TERRACE
Meals served outdoors, weather permitting.

</td></tr>
</table>

	CREDIT CARDS ACCEPTED	VEGETARIAN DISHES	GOOD WINE LIST	GARDEN OR TERRACE
KATOWICE: *Polska* ⓩⓩⓩ ul. Warszawska 37. **Road map** D5. ☎ *(0 32) 206 86 50.* Polska is an elegant restaurant specializing in Polish dishes, whose names are inspired by *Pan Tadeusz*, a poem by Adam Mickiewicz *(see p23)*. In the basement, *Piwnica u Marchołta* (Marchołt's Cellar) serves cheaper food, and for music enthusiasts there is live jazz or blues at weekends.	AE DC MC V			●
MYSŁOWICE: *Divertimento* ⓩⓩ ul. Krakowska 5. **Road map** D5. ☎ *(0 32) 222 24 59.* A very good Italian restaurant with a wide choice of wines and an interesting menu, offering excellent *eskalopki cielęce* (veal), *carpaccio* and various kinds of spaghetti. 🏃	AE DC MC V		■	●
SZKLARSKA PORĘBA: *Weneda* ⓩⓩ ul. Wzgórze Paderewskiego 12. **Road map** B5. ☎ *(0 75) 717 34 62.* @ weneda@weneda.dc.pl Ⓦ www.weneda.dc.pl Weneda is a small hotel with a good restaurant, located in an extended 19th-century guesthouse. The Argentine sirloin steak in pepper sauce is highly recommended. 🏃	AE DC MC V	●		●
ŚWIDNICA: *Park* ⓩⓩ ul. Pionierów 20. **Road map** B5. ☎ *(0 74) 853 70 98.* Ⓦ www.draconis.com.pl This is a good and not unduly expensive restaurant serving an interesting choice of dishes from different parts of the world.	AE DC MC	●	■	●
WAŁBRZYCH-KSIĄŻ: *Zamkowa* ⓩ ul. Piastów Śląskich 1a. **Road map** B5. ☎ *(0 74) 843 27 98.* Ⓦ www.wn.pl/ksiaz This restaurant, with a small hotel, is located in the great Książ Castle *(see p185)*, where a luxury complex is being built. The restaurant, not yet modernized, serves good, inexpensive traditional Polish dishes.	AE DC MC V	●		●
WOJNOWICE: *Restauracja Zamkowa* ⓩⓩ Wojnowice near Mrozowo. **Road map** B4. ☎ *(0 71) 317 07 26.* The restaurant and hotel in Wojnowice *(see p186)* are located in the magnificent Renaissance manor house on the island. The good traditional Polish cuisine includes excellent dripping with onion, homemade sausages and black pudding.	AE DC MC V	●		
WROCŁAW: *Vega* ⓩ ul. Sukiennice 1. **Road map** C4. ☎ *(0 71) 344 39 34.* A small vegetarian restaurant serving Hindu dishes. As you might expect, no alcohol is available.		●		
WROCŁAW: *Karczma Lwowska* ⓩⓩ ul. Rynek 4. **Road map** C4. ☎ *(0 71) 343 98 87.* A restaurant in a historical residence near the Market Square, with comfortable 19th-century-style interiors. The menu features dishes typical of the eastern borderland; the grilled meat, rubbed with aromatic herbs, and the stuffed veal are recommended. 🏃	AE DC MC V		■	●
WROCŁAW: *Karczma Piastów* ⓩⓩ ul. Kiełbaśnicza 6/7. **Road map** C4. ☎ *(0 71) 372 48 96.* @ dworpol@wr.onet.pl Ⓦ www.wroclaw.com/dworpol.htm The cheapest restaurant in the Dwór Polski hotel chain. The rustic interior is arranged in the style of a peasant's hut. The menu offers simple traditional Polish dishes, including *zrazy* (beef olives) with buckwheat, and pheasant in cranberry sauce.	AE DC MC V		■	●
WROCŁAW: *Magistracka* ⓩⓩ ul. Szewska 59. **Road map** C4. ☎ *(0 71) 341 75 70.* Magistracka is an exclusive restaurant with an elegant interior, serving Polish and international dishes. The speciality is meat in sweet and sour fruit sauces.	AE DC MC V	●	■	

WROCŁAW: *Casablanca*
ul. Włodkowica 8a. **Road map** C4. █ *(0 71) 344 78 17.*
The walls of this elegant restaurant are hung with photographs of
Humphrey Bogart and Ingrid Bergman. Among the fine Italian dishes, the
grilled salmon and the spaghetti with seafood are especially
recommended. Reservation is essential at weekends. 🏃

ⓩⓩ | AE DC MC V

WROCŁAW: *Czwartkowa* and *Królewska*
Rynek 5. **Road map** C4. █ *(0 71) 372 48 97.*
The Czwartkowa and Królewska are two different, relatively expensive
restaurants in the Dwór Polski hotel chain. Both have charming, tastefully
renovated interiors and are situated in the Market Square town house.
The menu is dominated by Polish dishes, such as *pierogi* (ravioli) and
bigos (sauerkraut), and the speciality is royal-style duck. 🏃

ⓩⓩⓩ | AE DC MC V

WROCŁAW: *Spiż*
Rynek, Nowy Ratusz 2. **Road map** C4. █ *(0 71) 344 72 25.*
In this restaurant in spacious vaulted cellars, Polish cooking
predominates but dishes from other countries are also served. The game
and spare ribs with Silesian dumplings are especially popular, as is the
beer made in the restaurant's own small brewery. The beer should ideally
be sampled with rye bread and homemade dripping. 🏃

ⓩⓩⓩ | AE DC MC V

WIELKOPOLSKA (GREATER POLAND)

GRABOWNO: *Dworek*
Grabowno near Piły. **Road map** C2. █ *(0 67) 287 41 28.*
This old manor house contains an excellent restaurant serving Polish and
other dishes. The *kołduny* (dumplings stuffed with meat) and the duck
with apples are recommended. 🏃

ⓩ | AE DC MC V

IWNO: *Zajazd Podbipięta*
Iwno. **Road map** C3. █ *(0 61) 817 85 49.*
This is one of the picturesque road-houses of the 1970s, with a restaurant
serving good, inexpensive meals. Gourmets from Poznań and elsewhere
come here to enjoy the "family joint of pork" for four people. 🏃

ⓩ | AE DC MC V

LESZNO: *Wieniawa*
Rynek 29. **Road map** C4. █ *(0 65) 529 50 58.* Ⓦ www.wieniawa.com.pl
This restaurant has period interiors, pleasant staff and good food – chiefly
Polish and French dishes – with mysterious names.

ⓩⓩ | AE DC MC V

ŁÓDŹ: *Hong Kong*
ul. Narutowicza 42. █ *(0 42) 630 46 56.*
A Chinese restaurant in the centre of the city. The menu includes good
vegetarian options.

ⓩ

ŁÓDŹ: *Dracena*
al. Kościuszki 68. **Road map** D4. █ *(0 42) 636 48 06.*
This is a good restaurant serving international cuisine. Apart from Polish
dishes, the menu includes dishes from China, Italy and Spain. The
speciality is roast wild boar in cranberry sauce.

ⓩⓩ | AE DC MC V

ŁÓDŹ: *Ziemia Obiecana*
ul. Wigury 4. **Road map** D4. █ *(0 42) 636 70 81.*
This good-quality, relatively inexpensive restaurant serves Polish and
international dishes. The liver on veal cutlets in wine and honey sauce and
the duck "à la Promised Land" (the restaurant's name) are recommended.

ⓩⓩ | AE DC MC V

OBORNIKI WIELKOPOLSKIE: *Delicja*
ul. Mostowa 22. **Road map** C3. █ *(0 61) 296 15 26.*
@ delicja@delicja.com.pl Ⓦ www.delicja.com.pl
This restaurant serves good European cuisine.

ⓩⓩ | AE DC MC

POZNAŃ: *Kresowa*
Stary Rynek 3. **Road map** C3. █ *(0 61) 853 12 91.* @ stochl@yoyo.pl
As the name ("the Borderland") suggests, the speciality of this restaurant is
the cuisine of the old Polish eastern borderlands. Excellent *pierogi* (ravioli)
and Wilno delicacies with cold borsch feature on the menu.

ⓩⓩ | AE DC MC V

POZNAŃ: *Valpolicella*
ul. Wrocławska 7. **Road map** C3. █ *(0 61) 855 71 91.*
The interior of this restaurant is in the style of an Italian taverna. The
menu features homemade pasta, a wide choice of starters and duck
dishes, the speciality of the house. 🏃

ⓩⓩ | AE DC MC V

Price categories are for a three-course meal for one without wine, including VAT (in PLN).

Ⓩ under 40
ⓍⓍ 40–70
ⓍⓍⓍ 70–100
ⓍⓍⓍⓍ over 100

CREDIT CARDS ACCEPTED
The following credit cards are accepted: American Express (AE), Diners Club (DC), MasterCard (MC), VISA (V).

VEGETARIAN DISHES
The menu includes dishes suitable for vegetarians.

GOOD WINE LIST
A wide choice of different wines.

GARDEN OR TERRACE
Meals served outdoors, weather permitting.

	CREDIT CARDS ACCEPTED	VEGETARIAN DISHES	GOOD WINE LIST	GARDEN OR TERRACE

POZNAŃ: *Czerwony Fortepian*   ⓍⓍⓍ
ul. Wroniecka 18. **Road map** C3. ☎ *(0 61) 852 01 74.*
@ catering@czerwony-fortepian.pl Ⓦ www.czerwony-fortepian.pl
This is a restaurant and jazz club combined. The restaurant serves sophisticated international dishes. In the evening, diners are entertained by the best-known Polish jazz players, some playing the red grand piano from which the establishment takes its name.

AE DC MC V		■	●

POZNAŃ: *Wenecja*   ⓍⓍⓍ
ul. Zamkowa 7. **Road map** C3. ☎ *(0 61) 853 04 89.*
This restaurant has charming air-conditioned period interiors and serves Italian food.

AE DC MC V		■	●

POZNAŃ: *Meridian*   ⓍⓍⓍⓍ
ul. Litewska 22. **Road map** C3. ☎ *(0 61) 847 15 64.* Ⓦ www.dial.com.pl/meridian
Situated by a small pond in the park, this ambitious restaurant specializes in Mediterranean cuisine, in particular French dishes. The menu includes frogs' legs, lobster and other kinds of seafood. On Sunday evenings in summer, concerts are given.

AE DC MC V	●	■	●

SĘPOLNO: *Zajazd Otwarte Wrota*   Ⓩ
Road map B3. ☎ *(0 61) 441 17 91.*
Zajazd Otwarte Wrota, one of many inns on the road from Świecko to Warsaw, is renowned for its pleasant service and its good, simple cooking. Polish dishes predominate, the speciality being fish and, in season, a variety of wild-mushroom-based dishes. The *żurek* (a sour soup based on soured rye flour) is recommended.

AE DC MC V			●

GDAŃSK

Cotton Club   ⓍⓍ
ul. Złotników 25/29. **Road map** D1. ☎ *(0 58) 301 88 13.* @ cotton@innet.pl
Named after the infamous New York nightclub, this is in fact a pub. Beer and good meals are served along with live jazz at quite reasonable prices.

AE DC MC V			

Kubicki   ⓍⓍ
ul. Wartka 5. **Road map** D1. ☎ *(0 58) 301 00 50.*
Founded in 1919, this legendary restaurant is still in the hands of the same family. The interiors are full of interesting old furniture. The food is typical of traditional port cities, with good starters, well-prepared fried trout and excellent cheesecake.

AE DC MC V			●

Towarzystwo Gastronomiczne   ⓍⓍ
ul. Korzenna 33/35 (in the basement of the Old Town Hall). **Road map** D1.
☎ *(0 58) 305 29 64.*
The French chef at Towarzystwo Gastronomiczne produces good lamb steak tartare, delicious kidneys in lemon sauce and duck à l'orange, Gdańsk-style. 🏃

AE DC MC V	●	■	●

U Szkota   ⓍⓍ
ul. Chlebnicka 9/12. **Road map** D1. ☎ *(0 58) 301 49 11.*
An intimate Victorian interior, waiters in kilts and a wide choice of English beers create a pleasantly themed atmosphere. The restaurant serves Gdańsk cuisine, including fish dishes. Of these, the fried trout deserves special recommendation.

AE DC MC V			

Milano   ⓍⓍⓍ
ul. Grunwaldzka 53. **Road map** D1. ☎ *(0 58) 341 11 53.*
The best Italian restaurant in Gdańsk, Milano has a cosy interior, an interesting choice of wines and excellent dishes from the southern Apennines. Of its many dishes, the *carpaccio*, steak in green pepper and tiramisu are particularly recommended.

AE DC MC V	●	■	●

Pod Łososiem

ul. Szeroka 52/54. **Road map** D1. ☎ *(0 58) 301 76 52.*

@ info@podlososiem.com.pl W www.podlososiem.com.pl

Because of its long-standing tradition, which dates back to the 17th century, this restaurant is almost an obligatory sightseeing point in Gdańsk. Excellent cuisine is served in a charming period interior. The fish-based house specialities – grilled salmon and salmon in crab sauce – are particularly recommended. Tables are quickly taken at lunchtime, so it is advisable to come early.

ZŁ ZŁ ZŁ | AE DC MC V

Tawerna

ul. Powroźnicza 19/20. **Road map** D1. ☎ *(0 58) 301 14 14.*

@ tawerna@tawerna.pl W www.tawerna.pl

An excellent fish restaurant, in the style of an old tavern, serving delicious *zrazy* (rolled and stuffed sole) and red mullet. Meat dishes, such as roast duck, are also available.

ZŁ ZŁ ZŁ ZŁ | AE DC MC V

POMERANIA

BYTÓW: *Zamkowa*

ul. Zamkowa 2. **Road map** C1. ☎ *(0 59) 822 20 95.*

@ hotzam@awinet.com.pl W www.awinet.com.pl/hotzam

This restaurant in the Teutonic castle serves traditional Polish dishes. The excellent *Talerz Zamkowy* (Castle Platter) consists of three different kinds of chops.

ZŁ | AE DC MC V

GDYNIA: *Jack Fish*

ul. Jana z Kolna 55. **Road map** D1. ☎ *(0 58) 661 75 34.*

This is a good fish restaurant whose menu includes flavoursome fish soups. All dishes are delicious, including the ones based on cod.

ZŁ ZŁ ZŁ ZŁ | AE DC MC V

GDYNIA: *Marco Polo*

ul. Śląska 21. **Road map** D1. ☎ *(0 58) 628 64 68.* @ vpryber@atomnet.pl

This sophisticated restaurant will satisfy the most discriminating tastes. The seafood includes lobster and crayfish.

ZŁ ZŁ ZŁ ZŁ | AE DC MC V

HEL: *Maszoperia*

ul. Wiejska 110. **Road map** D1. ☎ *(0 58) 675 02 97.* @ maszoperia@yahoo.com

This small restaurant is located in picturesque fishermen's houses. The menu ranges from simple dishes like Kashubian-style herring in cream with *pulki* (jacket potatoes) to more sophisticated dishes, such as sole with spinach and mozzarella.

ZŁ ZŁ | AE DC MC V

MALBORK: *Zamkowa*

ul. Starościńska 1. **Road map** D1. ☎ *(0 55) 272 33 67.*

This large restaurant with a knightly theme is located in the rebuilt wings of the castle outbuildings. It serves traditional Polish cuisine.

ZŁ ZŁ | AE DC MC V

MIELNO: *Meduza*

ul. Nabrzeżna 2. **Road map** B1. ☎ *(0 94) 318 99 66.* W www.hotels.inpoland.com

This hotel restaurant serves international cuisine. The menu features mainly French dishes, prepared by a French chef. 🛗

ZŁ ZŁ | AE DC MC V

MIĘDZYZDROJE: *Marina*

ul. Gryfa Pomorskiego 1. **Road map** A1. ☎ *(0 91) 328 04 49.*

@ marinahotel@az.pl W www.marinahotel.az.pl

The Marina is a small, pleasant hotel. Its Italian restaurant also serves French and Polish dishes. The dishes range from good fried fish to roast meat.

ZŁ ZŁ | AE DC MC V

SASINO: *Ewa Zaprasza*

Sasino 13. **Road map** C1. ☎ *(0 58) 676 33 39.*

Slightly off the beaten track, this restaurant is worth a detour. It is located in a charming, small manor house in a garden, and has a homely, original interior. The superb Polish cuisine includes delicious Polish-style trout and roast pork. 🛗

ZŁ ZŁ | AE DC MC V

SŁUPSK: *Zamkowa*

ul. Dominikańska 4. **Road map** C1. ☎ *(0 59) 842 04 79.*

This restaurant is considered to be the best in and around Słupsk, even though the interior is rather severe. On the menu are delicacies of the Kashubia region, such as nut soup with small meatballs and a Kashubian-style herring. For dessert, the Słowiński-style pear, served on a bed of rice, with raisins, nuts and almonds, topped with chocolate icing and whipped cream, is recommended.

ZŁ | AE DC MC V

Price categories are for a three-course meal for one without wine, including VAT (in PLN).

ⓩ under 40
ⓩⓩ 40–70
ⓩⓩⓩ 70–100
ⓩⓩⓩⓩ over 100

CREDIT CARDS ACCEPTED
The following credit cards are accepted: American Express (AE), Diners Club (DC), MasterCard (MC), VISA (V).
VEGETARIAN DISHES
The menu includes dishes suitable for vegetarians.
GOOD WINE LIST
A wide choice of different wines.
GARDEN OR TERRACE
Meals served outdoors, weather permitting.

	CREDIT CARDS ACCEPTED	VEGETARIAN DISHES	GOOD WINE LIST	GARDEN OR TERRACE
SMOŁDZINO: *Gościniec pod Rowokołem* ⓩ ul. Bohaterów Warszawy 26. **Road map** C1. 📞 *(0 59) 811 73 64.* 🌐 www.czasynawsi.com.pl This pleasant, unpretentious inn serves simple regional and traditional Polish dishes at reasonable prices. Meals are sometimes served in the restaurant patio. 👤				●
SOPOT: *Balzac* ⓩⓩⓩⓩ ul. 3 Maja 7. **Road map** D1. 📞 *(0 58) 551 77 00.* 🌐 www.balzac.com.pl This is the best French restaurant in Trójmiasto (the Tri-City of Gdańsk, Gdynia and Sopot). It offers a wide choice of meals, including frogs' legs and snails, many other gourmet dishes, a superb sirloin "Balzac" and delicious duck with apples.	AE DC MC V	●	■	
SOPOT: *Rozmaryn* ⓩⓩⓩⓩ ul. Ogrodowa 8. **Road map** D1. 📞 *(0 58) 551 11 04.* This Italian restaurant has a frequently changing menu.	AE DC MC V	●	■	
SOPOT: *Villa Hestia* ⓩⓩⓩⓩ ul. Władysława IV 3/5. **Road map** D1. 📞 *(0 58) 551 21 00.* @ villa@hestia.pl 🌐 www.villa.hestia.pl This comfortable restaurant is located in a beautiful villa in a garden setting. Its international cuisine includes good fish dishes, such as sturgeon with caviar and carp with ceps, as well as meat dishes, such as masterfully cooked sirloin. Expensive, but well worth a visit, both for the food and the surroundings.	AE DC MC V	●	■	●
STRZYŻAWA: *Jermir* ⓩⓩ Strzyżawa 48. **Road map** C2. 📞 *(0 52) 343 92 19, 381 74 53 or 381 74 54.* This motel restaurant has a dull interior but is worth a visit for the good food. The *jermir pieróg* (rolled loin of pork stuffed with rice and prunes) is superb. 👤	AE DC MC V	●		●
SZCZECIN: *Chief* ⓩⓩⓩ ul. Rayskiego 16. **Road map** A2. 📞 *(0 91) 434 37 65.* The Chief is without a doubt the best fish restaurant in Szczecin. Almost every kind of freshwater and sea fish features on the menu, making it an absolute must for fish lovers. 👤	AE DC MC V		■	
TORUŃ: *Zajazd Staropolski* ⓩⓩ ul. Żeglarska 10/14. **Road map** D2. 📞 *(0 56) 622 60 60.* @ zstaropolski@gromada.pl 🌐 www.gromada.pl A relatively cheap restaurant in a historic residence in the old town, the Zajazd Staropolski specializes in traditional Polish cuisine. The *żurek* (a sour soup) is excellent. 👤	AE DC MC V	●		●
TORUŃ: *Staromiejska* ⓩⓩⓩ ul. Szczytna 2/4. **Road map** D2. 📞 *(0 56) 622 67 25.* Although its name has no association with Italy, this pleasant, low-key little restaurant, located in a small street in the old town, serves a good range of standard Italian cuisine. The meat dishes and lasagne are particularly recommended.	AE DC MC V	●		

WARMIA, MAZURIA AND BIAŁYSTOK REGION

	CREDIT CARDS ACCEPTED	VEGETARIAN DISHES	GOOD WINE LIST	GARDEN OR TERRACE
AUGUSTÓW: *Hetman* ⓩ ul. Sportowa 1. **Road map** F2. 📞 *(0 87) 644 53 45.* This recently renovated hotel restaurant is situated on Lake Necko. Polish dishes are a speciality.	AE DC MC V			
BARTOSZYCE: *Stodoła* ⓩ ul. Bema 11. **Road map** E1. 📞 *(0 89) 762 55 01.* This restaurant is located in a beautifully renovated 18th-century granary, full of historic artifacts. The speciality is Polish cuisine.		●		●

BIAŁOWIEŻA: *Żubrówka*
ul. O. Grabiec 6. **Road map** G3. ☎ *(0 85) 681 23 03.*
This hotel restaurant specializes in game dishes. Precisely what is on the
menu on a particular day depends entirely on the results of the hunt, but
roast elk may well be featured.

BIAŁYSTOK: *Oaza*
ul. Świętojańska 4. **Road map** F2. ☎ *(0 85) 732 80 20.*
Oaza is a small, cosy and cheap Arab restaurant serving excellent *kofta*
(Greek or Middle Eastern kebabs), kebabs and shish kebabs.

BIAŁYSTOK: *Cristal*
ul. Lipowa 3 (in the Cristal Hotel). **Road map** F2. ☎ *(0 85) 742 50 61.*
@ cristal@cristal.com.pl W www.cristal.com.pl
This long-established and popular restaurant is well known for its Polish
cuisine, although the menu also features dishes from other countries –
France in particular. The duck with apples and the Polish-style steamed
pike are recommended.

ELBLĄG: *Słowiańska*
ul. Krótka 4. **Road map** D1. ☎ *(0 55) 232 42 78.*
The outer appearance of this restaurant may be dull but the interior is
comfortable, with antlers on the walls and unusual decorations on the
tables. The menu consists of traditional Polish dishes. Roast pig is
available as a special order.

IŁAWA: *Kormoran*
ul. Chodkiewicza 3. **Road map** D2. ☎ *(0 89) 648 59 63.*
The restaurant is situated by the lake, overlooking a beautiful landscape,
which compensates for the severity of the interior. The fish dishes
deserve special recommendation. The menu depends on the catch of the
day, although the delicious fried pikeperch is always available.

KADYNY: *Stara Gorzelnia*
Near Tolkmick (in the Kadyny Country Club). **Road map** D1. ☎ *(0 55) 231 61 20.*
This restaurant, located in the unusual setting of a renovated 19th-century
distillery, serves good international cuisine. Soups, such as asparagus
soup in season, are a speciality.

KĘTRZYN: *Zajazd Pod Zamkiem*
ul. A. Struga 3a. **Road map** E1. ☎ *(0 89) 752 31 17.*
This pleasant inn is situated next to the walls of a Teutonic castle. The
menu is interesting, featuring an exotic combination of traditional Polish
and Chinese dishes.

KRUTYŃ: *Krutynianka*
Road map E2. ☎ *(0 89) 742 12 19.*
This fish restaurant, which is open from the beginning of April until the
end of October, has a menu featuring almost every edible fish of the
Great Mazurian Lakes. Also recommended is nettle soup, a rare delicacy,
and for dessert, homemade honey liqueur.

MIKOŁAJKI: *Bar w kinie Wojtek*
pl. Wolności 9. **Road map** E2. ☎ *(0 89) 534 94 67.*
This popular, good-value restaurant, situated on the Market Square, is
open only in the summer. It is located in the atrium of the cinema, where
a film is shown every day. The cuisine includes freshly fried fish, *pierogi*
(ravioli), a wide choice of salads and superb hot apple pie, served with
ice cream and whipped cream. The restaurant is frequented by actors.

MIKOŁAJKI: *Mazur*
pl. Wolności 6. **Road map** E2. ☎ *(0 87) 421 69 41.*
This is a small hotel restaurant in the renovated town hall. Polish and
German dishes are on the menu.

OLSZTYN: *Eridu*
ul. Prosta 3/4. **Road map** E2. ☎ *(0 89) 534 94 67.*
This small restaurant serves Arab dishes, including delicious *kofta* and
shish kebabs.

OLSZTYN: *U Piotra*
ul. Pana Tadeusza 6. **Road map** E2. ☎ *(0 89) 533 50 77.* @ grobcio@pucta.onet.pl
This restaurant with an international menu, features Chinese dishes and
traditional Polish delicacies.

SHOPPING IN POLAND

POLAND is known first and foremost for its handicraft goods. Polish silver and amber jewellery are especially renowned, but hand-embroidered tablecloths, cut glass from Silesia, porcelain from Ćmielów and ceramics from Bolesławiec are also very popular. Thick, hand-knitted woollen sweaters and ornamented leather slip-pers are produced by the highlanders of Zakopane and its environs. CDs and cassettes of Polish classical and contemporary music are available all over the country. Large-format, lavishly illustrated books of the Polish landscape and on art, some of which are published in English, French or German, are other tempting souvenirs of a visit to Poland.

Ceramics from Bolesławiec

Amber jewellery and other goods displayed in a shop window

WHERE TO SHOP

ALTHOUGH THERE are retail shops everywhere, it often makes more sense to purchase goods from factory and established licensed shops. The most competitively priced handicraft goods can be bought direct from the manufacturers in the markets. Duty-free goods are also available at Warsaw airport.

SHOPPING IN WARSAW

MOST SHOPS ARE located in the city centre. There are many elegant boutiques in the Old Town, along Ulica Krakowskie Przedmieście and Ulica Nowy Świat. There are many clothes shops in Ulica Chmielna, Aleje Jerozolimskie and Ulica Marsza łkowska. Those interested in antiques should visit the Sunday morning market in the Koło district on the western side of Warsaw. Popular department stores are **Galeria Centrum, Arka** and **City Center**. Large shopping centres such as **Klif,**

Panorama and **Promenada**, are located away from the main tourist areas. Browsing for bargains and cheap goods is an attraction of large markets, for example those held in Plac Defilad, or Jarmark Saski, a bazaar located in Stadion Dziesięciolecia, on the eastern side of Warsaw.

OPENING HOURS

SHOPS ARE OPEN from 10am to 6pm Monday to Friday and, in the main, from 10am to 2pm on Saturdays. In the larger cities, shops usually close at 7pm, with most of the department stores staying open for an extra hour and closing at 8pm.

In the run-up to Christmas, the majority of shops are open much longer hours, and shopping centres open on the last Sunday before Christmas. Normal Sunday opening times are restricted to a few food shops and major shopping centres, although in summer souvenir shops in popular tourist resorts open as well.

On public holidays all shops are closed, with the exception of some pharmacies and food shops (those that are open at night). As a last resort, a 24-hour petrol station may fulfil any particularly pressing needs.

PAYING

ALTHOUGH CASH (in złote, of course) is always welcomed by Polish traders of all kinds, credit cards are nonetheless accepted in most shops in the big cities (this should be indicated by stickers on the door – if not, ask before making a purchase). However, small shops sometimes prefer to give a small discount for payment in cash rather than take a card, so there may be a little margin for haggling. Polish shops do not usually accept travellers' cheques, but it is perfectly easy to change them in banks (see pp348–9). There is VAT on the price of Polish goods, but a range of goods is tax free to foreign nationals, and on such goods (minimum value 200 PLN) a VAT refund can easily be obtained.

Atrium, Panorama shopping centre, Warsaw

An antiques market in Cracow's Main Market Square

BOOKS AND RECORDS

Well-stocked bookshops can be found in most towns and cities. The **EMPiK** chain of bookshops, with outlets in all big cities, offers the widest choice, and not only of books; there are music and CD-ROM sections as well. Guidebooks in foreign languages and glossy coffee-table books aimed at the tourist market are available from tourist information centres. Many second-hand bookshops, to be found in the old parts of big cities, often stock an interesting selection of old books.

Highlanders' sweaters and other local goods at a Zakopane market

HANDICRAFTS

Traditional handicraft products such as hand-woven tapestries, embroidered tablecloths and doilies, leather goods, decorative cut-outs, ceramics and even furniture are sold in **Cepelia** shops, which are to be found in all big cities. In Cracow, most of these shops are located in the **Sukiennice** in Main Market Square. In Gdańsk, the retail outlet Sklep Kaszubski specializes in artifacts made by folk artists from Kashubia. Local markets are also worth visiting. For example, one of the best places to buy highlanders' sweaters is at the market in Zakopane; embroidered tablecloths are on sale at stalls in Święta Lipka and Kashubian ceramics in pottery workshops in Chmielno.

A shop showroom with ceramics and other Polish handicraft goods

AMBER GOODS

Amber is a fossilized tree resin that ranges in colour from cream through translucent yellow and orange to rich brown. Most Polish amber comes from the Gulf of Gdańsk, and Polish amber goods are largely made in Gdańsk and its environs. Amber jewellery is extremely popular in Poland. It is sold at a range of outlets, but to avoid the risk of buying a fake it is best to go to an established shop. In Gdańsk there are several such shops, located chiefly in the Old City, particularly in Ulica Mariacka and Ulica Długie Pobrzeże – for example in **M&M**, the **Nord Amber Gallery** and the **Wydra Gallery**. The town of Mikołajki in the Great Mazurian Lakes region also offers a wide choice of amber artifacts.

MODERN ART

Some of the greatest attractions for tourists in Poland are contemporary paintings, prints and posters, which are available at very reasonable prices in galleries. Art galleries also sell original glass, ceramics and designer jewellery. Silver, in the form of sophisticated jewellery and various other artifacts, is relatively cheap.

Painting on glass also has a strong tradition in Poland, and small pieces, with traditional or modern designs, are offered for sale in many galleries around the country.

In Wrocław, the former meat market in **Kiełbaśnicza** has been taken over by artists. In Cracow, there are many galleries in the historic city centre – for example, **Kościół Artystyczny**. In Warsaw there is **Zapiecek** and **Art Gallery ZPAP** (Union of Polish Artists and Designers). There are small private galleries in many towns, even the smaller ones, and prices there are, as one might expect, usually lower than in Warsaw. All in all, the Polish arts and crafts scene is a thriving one, providing the visitor with a wide range of work at attractive prices.

Baskets for sale at the market in Sokółka

ANTIQUES

IN MOST TOWNS throughout Poland, antiques and collectables are sold in **Desa** shops. Second-hand goods, however, are sold in privately run shops that are to be found in both large and small towns and also in tourist spots. Visitors should bear in mind that there are special provisions pertaining to the export of objects made before 1945; under Polish customs regulations, such objects may not be exported, unless a special permit is obtained.

POTTERY AND PORCELAIN

POLAND HAS A long tradition of porcelain manufacture, and there are a few factories that still produce porcelain in both traditional and modern designs. The most renowned type is Ćmielów porcelain, which is available all over Poland. Just as attractive is the porcelain produced by the factory in Wałbrzych, which has its own retail shop situated in **Książ Castle** *(see p185)*. Popular also are traditional ceramics such as those made in Bolesławiec, especially the white and navy-blue crockery decorated with spots, circles and small stylized flowers.

GLASS AND CRYSTAL

HIGH-QUALITY GLASS, in both modern and traditional designs, is another Polish speciality, as is traditional cut glass, known as crystal. Designer glassware is also popular and in great demand. The most beautiful cut glass

Gdański Bówka, a shop in Gdańsk selling all sorts of souvenirs

comes from Silesia, where glass production dates back to the 14th century. The Julia glass factory in Szklarska Poręba, which was established in 1841 as Josephinenhütte, is also renowned.

Wedel, one of Warsaw's smartest sweet shops

CLOTHES AND ACCESSORIES

POLAND HAS never been synonymous with high-quality clothing, but in recent years the quality of clothes made in Poland has greatly improved, and many factories can now compete with Western European clothing manufacturers. Shirts from Wólczanka, suits from Bytom

and coats from **Próchnik** are in demand. They are available in department stores and from shops in big cities. Many Polish designers also have their own boutiques, which stock unique collections of suits and dresses.

Poland is well known for its high-quality leather goods, such as bags, belts and wallets. In Warsaw, Andrzej Kłoda's shop at the end of Krzakowskie Przedmieście and Maciej Batycki's shop on Ulica Złota, are well worth a visit.

FOOD AND DRINK

POLISH LIQUOR is internationally renowned, especially the pure vodkas, which – much like Scotch whisky – are available in a bewildering range of varieties. The most popular brands are *Premium* and *Chopin*, the latter sold in elegant, slender bottles decorated with a picture of the famous composer.

Another popular spirit is *żubrówka*, a vodka with a distinctive, slightly herbal flavour; it is obtained from hierchloe grass, which grows only in the Białowieska Forest. Another alcoholic drink is mead. Made with honey according to traditional recipes, it is the perfect accompaniment to desserts.

Many distilleries have their own retail outlets, where private buyers can taste the different specialities on offer. Such an establishment is **Polmos**, in Cracow. The vodka factory in Łańcut also houses a small museum.

Polish sweets are of a high quality. Chocolates made by the Warsaw firm **Wedel** and the Cracow firm **Wawel** are particularly esteemed.

A tasty present from Poland could be, for instance, a jar of dried ceps (porcini mushrooms), honey, smoked eel or dried sausage. The best places to buy such items are bazaars and markets. There are excellent markets in Warsaw in Hala Mirowska near Plac Mirowski, and Ulica Polna, in Cracow in Stary Kleparz, in Poznań in Plac Wielkopolski, and in the market halls of Wrocław and Gdańsk.

A flower stall in Cracow's Main Market Square

DIRECTORY

DEPARTMENT STORES AND SHOPPING CENTRES

Arka
Warsaw,
ul. Bracka 25.
(0 22) 692 14 00.

City Center
Warsaw,
ul. Złota 44/46.
(0 22) 625 15 24.

Galeria Centrum
Warsaw,
ul. Marszałkowska 104/122.
(0 22) 606 07 55.

Klif
Warsaw,
ul. Okopowa 58/72.
(0 22) 531 45 00.

Panorama
Warsaw,
ul. Witosa 31.
(0 22) 642 06 66.

Promenada
Warsaw,
ul. Ostrobramska 75c.
(0 22) 611 39 52.

BOOKS

EMPiK Megastore
Warsaw,
ul. Nowy Świat 15/17.
(0 22) 625 17 95.

EMPiK Salon Megastore "Junior"
Warsaw,
ul. Marszałkowska 104/122.
(0 22) 551 44 42.

Gdańsk
Gdańsk,
ul. Długa 62/63.
(0 58) 301 11 56.

Hetmańska
Cracow,
Rynek Główny 17.
(0 12) 430 24 53.

Suszczyński i S-ka
Cracow,
Rynek Główny 23.
(0 12) 421 68 99.
@ wydbis@krakow.cc

HANDICRAFTS

Cepelia
Gdańsk, ul. Długa 47/49.
(0 58) 301 27 08.

Bydgoszcz,
ul. Gdańska 17.
(0 52) 322 17 28.

Warsaw,
ul. Nowy Świat 35.
(0 22) 826 42 73.

Warsaw, pl. Konstytucji 5.
(0 22) 621 26 18.

Cracow, Dunajewskiego 6.
(0 12) 422 19 29.

Olsztyn, ul. Prosta 1/2.
(0 89) 527 25 97.

AMBER GOODS

M&M
Gdańsk, ul. Długie Pobrzeże 1.
(0 58) 346 27 17.

Nord Amber Gallery
Gdańsk, ul. Mariacka 44.
(0 58) 341 93 30.

Wydra Gallery
Gdańsk, ul. Mariacka 49.
(0 58) 301 77 79.

MODERN ART

Art Gallery ZPAP
Warsaw,
ul. Krakowskie Przedmieście 15/17.
(0 22) 827 64 14.

Galeria Art
Lublin,
ul. Krakowskie Przedmieście 62.
(0 81) 532 68 57.

Galeria Art T
Warsaw,
ul. Gałczyńskiego 5.
(0 22) 826 87 55.

Galeria Kwadratura Koła
Toruń,
Rynek Staromiejski 1.
(0 56) 622 62 12.

Galeria Sztuki Współczesnej

Wałbrzych, Zamek Książ,
ul. Piastów Śląskich 1.
(0 74) 843 13 00.

Łódź,
ul. Piotrkowska 113.
(0 42) 632 58 96.

Poznań,
ul. Wrocławska 10.
(0 61) 852 50 86.

Galeria ZPAP
Cracow,
Rynek Główny.1 lok.3
(0 12) 421 81 64.

Galeria Miejska
Wrocław,
ul. Kiełbaśnicza 28.
(0 71) 344 67 20.

Kocioł Artystyczny
Cracow,
ul. Mikołajska 6.
(0 12) 292 00 29.

Yam
Zakopane,
ul. Krupówki 63.
(0 18) 206 69 84.

Zapiecek
Warsaw,
ul. Zapiecek 1.
(0 22) 831 99 18.

ANTIQUES

Antyki
Toruń,
ul. Most Pauliński 2.
(0 56) 622 42 04.

Antykwariat
Wrocław,
pl. Kościuszki 15.
(0 71) 343 72 80.

Antykwariat pod Aniołem
Zakopane, ul. Kościuszki 8.
(0 18) 206 24 87.

Desa
Warsaw,
ul. Nowy Świat 48.
(0 22) 826 44 66.

Warsaw,
Rynek Starego Miasta.
(0 22) 831 16 81.

Bydgoszcz,
ul. Gdańska 12.
(0 52) 322 01 91.

Koneser
Lublin,
ul. Lubartowska 3.
(0 81) 534 41 60.

Salon Dzieł Sztuki i Antyków "Paga"
Kielce,
ul. Piotrkowska 2.
(0 41) 368 13 14.

Sklep ze starociami
Łódź, ul. Piotrkowska 101.
(0 42) 632 32 26.

CERAMICS AND GLASS

Aga 2
Elbląg, ul. Hetmańska 3e.
(0 55) 235 34 88.

Krosno
Krosno,
ul. Rynek 5.
(0 13) 436 26 71.

Salon Czasu
Przemyśl,
ul. Franciszkańska 31.
(0 16) 678 53 59.

Art-Crystal
Częstochowa,
ul. Popiełuszki 2.
(0 34) 324 70 01.

CLOTHES

Elux
Warsaw,
al. Solidarności 92
(0 22) 838 50 73.

Próchnik
Warsaw,
al. Jana Pawła II 18.
(0 22) 620 34 16.

Telimena
Warsaw,
ul. Marszałkowska 82.
(0 22) 622 63 37.

CONFECTIONERY

E. Wedel
Warsaw,
ul. Szpitalna 8.
(0 22) 827 29 16.

Wawel
Cracow,
Rynek Główny 33.
(0 12) 423 12 47.

What to Buy in Poland

Folk carvings

THE RANGE OF folk art and handicrafts in Poland is truly impressive. Almost every region has its own speciality. The production of Christmas tree ornaments, painted Easter eggs and Christmas crib figures is a distinctive folk industry. The work of Polish artists, in the form of paintings, prints, posters and sculpture, is also highly esteemed and can be found in commercial galleries. Designer jewellery, another high-profile Polish craft, and amber products, which are reasonably priced, are also attractive. Vodka, the national drink, is available in various flavours.

Dolls in Traditional Costume
Small dolls dressed in the traditional costume of the Cracow or Zakopane region make ideal gifts or souvenirs.

HIGHLANDERS' PRODUCTS

The Podhale region is famous for its original folk products. The hand-knitted socks and sweaters and the traditional leather *kierpce* (soft shoes with pointed toes) are very popular.

Oszczypek, sheep's milk cheese

Woollen socks

Patterned leather *kierpce*

Embroidered *serdak*

Hand-carved Christmas crib

Christmas Cribs
Christmas cribs are extremely popular, especially in southern Poland. The finest are hand-carved in wood. As well as a whole crib, it is possible to purchase individual figures.

Hand-painted Christmas decoration

Wooden angel

Easter Decorations
Easter eggs and lambs are essential on the Easter table. Not only are the eggs painted, but patterns are also created by scratching into the shell and applying paper and ribbons.

Sugar lamb

Decorated eggs

Jug made out of a hollow eggshell

Christmas Decorations
Traditional Polish Christmas decorations range from painted glass balls to ornaments made of wood, straw, paper or coloured ribbons.

Gingercake

Gingercake, a traditional delicacy from Toruń, is made using old moulds and is sometimes decorated with colourful frosting.

Toruń gingercake

FOLK ART

Folk art is deeply rooted in Polish tradition. It takes many forms – from painting, carving and embroidery to other skilled handicrafts. Painting on glass is a particularly vibrant aspect of the genre.

Colourful bas-relief

Wicker baskets from Kurpie

Silver rings

Jewellery

Silver jewellery is a speciality of Polish craftsmen. It is relatively cheap and comes in a variety of sophisticated modern designs.

Nativity scene painted on glass

Paper cut-out

Amber

Amber artifacts epitomize Polish craftsmanship. The translucent material is turned into original jewellery and ornaments and is also used for lampshades and such intricate pieces as model ships.

Amber ship

Art Nouveau-style lamp

Embroidered Doilies

Embroidered tablecloths, doilies and clothes are part of the folk art of many regions of Poland. The finest embroidery is that of Kashubia and Małopolska.

ALCOHOL

Pure vodka is a Polish speciality. High-grade vodkas, those with a mixture of herbal and other extracts – *żubrówka*, for example – are also very popular.

Pure vodkas: Cracovia   **Wyborowa**   **Goldwasser**

Cut Glass

Cut glass is made in many Silesian factories. The delicate hand-cut patterns on perfectly transparent glass are appreciated the world over.

ENTERTAINMENT IN POLAND

POLAND HAS A VIBRANT cultural life. In all the big cities there is an abundance of things to do: nightclubs, jazz clubs, casinos, theatres, opera, cinemas and concert halls. In summer, even the smaller tourist resorts have much to offer, and it is possible to chance upon many interesting and unusual events, such as a jousting tournament or a music festival. For those travellers who enjoy

A bill-post

taking part in more strenuous pastimes, there is much to satisfy, with trekking, rock-climbing, cycling, windsurfing, canoeing, ice sailing and many other sports *(see pp338–9)* on offer. There are also various spectator sports such as boxing, soccer, speedboat racing and dirt-track motorcycle racing. For animal lovers the country boasts a number of zoos.

José Carreras and Edyta Górniak singing at a charity concert

INFORMATION

FOR INFORMATION ON Poland's cultural events it is best to consult the local tourist information centres. In larger cities, information bulletins are also issued. In Warsaw, for example, there is *Informator Kulturalny Stolicy* and in Cracow, *Karnet*. The local supplement that is folded into the main copy of Friday's *Gazeta Wyborcza*, is another useful source of information. Details of cultural events are also published in the local press.

Bulletins printed in English are available in most large hotels and from tourist information centres. These are entitled *What, Where, When* and *Welcome to...* and form a series issued for Warsaw, Cracow, Poznań, Gdańsk, Wrocław and Upper Silesia. *The Warsaw Voice*, published in English, has a comprehensive guide to cultural events in and outside Warsaw.

TICKET RESERVATIONS

IN WARSAW, ADVANCE booking for plays, concerts and other cultural events in the capital is dealt with by the **ZASP box office**. In Cracow, tickets can be bought in advance at the

A giraffe in one of Poland's several zoos

Cultural Information Centre *(see p337)*. Theatre, cinema and concert hall box offices will also reserve tickets for their own performances, and these may be collected just before the performance begins. The larger hotels will book tickets for guests on request. Surcharges may be applied for agency bookings.

VENUES

MANY CULTURAL EVENTS, apart from theatrical perform-ances and classical concerts, take place in large public halls. In Warsaw, many spectacles are organized in the Sala Kongresowa in the Pałac Kultury. In Katowice, a hall called Spodek (The Flying Saucer) is the venue for both concerts and sports events. Wrocław has the Hala Ludowa (People's Hall) and Gdańsk the Hala Olivia. In summer, concerts and festivals are often organized in amphi-theatres, for example in the famous Opera Leśna (Forest Opera) in Sopot, the amphitheatre in Opole or in Mrągowo in the Great Mazurian Lakes region. In Szczecin and Olsztyn, artistic shows take place in the castle courtyard. Castles, palaces and churches all over Poland also host various cultural events.

THEATRES

IN POLAND, ALMOST all big cities have their own theatres – the country has, in total, over 80. Although theatrical companies move out of town for the summer holiday season, their

A theatrical production at the Teatr Wielki in Warsaw

premises are often used for festivals or theatre reviews. In Warsaw, the most popular theatres include **Ateneum**, Studio, Polski, **Współczesny**, **Powszechny**, **Narodowy** and Kwadrat, which specializes in comedy shows. The **Teatr Żydowski** (Jewish Theatre) presents spectacles in Yiddish; it is the only such place in Poland and attracts an international audience. In Cracow, the best theatres are considered to be **Teatr Stary** and **Teatr im. Słowackiego**. The major theatres in Wrocław are Teatr Polski and Współczesny (Contemporary Theatre).

Poland has enjoyed considerable fame for its avant-garde theatre. The productions of the Cracovian theatre company **Cricot 2** have become world classics; unfortunately, since the death of Tadeusz Kantor, its founder, performances by the company have seldom taken place. The experimental theatre of Jerzy Grotowski and his company, the Laboratorium, was also renowned. The Jerzy Grotowski (Theatrical-Cultural) Research Centre operates in Wrocław. The Pantomime Theatre, founded by Henry Tomaszewski and presenting Polish shows, is still active. Poznań has its famous **Teatr Ósmego Dnia**.

Musicals, Opera and Ballet

For those who do not understand the Polish language, musicals, opera and ballet can provide the best form of entertainment, and there is certainly much to choose from in these genres. Poland has many operetta companies. The **Teatr Muzyczny** in Gdynia puts on very popular shows. **Operettas** are performed in Cracow and Gliwice and at **Roma** in Warsaw, which also presents musicals. For opera lovers, the productions of the **Teatr Wielki** in Warsaw are recommended. There are also opera houses in Gdańsk, Wrocław, Bydgoszcz, Łódź, Poznań and Bytom, and operas are staged at the Teatr im. Słowackiego in Cracow. The **Warsaw Chamber Opera**, which specializes in Mozart operas, has won international recognition but performs only a few times a month. Poland's two best ballet companies can be seen in the **Teatr Wielki** (Great Theatre) in Warsaw and Poznań.

A concert in Warsaw's Concert Studio S1

Classical Music

There are over 20 classical orchestras in Poland and they perform in almost all the country's big cities. Particularly renowned are the **Filharmonia Narodowa** (National Philharmonic Orchestra) in Warsaw, **WOSPR** (Great Symphony Orchestra of Polish Radio) in Katowice and the Poznań Orchestra, which gives concerts in the University Hall. In Poznań there are performances by Poland's most famous choir, Poznańskie Słowiki (The Poznań Nightingales), founded by Stefan Stuligrosz.

Classical music is performed in museums, churches and palaces throughout the year. In the summer, concerts are given in the open air. Concerts of Chopin's music are given on Sundays in Żelazowa Wola and Łazienki Park in Warsaw.

Folk Music

In Poland there are many bands that perform the traditional folk music of individual regions, although it can be difficult to track down their concerts. The most likely occasions are the festivals and reviews that mostly take place in summer (see p336). Regional groups sometimes give concerts on public holidays or harvest festivals. Many singing and dancing groups perform especially for tourists in concerts organized by hotels or tourist agencies, but in most cases their shows have little in common with genuine folk traditions. Polish folk music and dance have been popularized outside Poland by such high-profile groups as *Śląsk* and *Mazowsze*. Their shows are professional spectacles based on folk traditions, rather than authentic performances.

The folk dance group *Mazowsze* in Cracovian folk costume

Musical performance at the Dominican Street Market in Gdańsk

ROCK, JAZZ AND COUNTRY MUSIC

STUDENT CLUBS AND music pubs are the best places to go to hear rock, jazz and country music in Poland. In most big cities it is quite easy to obtain information on current shows. Polish rock bands are on tour throughout the year, and in summer they usually perform in tourist resorts. There are many festivals for particular kinds of music, so whatever the visitor's taste it will very likely be catered for.

FESTIVALS, CONCERTS AND REVIEWS

POLAND HOSTS many festivals, both local and international. Two of the major drama festivals are **Malta International Drama Festival**, held from late June to early July in the streets and theatres of Poznań, and **Kontakt**, which takes place in Toruń from May to June. In Warsaw, there is also the **Garden Theatres Competition** (Konkurs Teatrów Ogródkowych), which lasts all summer, and the **International Festival of Street Theatre** (Międzynarodowy Festiwal Teatrów Ulicznych) in Jelenia Góra in late September. **Warsaw Theatre Meetings** (Warszawskie Spotkania Teatralne) are also among the most exciting theatrical events.

Opera festivals, such as the **Mozart Festival** in Warsaw, and ballet festivals, for example in Poznań are also popular. The most famous classical music festivals are the **Chamber Music Days**, organized in May in Łańcut Palace, the **Chopin Music Festival** in Duszniki Zdrój and the **Moniuszko Music Festival** in Kudowa Zdrój. Events of international renown include **Warsaw Autumn**, the great modern music festival, and the excellent **Wratislavia Cantans**, a religious song festival that takes place in Wrocław in September.

Lovers of church music gather in Hajnówka in June for the **Festival of Orthodox Church Music**. In summer, churches and cathedrals with especially fine organs host festivals of organ music; these take place in Gdańsk-Oliwa, Kamień Pomorski, Koszalin, Słupsk, Święta Lipka, Pasym, Warsaw, Cracow and other towns. Music lovers also enjoy such major international competitions as the Chopin Piano Competition, which takes place every five years in Warsaw in October, and the Wieniawski Violin Competition, which is held in Poznań every four years.

Song is celebrated at the **Polish Music Festival** in Opole in June and at the International Festival of Song in Sopot in August. **Country Picnic**, taking place in Mrągowo in July, is a country music festival. Jazz festivals are also very popular.

Major jazz events include the Warsaw **Jazz Jamboree** in late October, **Jazz on the Oder** in Wrocław in May, and **Jazz All Souls' Day** in Cracow in early November. The **International Festival of Mountain Folklore** in Zakopane and the **Festival of Folk Bands and Singers** in Kazimierz Dolny at the end of June are major showcases for folk music.

TOURNAMENTS AND STREET MARKETS

MANY OF THE tournaments and street festivals that take place in Poland are colourful events and are popular with tourists. Medieval **jousting tournaments** are organized in medieval castles, some of which – Bytów, Gniew and Golub-Dobrzyń – have witnessed dramatic though bloodless skirmishes. As well as the jousting tournaments and displays of archery, feasts of meat roasted on open-air fires may be enjoyed.

Church fairs, festivals, picnics and street markets also take place in towns and villages throughout Poland. The best-known include the **Dominican Street Market** held in Gdańsk at the beginning of August and **St John's Street Market**, which is held in Poznań. As well as the numerous stalls selling an extraordinary range of goods, there are concerts, games and other events to suit every taste.

A knight at a tournament at the castle in Gniew

DIRECTORY

INFORMATION AND TICKET SALES

Cultural Information Centre
Cracow, ul. św Jana 3.
☎ (0 12) 421 77 87.
w www.karnet.krakow2000.pl

Kasy ZASP (Central Box Office)
Warszawa,
al. Jerozolimskie 25.
☎ (0 22) 621 94 54.

THEATRES

Ateneum
Warsaw, ul. Jaracza 2.
☎ (0 22) 625 73 30.

Narodowy (National Theatre)
Warsaw, Plac Teatralny.
☎ (0 22) 692 06 04
or 692 06 64.
@ bow@teatr.pol.pl

Powszechny
Warsaw,
ul. Zamoyskiego 20.
☎ (0 22) 818 00 01.

Teatr im. J. Słowackiego
Cracow,
pl. Świętego Ducha 1.
☎ (0 22) 422 40 22.

Teatr im. St. Witkiewicza
Zakopane, Chramcówki 15.
☎ (0 18) 206 82 97.

Teatr Ósmego Dnia
Poznań, ul. Ratajczaka 44.
☎ (0 61) 855 20 86.

Teatr Stary
Cracow, pl. Szczepański 1.
☎ (0 12) 422 40 40.

Teatr Żydowski
Warsaw,
pl. Grzybowski 12/17.
☎ (0 22) 620 70 25.

Wrocławski Teatr Pantomimy
Wrocław, ul. Zapolskiej 3.
☎ (0 71) 337 21 03.

Współczesny (Contemporary Theatre)
Warsaw,
ul. Mokotowska 13.
☎ (0 22) 825 09 43.

MUSICALS, OPERA AND BALLET

Opera
Wrocław, ul. Świdnicka 35.
☎ (0 71) 341 40 81.

Opera i operetka
Cracow, ul. Lubicz 48.
☎ (0 12) 422 78 07.
w www.opera.krakow.top.pl

Opera Leśna
Sopot, ul. Moniuszki 12.
☎ (0 58) 551 18 12.
w www.sopot.pl/bart

Opera Śląska
Bytom, ul. Moniuszki 21.
☎ (0 32) 281 34 31.
w www.opera.silesia.top.pl

Teatr Muzyczny w Gliwicach
Gliwice, ul. Nowy Świat 55.
☎ (0 32) 232 11 01.
w www.teatry.art.pl/muzycznygli

Polski Teatr Tańca
Poznań, ul. Kozia 4.
☎ (0 61) 852 42 42.

Roma (Musical Theatre)
Warsaw,
ul. Nowogrodzka 49.
☎ (0 22) 628 03 60.

Studio-Buffo
Warsaw, Konopnickiej 6.
☎ (0 22) 625 47 09.
w www.studiobuffo.com.pl

Śląski Teatr Tańca
Bytom, ul. Żeromskiego 27.
☎ (0 32) 281 82 52.

Teatr Muzyczny
Poznań, ul. Niezłomnych 1a.
☎ (0 61) 852 17 86.

Teatr Wielki
Łódź, pl. Dąbrowskiego 1.
☎ (0 42) 633 99 60.

Teatr Wielki-Opera Narodowa
Warsaw, pl. Teatralny 1.
☎ (0 22) 826 32 88.
w www.teatrwielki.pl

CLASSICAL MUSIC

Filharmonia
Cracow, ul. Zwierzyniecka 1.
☎ (0 12) 422 09 58.

Filharmonia Bałtycka
Gdańsk, al. Zwycięstwa 15.
☎ (0 58) 305 20 31.

Filharmonia Częstochowska
Częstochowa,
ul. Wilsona 16.
☎ (0 34) 324 42 30.

Filharmonia im. M. Karłowicza
Szczecin, pl. Armii Krajowej 1.
☎ (0 91) 422 00 79.

Filharmonia im. Witolda Lutosławskiego
Wrocław,
ul. Piłsudskiego 19.
☎ (0 71) 342 20 01.
w www.filharmonia.an.pl

Filharmonia Łódzka im. A. Rubinsteina
Łódź, ul. Piotrkowska 243.
☎ (0 42) 637 26 52.
w www.lodz.pl/kultura/filharmonia.html

Filharmonia Narodowa
Warsaw, ul. Sienkiewicza 10.
☎ (0 22) 826 72 81.
w www.filharmonia.pl

Filharmonia Poznańska
Poznań, ul. św Marcin 81.
☎ (0 61) 852 22 66.
w www.filharmonia.poznan.pl

Studio Koncertowe S1 im. W. Lutosławskiego
Warsaw, ul. Woronicza 17.
☎ (0 22) 645 52 52.
w www.radio.com.pl

Teatr Muzyczny
Gdynia, pl. Grunwaldzki 1.
☎ (0 58) 620 95 21.
w www.trojmiasto.pl

NOSPR
Katowice,
ul. Sejmu Śląskiego 2.
☎ (0 32) 251 89 03.
w www.nospr.org.pl

ROCK, JAZZ AND COUNTRY

Cotton Club Café
Warsaw,
al. Jana Pawła II 52.
☎ (0 22) 831 08 43.

Jazz Club "Rynek"
Warsaw, Rynek Starego Miasta 2.
☎ (0 22) 831 23 75.
w www.sdk.bis.pl

Jazz Club u Muniaka
Cracow, ul. Floriańska 3.
☎ (0 12) 423 12 05.

Pod Jaszczurami
Cracow, Rynek Główny 8.
☎ (0 12) 422 09 02.

Tam-Tam
Warsaw, ul. Foksal 18.
☎ (0 22) 828 26 22.
w www.tamtam.com.pl

NIGHTCLUBS

Blue Note Club
Poznań, C.K. Zamek,
ul. Kościuszki.
☎ (0 61) 853 60 81.
w www.blue.info.poznan.pl

Cotton Club
Gdańsk,
ul. Złotników 25/29.
☎ (0 58) 301 88 13.
@ cotton@innet.pl

Ground Zero
Warsaw, ul. Spólna 62.
☎ (0 22) 625 39 76.

Park
Warsaw,
al. Niepodległości 196.
☎ (0 22) 825 71 99.

Riviera Remont
Warsaw,
ul. Waryńskiego 12.
☎ (0 22) 625 60 31.

Stodoła
Warsaw, ul. Batorego 10.
☎ (0 22) 825 60 31.

Vogue-Hybrydy
Warsaw, ul. Złota 7/9.
☎ (0 22) 827 66 01.
w www.stodola.pw.edu.pl

Sport and Leisure

TOURISTS IN POLAND – those, at least, who are interested in such things – are fortunate in the enormous range of open-air activities available to them. The possibilities – which range from strenuous rock climbing and exhilarating skiing at one end of the scale to serene sailing or peaceful mountain trekking at the other – are almost endless. Horse riding is very popular as Poland has a centuries-old reputation for its excellent stud farms. There are also lakeside fishing and long canoeing trips *(see pp288–9)*. Winter attractions include skiing and ice sailing on the frozen Mazurian Lakes.

A tourist information signpost

The caves in the Jurassic rocks of the Cracow-Częstochowa Upland

Rock climbing – a sport for the fit and courageous

ROCK CLIMBING

THE MOST DIFFICULT and dangerous climbing routes are in the Tatra Mountains. Climbing equipment is available in specialist shops. Although a licence is needed for climbing in the Tatra National Park, climbers have free access to the *skałki* (rocks) of the Karkonosze Mountains and of the Cracow-Częstochowa Upland.

In areas where there is a dearth of mountains, climbers can practise on concrete walls; early 20th-century fortifications have found a new use.

HORSE RIDING

POLISH STUDS HAVE long enjoyed high esteem for the quality of their horses. Even when they were nationalized under Communist rule, they were highly regarded. Horse riding is once again popular, attracting increasing numbers of enthusiasts. In addition to stables with long-standing traditions, more recent riding stables, both large and small, have been established. While some of these are open to all, others are quite exclusive.

HIKING

HIKING IS VERY popular in Poland. The most attractive areas with beautiful landscapes usually have specially marked hiking routes. Hiking maps are available both in specialist bookshops and in local stores and newsagents. Hikers can rest or stay overnight in tourist hostels, which are numerous in the mountains.

When hiking in the mountains, it is forbidden to stray off the marked track. Hiking can be done independently.

Alternatively, it is possible to join a hiking camp. Such camps are organized by travel agencies, usually student ones.

CYCLING

IT IS POSSIBLE to travel the length and breadth of Poland on a bicycle. However, tourist cycling tracks are not marked, so it is definitely advisable to buy one of the guidebooks for cyclists in Poland before setting out. Narrow, busy roads should be avoided. It is also difficult to cycle safely in big cities, as there are few cycle lanes.

HANG-GLIDING

THERE ARE NUMEROUS hang-gliding schools in Poland. While some operate throughout the year, others are open only in the tourist season. All

Hiking in the foothills of the Tatra Mountains *(see pp164–5)*

the schools have up-to-date, officially approved equipment. There are courses for individuals or small groups. Although hang-gliding is associated with mountains, it is also popular in lowland areas, on the coast or around the lakes.

SAILING AND WINDSURFING

THE LAKES AND rivers of northern Poland offer endless scope for sailing. Yachts and other boats can be hired from lakeside hostels. A stay in a sailing camp is a popular holiday. The longest and most attractive sailing routes are those on the Great Mazurian Lakes, the estuary of the Vistula and Szczecin Bay. Windsurfing – on the lakes, the coastal bays and the Baltic Sea – is an increasingly popular sport.

A windsurfing competition in the Gulf of Gdańsk

CANOEING

THE MOST ATTRACTIVE routes for canoeing trips are in the north of Poland, in the region of the Augustów Canal (see pp288–9), and in the Great Mazurian Lakes district. The most beautiful trips are those along the River Krutynia and on the Western Pomeranian Lakes. Most canoeing trips last from a few days to a fortnight, and travellers usually make overnight stops at campsites. Canoes can be hired at riverside hostels. Route maps are available in specialist bookshops or local stores. For the fit, this is a wonderful way to see the country.

Sailing is a popular summer sport

ICE SAILING

THE BEST PLACE in all of Poland for ice sailing is Lake Mamry, one of the Great Mazurian Lakes (see pp284–5). Lake Mamry happens to be one of the coldest lakes in Poland, and in winter, when it is frozen over, it is perfect for ice sailing. International ice-sailing competitions have been held here since the inter-war years.

SKIING

ZAKOPANE (see pp164–5), situated at the foot of the Tatra Mountains, is the winter capital of Poland. There are pistes both for beginners and experienced skiers. The longest and most difficult descents are on Mount Kasprowy, and include the Gąsienicowa run, 9.7 km (6 miles) long, and the Goryczkowa run, 5.25 km (3 miles) long. The skiing season runs from November to March. Pistes on Mount Nosal, 590 m (over 1,900 ft) high, are the most popular. Those on Mount Gubałówka, 1,600 m (5,250 ft) high, are less demanding. Beginners will find many easy pistes in the vicinity of Białka and Bukowina Tatrzańska. There are also many long, perfectly prepared ski runs in Szczyrk Brenna, Wisła and Ustroń in the Beskid Mountains of Silesia, and also in Szklarska Poręba in the Karkonosze Mountains and on the slopes of Mount Śnieżnik. The ski routes down Mount Jaworzyna near Krynica Górska are among the longest in Poland.

GOLF

GOLF DID NOT become popular in Poland until the late 1980s. It is a novel and exclusive sport. Most famous politicians, businessmen and those with a high profile in the arts frequent the 18-hole golf course at Rajszewo, near Warsaw. The best golf courses are in Pomerania and Warmia.

SURVIVAL
GUIDE

PRACTICAL INFORMATION

POLAND is a welcoming country and Polish people are well known for their hospitality. Since 1989, with the overthrow of Communist rule, tourism in Poland has greatly increased. Foreign visitors are drawn to the country for its history and folk culture, its great architecture, and the unique beauty of its natural environment. On a more practical note, new hotels have sprung up, petrol stations are more

Logo for a tourist information office

numerous and there are many more upmarket shops. The quality of service provided by post offices and banks has improved considerably, and cash dispensers can be found even in small towns. Phone cards can be used to make phone calls from almost any location. Poland is cheaper than most western European countries, although the best hotels and restaurants are expensive.

Museum ticket for the Royal Palace at Wilanów

provide professional advice, sell information bulletins and, occasionally, albums and books on the history of the town or region. Sometimes, information centres are found in railway stations.

For enquiries about accommodation, tickets and trains, Orbis agencies are preferable. Hotel employees may also be able to assist in providing essential tourist information if other sources fail.

The tourist information centre in Zakopane

WHEN TO GO

FOR THOSE who intend to travel around Poland, the best time to go is late spring or early autumn, when temperatures are usually pleasantly warm – although recently the weather in Poland has become quite unpredictable. At that time of year, tourist spots are not as crowded as during the long summer holiday period when coastal, lakeside and mountain resorts are packed with holiday visitors. Big cities, by contrast, are noticeably quieter in summer, so that moving around is easier and more relaxing. Summer is also when theatres close for the holiday break. After the summer holiday season, many guesthouses, hotels, clubs and restaurants in coastal resorts and other popular lakeside spots close. The skiing season runs from the end of November to mid-March.

TOURIST INFORMATION

FINDING AN information centre can be really difficult. Even in a big town, there is usually only one such centre. Their telephone numbers and addresses are listed in this guidebook, next to the name of each location. Tourist information centres

MUSEUMS AND MONUMENTS

DETAILS OF OPENING times for most galleries and museums mentioned in this guidebook are given on the relevant pages. Generally, museums are open from Tuesday to Friday, usually from 9am to 3 or 4pm. Entrance charges tend to be

quite reasonable. An extra charge may be made for admission to the more elaborate temporary exhibitions. In some institutions, admission is free on one day of the week.

VISITING CHURCHES

AS IN MANY Catholic countries, visitors to churches are expected to be appropriately dressed. Sleeveless shirts and

Tourists in a pedestrianized area of Międzyzdroje

◁ **Ulica Freta in Warsaw, enjoyed by tourists and locals alike**

Horse-drawn carriage in Main Market Square, Cracow

shorts, exposing bare arms and legs, are unacceptable.

Churches were once open from dawn to dusk, but crime has changed this. In big cities, churches are usually open all day, although visitors may not always be welcome during services. In small towns and villages, churches are likely to be locked; the priest may agree to let visitors in. Admission to churches is usually free.

FACILITIES FOR DISABLED PEOPLE

A LL RENOVATED or newly erected public buildings have ramps or lifts that have been installed especially for the convenience of disabled people. Even so, disabled people are quite likely to encounter difficulties. Only in a minority of cities, such as Gdańsk or Gdynia, do most of the shops have proper wheelchair access.

Sightseeing is a much more significant problem, since old churches, palaces and historic residences are, more likely than not, inaccessible to disabled people.

It is also worth noting that driving motorized wheelchairs along pavements can be highly problematical on account of parked cars. New buses, by contrast, are an unquestionable plus. Routes served by low-floor buses specially designed for wheelchairs are marked on timetables. There are also special taxis for disabled people. In general, disabled facilities in Poland continue to improve.

CUSTOMS INFORMATION

A VALID PASSPORT is required for admittance to Poland. For most European, and for many non-European, nationals, visas are not a requirement. However, check with the Polish embassy for entry requirements. Personal items may be brought into the country, but it is important to remember that limits are imposed on the import and export of alcohol and cigarettes. Guns brought into Poland and antiques exported from the country need a special permit. Gifts worth up to 70 Euros may be imported duty free.

MAGAZINES AND INFORMATION ON CULTURAL EVENTS

P OLAND HAS a lively programme of cultural events that take place throughout the year (see pp32–5, 334–7). Local bulletins providing information on upcoming events are useful

Parking sign for disabled people

2 miejsca

when planning a visit to a particular city or an itinerary in a certain area.

Local newspapers are another reliable source of information. Very useful is the Friday edition of *Gazeta Wyborcza*, which contains a local supplement, *What's on?*, giving details of cultural events. Newspapers also provide information on all regional events taking place in the week to come. The foreign-language edition of *What, Where, When*, which is regularly issued in big cities, is especially aimed at foreign visitors.

Information at the entrance to the Tatra National Park

Newsagent's kiosk, selling bus tickets as well as magazines

STUDENT AND YOUTH TRAVEL

Anyone who has an International Student's Card (ISIC) – and this should be obtained before arrival in Poland – is entitled to reduced admission to museums and cheaper accommodation in international student hostels, which operate during the summer holiday season. ISIC cardholders are also entitled to cheaper travel on international routes.

Within Poland, local authorities determine whether or not ISIC cards are valid for reduced fares on buses. In Warsaw, foreign students up to the age of 26, as well as secondary school pupils, are entitled to half-fare tickets. The International Youth Hostel Federation (IYHF) allows reduced charges for young travellers. Detailed information on student rates is available from the tourist agency Almatur. Holders of Euro<26 cards will obtain lower prices in many shops, pizzerias, bars and cultural institutions, so it is definitely worth the effort to procure a card before travelling.

ISIC and Euro<26 – useful cards to carry

LANGUAGE AND COMMUNICATION

In terms of nationality, Poland is a very uniform country, so that Polish is spoken everywhere. Because Polish is a western Slavonic language, it is usually possible to communicate with Poles quite easily in other Slavonic languages. The older sector of the population, however, is less likely to speak English, so that it is useful – as well as courteous – to master a few basic words and phrases *(see pp382–4)*. All those professionally involved in the tourist trade speak good, or at least adequate, English. German and French are much less widely spoken.

RELIGION

Over 90 per cent of Poles are Roman Catholic. Although Poles generally attach much importance to religion, most do not have a dogmatic attitude. Symbols and rituals are deeply rooted, as is evidenced by the wayside shrines and solitary crosses seen everywhere. Religious holidays are solemnly observed, and the cult of the Virgin Mary is particularly strong. Eastern Poland has a large Orthodox minority, while Silesian Cieszyn has many Augsburg Protestants. The places of worship of other religions and Christian denominations can be found in big cities. Visits to Catholic churches are often forbidden during services. On weekdays these take place in the morning and evening. On Sundays and religious holidays, visits are possible only during the short break between services in the early afternoon. On certain feast days, such as Corpus Christi, processions wind through the streets, and traffic problems can be expected.

EMBASSIES AND CONSULATES

Poland maintains diplomatic relations with most foreign countries, and these countries have their embassies in Warsaw. The United States and certain European countries also have consulates in Poland. In the case of serious problems, such as the loss of a passport, the relevant embassy or consulate will provide help.

Sign for a public toilet

PUBLIC TOILETS

The modernization of public toilets is one of the most conspicuous changes in Poland since the fall of Communist rule in 1989. Although the provision of public toilets still leaves something to be desired, they can be found in offices, railway stations, museums, galleries and restaurants. Most petrol stations also have customer toilets.

ELECTRICAL APPLIANCES

In Poland, the electric voltage is 220 V. Plugs are of the two-pin type, as is the case in most continental European countries.

TIME

Poland is in the Central European Time Zone, one hour ahead of Greenwich Mean Time. Summer time, two hours ahead of Greenwich Mean Time, applies from 21 March to 21 September.

PHOTOGRAPHY

PHOTOGRAPHIC FILM is widely available in Poland. It can be speedily developed in numerous film processing centres, where the service is a little cheaper than in Western Europe. With a few exceptions, photography inside churches is permitted. Some museums do not allow photography, while others only forbid the use of flash. In places where photography is allowed, filming with a camcorder is also usually permitted, although a small fee sometimes applies.

NEWSPAPERS, RADIO AND TELEVISION

THE MAINSTREAM foreign newspapers are available in most hotel shops and in some bookshops and newsgents, as well as EMPiK (International Book and Press Club) centres, which can be found in big cities. Among the most highly respected Polish national newspapers are *Gazeta Wyborcza* and *Rzeczpospolita*. *Superexpress*, at the more populist end of the market, also has a large circulation. The largest advertisement sections are to be found in *Gazeta Wyborcza* and local

What, Where, When: English-language editions for Warsaw and Cracow

newspapers. Outside Warsaw, where the major national newspapers are published, the local press is the most popular. *Gazeta Wyborcza*, however, also enjoys nationwide popularity on account of the local supplements that are folded into the main national newspaper. These are issued in several regions of Poland. Newspapers and magazines in the English language are also available. The most prominent include *The Warsaw Voice* and *Warsaw Business Journal*. For

cultural information, the anglophone leader in its field is *What, Where, When*.

The most popular television channels are the state-owned channels 1 and 2 (TVP1 and TVP2) and the commercial networks Polsat and TVN. There are also many local and satellite channels, received through cable or digital television. Of the national radio stations, Radio Zet, which broadcasts pop music (107.5 FM) and RFM FM (91.0 FM) are the most popular. Interesting music programmes are broadcast on Trójka, Polish Radio 3 (98.8 MHZ). Polish Radio 1 (223 kHZ, 92.0 FM) and Radio 2 (102.4 FM) also have a large following. Polish Radio 1 has a programme that runs between mid-summer's day and 31 August from 9am to 12pm called *"Lato z Radiem"*, *Summer with the Radio*. During this programme, the news and weather is broadcast on the hour in five foreign languages, including English. Local radio stations are based in every big city.

DIRECTORY

EMBASSIES

Austria
Warsaw, ul. Gagarina 34.
((0 22) 841 00 81.

Belgium
Warsaw,
ul. Senatorska 34.
((0 22) 827 02 33.

Canada
Warsaw,
ul. Matejki 1/5.
((0 22) 629 80 51.

China
Warsaw,
ul. Bonifraterska 1.
((0 22) 831 38 36.

Czech Republic
Warsaw,
ul. Koszykowa 18.
((0 22) 628 72 21.

Denmark
Warsaw,
ul. Rakowiecka 19.
((0 22) 848 26 00.

Finland
Warsaw,
ul. Chopina 48.
((0 22) 629 40 91.

France
Warsaw,
ul. Piękna 1.
((0 22) 628 84 01.

Germany
Warsaw,
ul. Dąbrowiecka 30.
((0 22) 617 30 11.

Holland
Warsaw, ul. Chocimska 6.
((0 22) 849 23 51.

Hungary
Warsaw,
ul. Chopina 2.
((0 22) 628 44 51.

Israel
Warsaw,
ul. Krzywickiego 24.
((0 22) 825 00 28.

Italy
Warsaw,
pl. Dąbrowskiego 6.
((0 22) 826 34 71.

Norway
Warsaw,
ul. Chopina 2a.
((0 22) 696 40 30.

Russia
Warsaw,
ul. Belwederska 49.
((0 22) 621 55 75.

Spain
Warsaw,
ul. Myśliwiecka 4.
((0 22) 622 42 50.

Sweden
Warsaw, ul. Bagatela 3.

((0 22) 843 33 51.

Switzerland
Warsaw,
al. Ujazdowskie 27.
((0 22) 628 04 81.

United Kingdom
Warsaw, al. Róż 1.
((0 22) 628 10 01.
W www.britishembassy.pl

United States
Warsaw,
al. Ujazdowskie 29/31.
((0 22) 628 30 41.
W www.usaemb.pl

STUDENT AND YOUTH TRAVEL

Almatur
Warsaw,
ul. Kopernika 15.
((0 22) 826 26 39.

Safety and Health

City guard sign in Warsaw

Tʜᴇ ꜱᴍᴀʟʟ ɴᴜᴍʙᴇʀ of policemen on the streets is the ongoing complaint of many Polish people. As elsewhere, crime has increased somewhat in recent years; organized crime is a new phenomenon. However, as long as they take reasonable care – avoiding certain districts of big cities, for example – tourists need have no real fears. Although the health service has been reformed, it still lags behind Poland's dynamically developing economy. State-run hospitals are ill-equipped and underfunded. Even so, first aid is free in Poland.

Police car

fraudsters, who prey on those naive enough to hand over money: the likelihood of being reimbursed if you win the game is rather small.

Drivers travelling at night should never react to signals given by anyone in plain clothes. Outside built-up areas, drivers can only be stopped by uniformed policemen standing near a marked police car – blue with a white stripe and a flashing light on the roof. Foreign visitors travelling around Poland should carry their passport with them at all times, or at the very least have some form of identification or the number of someone who should be contacted in the case of an emergency.

POLICJA

Police sign

Mɪɴᴏʀ Hᴀᴢᴀʀᴅꜱ

Mᴏꜱᴛ ᴠɪʟʟᴀɢᴇꜱ ᴀɴᴅ small towns in Poland are very quiet and peaceful. In resorts, especially during the summer months, youths under the influence of alcohol may be apparent – the best tactic is to avoid them discreetly.

Polish cities suffer from the same crime and security problems as most European capitals, so that vigilance and care are needed. In case of difficulties, the police are helpful. In big cities, visitors may walk quite safely during the day. Attacks on tourists in city centres are not unknown, but they happen very seldom. Every big town, however, has its shady districts. In Warsaw, it is advisable to avoid Ulica Brzeska and the surrounding Praga district; in Gdańsk, Ulica Orunia is best given a miss, while in Wrocław, Ulica Kościuszki, Ulica Traugutta and Ulica Krasińskiego are decidedly insalubrious. At night, robberies can occur even in city centres. In the Old Town and Main Town of Gdańsk, organized gangs

patrol the streets and it has been known for them to snatch a necklace from a tourist's neck or grab a bag despite the presence of witnesses. It is assumed that a tourist will not go to the trouble of reporting a crime and having to appear in court later on.

In market squares it is best to avoid all the games of dice or three-card tricks that go on. The players are usually

Policeman   **Traffic warden**

Aᴠᴏɪᴅɪɴɢ Tʜᴇғᴛ

Iɴ ᴄɪᴛɪᴇꜱ, pickpockets are responsible for many thefts. It is essential therefore always to keep bags and wallets safe, and never to carry a passport, wallet or other valuable item in a back pocket or open bag. Travellers should always be aware of the threat of theft, especially in railway and bus stations, in trams and at bus stops. In railway and bus stations, thefts mostly occur in an artificial crowd created by the thieves as people are boarding, so extra vigilance is required. On trams and buses thieves usually operate in groups, sometimes using such methods as crowding or "accidentally" running into a victim.

It is also inadvisable to leave any valuable or desirable items, particularly a radio, in a car. A car alarm may not discourage thieves, and it is best to park in one of the many supervised car parks. Car theft is conducted by increasingly daring means, and the police appear unable to prevent it. The thieves usually use one of two methods. One involves telling the driver about an imaginary puncture. When

An ambulance, with flashing blue lights

the driver gets out, the criminals threaten him or her with a weapon, get into the car and drive off. Another method is to provoke a collision so as to make the driver get out of the car.

It is advisable to take out insurance against theft before leaving for Poland, as this may be difficult to arrange once there. Although the theft of a car should be reported to the police immediately, there is little chance of it being recovered.

POLICE AND SECURITY SERVICES

SECURITY IN Poland is provided by policemen and policewomen from different forces, as well as private security organizations. Any problems encountered by the visitor should be reported to a policeman in uniform, at a police station. The state police are armed and have the right to arrest suspects. Policemen patrol streets on foot and in navy blue and white cars. Traffic wardens, who have fewer

powers, are primarily concerned with correct parking and the enforcement of traffic regulations. Traffic wardens wear different uniforms from town to town, and their cars carry plates bearing the town emblem.

Street traffic is the responsibility of the highway police. This includes the enforcement of speed limits and the control of drunken driving. Driving even after a small amount of alcohol is against the law. The police may ask drivers to take random breathalyzer tests; a positive result will incur a very steep fine indeed. Penalties for parking offences and speeding are also very high *(see pp358–9)*. In the event of a serious car accident, all three emergency services – police, fire brigade and ambulance – should be called.

In many towns, private security agents are hired to protect public buildings and private houses and keep order at various events. They usually wear black uniforms.

MEDICAL CARE

SHOULD MEDICAL attention be required, a doctor should be called or a visit made to the nearest hospital. Local daily newspapers carry up-to-date lists of hospitals. Poland has both public health service and private healthcare organizations. General health insurance is available only to Polish citizens, foreigners who hold residents' cards and political refugees. Citizens of those countries that have

appropriate agreements with Poland (and this includes the United Kingdom but not Commonwealth countries or the United States) are entitled to receive medical treatment until they can be safely repatriated. While first aid is administered free of charge, other kinds of treatment must usually be paid for on the spot. Travellers are strongly advised to take out health insurance before arriving in Poland. Foreign nationals should always carry a passport and keep money aside for medical emergencies. An invoice for medical treatment will be given on request.

PHARMACIES

PHARMACIES SELL a wide range of medication, but most of them will only be dispensed if prescribed by a doctor.

Pharmacy sign

Reduced rates only apply to prescriptions issued in Poland. Individuals who are receiving specialist treatment should take a sufficient supply of medicine with them or ask their doctor to make out several prescriptions with the international name of the drug.

In every town, at least one pharmacy should be on night duty. An up-to-date list of such pharmacies is published in local newspapers.

Entrance to a pharmacy in central Cracow

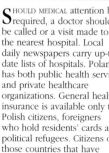

DIRECTORY

EMERGENCY NUMBERS

Police
997.

Fire brigade
998.

Ambulance
999.

Medical advice
94 39.

SOS for mobile phone owners
112.

Banking and Local Currency

Logo of Bank PKO

Prices in poland are still generally lower than in Western Europe, but hotels, restaurants and some imported articles tend to be expensive. In towns and tourist places, visitors should not have any problems exchanging currency in banks or exchange offices. Although it is by no means yet ubiquitous, credit and charge cards are accepted in more and more shops and restaurants. Cheques, however, should be cashed in banks as they are accepted as means of payment only in large hotels.

Cash dispensers are becoming increasingly common in Poland

Banking and Currency

In big cities, banks that will provide for all tourists' financial needs are easy to find, although lengthy queuing can be expected – especially at lunchtime, when many cashiers' windows are closed. Most banks are open from 8am right through to 6pm. Money can also be changed in the numerous bureaux de change, which sometimes offer better rates than banks and usually do not charge a commission, as banks commonly do. Money can also be changed at the cashier's desk of superior standard hotels, although rates there are definitely less favourable. An additional fee is also charged for changing money out of business hours. In tourist areas, near railway stations and in market squares you may come across touts offering what seems to be an advantageous street exchange. This is invariably an attempt at fraud: in exchange for foreign currency, the unlucky buyer will be duped with a wad of newspaper clippings, bank notes that have

KANTOR EXCHANGE

Bureau de change

been withdrawn from circulation or fake notes – any of which may result in a great deal of trouble for the hapless visitor.

Credit Cards

Credit cards are accepted in many places in Poland, especially now that Polish banks issue them to their customers. Credit cards are accepted in hotels, the better restaurants and clubs, car rental agencies and smart shops. Establishments usually post the logos of accepted cards on the door; however, it is wise to ask about any additional conditions for payment by

card, such as the minimum value of a purchase.

Privately owned shops are often willing to give a discount for cash payment, since they will in any case lose money in commission on a credit card transaction. As elsewhere, credit cards can also be used for withdrawing money in banks or from cash dispensers.

Entrance to the bank PKO in Cracow

Directory

Banks

Bank Polska Kasa Opieki SA
Warsaw, pl. Bankowy 2.
(0 22) 531 10 00.

Narodowy Bank Polski
Warsaw,
pl. Powstańców Warszawy 4.
(0 22) 653 10 00.

Bank Powszechna Kasa Oszczędności. Bank Państwowy
Cracow, Rynek Główny 21.
(0 12) 422 40 76.

Bureaux de Change

American Express
Warsaw,
ul. Krakowskie, Przedmiescie 11.
(0 22) 551 51 52.

Euro-Kantor
Cracow, ul. Szewska 21.
(0 12) 421 55 65.

Kantor
Warsaw, Rynek Starego Miasta 25.
(0 22) 635 79 88.

Lost and Stolen Cards

MasterCard and Visa
(0 22) 515 30 00.
www.polcard.com.pl

CURRENCY

THE OFFICIAL POLISH currency is the *złoty* (meaning "gold"). One złoty is divided into 100 *grosze*. In January 1997, four zeros were knocked off the złoty, so that 10,000 złote became 1 Polish New Złoty (PLN). The old banknotes were then withdrawn from circulation. They are no longer legal tender and can be exchanged only in banks, but unfortunately, they are used by criminals for fraudulent purposes; visitors beware.

10 PLN

20 PLN

50 PLN

100 PLN

200 PLN

Banknotes

Polish banknotes are issued in denominations of 10, 20, 50, 100 and 200 PLN. All bear the portrait of Polish rulers and are embossed to make them recognizable by blind people. In addition to standard protection against fraud, 100 and 200 złoty notes are also marked with holograms.

5 złote

2 złote

1 złoty

50 grosze

20 grosze

Coins

Polish coins are issued in denominations of 1, 2, 5, 10, 20 and 50 groszy, and 1, 2 and 5 złoty. The reverse bears the Polish eagle wearing a crown. The smallest coins – 1, 2 and 5 groszy pieces – are made of copper alloy. The 10, 20 and 50 groszy coins and the 1 złoty piece are made of nickel alloy. The 2 and 5 złoty pieces are gold- and silver-coloured.

10 grosze

5 grosze

2 grosze

1 grosz

Telephone and Postal Services

Post office logo

IN POLAND, POSTAL services are provided by Poczta Polska and telephone services by Telekomunikacja Polska. Telephone booths are easily found, even in the smallest towns, as well as in tourist spots and petrol stations. In smaller villages, however, the only public telephone may be in the local post office. Public telephones do not accept coins.

USING A PUBLIC TELEPHONE

IN RECENT YEARS, many new telephone boxes have been installed, and old ones have been replaced by more reliable machines that are operated by phonecard.

There are no coin-operated telephones in Poland, only token-operated ones, and these are being phased out. Tokens are available from post offices and newsagents. *Żeton "A"* (token "A") is just enough for a three-minute local call. For long-distance calls, *Żeton "C"* will be needed.

The easiest way to make a call is from one of the phonecard-operated machines. Phonecards are obtainable from post offices and newsagents. Some of the new generation of public telephones (which are a silver colour) also take credit cards and chip cards; these are specially marked. Calls can also be booked with a telephonist at a post office, with an advance for the first three minutes. If the call lasts more than three minutes, the balance is payable

Telephone box

afterwards. If the call does not go through, the prepayment is refunded.

Charges for long-distance national calls vary according to the time of day. The highest charges are for calls between 8am and 6pm on weekdays. From 6pm to 10pm on Saturdays, Sundays and public holidays, charges are lower. The lowest charges are for calls made between 10pm and 8am. Local call charges also vary, depending on the time of day – they are cheaper from 10pm to 6am. International call charges are fixed. When making a call to certain countries, it is possible to reverse the charges using the Direct Service. Information on country codes is available from Directory Inquiries *(see box)*.

On lifting the receiver, the caller should hear the

USING A TOKEN-OPERATED PUBLIC TELEPHONE

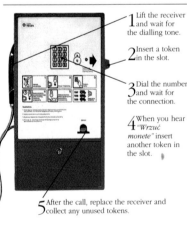

1 Lift the receiver and wait for the dialling tone.

2 Insert a token in the slot.

3 Dial the number and wait for the connection.

4 When you hear *"Wrzuć monetę"* insert another token in the slot.

5 After the call, replace the receiver and collect any unused tokens.

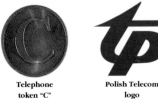

Telephone token "C"   **Polish Telecom logo**

USING A CARD-OPERATED PUBLIC TELEPHONE

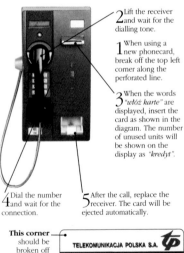

2 Lift the receiver and wait for the dialling tone.

1 When using a new phonecard, break off the top left corner along the perforated line.

3 When the words *"włóż kartę"* are displayed, insert the card as shown in the diagram. The number of unused units will be shown on the display as *"kredyt"*.

4 Dial the number and wait for the connection.

5 After the call, replace the receiver. The card will be ejected automatically.

This corner should be broken off before placing the card in the slot.

TELEKOMUNIKACJA POLSKA S.A.

← KARTA TELEFONICZNA

100

A 100-unit telephone card

The main post office in Warsaw

dialling tone. When the number has been dialled, there may be a vibrating sound as the connection is made. When it has been made, the caller will hear long, repeated signals. If the number is engaged, the sounds are short and frequent. Problems getting through may mean that the number has been changed. The process of modernization that the Polish telecommunications network is currently undergoing means that many subscribers' numbers are being extended to seven digits. In the event of

difficulties, help will be provided by *Biuro Numerów* (Directory Inquiries) *(see box)*.

MOBILE PHONES

POLAND HAS three mobile telephone networks, which operate on two wavelengths, 900 MHz and 1,800 MHz, and cover almost all of the country. Only in the more remote areas, far from the big cities and the major population centres, do users ever experience problems with connection.

POSTAL SERVICES

POCZTA POLSKA, the Polish postal service, provides a wide range of services. Post offices have been thoroughly modernized in recent years. Post offices are open from 8am to 8pm on

weekdays. In big cities, all main post offices (Poczta Główna) are open on Saturdays. However, the main post office in Warsaw, on the corner of Ulica Świętokrzyska and Ulica Jasna, is open day and night, seven days a week.

In many modernized post offices there is a ticketing system and customers are served in sequence. On entering the post office, customers take a numbered card from a machine and go to the appropriate desk when their number is displayed. The card also indicates roughly how long the customer is likely to have to wait before being served.

MAIL SERVICES

STAMPS ARE available from post offices and can also be obtained in shops and newsagents, although you often have to buy postcards too. While local correspondence should be posted in green boxes, letters for another town or a foreign country should be posted in a red box.

Letters to destinations within Poland usually arrive within 2 to 3 days of posting, while international mail may take up to a week, and inter-continental mail can take as long as three weeks to reach its destination.

For mail that is particularly urgent, Poczta Polska provides an express service and a courier service. Courier agencies such as DHL and UPS also operate in Poland, although all courier services are quite expensive.

A high letter box, which stands outside post offices

USING A CREDIT CARD-OPERATED SILVER PUBLIC TELEPHONE

1 Lift the receiver and wait for the dialling tone.

Display

3 Dial the number and wait for the connection.

Additional function key

2 When the words *"Włóż karte"* are displayed, insert the card.

4 After the call, replace the receiver and withdraw the card.

USEFUL INFORMATION ON TELEPHONE NUMBERS

- Directory inquiries (local numbers) – 911, 913
- Directory inquiries (regional) – 912
- To book a long-distance or international call – 900
- To make an international call: first dial 0, then wait for the tone; next, dial 0 again, followed by the country code, the area code (omitting the first 0) and lastly the telephone number.

Red post box, for regional and international mail

TRAVEL INFORMATION

POLAND HAS SEVERAL international airports, with flights to and from many European capitals, including London.
Warsaw, the hub of international air travel in Poland, has direct flights to many European and intercontinental destinations. Poland's major cities have international railway connections with neighbouring countries.

Plane from LOT's fleet

The country also has an extensive domestic rail network. One of the cheaper ways of travelling to Poland is by coach; there are departures from London, Paris and other European capitals. Polish ports are served by ferries to and from Scandinavian countries. Travelling to Poland by car is another attractive option.

Logo of LOT, the Polish national airline

ARRIVING BY AIR

POLAND IS WELL connected with the rest of the world. International flights from about 50 cities in 30 countries arrive in Warsaw. Polish airports also have connections with almost all the capitals of Western Europe as well as Prague, Budapest, Sofia, Bucharest and the capital cities of the Russian Federation, such as Vilnius, Riga, Mińsk and Kiev. Warsaw Okęcie airport is used by about 25 airlines, including British Airways, Air France, SAS and Lufthansa. Warsaw has direct international connections with such countries as Canada, the USA, Israel and Thailand.

The airports at Gdańsk, Katowice, Szczecin, Poznań, Wrocław and Cracow also have regular international flights. There are flights from London, Copenhagen, Hamburg and Visby to Gdańsk Rębiechowo airport. Regular connections link London, Paris, Rome, Vienna, Zurich, Dresden, Frankfurt and Copenhagen as well as Chicago and New York with Cracow Balice airport. It is possible to fly direct from Dresden, Hanover, Düsseldorf and Copenhagen to Poznań Ławica airport, and from Frankfurt, Copenhagen, Munich and Vienna to Wrocław Strachowice airport.

To reach Katowice it is usually necessary to fly via Düsseldorf, Frankfurt, Stuttgart or Vienna. Szczecin can be reached from Copenhagen.

Szymany airport in the Great Mazurian Lakes region is served by charter flights and has the status of an international airport. There are also domestic airports at Bydgoszcz, Łódź and Rzeszów, which are served by Eurolot planes.

WARSAW AIRPORT

WARSAW AIRPORT, at Okęcie, 6 km (4 miles) from the city centre, opened for business in 1933. The present passenger terminal, which opened in 1992, has both a national and an international section, with an arrivals hall on the lower level and departure lounge on the upper level. Although

Airport trolley for heavy luggage

the airport is not a particularly large one, it does provide everything that passengers are likely to need, from duty-free shops and a bureau de change on the one hand to a good restaurant and a coffee bar on the other.

A bus service runs between the airport and the city centre. Route 175 goes to the very centre of Warsaw; route 188 serves the eastern part of the city, on the right bank of the Vistula. Tickets can be bought at newsagents in town and at the airport, or they can be purchased directly from the bus driver – although in this case the exact fare, including a small handling charge, is required.

Taxi services also run to and from the airport. Visitors should exercise a degree of caution when booking a taxi.

Warsaw airport, hub of international flights

Information stands in the arrivals hall of the airport give the details of several taxi companies that are contracted directly by the airport. Although it is quite possible to order a taxi from another company by telephone, it is generally not advisable to use private taxis as the fare may be very high.

DIRECTORY

LOT
📞 952, 953.
🆆 www.lot.com

AIRPORTS

Gdańsk Rębiechowo
Road map D1.
📞 (0 58) 341 25 89/64 50.

Katowice Pyrzowice
Road map D5.
📞 (0 32) 285 34 87/30 41.

Cracow Balice
Road map D5.
📞 (0 12) 411 67 00.

Poznań Ławica
Road map C3.
📞 (0 61) 868 23 95.

Szczecin Goleniów
Road map A2.
📞 (0 91) 418 27 08 or 419 26 36.

Warsaw Airport
📞 (0 22) 650 41 00.

Wrocław Strachowice
Road map C4.
📞 (0 71) 357 70 03.

FERRY INFORMATION

📞 (0 58) 343 18 87.
🆆 www.polferries.com.pl

FERRY PORTS

Gdańsk, ul.Przemysłowa 1.
Road map D1.
📞 (0 58) 343 18 87/69 78.

Gdynia, Kwiatkowskiego 60.
Road map D1.
📞 (0 58) 665 14 14 or 660 92 00.

Świnoujście, ul. Dworcowa 1.
Road map A1.
📞 (0 91) 321 61 40.

Ferry terminal at Świnoujście

OTHER AIRPORTS

NEW TERMINALS have recently been built at the international airports in Wrocław, Gdańsk and Cracow. They are comfortable and well equipped, with restaurants, bureaux de change and car hire agencies. There are no duty-free shops. All these airports have regular bus connections with the city centre. From Gdańsk airport, at Rębiechowo, 14 km (9 miles) west of the city, buses B and 110 go to the Wrzeszcz district, where passengers can make other connections.

Cracow airport, at Balice, 12 km (7 miles) west of the city, is served by buses B, 208 and 152. While the B leaves every 15 minutes, the others are hourly. Poznań airport, at Ławica, 7 km (4 miles) west of the city, is connected with the centre by bus 78.

Connections between Wrocław airport, at Strachowice, and the city centre are provided by bus 406 and a LOT minibus. The airport has one drawback: there is a railway crossing with barriers on the access road, so

that passengers who have cut their travelling time too fine may be late for check-in.

Passengers travelling to and from central Szczecin and the airport are transported by a special LOT bus.

TICKET PRICES

THE CHEAPEST air fares to Poland are APEX-type tickets with a set return date. They have to be booked in advance and paid for two weeks before departure. In accordance with international agreements, most airlines operate a system of reduced rates for children, students, pensioners and tourist groups.

ARRIVING BY SEA

THREE POLISH FERRY ports have connections with Scandinavia. A service runs between Gdańsk and Nymäshamn in Sweden, and between Gdynia and Karlskrona in Denmark. Świnoujście has a regular connection with Ystadt and Malmö in Sweden, and with Copenhagen in Denmark.

Ferry entering Świnoujście harbour

Travelling by Train

Logo of PKP, the Polish railways network

POLAND HAS AN extensive railway network run by Polske Koleje Państwowe (Polish State Railways), with the result that it is possible to get almost everywhere by train. Big cities are served by fast InterCity trains, while international trains travel to many European cities. Journeys to smaller towns, however, may be easier to undertake by local bus, as bus services are likely to be more frequent than the train services.

A platform at Gdańsk Główny, the main railway station in Gdańsk

ARRIVING BY TRAIN

INTERNATIONAL train services run between all major European and Polish cities. The London-to-Warsaw route passes either through the Channel Tunnel or Ostend. The journey by fast InterCity trains from Prague or Berlin to Warsaw is just a few hours long. Szczecin is served by German regional railways. At the frontier town of Cieszyn it is possible to walk from the railway station on the Czech side of the border to a PKP railway station on the Polish side. The main rail route runs across Poland from east to west, connecting Russia with western Europe.

EXPRESS AND LONG-DISTANCE TRAINS

THE FASTEST and most convenient way of travelling around Poland is by express train. Express lines connect almost all big cities in Poland; the trains are fast and usually arrive on time. To travel by express train, it is necessary to reserve a seat as well as purchase a ticket. The most comfortable, but also the most expensive, are the InterCity express trains. On these trains, passengers are offered a free – if rather small – meal. Meals in restaurant cars are quite expensive.

The journey by express train from Warsaw to Cracow, Katowice, Poznań or Gdańsk takes from about three to four hours. Euro and InterCity trains have compartments especially for mothers with children and for disabled people. Long-distance trains, both fast and slow, are often delayed and can be dirty and crowded. Night journeys on these trains are neither comfortable nor safe. In Poland, there are two classes of carriage. Although travelling first class is more expensive, it is much more comfortable and is certainly worth the extra expense.

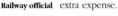

Railway official

SLEEPERS

LONG ROUTES ARE served by sleepers with couchettes and very comfortable sleeping cars. Trains leave Gdynia or Szczecin in the late evening, arriving at their destination the following morning. The standard of the compartments is not high; unfortunately, the same cannot be said of the fares.

TRAIN FARES

FARES FOR JOURNEYS on ordinary and fast trains are generally very reasonable. For journeys on express trains and in sleeping cars, however, fares are much higher. Teenagers and students up to the age of 26 who hold valid student cards are entitled to reduced fares.

Tickets are available direct from railway stations, and they can also be purchased in advance at any of the Orbis national travel agencies, which can be found in larger towns and cities.

Tickets can also be bought on the train, although in such cases passengers must report to the conductor when they board the train and an additional handling fee is charged. The fines for travelling without a valid ticket are punitively high. Reduced fares for excursion tickets are available on certain routes at weekends during the summer season.

An express InterCity train

Tickets for couchettes and sleepers can be booked via the Internet, on www.wars.pl, by telephone, on (0 801) 300 001, or by fax, on (0 22) 828 52 47. Travellers who choose to make their booking by one of these methods should pay the conductor for their tickets once they have boarded.

PERSONAL SAFETY

Kraków Główny, Cracow's historic main railway station

ACTS OF VANDALISM are not uncommon on suburban trains. Late at night, it is wise to choose a seat at the front of the train, where there are usually more people. If making an overnight journey

The main hall at Warszawa Centralna, Warsaw's central station

on any of the long-distance InterCity trains, it is safer to be seated in a compartment that is occupied by several other passengers. Money should be discreetly hidden away in pockets and definitely never left in an unattended bag or suitcase.

If in any doubt, travellers should also avoid drinking alcohol with strangers; of course, most people are trustworthy, but you are more vulnerable to theft if you have first been plied with drink. Theft is, not surprisingly, much rarer during the day than it is at night-time.

LEFT LUGGAGE

TRAVELLERS MAY LEAVE their luggage in the left luggage offices of railway stations if they want to go around town unencumbered. There is a charge for the left luggage service – often a kind of insurance, the price being dependent on the declared value of the luggage. Travellers should, of course, make sure that their luggage is fully insured before travelling to Poland.

The larger stations have a system of coin-operated luggage lockers.

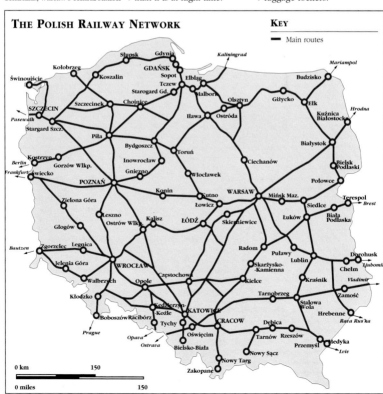

THE POLISH RAILWAY NETWORK

KEY

— Main routes

Map labels: Słupsk, Gdynia, Kaliningrad, Mariampol, Kołobrzeg, GDAŃSK, Sopot, Elbląg, Budzisko, Świnoujście, Koszalin, Tczew, Staragard Gd., Malbork, Olsztyn, Giżycko, Ełk, Hrodna, SZCZECIN, Szczecinek, Chojnice, Iława, Ostróda, Kuźnica Białostock, Pasewalk, Stargard Szcz., Piła, Białystok, Berlin, Kostrzyn, Bydgoszcz, Toruń, Ciechanów, Bielsk Podlaski, Frankfurt, Świecko, Gorzów Wlkp., Inowrocław, Gniezno, Włocławek, Połowce, POZNAŃ, Konin, Kutno, WARSAW, Mińsk Maz., Terespol, Zielona Góra, Łowicz, Siedlce, Brest, Leszno, Kalisz, ŁÓDŹ, Skierniewice, Łuków, Biała Podlaska, Głogów, Ostrów Wlkp., Bautzen, Zgorzelec, Legnica, Radom, Puławy, Lublin, Dorohusk, Jelenia Góra, WROCŁAW, Częstochowa, Skarżysko-Kamienna, Ljubomil, Wałbrzych, Opole, Kielce, Kraśnik, Vladimir, Kłodzko, Tarnobrzeg, Zamość, Kędzierzyn-Koźle, KATOWICE, Stalowa Wola, Hrebenne, Bobiszów Racibórz, Tychy, CRACOW, Dębica, Rata Rus'ka, Prague, Opava, Oświęcim, Tarnów, Rzeszów, Medyka, Ostrava, Bielsko-Biała, Nowy Sącz, Przemyśl, Lviv, Nowy Targ, Zakopane

0 km 150
0 miles 150

Travelling by Suburban Train or Bus

PKS logo

Suburban trains are the best means of getting around over short distances, and Warsaw is well served by its own underground system. The Fast City Railway runs between Gdańsk and Wejherowo. For rail enthusiasts narrow-gauge railways still operate in some areas. You will find almost all towns and villages served by local buses or coaches, with bus stations in big cities usually located near railway stations, and there are buses for longer international routes. Generally, the transport system in Poland is efficient and offers good value.

Fast City Railway in Trójmiasto

Suburban Trains

Suburban or commuter routes are served by electric trains, which sometimes consist of open-plan, double-decker cars. The service is frequent and trains stop at every station on the route. At station stops, the doors open automatically. Suburban trains are at their most crowded on weekdays before 8am and after 3pm.

Tickets

Tickets for journeys by suburban train can be bought at the station – either from the ticket office or sometimes from a newsagent within the station. Before boarding a suburban train, passengers are required to punch their ticket in a machine installed by the entrance to the platforms. Tickets are checked by conductors during the course of the journey.

The Warsaw Metro

The Warsaw metro, the only urban underground rail network in Poland, connects the city centre with the large housing estates in the southern part of the city.

The Warsaw metro is clean, safe and punctual. Entrances are marked by a stylized red M on a yellow background. Stations have lifts for disabled people. Tram and bus tickets are also valid in the metro. Passengers

Warsaw metro sign

should punch their ticket in a machine before crossing the yellow line marking the limit of the ticket-free zone.

Smoking on the metro is not allowed.

Station sign on a Fast City Railway route

Fast City Railway

Szybka kolej miejska, the Fast City Railway (SKM), operates in Trójmiasto, the Tri-City of Gdańsk, Sopot and Gdynia *(see p231)*. Trains depart punctually every few minutes and the destination is marked on the platform boards. A special ticket is needed to travel on these trains. The reverse is printed with all the stations at which the train stops. In Warsaw, a Fast City Railway service connects the western and eastern parts of the city.

Narrow-Gauge Railways

Until a few years ago, narrow-gauge railways were very common in Poland. Today only a few remain and these are solely a tourist attraction. Information about routes is obtainable in railway information offices in the major stations, or in tourist information centres. One of the most interesting narrow-gauge railway routes is the one that runs from Gąsawa to Żnin, near Bydgoszcz. Beside the track in Wenecja, there is a Museum of the Narrow-Gauge Railway.

A Warsaw underground station

The Western Bus Station in Warsaw

INTERNATIONAL COACH ROUTES

COACHES TO international destinations depart from all big cities in Poland, usually from coach stations near main railway stations or bus stations. For the cost-conscious, they provide a viable alternative to other forms of travel, and are operated by several different companies. Timetables are available in travel agencies; tickets for most international routes can be bought in Orbis tourist centres.

Coaches run from Polish frontier towns to the nearest towns of neighbouring countries. Przemyśl coach station has a stop for coaches going to major cities in the Ukraine, Slovakia and Romania. Przemyśl coach station is also a good place for starting excursions in the eastern Carpathian Mountains, which lie beyond the Polish borders.

COACHES

MOST LONG-DISTANCE routes within Poland are served by Polska Komunikacja Samochodowa (PKS), Polish Motor Transport. The coaches are not very comfortable and the journey times are usually longer than by train.

In bigger towns, coaches stop for a brief break so that passengers can get out and stretch their legs. Tickets are available in coach station ticket offices or from the driver. The seats are seldom numbered. On longer routes, it may be preferable not to sit at the back of the coach, as this is usually commandeered by rowdy passengers.

Polski Express is a competitor of PKS; its main coach stops are in Warsaw and it serves several routes out of the city. One of the Polski Express stops is at the junction of Ulica Złota and Aleje Jana Pawła II, close to Warsaw's Central Railway Station. The other is near Warsaw Okęcie airport.

Polski Express has cheaper fares, comfortable air-conditioned coaches and pleasant staff. The journey time to places distant from Warsaw, however, is long, as the route taken is not always the most direct.

A long-distance coach of the Polski Express company

LOCAL BUSES

BUSES ARE SOMETIMES the only means of getting to small towns and villages. The service is punctual and tickets are available from the driver.

Before 8am and in the afternoon local buses may be crowded. When planning to visit a small town or village, it is best to check connections in advance, as timetables at desolate bus stops are often vandalized and unreadable.

Information on local bus services is available from the PKS telephone information office and at all major bus stations.

Apart from PKS, private bus companies are becoming increasingly common. The best source of information about privately run services is by word of mouth in the particular locality.

An information board for travellers

MINIBUSES

MINIBUS SERVICES providing short-distance local connections run in many towns and tourist spots, and provide an extremely cheap and convenient way of getting about locally. Minibus fares are usually lower than those on PKS buses.

The minibus service runs frequently, but the number of seats is limited so, wherever possible, travellers should plan in advance. Minibus services are well-organized, particularly in Cracow. They stop near the Main Railway Station and serve most neighbouring villages, including Wieliczka and Niepołomice *(see p162)*.

The minibus is also a very convenient means of transport in Zakopane *(see pp164–5)*, Krościenko, the Karkonosze Mountains *(see pp182–3)* and in other highland regions.

A PKS bus, serving local routes

Travelling by Car

P OLAND HAS ACQUIRED something of a reputation as a dangerous place for foreign drivers, but this is largely undeserved. Car theft is a genuine problem, but it can easily be guarded against, and the pleasure of travelling independently is unbeatable. Renting a car is also quite straightforward. The only problem that driving in Poland presents is that of parking in big cities: they tend to be congested and there is rarely any parking space at all.

A Warsaw parking meter

A wheel clamp on an illegally parked car

A car rental agency at Warsaw airport

ARRIVING BY CAR

D RIVERS IN POLAND should at all times keep necessary documents about their person: these are a driving licence, registration documents and comprehensive insurance.

Foreign drivers are also required to carry a green card, and foreign cars should display the international symbol of their country of origin.

In Poland, driving licences for passenger cars can be obtained from the age of 17. Polish driving regulations are strict, but the roads are relatively safe.

CAR RENTAL

A LL THE MAJOR international car rental companies operate in Poland. It is best to book a particular make of car before arrival. Key conditions are a valid full driving licence and a minimum age of 21 or 25, depending on the hire company. Before signing the rental documents, it is also advisable to check the level of insurance cover provided.

PARKING

P ARKING REGULATIONS vary from city to city. In central Warsaw there are parking meters and many car parks where a fee is paid to an attendant, although the car park is unguarded.

In the main streets of Gdańsk and Gdynia, coin-operated parking meters have been installed.

Central Wrocław and Poznań have a system of

parking cards, obtainable from newsagents; the driver circles the date and time of parking and places the card in the windscreen.

In Cracow, driving and parking in the Planty area is difficult for foreign visitors. Without a special hotel permit, parking is in fact almost impossible. Elsewhere in Cracow, a system of parking cards similar to that in Wrocław applies.

REGULATIONS

D RIVERS MUST have their car headlights on at all times between 1 October and 1 March, as well as whenever it is raining or snowing. The national speed limit in built-up areas is 60 km/h (35 mph); on roads it is 90 km/h (55 mph) and on motorways it is 110 km/h (68 mph). Radar speed controls quite often operate. Foreign visitors should bear in mind that if they are caught speeding they cannot count on any leniency just because they are not Polish nationals: pleading ignorance is no

PARKING IN WARSAW

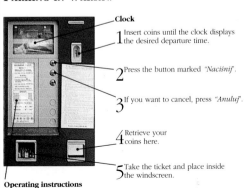

Clock

1 Insert coins until the clock displays the desired departure time.

2 Press the button marked *"Naciśnij"*.

3 If you want to cancel, press *"Anuluj"*.

4 Retrieve your coins here.

5 Take the ticket and place inside the windscreen.

Operating instructions

defence. A fine of up to 200 PLN must be paid on the spot, while larger amounts must be paid by postal order.

Poland has very strict drink-driving laws – tourists are best advised not to drink anything at all if they are driving. Breathalyzer tests are a regular part of roadside police checks; drivers can be stopped and tested by police even if they have committed no infringement.

The use of mobile phones while driving is also banned unless the phone is a hands-free model.

Children under the age of 12 must not be allowed to travel in the front seat, and small children must be strapped into special child seats at all times. All passengers sitting in the front seats – with the exception of heavily pregnant women – are obliged to travel with their seatbelts fastened.

It is obligatory for motorcyclists and their passengers always to wear helmets.

PETROL STATIONS

IN BIG CITIES, as well as on Poland's major roads, finding a 24-hour petrol station does not present a problem. In addition to selling fuel and motor accessories, petrol stations usually have shops. Those outside towns also have bars where travellers can drink coffee or have a hot meal.

Drivers planning journeys to certain remote areas,

however, should fill up in advance, as most small petrol stations in the countryside are open only on weekdays and close at 6pm.

Petrol in Poland is provided by multinational companies such as Shell, Esso, Aral and Neste. It is also provided by the national producers CPN, Rafineria Gdańska and Petrochemia Płocka.

ROAD MAPS

ALL THE TOWNS and cities mentioned in this guide appear on the map inside the back cover. Each chapter also features a more detailed regional map. Maps showing the most interesting excursion routes appear in the appropriate sections of the guide. For cycling or driving trips to other places, more detailed maps can be bought at tourist information centres and large petrol stations. There are now also Internet sites specializing in international route maps, and it may be helpful to consult one before setting out.

City sign

ROADS

POLAND HAS FEW motorways. Some were built before World War II and their condition is far from satisfactory. A modern motorway, for the use of which a toll is payable, connects Cracow and Katowice. A new network of highways is currently being planned. Other roads are usually reasonably good. The arterial roads used

by international traffic are often rutted by heavy trucks. They are a particular hazard in rainy conditions.

Signpost indicating traffic diversion

CAR THEFT

POLAND HAS an unenviable reputation for car theft. To avoid falling victim to theft, always leave your car at a guarded car park, even when planning only a short visit to a restaurant. For expensive vehicles, additional precautions should be taken. One way of securing a car is to attach a wheel clamp, which is a routine procedure for illegally parked cars. There are also other sensible rules. Keys should never be left in the ignition, even when the driver merely gets out to open the boot or check for a puncture. Luggage should not be left on the seats. Beware of anyone pointing out damage or some other problem with the car; this may be a ploy to tempt the driver to get out of the car. If you have to stop and get out, it is unwise to do so anywhere but in a well-lit public place.

DIRECTORY

CAR RENTAL AGENCIES

AVIS Poland
Gdańsk, Wały Jagiellońskie 2/4.
((0 58) 301 88 18.
Cracow, ul. Basztowa 15.
((0 12) 421 10 66.
Warsaw, lotnisko Okęcie.
((0 22) 650 48 72.
w www.avis.pl

Hertz Rent-a-Car
Cracow, al. Focha 1.
((0 12) 637 11 20.
Warsaw, Okęcie Airport.
((0 22) 650 28 96.
w www.hertz.com

ROADSIDE ASSISTANCE

(981

A Petrochemia Płocka petrol station

Getting around on Foot, by Taxi or Public Transport

TAXI

Taxi sign

THE EASIEST WAY of exploring most large city centres is on foot. Taking a taxi can be the quickest and most comfortable way of covering longer distances in towns. Most big cities have an efficient public transport system and fares are not high; this is also a good way of mixing with the local people.

ON FOOT

IN THE HISTORIC parts of towns and cities, motorized traffic is usually either limited or banned altogether. The Old Town in Warsaw and Cracow, the Main City in Gdańsk, the area around Main Market Square and the cathedral in Wrocław, and the old town in Lublin are best explored on foot. Distances between the historic sights are not great, but the condition of

The Royal Route, highlighted on an information panel in Cracow

the pavements may leave something to be desired. Because they are uneven, tripping and falling or spraining an ankle may be a hazard, especially when it is so easy to lose oneself and become focused on the beautiful towers of a historic building high above the ground. Road signs in old towns present another hazard; some are mounted so low that they threaten the heads of passing tourists.

CITY OF WARSAW INFORMATION (MSI)

Poczta Główna	200m
Ambasada Włoska / Ambasciata d'Italia	350m
Trakt Królewski	450m

Signposts for pedestrians, indicating the distance (in metres) to particular streets and buildings

Warsaw's information system facilitates circulation around the city, which has been divided into sectors. Blue signposts, information panels and other street signs give useful inform- ation and point the way to particular areas, buildings and other landmarks. Pictographs and arrows on signposts point to the nearest telephone box, police station or public toilet. Brown boards identify points of interest in the historic part of the city.

BY TAXI

IT IS ADVISABLE ONLY to use a taxi from a taxi company – identifiable by roof signs bearing the company's name and telephone number. Several such companies operate in every big town so flagging one down is easy.

There is no extra charge for a taxi ordered by phone. After 10pm, on Saturdays and Sundays and in remote parts of town, rates per kilometre are higher. Radio taxis (ordered by phone) are available 24 hours a day. Private taxis, which do not display a company name and phone number, should be avoided, as their charges may be several times the going rate.

A taxi from the fleet of one of Warsaw's licensed taxi companies

PUBLIC TRANSPORT IN TOWNS

THE MOST POPULAR form of public transport is provided by the bus network. Trams also run in many towns. Warsaw is the only Polish city to have a metro (see p356). Some towns have a trolleybus service, and in some areas, minibus transport is a cheap and popular alternative way of getting around town.

TICKETS

ALMOST EVERY TOWN – and this is also true of quite a few small villages as well – has its own system of ticketing. Fares also vary from place to place, and there may be an extra charge for luggage.

In most towns, tickets are universally valid for travel on buses, trams and trolleybuses. In Warsaw, tram, bus and trolleybus tickets are also valid on the metro.

In some cities, such as Gdańsk and Poznań, the price of a ticket depends on the journey time. There are fares for journeys of up to 10, 30 and 60 minutes. This can be a problem for anyone who is not familiar with the city. Journey times can, however, be estimated by consulting the timetable.

In big towns it is possible to buy a day ticket, or a group or weekend pass, which is designed for a group of five people travelling on Saturday and Sunday.

Reduced fares apply to children between the ages of 4 and 14 – so long as they appear on their parents' identity documents – and to holders of relevant cards. Small children (under 4) and people over the age of 75 travel free. Current fares are posted on special boards in prominent public places.

A fast city tram of the Pestka line in Poznań

TICKET PUNCHING

Bus, tram and trolleybus tickets can be purchased from newsagents. Passengers should punch them as they get on board.

Random checks are carried out by ticket inspectors – plain-clothes officials wearing a conspicuous badge. Passengers travelling without a valid ticket are fined.

Fines are either payable on the spot or within a week by banker's order. The latter option, however, is not applicable to foreign visitors, on the grounds that they might abscond without paying the fine. Those who refuse to pay may be taken to a police station.

Tram stop identification

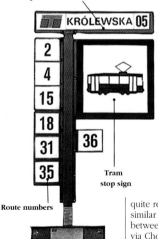

Route numbers

Tram stop sign

Timetable

A tram stop with timetable

PERSONAL SAFETY

Passengers on trams and buses should be on their guard against the pickpockets that operate on certain routes, especially in big cities, where there are many thefts.

Money should be put in a secure place before boarding. Keeping it in an open bag or pocket is asking for trouble.

BY TRAM

Trams are a convenient means of transport, especially during rush hours, when cars can cause serious congestion. They are also – relative to other road traffic, at least – quick, cheap and environmentally friendly.

Several of the largest cities have a tram network, and in the Upper Silesian Industrial Region (see p205), trams interconnect the neighbouring towns. Trams also link the centre of Łódź with four other towns of the Łódź agglomeration – Konstantynów Łódzki, Ozorków, Pabianice and Zgierz. Pestka, a fast city tram network with special tramlines, went into service quite recently in Poznań. A similar tram service is to run between Katowice and Bytom via Chorzów.

BY TROLLEYBUS

Trolleybuses run in Gdynia, Sopot, Lublin and other big cities. Itineraries and journey times are similar to those covered by buses. Trolleybuses are, however, losing their popularity.

BY MINIBUS

In some towns, suburban routes are served by minibuses (see p357). They provide a regular service and the timetables can be found at bus stops. Tickets are bought from the driver. City transport tickets are not valid on minibuses.

Standard local bus in Warsaw

BY BUS

Bus services run even in small towns, although the smaller the town, of course, the fewer bus routes there are likely to be. Big cities have several types of bus; the local buses, usually marked with black boards, call at every bus stop. The fast, or express buses, marked in red, usually serve long-distance routes. Night buses, which run in big cities, operate between 11pm and 5am. Because fares on the night buses are higher, it may be necessary to punch more than one ticket. The tickets can be bought from the bus driver. There is usually one night bus route in every town.

In many towns, the bus fleet has been modernized, and the old buses have been replaced by modern low-floor buses (see p343) that make public transport far easier to negotiate for disabled people and for those with small children in prams.

Index

Acknowledgments

DORLING KINDERLSLEY would like to thank the following people whose contributions and assistance have made the preparation of this book possible.

PUBLISHING MANAGER
Helen Townsend

MANAGING ART EDITOR
Kate Poole

ART DIRECTOR
Gillian Allan

DTP DESIGNER
Jason Little

PRODUCTION CONTROLLER
Marie Ingledew

DESIGN AND EDITORIAL ASSISTANCE
Ben Barkow, Arwen Burnett, Jo Cowen, Marcus Hardy, Marisa Renzullo, Emma Rose, Conrad Van Dyk, Stewart Wild.

PROJECT MANAGER
Tamiko Rex

ADDITIONAL CONTRIBUTORS
Beatrice Waller, Lucilla Watson, Chris Barstow, Alison Bravington, Matheusz Jozwiak, Joanna Hanson.

Special Assistance
Dorling Kindersley would like to thank the staff at the featured museums, shops, hotels, restaurants and other organizations in Poland for their invaluable help. Special thanks go to the following: Katarzyna Kolendo, Dorota Kuta, Jacek Łodziński and Zbigniew Kocyek.

Photography Permissions
"Piękna" Agency, Jagiellonian Library in Cracow, Kórnick Library of the Polish Academy of Sciences, Warsaw University Library, Central Photographic Agency, Central Maritime Museum in Gdańsk, Collegium Maius in Cracow, Film Library in Warsaw, Chancellory of the President of the Republic of Poland, Gniezno Cathedral, Poznań Cathedral, Metropolitan Police Headquarters in Warsaw, Czartoryski Museum in Cracow, Diocesan Museum in Tarnów, Łódź Historical Museum, Cracow History Museum, Jan Kochanowski Museum in Czarnolas, National Museum in Kielce, National Museum in Cracow, National Museum in Poznań, Regional Museum in Jelenia Góra, Art Museum in Łódź, Museum in Wilanów, Museum of Warmia and Mazuria in Olsztyn, Museum of the Polish Army in Warsaw, Museum of Arms in Liw, Zamoyski Museum in Kozłówka, Maria Pałasińska, Photography Editorship of the Polish Press Agency, Warsaw Traffic Police, Road Traffic Department of the Metropolitan Police Headquarters in Warsaw, J. Baranowski, Jacek Bednarczyk, Maciej Bronarski, Father Tadeusz Bukowski, Andrzej Chęć, Renata Cichocka, Mirosław Ciunowicz, Alicja Firynowicz, Maja Florczykowska, Michał Grychowski, Dorota and Mariusz Jarymowicz, Krzysztof Kapusta, Grzegorz and Tomasz Kłoszowski, Marek Kosiński, Beata and Mariusz Kowalski, Grzegorz Kozakiewicz, Jasusz Koziń, Stefan Kraszewski, Wojciech Kryński, Damazy Kwiatkowski, Janusz Mazur, Wojciech Mędrzak, Stanisław Micht, Jan Morak, Hanna and Maciej Musiał, Małgorzata Omilanowska, Henryk Pieczul, Tomasz Prażmowski, Ireneusz Radkiewicz, Wojciech Richter, Tomasz Robaczyński, Andrzej Rybczyński, Jakub Sito, Krzysztof Skalski, Andrzej Skowroński, Wojciech Stein, Wiesław Stępień, Wojtek Szabelski, Serge Tarasów, Jacek Urbański, Przemek Wierzchowski, Władysław Wisławski, Paweł Wójcik, Tadeusz Zagoździński, Jan Zych.

Picture Credits

Key: t=top; tl=top left; tlc=top left centre; tc=top centre; tr=top right; cla=centre left above; ca=centre above; cra=centre right above; cl=centre left; c=centre; bc=bottom centre; cr=centre right; bcr=bottom centre right; bcl=bottom centre left; bl=bottom left; b=bottom; bc=bottom centre; bcl=bottom centre left; br=bottom right.

Jagiellonian Library in Cracow 37t, 42bl; Warsaw University Library 22cla; Czartoryski Museum in Cracow 26tl; Diocesan Museum in Tarnów 38cl, 41cr; Cracow History Museum 29cl, 42tl, 51br, 144b; Jan Kochanowski Museum in Czarnolas 118bl; National Museum in Kielce 45tr, 150b; National Museum in Cracow 41tc, 48–49c, 51br, 131ca, 135cr, 137tr; Regional Museum in Jelenia Góra 184c; Museum in Wilanów 96cla, 97tc, bl; Museum of Warmia and Mazuria in Olsztyn 280tl, bl; Museum of the Polish Army in Warsaw 46tl, br, 51tl; Museum of Arms in Liw 116c; Zamoyski Museum in Kozłówka 122.

Phrase Book

Summary of Pronunciation in Polish

ą a nasal *"awn"* as in *"sawn"* or *"an"* as in the French *"Anjou"* but barely sounded

c *"ts"* as in *"bats"*

ć, cz *"ch"* as in *"challenge"*

ch *"ch"* as in Scottish *"loch"*

dz *"j"* as in *"jeans"* when followed by **i** or **e** but otherwise *"dz"* as in *"adze"*

dź *"j"* as in *"jeans"*

dż *"d"* as in *"dog"* followed by *"s"* as in *"leisure"*

ę similar to *"en"* in *"end"* only nasal and barely sounded, but if at the end of the word pronounced *"e"* as in *"bed"*

h *"ch"* as in Scottish *"loch"*

i *"ee"* as in *"teeth"*

j *"y"* as in yes

ł *"w"* as in *"window"*

ń similar to the *"ni"* in *"companion"*

ó *"oo"* as in *"soot"*

rz similar to the *"s"* in *"leisure"* or, when it follows **p**, **t** or **k**, *"sh"* as in *"shut"*

ś, sz *"sh"* as in *"shut"*

w *"v"* as in *"vine"*

y similar to the *"i"* in *"bit"*

ź, ż similar to the *"s"* in *"leisure"*

Emergencies

Help!	**pomocy!**	pomotsi
Call a doctor!	**zawołać doktora!**	zawowach doctora
Call an ambulance!	**zadzwonić po pogotowie!**	zadzvoneech po pogotovee
Police!	**policja!**	poleetsya
Call the fire brigade!	**zadzwonić po straż pożarną!**	zadzvoneech po stras posarnAWN
Where is the nearest phone?	**Gdzie jest najbliższa budka telefoniczna?**	gjeh yest nlbleezhsha boodka telefoneechna
Where is the hospital?	**Gdzie jest szpital?**	gjeh yest shpeetal
Where is the police station	**Gdzie jest posterunek policji?**	gjeh yest posterunek politsyee

Communication Essentials

Yes	**Tak**	tak
No	**Nie**	n-yeh
Thank you	**Dziękuję**	jENkoo-yeh
No thank you	**Nie, dziękuję**	n-yej jENkoo-yeh
Please	**Proszę**	prosheh
I don't understand	**Nie rozumiem**	n-yeh rozoom-yem
Do you speak English? (to a man)	**Czy mówi pan po angielsku?**	chi moovee pan po ang-yelskoo
Do you speak English? (to a woman)	**Czy mówi pani po angielsku?**	chi moovee panee po ang-yelskoo
Please speak more slowly	**Proszę mówić wolniej.**	prosh mooveech voln-yay
Please write it down for me.	**Proszę mi to napisać.**	prosheh mee to napeesach
My name is...	**Nazywam się...**	nazivam sheh

Useful Words and Phrases

Pleased to meet you (to a man)	**Bardzo mi miło pana poznać**	bardzo mee meewo pana poznach
Pleased to meet you (to a woman)	**Bardzo mi miło panią poznać**	bardzo mee meewo pan-yAWN poznach
Good morning	**Dzień dobry**	jen-yuh dobri
Good afternoon	**Dzień dobry**	jen-yuh dobri
Good evening	**Dobry wieczór**	dobri v-yechoor
Good night	**Dobranoc**	dobranots
Goodbye	**Do widzenia**	do veedzen-ya
What time is it..?	**Która jest godzina?**	ktoora yest gojeena
Cheers!	**Na zdrowie!**	na zdrov-yeh
Excellent!	**Wspaniale**	wspan-yaleh

Shopping

Do you have...? (to a man)	**Czy ma pan...?**	che ma pan
Do you have...? (to a woman)	**Czy ma pani...?**	che ma panee
How much is this?	**Ile to kosztuje?**	eeleh to koshtoo-yeh
Where is the... department?	**Gdzie jest dział z...?**	gjeh yest jawuh z
Do you take credit cards? (to a man)	**Czy przyjmuje pan karty kredytowe?**	chi pshi-yuhmoo-yeh pan karti kreditoveh
Do you take credit cards? (to a woman)	**Czy przyjmuje pani karty kredytowe?**	chi pshi-yuhmoo-yeh panee karti kreditoveh
bakery	**piekarnia**	p-yekarn-ya
bookshop	**księgarnia**	kshENgarn-ya
chemist	**apteka**	apteka
department store	**dom towarowy**	dom tovarovi
exchange office	**kantor walutowy**	kantor valootovi
travel agent	**biuro podróży**	b-yooro podroozhi
post office	**poczta, urząd pocztowy**	pochta, ooZHAWNd pochtovi
postcard	**pocztówka**	pochtoovka

stamp	**znaczek**	znachek
How much is a	**Ile kosztuje**	eeleh koshtoo-yeh
postcard to...?	**pocztówka do...?**	pochtoovka do
airmail	**poczta lotnicza**	pochta lotneecha

STAYING IN A HOTEL

Have you any	**Czy ma pan**	chi ma pan
vacancies?	**wolne pokoje?**	volneh poko-yeh
(to a man)		
Have you any	**Czy ma pani**	chi ma panee
vacancies?	**wolne pokoje?**	volneh poko-yeh
(to a woman)		
What is the charge	**Ile kosztuje**	eeleh koshtoo-yeh
per night?	**za dobę?**	za dobeh
I'd like	**Poproszę**	poprosheh
a single room.	**pokój**	pokoo-yuh
	jednoosobowy.	yedno-osobovi
I'd like a double	**Poproszę**	poprosheh
room.	**pokój**	pokoo-yuh
	dwuosobowy.	dvoo-osobovi
I'd like a twin	**Poproszę**	poprosheh
room.	**pokój z dwoma**	pokoo-yuh z dvoma
	łóżkami.	woozhkamee
I'd like a room	**Poproszę**	poprosheh
with a bathroom.	**pokój**	pokoo-yuh
	z łazienką.	z wazhenkAWN
bathroom	**łazienka**	wazhenka
bed	**łóżko**	woozhko
bill	**rachunek**	raHoonek
breakfast	**śniadanie**	shn-yadan-yeh
dinner	**kolacja**	kolats-ya
double room	**pokój**	pokoo-yuh
	dwuosobowy	dvoo-osobovi
full board	**pełne**	pewuhneh
	utrzymanie	ootzhiman-yeh
guest house	**zajazd**	za-yazd
half board	**dwa posiłki**	dva posheewuhkee
	dziennie	jen-yeh
key	**klucz**	klooch
restaurant	**restauracja**	restawrats-ya
shower	**prysznic**	prishneets
single room	**pokój**	pokoo-yuh
	jednoosobowy	yedno-osobovi
toilet	**toaleta**	to-aleta

EATING OUT

A table for one,	**Stolik dla jednej**	stoleek dla yednay
please.	**osoby proszę.**	osobi prosheh
A table for two,	**Stolik dla dwóch**	stoleek dla dvooh
please.	**osób proszę.**	osoob prosheh
Can I see	**Mogę prosić**	mogeh prosheech
the menu?	**jadłospis?**	yadwospees
Can I see the	**Mogę prosić**	mogeh prosheech
wine list?	**kartę win?**	karteh veen
I'd like...	**Proszę**	prosheh

Can we have the	**Proszę**	prosheh
bill, please?	**rachunek?**	raHoonek
Where is the toilet?	**Gdzie jest toaleta?**	gjeh yest to-aleta

MENU DECODER

baranina	mutton, lamb
barszcz czerwony	beetroot soup
bażant	pheasant
befsztyk	beef steak
bigos	hunter's stew (sweet and sour cabbage with a variety of meats and seasonings)
bukiet z jarzyn	a variety of raw and pickled vegetables
ciasto	cake, pastry
cielęcina	veal
cukier	sugar
cukierek	sweet, confectionery
dania mięsne	meat dishes
dania rybne	fish dishes
dania z drobiu	poultry dishes
deser	dessert
flaki	tripe
grzybki marynowane	marinated mushrooms
herbata	tea
jarzyny	vegetables
kabanos	dry, smoked pork sausage
kaczka	duck
kapusta	cabbage
kartofle	potatoes
kasza gryczana	buckwheat
kaszanka	black pudding
kawa	coffee
kiełbasa	sausage
klopsiki	minced meat balls
lody	ice cream
łosoś	salmon
łosoś wędzony	smoked salmon
makowiec	poppy seed cake
naleśniki	pancakes
piernik	spiced honeycake
pierogi	ravioli-like dumplings
piwo	beer
prawdziwki	ceps (type of mushroom)
przystawki	entrées
pstrąg	trout
rolmopsy	rollmop herrings
sałatka	salad
sałatka owocowa	fruit salad
sok	juice
sok jabłkowy	apple juice
sok owocowy	fruit juice
sól	salt
śledź	herring
tort	cake, gâteau
wieprzowina	pork
wino	wine

woda	water	
ziemniaki	potatoes	
zupa	soup	

HEALTH

I do not feel well.	**Źle się czuję**	zhleh sheh choo-yeh
I need	**Potrzebuję**	potzheboo-yeh
a prescription for…	**receptę na…**	retsepteh na
cold	**przeziębienie**	pshef-yENb-yen-yeh
cough (noun)	**kaszel**	kashel
cut	**skaleczenie**	skalechen-yeh
flu	**grypa**	gripa
hayfever	**katar sienny**	katar shyienny
headache pills	**proszki od**	proshkee od
	bólu głowy	booloo gwovi
hospital	**szpital**	shpeetal
nausea	**mdłości**	mudwosh-che
sore throat	**ból gardła**	bool gardwa

TRAVEL AND TRANSPORT

When is the	**Kiedy jest**	k-yedi yest
next train to…?	**następny**	nastENpni
	pociąg do…?	pochAWNg do…
What is the	**Ile kosztuje**	eeleh koshtoo-yeh
fare to…?	**bilet do…?**	beelet do
A single ticket	**Proszę bilet**	prosheh beelet
to … please	**w jedną**	v yednAWN
	stronę bilet do…	stroneh beelet do
A return ticket	**Proszę bilet**	prosheh beelet
to … please	**w obie**	v obye
	strony do…	strony do
Where is the	**Gdzie jest**	gjeh yest
bus station?	**dworzec**	dvozhets
	autobusowy?	awtoboosovi
Where is the	**Gdzie jest**	gjeh yest
bus stop?	**przystanek**	pshistanek
	autobusowy?	awtoboosovi
Where is the	**Gdzie jest**	gjeh yest
tram stop?	**przystanek**	pshistanek
	tramwajowy?	tramvl-yovi
booking office	**kasa biletowa**	kasa beeletova
station	**stacja**	stats-ya
timetable	**rozkład jazdy**	rozkwad yazdi
left luggage	**przechowalnia**	psheHovaln-ya
	bagażu	bagazhoo
platform	**peron**	peron
first class	**pierwsza klasa**	p-yervsha klasa
second class	**druga klasa**	drooga klasa
single ticket	**bilet w jedną**	beelet v jednAWN
	stronę	stroneh
return ticket	**bilet powrotny**	beelet povrotni
airline	**linia lotnicza**	leen-ya lotna-yeecha
airport	**lotnisko**	lotn-yeesko
arrival	**przylot**	pshilot
flight number	**numer lotu**	noomer lotoo

gate	**przejście**	pshaysh-cheh
coach	**autokar**	awtokar

NUMBERS

0	**zero**	zero
1	**jeden**	yeden
2	**dwa**	dva
3	**trzy**	tshi
4	**cztery**	chteri
5	**pięć**	p-yENch
6	**sześć**	shesh-ch
7	**siedem**	sh-yedem
8	**osiem**	oshem
9	**dziewięć**	jev-yENch
10	**dziesięć**	jeshENch
11	**jedenaście**	yedenash-cheh
12	**dwanaście**	dvanash-cheh
13	**trzynaście**	tshinash-cheh
14	**czternaście**	chternash-cheh
15	**piętnaście**	p-yEntnash-cheh
16	**szesnaście**	shesnash-cheh
17	**siedemnaście**	shedemnash-cheh
18	**osiemnaście**	oshemnash-cheh
19	**dziewiętnaście**	jev-yEntnash-cheh
20	**dwadzieścia**	dvajesh-cha
21	**dwadzieścia**	dvajesh-ch
	jeden	a yeden
22	**dwadzieścia dwa**	dvajesh-cha dva
30	**trzydzieści**	tshijesh-chee
40	**czterdzieści**	chterjesh-chee
50	**pięćdziesiąt**	p-yENchjeshAWNt
100	**sto**	sto
200	**dwieście**	dv-yesh-cheh
500	**pięćset**	p-yENchset
1,000	**tysiąc**	tishAWNts
1,000,000	**milion**	meel-yon

TIME

today	**dzisiaj**	jeeshl
yesterday	**wczoraj**	vchorl
tomorrow	**jutro**	yootro
tonight	**dzisiejszej nocy**	jeeshAYshay notsi
one minute	**jedna minuta**	yedna meenoota
half an hour	**pół godziny**	poowuh gojeeni
hour	**godzina**	gojeena

DAYS OF THE WEEK

Sunday	**niedziela**	n-yejela
Monday	**poniedziałek**	pon-yejawek
Tuesday	**wtorek**	vtorek
Wednesday	**środa**	shroda
Thursday	**czwartek**	chvartek
Friday	**piątek**	p-yAWNtek
Saturday	**sobota**	sobota

COUNTRY GUIDES

AUSTRALIA • CANADA • FRANCE • GREAT BRITAIN
GREECE: ATHENS & THE MAINLAND • THE GREEK ISLANDS
IRELAND • ITALY • JAPAN • MEXICO
PORTUGAL • SCOTLAND • SINGAPORE
SOUTH AFRICA • SPAIN • THAILAND
GREAT PLACES TO STAY IN EUROPE
TASTE OF SCOTLAND

REGIONAL GUIDES

BARCELONA & CATALONIA • CALIFORNIA
FLORENCE & TUSCANY • FLORIDA • HAWAII
JERUSALEM & THE HOLY LAND • LOIRE VALLEY
MILAN & THE LAKES • NAPLES WITH POMPEII & THE
AMALFI COAST • PROVENCE & THE COTE D'AZUR • SARDINIA
SEVILLE & ANDALUSIA • SICILY • VENICE & THE VENETO

CITY GUIDES

AMSTERDAM • BERLIN • BRUSSELS • BUDAPEST
CRACOW • DELHI, AGRA & JAIPUR • DUBLIN
ISTANBUL • LISBON • LONDON • MADRID
MOSCOW • NEW YORK • PARIS • PRAGUE • ROME
SAN FRANCISCO • STOCKHOLM • ST PETERSBURG
SYDNEY • VIENNA • WARSAW • WASHINGTON, DC

NEW FOR SPRING 2001

BALI & LOMBOK • BOSTON • CHICAGO
CRUISE GUIDE TO EUROPE AND THE MEDITERRANEAN
GERMANY • NEW ENGLAND • NEW ZEALAND

FOR UPDATES TO OUR GUIDES, AND INFORMATION ON
DK TRAVEL MAPS & PHRASEBOOKS

VISIT US AT
eyewitnesstravel.dk.com

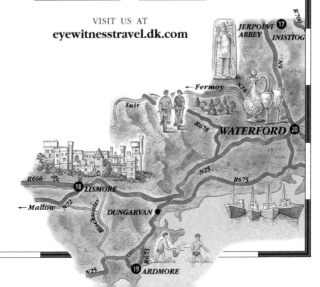

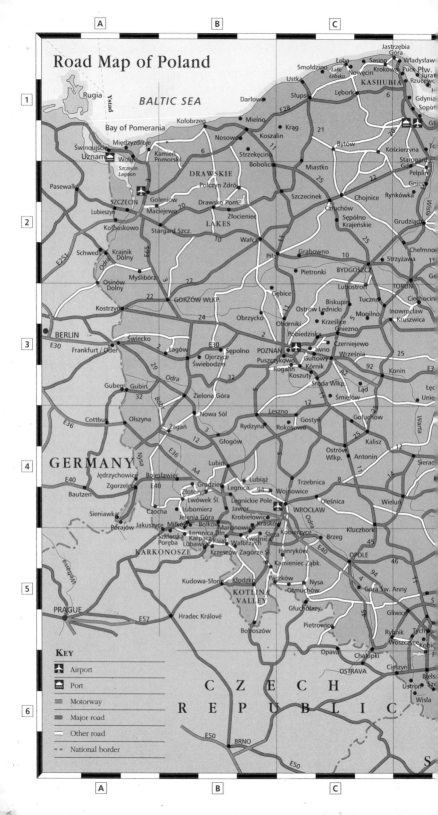